The Translator

ROBERT M. ADAMS was professor of English emeritus at the University of California at Los Angeles. A Columbia Ph.D., he also taught at Wisconsin, Rutgers, and Cornell. He was the author of many books, including *Ikon: John Milton and the Modern Critics*, *Strains of Discord*, *Surface and Symbol*, *The Land and Literature of England*, and *Shakespeare—The Four Romances*. He edited six Norton Critical Editions, including *The Prince* by Machiavelli, *Candide* by Voltaire, and *The Praise of Folly and Other Writings* by Erasmus, the texts of which he also translated. He was a contributing editor of *The Norton Anthology of English Literature*.

The Editor

SUSANNA LEE is associate professor of French at Georgetown University. A Yale Ph.D., she is the author of *A World Abandoned by God: Narrative and Secularism* and has written numerous articles on nineteenth-century narrative literature, the history of ideas, and crime fiction.

A NORTON CRITICAL EDITION

Stendhal

THE RED AND THE BLACK

SECOND EDITION

AUTHORITATIVE TEXT
CONTEXT AND BACKGROUNDS
CRITICISM

Translated by

ROBERT M. ADAMS

LATE OF THE UNIVERSITY
OF CALIFORNIA AT
LOS ANGELES

Edited by

SUSANNA LEE

GEORGETOWN
UNIVERSITY

First edition edited by

ROBERT M. ADAMS

W. W. NORTON & COMPANY

New York • London

W. W. Norton & Company has been independent since its founding in 1923, when William Warder Norton and Mary D. Herter Norton first published lectures delivered at the People's Institute, the adult education division of New York City's Cooper Union. The Nortons soon expanded their program beyond the Institute, publishing books by celebrated academics from America and abroad. By mid-century, the two major pillars of Norton's publishing program—trade books and college texts—were firmly established. In the 1950s, the Norton family transferred control of the company to its employees, and today—with a staff of four hundred and a comparable number of trade, college, and professional titles published each year—W. W. Norton & Company stands as the largest and oldest publishing house owned wholly by its employees.

This title is printed on permanent paper containing
30 percent post-consumer waste recycled fiber.

Composition by PennSet, Inc.
Manufacturing by Maple Press.
Book design by Antonina Krass.
Production manager: Benjamin Reynolds.

Library of Congress Cataloging-in-Publication Data
Stendhal, 1783–1842.
[Rouge et le noir. English]
The red and the black : authoritative text, context and backgrounds,
criticism / Stendhal ; translated by Robert M. Adams ; edited by Susanna
Lee. — 2nd ed.
        p.   cm. — (A Norton critical edition)
Includes bibliographical references.
ISBN 978-393-92883-9 (pbk.)
1. Young men—France—Fiction.   2. France—Social life and customs—
19th century—Fiction.   3. Stendhal, 1783–1842. Rouge et le noir.
4. Young men in literature.   I. Adams, Robert Martin, 1915–   II. Lee,
Susanna, 1970–   III. Title.
PQ2435.R7E5 2007
843'.7dc22

                                                      2007036467

W. W. Norton & Company, Inc., 500 Fifth Avenue, New York, N.Y. 10110
www.wwnorton.com

W. W. Norton & Company Ltd., 15 Carlisle Street, London W1D 3BS

2   3   4   5   6   7   8   9   0

Contents

Introduction to the Second Edition

In *Vie de Henry Brulard*, Stendhal pondered the staying power of his writing:

> The rhythmical, pretentious phrases of MM Chateaubriand and de Salvandy made me write *Le Rouge et le noir* in too jerky a style. It was a great folly, for in twenty years who will think of the hypocritical rigmaroles of these gentlemen? As for me, I am taking a ticket in a lottery in which the first prize amounts to this: to be read in 1935.[1]

Were Stendhal to see the reception that *The Red and the Black* has enjoyed through the twentieth century and into the twenty-first, he might be quite surprised at how much the modern audience has found to love in his "jerky style." Indeed, while Flaubert's *Madame Bovary* often gets top billing as the masterpiece of French nineteenth-century literature, *The Red and the Black* has become code for a reader's novel, and Stendhal a reader's author. The novel is an incomparably galloping, multilayered, labyrinthine adventure chronicling the inscrutable substance of character, the caprices of politics, the comforts and insincerities of religion, the ambiguities of the law, and the all-consuming, exhausting, and sometimes crazy-making vicissitudes of love. The pace and agility of the novel demand that the reader be sitting up, listening for the constant shifts in perspective, changes of mind, the minute details of action, reaction, and internal monologue. Indeed, as more than one student has remarked, first in fatigue and later in admiration, the demands of *The Red and the Black* are many, but the reward is an unforgettable journey into a society, a historical moment, a heart, a mind, a life.

Stendhal's original intention was to call his novel *Julien*, and indeed, more than anything, this is the story of an individual character. We follow Julien Sorel on his trajectory from Verrières to Besançon to Paris and through his numerous and contradictory in-

---

1. Stendhal, *The Life of Henri Brulard*, trans. Catherine Alison Phillips (New York: Knopf, 1925), p. 163.

carnations: Julien the son, the reader, the weakling, the hypocrite, the seducer, the student, the criminal, the philosopher, the egotist. He is remarkable for the simultaneity of his emotions, sensations, and actions, for this character does not just evolve, he divides, a sort of multicelled organism whose personality and fortunes split and shoot off in various directions. He is calculating but vulnerable, rational but mad, childish but perspicacious, innovative but imitative, grandiose but uncertain, red but black: The layers of his personality, the multitude of outside influence on that personality, all contribute to the richness of Julien as well as to the oft-repeated critical statement that Stendhal's *The Red and the Black* is the first psychological novel. But what does it mean to be a psychological novel, much less the first one? Other novels have certainly given us portraits of minds and souls in action. But this is perhaps the first novel in which the drama of self-invention is so utterly essential to the plot. Julien (and Mathilde) are to an unprecedented degree concerned with succeeding as characters—with *existing* with enough vigor and originality to merit a story. The obsession with existence and originality has much to do with the labile nature of circumstances social and political, the fragility of which forces characters to build and rebuild their own criteria. Unlike the social climbers of eighteenth-century novels, in other words, the characters in this novel are for the first time assailed with a double concern: not just how to function within the social and political and moral parameters of their world, but also how to determine what those parameters mean. Julien is steeped in these concerns, and to a large extent they drive his actions and define his personality. In this sense, he is the first existential hero: the first to encounter the specter of meaninglessness, both within himself and without. This is another way of saying that he is the first psychological hero, the first for whom questions of who he is are so fundamental, and so tormenting.

And yet, the question of who someone is was not as common in 1830 as it would become in the following century. French society might have been hypocritical and precarious, but it was nonetheless the playing field of the day. To disconnect from it would have been unthinkable, and identity was not something to conjure out of thin air. Rather than modern existential crises à la Jean-Paul Sartre, then, Julien's problems of self-definition were first and foremost problems of role-playing. He worries after a particularly noteworthy romantic encounter: "Did I play my role well?" (although the narrator is quick to add, "And what role was that?"[2]). For Julien as for

---

2. Stendhal, *The Red and the Black*, trans. Robert M. Adams, ed. Susanna Lee (New York: Norton, 2008). Abbreviated hereafter as *RB*.

Mathilde, questions of role have much to do with living in a society that is constantly changing and whose rules and norms can be endlessly manipulated. The main characters are concerned with fashioning themselves in the context of their surroundings even as they try to fashion those surroundings to serve as context. Whatever environment he finds himself in, be it mayoral home, seminary, or Paris mansion, Julien is intensely concerned with looking like what he believes he is supposed to be—the lover, the seminarian, the innocent, the scribe, and so on. At the same time, he is intensely worried about what others might think he looks like: a servant, a fool, Martin Luther, a pathetically out-of-his-league suitor. Dealing as it does with the voyage of self-discovery, then, the novel speaks not just to a volatility specific to its historical period, but also to a universal process of learning and shaping who one is.

The paradox of self-definition is that the only way to be original is to write one's own script, as it were. And yet, the most reliable way to know what makes a good story is to read one: thus Julien's obsession with Napoleon and other textual models. He constantly copies, from Rousseau and Molière, among others. So too with Mathilde, who, in a telling moment, braces herself against self-doubt with the phrase: "No matter! I can say like Medea: *Amid so many perils, still I have MYSELF.*"[3] The fact that the fictional Medea did not in fact say this underscores the precariousness of modeling oneself after literature. But nonetheless, it reminds us that a high consciousness of prescribed worlds is the foundation of the characters' imaginations. To fail to succeed is for them to fade into a story already written for their "type": a boring marriage for Mathilde, or a dinner at the servants' table for Julien. In many ways, then, this is a psychological novel in that it is about characters intensely aware of their existence *as* characters on the world stage, or on their own stage (which is starting to amount to the same thing), as we see in Julien's famous—and famously erroneous—line: "My novel is finished, and all the credit is mine."

With his posturings, his back-and-forths between imitation and originality, Julien is on a number of levels a rich hybrid of character types, combining shades of the epic hero with elements of the twentieth-century existentialist. His family tree, so to speak, begins with Homer, passes through Don Quixote, and continues on to include such troubled souls as Meursault, the dissociated center of Albert Camus' 1942 novel *The Stranger*. He also belongs (since this is a chronicle of 1830, after all) to that group of early nineteenth-century fictional *arrivistes* such as Balzac's Eugène Rastignac and Lucien de Rubempré, determined to find success in the big city.

3. *RB*, p. 267.

With his pale face and dark hair, there is also something of a Caspar Friedrich painting of a Byronic poet about him. His love of reading and his tendency to model his own life after those he sees in books also place him in a similar camp with that later, much more deluded and passive reader, Emma Bovary. Madame de Rênal, a sort of beautiful soul, also has something of the romantic heroine, but without the idealization that usually makes such characters boring or unreal. Mathilde de la Mole is in her turn one of the more unusual female characters of the French nineteenth century, containing ironized elements both of haughty eighteenth-century French aristocrats and virtuous heroines of English novels. And while adolescence as we understand it today was not really invented until the mid-twentieth century, Mathilde is very much a prototeenager, volatile, passionate, self-obsessed, rebellious. College students reading this novel often remark that they know someone like her, though they often don't like that someone. Actually, the same remark is often made about Julien, with his constantly changing affections, his looking out for number one, his occasional touching sincerity, his combination of willpower, perspicacity, and cluelessness.

Crossroads in Literary History

It is sometimes said that Stendhal's novel stands at the cusp of the epic and the novel; it also stands at other generic crossroads: those of the pastoral and the Bildungsroman, the religious and the secular, the romantic and the realist. With all these transitions, particularly the last, the novel marks an important moment in literary history—not just because it marks a historical transition, but also because it reveals an essential pretense in both romanticism and realism. To the contemporary reader, the romantic literary period seems a time of pure and unambivalent emotion. It is not an age or a style that seems to be aware of either neurosis or calculating self-involvement; to the contrary, the lilting cadences, bucolic scenes, and sentimental ruminations of, say, Chateaubriand and Lamartine suggest a starry-eyed generosity of spirit. *The Red and the Black*, written toward the end of but still well within the romantic period, keeps the reveries, the landscaped grounds of country estates, the scaling of stone walls for romantic assignations, the cutting-off a lock of hair as a sign of devotion. But in these pages, the ladder that scales the wall crushes the flowers beneath; the lock of hair becomes an entire clump hacked off with scissors, leaving the amorous woman half bald. And once the wall is scaled and the lovers meet, we see all the halting steps, the posing, the sometimes disingenuous movements that go into those meetings. Romance was work in 1830, we learn, and so was romanticism. *The Red and the Black* shows young people scrambling to keep up with the Joneses that their times, their books, or even just their own grasping imaginations have invented.

There is too much consciousness of romanticism in his novel—too much edge, too much trying too hard—for Stendhal to be entirely considered a romantic novelist, though the very trying, in a sense, becomes romantic through its pathos. Seeing the traces of irony that run through the novel, students, alerted that French novelistic style of the nineteenth century evolves from romanticism to realism, want to know, Is Stendhal then a realist? And the related, though rather impossible question, Is this novel realistic? On the one hand, the question is misplaced, as realism and romanticism are not really opposites. But talking about realism is important here, because it allows us to look at the historical importance of this novel, as well as the ways in which the narrator plays with history, with his characters, and with his readers.

Many of the events that take place in the novel, as well as the basic outline of Julien's adventures and misadventures, are in fact "ripped from the headlines!" The real-life escapades of one Antoine Berthet, combined with those of a woodworker named Lafargue, provided the foundation for the plot (an account of Berthet's trial is to be found in the "Backgrounds and Sources" section of this volume), More important, the political goings-on are in a broad sense real. And for this reason, the novel stands as a significant historical document. *The Red and the Black* gives us a close and ironic portrait of the French Restoration era, with its constant ideological upheaval and almost surreal public hypocrisy. Perhaps the second-best-known line in the novel is the narrator's aside: "Politics in the midst of imaginative activity is like a pistol shot in the middle of a concert. The noise is shattering without being forceful."[4] If the concert in question means an untroubled representation of life in a vacuum, life out of context, if there is such a thing, then Stendhal has fired his own shot, disrupting his own performance. But far from being the cacophonous pistol shot, of course, politics in this imaginative activity, as Sandy Petrey so wonderfully describes in his essay, is an imaginative activity of its own. Peter Brooks writes that Stendhal's novels "offer the first decisive representation of individuals plotting their lives in response to the sociopolitical dynamics of modern times." And just as no individual moment in this novel is immune to the intrusion of politics, so here, no political moment or event is immune to the intrusion of individual psychologies, de-

4. *RB*, p. 304.

sires, and egos. Society, family, government—these are monoliths, large-scale backdrops against which individuals define and position themselves. But as we are shown these monoliths, we are also constantly shown the component parts into which they are broken and the extent to which political systems depend on individuals playing their parts. Each part makes sense only relative to another part, and individuals are holding these roles up even as they fill them. In the end, while the showcasing of sociopolitical dynamics is new, so is the contingency and fragility, the very dynamism as it were, of those dynamics. For example, this is a society in which Julien's boss, wanting a man of his own social stature to converse with and knowing it would be out of the question to chat with a servant, arranges for Julien to dress up as an aristocrat. "Allow me, my dear Sorel, to make you a present of a blue suit: when you feel disposed to put it on and pay me a call, you will be, in my eyes, the younger brother of the Comte de Retz, that is to say the son of my friend the old duke."[5] It's an exhausting world for Stendhal's characters, not to mention for the readers who try to follow it all. The political background, the sociopolitical ground on which the characters stand, never really manages to *be* a ground, because it is itself shifting, and never settles into a reliable fixedness. Instead, it constantly and subtly slips into the foreground so that we may see the intricacies and fallibilities of its operation.

As a side note, we can remark that the political posturing in the novel is itself of particular interest to a contemporary English-reading audience. The portrait of politics driven by ego and caprice resonates mightily, as worsening cynicism greets the news of political dealings in twenty-first-century America. And just as no one in Stendhal's clever, jaded, and hypocritical 1830 expected politics to operate in some pure and unadulterated sphere, so increasingly, if sadly, few in our world expect politicians to rise above self-interest. The same sort of egocentric nervousness that pushes young Julien in love also drives M. de Rênal and Valenod in the political sphere. And so it is, many students remark, with the politicians of our time; the disingenuousness that permeated France in 1830 is more and more familiar—disturbingly, but also often, strangely, comfortingly so—to students of this early twenty-first American century.

Also of real social and historical interest is the complexity of treatment that the novel affords to religion. Religion is critically presented in all its permutations: as a profession, a spectacle, a consumable product, a social institution, and a political instrument, as well as a personal feeling and a spiritual force. All these depictions of religion are fraught with contradiction. On the one

5. *RB*, p. 219.

hand, an ironic doubt pervades the spiritual pursuit: We have Julien's cool musings on career and salary: "Nowadays, there are forty-year-old priests who draw salaries of a hundred thousand francs, three times as much as the famous division commanders of Napoleon . . . . The thing is to be a priest."[6] We also have the memorable scene of the young bishop of Agde practicing his benedictions in front of the mirror and experimenting with the best placement of his miter, among other scenes of posturing (the same theme appears in *The Charterhouse of Parma*, where handsome Fabrice becomes a sort of rock star of a preacher). And yet, on the other hand, men of religion are perhaps the most sincere characters in the novel; Abbé Pirard, that stern Jansenist, is in fact a kind and giving figure. We also see characters coming to surprising moments of spiritual clarity.

Some readers, finding the Abbé Pirard in charge of the Besançon seminary, wonder what the Jansenists, a religious group associated with the seventeenth century and excommunicated in 1719, are doing in the pages of this Chronicle of 1830. For one thing, the Jansenists serve as contrast to the Jesuits—selflessness to their materialism, severity to their flashiness. More than this, though, because Jansenism emphasizes salvation through divine grace, rather than through human will or action, the Jansenist/Jesuit conflict is a metaphor for the conflict within Julien's own experience. Julien wants to be master not only of his actions but of his entire destiny. But this mastery is largely an illusion, for even as he is writing his own script (deciding what he wants to do, whom he wants to seduce, where he wants to go), he is also following the script of others (studying Napoleon, parroting Tartuffe, copying Korosov's letters, and so on) and riding the tide of circumstance. Jesuits emphasized the idea of action and Jansenists emphasized the idea of grace. Similarly, Julien values the idea of action and the narrator values the idea not of grace, perhaps, but of chance, coincidence, good luck, good looks, the whims of other people—forces, that is, outside oneself. Julien, in other words, would like to take the world in hand, but has he? Can anyone? We are constantly confronted with the question of what precisely is driving this boat—a boat that contains the Jansenists, the Jesuits, religious institutions, Restoration politics, and Julien himself.

The issue of what (or who) makes the action happen in this story is an important one, because raising this question is one way Stendhal plays with the reader—one way he turns the reading of this novel into a highly entertaining game. Another way he does this is with a varied, nimbly shifting narrative point of view. Narra-

6. *RB*, p. 19–20.

tive point of view in this novel is a shape-shifting target, which in turn brings us back to the question of realism. Who is telling this story? The answer, of course, is our narrator. But while this narrator provides many points of access to his tale, many angles from which to approach it, he is also a rather tricky gatekeeper. A fictitious Stendhal fan in one modern novel says: "I love how Stendhal gets, you know, like, inside and outside Julien at the same time, so you can imagine doing what Julien's doing, and meanwhile you're thinking you would never do something like that."[7] That very dichotomy comes from an unparalleled narrative personality that simultaneously embraces Julien and detaches from him, embraces society and detaches from it, embraces reality and detaches from it—and expects the reader to do the same. At times, this narrator even invites us to wonder who he is and what he has to do with the entire business, and these moments are a monkey wrench thrown into the entire idea of the real.

Early on in the novel, the narrator muses: "How many times, my mind still dwelling on the balls of Paris which I left the night before, have I leaned on these great blocks of bluish-gray granite, gazing deep into the valley of the Doubs!" He seems at this point a resident of Verrières (though a frequent flier on the Paris party circuit), well placed to witness the goings on he describes. As if to support this role, he pauses in the middle of the action to insert the famous and often-quoted parenthetical aside: "A novel is a mirror moving along a highway. One minute you see it reflect the azure skies, next minute the mud and puddles of the road. And the man who carries the mirror in his pack will be accused by you of immorality! His mirror shows the mud and you accuse the mirror!"[8] Realism, indeed. But this same narrator, so insistent when defending the truth of his chronicle, continues: "Now that it's fully understood that a character like Mathilde's is impossible in our age, no less prudent than virtuous, I am less afraid of distressing the reader by describing further the follies of this attractive girl."[9] This sharp contradiction (my story is real/no it isn't) undermines the claim of realism. Or at least, it reminds us that realism is not primarily about being the real thing, but rather about not being reminded too harshly that we are not being shown the real thing—that we are in the land of fiction, of an author's creation.

Curiously, when the narrator concedes to us that a character like Mathilde's is impossible, she has done nothing terribly impossible or incredible: His comment serves mainly as an ironic reminder

7. Francine Prose, *Blue Angel* (New York: Harper Collins, 2000), p. 38.
8. *RB*, p. 289.
9. *RB*, p. 290.

that "our age" is neither prudent nor virtuous. And as the narrator abruptly abandons his aside and continues the story, we the readers are as caught up in Mathilde as ever, her "impossibility" never intended as an obstacle to our enjoyment of her (or annoyance with her). On the other hand, those acts in the novel that do seem the most outlandish and improbable are, ironically, the very ones cribbed from the real adventures of Lafargue and Antoine Berthet as reported in the *Gazette des Tribunaux*. Just as a novel that sets its characters at a remove from romanticism cannot be entirely romantic, so a narrator who stops his story to insist on (and then deny) his own realism cannot entirely be considered a realist. Or perhaps this is the highest form of realism—a real acknowledgment of the writing process. What one finds in this cryptic authorial aside, and what readers have always loved in Stendhal, is an author who thoroughly enjoys a vigorous give-and-take with the reader. His "jerky" narrative style, his occasional winking at the reader, his assumption of a common taste for rapid-fire shifts in perspective, for ironic historical and political asides, is Stendhal's signature, and an essential element of the novel's appeal. Many features of the novel show creative construction, a sense that writing is something of a game. Most of Stendhal's epigraphs, for instance, are misattributed. And this from the very beginning—from Danton's "Truth, bitter truth" (words not found among Danton's writing) to Hobbes's nonsensical "Put thousands together, less bad, but the cage less gay," in English, to the comically out-of-character: "The glance of a woman was enough to intimidate me. The harder I tried to please, the more awkward I became . . ." attributed to the philosopher, Immanuel Kant.[1] This is a narrator as well versed in ironic commentary as he is in compassion, in identification as in mockery, often in the same paragraph.

Forty-eight years old at the time of the novel's writing, in love with his mother whom he had lost at the age of seven, a veteran of Napoleon's army who had retired to Milan upon the general's exile, a short and squat man who lacked Julien's delicate features but had plenty of his impatience and infatuation, Stendhal had kept the soul of an adolescent enough to combine the wry perspective of the older man with a teenage sense of urgency. He was a romantic who disliked Romanticism, a French fan of Italian passion who described himself as Milanese in his self-authored epitaph, a Bonapartiste who nonetheless had considerable contempt for the bourgeoisie. He wrote an autobiography (*Vie de Henry Brulard*, excerpted in this volume) under a pseudonym, which demonstrates, at the least, a slightly fantastical relationship with the self. Sten-

1. *RB*, p. 192.

dhal (yet another pseudonym) is best known for his novels, starting
with *Armance* (1827), then *The Red and the Black* in the summer
of 1830, then *The Charterhouse of Parma* in 1839, as well as the
posthumously published (and unfinished) novels *Lamiel* and *Lucien Leuwen*. Stendhal also wrote the *Chroniques italiennes*, short
stories inspired by Italian Renaissance passion and violence, a biography of Rossini, biographies of Mozart, Haydn, and Métastase,
two travelogues (*Promenades in Rome* and *Rome, Naples and Florence in 1817*), and a two-volume history of Italian painting—this
last originally dedicated to Napoleon. In addition, though, distinguishing Stendhal from other great nineteenth-century novelists, is
a rich and moving autobiographical corpus. This contains *Vie de
Henry Brulard* and his treatise, "On Love" (1822), as well as *Memoirs of Egotism, The Private Diaries of Stendhal*, and the travelogues.
His autobiographical creations have inspired much public fondness
for the author, and even a subsequent of Stendhal fans called
Beylistes (for Stendhal's real name, Henri Beyle)—readers deeply
taken with the autobiographical writings and by extension with
Stendhal the person. The travelogues have even given us a psychiatric diagnosis: Stendhal Syndrome, a psychosomatic illness that
causes confusion and hallucinations when the sufferer is exposed
to art. This is not the only psychiatric syndrome that nineteenth-
century novels have given us—we have *bovarysme*, from Flaubert's
Madame Bovary, an inability to see oneself for who and what one
is—but Stendhal Syndrome is the only condition named after the
author himself. Flaubert might have claimed, "Madame Bovary,
c'est moi," but Stendhal put his own heart and soul (if not his real
name) on the page, making us particularly inclined to believe him,
and side with him.

Writing and Revolution

The Red and the Black was Stendhal's second novel, and it vies with
The Charterhouse of Parma for the distinction of being his greatest.
It has a particularly important role in the historiography of the
Restoration, as it was written in the summer of 1830 and is subtitled as a chronicle of that year—the year of the July Revolution,
which ended the Restoration period. The Restoration, meaning
restoration of the Bourbon monarchy deposed in the Revolution of
1789, had lasted since Napoleon's exile in 1815. At that time, Louis
XVIII, brother of the guillotined Louis XVI, assumed control of
France. When Louis XVIII died in 1824, a third brother, Charles X,
replaced him. The regime of Charles X was a reign of old men, a

veritable geriocracy that steadily became more and more repressive. The regime culminated in a series of measures (censorship of the press, dismantling of the chamber of deputies, restrictions on the electorate) that combined with economic insecurity to push the country into revolution. The resulting insurrection forced Charles X to abdicate, and France passed under the control of Louis-Philipe who, significantly, was not a Bourbon. With this transferal of power, the divine right of kings had given way to a "Popular" monarchy. This 1830 revolution, however, was not a revolution in the twentieth-century sense, nor in any particularly idealistic sense, and it certainly did not catapult the country into democracy. Louis Philipe's principal supporters were members of the wealthy middle class—indeed, they supported him because under his rule, money talked and the bourgeoisie rose in social status. The conditions of the working classes actually deteriorated under this elitist ruler, and in 1848, another revolution deposed him. But in 1830 these deteriorations were several years away, and the coming of revolution signified the opening of social doors, the end of the repressive, old-school *ancien régime*, and a new day in French history.

The Red and the Black is the most explicitly politically engaged of Stendhal's novels, but it is not entirely partisan. Stendhal was ambivalent about democracy. The good news of 1830 was that royal blood and aristocratic title were no longer the *sine qua non* of social and political influence: That influence was now theoretically open to anyone with money and connections. But that openness, of course, was also the bad news. The *ancien régime* standards were oppressive, but at least they were standards. And although Stendhal was an enthusiastic Bonapartiste, he nonetheless understood democracy in the Platonic sense, as a voice granted to the lowest common denominator. This did not please him: He was a clever man who wanted clever people to be in charge. Not surprisingly, then, there are various nostalgic musings on the elitism of the *ancien régime* in his novels and in his personal writings. In The Red and the Black, Mathilde laments the end of the exciting seventeenth century: "Civilization and policemen have eliminated danger, and the unexpected never happens."[2] And more to Stendhal's point: "Nothing is ridiculous, M. de La Mole used to say, in a country where there are two parties."[3] In order for there to be ridicule, there must be someone to do the ridiculing; someone with the intellectual and social authority to proclaim something ridiculous or to exile a ridiculous person from high society. Stendhal bemoaned

2. *RB*, p. 265–66.
3. *RB*, p. 253.

the occasional arbitrariness of social judgments but was also capable of lamenting the sort of level playing field that would allow anyone with money and influence an equal voice.

Because of its detailed description of the French Restoration and the revolutionary moment, because of its fine commentary on political hypocrisy, this novel stands as a historical as well as a literary document. One may therefore encounter it in a history rather than a literature course or, at the very least, find oneself deciphering the historical references in order to better "get" the literary picture. Because of the proliferation of political allusions, because of their sometimes daunting complexity, one very important element of this novel sometimes gets lost and should be mentioned here. Often, when wandering through the myriad political references, the comings and goings of Julien and company, the religious intrigue, the one-upmanship of romance, student readers miss an extremely important quality of *The Red and the Black*: its comedy! Yes, there is a great deal of humor in this novel. Mathilde wanders around in gravest mourning for an ancestor decapitated centuries earlier, to the bewilderment and eye-rolling of others in the house. Julien sends a series of borrowed, prewritten love letters to Madame de Fervaques, not even bothering to read them or edit their content. Madame de Fervaques then falls for those letters, even though the details they contain make no sense to her or to Julien. Julien at the seminary tries to make friends with a student who "lived in the odor of sanctity, listening submissively to some paralyzing drivel"; a storm begins, and the "saintly student" shoves Julien away so as not to be struck by lightning in case Julien is blasted by God.[4] The ironic eye in the midst of religious humorlessness is a staple of comedy—think of Dudley Moore's sleeping on a wooden pillow and jumping with the trampolining nuns in *Bedazzled*. So, too, is the act of posing, of pretending to be what the audience (readers or other characters) knows one is not.

Posing, or role-playing, is Julien's daily activity, rendered in an interior monologue so constant and darting as to seem slightly crazy. The humor of this monologue is particularly visible when one compares the novel with film versions thereof. In the 1997 film version, for instance, the interior monologue is rendered through dialogue—either through Julien's articulating a thought to another, or, sometimes, through another who speaks to him. In the novel, though, these labyrinthine dialogues are between Julien and himself, and remain within his overpopulated head. For this reason, film Juliens cannot have that strange combination of insincerity, haplessness, and furious intensity that both bewilders readers and

4. *RB*, p. 149.

invites their sympathy. The only place to find it is here, in the pages of the novel.

Critical Material

At the end of this edition, we have included a variety of critical and contextual material, as well as some of Stendhal's own writings. Among these latter are excerpts from his autobiography and from his treatise on love, in which he describes the phenomenon of "crystallization" that for him is essential to romance. The critical essays included in this edition speak to numerous facets of the novel, and one appears here in English translation for the first time: Shoshana Felman's "La Folie dans l' œuvre romanesque de Stendhal" was the first to find an undercurrent of madness in the methodical Julien Sorel. Also translated here for the first time is Jules Janin's 1830 review of Stendhal's novel, which found in the narrator (showing, in this case at least, that Stendhal was right to think that appreciation might have to wait until the twentieth century) a sort of antireligious nihilist. Other books excerpted, including Erich Auerbach's seminal *Mimesis* and Sandy Petrey's *Realism and Revolution*, provide various perspectives on Stendhal's novel, from the political to the feminist to the psychoanalytic. The purpose of these essays' inclusion is to suggest various critical angles and ways of reading, not to furnish the final word on interpretation. Indeed, as the pages of the novel itself reveal and as the critical essays here included concede, *The Red and the Black* resists such final words. The uncertainty and imagination that it generates ensures that Stendhal is more than winning his lottery, continuing to be read, and admired, in the twenty-first century.

The Text of
THE RED AND THE BLACK

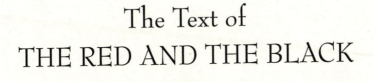

Translator's Note

The present translation was made from the 1960 edition prepared for Classiques Garnier by the late, great Henri Martineau. Only one edition of the *Rouge* was published during Stendhal's life (by Levavasseur, 1831), and no manuscript survives; M. Martineau was editing the text for the fourth time (previous editions were for Bossard, 1925; Le Divan, 1927; and La Pléiade, 1932). All this should make for a relatively straightforward text. Still, a modest problem remains. Before his death Stendhal made marginal annotations in a published copy of the novel, known as the Bucci copy, from its owner, Signor Clodoveo Bucci of Civitavecchia. In addition, two posthumous editions of the *Rouge* (that published by Hetzel in 1846 and that of Lévy in 1854) were supervised by Stendhal's good friend and literary executor, Romain Colomb. They contain various additions to, and modifications of, the 1831 text. The problem raised by all these variants is exacerbated by the fact that they cannot be accepted or rejected wholesale; it is a matter of the translator's individual judgment with regard to each individual change. Some of the Bucci corrections really and patently are Stendhal's afterthoughts and improvements. Some, however, are the author's idle comments and scribblings on his own fiction; they may indicate, for example, a general wish that he had done thus or so in a particular passage, but they offer no basis for amending the text. Similarly with the Hetzel and Lévy editions: Colomb made on his own initiative a great many moderate changes, mostly of verb tenses and pronoun references, in order to present his friend's work in what he considered its best light; but he made here and there a few other changes, for which it is evident he had some manuscript authority. According to his lights, and those of the day, he was a responsible editor and would not have revamped text or altered epigraphs (as in II, 6) without some sort of warrant from his author. So here too the translator must pick and choose.

As all these variants are recorded at large in the footnotes of the 1960 Martineau (Classiques Garnier) edition, I have not encumbered my text or apparatus by reproducing them in *extenso*. Where minor changes seemed both authentic and of literary advantage, I incorporated them silently, sometimes using an alternative reading merely to color the English equivalent. (For example, when Julien after long pleading triumphs over Mme. de Rênal's renascent virtue, in Book I, Chapter 30, the text says his reward, obtained thus by art, "*ne fut plus qu'un plaisir.*" The Bucci copy substitutes for *plaisir* the word *triomphe*. Running the two notions of "pleasure" and "complacency" together, one gets an English equivalent like "gratification.") Where the variants were more extensive (these instances are all from the Bucci copy), I supplied them within the identifying boundaries of square brackets.

Ravel is conservative
maybe even considered
reactionary

tension due to this

Valenod

CONSERVATIVE
want to maintain
status quo

REACTIONARY
want to go back
to how things
were, idea of

"Golden Age"

Reactionary →
more extreme

MODERATES

LIBERAL
want progressive
change that's
incremental

Chelan has more conservative
religious views, but is very
tolerant toward liberals

RADICAL
want a revolution /
immediate change

Most functioning countries would have most people in the middle positions, France
had such a reactionary leader that the political spectrum got pushed to the
extremes. Louise Phillipe moves radicals toward socialism + liberals want more
voting + more of a constitutional monarchy. Conservatives strengthen their action
to keep things the same.

Contents of *The Red and the Black*

The Red and the Black:[1]
Chronicle of 1830

Editor's Note[2]

This work was about to appear when the great events of July came along to give all our thoughts a turn away from the free play of imagination. We have reason to suppose the following pages were written in 1827.

Book I

Truth, bitter truth.
—Danton[3]

Chapter 1

A SMALL TOWN

Put thousands together
Less bad,
But the cage less gay.
—Hobbes[4]

The little town of Verrières must be one of the prettiest in the Franche-Comté. Its white houses with their steep, red tile roofs spread across a hillside, the folds of which are outlined by clumps

---

1. "Chronicle" implies a historical document: 1830 is the year of the great bourgeois revolution (the July days) during which the Bourbon regime (which since the Restoration of 1815 had comprised two brief kings, Louis XVIII and Charles X) was expelled and replaced by the bourgeois monarchy of Louis-Philippe. Stendhal's novels are carefully placed in time; *Armance*, for instance, is a novel of the early reaction; RB (as the present novel will be called in these notes) of the moment of insurrectional imbalance; while *Lucien Leuwen* deals with the doldrum days after the liberal "triumph."
2. This little disclaimer, like the more elaborate ones prefixed to the *Life of Henry Brulard* (henceforth in these notes simply *Brulard*), is intentionally misleading; the novel was written in 1829–30, as Stendhal explicitly said on several occasions.
3. Danton was a revolutionary leader, guillotined by Robespierre in 1794; the epigraph is in his spirit but has not been located among his writings.
4. The quotation from Hobbes, given in English in the original, is imaginary, but the attribution invokes a hard-minded cynic.

7

of thrifty chestnut trees. The Doubs flows a couple of hundred feet below the town's fortifications, built long ago by the Spaniards and now fallen into ruins.[5]

Verrières is flanked on the north by a lofty mountain, one of the spurs of the Jura. As soon as it grows cold in October, the ragged peaks of Verra are covered with snow. A brook which drops from the mountain-passes through Verrières before falling into the Doubs provides power for a number of sawmills; it is a simple industry and yields a certain prosperity for a fair number of the inhabitants, who are peasants rather than bourgeois. Still, the sawmills are not what has made this little town rich. The manufacture of so-called Mulhouse cotton prints is responsible for the general affluence that, since the fall of Napoleon, has resulted in new façades for almost all the houses of Verrières.

Scarcely inside the town, one is stunned by the racket of a roaring machine, frightful in its appearance. Twenty ponderous hammers, falling with a crash which makes the street shudder, are lifted for each new stroke by the power of a water wheel. Every one of these hammers makes, every day, I don't know how many thousand nails. The workmen are pretty, fresh-faced girls; they slip little slivers of iron into place beneath the sledge hammers, which promptly transform them into nails. A primitive factory like this provides one of those sights that most surprise the traveler as he enters for the first time the mountains separating France from Switzerland. If, when he gets into Verrières, the traveler asks who owns that handsome nail factory which deafens everyone on the main street, he will be told, in drawling tones: *Oh, that? It's the mayor's.*

And now let the traveler pause a few minutes in this main street of Verrières which rises from the bank of the Doubs to the peak of the hill; it's a hundred to one that he will see somewhere along it a big man looking busy and important.

The minute he appears, every hat is lifted. His hair is gray, and he is dressed in gray. He wears the ribbons of several orders; his features are impressive, his nose aquiline, and, all in all, his appearance does not fail of a certain regularity: at first glance one even finds that it combines, with the dignity of the town mayor, that sort of ingratiation still possible in a man of forty-eight or fifty years.

5. The Franche-Comté is a province in eastern France bounded on the north by Lorraine and on the south by Switzerland. After a turbulent medieval career as a semi-independent faction of the duchy of Burgundy, it became, early in the sixteenth century, tributary to Spain, but was captured for France by Louis XIV about two hundred years later. There are several little towns called Verrières in the valley of the Doubs (pronounced Dou), a river running close to the northern border of the Franche-Comté; but Stendhal took nothing from their various realities. Verrières has a few marks of a diminished Grenoble, Stendhal's native town (which he said was for him like the memory of a violent indigestion), but in reality Grenoble is 150 miles to the south of the Doubs, and Verrières is largely imaginary.

But shortly the visiting Parisian is struck with a certain air of self-satisfaction, perhaps of sufficiency, combined with something limited and unimaginative. One feels in the end that the talent of this man is confined to exacting every penny owing to him, and paying his own debts at the last possible minute.

Such is the mayor of Verrières, M. de Rênal. Having walked solemnly down the street, he enters the town hall and disappears from the view of the traveler. But, a hundred feet further on, if our traveler continues his stroll, he will see a fine house and, through an iron grating next to the house, magnificent gardens. Beyond, the broken horizon formed by the Burgundian hills seems outlined on purpose to give delight to the eye. This view makes the traveler forget the pestilent atmosphere of petty financial worries in which he has been close to stifling.

He learns that the house belongs to M. de Rênal. Thanks to the profits from his great nail factory, the mayor of Verrières now owns this fine mansion of cut stone, which has just been completed. They say that his family is Spanish, ancient, and (at least, this is how the report runs) was established in the land long before the conquest of Louis XIV.

Since 1815 he has been ashamed of being in trade: 1815 made him mayor of Verrières.[6] The terrace walls holding up various parts of that magnificent garden which descends in stages to the Doubs are also the reward of M. de Rênal's dexterity in the iron trade.

Never expect to find in France those picturesque gardens that surround the handicraft towns of Germany, such as Leipzig, Frankfurt, and Nuremberg. In the Franche-Comté, the more walls one builds, the more one covers the land with rocks placed atop each other, the more one is entitled to the neighbors' respect. M. de Rênal's gardens, encumbered with walls, are still admired because he purchased, for their weight in gold, certain minute scraps of land which they cover. For example, that sawmill, so singularly situated on the bank of the Doubs, which struck you as you entered Verrières, and on which you read the name SOREL, written in gigantic letters on a board nailed to the rooftree—six years ago, it stood precisely where the wall for the fourth terrace of M. de Rênal's gardens is going up.

For all his pride, the mayor had a hard time with old Sorel, a tough, stubborn peasant; he had to pay over plenty of good gold louis to get the old man to move his sawmill elsewhere. As for the *public* sluice which powered the saw, M. de Rênal, by means of his

6. 1815, the date of Napoleon's defeat at Waterloo, marks a decisive victory, in Stendhal's mind, for reaction over rationality.

special influence at Paris, got it turned aside. This favor came his way after the elections of 182__.

He gave Sorel four acres further down the Doubs, for one. And though the new position was much better for his trade in pine planks, old Papa Sorel (as they call him since he has been rich) had the shrewdness to extract from his neighbor's impatience and *land owning mania* the sum of six thousand francs.

It is true that this deal was criticized by the local wiseacres. One Sunday about four years ago, M. de Rênal was returning from church in his official uniform when he saw in the distance old Sorel, surrounded by his three sons, and smiling upon him. That smile marked a fatal moment in the mayor's mind; ever since, he has been sure he could have got the land for less.

To stand well in Verrières the essential thing is to build plenty of walls, but not to adopt any of those plans brought from Italy by masons who each spring pass through the gorges of the Jura on their way to Paris.[7] Any such innovation would gain for the rash builder a permanent reputation as a *hothead*, and he would be lost forever in the judgment of those wise and moderate folk who make public opinion in the Franche-Comté.

As a matter of fact, these folk wield the most wearisome *despotism*: and this is why, for anyone who has lived in the great republic called Paris, life in the provinces is insupportable. The tyranny of public opinion—and what an opinion!—is as *stupid* in the small towns of France as it is in the United States of America.[8]

Chapter 2

A MAYOR

Importance! Well, sir, is it worth nothing at all? Respect from fools, awe from children, envy from the rich, and disdain from the wise.

—Barnave[9]

Happily for M. de Rênal's reputation as an administrator, an immense *containing wall* was required by the public terrace that runs along the hillside a hundred or so feet above the Doubs. This admirable site gives the town one of the finest views in France. But every springtime, rains used to silt up the promenade, cut little gul-

---

7. Stendhal as a freemason and a lover of Italy alludes here to an international traffic in liberal ideas.
8. For Stendhal, as for many Europeans, America represented a shopkeeper's civilization, the last word in mean and petty values.
9. Antoine Barnave (1761–1793) was, with Mirabeau, one of the great orators of the French Revolution; he came from Grenoble and had been known to members of Stendhal's family (see *Brulard*, Chap. 5).

[handwritten margin note: Sentence rewrite: The tyranny of Elvis – and what a chapter! – is as stupid in the small town of Sesame Street as it is in Telletubby land]

lies into it, and render it impassable. This difficulty, which was felt by all, put M. de Rênal under the happy necessity of immortalizing his administration with a wall twenty feet high and thirty or forty rods long.

The parapet of this wall, for which M. de Rênal had to make three special trips to Paris, since the previous minister of the interior was a declared enemy of the terrace at Verrières—this parapet now rises four feet above ground level. And, as if in defiance of all ministers past and present, it is even now being capped with a layer of cut stone.

How many times, my mind still dwelling on the balls of Paris which I left the night before, have I leaned on these great blocks of bluish-gray granite, gazing deep into the valley of the Doubs! Over yonder, on the left bank, wind five or six valleys, at the bottom of which the eye distinguishes little brooks. They leap from falls to falls and disappear into the Doubs. The sun is hot in these mountains; when it stands overhead, the meditative traveler is shaded on this terrace by magnificent plane trees. Their rapid growth and greenish-blue foliage are due to the fill the mayor has poured in behind his immense containing wall, for, in spite of opposition from the municipal counsel, he has widened the terrace by more than six feet (though he's a conservative and I'm a liberal, I give him credit); and this is why, in his opinion, and in the opinion of M. Valenod, fortunate director of the Verrières poorhouse, this terrace can fairly be compared with that of Saint-Germain-en-Laye.[1]

For my part, I can find only one thing to criticize on LOYALTY SQUARE; this official name is to be seen in fifteen or twenty places on marble plaques which earned an extra cross for M. de Rênal. What I would criticize on Loyalty Square is the barbaric way the administration clips and snips these vigorous plane trees back to the very quick. They stand there, with heads held low, shaved and flattened like the most vulgar of domestic vegetables, when they would like nothing better than to assume those splendid shapes they are free to take in England. But the mayor's will is supreme, and twice a year all the trees belonging to the town are pitilessly pruned back. The liberals of the district claim, but they exaggerate, that the official gardener wields a heavier hand since Vicar Maslon has started to engross for himself the products of the shearing.

This young ecclesiastic was sent down from Besançon some

---

1. The poorhouses, established by Louis XVI and abolished by Napoleon, were reintroduced by the Bourbons in 1815; a clever, unscrupulous man could make a good deal of money running one, both from the labor of the inmates and on public contracts for their maintenance. The terrace of St. Germain-en-Laye, a few miles from Paris, was built in the late seventeenth century; as it is a hundred feet wide and a mile and a half long, comparison with that at Verrières is a bit generous.

years ago to keep an eye on Abbé Chélan[2] and several other priests of the district. An old surgeon-major from the army of Italy, retired at Verrières, and who, according to the mayor, had been both a Jacobin and a Bonapartist, had the audacity one day to complain about the periodic mutilation of these fine trees.

—I'm very fond of shade, replied M. de Rênal, with that touch of disdain which is so appropriate when one is talking to a surgeon and a member of the Legion of Honor; I'm very fond indeed of the shade; I have *my* trees trimmed in order to give shade; I don't suppose a tree is really good for anything else, unless, like the useful walnut, *it yields a return.*

There now is the grand phrase that decides everything at Verrières: YIELD A RETURN. That phrase alone represents the mental life of three quarters of the townspeople.

Yielding a return decides everything in this little town which at first seemed so attractive to you. The stranger, as he arrives, is so entranced by the beauty of the cool, deep valleys that he imagines the natives are themselves responsive to beauty. It is true they talk, even to excess, of how beautiful their town is; they make a great to-do over it. But the reason is simply that the scenery attracts various outsiders, whose money enriches the hotel keepers and thus, through the tax-collecting machinery, *yields a return to the town.*

One fine autumn day M. de Rênal was strolling on Loyalty Square, with his wife by his side. Even as she listened to the grave discourse of her husband, Mme. de Rênal was watching anxiously the gyrations of three little boys. The eldest, who might be as much as eleven, kept wandering over to the parapet and seemed about to climb on top of it. A gentle voice then called the name of Adolphe, and the youngster turned back. Mme. de Rênal seemed a woman in her thirties, but still quite handsome.

—Oh, he'll regret it, this fine Paris gentleman, said M. de Rênal with indignation, his cheek a little paler than usual. I'm not without a certain number of friends at the castle. . . .[3]

But though I intend to speak of provincial life for two hundred pages, I shall not be so cruel as to inflict on you the full dimensions, and all the *clever turns*, of a provincial dialogue.

2. *Abbé*: This term is use loosely on the Continent especially in France, for almost any clergyman, whether beneficed or not, François I, by agreement with Pope Leo X, first got the right to appoint abbots *in commendam* (that is, provisionally, and without duties) to most of the abbeys in France. Many young gentlemen of very secular tastes (for example, the author of *Manon Lescaut*, Abbé Prévost) took a short course in theology, assumed a modified tonsure, wore a special violet coat, practiced a sort of celibacy, and were known as abbés. These completely secularized abbés are not to be found in the nineteenth century; but the word continued to be used loosely of anyone who had a sort of connection with the church (a tutor, a theological student), as well as of regular clergymen.
3. Charles X and his court lived at the Château de St. Cloud, and were thus referred to familiarly as the castle.

This fine Paris gentleman, so distressing to the mayor of Verrières, was no other than M. Appert, who two days before had
found means to get into the prison and the poorhouse of Verrières,
and even into the free hospital run by the mayor and the principal
gentry of the district.[4]

—But after all, said Mme. de Rênal timidly, what harm can this
Paris gentleman do, since you look after the welfare of the poor
with the most scrupulous honesty?

—He comes only to find fault, and afterward he'll have articles in
all the liberal newspapers.

—But you never read them, my dear.

—People will talk to us about these Jacobin articles; the whole
business distracts us, and *prevents us from doing good*.[5] Personally,
I'll never forgive that priest.

Chapter 3

THE WELFARE OF THE POOR

> A priest who is virtuous and no intriguer is a blessing upon his vil-
> lage.
>
> —Fleury[6]

Though eighty years old, the priest of Verrières, thanks to the
sharp air of these mountains, had a character and a constitution of
iron; he also had the right to visit, at any time of day, the prison,
the hospital, and even the poorhouse. M. Appert, who had been
commended to the priest from Paris, had been prudent enough to
arrive in a small town eaten up with curiosity at six in the morning.
He went directly to the presbytery.

As he looked over the letter written to him by the Marquis de La
Mole, peer of France and the richest landowner of the province,
the priest, M. Chélan, grew pensive.

—I have grown old here, and am well loved, he murmured at
last; they would never dare! And he turned abruptly on the gentleman from Paris, with eyes in which, despite old age, there glittered
that sacred fire which accompanies the pleasure of performing a
fine deed that is at the same time a bit dangerous.

—Come with me, sir, and remember, in the presence of the jailer

---

4. Benjamin Appert (1797–1847) was a philanthropist and prison reformer of the day. He
   visited Antoine Berthet (whose story provided one of the models for Julien Sorel's) during his trial at Besançon, to make sure he was properly defended.
5. Historic [Stendhal's note].
6. Fleury was an early eighteenth-century cardinal and statesman whom Stendhal uses
   here as an example of the authentic, old, uncorrupted clergy. His *Ecclesiastical History*
   was placed on the Index as tainted with Gallicanism, that is, the doctrine that would
   limit papal authority (see *Brulard*, Chap. 10).

and above all of the poorhouse wardens, you must express no opinion about the things we shall see. M. Appert understood that he
had to do with a man of feeling: he accompanied the old priest, visited the prison, the clinic, the poorhouse, asked plenty of questions, and in spite of some very strange answers, gave not the
slightest sign of disapproval.

The visit lasted for several hours. The priest asked M. Appert to
dinner, but he claimed to have letters to write; he did not want to
compromise any further his generous friend. About three o'clock,
they returned to complete their inspection of the poorhouse, and
then went on to the prison. In the doorway there they found the
jailer, a kind of giant six feet tall and bowlegged; his coarse features
had become hideous with terror.

—Ah, sir, said he to the priest as soon as he saw him, this gentleman with you here, isn't he M. Appert?

—Why do you ask? said the priest.

—Because I received just yesterday the most precise orders, sent
by a police officer from the prefect himself, and he had to gallop all
night long, *not* to let M. Appert into the jail.

—Well, Monsieur Noiroud, said the priest, I can assure you that
this visitor with me is in fact M. Appert. Now do you remember
that I am free to enter the jail at any hour of the day or night, and
to bring with me anyone I want?

—Yes, your reverence, grumbled the jailer, lowering his head like
a bulldog yielding reluctantly to the menace of a club. Only, your
reverence, I've got a wife and children; if there's a complaint, I'm
out; and I've got nothing to live on but this job.

—I should be just as unhappy to lose my own, said the priest,
with feeling.

—What a difference! the jailer replied quickly; you, your reverence, everyone knows you've got eight hundred florins[7] a year of
your own, free and clear. . . .

Such were the events that, embroidered and distorted in twenty
different ways, had been stirring up over the past two days all the
hateful passions of the little town of Verrières. At this very moment,
they were serving as the theme of M. de Rênal's conversation with
his wife. He had gone that morning, accompanied by M. Valenod,
director of the poorhouse, to call on the priest and express furious
disapproval of what he had done. M. Chélan had no protector; he
bore by himself the full brunt of their words.

—Well, gentlemen! I shall be the third eighty-year-old priest in
this district to be deprived of my position. I've been here for fifty-six

---

7. Eight hundred florins (*livres*) would be worth approximately $5,300, or 4,000 euros to-
day.

years; I have baptized nearly every person in this town, which was nothing but a crossroads when I came here. Every day I marry young people whose grandparents I married in the old days. Verrières is my family; but [fear of having to leave it will never make me traffic with my conscience or grant another person authority over my actions:] when I saw that visitor, I said to myself: "This man from Paris may really be a liberal, there are only too many of them; but what harm can lie do our paupers and prisoners?"

The outcries of M. de Rênal, and especially of M. de Valenod, the poorhouse director, became even louder:

—All right, gentlemen, cried the old priest in a quavering voice, go on, have me thrown out. I'll live here just the same. Forty-eight years ago, it's well known, I inherited an estate that brings in eight hundred florins: I'll live on that. I haven't used my position to graft, gentlemen, and maybe that's why I'm not terrified at the prospect of losing it.

Though M. de Rênal was extremely considerate of his wife [who had a very rich aunt:], he did not know how to answer her timidly repeated question, "But what harm could that man from Paris possibly do the prisoners?" and was on the point of losing his temper when she suddenly cried aloud. The second of her sons had just climbed up on the parapet and was running along it, though the drop to a vineyard on the other side was more than twenty feet. Fear of startling her son and making him fall kept Mme. de Rênal from calling out to him. Finally the boy, laughing at his own adroitness and looking to his mother, saw her pallor, leaped to the ground, and ran to her. He was thoroughly scolded.

This little episode changed the course of the conversation.

—I've really decided to take on young Sorel, the carpenter's son, said M. de Rênal; he will look after the children, who are starting to be too much for us. He's a young priest, or just as good as, he's clever at Latin and will keep the children at their lessons, for the priest says he's strong willed. I'll let him have three hundred francs[8] and his board. On the score of morality. I had some doubts; for he was the protégé of that old surgeon, member of the Legion of Honor, who came to live with the Sorels, under pretext of being their cousin. Down deep that man may very well have been nothing but a secret agent of the liberals; of course, he said the mountain air was good for his asthma, but there's no proving that. He was with *Buonaparté*[9] on all his Italian campaigns and, they even say, once, long ago, signed something against the empire. This liberal taught Latin to young Sorel and left him some of his books. Ordi-

8. Three hundred francs would be worth approximately $2,000, or 1,500 euros today.
9. In giving Napoleon his Corsican, semi-Italian name, M. de Rênal is trying to repudiate him as a foreigner.

narily, I would never consider putting a carpenter's son in charge of our children. But the priest told me, just the night before that last quarrel of ours, that young Sorel has been studying theology for the last three years, hoping to enter the seminary; so he isn't a liberal, and he does know Latin.

—This arrangement works out in several different ways, M. de Rênal went on, glancing at his wife with the air of a diplomat; that fellow Valenod is proud of the two Norman horses he's just bought for his carriage. But he doesn't have a tutor for his children.

—He might very well get this one away from us.

—Then you approve of my plans? said M. de Rênal, thanking his wife with a quick smile for the excellent insight she had just had. Fine, then it's all decided.

—Good Lord, my dear! you're so sudden in your decisions!

—That's because I have a bit of character, I do, and I let that priest see the edge of it. Let's not fool ourselves, we're surrounded by liberals here. All these cotton merchants are envious of me, I'm certain of it; two or three of them are getting really rich. All right, I want them to see the children of M. de Rênal passing by, going for a walk *with their tutor*. That will make an impression. My grandfather often told us that in his youth he had a tutor. He may very well cost me a hundred crowns,[1] but it's simply one of those expenses that are necessary to keep up a social position.

This sudden decision left Mme, de Rênal quite pensive. She was a tall woman, and well proportioned, who had been the beauty of the countryside, as they say in this mountainous district. She had a certain air of simplicity, and the spring of youth in her step. In the mind of a Parisian, this simple elegance, full of innocence and liveliness, might even have roused notions of sensual pleasure. If she had realized that she was attractive in this way, Mme. de Rênal would have been deeply ashamed. Neither coquetry nor affectation had ever touched her heart. M. Valenod, the rich poorhouse director, was reputed to have sighed for her, but without success, a story that lent particular luster to her virtue; for this M. Valenod was a bluff young man, strongly built, highly colored, with big black whiskers—one of those gross, bold, loud fellows who in the provinces are known as handsome men.

Mme. de Rênal, who was quite timid and apparently of retiring character, was particularly distressed by M. Valenod's continual abrupt motion and bursts of noise. Her dislike of everything that in Verrières is considered fun had caused her to be thought a snob. She never gave the matter a thought, but was very glad to find the

---

1. One hundred crowns (*écus*)—six hundred francs—would be worth approximately $4,000, or 3,000 euros today.

townspeople calling upon her less often. We shall not hide the fact that *those* ladies thought her a fool because she often overlooked occasions to get herself fancy hats from Paris or Besançon. Provided people left her free to wander alone in her fine garden, she never thought herself ill used.

She was an innocent soul who had never risen even to the point of passing judgment on her husband and admitting that she was bored. Without saying so directly, she supposed things were always about this way between husbands and wives. She was particularly fond of M. de Rênal when he talked about his plans for their children, one of whom was to be a soldier, the second a magistrate, and the third a churchman. In a word, she found M. de Rênal a good deal less boring than most men of her acquaintance.

This conjugal opinion was perfectly sensible. The mayor of Verrières owed his reputation for wit and social poise to a half dozen jokes he had inherited from an uncle [and brought out on state occasions]. Old Captain de Rênal had served before the Revolution in the Duc d'Orleans' infantry regiment, and when he visited Paris used to be admitted to the salons of the prince. There he had observed Mme. de Montesson, the famous Mme. de Genlis, and M. Ducrest, the redesigner of the Palais Royal. These figures turned up, all too often, in the anecdotes of M. de Rênal. But gradually the recollection of things so hard to put into exact words had become a chore for him, and for some time now it was only for special events that he trotted out his anecdotes concerning the House of Orleans. As he was generally a very polite man, except when the talk turned to money, he passed with good reason for the most aristocratic personage in Verrières.

Chapter 4

FATHER AND SON

And is it my fault
If that's how things are?
            —Machiavelli[2]

—My wife is really pretty shrewd, said the mayor of Verrières to himself, about six o'clock the next morning, as he strolled down to old Sorel's sawmill. Though I saw it was important to keep up our social position, I hadn't really considered that if I don't pick up this little Abbé Sorel—they say he knows Latin like an angel—the director of the poorhouse, who's always up to something, might get the

2. The quotation is not word for word anywhere in Machiavelli, but the spirit behind it is authentic.

same idea and snatch him away from me. And wouldn't he be complacent, talking to me about his children's tutor! . . . Once he's in my house, will this tutor wear a cassock, I wonder?

M. de Rênal was working over this question when he saw in the distance a peasant, nearly six feet tall, who seemed to have been busy since the first light of dawn measuring some tree trunks which had been laid alongside the Doubs on the towpath. The peasant was not particularly pleased to see the mayor approach; for his tree trunks blocked the path, and were laid there illegally.

Old Sorel, for it was he, was much surprised and even more pleased with the unusual proposal M. de Rênal made regarding his son Julien. But all the same he listened to it with that air of peevish discontent and indifference which these mountaineers know so well how to cast over their shrewdness. Slaves in the days of the Spanish dominition, they still retain in their features this trait of the Egyptian fellah.

At first Sorel replied by reciting at length all the formulas of polite conversation he knew by heart. While he was repeating these empty phrases with an awkward smile which emphasized the air of falsity and almost of trickery natural to his features, the old peasant's quick wit was trying to imagine why such an important man would want to take into his house that good-for-nothing son. He had no use for Julien, yet it was for him that M. de Rênal was offering the unexpected salary of three hundred francs a year, plus board and even a clothing allowance. This last request, which old Sorel had had the genius to put forward at the very beginning, had been granted at once by M. de Rênal.

This demand put M. de Rênal on the alert. He thought: Since Sorel is not overwhelmed with joy at my proposal, as he ought to be, it's clear that he has been receiving offers from some other quarter; and where could they come from, if not from Valenod? In vain did the mayor press old Sorel to reach a decision then and there; the peasant refused shrewdly and stubbornly, saying he had to talk it over with his son—as if, in the provinces, a rich father ever consulted a poor son except for form's sake.

A sawmill consists of a shed beside a stream. The roof rests on a frame, supported by four heavy wooden columns. In the middle of the shed, rising to the height of eight or ten feet, is the saw, going steadily up and down, while a simple mechanism pushes against it a piece of wood. A water wheel turned by the stream powers this double mechanism—the saw that goes up and down, the carriage that moves the wood gradually against the saw, so that it can be split into planks.

Approaching his mill, old Sorel bellowed for Julien; nobody answered. He saw only his elder sons, a couple of giants who were working with heavy axes, squaring off some pine trunks they were preparing for the saw. They were intent on following exactly the black lines drawn on the wood; at every blow of their axes huge chips flew through the air. They did not hear their father's voice. He turned toward the shed, entered, and looked vainly for Julien at the station where he should have been, beside the saw. At last he saw him, five or six feet higher, astraddle one of the roof beams. Instead of keeping close watch on the working of the machine, Julien was reading a book. Nothing could have been more disagreeable to old Sorel; he might perhaps have pardoned Julien his slender figure, unsuited to hard labor and unlike his elder brothers'; but this passion for reading was hateful to him, as he didn't know how to read himself.

He called Julien, vainly, two or three times. The young man's absorption in his book, much more than the roar of the saw, prevented him from hearing his father's terrible voice. Finally, despite his age, the old man jumped lightly onto the tree trunk which was being sawed and from there to the crossbeam which helped support the roof. A violent blow sent Julien's book flying into the stream; a second cuff, just as heavy, fell on his head and caused him to lose his balance. He was about to fall a distance of ten or fifteen feet into the middle of the machinery, which would have ground him up, but his father caught him, with his left hand, just as he was falling:

—All right, loafer! still reading your damn books while you're supposed to be watching the saw? Read them after work, when you're wasting your time with the priest, why don't you?

Julien, though stunned by the force of the blow and bleeding slightly, went to his proper station alongside the saw. His eyes were full of tears, less from physical pain than for the loss of his book, which he worshipped.

—Get down from there, animal, I want to talk to you.

The roar of the machinery still prevented Julien from hearing this order. His father, who had returned to the floor and didn't want to bother climbing up on the machinery again, took a long pole used for knocking down nuts and struck him across the shoulder with it. Scarcely was Julien on the ground when his father, driving his son before him, set out for the house. God knows what he's going to do to me! thought the young man. As they passed the stream into which his book had fallen, he glanced, sadly aside; it had been his favorite book, the _Mémorial de Sainte-Hélène_.[3]

He walked on, with flushed face and lowered eyes. He was a

3. Emanuel Las Cases (1766–1842) had been an émigré in the early years of the Revolution but joined Napoleon just in time to accompany him in his final exile on St. Helena. He wrote there the long and richly rhetorical _Mémorial_, which is a keystone of the Napoleonic legend.

slightly built young man, eighteen or nineteen years old, feeble in appearance, with irregular but delicate features, and an aquiline nose. Big dark eyes, which in repose expressed fire and reflection, were filled at this moment with the most ferocious hatred. Dark brown hair growing low over his forehead gave him, in moments of anger, an ugly look. Among the innumerable varieties of human expression, there is perhaps no other that is so striking. A slender and finely molded figure suggested a man of more nerve than strength. The pensive air and extreme pallor which had marked him from early youth convinced his father that he would not live long, or would prove merely a drag on the household. An object of scorn to the entire family, he hated his brothers and his father; and in the Sunday games on the public square he was invariably beaten.

About a year ago his handsome features had started to give him a few friendly voices among the girls. Scorned by everyone as a weakling, Julien had worshipped that old surgeon-major who one day dared to address the mayor on the subject of the plane trees.

This surgeon sometimes paid old Sorel a day's wages for his son's time, and then taught him Latin and history, that is, all the history he knew, the Italian campaign of 1796. When he died he left Julien his cross of the Legion of Honor, the arrears of his half pension, and thirty or forty volumes, the most precious of which had just been pitched into the *public water supply*, diverted by the mayor's influence.

Scarcely was he in the house when Julien felt his shoulder gripped by his father's powerful hand; he shuddered, expecting more blows.

—Answer me now, and no lies! The old peasant's voice grated in his ears, while his heavy hand spun Julien about like a child playing with a tin soldier. Raising his great black eyes filled with tears, Julien stared into the little, gray, suspicious eyes of the old sawyer, who seemed intent on reading the very depths of his soul.

Chapter 5

HAGGLING

Cunctando restituit rem.
(By stalling he gained his point.)
—Ennius?[4]

—Answer me now, and no lies, if you can manage that, you little hound; how do you know Mme. de Rênal, when did you talk with her?

---

4. Cato the Elder (234–149 B.C.E.) quotes these line from the Roman poet Ennius (239–169 B.C.E.), whose work survives largely in quoted snippets like this.

—I've never talked with her, said Julien, the only time I've seen the lady is at church.

—But you've ogled her there, you shameless scoundrel?

—Never! You know that at church I see only God, said Julien with a little hypocritical look which he thought quite the best way to prevent another cuff.

—Just the same, there's something behind all this, said the surly peasant, and paused a moment; but I'll never get anything out of you, you confounded hypocrite. The fact is, I'm going to get rid of you, and my saw will run all the better for it. You've worked the priest, or somebody else, into fixing you up with a soft job. Go get your things together, and I'll take you to M. de Rênal's house, where you will be a tutor for his children.

—And what will I be paid?

—Food, clothing, and three hundred francs wages.

—I don't want to be a servant.

—Stupid animal, who's talking about being a servant? You suppose I'd want my son to be a servant?

—Well then, whom will I eat with?

This question upset old Sorel; he felt that if he said anything he might compromise himself; so he got angry with Julien, poured insults on him, accused him of softness, and left him to go talk it over with his other sons.

Julien saw them soon after, leaning on their axes, and holding a family council. He watched them for a long time, but then, seeing he could not guess what was going on, went around to the other side of the saw, so that they shouldn't come on him unexpectedly. He wanted to think over this unforeseen news, which was about to change his destiny, but found himself incapable of prudence; his imagination was wholly occupied in picturing what he would find in M. de Rênal's fine house.

Still, I must give it all up, said he to himself, rather than sink to eating with the household servants. My father will try to push me into it; I'd sooner die. I've saved fifteen francs and eight sous.[5] I can run away tonight; in two days, using the back roads where I won't meet with policemen, I'll be at Besançon; there I'll enlist, and if necessary, I'll cross over into Switzerland. But no future there, no more moving up in the world, no more chance at the priesthood, that leads to all good things.

This horror of eating with servants was by no means natural to Julien; in order to make his fortune he would have done other things much more painful in themselves. He had picked up this notion from Rousseau's *Confessions*. It was the only book his imagina-

---

5. Fifteen francs and eight sous would be worth approximately $113, or 85 euros today.

tion had made use of in constructing a picture of the social world. A collection of bulletins from the Grande Armée and the *Mémorial de Sainte-Hélène* filled out his Koran.[6] He would have gone to the stake for these three works. He never believed in any other. Taking his hint from the old surgeon-major, he looked upon all the other books in the world as lies written by rascals to gain advancement.

With a fiery spirit Julien united one of those astounding memories which are so often joined to complete stupidity. Seeing that his future depended on the old priest Chélan, he had won him over by learning the whole New Testament verbatim in Latin; he also knew M. de Maistre's book *On the Pope*,[7] and believed as little of one as of the other.

As if by common consent, Sorel and his son avoided talking to one another for the rest of the day. When evening fell, Julien went off to take his lessons in theology from the priest, but he thought best to tell him nothing at all of the strange proposal made to his father. Perhaps it's a trap, said he to himself; I'd better pretend to have forgotten it.

Early next morning, M. de Rênal sent for old Sorel, who, after delaying an hour or two, finally arrived and immediately started to make a hundred different excuses all mixed up with as many compliments. After working his way through all sorts of objections, Sorel was given to understand that his son would eat with the master and mistress of the house, and that when there was company, he would eat alone in a separate room with the children. The more he observed the mayor's impatience, the more Sorel was disposed to raise difficulties, and besides he was mistrustful and surprised; he asked to see the room where his son would sleep. It was a large room, finely furnished, into which men were already carrying the beds of the three children.

This incident was a gleam of light for the old peasant; at once he asked boldly to see the suit of clothes that would be his son's. M. de Rênal opened his desk drawer and took out a hundred francs.

—With this sum your son can go to M. Durand the tailor and get a complete black suit.

6. The Koran used to suggest a pagan creed. Stendhal himself used to sharpen his style for the *Rouge* by reading the Code Napoleon. His admirations for the laconic precision of an army bulletin, for the psychological subtlety and truth-at-the-expense-of-meanness of Rousseau, and for the noble resignation of Las Cases' *Mémorial*, make up for Julien a literary trinity.
7. Joseph de Maistre (1753–1821), one of the anti-philosophical Catholic reactionaries inspired by opposition to Napoleon, published his two-volume treatise *On the Pope* in 1819; it took the highest conceivable view of papal absolutism. Stendhal's own early education (described in *Brulard*, Chap. 10) consisted in good part of memorizing certain Latin texts without any real understanding of what they said or even of the language in which they were written. Among other things, he tells us he learned the Latin New Testament by heart (*Brulard*, Chap. 20).

—And even if I take him home again, said the peasant, who had suddenly forgotten all his obsequious expressions, he'll still keep the black suit?

—Of course.

—All right, said Sorel, in drawling tones, then there's only one thing left to settle between us, how much money will you give him?

—What's this? cried M. de Rênal in a rage, we agreed on that yesterday. I'm giving three hundred francs. In my opinion, it's a great deal of money and maybe even too much.

—That was your offer, I won't deny it at all, said old Sorel, talking still more slowly; and then, by a stroke of genius which will astonish those who do not know the peasants of the Franche-Comté, he looked straight at M. de Rênal and said: *We can do better elsewhere.*

At these words the mayor appeared stunned. But he recovered, and after a masterly conversation of two long hours, during which not a word was said without its purpose, peasant shrewdness won out over rich-man's shrewdness, which is not needed for survival. All the various clauses that would control Julien's future existence were settled; not only was his pay set at four hundred francs but he was to receive it in advance, on the first of each month.

—All right, I'll send him thirty-five francs, said M. de Rênal.

—Just to make a round figure, a rich and generous gentleman like our mayor, said the peasant in a coaxing tone, will surely make it thirty-six francs.[8]

—Yes, said M. de Rênal, but that's the end.

At that moment his rage gave him the tone of a decisive man. The peasant saw there was no more progress to be made; and then M. de Rênal, in his turn, began to forge ahead. He absolutely refused to give the first month's thirty-six francs to old Sorel, who was very anxious to bring them to his son. It occurred to M. de Rênal that he might have to describe to his wife the part he had played in all this bargaining.

—Give me back those hundred francs I gave you, he said crossly. M. Durand owes me some money. I'll go with your son to pick up the black suit.

After this vigorous gesture old Sorel wisely fell back upon his formulas of respect; they took up a good quarter of an hour. Finally, seeing that there was really nothing more to be gained, he took his leave. His final compliment finished with these words:

—I shall send my son up to the manor house.

This was the term the mayor's subordinates applied to his house when they wanted to flatter him.

---

8. If one paid in *écus* (crowns) worth six francs apiece, thirty-six francs would make a round sum.

When he got back to his mill, Sorel looked about vainly for his son. Uneasy about what might happen, Julien had slipped out in the middle of the night to find a safe place for his books and his cross of the Legion of Honor. He had taken everything to a young lumberman, his friend, a man named Fouque who lived up on the big mountain that stands over Verrières.

After his return: —God knows, said his father, if a lazy loafer like you will ever have the grace to repay me all the money. I've been laying out for your food all these years. Pack up your rubbish and get over to the mayor's.

Surprised that he hadn't been beaten, Julien hastened to leave. But scarcely out of sight of his terrible father, he slackened his pace. He thought it might be useful to his hypocrisy to stop off in the church.

The word surprises you? Before reaching this horrible expression, the soul of the young peasant had passed through a long development.

When he was a mere child he had seen certain dragoons of the 6th, with their long white cloaks and helmets decked with long black horsehair, on their way back from Italy. Julien watched them tie their horses to the grilled windows of his father's house, and grew wild to be a soldier. Later, he listened with passionate excitement to those stories about the battles at the bridge of Lodi, of Arcola and Rivoli, which he heard from the old surgeon-major.[9] He noted the pride and enthusiasm with which the old man kept glancing at his cross.

But when Julien was just fourteen, they began to build at Verrières a church which could fairly be called magnificent for such a small town. There were four columns of marble, in particular, the sight of which struck Julien; they became famous throughout the countryside, by reason of the deadly feud they caused between the justice of the peace and the young vicar, sent from Besançon, who was thought to be a spy for the congregation.[1] The justice of the peace was sure to lose his post, or such at least was the general impression. Hadn't he dared to quarrel with a priest who every two weeks went to Besançon, where, people said, he visited the bishop himself?

9. Lodi (May 10, 1796), Arcola (November 15–17, 1796), and Rivoli (June 14, 1797) were classic battles of Napoleonic strategy.
1. A congregation is any of a variety of pious, voluntary organizations that existed after the seventeenth century in France. They might include laymen as well as ecclesiastics, and they had to have the approval of the diocesan bishop and sometimes of the pope. They ordinarily grew up around a religious figure (the Virgin), symbol (the Sacred Heart), or order (the Jesuits). Stendhal's imagination regarding clerics may have attributed to them a sinister power they did not always possess; yet there can be no doubt that in small provincial towns they wielded great influence.

Meanwhile, the justice of the peace, who was father of a numerous family, rendered a number of decisions that seemed unjust; they all seemed to bear against townspeople who read the *Constitutionnel*.[2] The party of virtue was triumphant. The fines never amounted, it's true, to more than three or five francs; but one of these petty mulcts fell on a nailmaker, Julien's godfather. In his rage this man declared:—What a change! And to think that for twenty years and more everybody thought that justice was an honest man! The surgeon-major, Julien's friend, was dead.

Quite suddenly Julien stopped talking of Napoleon; he declared that he wanted to become a priest, and he was constantly observed about his father's sawmill, memorizing a Latin Bible the priest had loaned him. That good old man, amazed at his progress, devoted whole evenings to teaching him theology. Julien never displayed before him any but pious sentiments. Who could have guessed that that girlish face, so pale and soft, concealed an unshakable resolution to die a thousand deaths rather than fail to make his fortune!

For Julien, making his fortune meant, first of all, getting out of Verrières; he loathed his home town. Everything he saw there chilled his imagination.

Ever since he was a boy, he had had moments of secret exultation. He dreamed with joy of one day being introduced to the pretty women of Paris; he would, of course, attract their admiration with some brilliant action. Why should he not win the love of one of them, just as Bonaparte, when still young, had been loved by the brilliant Mme. de Beauharnais?[3] Over the past several years, Julien had scarcely passed an hour without reminding himself that Bonaparte, starting as a poor and obscure lieutenant, had made himself master of the world, with his sword alone. This idea consoled him amid his sorrows, which he considered great, and multiplied his joys when he had any.

The building of the church and the sentences imposed by the justice of the peace illuminated him, as by a flash; an idea that came to him rendered him for several weeks almost mad, and finally took possession of him with the irresistible power which his first-born idea exercises over every passionate soul.

—When Bonaparte made his name, France was in danger of invasion; the soldier's trade was necessary and fashionable. Nowadays, there are forty-year-old priests who draw salaries of a hundred

---

2. Though not avowedly liberal itself, the *Constitutionnel* became a rallying point after the Restoration for whatever liberal opinion the Bourbons permitted.
3. Mme. de Beauharnais (1763–1814) later became the Empress Josephine; it would seem she was not at first much impressed with the scrawny, penniless, provincial young man who was destined to make himself emperor—and her an empress.

thousand francs,[4] three times as much as the famous division commanders of Napoleon. They need subordinates. Think of that justice of the peace, once a good judge and an honest man, and now grown old, who covers himself with disgrace, for fear of displeasing a young vicar thirty years old. The thing to be is a priest.

Once, in the midst of his new piety, when Julien had been studying theology for two years, he was betrayed by a sudden outburst of the passion that was devouring him inwardly. It was at M. Chélan's, at a dinner of clerics to whom the old priest had presented him as a prodigious scholar: he found himself babbling frantic praises of Napoleon. He strapped his right arm to his chest, pretended that he had dislocated it while shifting a tree trunk, and carried it in this painful position for two months. After this judicial penalty, he pardoned himself. Such was the young man, nineteen years old, but so frail that he would never have been thought more than seventeen, who entered the splendid church of Verrières with a little parcel under his arm.

He found the church dark and deserted. Because of a festival, all the windows of the building had been covered with scarlet cloth. As a result, the sun struck through in shafts of brilliant light, creating an impressive and religious atmosphere. Julien shivered. All alone in the church, he took a seat in the finest pew. It bore M. de Rênal's coat of arms.

On the lectern, Julien noted a scrap of printed paper, set out there as if for him to read. He glanced at it and saw:

> Details of the execution and last moments of Louis Jenrel, executed at Besançon, on the ____

The paper was torn. On the other side were the first words of a line: *The first step. . . .*

Who could have left this paper here? thought Julien. Poor fellow, he added with a sigh, his name has the same ending as mine. . . . He crumpled up the paper.

As he went out, Julien imagined he saw a pool of blood by the baptismal font; it was merely some holy water which had been spilled; the red curtains covering the windows made it look like blood.

At last, Julien grew ashamed of his secret terrors.

—Am I going to be a coward? he said. *To arms!*

This phrase, so often recurring in the battle stories of the old surgeon, was a heroic word for Julien. He rose and walked swiftly toward the house of M. de Rênal.

---

4. One hundred thousand francs would be worth approximately $665,500 or 500,000 euros today.

In spite of his fine resolutions, as soon as he was within twenty feet of it he was overcome by timidity. The iron gate was open, it seemed magnificent to him, and he had to go inside it.

Julien was not the only person deeply disturbed by his arrival in this house. Mme. de Rênal's modesty was much distressed by the idea of this outsider, whose work would continually bring him between her and her children. She was used to having her children sleep in the same room with her. That morning tears had flowed freely when she saw their little beds carried off into the room set aside for the new tutor. She had implored her husband in vain that the bed of Stanislas-Xavier, her youngest, might be returned to her room.

Feminine delicacy was carried to an extreme in Mme. de Rênal. She had formed in her mind a most disagreeable picture of a gross and slovenly creature, whose duty it would be to scold her children simply because he knew Latin, a barbarous language on account of which her children would be whipped.

Chapter 6

BOREDOM

What I am I no longer know,
Nor what I'm doing.
—Mozart (*Figaro*)[5]

With the swift grace that was natural to her when unconstrained by the sight of men, Mme. de Rênal was going out the living room door that gave onto the garden when she noticed by the main entry a young peasant, scarcely more than a child, very pale and showing traces of recent tears. He wore a white shirt and was carrying under his arm a cotton jacket of violet color, neatly folded.

The complexion of this little peasant was so pale, his eyes so soft, that Mme. de Rênal's somewhat romantic disposition took him at first for a girl in disguise who might have come to beg some favor of the mayor. She felt an impulse of pity for this poor creature, hesitating in the doorway, and apparently fearful of lifting her hand to ring the bell. Diverted a moment from her own bitter distress over the arrival of the tutor, Mme. de Rênal came closer. Julien, his eyes fixed on the door, did not notice her approach; he started when a gentle voice, speaking close beside his ear, said:

—What do you want here, my child?

Julien turned suddenly, and was so struck by the kind glance of

---

5. The phrase is from Cherubino's aria in Act I and describes young Cherubino's intense erotic fantasies.

Mme de Rênal that he forgot part of his timidity. Then, astonished
by her beauty, he forgot everything else, including his purpose in
coming. Mme. de Rênal had repeated her question.

—I've come to be the tutor, madame, he said at last, covered with
shame for the tears he was trying his best to efface.

Mme. de Rênal was overcome with surprise; they stood quite
close and looked at one another. Julien had never seen anyone so
well dressed, nor a woman with so fine a complexion, who spoke to
him so gently. Mme. de Rênal looked at the great tears standing on
the cheeks, once so pale and now so pink, of the young peasant.
Then she began to laugh, with all the absurd gaiety of a young girl,
laughing at herself and yet unable to think why she felt so happy.
So this was the tutor whom she had imagined as an unwashed,
slovenly priest who would scold her children and whip them!

—Well, sir, she said at last, so you know Latin?

This word "sir" surprised Julien so much that he hesitated for an
instant.

—Yes, madame, he said timidly.

Mme. de Rênal was so happy, she dared to say to Julien:

—You won't scold the poor children too much?

—Scold them? said Julien, in astonishment. I scold them? Why
should I?

—Then, sir, she added after a short silence, and in a voice that
grew every instant more emotional, then you will be kind with
them, you promise it?

Hearing himself called "sir" again, in perfect seriousness, and by
a finely dressed lady, was altogether beyond Julien's expectations; in
none of the splendid fantasies of his youth had he ever imagined
that a lady of fashion would deign to say a word to him before he
had a fancy uniform. Mme. de Rênal, for her part, was completely
deceived by the fresh complexion, the great dark eyes of Julien, and
his fine head of hair which curled a little more than usual, because,
in order to cool off, he had just ducked his head in the public fountain. To her great joy, she discovered the timid manner of a young
girl in this terrible tutor whose fierce look and surly manners had
seemed to threaten such terrors for her children. For Mme. de Rênal's placid disposition, the contrast between her fears and what
she actually saw was a great event. At last she recovered from her
surprise. She was astonished to find herself at the doorstep of her
own house, with this young man, almost in his shirt, and standing
so close to him.

—Come in, sir, said she, in some embarrassment.

In her whole lifetime a completely pleasant experience had never
struck Mme. de Rênal so profoundly; never had such a gracious

event succeeded such disturbing fears. So her pretty little children, over whom she had watched so carefully, were not to pass into the dirty hands of a grumbling old priest. Scarcely were they in the hallway when she turned back toward Julien, who was following her timidly. His look of astonishment at such a beautiful house was one more charm in the eyes of Mme. de Rênal. She could hardly believe her eyes; it seemed to her particularly strange that the tutor was not dressed in black.

—But is it true, sir, she said, stopping again and mortally afraid of having made a mistake, for she was so happy in her illusions, is it true that you know Latin?

These words struck at Julien's pride, and dispelled the charm in which he had been floating for the past quarter hour.

—Yes, indeed, madame, said he, seeking to assume a chilly tone; I know Latin as well as the priest does, and, as he is occasionally kind enough to say himself, perhaps even better.

Mme. de Rênal noted that Julien had a particularly cruel expression; he had stopped two paces from her. She moved toward him and said softly.

—But these first days, you will promise not to beat my children, even if they don't know their lessons?

This gentle, almost supplicating tone on the part of a fine lady suddenly caused Julien to forget his reputation as a Latinist. Mme. de Rênal stood very close to him; he breathed the perfumed scent of a woman in light summer clothing—an astonishing thing for a young peasant. Julien blushed deeply, sighed, and said faintly:

—Have no fear, madame, you shall be obeyed in everything.

Only at this moment, when her fears on behalf of her children were completely relieved, did Mme. de Rênal notice that Julien was extremely handsome. The almost feminine delicacy of his features and his awkward air seemed in no way ridiculous to a woman who was herself extremely timid. The blunt, masculine air commonly considered necessary to male beauty would have frightened her.

—How old are you, sir? she asked Julien.

—Nearly nineteen.

—My oldest son is eleven, said Mme. de Rênal, quite at her ease; he will be almost like a friend for you, you can reason with him. Once his father had occasion to whip him and the boy was sick for a whole week, yet he was not hit hard at all.

How different from me, thought Julien. Only yesterday my father beat me up. Don't these rich people have it easy!

Mme. de Rênal was already reaching after the slightest subtleties of reaction within the tutor's soul; she took his look of grief for further timidity, and tried to encourage him.

—What is your name, sir? she asked, in a tone and with an expression whose full charm Julien experienced without being able to explain it.

—I am Julien Sorel, madame; I am terrified at entering a strange household for the first time in my life; I shall need your protection and your pardon for many faults during the first days. I have never gone to college, I was too poor; I have never talked with other men except for my cousin, the surgeon-major, who was a member of the Legion of Honor;[6] and M. Chélan, the priest. He can give you a good account of me. My brothers have always beaten me up; you must not believe them if they say evil things about me; pardon my faults and errors, madame, I shall never mean any harm.

Julien gained in confidence during this long speech, and he examined Mme. de Rênal. Grace is perfect when it is natural and un–self-conscious; Julien, who had distinct ideas about feminine beauty, would have sworn at that moment that she was only twenty years old. All of a sudden the wild idea occurred to him of kissing her hand. At first he was afraid of his own idea; an instant later he said to himself: It will be cowardice on my part not to carry out a scheme that may be useful to me, and cut down this fine lady's contempt for a laborer just liberated from his sawmill. Perhaps Julien was somewhat encouraged by that phrase, *good-looking boy,* he had been hearing every Sunday for the past six months or so from several girls. While these inner debates were going on, Mme. de Rênal gave him a few words of advice on the way to win the confidence of the children. The violence of Julien's inner struggles rendered him pale again; he said, with an air of constraint:

—Never, madame, shall I lift a hand against your children; I swear it before heaven.

And as he said these words, he had the audacity to take Mme. de Rênal's hand and carry it to his lips. She was astonished at this action, and on thinking it over, shocked. As it was quite hot, her arm was completely bare beneath her shawl, and Julien's action of raising the hand to his lips uncovered it entirely. A few moments later she scolded herself for not having grown indignant quickly enough.

M. de Rênal, who had heard their talk, emerged from his study; with the same majestic and paternal air he assumed when he married people at the mayor's office, he said to Julien:

—It is imperative that I have a word with you before the children see you.

He invited Julien into a room and brought his wife along, though she wanted to leave them alone together. When the door was

---

6. The Legion of Honor, created by Napoleon in 1802, is the premier order of the French republic.

closed, M. de Rênal seated himself and put on a solemn expression.

—The priest has assured me that you are a worthy person; everyone here will treat you with respect, and if I am satisfied, I may well help you toward a modest but respectable position. I desire that you see no more of your parents or your friends, their tone can scarcely be suitable for my children. Here are thirty-six francs[7] for your first month's pay; but I require your word of honor that not a single sou of it shall go to your father.

M. de Rênal was furious with the old man, who in this bargain had got the better of him.

—Now, *sir*, for by my orders everyone here will address you as "sir," and you will find the advantages of living in a well-ordered household; now, sir, it is by no means suitable that the children see you in a workman's jacket. Did any of the servants see him? M. de Rênal asked his wife.

—No, my dear, she replied, as if deep in thought.

—So much the better. Put on this, said he to the surprised young man, handing over one of his own coats. Now let us pay a visit to M. Durand, the tailor.

An hour later, when M. de Rênal returned with the new tutor all dressed in black, he found his wife still sitting in the same room. She felt calmer in the presence of Julien, and as she watched him she forgot to be afraid. Julien gave her not a thought; for all his lofty views of destiny and humankind, his soul at that moment was a child's; he felt he had lived for years in the three hours since he stood trembling in the church. He took note of Mme. de Rênal's chilly attitude and understood that she was angry at his boldness in kissing her hand. But the sense of pride he felt at wearing clothes so different from his usual garb distracted him, and he was so hard put to repress his delight that all his gestures became abrupt, almost wild. Mme. de Rênal looked upon him with astonished eyes.

—A little gravity, sir, M. de Rênal said to him, if you wish to be respected by my children and my servants.

—Sir, Julien replied, I feel ill at ease in these new clothes. I am a poor peasant and have never worn anything but a jacket. With your permission, I shall retire to my room.

—What do you think of our new acquisition? M. de Rênal asked his wife.

By an instinctive reflex, the meaning of which she never declared to herself, Mme. de Rênal masked the truth from her husband.

—I am by no means as delighted as you are with this little peasant, she said; your kindness will make him impertinent, and then you'll have to turn him off within a month.

---

7. Thirty-six francs would be worth approximately $240, or 180 euros today.

—So be it, then! I'll turn him off; we may be out a hundred francs or so, and Verrières will be in the habit of seeing a tutor with M. de Rênal's children. We would not have gained that point if I had left Julien in a workman's blouse. If I turn him off, naturally I'll keep the black suit I just got at the tailor's. He will keep only what I picked up for him off the ready-made rack.

The hour during which Julien kept to his room seemed an instant to Mme. de Rênal. The children, who had heard of their new tutor's arrival, overwhelmed their mother with questions. At last Julien came forth. He was an entirely new man. To say that he was grave would be absurd; he was gravity incarnate. He was introduced to the children and spoke to them with an air that astonished M. de Rênal himself.

—I am here, young gentlemen, said he at the end of his allocution, to teach you Latin. You know what it means to recite your lessons. Well, here is the Holy Bible, said he, showing them a little black-bound duodecimo. It is, specifically, the story of our Lord Jesus Christ, the part known as the New Testament. I shall often ask you to recite your lessons; now I want you to make me recite mine.

Adolphe, the eldest of the children, had taken the book in his hand.

—Open it at random, said Julien, and read off the first three words of a verse. I shall repeat from memory the sacred book, guide of conduct for us all, until you stop me.

Adolphe opened the book and read a couple of words; Julien recited the entire page as fluently as if he had been speaking French. M. de Rênal cast toward his wife a look of triumph. The children, seeing that their parents were astonished, opened their own eyes wide. A servant came through the doorway; Julien continued to recite Latin. The servant stopped still for a moment, then disappeared. Soon madame's maid and the cook appeared in the doorway and stood there; by then Adolphe had opened the book in eight different places, and Julien was still reciting as glibly as ever.

—Oh, good Lord, what a pretty little priest! the cook said aloud; she was a good girl and very devout.

M. de Rênal's self-esteem was aroused; far from dreaming of examining the tutor, he was busy rummaging through his memory for a few Latin tags; at last he succeeded in repeating a verse of Horace. Julien knew no Latin outside the Bible. He answered with a frown:

—The holy ministry for which I am destined precludes my reading so profane an author.

M. de Rênal cited a pretty liberal number of pretended verses from Horace. He explained to his children who and what Horace was; but the children, struck with admiration, paid scarcely any attention to what he was saying. They were watching Julien.

As the servants were still crowding into the doorway, Julien felt he had to prolong the test:

—And now, said he to the youngest child, I should like M. Stanislas-Xavier to select for me a passage of holy writ.

Little Stanislas, flushed with pride, read as well as he could the first word of a verse, and Julien recited the whole page. That nothing should be lacking to M. de Rênal's triumph, as Julien was reciting there entered M. Valenod, owner of those fine Norman horses, and M. Charcot de Maugiron, subprefect of the district. This scene earned Julien the title of "sir"; henceforth not even the servants dared refuse it.

That evening all Verrières poured in upon M. de Rênal to witness the marvel. Julien replied to everyone with an air of gloom that kept them at a distance. His glory spread through the town so rapidly that, a few days later, M. de Rênal, who feared that somebody might woo him away, proposed that he sign a contract for two years.

—No, sir, Julien replied coldly, should you decide to dismiss me, I would be obliged to leave. A contract that binds me but commits you to nothing is altogether unfair; I must decline it.

Julien managed so cleverly that within a month of his arrival M. de Rênal himself respected him. Since the priest had quarreled with Messieurs de Rênal and Valenod and nobody could reveal Julien's former admiration for Napoleon, he never spoke of him without horror.

Chapter 7

ELECTIVE AFFINITIES[8]

They can touch the heart only by bruising it.
—A Modern Man

The children worshipped him, he liked them not at all; his thoughts were elsewhere. What the little ones did had no power even to make him impatient. Cool, judicial, impassive and yet beloved, because his coming had in some degree relieved the boredom of the household, he was a good tutor. On his own account, he felt only hatred and horror for the high society to which he was now admitted, if only at the foot of the table—a circumstance which may explain his hate and horror. At certain formal dinners he could hardly contain his hatred of everything that surrounded him.

8. The chapter title is the name of a novel by Goethe that Stendhal had read many years before.

One day in particular of the festival of St. Louis,[9] when M. Valenod was dining with M. de Rênal, Julien almost gave himself away; he fled into the garden, on the pretext of looking after the children. What harangues about honesty, he cried; you'd think it was the only virtue there is; and yet, what consideration, what fawning respect, for a man who's obviously doubled and tripled his estate since he's been in charge of the poorhouse! I'll bet he even makes a profit out of the orphans, paupers whose misery is specially sacred. Ah, monsters, they're all monsters! And I'm a sort of orphan myself, hated by my father, my brothers, my whole family.

A few days before the festival of St. Louis, Julien had been walking alone and saying his breviary in a little park called the Belvedere, which stands above Loyalty Square, when he saw his two brothers approaching along a deserted path. His first impulse was to avoid them. These clumsy oafs were so provoked by the fine black suit of their brother, by his look of extreme cleanliness, and by the sincere contempt he felt for them that they beat him up and left him on the ground bloody and unconscious. Mme. de Rênal, strolling with M. Valenod and the subprefect, arrived by accident in the little park; she saw Julien stretched on the ground and supposed him dead. Her anguish was such as to rouse M. Valenod's jealousy.

His alarm was premature. Julien thought Mme. de Rênal very lovely, but he hated her for her beauty; it was the first reef on which his career had almost run aground. He talked to her as little as possible, hoping to make her forget the folly that had led him, the first day, to kiss her hand.

Elisa, Mme. de Rênal's maid, had not failed to fall in love with the young tutor, and often talked of him with her mistress. Mlle. Elisa's affection earned Julien the hatred of one of the valets. One day he heard this man saying to Elisa: You never talk to me any more since that greasy tutor's been in the house. Julien deserved no such epithet; but with the instincts of a good-looking young fellow he paid extra attention to his appearance. M. Valenod's dislike of him redoubled as well. He said publicly that such elegance was unbecoming in a young abbé. Except for the cassock, that was the dress that Julien wore.

Mme. de Rênal noted that he talked frequently with Mlle. Elisa; she learned that these talks were occasioned by the extreme meagerness of Julien's wardrobe. He had so little linen that he was often obliged to have it laundered outside the house, and it was in these little arrangements that Elisa served him. Such extreme

---

9. The festival of St. Louis falls on August 25; this date makes some trouble for the chronologist of the novel, since according to indications it should be later in the year at this point.

poverty, of which she had never had a suspicion, touched Mme. de Rênal; she would have liked to give him a present, but did not dare; this inner resistance was the first painful sensation that Julien caused her. Until then, his name and the sense of a pure and spiritual joy had been synonymous for her. Tormented by the thought of Julien's poverty, Mme. de Rênal spoke to her husband about making him a present of some linen:

—What foolishness! he told her. That's some idea, giving presents to a man who's serving us perfectly well already. We might do it if he were slacking off and we wanted to rouse his eagerness again.

Mme. de Rênal was humiliated by this way of looking at things; before Julien came she would never have noticed it. She never saw his costume, very neat but very simple, like that of a young abbé, without thinking to herself: poor boy, how can he possibly manage?

Gradually she came to feel pity instead of shock at all the things Julien lacked.

Mme. de Rênal was one of those provincial women whom you might very well take for fools the first two weeks of your acquaintance. She had no experience of life and made no effort at small talk. Since she was gifted with a delicate and lofty soul, her instinct for happiness, which is natural to all living creatures, provided that mostly she paid no attention to the behavior of the gross creatures amid whom fortune had thrust her.

She would have been noted for the instinctive quickness of her wit if she had received the least education. But as an heiress she had been raised among devotional nuns with a passion for the *Sacred Heart of Jesus*[1] and a violent hatred for those Frenchmen who were assumed to be enemies of the Jesuits. Mme. de Rênal had the good sense to forget immediately, as ridiculous, whatever she had been taught in the convent; but she put nothing in its place, and ended by knowing nothing. The premature flatteries to which she had been subjected as heiress to a great fortune, and a distinct leaning toward passionate devotion, had given her a whole inner life of her own. With the most perfect air of condescension and a self-sacrificing manner which all the Verrières husbands cited to their wives as exemplary and which was M. de Rênal's chief pride, she still managed her existence on the principle of the most lofty disdain. Any princess distinguished for her pride pays infinitely more attentions to what her attendants do than did this lady, so gentle and modest in appearance, to the words or deeds of her hus-

---

1. Marie Alacoque (1647–1690), a nun of the Visitation, was chosen by the Jesuits to inspire the cult of the Sacred Heart. After a period of decline, Adoration of the Sacred Heart of Jesus again became widespread during the Restoration.

band. Until Julien came she had really paid no attention to anyone
except her children. Their little ailments and pains, their little
pleasures, had occupied the entire consciousness of this soul who
in her whole life had never adored anyone but God when she was
in the *Sacred Heart* of Besançon.

Though she would not have ventured to say a word to anyone, a
feverish spell on the part of one of her children could reduce her
almost to the same condition as if the child had died. A burst of
crude laughter and a shrug of the shoulders accompanied by some
trivial proverb about the folly of women were the only sort of welcome she ever got when the need to open her heart led her, in the
first years of her marriage, to discuss troubles of this sort with her
husband. His variety of humor, especially when it concerned the ill-
nesses of her children, twisted the knife in Mme. de Rênal's heart.
And it was for this that she had exchanged the obsequious and honeyed flatteries of the Jesuit convent where she had passed her
youth. She achieved her education through grief. Too proud to talk
openly about troubles of this sort, even to her friend Mme.
Derville, she supposed that all men were like her husband, like
M. Valenod, like the subprefect de Maugiron. Coarseness and brutal indifference to everything that was not money, promotion, or a
cross; a blind hatred for any sort of thought that went against their
interests—these qualities seemed to her as natural to the sex as
wearing boots and felt hats.

After many years Mme. de Rênal was not yet accustomed to
these money men among whom it was her fate to live.

Hence the success of the young peasant, Julien. She found many
sorts of pleasure, all bright with the charm of novelty, in the sympathy accorded by his proud and noble spirit. Mme. de Rênal quickly
forgave him his extreme ignorance, which was only one grace more
in her eyes, and the rudeness of his manners, which she succeeded
in correcting. She found that he was worth listening to, even when
the talk ran on the most ordinary topics, even in the matter of a
wretched dog, crushed as it was crossing the street by the cart of a
peasant going by at a trot. The sight of such suffering provoked her
husband to his coarse laughter, whereas she noted that Julien's
dark, finely arched eyebrows contracted in a frown. Gradually, it
seemed to her generosity, nobility of spirit, and humanity existed
only in the person of this young abbé. She felt for him all the sympathy, and even worship, that these virtues arouse in well-born na-
tures.

In Paris, Julien's position with regard to Mme. de Rênal would
quickly have been simplified; but in Paris, love is the child of novels. The young tutor and his timid mistress would have found in
three or four novels, or even in the couplets of the Gymnase, a clar-

ification of their position.[2] The novels would have outlined for them the roles to be played, provided them with a model to imitate; and this model, sooner or later, though without the least pleasure and perhaps even reluctantly, vanity would have forced Julien to follow.

In a little village of the Aveyron or the Pyrenees, the slightest incident would have been rendered decisive by the heat of the climate. Under our darker skies, a poor young man who is ambitious only because the delicacy of his heart makes absolutely necessary for him some of those pleasures that money bestows can see every day a woman of thirty, sincerely virtuous, devoted to her children, and who never thinks of looking in novels for examples of conduct. Everything progresses slowly, things are done gradually in the provinces, behavior is more natural.

Often, as she thought of the young tutor's poverty, Mme. de Rênal was moved almost to weep. Julien came upon her one day when she was actually in tears.

—Ah, madame, have you had some misfortune?

—No, my friend, she answered; call the children, we'll go for a walk.

She took his arm, and leaned on it in a way that seemed extraordinary to Julien. This was the first time she had called him "my friend."

Toward the end of the stroll Julien noted that she was blushing deeply. She slowed her steps.

—You will perhaps have heard, she said, without looking at him, that I am the only heiress of a rich aunt who lives near Besançon. She loads me down with presents . . . . My boys are making such progress . . . such amazing progress . . . that I would very much like to ask you to accept a little present as a token of my gratitude. It is only a matter of a few louis so you can get some linen. But . . . she added, blushing even more deeply, and she fell silent.

—What, madame? asked Julien.

—It would be unnecessary, she continued, lowering her head, to speak of this to my husband.

—I may be humble, madame, but I am not base, Julien replied, stopping and drawing himself up to his full stature, while his eyes sparkled with anger; perhaps you have not thought about that enough. I should be worse than a menial if I put myself in the position of concealing from M. de Rênal anything having to do *with my money.*

Mme. de Rênal was crushed.

—His honor the mayor, Julien went on, has made five payments

2. The Gymnase Dramatique, a theater erected in 1820, was largely given over to vaudeville comedies in couplets.

of my thirty-six-franc salary since I have been in his household. I am ready to display my account book to M. de Rênal, or to anybody else, even to M. Valenod, who hates me.

After this outburst, Mme. de Rênal remained pale and trembling and the walk ended without either one of them finding any pretext for renewing the discussion. Love for Mme. de Rênal became more and more impossible in Julien's haughty heart; on her side, she admired, she respected him; she had been scolded by him. Under pretext of atoning for the humiliation she had unintentionally caused him, she allowed herself to pay him the most delicate attentions. The novelty of these maneuvers provided a week's happiness for Mme. de Rênal. They had the further effect of partially soothing Julien's anger; he was far from seeing in them anything that could resemble personal affection.

That's how rich people are, he told himself; they humiliate you and then think they can set things right with a few monkey tricks!

Mme. de Rênal's heart was so full, and still so innocent, that in spite of her resolutions on this point she told her husband about the offer she had made to Julien and the way in which he had rejected it.

—How in the world, said M. de Rênal in great indignation, could you endure a refusal on the part of a *servant*?

And when Mme. de Rênal exclaimed against this term:

—I speak, madame, as the late Prince of Condé did when introducing his courtiers to his new wife: "*All these people*, said he, *are our servants.*" I read you the passage from Besenval's *Memoirs*,[3] it's important in these matters of precedence. Anyone who isn't a gentleman, who lives in your house and receives a salary, is your servant. I'll have a few words with this M. Julien, and give him a hundred francs.

—Ah, my dear, said Mme. de Rênal, trembling, at least you must not do it in front of the other servants!

—You are right, they might be jealous, and rightly so, said her husband, and he took himself off, much impressed by the vastness of the sum.

Mme. de Rênal dropped into a chair, almost fainting with grief. He is going to humiliate Julien, and it will be my fault! She felt a horror of her husband, and buried her face in her hands. She swore then never to confide in him again.

When she saw Julien again, she was all atremble, her throat so

---

3. Besenval de Bronstatt (1722–1794), a Swiss officer in service of the French king during the eighteenth century, left behind some (unreliable) memoirs and a novel which Stendhal prized as representations of life under the old regime. M. de Rênal endeavors to copy aristocratic manners at very long range.

choked that she could hardly manage to say the least word. In her embarrassment, she took his hands and wrung them.

—Well, my friend, she managed to say at last, are you pleased with my husband?

—Why not? said Julien, with a bitter smile, he just gave me a hundred francs.

Mme. de Rênal looked hesitantly at him.

—Give me your arm, she said to him, finally, with an accent of decision Julien had never noted in her before.

She ventured to go to the bookseller of Verrières, in spite of his frightful reputation for liberalism.[4] There she selected books to the value of ten louis which she presented to her sons. But the books were just those that she knew Julien wanted. She demanded that each of her sons write his name in the books that had been selected for him, and do it immediately, in the bookseller's shop. While Mme. de Rênal was happy in making this sort of audacious reparation to Julien, he was lost in amazement at the number of books to be seen in a bookstore. Never had he dared to set foot in such a profane place; his heart was thumping. Far from even trying to think what was going on in Mme. de Rênal's heart, he was lost in thought about how it would be possible for a young theological student to get hold of some of these books. The idea occurred to him at last that with some cleverness one might persuade M. de Rênal that it would be good for his sons to write themes based on the lives of celebrated gentlemen born in the district. After a month of managing, Julien got this idea across, and to such effect that shortly afterward he ventured, in a conversation with M. de Rênal, to propose an action that would otherwise have been very painful for the noble mayor; it was a matter of contributing to the prosperity of a liberal by taking out a subscription to the lending library. M. de Rênal agreed, indeed, that it would be wise to give his elder son *a visual impression* of various books he might hear mentioned when he went off to the military academy; but Julien saw that his honor refused stubbornly to go a step farther. He suspected a secret motive, but could not guess at it.

—I was thinking, sir, he remarked one day, that it would be highly inappropriate for the name of a gentlemen, a name like Rênal, to appear in the dirty ledgers of a bookseller.

M. de Rênal's brow cleared.

—It would also be a very bad business, Julien continued in even humbler tones, for a poor student of theology, if someone some day

---

4. The only bookstore in Stendhal's Grenoble was a center of liberal thought, hence bookstores in the Stendhalian fiction are generally centers of leftist influence, despised by "good" society.

should find that his name had been in the accounts of a bookseller who keeps a lending library. The liberals could accuse me of having asked for the most infamous books; who knows, they might go so far as to write in after my name the titles of these perverse volumes.

But Julien was off the track. He saw the mayor's face resume its expression of embarrassment and ill temper. Julien fell silent. I have him on the hook, said he to himself.

A few days later the elder boy asked Julien about a book that had been advertised in the *Quotidienne*;[5] M. de Rênal was present.

—In order to avoid all occasions for triumph by the Jacobin party, and yet to provide me with a way to answer M. Adolphe, said the young tutor, it might be possible to take out a subscription at the library in the name of the lowest of your servants.

—Not a bad idea at all, said M. de Rênal, in great good humor.

—Yet it must be specified, Julien added, with that grave and almost unhappy expression which suits certain people so admirably when they see that something they have desired for a long time is about to come true, it must be specified that the servant shall not withdraw any novel. Once in the house, these dangerous books may corrupt madame's maids and the very servant himself.

—You are forgetting to ban political pamphlets as well, added M. de Rênal with a haughty air. He was trying to conceal his admiration for the shrewd middle course discovered by his children's tutor.

Julien's life was composed of a series of such petty negotiations; and his success in them counted much more, with him, than the sentiment of marked personal preference which he could have seen, if he had only looked, in the heart of Mme. de Rênal.

The moral position he had occupied all his life repeated itself in the household of the mayor of Verrières. As in his father's sawmill, he despised in his heart the people among whom he lived, and they hated him. Every day he observed, from the stories told by the subprefect, by M. Valenod, by the other acquaintances of the family, when they talked about things that had just taken place beneath their very eyes, how little their ideas corresponded with reality. If an action seemed admirable to him, that was precisely the deed which called forth blame from the people around him. His inward comment on them was always: What monsters, or what fools! The joke is that with all his pride, he often did not understand the first thing of what was being talked about.

In his whole life he had spoken sincerely with only one person, the old surgeon-major; the few ideas he had all bore on Bonaparte's campaigns in Italy or the practice of surgery. His youthful courage

5. The legitimist, that is, the royalist and authoritarian newspaper. The *Quotidienne* stood in diametrical opposition to the *Constitutionnel*.

was fired by detailed accounts of extremely painful operations; he used to tell himself: I wouldn't have flinched.

The first time that Mme. de Rênal tried to talk with him on some topic other than the education of children, he began to talk about surgical operations; she turned pale, and begged him to stop.

Julien knew nothing else. And so, as he spent much time in the company of Mme. de Rênal, the most extraordinary silence sprang up between them as soon as they were alone together. In the drawing room, though his deportment was always humble, she noted in his eyes an air of intellectual superiority over whatever company came to the house. Finding herself alone with him for a minute, she saw him grow visibly embarrassed. She was disturbed by it, for her woman's instinct warned her that this embarrassment was in no way sentimental.

As a result of an odd idea picked up from some tale of good society told by the old surgeon-major, Julien felt humiliated as soon as there was a moment's silence anytime he was in the company of a woman, as if this silence were bound to be his personal fault. When they were alone together, the sensation was a hundred times more painful. His imagination was full of the most exaggerated, the most Spanish, ideas about what a man should say when he is alone with a woman; it offered him, in his difficulties, only unacceptable ideas. His soul might be in the clouds, but he could not break out of this humiliating silence. Thus the severe air he assumed during his long walks with Mme. de Rênal and the children was intensified by the most cruel sufferings. He despised himself horribly. If, unhappily, he forced himself to talk, he always managed to say the most ridiculous things conceivable. To complete his misery, he saw and exaggerated his own absurdity; but what he did not see was the expression of his eyes; they were so fine and expressed so ardent a spirit that sometimes, like good actors, they gave meaning to words which in themselves had none. Mme. de Rênal noticed that when he was alone with her he never succeeded in saying anything good except when he was distracted by some unforeseen event and forgot about turning a neat compliment. As the friends of the family did not spoil her with an excess of new and brilliant ideas, she took great pleasure in the flashes of Julien's wit.

Since Napoleon fell, every semblance of gallantry has been strictly banished from the manners of the provinces. People are afraid for their jobs. Rascals seek support from the congregation; and hypocrisy has made splendid headway even among the liberal classes. Boredom is thicker than ever. The only pleasures left are reading and farming.

Mme. de Rênal, rich heiress of a pious aunt, married at sixteen to a respectable gentleman, had never in her life seen or experienced anything that resembled in any way whatever the passion of love. Her confessor, the good Curé Chélan, was almost the only man who had ever mentioned the topic to her, in connection with M. Valenod's advances, and he had given her such a disgusting picture of it that the word represented nothing, in her mind, but the most depraved libertinage. She regarded as wholly exceptional, and perhaps even as unnatural, love as it had been presented to her in the very moderate number of novels that had chanced to meet her eyes. Thanks to this ignorance, Mme. de Rênal, in perfect happiness, occupied herself continually with Julien, and was far from blaming herself in any way.

Chapter 8

SMALL HAPPENINGS

Then there were sighs, the deeper for suppression,
And stolen glances, sweeter for the theft,
And burning blushes, though for no transgression.
—*Don Juan*, Canto I, stanza 74

Mme. de Rênal's angelic temper, which was due to her character and her present happiness, was disturbed a little only when she came to think of her maid, Elisa. The girl came into a legacy, made her confession to Abbé Chélan, and told him she wanted to marry Julien. The priest was really delighted at his friend's good fortune; but he was greatly surprised when Julien told him, in a decisive tone, that Mlle. Elisa's offer was by no means acceptable to him.

—Keep watch, my son, said the priest with a frown, over this disposition of yours. You are turning down a very adequate fortune; if it is simply because of your priestly vocation, let me congratulate you. For fifty-six years I have been priest of Verrières, yet now, it seems, I am going to be turned out. Even though I have an income of eight hundred florins, I find this distressing. I remind you of this detail simply so you will have no illusions about your future as a priest. If you expect to make your way with the men of power, the fate of your soul is sealed. Perhaps you can make a fortune, but you will have to trample on the wretched while flattering the subprefect, the mayor—the important man, whoever he is—by playing on his passions. Such conduct, known in the world as shrewd policy, may not, in the case of a layman, be absolutely destructive of every hope of salvation; but in our condition, we must choose to flourish in this world or the next one; there is no middle course. Go along with you now; my dear boy, think it over, and three days from now come back with a final answer. At the root of your character, I seem to see (and I am sorry for it) a sort of gloomy energy which does not suggest the moderation and perfect indifference to earthly advantage that is proper to a priest. I expect great things of your intellect; but let me tell you (added the good man, with tears in his eyes) that if you are a priest, I shall fear for your salvation.

Julien was ashamed of his emotion; for the first time in his life he saw that someone loved him; he wept with joy, and went off to hide his tears in the deep woods above Verrières.

—Why am I in this state? he said to himself at last; I feel I would give my life a hundred times over for this good priest Chélan, and yet he's just demonstrated to me that I'm a fool. He is the man above all others that I must deceive, and he's seen through me. That secret energy which he talks about is my plan to get ahead in the world. He thinks me unworthy of the priesthood, and just at the moment when I thought my rejecting a fifty-louis income[6] would give him the grandest impression of my pious vocation.

—From now on, Julien continued, I must rely only on those parts of my character that I've thoroughly tested. Who would have supposed that I would find pleasure in tears, that I would love the man who proves to me that I'm only a fool!

Three days later Julien had discovered the pretext he should have had ready from the beginning; it happened to be a slander, but what matter? He made known to the priest, with many hesitations, that a certain reason, which he could not explain because it would implicate a third party, had set his mind against the proposed marriage. It amounted to an accusation against Elisa. M. Chélan noted in his behavior a certain worldly passion quite different from that which ought to inspire a young levite.

—My boy, he said again, be a respectable tradesman in the provinces, well liked and well educated, rather than a priest without conviction.

Julien replied to these new warnings rather well, as far as words went; he found just the expressions that an ardent young seminarian would have used, but the tone in which he pronounced them, the ill-concealed fire that glittered in his eyes, alarmed M. Chélan.

Let us not think too poorly of Julien's future; he was inventing, with perfect correctness, the language of a sly and prudent hypocrisy. At his age, that's not bad. In the matter of tone and gestures, he lived among yokels, and so had never studied the great models. Later, circumstances permitted him to approach closer to fine gentlemen; no sooner had he done so than he was as skillful with gestures as with words.

Mme. de Rênal was surprised that her maid's stroke of good for-

---

6. Fifty louis—one thousand francs—would be worth approximately $6,700; or 5,000 euros today.

tune didn't make her any happier; every day the girl went off to the priest and returned in tears; finally Elisa spoke to her of her marriage.

Mme. de Rênal thought herself ill; a sort of fever kept her from sleeping; she was alive only when she had either Julien or her maid under surveillance. They were all she could think of, and she dreamed of the happiness they would find together. That meager little house where they would have to live on fifty louis a year seemed altogether heavenly to her. Julien might very well become a lawyer at Bray, the subprefecture a couple of leagues from Verrières; in that case, she might possibly see him from time to time.

Mme. de Rênal really, thought she was going mad; she said so to her husband, and at last actually fell ill. That evening, as her maid was serving her, she noticed that the girl was weeping. She was feeling angry with Elisa, and had just spoken sharply to her; now she begged her pardon. Elisa's tears flowed afresh; with her mistress' permission, she said, she would tell the whole story.

—Speak up, said Mme. de Rênal.

—Well, madame, he has refused me; people have told him nasty tales about me, and he believes them.

—Who has refused you? said Mme. de Rênal, scarcely able to breathe.

—Who else, madame, who else but M. Julien? the maid replied, through her tears. The priest can't talk him out of it; for the priest doesn't think it's right for him to turn down a good girl just because she was a chambermaid. After all, M. Julien's father is nothing but a carpenter; and how did he himself earn his living before he came here?

Mme. de Rênal was no longer listening; overcome by joy, she was almost out of her mind. She insisted on hearing, several times over, that Julien had refused in a most positive manner which absolutely precluded a more sensible reconsideration.

—I will make a last effort, she said to her maid, I will talk to M. Julien myself.

The next day after lunch Mme. de Rênal indulged in the delicious pleasure of pleading her rival's cause, and of seeing Elisa's hand and fortune turned down, again and again, for an entire hour.

Gradually Julien passed beyond merely shrewd responses, and ended by answering Mme. de Rênal's prudent suggestions with wit and intelligence. She could not support the torrent of joy that flooded her soul after so many days of despair, and became really unwell. When she was revived and taken to her room she sent everyone away.

—Can I be in love with Julien? she said to herself at last.

This discovery, which at any other time would have plunged her in remorse and deep distress, was at the moment merely an unusual spectacle to which she remained quite indifferent. Her soul, worn out by all it had endured, could no longer respond to her feelings.

Mme. de Rênal tried to work but fell into a deep sleep; when she awoke she was not as much afraid as she should have been. She was too happy to suspect the turn of events. Simple and innocent, this good provincial lady had never plagued her mind to work up a new response for each new shade of passion or of grief. Before Julien came she had been wholly absorbed in that mass of work which, outside of Paris, falls to every good mother of a family; Mme. de Rênal thought of the passions as we think of the lottery—inevitable delusion, a path to happiness taken only by madmen.

The dinner bell sounded; Mme. de Rênal blushed deeply as she heard the voice of Julien, bringing in the children. Being a little cleverer since she fell in love, she explained her flushed features by pleading a frightful headache.

—That's women for you, M. de Rênal struck in with a guffaw; there's always something out of order in those machines!

Though she was used to this sort of wit, the tone of voice shocked Mme. de Rênal. To divert her mind, she looked toward Julien; had he been the ugliest man in the world, at that moment he would have been pleasing to her.

Always intent on copying court manners, M. de Rênal moved out to the country during the first fine days of spring, to Vergy; it is the little town rendered famous by the tragic story of Gabrielle.[7] A few hundred feet from the picturesque ruins of the old Gothic church, M. de Rênal owned an old country house, with its four corner towers and a garden designed like that of the Tuileries, with plenty of box hedges and rows of chestnut trees which were clipped twice a year. Eight or ten magnificent walnut trees marked the edge of the orchard; their immense masses of foliage rose to a height of nearly eighty feet.

—Every one of those damn walnut trees, said M. de Rênal to his wife when she admired them, costs me the yield of a quarter acre of ground; wheat won't grow in the shade.

To Mme. de Rênal, the countryside seemed altogether fresh and

---

7. Gabrielle de Vergy is the heroine of a late-thirteenth-century romance popular in the Renaissance and since translated to the tragic and operatic stage. Briefly, it tells how the Duchess of Burgundy falls in love with a man who is already in love with Gabrielle, chatelaine of the castle of Vergy; the duchess, enraged by his rejection, complains to the duke that he has assaulted her. He exculpates himself without difficulty, but in the process reveals his love for Gabrielle. The duke betrays this confidence, and the duchess is furious with Gabrielle. As a result, Gabrielle commits suicide, and her lover, remorseful, stabs himself over her body. Vergy itself is in the right general area for Stendhal's story, not far from Dijon.

new; her admiration reached almost to transports. Her enthusiasms gave her new spirit and resolution. The day of their arrival at Vergy, when M. de Rênal had returned to town on official business, Mme. de Rênal hired some workmen. Julien had given her the idea of a little gravel path that would pass through the orchard and under the walnut trees, on which the children could walk during the early morning without getting their shoes soaked in the dew. The idea was given shape less than twenty-four hours after being conceived. Mme. de Rênal passed a merry day with Julien supervising the workers.

When the mayor of Verrières returned from town, great was his surprise to find the path already completed. His return was a surprise for Mme. de Rênal as well; she had quite forgotten his existence. During the next two months he never ceased talking sulkily about the boldness of some people who, without consulting him, had executed such an important piece of *repair work*; but as Mme. de Rênal had done it at her own expense, that consoled him a bit.

She passed the days playing with her children in the garden and chasing butterflies. They made themselves great nets of gauze with which to capture the poor *Lepidoptera*—that was the barbarous name that Julien taught Mme. de Rênal. For she had ordered from Besançon the handsome treatise of M. Godart;[8] and Julien read to her from it accounts of these insects and their remarkable habits.

They pinned them pitilessly to a mounting board of stiff paper, also designed by Julien. And thus at last there came to be, between Mme. de Rênal and Julien, a subject of conversation; he was no longer exposed to the frightful sufferings imposed upon him by moments of silence.

They talked continually, and with great animation, though always of perfectly innocent matters. This active, bustling, cheerful life was much to the taste of everyone except Mlle. Elisa, who found herself badly overworked. Even during carnival time, said she, when there are dances at Verrières, madame never takes such pains over her toilette; here she changes dresses two or three times a day.

As we have no intention of flattering anyone, we shall not deny that Mme. de Rênal, who had a splendid complexion, took pains to wear dresses that liberally exposed her arms and throat. She had an admirable figure, and this manner of dress suited her to perfection.

—You've *never been so young*, my dear, said all her friends from Verrières when they came out to dine at Vergy. (It's an idiom of the country.)

A remarkable fact, which every few of us will believe, is that

8. J. B. Godart wrote a standard account of French butterflies early in the nineteenth century.

Mme. de Rênal took all these pains without any real conscious purpose. It pleased her to do so; and without thinking about it, whenever she was not chasing butterflies with the children and Julien, she worked with Elisa on her wardrobe. Her one trip to Verrières was made in order to buy new summer dresses just arrived from Mulhouse.

She brought back with her to Vergy a young lady to whom she was distantly related. Since her marriage, Mme. de Rênal had gradually grown attached to Mme. Derville, with whom she had formerly attended the Convent of the Sacred Heart.

Mme. Derville laughed a great deal at what she called the crazy notions of her cousin: by myself, she said, I'd never think such thoughts at all. When she was with her husband, Mme. de Rênal was ashamed of these odd notions, which in Paris are called sallies of wit, as if they were something stupid; but in the presence of Mme. Derville she took courage. At first she expressed her thoughts only timidly; but when the ladies had been alone together for a while, Mme. de Rênal grew more spirited, and a long, solitary morning passed in an instant, leaving the two friends perfectly merry. On this particular trip, reasonable Mme. Derville found her cousin much less witty and much more happy.

Julien, for his part, had lived like a perfect child ever since they moved to the country, as happy to run after butterflies as his pupils. After all that constraint and crafty managing, now that he was alone, far from the sight of men and instinctively unafraid of Mme. de Rênal, he yielded to the sheer pleasure of existing, which is so vital at his age, and to the pleasures of the most beautiful mountains in the world.

When Mme. Derville arrived Julien was at once convinced that she was his friend; he hastened to show her the panorama that opens up at the end of the new walk under the walnut trees. It's really equal, if not superior, to the finest landscapes of Switzerland and the Italian lake country. If one climbs the steep slope which begins a few paces further on, one comes suddenly on a series of great precipices crowned with oak trees which fall away almost to the river. Atop these tumbled rocks, Julien, happy, free, and, moreover, king of the household, guided the two ladies and delighted in their admiration of the magnificent view.

—There's something about it that reminds me of Mozart's music, said Mme. Derville.

The jealousy of his brothers, the continual presence of his despotic, angry father, had spoiled the countryside around Verrières for Julien. At Vergy, he had no such bitter thoughts; for the first time in his life, when he looked about him he saw no enemy. When M. de Rênal was in town, as frequently happened, he was free to read; soon, instead of reading at night (and taking pains to hide his lamp under an overturned flowerpot), he could go to sleep; for during the day, between the children's lessons, he could come to these rocks with the one book which served as the rule of his conduct and the object of his passion. At different times he found in it happiness, ecstasy, and consolation for momentary discouragement.

Certain things that Napoleon says on the topic of women and various discussions on the merits of novels fashionable during his reign now gave Julien for the first time certain ideas which any other young man of his age would have had years ago.

The dog days came; they got in the habit of spending the evening under an immense linden tree a few feet from the house. It was very dark there. One evening Julien was talking animatedly and enjoying the very real pleasures of talking well, and to young women, when, in the course of a gesture he touched the hand of Mme. de Rênal, which was lying on the back of a painted wooden garden chair.

The hand was swiftly withdrawn; but Julien thought it was his *duty* to make sure that the hand was not withdrawn when he touched it. The idea of an obligation to fulfill, and of ridicule, or at least a sense of inferiority, to be endured if one did not succeed, immediately drove the last trace of pleasure from his heart.

Chapter 9

AN EVENING IN THE COUNTRY

The Dido of M. Guerin, a charming sketch!
—Strombeck[9]

His glances the next morning, when he saw Mme. de Rênal, were remarkable; he looked her over like an enemy with whom he was bound to fight. These glances, so different from those of the evening before, drove Mme. de Rênal to distraction; she had been kind to him, and he seemed annoyed. She could not turn her eyes from his.

Mme. Derville's presence permitted Julien to talk less and think more about his preoccupation. The only thing he did all day was to strengthen himself by reading the inspired book in which his soul was to be tempered.

He cut short the children's lessons, and then when reminded of

9. A German friend whom Stendhal met at Brunswick when he was there on military assignment in 1806–08 and with whom he kept in touch. Strombeck had fought in the Reserves at the Battle of Waterloo. Pierre Guerin was a popular painter of the Napoleonic era; his *Aeneas Relating to Dido the Disasters of Troy* was a great success in 1817 and now hangs in the Louvre.

his need for glory by the presence of Mme. de Rênal, he decided it was absolutely necessary that his hand should remain in hers that very evening.

As the sun sank slowly and the decisive moment approached, Julien's heart began to beat furiously. Night fell. With a joy that seemed to lift an immense weight from his heart he saw that it would be very dark. The sky, heavy with thick clouds driven forward by a hot wind, seemed to promise a storm. The two ladies strolled about for a long time. Everything they did that evening seemed peculiar to Julien. They were enjoying that time of the day which, for certain delicate souls, seems to augment the pleasure of loving.

At last they sat down, Mme. de Rênal next to Julien, Mme. Derville on the other side of her friend. Preoccupied with his great attempt, Julien found nothing to say, and the conversation languished.

Will I be cringing and miserable like this at the first duel that befalls me? Julien asked himself—for he was too suspicious, of himself and others, not to be aware of his own state.

In his anguish of soul any danger would have seemed preferable. How often did he pray that some little piece of business would come up which would oblige Mme. de Rênal to go back into the house and leave the garden! The violence of his inner struggle had its effect on his voice; soon the voice of Mme. de Rênal began to tremble too, though Julien was unable to notice it. The frightful struggle between his sense of duty and his timidity was too absorbing for him to notice anything outside himself. Quarter of ten had just struck on the house clock, and still he had not dared to make a move. Furious at his own cowardice, Julien said to himself: At the stroke of ten either I will do what I have been promising myself to do all day or I'll go upstairs and blow out my brains.

After a final moment of anxious waiting, during which his excess of emotion nearly drove Julien out of his mind, the hour of ten began to sound on the clock above his head. Every stroke of that fatal gong reverberated through his body, causing something like a convulsion.

Then, as the last stroke of ten was still sounding, he reached forth his hand and grasped that of Mme. de Rênal, who immediately withdrew it. Julien, without knowing very clearly what he was doing, grasped it again. Though deeply agitated himself, he was struck by the icy chill of the hand he held; he wrung it with convulsive force; a last effort was made to withdraw it, but at last it remained in his possession.

His soul was flooded with joy, not because he loved Mme. de Rênal but because an atrocious torment had ceased. To prevent Mme. Derville from noticing anything, he supposed himself obliged to talk; his voice was now strong and and resonant. Mme. de Rênal's, on the other hand, was so full of emotion that her friend supposed she was ill and suggested that they go in. Julien sensed the danger: if Mme. de Rênal goes back to that drawing room, I fall back on the frightful posture in which I passed the entire day. I haven't held onto the hand long enough to count it a definite conquest.

As Mme. Derville renewed her suggestion that they go in, Julien pressed vigorously the hand that had been abandoned to him.

Mme. de Rênal was already getting up, but sat down again, saying in a languid voice:

—I really do feel a little ill, but the fresh air is doing me good.

These words confirmed Julien's happiness, which in that instant was at its peak: he talked, he forgot to pretend, he seemed, to the two listening ladies, the world's most amiable man. And yet there was a little cowardice behind this eloquence which suddenly came flooding over him. He was in mortal terror that Mme. Derville, wearied by the wind which was starting to blow as a prelude to the storm, might go indoors by herself. Then he would be left alone with Mme. de Rênal. He had found, almost by accident, enough blind courage to take a single action; but he felt utterly incapable of saying the simplest word to Mme. de Rênal. However mild her reproaches, he would be beaten down by them and his newly gained advantages canceled.

Happily for him, that evening his earnest, eager speeches found favor with Mme. Derville, who often considered him childishly awkward and rather dull. As for Mme. de Rênal, with her hand in Julien's, she thought of nothing at all; she allowed herself to live. The moments passed under that great linden tree, which local tradition says was planted by Charles the Bold,[1] were for her a whole age of happiness. She listened with delight to the sighs of the wind in the thick foliage, and the noise of a few scattered raindrops which were starting to fall on its lower leaves. Julien failed to notice one circumstance which would have much relieved him; Mme. de Rênal, who had been obliged to take back her hand in order to help her cousin right a flowerpot overturned at their feet by the wind, as soon as she sat down again returned her hand to his almost without difficulty, as if the whole matter were now settled between them.

Midnight had long struck; it was time to go in, and the little group at last broke up. Mme. de Rênal, overwhelmed with the sensation of being in love, was so ignorant as scarcely to reproach herself at all. Her happiness kept her awake. But Julien slept like a log;

---

1. Charles the Bold (1433–1477) was the last reigning duke of Burgundy. He was killed by the Swiss and the Lorrainers in battle at Nancy.

he was exhausted by the struggles which pride and timidity had been waging all day in his heart.

Next morning he was awakened at five; and it would have been a bitter blow for Mme. de Rênal if she had known that he scarcely gave her a thought. He had carried out *his duty, and a heroic duty*. Overjoyed at this thought, he locked himself into his room and surrendered himself with a new sort of pleasure entirely to reading of the exploits of his hero.

When the bell sounded for lunch he had forgotten, in the course of reading bulletins of the Grande Armée, all his advantages of the night before. He said to himself blithely, as he descended the staircase: I've got to tell this woman I love her.

Instead of glances charged with affection, which he was expecting, he found the stem features of M. de Rênal, who had arrived two hours ago from Verrières, and made no effort to hide his displeasure that Julien had spent an entire morning without paying any attention to the children. Nothing could have been uglier than this important man in an angry mood and feeling free to express his anger.

Every sharp word her husband uttered pierced the heart of Mme. de Rênal. Julien, on the other hand, was so deeply plunged in reverie, still so preoccupied by the mighty events that had been passing before his eyes during the last hours, that he could scarcely bring his mind down to the harsh words being addressed to him by M. de Rênal. At last he said brusquely:

—I was sick.

The tone of this phrase would have wounded a man much less touchy than the mayor of Verrières; for a moment he thought of answering Julien by dismissing him on the spot. He was restrained only by the maxim he had set for himself, never to act hastily in business.

This young fool, he said to himself, has picked up a sort of reputation in my house; either Valenod will take him in or else he can marry Elisa; in either case, he can afford to make light of me.

For all the wisdom of his thoughts, M. de Rênal's ill humor did not subside without a series of grumbles and insults which gradually infuriated Julien. Mme. de Rênal was on the point of bursting into tears. When lunch was over she asked Julien to lend her his arm for a stroll; and she leaned closely upon him. To everything she said Julien replied only by murmuring:

—*That's how rich people are!*

M. de Rênal walked beside them; his presence added to Julien's wrath. Suddenly he noticed that Mme. de Rênal was leaning markedly upon his arm; under an impulse of horror he shook her violently off and freed his arm.

Happily, M. de Rênal did not observe this fresh impertinence; only Mme. Derville noted it; her friend burst into tears. Meanwhile M. de Rênal rushed off, throwing stones at a little peasant girl who in taking a short cut had passed through a corner of his orchard.

—Monsieur Julien, be a little calmer, if you will, Mme. Derville said rapidly, remember we all have moments of ill humor.

Julien glanced at her coldly, with eyes in which appeared the most sovereign contempt.

This glance astonished Mme. Derville, and would have surprised her even more if she could have guessed its true meaning; she would then have seen in it a still-vague hope of the most atrocious vengeance. No doubt it is moments of humiliation like this one that are responsible for figures like Robespierre.

—Your Julien has a violent temper, he frightens me, Mme. Derville murmured to her friend.

—He is right to be angry, replied the other; after the extraordinary progress the children have made with him, what matter if he takes off a morning? Men are very strict about these things, we must agree.

For the first time in her life Mme. de Rênal felt a sort of desire for vengeance upon her husband. Julien's furious hatred of the rich was about to break out openly; but happily M. de Rênal called for the gardener and busied himself with the latter in building a barrier of thorny sticks across the shortcut at the corner of the orchard. During the rest of the walk, Julien answered not a word to the various advances that were made in his direction. Scarcely had M. de Rênal disappeared when the two ladies, pleading fatigue, both demanded the support of his arm.

Standing between these two women, whose cheeks were flushed with distress and embarrassment, Julien, with his lofty pallor, his gloomy and determined air, provided a strange contrast. He despised these women and all their sensitive feelings.

What! he exclaimed mutely, not even five hundred francs with which to finish my courses! Ah, how I'd love to tell him off!

Absorbed as he was in these bitter thoughts, the little he deigned to hear of the ladies' kind words displeased him as foolish, inane, feeble, in a word, *feminine*.

As she continued to chatter, merely to keep the conversation alive, Mme. de Rênal chanced to say that her husband had come from Verrières because he had bought some wheat straw from one of his farmers. (In this district they use wheat straw to fill the mattresses.)

—My husband won't be back, added Mme. de Rênal; he'll be busy with the gardener and his valet; they're changing all the mattresses in the house. This morning they put new straw in all the beds on the first floor, this afternoon they'll do the second.

Julien grew pale; he glanced at Mme. de Rênal with a singular expression, and shortly took her a little aside by stepping out somewhat faster. Mme. Derville let them go.

—Save my life, Julien said to Mme. de Rênal; only you can do it; for you know that valet is my mortal enemy. I must confess to you, madame, that I have a portrait, and I have hidden it in my mattress.

At this word Mme. de Rênal became pale in her turn.

—Only you, madame, only you can go to my room at this moment, look, but without leaving any traces, in the corner of the mattress closest to the window; you'll find there a little box of black cardboard, quite smooth.

—It contains a portrait, said Mme. de Rênal, scarcely able to hold herself erect.

Her air of discouragement was apparent to Julien, who promptly took advantage of it.

—I have a second favor to beg of you, madame; I beg you not to look at the portrait, it is my secret.

—It is a secret! repeated Mme. de Rênal in a suffocated voice.

But though she had been raised among people proud of their fortune and with a single-minded interest in money, love had already introduced some generosity into her soul. Cruelly wounded though she was, Mme. de Rênal questioned Julien with an air of the purest devotion about the things she must know to fulfill her mission.

—And so, she said as she left him, it is a little round box, of black cardboard and rather smooth.

—Yes, madame, said Julien with that hard, abrupt tone that men assume in the presence of danger.

She climbed to the second floor of the house, pale as if she were going to her death. To heighten her misery, she felt that she was about to faint; but the need to help Julien restored her strength.

—I must have that box, she said, hastening forward.

She heard her husband talking to the valet in Julien's very room. Happily, they passed on into the children's. She snatched the mattress and plunged her hand into the straw so violently that she scratched her fingers. But though generally sensitive to minor griefs of this nature, she was not even aware of the pain, for just at this moment she felt the cardboard box. She grasped it and fled.

Scarcely was she delivered from the fear of being surprised by her husband when the sense of horror which this box caused her was on the point of really making her faint.

Julien then is in love, and I have here the portrait of the woman he loves!

Seated on a chair in the antechamber of the upstairs apartment, Mme. de Rênal fell prey to all the horrors of jealousy. Her remarkable ignorance was particularly useful to her at this point, since as-

tonishment tempered her grief. Julien appeared, snatched the box
without a word of thanks or a word of any sort, and ran to his room
where he lit a fire and burned it on the spot. He was pale and haggard; he exaggerated the extent of the danger he had just run.

The portrait of Napoleon, he said to himself, shaking his head;
and found on a man who professes such hatred for the usurper!
Found by M. de Rênal, a black reactionary and in a bad humor!
And to top it all, on the cardboard mounting of the portrait, phrases
written in my hand which leave no doubt of the depth of my admiration! Each one of these transports was dated, too, and the last
one just yesterday!

My whole reputation would have fallen, blasted in a minute! said
Julien as he watched the box burn; and my reputation is my fortune, it's all I have to live by—and, good God, what a way to live!

An hour later weariness and self-pity disposed him to more tender sentiments. Meeting Mme. de Rênal, he took her hand and
kissed it with more sincerity than he had ever showed her before.
She blushed with happiness, and almost at the same instant pushed
Julien away with a gesture of anger and jealousy. Julien's pride, so
recently wounded, made a fool of him at that moment. He saw
nothing in Mme. de Rênal but a rich woman, dropped her hand
with disdain, and walked away. After strolling pensively in the garden for a few minutes, he began to smile bitterly.

Here I am walking about like a man whose time is his own! I'm
not busy with his children! I'll have more harsh words from M. de
Rênal, and he will be right. He ran at once to the children's room.

The caresses of the younger, of whom he was fond, did something to calm his black mood.

This little one doesn't despise me yet, Julien thought. But shortly
he felt that this comfort was merely a new weakness. These children are fond of me just as they're fond of that new puppy who was
bought yesterday.

Chapter 10

LOFTY HEART AND LITTLE FORTUNE

> But passion most dissembles, yet betrays,
> Even by its darkness; as the blackest sky
> Foretells the heaviest tempest.
> —*Don Juan*, Canto 1, stanza 73

M. de Rênal, who was going through all the rooms of the house,
returned to the children's room with the servants who were bringing back the mattresses. The sudden appearance of this man was
for Julien the last straw.

Paler than usual, and more gloomy, he strode toward him. M. de Rênal stopped and glanced toward his servants.

—Sir, Julien said to him, do you suppose that with any other tutor your children would have learned as much as they have with me? If you suppose not, Julien continued, without allowing M. de Rênal a single word, then how do you dare to accuse me of neglecting them?

M. de Rênal, scarcely recovered from his first fear, concluded that the strange tone being taken by this little peasant came from his having in hand another offer, and that he was going to resign. As Julien continued to talk, his wrath increased:

—I can live without you, sir, he added.

—I am very sorry to see you so upset, replied M. de Rênal, stammering slightly. The servants were a few feet apart, busily rearranging the beds.

—This isn't my style, sir, Julien went on, beside himself; just think of the abominable things you said to me, and in the presence of ladies, too!

M. de Rênal understood only too clearly what Julien was demanding, and a painful struggle took place in his heart. Finally, Julien, in an access of rage, cried:

—I know where to go, sir, when I leave your house.

At that moment, M. de Rênal had a vision of Julien in the service of M. Valenod.

—Well, sir, he finally said, with a sigh and the sort of expression he would have put on when asking the surgeon to perform a hideous operation, I grant your request. After tomorrow, which is the first of the month, your salary will be fifty francs a month.

Julien felt an impulse to laugh and then stood stupefied; all his anger disappeared.

I didn't despise this animal sufficiently, he said to himself. No doubt he's just made the best apology of which his degraded mind is capable.

The children, who had been listening open-mouthed to this conversation, dashed off to the garden to tell their mother that M. Julien was furious but that he was going to have fifty francs a month.

Julien followed them mechanically, without even glancing at M. de Rênal, whom he left in a state of profound irritation.

That's a hundred and sixty-eight francs, muttered the mayor to himself, that M. Valenod has cost me. I really will have to say a few firm words to him about his scheme for the foundlings.

An instant later Julien again confronted M. de Rênal:

—I must consult with M. Chélan on a matter of conscience; I should like to advise you that I shall be absent for several hours.

—Eh, my dear Julien! said M. de Rênal, with a hollow laugh, all day if you wish, all day tomorrow too, my dear fellow. Take the gardener's horse for the trip to Verrières.

Now there he goes, said M. de Rênal to himself, off to give his answer to Valenod; he didn't promise anything—but we'll have to let that hot young head cool off.

Julien departed at once, climbing along the forest trails that lead from Vergy to Verrières. He had no wish to arrive too soon at M. Chélan's. Far from wanting to undertake another scene of hypocrisy, he had a need to see more clearly into his own soul, and to give audience to the crowd of feelings agitating him.

I've won a battle, he said to himself, as soon as he was into the woods and away from people; so I've won a battle!

The phrase described his position clearly enough, and restored to his mind some of its tranquillity.

Here I have a salary of fifty francs a month; so M. de Rênal must have been thoroughly frightened. But of what?

What could have frightened that contented and powerful man against whom, an hour before, he had been boiling with rage? Thinking about this problem restored Julien's calm. For a moment he was almost aware of the amazing beauty of the forests through which he was passing. Enormous bare boulders of rock had once fallen from the mountainside into the middle of this forest. Beside these great rocks, and almost as tall, rose beech trees whose shade kept the path deliciously cool three feet from spots where the heat of the sun would have made it impossible to stop.

Julien paused to catch his breath for a moment in the shadow of the great rocks, then resumed his climb. Soon, by a narrow pathway, almost unmarked and used chiefly by goatherds, he found himself poised on an immense rocky crag, where he could be sure of standing apart from everyone. This physical stance made him smile, it indicated so clearly the position he wanted to attain in morality. The pure mountain air filled his soul with serenity and even joy. The mayor of Verrières was, and always would be, in his eyes, the representative of the rich and insolent of this earth; but Julien sensed that his hatred for this man, despite its recent violence, was in no way personal. If he had stopped seeing M. de Rênal, in a week he would have forgotten him, his house, his dogs, his children, and his whole family. Without knowing quite how, I've forced him into the greatest sacrifice of which he is capable. What! more than fifty crowns a year! And yet just an instant before, I had barely escaped the gravest dangers. There are two victories in one day. The second was undeserved; I'll have to figure out the reason for it. But I'll go into that dreary business tomorrow.

Julien, standing atop his great rock, looked up into the sky, heated by an August sun. Locusts were chirring in the field below the rock; when they paused, all was silence around him. At his feet lay twenty leagues of countryside. A solitary eagle, risen from the rocks over his head, appeared from time to time, cutting immense silent circles in the sky. Julien's eye followed mechanically the bird of prey. Its calm, powerful movements struck him; he envied this power, he envied this isolation.

Such had been the destiny of Napoleon; would it someday be his?

Chapter 11

AN EVENING

> Yet Julia's very coldness still was kind
>> And tremulously gentle her small hand
> Withdrew itself from his, but left behind
>> A little pressure, thrilling, and so bland
> And slight, so very slight that to the mind
>> 'Twas but a doubt.
>> —*Don Juan*, Canto I, stanza 71

But he had to put in an appearance at Verrières. As he left the presbytery a lucky accident brought Julien into the presence of M. Valenod, whom he hastened to inform of his new raise in pay.

Once back at Vergy, Julien did not descend into the garden until night was falling. His spirit was weary from the many powerful passions that had stirred it in the course of the day. What shall I say to them? he asked uneasily, as he thought of the ladies. He was quite unable to see that his soul was precisely on the level of those petty circumstances that generally absorb the full interest of women. Julien had often been incomprehensible to Mme. Derville and even to her friend; and he himself often only half understood what they said to him. This resulted from the force, and, if I may say so, grandeur of the passions in this ambitious young man. For this extraordinary being, almost every day was bound to be stormy.

As he entered the garden that evening Julien was quite prepared to concern himself with the ideas of the attractive cousins. They were awaiting him impatiently. He took his regular seat beside Mme. de Rênal. Soon the darkness deepened. He sought to grasp a white hand which had for some time been in view, resting on the back of a chair. There was a moment of hesitation, but the hand was then withdrawn, not without some indications of ill humor. Julien was disposed to consider the matter closed and continue with a pleasant conversation when he heard M. de Rênal approaching.

Julien still heard, ringing in his ears, the insulting words of the morning. Now, said he to himself, wouldn't it be a good way of mocking this creature, who has all the advantages of fortune, if I should take possession of his wife's hand, right in his presence? Yes, I'll do it, the very person he treated with so much contempt.

M. de Rênal talked angrily of politics: two or three Verrières manufacturers were becoming noticeably richer than he and were preparing to stand against him in the next elections. Mme. Derville was listening to him. Julien, irked by the harangue, shifted his own chair closer to Mme. de Rênal's. The darkness hid all his gestures. He had the boldness to put his hand close to that pretty arm half concealed under drapery. His head was in a whirl, he could no longer control himself; he bent over the pretty arm and brushed it with his lips.

Mme. de Rênal shuddered. Her husband was four paces away; she hastened to give her hand to Julien and at the same time to push him away slightly. As M. de Rênal continued to denounce the upstarts and rich radicals, Julien covered the hand that had been granted him with passionate kisses, or at least they seemed such to Mme. de Rênal. And yet in the course of that tragic day the poor woman had had proof that the man she adored (without admitting it to herself) loved somebody else! Throughout the period of Julien's absence she had been subject to a profound depression, which caused her to reflect on her situation.

Good Lord, she said to herself, it seems I'm in love! A married woman and yet I'm in love! Well, she said, but I never felt anything for my husband like this morbid folly which keeps me from thinking of anything but Julien. He's only a child, of course, and feels nothing but respect for me! I'll get over it. How can it matter to my husband that I have feelings for this young man? M. de Rênal would be bored by the topics I discuss with Julien; they're only things of the imagination. He's got his business to think about. I'm not taking anything from him to give to Julien.

No hypocrisy clouded the purity of this innocent spirit, haunted by a passion it had never known before. She was deceived but unknowingly, and yet an instinct of virtue had been terrified. These were the torments that racked her when Julien made his appearance in the garden. She heard him speak; almost at the same instant she saw him sitting by her side. Her soul was carried away by that charming sense of delight that for the past two weeks had been surprising her more even than it enchanted her. Everything for her was unexpected. Yet after a few moments she said to herself. Well!

so all Julien has to do is appear for a few minutes and all his faults are forgotten? She was struck with terror; and that was the moment when she withdrew her hand.

The passionate kisses, such as she had never received before, made her forget suddenly that he might possibly love another woman. The end of her agony born of suspicion, the presence of a joy such as she had never dreamed of, inspired in her transports of affection and wild gaiety. The evening was delightful for everybody except the mayor of Verrières, who was incapable of forgetting his upstart manufactures. Julien gave no further thought to his black ambition or to his projects, so difficult to realize. For the first time in his life he was carried away by the power of beauty. Lost in a vague delightful dream, wholly foreign to his character, gently pressing that hand which seemed to him perfectly beautiful, he only half heard the rustling of the linden tree in the light night wind and the distant barking of dogs by the mill on the Doubs.

But this emotion was a pleasure, not a passion. Returning to his room, he thought only of one happiness, of getting back to his favorite book; at the age of twenty, the idea of the world and the effect to be produced there is more important than anything else.

Soon, however, he set aside the book. In thinking over the victories of Napoleon, he had learned something about his own. Yes, I've won a battle, he told himself, but I must press my advantage and crush the pride of this fine gentleman while I have him on the defensive. That's Napoleon, that's his style. [He charges me with neglecting his children.] I'll ask for a leave of three days in order to visit my friend Fouqué. If he refuses, I'll threaten to leave, but he won't refuse.

Mme. de Rênal could hardly sleep a wink. She felt that until this moment she had never really been alive; and she could not stop thinking about the pleasure of feeling Julien covering her hand with hot kisses.

Suddenly the frightful word *adultery* came to her mind. All the most disgusting images that vile debauchery can attach to sensual love came thronging into her imagination. All these ideas sought to blacken the tender and sacred image she was forming of Julien and the joy of loving him. The future drew itself up before her in horrible colors. She saw herself the object of contempt.

It was a terrible moment; her soul was moving toward unknown lands. During the evening she had experienced delights never known before; now she found herself plunged unexpectedly into atrocious suffering. She had had no conception of such misery; it attacked her very reason. For an instant the thought crossed her mind of telling her husband that she was afraid she loved Julien. It would have been, at least, an occasion to talk about him. Happily she recalled a precept once given her by an aunt on the day before her wedding; it warned of the dangers of confiding in a husband, who after all is a master. In the agony of her distress, she could only wring her hands.

She was dragged this way and that by contradictory images, all painful. At one moment her fear was that he did not love her; the next moment she was tortured by the frightful thought of her crime, as if on the morrow she was to be exposed in the pillory, on the public square of Verrières, with a placard explaining her adultery to the populace.

Mme. de Rênal had no experience of life; even in broad daylight and when completely rational she would have seen no difference between being guilty in the sight of God and being publicly covered with all the most humiliating marks of general contempt.

When the terrible idea of adultery and the life of shame which she considered its necessary consequence had ceased to torture her and she began to dream of living with Julien in perfect innocence, just as before, she was seized by the horrible idea that Julien loved another woman. She recalled his sudden pallor when he thought he might lose her portrait, or might compromise her by letting it be seen. For the first time then she had surprised a trace of fear on that lofty, emotionless face. Never had he showed himself in such distress for her or for her children. This excess of misery attained the absolute limit of anguish which the human soul can endure. Without being aware of what she was doing, Mme. de Rênal gave a shriek that awakened her maid. Suddenly she saw the glow of a lamp approaching her bed and recognized Elisa.

—So it's you he loves? she cried out, in her madness.

The maid, wholly astonished to find her mistress in such a distracted state, fortunately paid no attention to this extraordinary expression. Mme. de Rênal became aware of her imprudence: "I feel feverish," she said, "and perhaps I have a touch of delirium; stay with me." Being now quite awakened by the necessity for concealment, she found herself less miserable; reason resumed the sway her drowsiness had canceled. To escape the maid's attentive eye she asked her to read aloud from the newspaper, and it was to the monotonous accompaniment of the girl's voice, reading a long article from the *Quotidienne*, that Mme. de Rênal finally reached the virtuous resolution that when she next saw Julien she would treat him with chilly correctness.

Chapter 12

TRAVEL

At Paris you will find elegant folk, in the provinces there may be people with character.

—Sieyès[2]

Next morning, when it was barely five o'clock, before Mme. de Rênal was about, Julien had obtained from her husband permission to be gone for three days. Unexpectedly, Julien found himself wanting to see her again; he was dreaming of her pretty hand. Though he waited in the garden, Mme. de Rênal was slow in appearing. But if Julien had been in love with her, he would have seen her behind the half-drawn shutters of an upstairs window, her brow resting against the glass. She was watching him. Finally, in spite of her resolutions, she determined to go into the garden. Her customary pallor was replaced by a rosy coloring. This innocent woman was evidently distressed: a sense of constraint, and even of anger, had replaced her expression of profound serenity and of superiority to the vulgar interests of life, an expression that gave added charm to her heavenly features.

Julien approached her hastily; he was admiring those beautiful arms which could be seen beneath a hastily thrown-on shawl. The fresh morning air seemed to heighten further the brilliance of a complexion rendered sensitive by the agitations of the night. This modest and appealing beauty, which was nonetheless full of thoughts never found among the lower orders, seemed to reveal to Julien an aspect of his own soul of which he had never been aware. Completely absorbed in admiring the charms uncovered to his avid glance, Julien never doubted of the friendly greeting he was expecting to receive. All the more, then, was he shocked at the glacial chill with which he was met, and behind which he even seemed to sense an intention of putting him in his place.

The smile of pleasure faded on his lips; he thought of the rank he really occupied in society, especially in the eyes of a rich and noble heiress. Instantly there appeared on his face only arrogance and self-contempt. He felt an access of scorn for himself at having delayed his departure more than an hour for a humiliation like this.

Only a fool, said he to himself, would be angry with other people: a stone falls because it's heavy. Am I going to be a child forever? When did I get into the habit of giving these people my soul in ex-

---

2. Shrewd, lean, and subtle, Abbé Sieyès (1748–1836) rose to be a vicar general in the church before abjuring his faith during the Revolution and becoming a diplomat, politician, and all-purpose conniver.

change for their money? If I want to be respected by them, and by myself, I have to show them that it's my poverty that trades with their wealth, but that my heart is a thousand leagues from their insolence, and in a sphere too lofty to be touched by their petty marks of favor or disdain.

While these thoughts were crowding through the mind of the young tutor, his features took on an expression of angry pride and ferocity. Mme. de Rênal was distressed by it. The look of chilly virtue she had sought to impose on her greeting gave place to an expression of interest, an interest motivated by surprise at the sudden change she had just seen. The empty words that are usually exchanged in the morning on such topics as one's state of health and the lovely weather perished on both their lips. Julien, whose judgment was clouded by no passion whatever, quickly hit upon a way of showing Mme. de Rênal how little he supposed himself on terms of friendship with her: he neglected to tell her anything of the little trip he was taking, bowed, and departed.

As she watched him going, thunderstruck at the gloomy arrogance of his glance, so amiable the night before, her elder son came running up from the end of the garden, kissed her, and said:

—We have a vacation, Julien is going on a trip.

At these words Mme. de Rênal felt herself seized by a mortal chill; she was wretched in her virtue and even more so in her weakness.

This new incident quickly took possession of her whole imagination; she was carried far beyond the virtuous resolutions derived from her terrible midnight meditations. Her problem was not how to resist this agreeable lover, it was the peril of losing him forever.

She had to go in to breakfast. To climax her misery, M. de Rênal and Mme. Derville chose to talk of nothing but Julien's departure. The mayor of Verrières had noted something unusual in the firm tone with which the leave had been demanded.

—No doubt this little peasant has in pocket an offer from somebody else. But this somebody, even if it's M. Valenod, is going to be a bit discouraged by the sum of six hundred francs, which is what the annual expense is going to be now. Yesterday, at Verrières, he must have asked for three days to think over the offer; and now, this morning, in order to avoid giving me a straight answer, our little gentleman takes off for the mountains. Having to haggle with a miserable workman who plays hard to get—that's what we've come to nowadays!

Mme. de Rênal said to herself: Since my husband, who doesn't understand how deeply he's insulted Julien, thinks he's going to leave, what hope can I have myself? Ah, it's all finished now!

So that she could at least weep freely and evade the questions of

Mme. Derville, she pleaded a frightful headache and went to bed.

—That's a woman for you, M. de Rênal repeated, there's always something wrong with their complicated machinery. And he went off in rare good humor.

While Mme. de Rênal was suffering the cruelest pangs of the terrible passion in which misfortune had entrapped her, Julien followed cheerfully along his path amid the most beautiful scenery our mountains can afford. He had to cross the great chain lying to the north of Vergy. The path he followed, rising gradually through great forests of beech trees, scribes an infinity of zigzags along the slope of the lofty mountain that outlines on the north the valley of the Doubs. Soon the glances of the traveler, rising above the lower hills which hedge in the Doubs to the west, extended over the fertile plains of Burgundy and Beaujolais. However insensitive this ambitious young man naturally was to this sort of beauty, he could not help stopping from time to time in order to survey a panorama so vast and so impressive.

At last he rose to the crest of the great ridge he had to cross in order to reach, by this cross-country path, the lonely valley where lived his friend Fouqué, the young dealer in wood. Julien was in no hurry to see him, nor for that matter any other human being. Lurking like a bird of prey among the naked rocks which cap the great mountain, he could watch the distant ascent of any man who tried to come near him. In the almost vertical face of one of the cliffs he discovered a little grotto, clambered up to it, and was soon established in his retreat. Here, said he—his eyes shining with pleasure—here people will never be able to get at me. He had the notion of indulging himself by writing down those ideas which, everywhere else, were so dangerous for him. A square block of stone served as a desk. His pen flew; he forgot his surroundings entirely. At last he noted that the sun was setting behind the distant mountains of Beaujolais.

Why not spend the night here? he asked himself; I have a bit of bread, and *I am free*! His soul exulted in this grand phrase, his hypocrisy prevented his feeling free even with Fouqué. Cradling his head in his hands [and looking out over the plain], Julien sat still in his cave, happier than he had ever been in his life, stirred only by his dreams and the delight of feeling free. Idly he watched the last rays of the sunset fade one by one from the heavens. In the midst of an immense darkness his soul wandered, lost in the contemplation of what awaited him someday in Paris. It would be, first of all, a woman, far more beautiful and of a more exalted genius than any he had ever been able to see in the provinces. He adored her; he was beloved in return. If he left her for only a few moments it was to cover himself with glory and thus merit even more of her devotion.

Even if possessed of Julien's imagination, a young man raised amid the sad actuality of Paris society would have been awakened at this point in his daydream by a touch of chilly irony; heroic actions, and the hope of performing them, would have been supplanted by the familiar maxim; Leave your mistress alone and you'll be betrayed, alas, two or three times a day. This young peasant saw no gap between himself and the most heroic achievements except the want of opportunity.

Meanwhile thick darkness had fallen, and he still had two leagues to cover before reaching the little hamlet where Fouqué lived. Before leaving his grotto Julien struck a light and carefully burned everything he had written.

He rather startled his friend by rapping on his door at one o'clock in the morning. Fouqué was busy over his ledgers. He was a tall young man, ungainly and rather hard-faced, with an immense nose and a warm supply of good humor hidden beneath this rather repellent exterior.

—I suppose you've had a fight with M. de Rênal, the way you drop in on me without any notice?

Julien recounted to him, but with due discretion, the events of the day before.

—Stay with me, Fouqué told him, I see you know M. de Rênal, M. Valenod, the subprefect Maugiron, and Abbé Chélan; you understand the fine points of character in gentry like these; that makes you very fit to negotiate contracts with them. Your mathematics is better than mine; you can keep my accounts. I make good money in this trade. But I can't do everything myself, and if I take in a partner I'm afraid of getting a rascal; so every day I'm forced to pass up some excellent deal. Not a month ago. I put Michaud de Saint-Amand in the way of making six thousand francs—I hadn't seen him for six years, and I met him only by accident at the auction in Pontarlier. Why shouldn't you have made those six thousand francs, or at least three thousand of them? For if I'd had you with me that day I'd have put in my own bid for that stand of wood, and I'd have got it too. So be my partner.

This offer disturbed Julien; it interfered with his crazy dreams. Throughout the supper which the two friends prepared for themselves like Homeric heroes (for Fouqué lived all alone), he went over his books with Julien and showed him the advantages of his trade in wood. Fouqué had the loftiest notion of Julien's character and intelligence.

When Julien was at last alone in his little pine-paneled bedroom, he took stock. It is true, he told himself, I can make a couple of thousand francs here, and then be in a good position to take up the soldier's trade, or the priest's, depending on which is then fashion-

able in France. The little bit of money I can save up here will
smooth the way in either line of work. Even though living alone in
the mountains, I can do something to dissipate my frightful ignorance of the things that occupy society people. But Fouqué, though
he's decided not to marry, keeps telling me that loneliness makes
him wretched. It's obvious that if he takes in a partner who has no
capital to put into the business he hopes to find a friend who will
never leave him.

And shall I betray my friend? Julien said angrily to himself. This
creature, for whom hypocrisy and cold calculation were the ordinary
means of refuge, could not on this occasion endure the idea of even
the slightest dishonorable act toward a man who was fond of him.

But suddenly Julien was happy; he had a reason for his refusal.
What! to squander in base pursuits seven or eight years! In that way
I should reach the age of twenty-eight; and by that age Bonaparte
had already performed his finest actions. Even if I make a little devious money by running around to wood auctions and currying the
favor of some subordinate scoundrels, how can I suppose I'll still
have the sacred fire with which one makes oneself a name?

Next morning Julien spoke to the good Fouqué, who was already
taking the partnership for granted, and told him, with the greatest
coolness, that his sacred vocation would not allow him to accept
the other's offer. Fouqué was thunderstruck.

—But just think, he kept repeating, I put you in the way of four
thousand francs a year, or if you prefer it this way, I give them to
you. Yet you want to go back to M. de Rênal, who despises you like
the dirt on his shoes! After you've piled up a couple of hundred
louis of your own, what prevents you from entering a seminary? I'll
tell you something else; I can guarantee to get you the best vicarage
in the countryside. For, listen here (Fouqué added, lowering his
voice), I supply firewood to M. le _____, M. le _____, and M.
_____. What I give them is first-quality oak wood, what I charge
them for is ordinary pine, but money was never better invested.

No arguments could overcome that of Julien's vocation. Fouqué
finally decided he was a little crazy. Early on the morning of the
third day Julien left his friend, to spend the day among the rocks of
the high mountains. He sought out his little grotto again, but peace
of mind had left him, driven away by his friend's offers. Like Hercules, he found himself faced with a choice, not between vice and
virtue but between comfortable mediocrity and the heroic dreams
of youth. Well, he said to himself, I don't really have a firm character after all—and this was the thought that caused him deepest
pain. I'm not made of the stuff that goes into great men, since I'm
afraid that eight years spent in money making will rob me of the
sublime energy that goes into the doing of extraordinary deeds.

Chapter 13

NET STOCKINGS

A novel: it's a mirror being carried along a highway.
—Saint-Réal[3]

When Julien caught sight of the picturesque ruins of the old church of Vergy, he reflected that not once in the last two days had he given a thought to Mme. de Rênal. The other day as we said good-bye that woman reminded me of the distance that divides us; she treated me like the child of a workman. No doubt she wanted to show me her regret at having granted me her hand the previous evening. . . . Still, that's a very pretty hand! And what charm, what nobility in the glances of that woman!

His chance of getting ahead in the world with Fouqué gave a certain fluency to Julien's speculations; they were not now spoiled so often by irritation and a bitter sense of poverty and contempt in the eyes of the world. Placed as it were on a lofty promontory, he could judge and exercise dominion, so to speak, over the alternatives of extreme poverty and the comparative comfort he called wealth. He was far from taking stock of his position like a philosopher, but he had enough insight to feel that he was *different* after his brief trip through the mountains.

He was struck by the air of deep anxiety with which Mme. de Rênal listened to the little story of his trip which she asked him to tell her.

Fouqué had had various projects of marrying, but his love affairs had been unhappy; long exchanges on this topic had filled the conversations of the two friends. Having found happiness too quickly, Fouqué had discovered that he was not without rivals. All his stories had astonished Julien; he learned a great deal that was new to him. His solitary life compounded of imagination and mistrust had distanced him from everyone who could enlighten him.

While he was away life had been nothing for Mme. de Rênal but a succession of different torments, all intolerable, she was really ill.

—Above all, said Mme. Derville when she saw Julien returning, sick as you are, you won't sit out in the garden this evening; the night air will make you worse than ever.

Mme. Derville noted with amazement that her friend, who was always being scolded by M. de Rênal for the excessive simplicity of her dress, had put on net stockings and a pair of charming little

---

3. César de Saint-Réal (1639–1692), French novelist and historian, probably never made this statement about novels—a statement that is, moreover, perhaps less true of Stendhal's own novels than of most others.

slippers direct from Paris. For the past three days Mme. de Rênal's only amusement had been in having Elisa make for her, as quickly as possible, a summer dress; it was of a very pretty material, quite in the latest style. The dress was finished only a few minutes after Julien's return; Mme. de Rênal put it on at once. Her friend had no further doubts. She's in love, poor thing! said Mme. Derville to herself. She now understood all the symptoms of her friend's malady.

She watched her talking with Julien. Pallor alternated with blushes. Her anxious eyes were fastened on those of the young tutor. Mme. de Rênal expected that at any moment he would explain his position and announce that he was leaving the house, or would stay. Julien was far from saying any such thing; he never gave this matter a thought. After frightful inner struggles Mme. de Rênal finally brought herself to say to him, in a voice that trembled and revealed all her feeling:

—Will you be leaving your pupils and taking a position somewhere else?

Julien was struck by Mme. de Rênal's quavering voice and glance. This woman is in love with me, he said to himself; but after this moment of weakness, which her pride is already ashamed of, as soon as she no longer fears my leaving, she'll turn arrogant again. This survey of his position took place, in Julien's mind, with the speed of light; he replied cautiously:

—I should be much distressed to leave children who are so attractive and *so well born*, but perhaps I will have to. One has duties toward oneself, as well.

As he pronounced the words *so well born* (it was one of those aristocratic phrases Julien had recently picked up), he was stirred with a deep sense of hostility.

In the eyes of this woman, he reflected, I myself am not well born.

Mme. de Rênal as she listened to him admired his spirit, his charm; her heart was lacerated at the thought of the separation he was forcing her to contemplate. All her friends from Verrières, who during Julien's absence had come to dinner at Vergy, had complimented her lavishly on this astonishing man whom her husband had been lucky enough to discover. It wasn't that anyone knew whether the children were learning anything. The fact that he knew the Bible by heart, and actually in Latin, had inspired in the people of Verrières an admiration that will probably last a hundred years.

Julien, who talked to nobody, was unaware of all this. If Mme. de Rênal had had the least self-composure, she would have complimented him on the reputation he had earned, and when Julien's pride had been set at rest, he would have been gentle and agreeable to her, especially since the new dress seemed delightful to him.

Mme. de Rênal, who was also pleased with her pretty dress, and with the things Julien said about it, wanted to stroll in the garden; soon, however, she had to confess that she could go no further. She seized his arm, and far from restoring her strength, contact with his arm took away her last remaining energy.

It was evening; scarcely were they seated when Julien, resuming his former privilege, ventured to bring his lips close to the arm of his pretty neighbor and to grasp her hand. He was thinking of the boldness Fouqué had demonstrated in his love affairs and not at all of Mme. de Rênal; the phrase *well born* still weighed heavily on his spirit. His hand was grasped warmly, but it gave him no pleasure. Far from being proud of or even grateful for the feelings that Mme. de Rênal revealed all too openly that evening, her beauty, elegance, and freshness left him completely cold. There can be no doubt that purity of spirit and freedom from hateful passions prolong one's youth. With most pretty women it's the features that first harden into age.

Julien was sullen all evening; hitherto, he had been angry only with his destiny and with society, but since Fouqué had offered him a vulgar way to wealth, he was angry with himself as well. Absorbed in his own thoughts, though from time to time he spoke a few words to the ladies, Julien ended by thoughtlessly releasing the hand of Mme. de Rênal. The poor woman was devastated by this act; she saw in it a foreshadowing of her own fate.

Had she been confident of Julien's affection, perhaps her virtue might have found strength against him. But she was fearful of losing him forever, and her passion drove her to the point of reaching out for Julien's hand, which in his distraction he had rested momentarily on the back of a chair. Her action reawoke the ambition in Julien: he would have liked to be seen by all those arrogant gentry who, at dinner when he sat at the foot of the table with the children, looked upon him with complacent smiles. This woman can't despise me any more: very well, in that case, said he to himself, I ought to be aware of her beauty; indeed, I owe it to myself to become her lover. Such an idea would never have occurred to him before he had heard the naïve confessions of his friend.

The abrupt decision he had just reached provided an agreeable distraction. He said to himself: I must have one of these two women; and then he was aware that he would much have preferred to make his advances to Mme. Derville—not that she was more attractive, but she had always seen him as a tutor honored for his learning, not as a journeyman carpenter, with his rough vest folded under his arm, as he had appeared before Mme. de Rênal.

It was precisely as a young workman, blushing to the whites of his eyes, pausing before the house door and not daring to ring, that

Mme. de Rênal remembered him most fondly. [This woman, whom the shopkeepers of the district considered so arrogant, rarely thought of social status at all, and the slightest assurance in a man's character impressed her more than all the promises held out by his rank. A cart driver who had showed some real bravery would have stood higher, in her eyes, than a fearful captain of hussars, complete with moustache and pipe. She thought Julien's soul nobler than those of all her relatives, though they were all gentlemen of the blood and several of them titled.]

As he continued the summary of his position, Julien saw that he must not dream of the conquest of Mme. Derville, who was no doubt aware of Mme. de Rênal's attraction to him. Forced, then, to consider the latter, Julien asked himself: What do I really know about the character of this woman? Only one thing: before I went away I took her hand and she withdrew it, now I withdraw my hand and she reaches after it. A fine chance to pay her back for all her contempt of me. God only knows how many lovers she's had! She's probably interested in me only because the arrangements are so easy.

Such, alas, is the unhappy effect of too much civilization! At the age of twenty a young man's spirit, if he has any education at all, is a thousand miles from that ease without which love is often only the most laborious of obligations.

I'm all the more duty-bound to succeed with this woman, Julien's petty vanity pursued, since if ever I make my fortune and someone throws up at me that I held the low post of a tutor, I can let it be understood that love alone induced me to accept such a position.

Once again Julien let fall the hand of Mme. de Rênal, then took it up and clasped it warmly. As they were returning to the drawing room about midnight, Mme. de Rênal said to him in an undertone:

—Are you going to leave us, will you go away?

Julien answered with a sigh:

—I must go, indeed, for I love you passionately, and that is a crime . . . what a crime for a young priest!

Mme. de Rênal leaned upon his arm, and with so little constraint that her cheek felt the warmth of Julien's.

These two beings passed very different nights. Mme. de Rênal was exalted by transports of the most exalted moral pleasure. A flighty young girl who learns the ways of love early gets accustomed to its troubles; when she reaches the age of real passion the charm of novelty is altogether missing. As Mme. de Rênal had never read any novels, all the subtleties of her happiness were new to her. No gloomy truths could freeze her spirit, not even the specter of the future. She looked forward to being as happy ten years hence as she was at that moment. Even the notion of her virtue, and the fidelity she had pledged to M. de Rênal, which had so much disturbed her several days before, knocked vainly on her consciousness; it was sent away like an unwanted guest. Never will I accord any favor to Julien, Mme. de Rênal told herself, we will live in the future exactly as we have lived the past month. He will be a friend.

Chapter 14

ENGLISH SCISSORS

A girl of sixteen had a rose-petal complexion and wore rouge.
—Polidor[4]

In effect, Fouqué's offer had robbed Julien of all happiness; he couldn't settle on any line of action. Alas! perhaps I'm lacking in character; I would have made a poor soldier for Napoleon. At least, he added, my little intrigue with the lady of the house will distract me for a while.

Happily for him, even in this minor episode the depths of his soul bore little relation to his crude language. He was afraid of Mme. de Rênal because her dress was so pretty. In his eyes this dress constituted the advance guard of Paris itself. His pride would not allow him to leave anything to chance or to the inspiration of the instant. Relying on the confidences made him by Fouqué and the little he had read about love in the Bible, he drew up a highly detailed plan of campaign. And as he was much worried, though unable to admit it, he wrote down this plan.

Next morning in the drawing room Mme. de Rênal was for an instant alone with him.

—Don't you have any other name besides Julien? she asked him.

The question was flattering, but our hero knew not what to answer; there was no room for this episode in his plan. If he had not been so stupid as to make up a strategy beforehand, Julien's quick wit would have served him very well; his surprise would only have added to the brilliance of his phrases.

He was awkward, and exaggerated his awkwardness. Mme. de Rênal pardoned him quickly enough; she saw in his clumsiness the effect of a delightful simplicity. And the only thing she had found lacking in this man, to whom everyone else attributed a great genius, was precisely an air of candor.

—I don't trust your little tutor, Mme. Derville sometimes said to

---

4. John William Polidori (1795–1821) was Lord Byron's physician and secretary. Stendhal met them both in Milan in October, 1816. The epigraph reappears in different forms, as part of the text of Book I, Chap. 15, and as the epigraph to Book II, where it is attributed to Sainte-Beuve. Chances are it was neither Polidori's nor Sainte-Beuve's remark, but an invention of Stendhal's.

her. He always seems to be calculating and to act only out of craft. He's a sly one.

Julien remained deeply humiliated by his failure to find an answer for Mme. de Rênal.

A man like me must redeem a failure like that, he thought; and seizing the moment when they were passing from one room to another, he felt it his duty to try to give Mme. de Rênal a kiss.

Nothing could have been less suave, nothing less agreeable for either of them, and nothing more imprudent. They were nearly overseen. Mme. de Rênal thought him mad. She was frightened and above all shocked. This crudity reminded her of M. Valenod.

What would happen to me, she asked herself, if I were left alone with him? All her virtue returned, because her love was in eclipse.

She arranged things so one of her children would always be at her side.

The day was a complete bore for Julien; he spent it carrying clumsily forward his scheme of seduction. He never once glanced at Mme. de Rênal without a question in his eyes. Still, his folly did not prevent him from seeing that he had not succeeded in being agreeable, much less seductive.

Mme. de Rênal could not get over her astonishment at finding him both so bashful and so bold. It is the timidity of first love in a man of wit! she finally told herself, with immense delight. Is it possible that he was never loved by my rival!

After lunch Mme. de Rênal returned to the drawing room to receive a visit from M. Charcot de Maugiron, the subperfect of Bray. She was working on a little raised tapestry loom, with Mme. Derville by her side. It was under these circumstances, and in full daylight, that our hero found it appropriate to reach forth his foot and press it against the pretty foot of Mme. de Rênal, whose net stockings and pretty Paris slippers were actually drawing admiring glances from the gallant subperfect.

Mme. de Rênal was terrified; she dropped her scissors, her ball of yarn, and her needles; thus Julien's gesture could pass as an awkward effort to prevent the scissors from falling—as if he had seen them slipping. Happily these little scissors of English steel were broken in their fall, and Mme. de Rênal was lavish in deploring the fact that Julien had not been nearer to her.

—You saw them falling before I did, you might have caught them; as it is, your eagerness has brought me nothing but a kick on the ankle.

All this business deceived the subprefect, but not Mme. Derville. This pretty boy has awfully crude manners, she thought to herself; even in a provincial capital this sort of clumsiness won't pass. Mme. de Rênal found occasion to say to Julien:

—Be more careful, I command you.

Julien was aware of his own clumsiness and grew angry. He spent a long time debating inwardly whether he ought to be angry over that expression: *I command you.* He was stupid enough to think: she might very well say *I command* if it was a question involving her children's education, but in a love affair we presuppose equality. Without *equality* love is impossible . . . ; and his mind lost itself in the recitation of commonplaces about equality. Wrathfully he repeated to himself a verse of Corneille that Mme. Derville had taught him a couple of days before:

> . . . Love
> Makes its equalities, it does not seek them out.

Since Julien persisted in playing the role of a Don Juan, he who had never in his life had a mistress, he was paralyzingly dull all day. He had only one sensible idea; bored with himself and Mme. de Rênal, he was terrified at the approach of evening and the prospect of sitting beside her in the garden and the gathering dusk. So he told M. de Rênal that he was going to Verrières to see the priest, left after dinner, and came back only late at night.

At Verrières Julien found M. Chélan busy moving out; he had in fact been removed from his position; Vicar Maslon was replacing him. Julien helped the good curé with his things, and even got the idea of writing to Fouqué that his irresistible impulse toward a sacred calling had recently kept him from accepting certain kind offers, but now he had just seen such a shocking example of injustice that perhaps it would be safer for his salvation not to enter holy orders.

Julien was much pleased with his own cleverness in using the dismissal of the curé to provide himself with an easy retreat to the world of commerce just in case melancholy prudence should win out in his soul over heroism.

Chapter 15

COCKCROW

> *Love* in Latin is *amor,*
> And in this love we find the source
> Of danger, death, and biting cares,
> Tears, sorrows, traps, grief, and remorse.
> —Love's Heraldry

If Julien had had a bit of the shrewdness he so liberally ascribed to himself, he might have been able to congratulate himself the next morning on the effect produced by his visit to Verrières. His absence had caused his clumsiness to be forgotten. Even on this next day, however, he was still fairly sullen; but in the evening a ridiculous idea occurred to him, and he communicated it to Mme. de Rênal with a singular boldness.

Scarcely were they seated in the garden when Julien, without even waiting for dusk to fall, leaned toward the ear of Mme. de Rênal and, at the risk of compromising her terribly, whispered:

—Madame, tonight at two o'clock I must come to your room; I have something to tell you.

Julien was in an agony of fear lest his demand be granted; his role of seducer weighed on him so horribly that if he had been free to follow his own instincts, he would have retired to his own room for a few days and seen no more of these ladies. He understood that by his masterful policy yesterday he had spoiled all the prospects that seemed so fine the day before, and he no longer knew which way to turn.

Mme. de Rênal replied to Julien's impudent proposal with genuine indignation, which was in no way exaggerated. He thought he caught a note of scorn in her curt response. It's beyond question that in this answer, which was only whispered, the expression *for shame* appeared. Pretending that he had something to tell the children, Julien went to their room, and when he came back placed himself beside Mme. Derville and at a distance from Mme. de Rênal. He thus eliminated all possibility of grasping her hand. The discussion was serious, and Julien came off very well, apart from several moments of silence during which he groped desperately for a phrase. Why can't I invent some fine maneuver, he asked himself, that would force her to repeat those signs of tender feeling that convinced me, a few days ago, that she was mine for the taking!

Julien was greatly distressed by the almost desperate posture into which he had guided his affairs. And yet nothing would have embarrassed him more than success.

When the party broke up at midnight, his pessimism convinced him that Mme. Derville despised him, and that probably he was no better off with Mme. de Rênal.

Badly out of humor, and much disgruntled, Julien was unable to sleep. He was not far from giving up on all his efforts,[5] all his schemes, and living from day to day with Mme. de Rênal in the childish happiness each hour would bring him.

He exhausted his mind in inventing elaborate strategies that, an

---

5. Stendhal's sentence actually says, "He was a thousand leagues [i.e., very far indeed] from giving up," etc. One might read the sentence as saying, then, "He rejected with horror an idea which he yearned for instinctively" Accordingly, I have rationalized the sentence to conform with its major element. [Translator's Note].

instant later, he found absurd; in a word, he was most unhappy
when two o'clock struck on the farmhouse clock.

The sound roused him as the cockcrow roused Saint Peter.[6] He
saw himself on the verge of a terrifying venture. Since the moment
when he made it, he had not given another thought to his impertinent proposal: it had been so unfavorably received!

I told her that I would come to her room at two o'clock, he said
to himself as he got up; I may be inexperienced and boorish like the
son of a peasant—Mme. Derville has made that perfectly clear to
me. But at least I shan't be a weakling.

Julien was perfectly right in admiring his own courage; never had
he undertaken a more disagreeable task. As he opened the door he
trembled so violently that his legs gave way beneath him, and he
had to lean against the wall.

He was barefoot. For a moment he paused outside the bedroom
of M. de Rênal, who could be heard snoring away. Julien was distressed to hear it; he had no other pretext to prevent him from going to her. But good God! what would he ever do there? He had no
strategy worked out, and even if he had; he felt himself too distressed ever to carry it out.

At last, suffering a thousand times worse than if he had been
marching to his execution, he crept into the little corridor leading
to Mme. de Rênal's room. With trembling hands he opened the
door; it made a frightful noise.

The room was lit; a night lamp was burning on the mantle. He had
not expected this particular misfortune. As she saw him come in
Mme. de Rênal flung herself angrily out of bed. Wretch! she cried.
There was a moment of confusion. Julien forgot all his empty projects and recovered his natural self; to fail of pleasing such an attractive woman seemed to him the blackest of misfortunes. He answered
her scoldings only by falling at her feet and catching her about the
knees. As she talked to him extremely harshly, he burst into tears.

Several hours later, when Julien left Mme. de Rênal's room, one
might have said, after the fashion of novelists, that he had nothing
further to desire. Actually, he owed to the love he had previously inspired, and to the unexpected impression produced on him by feminine charms, a victory to which all of his clumsy subtleties would
never have conducted him.

But in the moments of supreme delight, victim of his own
strange pride, he insisted on playing the role of a man accustomed
to triumph over women: he made incredible efforts to spoil the effect of all his own charm. Instead of paying attention to the transports of delight he aroused and to the remorse that sharpened

6. See Mark 14.

them, he focused his attention entirely on the idea of *duty*. He feared that he would be the victim of a fearful disgrace and of perpetual ridicule if he departed from the ideal of behavior he had set himself. In a word, what made Julien a superior being was precisely the quality that prevented him from seizing a pleasure that lay directly in his path. He was like a young girl of sixteen with a charming complexion, who, when she's going to a dance, is foolish enough to cover her cheeks with rouge.

Mortally terrified when Julien actually appeared, Mme. de Rênal was quickly overwhelmed with other griefs. Julien's tears and unhappiness distressed her deeply.

Even when she had nothing further to refuse, she spurned Julien from her presence with genuine indignation, and the next instant flung herself into his arms. There was no policy behind this conduct. She saw herself damned without pardon and sought to hide her vision of hell by covering Julien with the most ardent caresses. In a word, nothing was lacking to our hero's happiness, not even a passionate sensitivity on the part of his beloved, if he had only known how to enjoy it. Not even Julien's departure put a stop to her transports of uncontrollable joy and to the attacks of bitter remorse that tore at her conscience.

Good Lord! being happy, being in love, is that all it is? This was the first thought of Julien as he regained his bedroom. He was in that condition of astonishment and uneasy discontent which generally overtakes the soul that has just obtained its heart's desire. Such a soul is accustomed to yearning, no longer has anything to yearn after, and has no memories as yet. Like a soldier just back from review, Julien was intent on examining all the details of his conduct.

—Did I fail in any of my responsibilities to myself? Did I play my role well?

And what role was that? The role of a man accustomed to shine before women.

Chapter 16

THE MORNING AFTER

> He turned his lip to hers, and with his hand
> Call'd back the tangles of her wandering hair
> —*Don Juan*, Canto 1, stanza 170

Fortunately for Julien's glory, Mme. de Rênal had been too disturbed and too astonished to observe the stupidity of this man who in an instant had become the whole world to her.

As she was begging him to leave her, just as day was beginning to break:

—Oh, Lord! she said, if my husband has overheard anything, I'm ruined forever.

Julien, who had time to make fine phrases, thought of this one:

—Should you regret losing your life?

—Ah, terribly, just now; but I should never regret having known you.

Julien found it accorded with his dignity to return deliberately to his room in broad daylight and with the greatest indiscretion.

The minute care with which he studied his own behavior, in the foolish expectation of appearing a man of experience, had only one good result; when he saw Mme. de Rênal at lunch his comportment was a masterpiece of prudence.

As for her, she could hardly look at him without blushing furiously, and she looked at him all the time. Becoming aware of her own distress, she made extra efforts to conceal it. Julien raised his eyes to hers only once. At first Mme. de Rênal admired his discretion. But then, seeing that single glance was not repeated, she grew alarmed: "Perhaps he no longer loves me," she told herself; "alas, I'm much too old for him, I must be ten years older."

As they strolled from the dining room out into the garden she clasped Julien's hand. In the moment of surprise caused by such an open mark of affection he glanced at her with passion, for she had in fact seemed beautiful to him at lunch, and even as he lowered his eyes he had passed the time by thinking of her charms. This glance brought some comfort to Mme. de Rênal; it did not relieve all her disquiet, but then her disquiet served to efface almost entirely any remorse she might have felt concerning her husband.

At lunch the husband noticed nothing; neither did Mme. Derville, who thought Mme. de Rênal was simply in danger. Throughout the day her bold and incisive friendship took the form of hints and allusions designed to paint in the most hideous colors the danger her friend was running.

Mme. de Rênal was furiously impatient for a moment alone with Julien; she wanted to ask if he still loved her. Despite the unshakable sweetness of her character, she was several times on the point of letting her friend understand how troublesome she was being.

In the garden that evening, Mme. Derville arranged matters so well that she got herself stationed between Mme. de Rênal and Julien. Mme. de Rênal, who had built up a delicious expectation of holding Julien's hand and raising it to her lips, was unable even to address a word to him.

This maneuvering increased her distress. She was haunted by one regret in particular. She had reproached Julien so bitterly for his audacity in visiting her the night before that now she was in terror he might not come again. She left the garden early, and retired to her bedchamber. But, unable to control her impatience, she came and pressed her ear against Julien's door. In spite of the uncertainty and violent passions that were devouring her, she dared not enter. Such an action seemed to her the last word in crude behavior, simply because it provides the text of a provincial proverb.

The servants were not yet all abed; discretion finally forced her to retire to her own room. Two hours of waiting were two centuries of torment.

But Julien was too faithful to what he called *his duty* to fail of executing, point by point, the program he had laid down for himself.

As the clock tolled one he slipped silently from his room, made sure that the master of the house was fast asleep, and appeared before Mme. de Rênal. That night he experienced more real pleasure with his mistress, for he thought less continually about the role he was playing. He had eyes to see and ears to hear. What Mme. de Rênal told him of her age helped to give him some assurance.

—Alas, I'm ten years older than you! How can you possibly love me? She repeated these words without ulterior motive, simply because the idea oppressed her.

Julien could form no idea of her grief, but he saw that it was real, and he forgot almost all his fears of seeming ridiculous.

The silly notion that he might be regarded as a hired lover, because of his low birth, disappeared as well. As gradually Julien's transports gave new confidence to his timid mistress, she recovered both a little happiness and the power of judging her lover. Fortunately that night he had little of that artificial manner that had made the previous night's encounter a victory but not a pleasure. If she had become aware of his efforts to play a part, the discovery would have destroyed her happiness forever. She could have seen in it only a bitter consequence of the difference in their ages.

Although Mme. de Rênal had never reflected on the theories of love, disparity of age is, after disparity of fortune, one of the great commonplaces of provincial humor whenever love is mentioned.

Within a few days Julien, quite restored to the natural ardor of his age, was desperately in love.

No one can deny, said he to himself, the angelic beauty of her soul, and they don't come any prettier.

He had almost entirely dismissed the idea of a role to be played. In a moment of self-abandon, he even told her of his anxieties. This confession lifted even higher the passion he inspired. So I never had a successful rival, Mme. de Rênal told herself joyously. She ventured to ask him about the portrait by which he placed such store; Julien swore to her that it was the portrait of a man.

When Mme. de Rênal had enough self-possession to meditate,

she could not get over her astonishment that such happiness should exist and that she should never have suspected it.

Ah! she told herself, if only I had known Julien ten years ago, when I could still pass for pretty!

Julien was far from sharing these thoughts. His love was still a form of ambition; it was his joy in possessing—he, a wretched and despised creature—such a noble and beautiful woman. His acts of adoration, his transports of delight at the attractions of his mistress, succeeded at last in reassuring her slightly about the disparity in their ages. If she had had a touch of that worldly wisdom which, in the more civilized nations, women of thirty normally have, she would have shuddered for the future of a love that seemed to depend altogether on novelty and the flattery of self-esteem.

At times when his ambition was forgotten, Julien admired with ecstasy Mme. de Rênal's very hats and dresses. He never tired of their perfume. He opened her mirrored closet and spent hours on end wondering at the beauty and order of everything he found there. His mistress, leaning against him, watched his face while he admired all the jewels and frippery which on the occasion of a marriage fill a hope chest.

And I might have married such a man! Mme. de Rênal sometimes reflected; what a fiery spirit! what a marvelous life with him!

As for Julien, he had never found himself so close to these terrible weapons of feminine artillery. It's impossible, said he to himself, that even in Paris there should be anything more beautiful! And at that point he found nothing to object to in being happy. Frequently his mistress's sincere admiration and transports of pleasure caused him to forget the empty theory that had made him so affected and almost absurd in the first moments of their affair. There were even instants when, in spite of his habitual hypocrisy, he found great joy in admitting to this great lady who so admired him his unfamiliarity with a whole mass of little forms. The rank of his mistress seemed to lift him out of his own. For her part, Mme. de Rênal found it the most delicate of moral pleasures to instruct in the niceties of behavior a young man of genius who, as everyone agreed, would some day go far. Even the subprefect and M. Valenod could hardly refrain from admirring him; because they did so, she thought them less stupid. As for Mme. Derville, she was far from sharing these feelings. Desperate over the things she guessed, and seeing that her good advice was odious to a woman who had, in fact, lost control of herself, Mme. Derville left Vergy without offering any explanation and without being asked for one. Mme. de Rênal shed a few tears over her departure and soon felt twice as happy without her. In her friend's absence she could be alone almost every day with her lover.

Julien abandoned himself all the more fully to the sweet society of his mistress because, whenever he was too long by himself, the fatal proposal of Fouqué returned to disturb him. In the first days of this new life there were moments when he, who had never loved or been loved by anybody, found such delicious pleasures in sincerity that he was on the point of confessing to Mme. de Rênal the ambition that had been, up to this point, the secret essence of his existence. He would have liked to consult her on the strange attractiveness of Fouqué's offer, but a little episode occurred that blocked all thoughts of frankness.

Chapter 17

THE FIRST DEPUTY

> O, how this spring of love resembleth
> The uncertain glory of an April day;
> Which now shows all the beauty of the sun
> And by and by a cloud takes all away!
> —*Two Gentlemen of Verona*

One evening at sunset he was sitting by his mistress at the foot of the orchard, far from any intruder, sunk in deep reverie. Can such delectable moments, he asked himself, possibly last forever? His thoughts were caught up with the difficult necessity of finding a position; he lamented that sudden burden of unhappiness which puts an end to childhood and spoils the young manhood of anyone born poor.

—Ah, he exclaimed, Napoleon was really the man sent by God to the youth of France! Who can take his place? What will those wretches do who are even richer than me, who have just the meager sum needed to get a good education, but not enough money to buy a man and get started in a career at twenty![7] Whatever becomes of us, he added with a sigh, this fatal memory will prevent our ever being really happy!

Suddenly he noted that Mme. de Rênal was frowning, had assumed a cold and disdainful air; this way of thinking seemed to her suitable only to a servant. Brought up in the consciousness of wealth, she took it for granted that Julien was too. She loved him more than life itself. She would have loved him had he proved unkind or betrayed her and money was a matter of no moment to her.

Julien was far from guessing what was in her mind. Her frown brought him back to earth. He had enough presence of mind to

---

7. "Buying a man" indicates a normal procedure for a commercial career; it entails bribing an official or purchasing someone's favor.

modify his terms and convey to this noble lady seated beside him on a grassy bank that the speech he had just delivered was one he had overheard on his recent visit to the wood dealer; that was how wicked worldlings talked.

—All right, just don't get yourself mixed up with that lot, said Mme. de Rênal, still with that glacial air that had abruptly replaced a manner of melting [and intimate] tenderness.

This frown of hers, or rather regret at his own imprudence, was the first setback for the illusion that was carrying Julien away. He said to himself: She is good, she is sweet, she is fond of me, but she has been raised in the enemy camp. They are bound to be afraid of spirited men, well educated, who don't have enough money to take up a career. What would happen to these noblemen if ever we were matched with them in even fight? If I, for example, were mayor of Verrières, honest and well meaning as I suppose M. de Rênal is at bottom! Wouldn't I get rid of the vicar, of M. Valenod, and their whole bag of tricks! Justice would really triumph in Verrières! It's not talents like theirs that would know how to stop me. They're born bumblers.

Julien's happiness that day was on the verge of becoming lasting. Our hero simply lacked the audacity to be sincere. It required bold-ness to give battle, and on the spot; Mme. de Rênal had been sur-prised by Julien's words because the men she knew always said a Robespierre might arise any minute precisely from among those well-educated, ambitious young men of the lower orders. Her se-vere expression lasted a long time, and to Julien seemed particu-larly marked. But the reason was that her first dislike of the idea was followed by regrets at having said something indirectly dis-agreeable to him. Unhappiness made itself quickly apparent on those features, which were so pure and innocent when she was happy and unworried.

Julien no longer dared meditate openly. Growing more calm and less passionate, he found that it was impractical to continue meet-ing Mme. de Rênal in her bedroom. It was better that she should come to his; if a servant saw her wandering about the house, there were twenty different pretexts at hand to explain it.

But this arrangement too had its inconvenient side. Julien had received from Fouqué various books which he himself, as a student of theology, could never have requested in a bookstore. The only time he dared open them was at night. Very often he would have been glad enough not to be interrupted by a visit; before the little scene in the orchard, mere expectation of such a visit would have rendered him incapable of reading.

Because of Mme. de Rênal, he now understood books after a wholly new fashion. He had ventured to ask her about a whole throng of little matters, ignorance of which stops short the under-standing of a young man brought up outside society, however intel-ligent we suppose him to be.

This education in love, conducted by an extremely ignorant woman, was sheer delight. Julian moved directly to an understand-ing of society as it really is today. His intelligence was not clouded by recitals of what it used to be two thousand years ago, or just sixty years ago in the era of Voltaire and Louis XV. To his indescribable joy, the scales fell from his eyes and he understood at last what was going on in Verrières.

In the foreground, various complicated intrigues had been in process for some two years now around the prefect of Besançon. They were supported by letters written from Paris and signed by all the most distinguished names in the land. And the purpose of all this was to make M. de Moirod, the most devout man in the coun-tryside, first rather than second deputy of the mayor of Verrières.

His rival was a rich manufacturer whom it was of the utmost im-portance to push down into the position of second deputy.

At last Julien understood the allusions he had overheard when good company came to dine at M. de Rênal's. This privileged group was profoundly involved in the selection of the first deputy—a process of which the rest of the town, and above all the liberals, were wholly unaware. What made it all so important was that, as is well known the main street of Verrières had to be widened, on its eastern side, by more than nine feet, since the street was declared a royal road.

But, if M. de Moirod, who had three houses in the way of the new improvement, should become first deputy and thus mayor in the event of M. de Rênal's being named representative, he would look in the other direction and people could make imperceptible repairs on houses that were blocking the new road, and by this means they would last another hundred years. In spite of M. de Moirod's lofty piety and recognized probity, everyone was sure he would be *under-standing*, for he had several children. Of the houses that had to be moved back, nine belonged to the top circles of Verrières society.

In Julien's eyes this intrigue was far more important than the his-toric battle of Fontenoy,[8] the name of which he had just seen for the first time in one of the books sent him by Fouqué. There were some things that had puzzled Julien for five years, ever since he started to study evenings with the curé. But discretion and spiritual humility are the chief qualities of a theological student, so it had been impossible for him to make inquiries.

---

8. At the battle of Fontenoy (May 11, 1745) the French, aided by a brigade of Irish exiles, defeated a British and allied army.

Renals are paying off Free Masons so they don't get attacked in the next revolution

Free Masons

Free Masons were radical + wanted egalitarianism - treated all people in their meeting the same

One day Mme. de Rênal gave an order to her husband's valet, who was Julien's enemy.

—But, madame, this is the last Friday of the month, replied the man, putting on a peculiar expression.

—Off with you, said Mme. de Rênal.

—So that's it! said Julien, he's going to that hay warehouse that used to be a church and was recently restored to the uses of religion. But what do they do there? That's one of the mysteries I never could solve. *Mme de Renal is playing dumb, she knows more about it then her husband* —It's a very useful institution, but also a very odd one, replied Mme. de Rênal; women aren't admitted. All I can learn is that all the people who go there are on very familiar terms. For example, this servant will meet M. Valenod there, and that arrogant, stupid fellow will not be at all distressed when Saint-Jean talks to him as an equal; he'll answer in the same tone. If you really want to know what they do there, I'll ask M. de Maugiron and M. Valenod.[9] We pay twenty francs for every servant, to prevent them from cutting our throats some day [in case the Terror of '93 returns].

Time fled by. Thinking of his mistress's charms distracted Julien from his black ambition. His inability to talk with her about gloomy, reasonable things, because they were of opposite parties, increased (though he never suspected it) the happiness she gave him and her power over him.

At times, when the presence of too-understanding children reduced them to talking the language of cold reason, Julien sat with perfect docility, watching her with eyes in which love glittered, while she explained to him the way of the world. Often in the midst of telling about some clever bit of rascality in connection with a road or a purchasing order Mme. de Rênal grew ecstatic with joy; Julien had to warn her she was allowing herself to use with him the same intimate gestures she used with her children [she ran her hand through his hair]. There were in fact days when she had the illusion of loving him like her own child. Didn't she have to reply constantly to his simple-minded questions about a thousand elementary things a well-born child knows by the age of fifteen? A moment later, she worshipped him as her master. His genius came close to terrifying her; she could see more clearly every day, so she thought, the future great man in this young cleric. She saw him as the pope, she saw him as a great minister, like Richelieu.[1]

—Will I live to see you in your glory? she said to Julien; the time

9. The congregations, which began as voluntary devotional organizations, were particularly apt to be transformed during times of social stress into vigilante and espionage groups. Stendhal's contempt for the fraternizing of servants and masters in these groups contrasts with his fitfully egalitarian sentiments elsewhere.
1. Cardinal Richelieu (1585–1642) was the supreme architect of French royal power.

is ripe for a great man; church and monarchy are in need of one. [Our gentlemen say every day: if some Richelieu doesn't cut off the torrent of personal judgment, all will be lost.]

Chapter 18

A KING AT VERRIÈRES

Are you good for nothing but to lie there like a corpse of a people, inanimate and bloodless?
—Speech of the bishop, in St. Clement's.

On the third of September at ten o'clock at night a police officer roused all Verrières by charging up the main street at a gallop; he brought news that his majesty the king of _____ would arrive the following Sunday, and here it was already Tuesday. The prefect authorized, that is to say, ordered, formation of a guard of honor; the show must be as big as possible. A courier was dispatched to Vergy; M. de Rênal arrived that same night and found the town in turmoil. Every man had his pretensions; the least important people were renting balconies from which to view the king's entry.

Who will command the guard of honor? M. de Rênal saw instantly how important it was, in view of those houses that might have to be moved back, that M. de Moirod should be in command. That might open his way to the office of first deputy. There was nothing to be said against M. de Moirod's devotion, it was quite unparalleled, but he had never sat upon a horse. He was thirty-six years old, timid in every way, fearful alike of falling off his horse and of making himself ridiculous.

The mayor summoned him at five o'clock in the morning.

—Look here, sir, I'm asking your advice today as if you already held the post for which all right-thinking men support you. Now, in this unfortunate town industry is flourishing, the liberals are all becoming millionaires, their group aspires to power and will make a weapon of anything. Let us safeguard the interests of the king, of the monarchy, and above all of our holy religion. Now who do you think, my dear sir, should be entrusted with command of the guard of honor?

Despite his horrible fear of horses, M. de Moirod finally accepted this distinction like a martyr. "I shall be able to give the occasion a proper style," he told the mayor. There was barely time to get ready the uniforms that seven years before had served for the arrival of a royal prince.

At seven Mme. de Rênal arrived from Vergy with Julien and the children. She found her drawing room filled with liberal ladies, all preaching the reconciliation of parties and all come to beg from her husband a place for their husbands among the guard of honor. One of them suggested that if her husband was not chosen, out of sheer humiliation he would go bankrupt. Mme. de Rênal quickly sent this crowd packing. She seemed very thoughtful.

Julien was surprised and angry that she kept from him the reason for her concern. Just as I thought, he said bitterly to himself, her love is eclipsed by the joy of having a king in her house. This whole uproar has overwhelmed her. Perhaps she'll love me again when the ideas of her caste no longer disturb her mind.

An astonishing thing: he loved her all the more for this behavior.

Upholsterers were starting to flood through the house; he sought long and vainly for an occasion to have a word with her. Finally he found her, coming out of his room, Julien's own room, carrying one of his suits. They were alone. He tried to speak with her. She turned away, and refused to listen to him.—I'm a fool to be in love with such a woman; ambition has driven her just as crazy as her husband.

But she was even crazier; one of her great desires, which she had never admitted to Julien for fear of shocking him, was to see him put off, if only for a day, his gloomy black suit. With a subtlety really to be admired in a woman who was so natural, she obtained, first from M. de Moirod, and then from the subprefect de Maugiron, the nomination of Julien for the guard of honor, in preference to five or six young men, sons of wealthy manufacturers, of whom two at least were distinguished for their piety. M. Valenod, who had expected to make his carriage available to the town's prettiest women and to have his fine stallions admired, agreed to lend one of his horses to Julien, whom he hated above all other beings. But all the guards of honor either owned or had borrowed one of those sky-blue uniforms with the two silver stars of a colonel which had glittered so splendidly seven years before. Mme. de Rênal wanted a new uniform altogether, and she had only four days in which to send to Besançon and get back the uniform, side arms, cocked hat, and so forth—everything that makes an honor guard. What is most amusing is that she thought it imprudent to have Julien's outfit made at Verrières. She wanted to surprise him, him and the town.

His duty having been done with respect to the honor guard and the expressions of public joy, the mayor had now to concern himself with a great religious ceremony; the king of _____ did not want to pass Verrières without seeing the great relic of St. Clement, which is preserved at Bray-le-Haut, only one short league from the town. The clergy must be well represented; this was the hardest matter of all to arrange, since M. Maslon, the new priest, wanted above all to avoid the presence of M. Chélan. In vain did M. de Rênal object to him the rashness of this procedure. The Marquis de La Mole, whose ancestors had been for many years governors of the district, had been appointed to accompany the king of _____. For at least thirty years he had been acquainted with Abbé Chélan. He would certainly ask for news of him, immediately upon reaching Verrières, and if he found him disgraced would be capable of going, with all the dignitaries he could summon, to look him up in the humble cottage to which he had retired. What an insult!

—I am disgraced, both here and in Besançon, replied Abbé Maslon, if he makes an appearance among my clergy. A Jansenist, Good God![1]

—Whatever you say, my dear abbé, replied M. de Rênal, I shall not expose the whole administration of Verrières to an affront from M. de La Mole. You don't know him, he's a sound man at court, but down here in the provinces he has a wicked satiric wit; he's a mocker who tries only to embarrass people. Simply to amuse himself, he's capable of covering us with ridicule in the eyes of the liberals.

It was only in the course of the night between Saturday and Sunday, after three days of negotiation, that the pride of Abbé Maslon yielded before the mayor's fears as they gradually changed to courage. It was necessary to write a honeyed letter to Abbé Chélan, begging him to attend the ceremony of the relic at Bray-le-Haut, if indeed his advanced years and infirmities allowed him to do so. M. Chélan requested and obtained a letter of invitation for Julien, who was to accompany him as subdeacon.

Sunday morning thousands of peasants arriving from the mountains flooded through the streets of Verrières. The sun shone brilliantly. Finally, about three o'clock, the whole crowd was stirred by the sight of a great beacon fire atop a peak two leagues from Verrières. This signal made known that the king had entered upon the territory of the district. At once the sound of all the bells pealing and repeated shots from an old Spanish cannon belonging to the town gave evidence of the population's joy at this great event. Half the people climbed to the rooftops. All the women crowded onto balconies. The honor guard stirred itself. There was admiration for the brilliant uniforms; everyone recognized a relative or a friend.

1. In the middle of the seventeenth century the French church divided between factions calling themselves Jansenists (after Cornelis Jansen [1585–1638], whose book on St. Augustine, posthumously published in 1640, was deeply influential) and anti-Jansenists, the leaders of whom were generally Jesuits. Temperamentally and by conviction the Jansenists tended to be austere, rigorous, inflexible types who emphasized the soul's intimate and personal relation to God; thus they were often accused of sympathy with Protestantism, and especially Calvinism. The Jesuits, on the other hand, were popularly supposed to be supple intriguers whose failings tended to be in the direction of worldliness.

There was laughter at the timidity of M. de Moirod, who kept a prudent hand ready at every instant to clutch the saddle bow. But one spectacle caused all the others to be forgotten: the first horseman of the ninth file was a handsome boy, very slender, whom at first nobody recognized. Shortly a cry of indignation from some, and an astonished silence from others, bore witness to a general sensation. This young man, astride one of M. Valenod's Norman horses, was recognized as young Sorel, the carpenter's boy. With one voice everyone cried out against the mayor, especially the liberals. So that was it, just because this little workman disguised as an abbé gave lessons to his brats, he had presumed to name him to the guard of honor, over the candidates of Messieurs So and So, wealthy manufacturers! All the other ones, said a lady banker, ought to throw out that little brat, born on a dunghill.—He's sneaky, and he has a saber, replied her neighbor; he'd be just crooked enough to give them a slash across the face.

The comments of the well-born were more dangerous. The ladies asked one another if the mayor alone was responsible for this striking indecorum. In general, they did ample justice to his scorn for those of low birth.

While he was the center of all these comments, Julien was the happiest of men. Naturally bold, he sat a horse better than most young men in this mountain village. He saw from the glances of the women that he was the center of attention.

Because they were new, his epaulets were more brilliant than anyone else's. His horse reared at every moment; he was in his glory.

His joy exceeded all measure when, as they passed by the old rampart, the noise of the little cannon caused his horse to shy out of line. By great good luck, he did not fall off, and from that moment on he felt himself a hero. He was one of Napoleon's orderlies in the act of charging a battery.

One person was happier than he. She had seen him first from one of the windows of the town hall; getting into her coach then, and swiftly accomplishing a wide detour, she arrived in time to tremble for him when his horse shied out of the column. Then, her carriage galloping furiously out another one of the town's gates, she was able to regain the road along which the king would pass, and to follow the honor guard at a distance of twenty paces amid a noble cloud of dust. Ten thousand peasants cried: Long live the king! when the mayor had the honor to harangue his majesty. An hour later, all the speeches being finished, the king was about to enter the town and the little cannon began to fire hasty shots. But an accident occurred, not to the artillerymen who had served their guns at Leipzig and Montmirail[2] but to the future first deputy, M. de Moirod. His horse lowered him gently into the only mud puddle on the broad highway, and this made for some disorder, since he had to be pulled out before the king's carriage could pass.

His majesty alighted at the fine new church, which that day was arrayed in all its crimson draperies. The king was to dine and then shortly return to his carriage in order to go and worship at the famous relic of St. Clement. Scarcely was the king at the church when Julien was galloping toward the house of M. de Rênal. There, he put off with a sigh his fine sky-blue uniform, his saber and epaulets to resume his seedy little black outfit. Once more he took to horse, and in a few moments was at Bray-le-Haut, which occupies the summit of a very pretty hill. Enthusiasm brings out these peasants in swarms, Julien thought. There's scarcely room to turn around in Verrières, and here are ten thousand more of them around the old abbey. Half ruined by vandalism during the Revolution, it had been magnificently rebuilt since the Restoration, and people were starting to talk of miracles. Julien sought out Abbé Chélan, who scolded him sharply and gave him a cassock and surplice. He dressed at once, and followed M. Chélan, who was to wait upon the young bishop of Agde. This was a nephew of M. de La Mole, recently named to the post, and now charged with displaying the relic to the king. But the bishop could not be discovered.

The clergy grew impatient. They were waiting for their leader in the dark gothic cloister of the old abbey. Eighty curés had been assembled to represent the former chapter of Bray-le-Haut, composed before 1789 of eighty canons.[3] Having deplored for three quarters of an hour the extreme youth of the bishop, the curés thought fit that their dean should seek out monsignor and advise him that the king was approaching and it was time to enter the choir. M. Chélan's great age had made him dean; despite his crossness with Julien, he made a sign for him to follow. Julien wore his surplice very gracefully. By some sort of ecclesiastical toiletry he had flattened out his fine head of hair; but, by an oversight which irked M. Chélan even further, under the long folds of his cassock appeared the spurs of an honor guard.

When they reached the bishop's apartment various lace-covered lackeys barely deigned to explain to the old curé that monsignor

2. Leipzig (October 1813) and Montmirail (February 1814) were Napoleonic battles of the last days of the First Empire.
3. Eighty canons, before the Revolution, would have involved eighty ceremonial posts of great magnificence, eighty sinecures probably held by younger sons of important families.

was not to be seen. They disregarded him when he tried to explain that as dean of the noble chapter of Bray-le-Haut he was entitled at all times to be admitted to the presence of the officiating bishop.

Julien's lofty mood was shocked by the insolence of these lackeys. He began to run through the dormitories of the ancient abbey, opening every door he saw. A particularly little one opened to his efforts, and he found himself in a room full of the bishop's valets, all dressed in black with gold chains about their necks. Supposing from his anxious expression that he was on an errand for the bishop, these gentry let him pass. He took a few steps and found himself in an immense and very dark gothic hall, paneled in dark oak; all the pointed windows, except for one, had been bricked up. Nothing concealed the crudity of this masonry, and it formed a melancholy contrast with the magnificence of the wood paneling. The two long sides of this room, famous among scholars of Burgundian antiquities and built by Charles the Bold about 1470 in expiation of some sin or other, were lined with wooden stalls, richly carved. In varicolored woods were to be seen there all the mysteries of the Apocalypse.

This gloomy magnificence, degraded by the presence of raw bricks and naked plaster, stirred Julien's heart. He stopped and stood silent. At the other end of the hall, near the only window that admitted light, he saw a portable mirror framed in mahogany. A young man in violet robes and lacy surplice, but bareheaded, was standing a few feet from the mirror. It seemed a strange piece of furniture for such surroundings; doubtless it had been brought from town. Julien thought the young man seemed irritated; with his right hand he kept bestowing benedictions in the direction of the mirror.

What's all this about? thought Julien. Is there some sort of preliminary ceremony that this young priest is performing? Perhaps it's the bishop's secretary . . . he'll be arrogant like the lackeys . . . well, never mind, let's give it a try.

He stepped forward and walked slowly the length of the room, always looking toward the single window and the young man, who continued to mime benedictions, slow but numerous and executed without a moment's pause.

As he approached he was better able to distinguish the angry look of the other. The richness of his lace-lined surplice stopped Julien involuntarily a few paces from the splendid mirror.

It's my duty to speak first, he said to himself at last; but the beauty of the hall had touched him, and in anticipation he was already wounded at the harsh words that he expected.

The young man saw him in the glass, turned, and abruptly putting off his angry air, said to him in the gentlest of tones:

—Very well, my dear sir, has it finally been set to rights?

Julien was thunderstruck. As the young man turned toward him, Julien saw the pectoral cross about his neck; it was the bishop of Agde. So young, thought Julien; at most, six or eight years older than me!

And he was ashamed of his spurs.

—Monsignor, he replied timidly, I am sent by the dean of the chapter, M. Chélan.

—Ah, he's been warmly recommended to me, said the bishop in a polite tone that completed Julien's enchantment. But I beg your pardon, sir, I mistook you for the person who is supposed to bring back my miter. They packed it so clumsily in Paris that the silver star on top has been horribly twisted. That will make a very ugly impression, the young bishop added gloomily, and I'm still waiting for it to come back.

—Monsignor, I will go look for the miter, if your eminence permits.

Julien's fine eyes had their effect.

—Please do so, my dear sir, the bishop replied, with charming courtesy, I really need it right away. I am deeply distressed to keep the gentlemen of the chapter waiting.

When Julien was in the middle of the hall, he glanced back toward the bishop and saw that he had begun to deliver his benedictions again. What can that possibly be? Julien asked himself; no doubt it's some sort of ecclesiastical preparation required by the ceremony which is going to take place. As he reached the anteroom where the valets were gathered, he saw the miter among them. Yielding involuntarily to Julien's imperious glance, these gentlemen placed monsignor's miter in his hands.

He felt proud to be carrying it. As he crossed the long hall he walked slowly; he held it with respect. He found the bishop seated before the mirror; from time to time his right hand still gestured, though wearily, a benediction. Julien helped him to put on the miter. The bishop shook his head.

—Ah, that will do, he said to Julien contentedly. Would you be good enough to step away a few feet?

The bishop strode swiftly to the center of the room, then walked very slowly toward the mirror, resumed his cross expression, and made a series of solemn benedictions.

Julien stood motionless with surprise; he was tempted to understand, but did not dare. The bishop paused, and glancing at him with an expression from which gravity rapidly faded, asked:

—What do you think of my miter, sir, does it fit me properly?

—Very well indeed, monsignor.

—It's not too far back? That would look pretty silly; but then you can't wear it down over your eyes, either, like an officer's cap.

—It seems to me exactly right.

—The king of _____ is used to a venerable and no doubt extremely grave clergy. Particularly because of my age, I shouldn't like to give too casual an impression.

And the bishop began to walk about again, bestowing benedictions.

It's perfectly clear, thought Julien, daring at last to understand, he's practicing his benedictions.

After a few more minutes, the bishop said:—I'm ready now. Would you go, sir, and give notice to the dean and the gentlemen of the chapter.

Shortly M. Chélan, followed by the two senior curés, entered through a vast and magnificently sculptured doorway, which Julien had not noticed before. But this time he remained in his proper position, in the last rank of all, and could see the bishop only over the shoulders of the ecclesiastics as they crowded through the doorway.

Slowly the bishop walked down the hall; as he reached the threshold, the curés formed a line of march behind him. After an instant of disorder the procession moved forward, intoning a psalm. The bishop walked last between M. Chélan and another very elderly cleric. Julien, as an adjunct of Abbé Chélan, managed to get quite close to monsignor. They walked down the long corridors of the abbey of Bray-le-Haut; despite the brilliant sunshine outside, the walls were dark and dank. At last they reached the gate of the cloister. Julien was overcome with admiration for such a splendid ceremony. Ambition, stirred by the youth of the bishop, disputed in his heart with admiration for his sensitivity and exquisite courtesy. His politeness was quite another thing from that of M. de Rênal, even on one of his good days. The higher one rises in society, Julien thought to himself, the more one finds these charming good manners.

They entered the church by a side portal. Suddenly a frightful noise caused the ancient vaults to reverberate; Julien thought they would fall down. It was that little cannon again; it had just arrived, drawn at a full gallop by eight horses; and no sooner arrived than it went into action, with the cannoneers of Leipzig firing five shots a minute just as if they had the Prussians in their sights.

But this glorious racket made no impression on Julien; he had no more dreams of Napoleon and military glory. So young, he thought, to be bishop of Agde! But where is Agde? And how much does it bring in? Two or three hundred thousand francs, probably.

Monsignor's lackeys appeared with a magnificent canopy; M. Chélan grasped one of the poles, but in fact Julien supported it. The bishop took his place beneath it. He had actually succeeded in giving himself the appearance of an old man; our hero's admiration knew no bounds. What can't be done with a little cunning! he thought.

The king appeared. Julien had the privilege of seeing him from quite close. The bishop harangued him with great unction, not forgetting to add a little touch of extremely polite reproof to his majesty.

We shall not describe at length the ceremonies of Bray-le-Haut; for two weeks they filled all the columns of all the newspapers in the district. Julien learned from the bishop's speech that the king was a descendant of Charles the Bold.

Later it became part of Julien's duties to check over the accounts detailing what this ceremony had cost. M. de La Mole, who had made his nephew a bishop, undertook the additional gesture of paying for the whole show. The ceremony of Bray-le-Haut alone cost three thousand eight hundred francs.

After the bishop's speech and the king's response, his majesty placed himself beneath the canopy, where he kneeled very devoutly on a cushion placed by the altar. The choir was lined with stalls and the stalls were raised two steps above the floor. On the upper of these two steps sat Julien at the feet of M. Chélan, almost like a train bearer with his cardinal, in the Sistine Chapel at Rome. There was a *Te Deum*, clouds of incense, infinite volleys of musketry and artillery; the peasants were delirious with joy and piety. One such day undoes the work of a hundred issues of Jacobin newspapers.

Julien was six feet from the king, who was in fact praying earnestly. For the first time he noticed a short man with a sharp glance wearing a perfectly plain suit. But on this very simple costume he wore a sky-blue ribbon. He was a good deal closer to the king than numerous other gentlemen, whose costumes were so covered with gold braid that, as Julien said to himself, one could hardly see the basic material. A few moments later he learned that this was M. de La Mole. He seemed to have a lofty, even insolent, manner.

This marquis wouldn't be courteous like my fine bishop, thought he. Ah, doesn't a job in the church render a man bland and good! But the king came here to worship the relic, and I don't see any relic. Now where can St. Clement be?

A little cleric beside him made known that the venerable relic was in an upper part of the building in a *chapelle ardente*.

What's a *chapelle ardente*? Julien asked himself.[4]

But he did not want to ask for an explanation of the phrase. He watched more closely than ever.

---

4. Actually, a *chapelle ardente* (for which English has no brief equivalent) is a chapel lit with candles where, ordinarily, a corpse is laid out before burial. The candles are what make it *ardente*, a "burning" chapel.

When a reigning prince visits, etiquette requires that the canons not accompany the bishop. But as he set out for the *chapelle ardente*, the bishop of Agde asked Abbé Chélan to accompany him, and Julien ventured to follow.

Having mounted a long staircase, they reached an extremely narrow doorway, the frame of which was splendidly gilded. This work seemed to have been done yesterday.

Before the door was kneeling a group of twenty-four girls belonging to the most distinguished families of Verriéres. Before opening the door, the bishop kneeled for a moment among the girls, all of them pretty. While he was praying loudly they were lost in admiration of his fine laces, his graceful gestures, his youthful, sensitive face. This spectacle deprived our hero of what remained of his reason. At that moment he would have fought for the Inquisition, and with full conviction. Abruptly the door opened and the chapel appeared, glowing with light. On the altar were visible more than a thousand candles divided into eight tiers, with bouquets of flowers in between. The strong odor of fine incense rose in clouds from the doorway of the sanctuary. The newly gilded chapel was narrow but lofty. Julien observed that on the altar there were some candles more than fifteen feet high. The girls could not repress a cry of admiration. No one had been admitted into the little vestibule of the chapel except the twenty-four girls, the two curés, and Julien.

Shortly the king arrived, followed by M. de La Mole and by his grand chamberlain. The guards themselves remained outside, kneeling and presenting arms.

His majesty flung himself, rather than placing himself, on a low stool. Only then did Julien, drawn back against the gilded door, perceive, under the bare arm of a girl, the enchanting statue of St. Clement. He was concealed beneath the altar, wearing the costume of a young Roman soldier. A wide wound appeared on his neck, from which blood seemed to flow. The artist had quite outdone himself; the Saint's dying eyes, still full of grace, were half closed. A budding moustache adorned that charming mouth, which, though half closed, still seemed to be praying. Seeing this, the girl beside Julien wept bitterly; one of her tears fell warm on Julien's hand.

After a moment of silent prayer, broken only by the distant sound of bells tolling in all the villages for ten leagues around, the bishop of Agde begged permission of the king to speak. He concluded his short but very moving talk with these words, the more effective for their simplicity.

—Never forget, young Christians, that you have seen one of the greatest kings on earth kneeling before the servants of an omnipotent and terrible God. These servants, though weak, persecuted, and done to death on earth, as you see from the still-bleeding wounds of St. Clement, have their triumph in heaven. Do you promise, young Christians, to hold this day in remembrance? You must hate impiety, then. Forever you must remain true to a God who is great, who is terrible, and who is also good.

At these words the bishop rose with an air of authority.

—You promise me? said he, holding up his arms like one inspired.

—We promise, cried the girls, melting into tears.

—I receive your promise in the name of almighty God! said the bishop in a voice of thunder. And that was the end of the ceremony.

The king himself was weeping. Only much later did Julien regain enough coolness to ask where were the saint's bones, sent from Rome to Philip the Good, Duke of Burgundy. He was told that they were hidden inside the charming wax figurine.[5]

His majesty graciously permitted the young ladies who had been with him in the chapel to wear a red ribbon on which were embroidered these words: DOWN WITH IMPIETY, ADORATION FOREVER.

M. de La Mole ordered a distribution among the peasantry of ten thousand bottles of wine. That night, at Verrières, the liberals found it appropriate to light up their houses a hundred times brighter than the royalists. Before he left, the king paid a call upon M. de Moirod.

Chapter 19

TO THINK IS TO SUFFER

The grotesque quality of everyday life conceals from you a real misery of the passions.

—Barnave[6]

As he was replacing the everyday furniture in the room which had been occupied by M. de La Mole, Julien came across a sheet of heavy paper folded in four. At the foot of the sheet he read:

To His Excellency, M. le Marquis de La Mole, peer of France, knight of the orders of the king, etc.

It was a petition, in the clumsy handwriting of a cook.

Monsieur le marquis,
I have had good religious principles all my life. I was in Lyon exposed to bombs during the siege of '93 of detestable memory. I take communion. I go Sundays to mass at the parish church.

---

5. Philip the Good (1396–1467) was a fifteenth-century Duke of Burgundy. He was the father of Charles the Bold.
6. See p. 10, note 9.

I never missed my Easter duty, not even in '93 of detestable memory. My cook, before the Revolution I had servants, my cook has orders that we fast on Friday. I have an excellent reputation in Verrières, and make bold to say I deserve it. I walk under the canopy in the processions beside his honor the priest and his honor the mayor. I carry at big festivals a fat candle bought at my own expense. Concerning which matters certificates are at Paris at the ministry of finance. I request of M. le marquis the lottery office at Verrières,[7] which cannot fail to be available soon, one way or another, the incumbent being very sick and besides voting badly in the elections, etc.

De Cholin.

In the margin of this petition was an endorsement signed *De Moirod*, which began with this line:

I had the honor to speak *yessturday* of the good subject who makes this request, etc.

So even that imbecile de Cholin shows me the path to be taken, said Julien to himself.

A week after the king of _____ passed through Verrières, the one topic of discussion that survived innumerable lies, stupid explanations, ridiculous opinions, etc., etc., which fastened successively on the king, the bishop of Agde, the Marquis de La Mole, the ten thousand bottles of wine and poor tumble-down de Moirod, who, in hopes of a cross,[8] left his house only a month after his fall—the one topic was the frightful impropriety of having *hoisted* into the honor guard Julien Sorel, the carpenter's son. You should have heard on this topic the rich manufacturers of figured cloth who night and day bawled themselves hoarse in the cafés on the subject of equality. That snob Mme. de Rênal was responsible for the abomination. And why? The bright eyes and fine complexion of little Abbé Sorel were reason enough.

Scarcely were they back in Vergy when Stanislas-Xavier, the youngest of the boys, came down with a fever; Mme. de Rênal fell victim at once to a frightful remorse. For the first time she looked upon her love affair in a coherent, consecutive way; she seemed to understand, as by a miracle, the enormity of the fault into which she had let herself be carried. Though profoundly religious by nature, she had never until this moment thought of her crime as it must appear in the eyes of God.

Years ago, in the Convent of the Sacred Heart, she had loved God passionately; in her present circumstances she feared him

---

7. A national lottery was operated in France during the last quarter of the eighteenth and the first quarter of the nineteenth century.
8. "Cross" stands for the ribbon and medal of an honorary order.

equally. The conflicts that ravaged her spirit were all the worse because there was nothing reasonable about her terror. Julien soon found that the least trace of logic infuriated rather than calmed her; she saw in it the language of hell. So that, as Julien was himself very fond of little Stanislas, it seemed better to talk to her about his sickness; then she quickly assumed a grave calm. But continual remorse prevented Mme. de Rênal from sleeping; she never broke her somber silence; if she had opened her mouth, it would have been to proclaim her guilt to God and man.

—I implore you, Julien told her, let me be the only one to whom you tell your troubles. If you still love me, don't talk to anyone else; your words can never relieve our Stanislas of his fever.

But his consolations were fruitless; he did not know Mme. de Rênal had got it into her head that her jealous God would be satisfied only if she hated Julien or suffered the loss of her son. It was because she knew she could never hate her lover that she was so wretched.

—Go away, she said one day to Julien; in the name of God, leave the house; it's your being here that's killing my son.

God is punishing me, she added in a whisper, he is a just God, I worship his justice; my crime was horrible and I felt no remorse! It's the first sign that God has given me up; I shall be doubly punished, and I deserve it.

Julien was deeply moved. He saw neither hypocrisy nor exaggeration in her remorse. She thinks that in loving me she is killing her boy, and yet the poor woman loves me better than her own son. No doubt about it, that's the grief which is killing her; and that's real magnificence of feeling. But how could I give rise to such a passion, poor as I am, ill taught, ignorant, sometimes crude in my manners?

One night the child was in crisis. About two in the morning M. de Rênal came to see him. Flushed with fever, the boy could not recognize his father. Suddenly Mme. de Rênal threw herself at the feet of her husband: Julien saw she was going to tell everything and ruin herself forever.

Fortunately, her dramatic gesture irked M. de Rênal.

—Good-bye, good-bye! he cried, and turned to go.

—No, no, listen to me, cried his wife, kneeling before him and trying to hold him back. Here is the whole truth. I am killing my own son. I gave him life and I'm taking it away from him. Heaven is punishing me, in the eyes of God I am guilty of murder. I must destroy and abase myself; perhaps that sacrifice will appease the Lord.

If M. de Rênal had been a man of imagination, he would have understood everything.

—Romantic ideas, he cried, pushing away his wife as she tried to clutch his knees. All romantic notions, that stuff! Julien, call the doctor as soon as it's morning.

And he went back to bed. Mme. de Rênal fell to her knees, half fainting, and repelling Julien with a convulsive gesture as he offered to come to her aid.

Julien stood amazed.

So this is adultery, he said to himself. . . . Is it possible that those knavish priests . . . . could be right? Can they, who commit so many sins themselves, have the special privilege of understanding the real principle of sin? What a fantastic thought!

For twenty minutes after M. de Rênal left, Julien watched the woman he loved resting her head on the child's little bed, motionless and almost unconscious. Here is a woman of superior spirit reduced to the pit of misery because she has known me, he said to himself.

Hours passed swiftly. What can I do for her? I must decide. There's no question of my interests here. What do I care about men and their stupid shows? What can I do for her? . . . leave her? But I leave her alone, in prey to the most atrocious griefs. That automaton husband of hers does more harm than good. He'll say something crude to her, out of sheer clumsiness; she may go mad, throw herself out of a window.

If I leave her, if I no longer watch over her, she'll tell him everything. And who knows, maybe, in spite of the fortune she must have brought him, he'll make a scandal. She might tell everything, Good God! to that b_____ Abbé Maslon who's been using the illness of a six-year-old as a pretext for sticking close to this house, and not without his own purposes. In her grief, and with her fear of God, she will forget everything she knows about this man; she'll see in him only a priest.

—Go away, Mme. de Rênal said to him, suddenly opening her eyes.

—I would give my life a thousand times over to know how to serve you best, Julien replied; never have I loved you so much, my darling, or rather, it's only at this moment that I've begun to love you as you deserve. What would become of me far from you, and knowing that you are unhappy because of me! But let's not talk of my troubles. I'll go, indeed I will, my love. But if I leave you, if I cease to watch over you, to be between you and your husband, you'll tell him everything, you'll ruin yourself. Only think, he'll drive you out of his house in disgrace; all Verrières, all Besançon, will be buzzing with the scandal. They'll put all the blame on you; you'll never be able to live it down . . .

—That's just what I want, she cried, leaping up. I'll suffer; so much the better.

—But this horrible scandal will make him miserable too!

—But I humiliate myself, I drag myself in the mud; and perhaps in that way I'll save my son. This humiliation before the whole town may be a form of public penance. As far as I can judge, and I'm a weak woman, isn't this the greatest sacrifice I can make to God? Perhaps He in his mercy will accept my humiliation, and leave me my son! Tell me of a more painful sacrifice and I'll perform it.

—Let me punish myself, as well. I too am guilty. Shall I enter a Trappist monastery? The austerity of that life may appease your God. . . . Ah, God, why can't I take on myself the sickness of Stanislas. . . .

—Ah! you love him too, cried Mme. de Rênal, rising and throwing herself into his arms.

At the same time she pushed him away with horror.

—I believe you! I believe you! she continued, once more back on her knees; oh, my only friend, oh, why aren't you the father of Stanislas? Then it would not be a horrible sin to love you better than your son.

—Will you let me stay if in the future I love you only as a brother? It's the only sensible form of expiation, perhaps that will appease God's anger.

—And how about me? she cried, rising, taking Julien's head between her two hands, and holding it before her eyes at a little distance; how about me? Shall I love you as a brother? Do you think it's in my power to love you like a brother?

Julien broke into sobs.

—I obey you, he said, falling at her feet, I obey you in everything you decree; it's all that's left for me to do. My mind is blinded; I see no way out. If I leave, you'll tell everything to your husband, destroy yourself and him with you. After such a scandal, he'll never be named deputy. If I stay, you'll think me responsible for your son's death, and you'll die of grief. Shall we try the consequences of my leaving? If you wish, I'll punish myself for our sin by leaving you for a week. I'll spend it in some retreat, wherever you say. At the abbey of Bray-le-Haut, for example; but you must swear that while I'm away you won't say anything to your husband. Remember, I'll never be able to return if you talk.

She promised; he left, but two days later she called him back.

—Without you I'll never be able to keep my vow. I'll tell my husband if you're not continually here to silence me with your glances. Every hour of this horrible existence seems to last a whole day.

At last the clouds lifted for the wretched woman. Little by little Stanilas began to recover. But the glass was cracked; her reason had measured the extent of her sin, and she could no longer regain her balance. Remorse remained, and became what it should be in a deeply sincere heart. Her life was heaven and hell; hell when Julien was out of her sight, heaven when she was at his feet. I'll never delude myself again, she said to him, even at the moments when her love was at its highest pitch. I am damned, damned without hope of pardon. You are young, you yielded to my seductions, you may be pardoned; but for me, it is damnation. I know it, beyond any question. I'm afraid; who wouldn't be terrified at the prospect of hell? But really, I have no regrets. I would sin again, if my sin were still before me. Let God simply forbear to punish me in this world, and through my children, and I'll have more than I deserve. But you, at least, Julien, she cried at other moments, are you happy? Do you think I love you enough?

Julien's suspicion and anxious pride, which required above all a love built on sacrifice, could not hold out against a sacrifice so vast, so unquestionable, so continual. He adored Mme. de Rênal. What matter if she is noble, and I the son of a workman, she loves me. . . . In her eyes, I am no valet employed on the side as a lover. Once this fear was destroyed, Julien fell into all the madness of love, all its mortal uncertainties.

—At least, she said, seeing his doubts about her love, at least let me make you happy during the few days we have together! We must hurry; tomorrow, perhaps, I can no longer be yours. If God strikes at me through my children, it will be useless for me to try to live only in your love, to forget that my crime killed them. I shall never survive them. Even if I wanted to, I wouldn't be able; I should go mad.

—Oh, if only I could take on myself the blame for your crime, as you in your generosity wanted to assume the fever of Stanislas!

This great moral crisis changed entirely the nature of the bond that united Julien to his mistress. His love was no longer simply an admiration for her beauty compounded with pride of possession.

Henceforth, their happiness was of a finer grain; the passion that devoured them was more intense. They underwent transports of total folly. In the eyes of the world, perhaps, their happiness would have seemed greater than it was before. But they never could recover that delicious serenity, that cloudless felicity, that easy joy of their first falling in love, when Mme. de Rênal's only fear was that Julien might not love her enough. Their happiness now wore sometimes the expression of a crime.

In their moments of greatest happiness, when things seemed on the surface most tranquil: —Oh, great God, I see hell before me! Mme. de Rênal would cry suddenly, clutching Julien's hand convulsively. What horrible torments! yet I've deserved them all! She drew him to her, as ivy clutches a wall.

Julien tried vainly to calm this tormented spirit. She grasped his hand, covered it with kisses. Then, falling into a gloomy reverie, she said: Hell, now, real hell, would be a relief to me; on earth I would still have some time to spend with him, but to have hell in this world as well, the death of my children. . . . Yet, after all that suffering, perhaps my crime would be pardoned. . . . Oh, almighty God, don't pardon me at that price. My poor children have done you no harm; I'm the guilty one, I alone; I love a man who is not my husband.

Then it seemed to Julien that Mme. de Rênal had reached a stage of calm. She was striving to gain control of herself because she did not want to embitter the life of the man she loved.

Amid these alternatives, the remorse and pleasure of love, time passed for them with the speed of light Julien lost the habit of reflection.

Mlle. Elisa went to Verrières, where she had a little legal business to attend to. There she found M. Valenod much irritated with Julien. She hated the young tutor, and often talked of him with his enemy.

—You would be scandalized at me, sir, if I told you the truth! . . . she said one day to M. Valenod. When it's anything important, the masters all see eye to eye. . . . There are certain things they'll never pardon a poor servant for mentioning. . . .

After these routine phrases, which the impatience and curiosity of M. Valenod found ways of shortening, he managed to learn certain things most distressing to his self-esteem.

This woman, the most distinguished of the district, whom for six years he had been assiduously plying with attentions, and unhappily in the sight of the whole world; this proud woman, whose lofty disdain had so often put him to the blush, had just accepted as her lover a little workman disguised as a tutor. And to add the crowning touch to the indignity of the poorhouse director, Mme. de Rênal adored this lover.

—And, what's more, the maid added with a sigh, M. Julien made no special effort to achieve this conquest; he never even altered for madame his usual coldness.

Elisa had been convinced only by events in the country, but she suspected the intrigue had been going on longer than that.

—I'm sure that was the reason, she said angrily, that he refused to marry me that time. And I, like a fool, I went to Mme. de Rênal; I begged her to talk to that little tutor.

That very evening M. de Rênal received from town, along with his newspaper, a long anonymous letter that informed him in the very greatest detail of what was happening in his house. Julien saw him grow pale as he read this letter, written on bluish paper; and he noted several surly glances. For the rest of the evening the mayor remained in distress; Julien tried vainly to flatter him by inquiring about the genealogies of all the best families of Burgundy.

Chapter 20

ANONYMOUS LETTERS

Do not give dalliance
Too much the rein; the strongest oaths are straw
To the fire i' the blood.
　　　　　　　　　—*The Tempest*

As they left the drawing room about midnight, Julien found an instant to tell his mistress:

—Let's not meet this evening, your husband is suspicious; I'm sure that letter he was grumbling over tonight was a denunciation.

By good fortune Julien was in the habit of locking his bedroom door from within. Mme. de Rênal had the crazy notion that this warning was only a pretext not to see her; she lost her head completely, and at the regular hour came to his room. Julien, who heard noises in the hallway, put out his light at once. Efforts were made to open his door; was it Mme. de Rênal or was it a jealous husband?

Next morning quite early the cook, who was fond of Julien, brought him a book, on the cover of which he read these words in Italian: *Guardate alla pagina* 130.

Julien shuddered at such indiscretion, turned to page 130, and found pinned to it the following letter, written in haste, stained with tears, and full of misspellings. Ordinarily Mme. de Rênal wrote very correctly; he was touched by this detail, and forgot for a moment her terrifying rashness.

> You wouldn't let me in last night? There are times when I'm sure I don't know you at all. Your looks terrify me. I'm afraid of you. Good God, perhaps you never even loved me! In that case, I hope my husband discovers everything and shuts me away forever in some solitary place deep in the country and far from my children. Perhaps that is what God wishes. I shall die soon. But you will be a monster.
>
> Don't you love me any more? Are you tired of my folly, of my remorse, wretch that you are? Would you like to ruin me? I'll give you an easy weapon. Go, show this letter throughout Verrières, or instead just show it to M. Valenod. Tell him I love you; but no, that's blasphemy, don't say that, tell him I adore you, that life only began for me the day I saw you, that in my craziest childish dreams I never imagined such happiness as

I've had with you, that I sacrifice my life to you, my soul. And you know that I've sacrificed even more than that.

But what does he know about sacrifices, that man? Tell him, tell him just for spite that I defy all evil tongues, that there's only one sorrow left in my world, when I see a change of heart in the only man for whom I want to live. What happiness for me to give up my life, to offer it as a sacrifice, and have nothing further to fear for my children!

Never doubt it, my dearest, if there is an anonymous letter it comes from that odious man who for six long years has been persecuting me with his loud mouth, his great deeds as a horseman, his fatuity, his endless enumeration of his own advantages.

Is there an anonymous letter? Wretch, that's what I wanted to talk about with you; but no, you were right. If I held you in my arms, perhaps for the last time, I would never have been able to talk cold policy with you, as I can when alone. From now on, our happiness will not come so easily. Will that distress you? Yes, probably on the days when you haven't received some amusing book from M. Fouqué. But the die is cast; tomorrow, whether there's an anonymous letter or not, I'm going to tell my husband that I myself have received such a letter, and that he must immediately pay you off lavishly, find some decent pretext, and send you back at once to your own people.

Alas, my darling, we shall be separated for a couple of weeks, perhaps even a month! Go, then, I'm sure you will be as unhappy over this as I am. But after all, this is the only way to ward off the effect of that anonymous letter; it's not the first one my husband has received, and on my account too. Alas! How I laughed at the others!

The whole point of my acting is to make my husband think the letter comes from M. Valenod, as I don't doubt if does. If you have to leave this house, don't fail to settle yourself in Verrières somewhere. I'll arrange for my husband to get the idea of spending a couple of weeks there in order to show the fools that there's no estrangement between him and me. Once at Verrières, make yourself the friend of everyone, even the liberals. I know you'll be a favorite with all the ladies.

Don't quarrel with M. Valenod or slice his ears as you threatened to do once; on the contrary, court his favor. The big thing is to make everyone in Verrières think you are going to enter his household, or some other such, as tutor to the children.

That's what my husband will never endure. Even if he brings himself to allow it, well, at any rate, you'll still be in Verrières and I'll be able to see you. My children, who love you so much, will go to see you. My God, it seems to me I love my children more because they love you. What unhappiness! Where will it all end? . . . I'm bewildered . . . Well, you see how to act; be courteous, be polite, don't be in any way lofty with these clods, I beg of you on bended knee; they are going to be the masters of our fate. Never suppose for a minute that my husband won't conform, in every detail concerning you, to the program that *public opinion* will prescribe for him.

Now you must furnish me with my anonymous letter; you'll need patience and a pair of scissors. Cut out of a book the words with which I'll furnish you; then glue them on the sheet of blue notepaper enclosed here; it was sent me by M. Vale-nod. Anticipate that your room will be searched; burn the remaining pages of the book you've cut up. If you don't find the exact words, take time to form them letter by letter. To ease your task, I've cut the letter short. Alas, if you don't love me any more, as I fear, how long my own letter will seem to you.

Madame,

All your little tricks are known; but the people who will want to prevent them have been told. In the name of our old friendship, I implore you to get rid of the little peasant for good. If you can manage that, your husband will think the note he has received was false, and he can be left to think it. Keep in mind, I have your secret, tremble for your guilt; from this moment on, you must *walk the straight and narrow* under my eyes.

As soon as you have finished piercing this letter together (do you recognize the director's habits of speech in it?), leave the house, and I'll meet you.

I'll go to town and return looking troubled—as in fact I will be. My God, what risks I'm running, and all because you *thought you suspected* an anonymous letter. Finally, with an incredulous look, I'll give my husband this letter, which will have been handed to me by an unknown man. You, meanwhile, will walk out along the forest road with the children, and come back only at dinnertime.

From the rocky part of that road you can easily see the dovecote. If our business succeeds, I'll put a white handkerchief in the window, otherwise nothing.

Perhaps your thoughtless heart will find a means of telling me that you love me before you leave on your walk? Whatever happens, you may be sure of one thing: I shall never survive our final separation, not for a day. Ah, what a wicked mother! Two empty words I have written there, dear Julien. They have no meaning for me; at this moment I can think only of you, and I wrote them only to forestall your blame. Now that I see myself about to lose you, why pretend? Let my soul seem horrible in your eyes, all right, but I don't want to lie to the man I adore! My life has been too full of lies. Go now. I forgive you if you no longer love me. I have no time to reread this letter. It's no great matter, I think, if I have to pay with my life for the days of joy I've spent in your arms. You know they will cost me more than that.

Chapter 21

DIALOGUE WITH THE MASTER OF THE HOUSE

Alas, our frailty is the cause, not we:
For such as we are made of, such we be.
—*Twelfth Night*

With childish pleasure Julien spent an hour assembling words. As he left his room, he met his pupils and their mother; she took the letter with a simplicity and courage so unruffled that he was terrified by it.

—Is the paste dry enough? she asked him.

And is this the woman whom remorse was almost driving to distraction? he thought. What is she planning to do now? He was too proud to ask her; but never before, perhaps, had she pleased him more.

—If this turns out badly, she added, as coolly as ever, I lose everything. Hide these things out on the mountain somewhere; they may one day be all I have.

She handed him a red morocco case with a glass top, filled with gold and some diamonds.

—Now go, she said.

She kissed her children, the younger twice. Julien stood still. She walked swiftly away without looking back.

From the moment when he opened the anonymous letter M. de Rênal had led a frightful existence. He had not been so upset since a duel he nearly had in 1816, and to do him justice, the prospect of getting shot on that occasion had made him less unhappy than now. He went over the letter from every point of view: Isn't it a woman's hand? he asked himself. In that case, what woman could have written it? He reviewed mentally all the women he knew in Verrières without being able to settle his suspicions. Could a man have dictated the letter? Then what man? The same uncertainty here; he was envied, and no doubt hated, by most of the men he knew. I'll have to ask my wife, he said out of sheer habit, rising from the chair in which he had sunk.

But scarcely was he up—Great God! he cried, striking his brow, she's the person I have to mistrust more than anyone; from now on, she's the enemy. And tears of sheer rage came to his eyes.

It was due retribution for that dryness of heart that is known in the provinces as practical wisdom that the two men whom M. de Rênal suspected most, at this moment, were his two most intimate friends.

After that pair, I have maybe ten friends, and he numbered them over, estimating for each one how much consolation might be had from him. Every one of them, every last one, he cried in a rage, would be delighted at my trouble! Fortunately, he thought himself envied by one and all—not wholly without reason. Apart from his superb town house, which the king of _____ had just distinguished forever by sleeping in it, he had made a fine thing out of his country house at Vergy. The front was painted white, the windows furnished with fine green shutters. For an instant he was consoled by the thought of this magnificence. The fact is that his house was visible at a distance of three or four leagues, much to the discredit, of all the other country houses or so-called *châteaux* of the district, which had been allowed to fade into the humble gray tones imposed by time.

M. de Rênal could indeed count on the tears and sympathy of one friend, the church warden of the parish; but this man was an imbecile who had sympathy for everyone. Yet he was the mayor's only recourse.

What misery like mine! he cried, furiously; what loneliness!

Can it possibly be, this really wretched man asked himself, is it actually possible that in my misfortunes I don't have a single friend to talk to? My reason is giving way, I'm sure of it. Ah, Falcoz! ah, Ducros! he cried bitterly. They were two childhood friends whom he had estranged by his arrogance in 1814. They were not noble, and he had tried to change the terms of equality on which they had lived since childhood.

One of them, Falcoz, a man of spirit and feeling who sold paper in Verrières, had bought a print shop in the district capital and undertaken a daily newspaper. The congregation set out to ruin him: his paper had been condemned and his license to print withdrawn. In these bitter circumstances he undertook to write to M. de Rênal for the first time in ten years. The mayor of Verrières felt obliged to reply like an ancient Roman: "If the king's minister did me the honor to ask my advice, I should tell him: Ruin without mercy every printer in the province, and make printing a government monopoly like tobacco." Such a letter to an intimate friend, which all Verrières had admired at the time, now caused M. de Rênal to shrink in horror. Who would have thought that with my rank, my fortune, and my decorations I should someday regret it? It was in transports of rage like these, directed now against himself, now against his surroundings, that he passed a night of torture; but, by good fortune, he did not get the idea of spying on his wife.

I am used to Louise, he said to himself, she knows all my business; if I were free to remarry tomorrow, I wouldn't find anyone to replace her. And then he consoled himself with the idea that his wife might be innocent; seeing things in this light saved him from the necessity of displaying some character, and pleased him much better; after all, everyone knows women are often subjected to calumny!

But then, he exclaimed suddenly, walking convulsively about, why do I have to act like an ordinary nobody, a ragamuffin, while she makes game of me with her lover! Do I have to see all Verrières sniggering over my complacency? What haven't they said about Charmier (he was a notoriously deceived husband of the district)? Anytime his name is spoken, there's a grin. He's a good lawyer, but who ever talks about his professional qualities? Ah, Charmier, they say, Bernard's Charmier, they call him by the name of the man who brought about his disgrace.

Thanks be to God, said M. de Rênal at other moments, I have no daughter, and the way in which I shall punish the mother won't hold back my sons in their careers. I can catch the little peasant with my wife and kill them both; that way the tragic ending of the story will soften the absurdity of it. This idea pleased him; he worked it out in all its details. The penal code is on my side, and, whatever happens, our congregation and my friends in the jury will protect me. He examined his hunting knife, and it was very sharp; but the idea of blood terrified him.

I can have this insolent tutor beaten up and driven out of the house; but what a scandal in Verriéres and throughout the department! After we smashed Falcoz's paper, when his editor-in-chief got out of prison, I helped to have him fired from a job worth six hundred francs. They say that scribbler has had the boldness to turn up again in Besançon; he can lampoon me from there, and so cleverly that I'll never get him into a court. Get him before a court! The scoundrel will suggest in a thousand ways that he's told nothing but the truth. A man of good birth who upholds his rank as I do gets hated by all the common ruck. I'll see my story in those horrible Paris newspapers. Oh, good God! what a sewer! to see the ancient name of Rênal dragged in the mud of derision. . . . If ever I take a trip, I'll have to use another name, yes, abandon this name which makes up my strength and my glory. What a ghastly thought!

If I don't kill my wife, just drive her out in disgrace, she has her aunt at Besançon, who will hand over her whole fortune. My wife will go to Paris where she'll live with Julien; everyone will know it at

Supposed love as an economic + societal structure [handwritten margin note]

Verrières, and once again I'll be thought a dupe. At this point the miserable man noted by the paling of his lamp that dawn was starting to break; he decided to go out into the garden for a bit of fresh air. He had almost decided not to make a scandal, largely as a result of the idea that a scandal would overjoy his good friends in Verrières.

A stroll in the garden calmed him somewhat more. No, he exclaimed, I shall not break with my wife, she's too useful to me. He imagined with horror what his house would be like without his wife; his only female relative was the Marquise de R____, old, imbecilic, and mean.

An extremely sensible idea occurred to him, but carrying it out required force of character far greater than the poor man possessed. If I keep my wife, he said, I know my own character; one day when I'm impatient with her I'll accuse her. She's proud, we'll quarrel, and all that is bound to happen before she's inherited from her aunt. Then what fun they'll make of me! My wife loves her children; her whole fortune will end up going to them. While I, I will be the laughing stock of Verrières. Some man, they'll say, he didn't even know how to get back at his own wife! Wouldn't it be better to sit on my suspicions and not try for certainty? Then I tie my own hands; I can never reproach her again.

An instant later M. de Rênal, still in the grip of his wounded vanity, was laboriously repeating to himself all the terms used in the billiard parlor of the *Casino* or the *Noble Circle*[9] in Verrières, when some fine talker interrupted a round of pool to divert himself at the expense of a betrayed husband. How cruel, at this moment, such raillery seemed to him!

Good God! Why isn't my wife dead? Then I would be safe from ridicule. I wish I was a widower! I could go and spend six months at Paris in the best society. After this moment of happiness at the idea of being a bereaved husband, his imagination returned to the question of finding out the truth. At midnight, when everyone was abed, he might sprinkle a thin layer of bran before the door of Julien's bedroom; the next morning, when day broke, he could look for footprints.

But this scheme is no good, he exclaimed with sudden anger, that bitch Elisa would notice, and it would be all over the house that I'm jealous.

In another story told around the *Casino* a husband had verified his sad state by using a bit of wax to fasten a hair that closed, as with a seal, his wife's door and that of the gallant.

---

9. Social clubs in French provincial towns were engines of social snobbery. Stendhal's uncle Romain Gagnon had belonged to the extreme right-wing club in Grenoble, known as the *Casino*.

After so many hours of uncertainty this method of gaining certainty seemed to him by all odds the best, and he was thinking of
how to put it in practice when, at the intersection of a path, he encountered the very woman he wanted to see dead.

She was on her way back from town. She had gone to hear mass
in the church of Vergy. A tradition, very dubious in the eyes of a
cold historian, but which she believed, had it that the little church
in use today was once a chapel attached to the castle of the lord of
Vergy. This idea obsessed Mme. de Rênal all the while she had
spent trying to pray in the church. She continually imagined her
husband killing Julien while out hunting, killing him as if by accident and then that evening forcing her to eat his heart.

My fate, she told herself, will depend on what he thinks when he
hears me. After that fatal fifteen minutes, I may never again have a
chance to speak with him. He is not a wise or reasonable man. If he
were, I might with my own feeble reason foresee what he's likely to
do or say. He will decide both our fates; he has the power to do it.
But really that fate lies in my hands, in my skill at directing the
ideas of this harebrain, who's blinded by his own anger and incapable of seeing half of what's happening. My God, I need skill, I
need coolness, and where to find them?

Calm possessed her as if by magic as she entered the garden and
saw her husband in the distance. His rumpled hair and disordered
dress showed that he had not slept all night.

She handed him a letter which had been unsealed but folded up
again. Without opening it, he stared wild-eyed at his wife.

—Here is an abominable thing, she said, which was given to me
behind the notary's garden by an ugly man who pretended to know
you and to owe you some gratitude. I demand just one thing of you,
that you send this Julien back to his own people without an instant's delay. Mme. de Rênal hastened to make this speech, getting
to the point perhaps a little prematurely, in order to escape the
hideous prospect of having to say it.

She was overwhelmed with joy at seeing the pleasure it caused
her husband. From the fixed gaze he bent upon her, she grasped
that Julien had guessed right. Instead of being disturbed by her
present troubles, she thought of him: What genius! What perfect
tact! And in a young man still without experience of the world!
What won't he accomplish in the future? But then, alas, his successes will cause him to forget me.

This instant of admiration for the man she adored relieved her
distress entirely.

She applauded her own policy. I have not been unworthy of
Julien, she told herself, with a sweet and intimate pleasure.

Not saying a word, for fear of committing himself, M. de Rênal

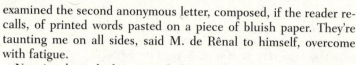
examined the second anonymous letter, composed, if the reader re-
calls, of printed words pasted on a piece of bluish paper. They're
taunting me on all sides, said M. de Rênal to himself, overcome
with fatigue.

New insults to look into, and always on account of my wife! He
was on the point of assailing her with gross abuse, but the prospect
of the Besançon inheritance barely restrained him. Feeling obliged
to vent his rage on something, he ripped the paper of this second
anonymous letter to shreds and began to stride off; he absolutely
had to get away from his wife. A few minutes later he returned to
her side, somewhat calmed.

—We have to take immediate steps and send Julien away, she
said to him at once; after all, he's nothing but a workman's son. You
will pay him off with a few crowns, and besides, he's clever and will
easily find a place, for example, with M. Valenod or the subprefect
de Maugiron, both of whom have children. Thus you won't be
harming him. . . .

—Now you're talking like the fool you really are, shouted M. de
Rênal in a bellow. What good sense ever comes out of a woman?
You pay no attention to what's reasonable; how do you expect to
know anything? You're sloppy, you're lazy, you're good for nothing
but chasing butterflies—feeble creatures, who bring misfortune
with you when you enter our families! . . .

Mme. de Rênal let him talk, and he talked on for a long time; he
was *passing his anger*, as they say in the country.

—Sir, she answered him at last, I speak as a woman outraged in
her honor, that is, in her most precious possession on earth.

Mme. de Rênal preserved a cool, fixed calm throughout this disagreeable conversation, on which depended all her chances of ever
living again under the same roof with Julien. She sought out all the
ideas she considered most suitable to guide her husband's blind
rage. She had been unmoved by all the insults he hurled at her; she
never heard them; she was thinking of Julien. Will he be pleased
with me?

—This little peasant whom we have covered with kindness and
showered with gifts may be innocent, she said at last, but nonetheless he is the occasion of the first affront I ever received. . . . Sir,
when I read that abominable letter, I vowed that either he or I must
leave your house.

—Do you want to make a scandal, to dishonor me and yourself
as well? You'll gratify every scandal-monger in Verrières.

—It's true, they're all envious of the prosperity your wise management has created for yourself, your family, and the town. . . . All
right! I shall require Julien to ask a month's leave of you, which he

will spend with that mountaineer wood-seller of his, fit companion for this little mechanic.

—Restrain yourself, said M. de Rênal, speaking with a fair measure of calm. What I require of you, mainly, is not to talk with him. You'd lose your temper and involve me in a quarrel with him; you know how touchy this little gentleman is.

—He's a young man altogether without tact, replied Mme. de Rênal; maybe he's learned, you know about that, but at bottom he's nothing but a peasant. For my part, I've never thought well of him since he refused to marry Elisa, who was a proper fortune ready-made for him; and all on the pretext that sometimes she makes secret visits to M. Valenod.

—Aha! said M. de Rênal, lifting an exaggerated eyebrow, is that it, did Julien tell you that?

—No, not exactly; he always talked about his calling to the holy ministry; but, believe me, the real calling for all these little people is always filling their bellies. He gave me to understand that he was not in the dark about these secret visits.

—And I was, I was! cried M. de Rênal, returning to rage and emphasizing every word. Things go on in my house that I don't know about. . . . What's this now, something going on between Elisa and Valenod?

—Pooh! that's ancient history, my dear, said Mme. de Rênal with a laugh, and perhaps there's no harm in it after all. It began at a time when your good friend Valenod would not have been unhappy to have it said in Verrières that he and I enjoyed a little, perfectly platonic, relationship.

—I once had that idea myself, cried M. de Rênal, smiting his brow and striding furiously from discovery to discovery; but you never said a word to me.

—And was I to stir up trouble between two friends on account of a little puff of vanity in our dear director? Where is there a woman of society to whom he hasn't addressed a few letters, very witty indeed and maybe even a bit gallant?

—Has he written to you?

—He writes a great deal.

—Show me those letters at once, I command you; and M. de Rênal drew himself up six feet taller than usual.

—I certainly will not, she told him with a gentleness that verged almost on indifference; I'll show them to you some other day when you are less distressed.

—This very instant, damn it! shouted M. de Rênal, drunk with rage, yet happier than he had been any time in the last twelve hours.

—Will you give me your word, Mme. de Rênal said gravely, never to quarrel with the director of the poorhouse over the matter of these letters?

—Quarrel or no, I can put him out of the orphan business; but, he went on furiously, I want those letters this very minute; where are they?

—In a drawer of my desk; but I certainly shan't give you the key.

—I can break it, he shouted, rushing off toward his wife's room.

And, in fact, he broke with an iron bar a precious desk of fine-grained mahogany, brought from Paris, which formerly he used to polish with his coat tails whenever he thought there was a spot on it.

Mme. de Rênal climbed at a run the hundred twenty steps to the dovecote and tied a white handkerchief by its corner to one of the iron bars of the little window. She was the happiest of women. Tears in her eyes, she looked out toward the great forests of the mountainside. No doubt, she said to herself, Julien can see this happy signal from his post under one of those spreading beeches. For a long time she listened, cursing the monotonous song of the cicadas and the chatter of the birds. Without their irksome noise, a cry of joy, rising from the steep rocks, might have been audible. Her eye moved greedily across that immense slope of dark verdure, thick and solid as a meadow, formed by the tree tops. Why doesn't he think, she asked in a mood of sudden tenderness, of making some signal to show that his joy is equal to mine? She came down from the dovecote only when she began to fear that her husband would come looking for her there.

She found him in a rage. He was running through the insipid phrases of M. Valenod, never before perused with so much emotion.

Seizing a moment when her husband's exclamations had subsided enough for her to be heard:

—I still think my first idea is best, said Mme. de Rênal; Julien had better take a trip. He may know Latin, but he's no better than a peasant; he's often clumsy and lacking in tact; every day, thinking that he's being polite, he offers me exaggerated compliments in very bad taste, which he's learned by heart out of some novel . . . .

—He never reads novels, exclaimed M. de Rênal; I'm sure of that. Do you think I'm a blind master who knows nothing of what goes on under his own roof?

—All right, if he doesn't read these ridiculous compliments in a book, he makes them up, and that's no better for him. He must have talked about me in this vein around Verrières . . . ; and even if he didn't go that far, said Mme. de Rênal with the air of making a discovery, he must have talked this way before Elisa, which is all one as if he had talked to M. Valenod.

—Aha! roared M. de Rênal, shaking the table and the whole

room with a mighty blow of his fist, the printed anonymous letter
and these other letters of Valenod are written on the same paper!

—At last! thought Mme. de Rênal; she appeared stunned by this
conclusion, and without having courage to add a single word took a
seat on the sofa at the far end of the room.

The battle had now been gained; but she had some trouble in
keeping M. de Rênal from going to confront the supposed author of
the anonymous letter.

—How can you fail to see that provoking a scene with M.
Valenod, without having sufficient proof on your side, is the greatest blunder in the world? You are the victim of envy, my dear; whose
fault is it? It's because of your talents: your wise policies, your
handsome properties, the fortune I brought you, and then there's
the very considerable inheritance that we can expect from my good
aunt, an inheritance that has, of course, been immensely exaggerated—all these things have made you the most important person in
Verrières.

—You didn't mention my noble birth, said M. de Rênal with a
small smile.

—You are one of the most distinguished gentlemen in the district,
Mme. de Rênal said with fresh enthusiasm; if the king was free and
could do justice to distinguished birth, you would doubtless sit in
the house of peers, . . . and so forth, and so on. And now, given your
splendid position, do you want to give envy an incident to work on?

Accusing M. Valenod of his anonymous letter is like proclaiming
to all Verrières, or rather to Besançon, to the whole district, that
this petty bourgeois, once admitted (no doubt incautiously) to intimacy with *a Rênal*, has found a way to offend him. Suppose these
letters you have just discovered contained proof that I had responded to M. Valenod's proffered love; then you should kill me. I
would have deserved it a hundred times over, but you should not
show anger toward him. Keep in mind that all your neighbors are
only looking for a pretext to be revenged for your superiority; remember that in 1816 you had a hand in various arrests. That man
who took refuge on the roof of your house. . . .[1]

—What's clear is that you have neither respect nor kindness for
me, cried M. de Rênal in the full bitterness of these memories; and
what's more, I haven't been made a peer! . . .

—My own opinion, dear friend, said Mme. de Rênal with a
smile, is that I shall be richer than you, that I have been your associate for twelve years, and that on both these scores I should have a

---

1. A Grenoble scandal from the days of 1816 is glanced at here: A liberal named Tabaret
   took refuge from some infuriated conservatives on the roof of a neighbor's house and
   was shot to death there.

voice in your decisions, especially in today's business. If you prefer someone like M. Julien to me, she added, with ill-concealed scorn, I am quite prepared to go and spend a winter with my aunt.

This phrase was *happily* turned. Though cloaked in polite forms, it had a latent firmness that settled M. de Rênal's judgment. But after the provincial fashion, he continued to talk for a long time, going back over his arguments; his wife let him talk; there was still anger in his expression. At last, two hours of useless babble exhausted the energies of a man who had been in spasms of rage all night long. He settled the lines of policy to be followed with regard to M. Valenod, Julien, and even Elisa.

Once or twice in the course of this great scene, Mme. de Rênal was on the verge of feeling some sympathy for the very real sufferings of this man who for twelve years had been her husband. But real passions are selfish. And besides, she kept expecting that at any minute he would say something about the anonymous letter received the day before, and this he never did. Mme. de Rênal could not have been sure of her position without knowing what ideas had been suggested to the man on whom her whole fate depended. In the provinces husbands are the masters of public opinion. A husband who complains against his wife covers himself with ridicule, a fate that is becoming less and less dangerous in France; but his wife, if he refuses to supply her with money, falls to the condition of a workingwoman at fifteen sous a day, and even at that price the respectable will make scruples of employing her.

An odalisque in a harem had better love the sultan at all hazards; he is all-powerful, she has no hope of diminishing his authority by a series of petty diplomacies. The master's punishment is terrible, bloody, but military, noble; a dagger stroke finishes everything. It is with blows of public contempt that a husband kills his wife in the nineteenth century; it is by closing all the drawing rooms to her.

The sense of her danger was sharply revived in Mme. de Rênal when she retired to her room; she was shocked at the disorderly state in which she found it. The locks of all her pretty little jewel chests had been smashed; several squares of the parquet floor had been ripped up. He would have had no mercy on me, she said. To ruin in this way an inlaid floor of which he was so proud! When one of the children stepped on it with dirty shoes, he used to be purple with rage. And now it's ruined forever! The spectacle of this violence dissipated at once the last regrets she felt for her too-easy victory.

A little before the bell sounded to dinner, Julien returned with the children. Over dessert, when the servants had withdrawn, Mme. de Rênal said to him in a very dry tone:

—You've indicated a desire to spend a couple of weeks at Verrières; M. de Rênal has kindly granted you a leave. You may depart when you choose. But, to be sure the children don't waste their time, we will send their themes to you every day, and you can correct them.

—I shall certainly not grant you more than a week, M. de Rênal added in his sourest tone.

Julien noted on his features the uneasiness of a man in profound torment.

—He has not yet settled on what he's going to do, said he to his mistress, during a moment when they were alone together in the drawing room.

Mme. de Rênal told him briefly what she had been doing since morning.

—The details tonight, she added with a smile.

Perversity of women! thought Julien. What pleasure, what instinct leads them to deceive us?

—It seems to me you're both inspired and blinded by your love, he told her with some coolness; your conduct today was admirable; but is it sensible for us to try to meet tonight? This house is swarming with enemies; think of Elisa's bitter hatred for me.

—That hatred is much like your own passionate indifference to me.

—Even if I were indifferent, I should be bound to save you from dangers in which I involved you. If by chance M. de Rênal talks to Elisa, a word from her may disclose everything to him. Why couldn't he hide himself near my room with a weapon. . . .

—What's this? Not even courage! said Mme. de Rênal, with all the disdain of a woman of quality.

—I shall never lower myself to talk about my courage, said Julien coldly, that's vulgar. Let the world judge from events. But, he added, taking her by the hand, you cannot imagine how deeply I'm attached to you and what a joy it will be to have a chance to take leave of you before this cruel separation.

Chapter 22

WAYS OF ACTING IN 1830

Speech was given to man to conceal his thought.
—R. P. Malagrida[2]

Scarcely had he reached Verrières when Julien began reproaching his injustice toward Mme. de Rênal. I would have despised her as a silly female if, through weakness, she had mishandled her scene with M. de Rênal! She carried it off like a diplomat, and now I sympathize with the loser, who is my enemy. There's something middle-class about my attitude; my vanity is offended because M. de Rênal is a man! An immense and magnificent corporation, this, of which I happen to be a member! Really, I'm no better than a fool.

M. Chélan had refused various offers of lodging made him by the most eminent liberals of the district at the time when he was forced out of his presbytery. The two rooms he had rented were crowded with his books. Julien, wanting to show Verrières what it was to be a priest, went to his father for a dozen pine planks, which he carried on his own back the length of the main street. Then he borrowed tools of a former friend and had soon built a sort of bookcase, in which he arranged the books of M. Chélan.

—I thought you would be corrupted by the vanity of the world, said the old man, with tears of joy; but here's an action that fully redeems that childish business with the honor guard and the gaudy uniform, which made you so many enemies.

M. de Rênal had told Julien to stay in his house. Nobody suspected what had happened. The third day after his arrival Julien saw coming up to his room no less a personage than the subprefect, M. de Maugiron. It was only after two long hours of insipid gossip and tedious jeremiads about the evil habits of men, the dishonesty of public officials, the perils confronting our poor France, etc., etc., that Julien finally caught a glimpse of the point of the visit. They were already at the head of the staircase, and the poor tutor half in disgrace was leading to the door with all appropriate respect the future prefect of some fortunate province, when the latter decided to concern himself with Julien's prospects, to praise his splendid mod-

2. R. P. (Révérend Père) Gabriel Malagrida was an Italian Jesuit who served nearly thirty years as a missionary in Brazil. He returned to Portugal in time to help the victims of the Lisbon earthquake (1755) but was accused of complicity in an attempt to assassinate the king and was burned alive on September 21, 1761. He did not make the statement about human speech attributed to him here: Talleyrand, a French diplomat, perhaps did, or at least abundantly exemplified it. Stendhal probably heard of Malagrida through Voltaire's *Siècle de Louis XV.*

eration in matters affecting his own interests, etc., etc. At last M. de Maugiron, clasping him in his arms with the most paternal affection, suggested that he should leave M. de Rênal and take service with an official who had children to raise and who, like King Philip,[3] would thank God not so much for the children themselves but for being allowed to have them in due proximity to M. Julien. Their tutor would receive an income of eight hundred francs, payable not on a monthly basis (which is not noble, said M. de Maugiron), but quarterly, and what's more, in advance.

Now it became Julien's turn; for an hour and a half he had been waiting for the other to get to the point. His reply was perfect, and as long as an episcopal sermon; it let everything be understood, and yet said nothing clearly. There appeared in it, all at the same time, respect for M. de Rênal, veneration for the public of Verrières, and gratitude to the illustrious subprefect. The subprefect, astonished to find a bigger Jesuit than himself, struggled vainly to get out of him something clear. Julien in high glee seized the occasion to exercise his wits, and began his reply all over again, using other terms. Never did an eloquent minister, trying to talk his way through the last hours of a session when the house is threatening to wake up, use more words with less substance. Hardly was M. de Maugiron out the door when Julien began to laugh like a maniac. While his Jesuitical vein was flowing, he wrote a nine-page letter to M. de Rênal in which he described everything that had been said to him, and humbly begged his advice. And yet that scoundrel never told me the name of the person who's making the offer! Of course, it must be M. Valenod, who sees my exile to Verrières as the effect of his anonymous letter.

When his letter had been dispatched, Julien, as happy as a hunter who marches forth at six in the morning of a fine autumn day onto a plain teeming with game, set forth to seek counsel of M. Chélan. But before he reached the good cure's house, fate, which was being lavish in dispensing pleasures to him, threw into his path M. Valenod, from whom he did not conceal that his heart was sorely torn; a poor boy like himself should devote himself wholly to the vocation that heaven had written in his heart, but in this fallen world one's vocation wasn't everything. To labor worthily in the Lord's vineyard, and not to disgrace one's many learned coworkers, instruction was necessary; one must spend two years in the seminary at Besançon, and very costly they would be; it was therefore indispensable [and one might even say, after a certain sort, one's duty] to save up a sum of money, which would be much easier to do

---

3. King Philip of Macedon (382–336 B.C.E.) was glad not only to have a son (Alexander the Great) but to have a son whom Aristotle could educate.

on a salary of eight hundred francs paid quarterly than with six hundred francs paid from month to month. On the other hand, didn't heaven, when it placed him in charge of the Rênal children, and inspired him with a particular affection for them, show that it would not be fitting to abandon this task for another? . . .

Julien attained such perfect skill in this sort of eloquence, which has replaced the decisive action of the empire, that he ended by boring himself with the sound of his own words.

Back at the house he found a servant of M. Valenod's, in full livery, who had been looking for him throughout the town with an invitation to dinner that very day.

Julien had never been in this man's house; just a few days before he had been thinking only of how to give him a good cudgeling without risk from the police. Though dinner was announced for one o'clock, Julien thought it more respectful to present himself about twelve-thirty in the office of the director of the poorhouse. He found him exercising his importance in the midst of a pile of papers. His thick black whiskers, his enormous head of hair, his Phrygian cap cocked crossways on his head, his huge pipe, his embroidered slippers, the thick gold chains strung every which way across his chest, and all that apparatus of a provincial money man who thinks himself a lady-killer made no impression on Julien; he thought all the more of that cudgeling which was due him.

He requested the honor of meeting Mme. Valenod; she was in her dressing room and could not see him. By way of compensation, he was privileged to attend the poorhouse director in his dressing room. Then they met with Mme. Valenod, who introduced her children with tears in her eyes. This lady was one of the most respectable in Verrières; she had a broad, mannish face to which she had applied rouge for this great occasion. She displayed a good deal of maternal pathos.

Julien thought of Mme. de Rênal. His habitual suspicion scarcely left him susceptible to anything but those memories that are called up by contrasts, but then he could be touched to the point of tenderness. This mood was augmented now by the look of the poorhouse director's establishment. Everything in it was splendid and new, and he was told the price of each piece of furniture. But Julien found something ignoble about it, as if it stank of stolen money. Everyone there, even the servants, had the look of hardening his features against contempt.

The tax collector, the assessor, the chief of police, and two or three other public officials arrived with their wives. They were followed by a number of rich liberals. Dinner was announced. Julien, already ill at ease, was struck with the idea that on the other side of the dining room wall were the poor prisoners, whose allotments of food had perhaps been *chiseled* in order to buy all this ostentatious luxury with which people were trying to astonish him.

Perhaps they are suffering from hunger at this very moment, said he to himself; his throat choked up, he found it impossible to eat and almost to talk. It was much worse a quarter of an hour later; in the distance there were heard various phrases of a popular song, rather vulgar it must be admitted, being sung by one of the inmates. M. Valenod cast a glance at one of his servants in full livery, who disappeared; shortly thereafter the song stopped. At that moment a valet offered Julien some Rhine wine in a green glass, and Mme. Valenod seized the occasion to observe that this wine cost nine francs a bottle direct from the grower. Julien, holding his green glass, said to M. Valenod:

—They're not singing that miserable song anymore.

—Blast 'em, I should think not, replied the director in triumph, I've had the beggars shut up.

The phrase was too much for Julien; he had the manners, but not yet the feelings, of his social position. Despite all his much-practiced hypocrisy, he felt a tear flow down his cheek.

He tried to conceal it with his green glass, but found it absolutely impossible to do honor to the Rhine wine. *Stop the man from singing!* he murmured to himself, Oh my God! And you permit it!

Fortunately nobody noticed his moment of ungentlemanly emotion. The assessor had struck up a royalist song. During the uproar of the refrain, which was sung in chorus: There now, Julien's conscience said to him, that's the dirty fortune you're going to attain, and you'll enjoy it only under these circumstances and in this sort of company! Maybe you'll get a place worth twenty thousand francs, but while you gorge yourself on rich foods, you'll have to shut the mouth of a poor prisoner who's trying to sing. You'll give banquets with the money you've stolen from his miserable pittance, and while you're eating he'll be made more miserable than ever! Oh Napoleon! What a joy it was in your day to rise through the perils of the battlefield; but to feed like a coward on the misery of the helpless!

I confess that the weakness which Julien displays in this monologue gives me a poor opinion of him. He would be a worthy colleague of those conspirators in yellow gloves who pretend to change the whole way of life of a great nation but don't want to be responsible for inflicting the slightest scratch.[4]

Abruptly Julien was recalled to his role. It was not to dream and be silent that he had been invited to dinner in such good company. A retired manufacturer of calico prints, corresponding member

4. Conspirators in yellow gloves are in effect parlor liberals.

of one academy at Besançon and another at Uzès, called to him down the full length of the table to ask if it was true that he had made such astonishing progress as people were saying in his study of the New Testament.

At once complete silence was established; a Latin New Testament appeared, as if by magic, in the hands of the learned member of two academies. No sooner had Julien agreed than a half sentence of Latin, chosen at random, was read to him. He recited: his memory served, and this prodigous feat was admired with all the clamorous energy of an after-dinner performance. Julien noted the candlelit features of the ladies; several were not bad-looking. He picked out the wife of the assessor who sang so loudly.

—But really I'm ashamed to talk Latin before these ladies for so long, he said with a glance at her. If M. Rubigneau (that was the member of the two academies) will be kind enough to read a Latin sentence at random, instead of repeating the Latin text that follows, I'll try to translate it impromptu.

This second display raised his glory to its peak.

There were in the group several rich liberals, fortunate fathers of children capable of winning scholarships, and as such suddenly converted since the last mission.[5] In spite of this neat political stroke, M. de Rènal had never been willing to receive them in his house. These fine gentry, who knew Julien only by reputation and from seeing him on horseback when the king of _____ came to town, were his most enthusiastic admirers. When will these fools get tired of listening to this Biblical style, which they can't understand at all? he thought. Quite the contrary, this style amused them because it was strange; they laughed at it. But Julien grew tired.

He rose with a serious expression as six o'clock struck and spoke of a chapter in the new theology of Ligorio which he had to learn in order to repeat it on the morrow for M. Chélan. For it's my trade, he added jovially, to make other people recite lessons and to recite them myself.

They laughed a good deal; they admired him; this is wit as they understand it in Verrières. Julien was already on his feet, and everyone else rose, regardless of decorum; such is the power of genius. Mme. Valenod kept him for another quarter hour; he simply must hear her children recite their catechism. They made the most comical errors, which he was the only one to notice. He made no effort to correct them. What ignorance of the first principles of religion!

5. Missions within France itself were essentially revivalist movements propagated after 1815 by Abbés Rauzon, Forbin-Janson, Fayet, and their ilk, with the approval of the parish priest and his bishop, in the hope of reviving the zeal of the faithful.

he thought. At last he said good night, and hoped to make his escape; but he had to undergo a fable of Lafontaine.

—This author is thoroughly immoral, said Julien to Mme. Valenod; one of his fables on Messire Jean Chouart[6] ventures to asperse with ridicule the most venerable matters in the world. He is sharply reproved for this by the best commentators.

Before he left, Julien had received four or five other invitations to dinner. This young man does great credit to our district, all the diners cried unanimously, in high good humor. They went so far as to discuss a pension, to be voted out of municipal funds, which would enable him to continue his studies in Paris.

While this rash idea was resounding through the dining room, Julien had made his way hastily to the carriage entry. Ah, the swine! the swine! he murmured three or four times over, drinking in the fresh air with pleasure.

At this moment he saw himself as a complete aristocrat, he who for so long had been irked by lofty smiles and arrogant airs which he sensed behind all the polite phrases addressed to him at M. de Rênal's. He could not fail to notice the extraordinary difference. I won't consider, said he to himself as he left, that all this money was stolen from the poor inmates, who are even forbidden to sing! But would M. de Rênal ever take it on himself to tell his guests the price of every bottle of wine he set before them? And this M. Valenod, when he counts up his belongings, as he's always doing, can never talk of his house, his grounds, and so on, when his wife is present without saying *your* house, *your* grounds, and so on.

This lady, who seemed so responsive to the pleasures of possession, had just made an abominable scene during dinner because one of the servants had broken a piece of stemware and *spoiled one of her sets*; and the servant had answered her back with supreme insolence.

What a crowd! said Julien to himself; they could give me half their haul and I still wouldn't want to live with them. One fine day I'd give myself away; I couldn't keep from showing the scorn I feel for them.

He was required, however, on orders from Mme. de Rênal, to attend several dinners of the same sort; Julien was the fashion; people excused his donning the guard-of-honor uniform, or rather that act of folly was the real cause of his success. Before long the only question discussed in Verrières was who would win out in the struggle to obtain this learned young man, M. de Rênal or the director of the poorhouse. These gentlemen formed with M. Maslon

6. La Fontaine's fable of the Curé and the Corpse (VII, 11) is a satire on clerical greed.

a triumvirate which for some years now had been tyrannizing over the town. There was jealousy of the mayor, all the liberals complained of him; but after all, he was noble and trained for lofty positions, while M. Valenod's father had not left him an income of six hundred florins. He had had to rise from being pitied for the mean apple-green jacket in which everyone had seen him when he was young to the stage of being envied his Norman horses, golden chains, Paris suits, and all his present prosperity.

In the flood of this society, all new to Julien, he thought he had discovered an honest man; this was a geometer named Gros, considered a Jacobin. Julien, who had sworn an oath never to say anything except what seemed false to him, was obliged to maintain suspicions with regard to M. Gros. Fat packets of themes kept arriving from Vergy. He was counseled to see his father frequently, and submitted to this sad necessity. In a word, he was patching up his reputation rather nicely when one morning he was startled to be wakened by a pair of hands held over his eyes.

It was Mme. de Rênal, who had come to town, climbed the stairs in great haste, leaving her children to bring along a favorite rabbit who had made the trip with them, and thus reached Julien's room an instant before they did. It was a delicious moment, but very short: Mme. de Rênal was out of sight when the children came in with the rabbit, which they wanted to show to their friend. Julien welcomed everyone warmly, even the rabbit. He seemed to be back with his own family; he felt that he loved these children, that he enjoyed chattering with them. He was struck by the gentleness of their voices, the simplicity and dignity of their little ways; his imagination had to be washed clean of all the vulgar manners and disagreeable thoughts he breathed in every day at Verrières. Everywhere was the fear of failure, everywhere luxury and misery were at one another's throat. The people with whom he dined, when they talked about the roast, made confidential statements humiliating for themselves and disgusting for anyone who listened.

—You others, who are noble, you have good reason to be proud, he told Mme. de Rênal. And he described the many dinners he had endured.

—So, then, you're all the rage! And she laughed heartily at the thought of all that rouge which Mme. Valenod felt obliged to use whenever Julien was coming. I daresay she has designs on your heart, she added.

Lunch was delightful. The presence of the children, though apparently a constraint, actually increased the general happiness. These poor children did not know how to express their joy at seeing Julien again. The servants had not failed to tell them that he was being offered two hundred francs more to *raise* the young Valenods.

In the midst of lunch Stanislas-Xavier, still pale from his terrible illness, suddenly asked his mother how much the silverware at his place and the goblet from which he was drinking were worth.

—Why do you want to know?

—I want to sell them and give the money to M. Julien, so he won't be a *dupe* for staying with us.

Julien kissed him, with tears in his eyes. His mother wept openly, while Julien, who had taken Stanislas on his knee, explained to him that he shouldn't use the word *dupe*, which, when used in this sense, is a vulgar expression for servants. Seeing the pleasure this gave to Mme. de Rênal, he tried to explain by means of picturesque examples that would amuse the children what a *dupe* really is.

—I understand, said Stanislas, it's the crow who's stupid and drops his cheese so the fox can take it, who's a flatterer.

Mme. de Rênal, delirious with happiness, covered her children with kisses, which she could scarcely do without leaning somewhat on Julien.

Suddenly the door opened; it was M. de Rênal. His severe, sour face made a strange contrast with the simple happiness which he drove from the room. Mme. de Rênal grew pale; she felt herself incapable of denying anything. Julien began to talk, and speaking loudly, repeated to his honor the mayor the story of the silver goblet that Stanislas wanted to sell. He was certain this story would be unwelcome. In the first place, M. de Rênal tended to frown out of sheer habit at the mention of silver.[7] The very name of that metal, said he, is always a prelude to some demand on my pocketbook.

But here there was more than a matter of money, there was an increase of suspicion. The happy atmosphere that surrounded his family in his absence did nothing to smooth things over, especially with a man whose vanity was so touchy. As his wife was describing to him the graceful, witty way in which Julien introduced his pupils to new ideas:

—Sure, sure, I know; he makes me hateful to my own children. It's easy enough for him to be a hundred times more agreeable than I am, just because I'm the master. Everything in this century works to make *legitimate* authority odious. Ah, poor France!

Mme. de Rênal did not pause to examine the subtleties of her husband's attitude. She had just glimpsed the possibility of passing half a day with Julien. She had a long list of purchases to make in town and said she absolutely insisted on eating dinner in a tavern; whatever her husband might do or say, she stuck to that idea. The children were ecstatic at the very word *tavern*, which modern prudery pronounces with such pleasure.

---

7. In French, *argent* is the normal word for both silver and money.

M. de Rênal left his wife at the first notion shop she entered, say-ing he had some calls to make. He came back even gloomier than he had been in the morning; he was convinced that the whole town was talking of him and Julien. As a matter of fact, nobody had so much as insinuated to him the offensive part of the public gossip. What he had heard dealt simply with the question of whether Julien would stay with him at six hundred francs or would accept the eight hundred offered by the poorhouse director.

Said director, when he met M. de Rênal in society, was very much the *cold fish*. His comportment in this matter was not with-out its clever side; there's very little unconsidered behavior in the provinces; impulses are so rare that they're easily suppressed.

M. Valenod was what they call, at a hundred leagues from Paris, a boldfaced slob.[8] It's a species that is pompous and stupid by na-ture. His triumphant career, since 1815, had added emphasis to his natural gifts. At Verrières he reigned, so to speak, under the dispen-sation of M. de Rênal; but being much more active, ashamed of nothing, mixed up in everything, continually on the go, writing, talking, shaking off humiliations, and laying claim to no personal dignity, he ended up by seeming, at least to the ecclesiastical power, the mayor's equal. M. Valenod had as good as said to the business-men in town: Give me your two biggest fools; to the lawyers he'd said, pick out a pair of your dumbest; and to the medical men, name me your two biggest charlatans. When he had assembled the most shameless members of every trade, he said to them, let's get together and make a government.

The manners of these people disturbed M. de Rênal. M. Valenod was too gross to be offended by anything, even when young Abbé Maslon called him a liar in public.

But in the midst of this prosperity M. Valenod had constantly to reassure himself by acts of petty insolence designed to ward off the hard truths that he very well knew everyone could cast up to him. He had been doubly active as a result of the fears inspired by M. Appert's visit; he had made three trips to Besançon; he wrote three letters by every post; he sent others off by unknown couriers who stopped by his house during the night. Perhaps he had been wrong in securing the dismissal of the old curé Chélan; for this vindictive step had earned him, among several pious ladies of good birth, a reputation as a wicked man. Besides, this favor received had made him absolutely dependent on the grand vicar de Frilair, from whom he received some rather odd instructions. His intrigues had reached this stage when he yielded to the pleasure of writing an anonymous letter. To add to his problems, his wife had declared

8. In the original, *faraud*.

that she must have Julien in her household; her vanity was intoxicated at the very thought.

Under these circumstances M. Valenod foresaw a decisive scene with his old colleague M. de Rênal. The latter might storm and bluster; no matter; but he might write to Besançon and even to Paris. The cousin of some minister might drop down upon Verrières all of a sudden and take the directorship of the poorhouse. M. Valenod thought of reaching an arrangement with the liberals: that was why several of them had been invited to the dinner at which Julien recited. He might, with their help, have held his own against the mayor. But elections might be called for, and it went without saying that a post in the poorhouse and a wrong vote were incompatible. These schemes, shrewdly reconstructed by Mme. de Rênal, had been sketched for Julien's benefit as he was escorting her from one shop to another, and had gradually led them to LOYALTY SQUARE, where they passed several hours almost as peacefully as at Vergy.

During this period M. Valenod was at work, stalling off a decisive break with his former chief by himself assuming a lofty tone. On this particular day the strategy worked, but it increased the mayor's ill humor.

Never did vanity at odds with mean and bitter cupidity reduce a man to a state more wretched than that of M. de Rênal as he entered the tavern. On the other hand, never had he seen his children more cheerful and joyous. The contrast completed his pique.

—So far as I can see, I'm not wanted in my own family! he said as he came in; he was trying to be impressive.

For her only answer, his wife took him aside and told him that Julien must be sent away. The hours of happiness she had just enjoyed gave her the strength and firmness of purpose necessary to carry out the plan she had been meditating for the last two weeks. What put the poor mayor of Verrières to the ultimate torture was the knowledge that people were making jokes throughout the town about his excessive fondness for *ready money*. M. Valenod had the generosity of a crook, but he, the mayor, had performed in a manner more prudent than brilliant in the last five or six collections for the Confraternity of St. Joseph, the Congregation of the Virgin Mary, the Congregation of the Holy Sacrament, etc., etc.

Among the country gentry of Verrières and vicinity, neatly listed on the books of the collecting friars in order of generosity, it had more than once been noted that the name of M. de Rênal occupied the very last line. In vain did he protest that he *earned nothing*. The clergy allow no jokes on this score.

Chapter 23

SORROWS OF AN OFFICIAL

> The pleasure of holding high one's head all year is amply repaid by
> certain quarter hours one must live through.
>
>   Casti[9]

But let's leave this little man to his little fears; why did he take into his household a man of feeling when what he wanted was the spirit of a valet? Why doesn't he know how to choose his people? It's a general rule in the nineteenth century that when a man of power and position meets a man of feeling, he kills him, exiles him, imprisons him, or humiliates him until the other is stupid enough to die of grief from it. By good fortune, in the present instance it's not yet the man of feeling who is suffering. The great unhappiness of little French towns, and of elective governments like that in New York, is that there one can't forget the existence of creatures like M. de Rênal. In a town of twenty thousand inhabitants these people make public opinion, and public opinion has terrible power in a country with the charter.[1] A man with a noble, generous spirit, who might have been your friend but who lives a hundred leagues away, judges of you by the public opinion of your town, which is formed by fools whom fortune has created respectable, rich, and moderate. Woe to the man who distinguishes himself!

Shortly after dinner they left for Vergy; but on the second day after Julien saw the whole family return to Verrières.

An hour had not passed when, to his great surprise, he found that Mme. de Rênal was keeping something from him. As soon as he appeared she broke off conversations with her husband, and she almost seemed to wish him away. Julien asked for no second hint. He became cold and withdrawn; Mme. de Rênal took note of the fact and sought no explanations. Is she going to supply me with a successor? Julien thought: Only the day before yesterday, so intimate with me! But they say this is how fine ladies are. It's like kings, who never show more kindness than to the minister who when he goes home finds his letter of dismissal.

Julien observed that in these conversations that faded suddenly at his approach there was frequent mention of a big house belonging to the commune of Verrières, old but vast and comfortable, which stood opposite the church in the best commercial section of the town. What's the connecting link between that house and the

9. G. B. Casti (1724–1803) was an Italian poet of rather licentious tastes. It is reasonably certain that he never said anything like what the epigraph attributes to him.
1. A "country with a charter" is one with a constitution—and, by implication, a representative government. The opposite would be an absolute monarchy.

new lover! Julien asked. In his distress he repeated to himself those pretty verses of François I, which seemed new to him because it was only a month since Mme. de Rênal had taught them to him. At that time how many vows, how many caresses were ready to deny each one of these verses:

> *Souvent femme varie,*
> *Bien fol qui s'y fie.*
> [Woman's a constant deceiver,
> And men are great fools that believe her.]

M. de Rênal left by the mail coach for Besançon. The trip was taken on two hours' notice; he seemed much agitated. When he came back he flung onto the table a thick packet wrapped in gray paper.

—And so much for that stupid business, he said to his wife.

An hour later Julien saw the bill sticker take away the packet; he followed him eagerly. I'll know the secret at the first street corner.

He waited impatiently behind the bill sticker while the latter slathered paste on the back of the notice with his big brush. Scarcely was it stuck up when Julien, in his curiosity, was busy reading a detailed announcement of the sale, by public auction, of a lease to that big old house that was so often being discussed by M. de Rênal and his wife. The awarding of the lease was announced for the following day at two o'clock, in the town hall, at the extinction of the third light. Julien was much disappointed; he thought the notice given was rather short: how could all the possible bidders be notified in time? But for the rest, this notice, which was dated two weeks earlier, and which he read all the way through in three different places, told him nothing.

He went to visit the house that was for sale. As he approached unobserved, the doorman was speaking mysteriously to a neighbor:

—Bah! Bah! It's a waste of time. M. Maslon has told him he'll have it for three hundred francs; and when the mayor kicked up a fuss, he was sent up to the bishop by the grand vicar de Frilair.

Julien's arrival seemed very distressing to the two friends, who cut short their conversation.

Julien did not fail to attend the auction. There was a crowd gathered in an ill-lit room; but people kept *eyeing one another* in an extraordinary way. Everyone was looking at a table where Julien saw three bits of candle end flickering in a tin plate. The bailiff cried aloud: *Three hundred francs, gentlemen!*

—Three hundred francs! That's going too far, one man murmured to his neighbor. And Julien was between the two of them. The house is worth more than eight hundred; I'm going to raise it.

—You're wasting your breath. What's the good of getting yourself in trouble with Maslon, Valenod, the bishop, and his terrible grand vicar de Frilair, and the whole crowd?

—Three hundred twenty francs, cried the other.

—Stubborn brute! said the other; and then he added, pointing to Julien, and here's the mayor's spy, right on the spot.

Julien swung around to answer this charge; but the two country-men were no longer aware of him. Their cool indifference restored his. At that moment the last candle end flickered out, and the drawling voice of the bailiff awarded the house for nine years to M. de Saint-Giraud, section chief in the prefecture of _____, at a rental of three hundred and thirty francs.

As soon as the mayor left the room conversation opened up.

—There's thirty extra francs for the town because Grogeot spoke up, said one man.

—But M. de Saint-Giraud will get back at Grogeot, said another, he'll know how to pass it along.

—What a disgrace! said a fat man on Julien's left: there's a house for which I personally would have given eight hundred francs for my business, and at that I'd have had a good bargain.

—Bah! said a young manufacturer of the liberal party, isn't it clear that M. de Saint-Giraud is in the congregation? Aren't his four children a great expense? Poor fellow! The town of Verrières just has to pitch in and provide him with an extra five hundred francs, that's all.

—And to think that the mayor couldn't prevent it! remarked a third. For he may be a <u>reactionary</u>, if you like, but a thief he isn't.

—Not a thief? said another, no, of course not, it's the little birds that take everything. The whole thing goes into one big pile, and they divide it up at the end of the year. But here's young Sorel: let's get out of this place.

Julien returned home very much out of sorts; he found Mme. de Rênal in a melancholy mood.

—You're just back from the auction? she asked.

—Yes, madame, where I had the pleasure of being taken for the mayor's spy.

—If he'd followed my advice, he would have been out of town to-day.

At that moment M. de Rênal appeared; he too was gloomy. Din-ner was eaten in complete silence. M. de Rênal ordered Julien to take the children to Vergy; the trip was somber. Mme. de Rênal comforted her husband:

—You must get used to these things, my dear.

That evening they were seated silently around the hearth; only the crackle of a burning beech log served to distract them. It was

clearly defined political stance other than conservative for M. de Rênal

one of those moments of desolation that occur in the most closely
knit families. One of the children cried joyfully:

—There's somebody at the door!

—By God! if that's M. de Saint-Giraud come to put me down by
pretending to thank me, cried the mayor, I'll tell him what's what.
He's gone too far. It's that Valenod he ought to be thanking, I'm just
the one who gets the blame. What am I going to do if these damned
Jacobin newspapers get hold of the story and try to turn me into a
M. Nonante-cinq?[2]

An extremely handsome man with big black whiskers entered at
this moment, behind the servant.

—Mr. Mayor, I am Signor Geronimo. Here is a letter for you,
given me when I left by M. le Chevalier de Beauvaisis, adjutant at
the Neapolitan embassy; that was only nine days ago, added Signor
Geronimo, glancing gaily at Mme. de Rênal. Signor de Beauvaisis,
who is your cousin and my good friend, madame, tells me you know
Italian.

The good humor of the Neapolitan changed a melancholy
evening to a gay one. Mme. de Rênal insisted on his having a late
supper. She set the whole household to bustling; she wanted to distract Julien at any cost from the insult of being called a spy, a word
that had twice been applied to him that day. Signor Geronimo was
a celebrated singer, a man used to good society and yet very cheerful himself, qualities that in France are hardly compatible any
more. After supper he sang a little duet with Mme. de Rênal. He
told a number of delightful anecdotes. At one o'clock in the morning the children protested when Julien told them it was bedtime.

—Just this one story, said the eldest.

—It's my own personal story, young sir, replied Signor Geronimo.
Eight years ago, I was like you, I was a young student in the conservatory of Naples; I mean, I was just your age, for I didn't have the
honor of being the son of the illustrious mayor of the beautiful
town of Verrières.

The phrase drew a sigh from M. de Rênal; he glanced at his wife.

—Now Signor Zingarelli, the young singer went on, exaggerating
his accent in a way that made the children burst out laughing,
Signor Zingarelli is an excessively severe teacher. He is not well
liked at the conservatory; but he insists on being treated as if he is
very well liked indeed. I sneaked out as often as I could; I used to
go to the little theater of San Carlino, where I heard music fit for

---

2. A Marseilles magistrate, M. Mérindol, who hated liberals, used the phrase *nonante-cinq*
for the number 95 (properly *quatre-vingt-quinze*) and was ridiculed for it by all the liberal journals.

the gods: but, oh, good heavens! how to scrape up the eight sous for a seat in the orchestra? An enormous sum, he said, goggling at the children until they laughed. Signor Giovannone, director of the San Carlino, heard me sing. I was sixteen years old: This child is a treasure, says he.

—How would you like a job, my friend? he asks.

—What'll you pay?

—Forty ducats a month. (That, gentlemen, would be a hundred and sixty francs.) I thought the sky was falling down.

—But, said I to Giovannone, how am I going to arrange it so that tyrant Zingarelli lets me go?

—*Lascia fare a me.*

—Leave it to me! cried the older boy.

—Exactly, young man. Signor Giovannone says to me: First of all, dear boy, a little bit of a contract. I sign: he gives me three ducats. I'd never seen so much money in my life. Then he tells me what to do.

Next morning I ask to see the terrible Signor Zingarelli. His old servant brings me in.

—What do you want, you imp? says Zingarelli.

Maestro, say I, I'm sorry for all my faults. I'll never sneak out of the conservatory again by climbing over the iron railings. I'll work twice as hard as ever.

—If I wasn't afraid of spoiling the best bass voice I ever heard, I'd put you in jail on bread and water for two weeks, you little ruffian.

—Maestro, I said, I'm going to be a model pupil for the whole school, *credete a me.* But I want to ask one favor, if anyone comes to offer me a job singing outside, please tell them no. I beg of you, tell them it's impossible.

—And who the devil do you think is going to ask for a bad lot like you? Do you think I'll ever let you leave the conservatory? Are you trying to make fun of me? Out, out, get out of here! he shouted, trying to give me a kick in the pants, or it will be dry bread and close quarters for you.

An hour later Signor Giovannone appears in the director's office:

—I want you to help me be a rich man, says he; let me have Geronimo. If he sings in my theater, I'll be able to marry off my daughter this winter.

—What do you want with that trash? says Zingarelli. I won't consent; you shan't have him. And besides, even if I consented, he'll never leave the conservatory; he just told me so.

—If all we're worried about is his consent, says Giovannone solemnly, pulling my contract out of his pocket, well, *carta canta!*[3] here's his signature.

---

3. *Carta canta:* paper talks (literally, sings).

At that Zingarelli, in a rage, rushes to the bell pull: Throw Geronimo out of the conservatory, he roars, boiling with rage. So they threw me out, helpless with laughter, and that night I sang the aria *del Moltiplico*. Pulchinello had his mind on an approaching marriage that evening and spent it counting up on his fingers all the different things he would need to set up housekeeping, and losing track at every count.

—Oh, won't you please sing us that aria, begged Mme. de Rênal.

Geronimo sang, and everyone laughed until the tears came. It was two in the morning before Signor Geronimo went off to bed, leaving the family enthralled with his good manners, his good nature, and his good humor.

Next morning, M. and Mme. de Rênal gave him various letters that would be useful to him at the court of France.

So it goes, dishonesty everywhere, said Julien. Signor Geronimo is going to London with engagements worth sixty thousand francs. If it hadn't been for the shrewdness of the director of San Carlino, very likely his wonderful voice would have been known and appreciated only ten years later. . . . My word, I'd rather be a Geronimo than a Rênal. He's not so much respected by society, but he doesn't have the shame of presiding over deals like that one yesterday, and his life is a merry one.

One thing surprised Julien; the weeks he had spent alone at Verrières in M. de Rênal's house had been a happy period for him. He had experienced melancholy thoughts and disgust only at the dinners that were given for him; but, alone in the house, he had been free to read, write, and think without disturbance. He was not being distracted from his glittering dreams at every instant by the need to study some low mind which then he would have to deceive by tricks or hypocritical words.

Is happiness really so near at hand? . . . There's no expense to such a life; I could, just as I please, marry Mlle. Elisa or become a partner with Fouqué. . . . But the man who's just climbed a mountain sits down at the top, and finds perfect satisfaction in resting there. Would he be just a happy if forced to rest all the time?

Mme. de Rênal's mind had reached a new stage of self-doubt. In spite of a resolve not to do so, she had told Julien the whole story of the crooked lease. In the same way, he'll make me forget all my resolutions, she thought.

She would have sacrificed her own life unhesitatingly to save that of her husband, if she had seen it endangered. She was one of those noble, romantic souls for whom a generous action unperformed gives rise to remorse as bitter as that for an actual crime. Yet there were dark days when she could not get out of her mind the thought of the joy that would be hers if she were suddenly widowed and could marry Julien.

He loved her children much more than their own father did: though his justice was strict, they adored him. She realized that if she married Julien they would have to leave Vergy, whose leafy shades were dear to her. But she would live at Paris, and continue to provide her children with that education which everyone so admired. Her children, she, Julien, everybody would be perfectly happy.

Strange effect of marriage, as the nineteenth century has created it! The boredom of married life is sure to destroy love, whenever love has preceded the marriage. Indeed, a philosopher would say, it even leads (where people are rich enough not to have to work) to a profound boredom with all tranquil satisfactions. Yet among women it is only the dried-up souls whom it does not predispose to love.

The philosopher's reflection makes me excuse Mme. de Rênal, but nobody excused her in Verrières, and without her suspecting it the whole town was occupied with nothing but the scandal of her affair. Because of this great scandal, people were less bored that fall than usual.

Autumn, and part of winter, passed quickly; it was time to leave the woods of Vergy. Respectable society in Verrières began to grow indignant that its anathemas had made so little impression on M. de Rênal. In less than a week various grave personages who atone for their habitual seriousness with the pleasure of running certain errands inspired in him the most cruel suspicions while still making use of the most circumspect language.

M. Valenod, who was playing it close to the vest, had placed Elisa in an aristocratic and well-considered family where there were five ladies. Elisa was afraid, she said, that she might not find a post for the winter, and so asked of this family only about two thirds of what she had received from the mayor. Of her own accord, this girl got the excellent notion of going to confess to the old curé, Chélan, and at the same time to the new curé, in order to inform them both of the latest details of Julien's love life.

The day after his return, at six o'clock in the morning, Abbé Chélan called Julien to him:

—I ask you no questions, he said; I beg of you and if necessary I order you to tell me nothing. I demand that within three days you leave, either for the seminary at Besançon or for the home of your friend Fouqué, who is still ready to provide a magnificent future for you. I have foreseen everything, arranged everything, but you must leave, and not come back to Verrières for at least a year.

Julien made no answer; he was wondering whether his honor

shouldn't take offense at all the pains that M. Chélan, who after all wasn't his father, had lavished on him.

—Tomorrow at this same time I shall have the honor of calling on you again, he said at last.

M. Chélan, who had counted on carrying the day by main force over so young a man, talked a great deal. Drawn into the humblest possible posture and expression, Julien never opened his mouth.

At last he got away and ran to tell Mme. de Rênal, whom he found in despair. Her husband had just talked to her with a certain frankness. The natural weakness of his character, sustained by a prospect of the Besançon inheritance, had induced him to consider her perfectly innocent. He had just told her of the strange condition in which he found the public opinion of Verrières. This public was mistaken, misled by envious men, but what, after all, were they to do?

For a moment Mme. de Rênal had the illusion that Julien might accept the offers of M. Valenod and remain in Verrières. But she was no longer the simple, timid woman of the year before; her fatal passion, her attacks of remorse, had enlightened her. To her grief, she was soon convinced, as she listened to her husband, that a separation, at least for the moment, had become necessary. Far from me Julien will take up again those ambitious projects which are so natural when one is penniless. And as for me, good God, I'm so rich! And it's so useless for my happiness! He'll forget me. Admirable as he is, he will love and be loved. Ah, unhappy woman! . . . But what am I complaining about? God is just; I have not been able to forsake the crime, therefore he destroys my judgment. It was up to me to shut Elisa's mouth with money; nothing would have been easier. I didn't take enough trouble to think for a minute, those mad dreams of love absorbed all my time. And so I'm lost.

Julien was struck by one thing when he heard from Mme. de Rênal the terrible news of his departure; she raised no selfish objections. She seemed to be making great efforts not to weep.

—We must be strong, my friend.

She cut a lock of his hair.

—I don't know what will become of me, she said, but if I die, promise never to forget my children. Whether from far or near, you must try to make honest men of them. If there's a new revolution, the aristocrats will all have their throats cut, and their father will emigrate no doubt, because of that peasant who was killed on his rooftop. Watch over the family. . . . Give me your hand. Goodbye, my friend: These are our last moments together. Once this great sacrifice is made, I hope that in public I'll be brave enough to think only of my reputation.

Julien had been anticipating despair. The simplicity of these farewells affected him.

—No, I won't accept your good-byes in this way. I'll go away; they want me to, and so do you yourself. But three days after I leave I'll come back to visit you at night.

Mme. de Rênal's existence was changed. Julien must love her since he had had, on his own, the idea of coming back! Her frightful grief changed into one of the sharpest impulses of joy she had ever experienced in her life. Everything became easy for her. The certainty of meeting her lover again took away from these last moments all their anguish. From this instant the conduct of Mme. de Rênal, like her expression, was noble, firm, and perfectly conventional.

Shortly M. de Rênal returned; he was beside himself. He finally talked to his wife of the anonymous letter he had received two months before.

—I'm going to take it to the Casino and show everyone it came from that villain Valenod, who was a beggar when I took him up and made him one of the richest men in Verrières. I'll shame him in public, and then challenge him to a duel. This has gone too far.

I could be a widow, great heavens! thought Mme. de Rênal. But almost at the same instant, she told herself: If I don't stop this duel, and it's certainly in my power to do so, I'll be my husband's murderer.

Never had she managed his vanity with so skilled a hand. In less than two hours she had made him understand, and always for reasons that he had discovered, that he must be more friendly than ever with M. Valenod, and even take back Elisa into his household. Mme. de Rênal needed great courage to call back this girl, cause of all her misfortunes. But the idea came from Julien.

At last, after being set back on the proper path three or four times, M. de Rênal arrived under his own power at the idea, extremely painful to him from a financial point of view, that the most disagreeable thing for him would be to have Julien staying amid the gossippy talkers of Verrières as tutor to M. Valenod's children. Julien's evident interest lay in accepting the offers of the director of the poorhouse: it served M. de Rênal's reputation much better that he should leave Verrières altogether and enter the seminary at Besançon or that at Dijon. But how to bring him to that decision, and after that how would he live there?

M. de Rênal, seeing that a financial sacrifice was imminent, suffered worse than his wife. For her part, after this conversation she was in the state of a man of feeling who has grown tired of life and taken a dose of stramonium;[4] he acts only automatically, so to

4. Stramonium: a poisonous narcotic derived from the Jimson weed.

speak, and takes no interest in anything. Thus it happened, when Louis XIV lay dying, that he said: *When I was king.* A wonderful expression!

Early next morning M. de Rênal received an anonymous letter. This one was in the most insulting style. The grossest words applicable to his position appeared in every line. It was the work of some envious inferior. This letter brought back to his mind the thought of a duel with M. Valenod. Soon his courage had reached the point where he was contemplating immediate action. He went out by himself and went to the gun shop to get some pistols, which he loaded.

After all, he said to himself, suppose the strict rule of the Emperor Napoleon is reinstated; I can't be blamed for a penny of actual theft. At most I've turned a blind eye now and then, but my desk is full of excellent letters authorizing me to do so.

Mme. de Rênal was terrified at her husband's cold rage; it reminded her of that possible widowhood which she had been at such pains to put out of her mind. She closeted herself with her husband. For several hours she talked to him in vain; the new anonymous letter had decided him. But finally she succeeded in transforming the courage to slap M. Valenod's face into the courage to offer Julien six hundred francs for a year's board in a seminary. M. de Rênal, cursing a thousand times over the day when he had the fatal notion of taking a tutor into his house, forgot the anonymous letter.

He was a little consoled by a notion he didn't mention to his wife: with a little clever management, and by playing on the young man's romantic notions, he hoped to dissuade him a little more cheaply from taking up M. Valenod's offer.

Mme. de Rênal had much trouble proving to Julien that, since he was setting her husband's mind at rest by giving up a post worth eight hundred francs a year, a post that had been publicly offered him by the director of the poorhouse, he could accept a sum of money in compensation without loss of honor.

—But, Julien kept repeating, I never had for an instant any intention of accepting that offer. You've got me too used to an elegant life; the crudity of those folk would kill me.

Harsh necessity, with fist of steel, bent Julien's will. His pride allowed him to accept the sum offered by the mayor of Verrières, but only as a loan; he made out a note promising repayment in five years, and with interest.

Mme. de Rênal still had several thousand francs hidden out on the mountainside.

She offered them to him, trembling, and all too certain of meeting with an angry refusal.

—Are you trying to render the memory of our love abominable? Julien asked her.

At last Julien left Verrières. M. de Rênal was completely happy; at the fatal moment of taking his money, Julien found it was too great a sacrifice. He refused point blank. M. de Rênal fell on his neck, with tears in his eyes. Julien having asked for a certificate of good conduct, he was unable in his enthusiasm to find expressions magnificent enough to describe that conduct. Our hero had five louis in his savings account and anticipated being able to borrow a similar sum from Fouqué.

He was deeply moved. But when he had gone a league from Verrières, where he was leaving behind him so much love, he was no longer thinking of anything except the pleasure of seeing a capital city, a great military center like Besançon.

During this short absence of three days Mme. de Rênal fell victim to one of the cruelest deceptions of love. Her life was bearable; between her and ultimate grief stood always that final meeting with Julien. She counted the hours, the minutes, that separated them. At last, during the night of the third day, she heard in the distance the prearranged signal. After passing through a thousand dangers, Julien appeared before her.

From this moment forward she had only one thought, and that was, I am seeing him for the last time. Far from responding to her lover's ardors, she was like a barely animate corpse. If she forced herself to tell him she loved him, it was with an awkward air which came close to proving the contrary. Nothing could distract her from the bitter thought of their eternal separation. Julien, in his mistrust, thought for a while that he was already forgotten. The hints he cast forth of this possibility were met only with silent tears and almost convulsive handclasps.

—But, good God, what do you expect me to believe? Julien replied to his mistress's cold protestations; you would show a hundred times more sincere feeling for Mme. Derville, for a simple acquaintance.

Mme. de Rênal, petrified, had no answer but this:

—It's impossible to be more wretched . . . I hope I shall die . . . I feel my heart is frozen . . . .

These were the longest answers he could obtain from her.

When daybreak rendered it necessary for him to leave, Mme. de Rênal's tears ceased altogether. She watched him tie a knotted cord to the window without saying a word, without returning his kisses. In vain did Julien say to her:

—Here we are in the condition for which you've been longing. Henceforth you'll be able to live without remorse. When your children have a minor ailment, you'll no longer see them already in the grave.

—I am sorry you could not kiss Stanislas good-bye, she told him coldly.

In the end, Julien was deeply struck by the icy kisses of this living corpse; he could think of nothing else for several leagues. His soul was unstrung, and before passing over the mountain, as long as he could see the church steeple of Verrières, he kept turning to look back.

Chapter 24

A CAPITAL CITY

What a racket, what a lot of busy people! what a lot of ideas for the future in a twenty-year-old head! what a lot of distractions from love!

—Barnave

At length he saw on a distant mountain some dark walls; it was the fortress of Besançon. What a difference for me, said he with a sigh, if I were coming into this splendid military town in order to serve as a sublieutenant in one of the regiments charged with defending it!

Besançon is not only one of the prettiest towns in France, it's full of people of feeling and wit. But Julien was only a little peasant and he had no sort of access to distinguished men.

He had borrowed from Fouqué a shopkeeper's jacket, and it was in this guise that he passed over the drawbridges. Preoccupied with the story of the siege of 1674,[5] he wanted to see the ramparts and the fortress before shutting himself up in the seminary. Two or three times he was on the point of being arrested by sentinels; he was able to get into places which the military close to the public, so that they can sell the hay raised there for twelve or fifteen francs a year.

The high walls, deep moats, and terrible aspect of the cannon had preoccupied him for several hours when he passed by the main café on the boulevard. He stopped stock still in admiration; though he could read the word *café* in huge letters over the two immense doors, he could hardly believe his eyes. He tried to overcome his timidity; he ventured to go in, and found himself in a room thirty or forty feet long, with a ceiling at least twenty feet high. On that day everything seemed enchanting to him.

---

5. In the war to liberate the Franche-Comté from Spain, Besançon was twice besieged and captured by the French—in 1660 and then in 1674.

Two games of billiards were being played. The waiters called out the scores; the players moved about the tables through numerous onlookers. Clouds of tobacco smoke pouring from every mouth filled the room with a blue haze. The tall stature of these men, their round shoulders, heavy strides, enormous whiskers, and the long overcoats that enveloped them, all attracted Julien's attention. These noble offspring of ancient Byzantium conversed only in bellows; they acted the part of terrible warriors. Julien admired the furnishings; he was thinking of the immensity and magnificence of a capital city like Besançon. He felt himself absolutely devoid of the courage necessary to ask for a cup of coffee from one of those lofty gentlemen who were calling out the billiard scores.

But the young lady behind the bar had noted the charming features of this young countryman who had stopped three feet from the stove, and, still holding his little parcel under his arm, was studying a fine white plaster bust of the king. This young lady, a robust product of the Franche-Comté with an admirable figure and the sort of dress one needs to be noticed in a café, had already twice called in a modest voice intended only for Julien's ears: Monsieur! Monsieur! Julien glanced into a pair of big blue eyes with a gentle expression and understood that he was being addressed.

He stepped briskly up to the counter and the young lady, as if he were charging an enemy. As he executed this maneuver, his parcel fell to the floor.

What pity will be felt for our bumpkin by those Paris schoolboys who at fifteen already know how to enter a café in such distinguished style! But these children, so modish at fifteen, turn to the *common* at eighteen. The impassioned timidity one sees in the provinces occasionally transcends itself, and then becomes a pathway to will. As he approached this beautiful girl who was kind enough to speak a word to him, I must tell her the truth, thought Julien, whose courage was thriving on conquered timidity.

—Madame, for the first time in my life I've come to Besançon; I should like to have, to purchase for money, that is, a roll and a cup of coffee.

The girl smiled a little and then blushed; she feared this handsome young fellow would draw ironic commentary from the billiard players. He would be terrified by that and would never come back.

—Sit here beside me, she said, showing him to a marble table almost entirely concealed behind the enormous mahogany bar which stood out in the room.

The young lady leaned across this counter, an action that gave her occasion to display a superb figure. Julien took notice; all his ideas changed. The pretty girl had just set before him a cup, a sugar bowl, and a roll. She paused before calling a waiter to bring coffee, because she foresaw that the coming of the waiter would put to an end her private conversation with Julien.

Julien, in thoughtful mood, was comparing this blond, gay beauty with certain memories that often disturbed him. The idea of the passion he had inspired drove away almost all his timidity. The pretty girl had only a minute; she read something in Julien's eyes.

—This tobacco smoke makes you cough; come for breakfast tomorrow before eight; at that time I'm almost alone.

—What's your name? Julien asked, with the caressing smile of timidity set at ease.

—Amanda Binet.

—Will you let me send you within an hour a little parcel about as big as this one?

The fair Amanda thought for a bit.

—I have to be careful of the boss; what you're asking may get me in trouble; but no matter, I'll write my address on a card, which you can put on your parcel. You can send it to me without fear.

—My name is Julien Sorel, said the young man; I have no relatives or friends in Besançon.

—Ah, so that's it! she said joyfully, you're coming to the law school?

—Alas, no, Julien replied, they're sending me to the seminary.

Darkest discouragement overspread Amanda's features and she called the waiter; she was decisive enough now. The waiter poured Julien's coffee without so much as seeing him.

Amanda took in money at the bar; Julien was proud of himself for having dared to speak up: a quarrel was in process at one of the billiard tables. The shouted charges and denials of the players echoed through the enormous room, making an uproar that almost stunned Julien. Amanda was dreamy and her eyes downcast.

—If you prefer, mademoiselle, he said to her suddenly with assurance, I can say that I'm your cousin.

This little air of authority pleased Amanda. This young man isn't a nobody, she thought. And she said to him very quickly, without looking at him, for she had to keep an eye out lest anybody come up to the counter.

—I come from Genlis near Dijon; say that you're from Genlis too, and my mother's cousin.

—I won't forget.

—Every Thursday at five o'clock during the summer all the young gentlemen from the seminary come past the café here.

—If you're thinking of me when I come past, have a bouquet of violets in your hand.

Amanda looked at him in amazement; this look converted Julien's courage to rashness; but he blushed deeply as he said to her:

—I feel that I love you with an overwhelming passion.

—Don't talk so loud then, she said with a frightened glance.

Julien had the idea of summoning up the phrases of a volume of
La Nouvelle Héloïse which he had read at Vergy.[6] His memory
served him well; for ten minutes he recited *La Nouvelle Héloïse* to
Mlle. Amanda Binet, who was in ecstasies; and he was pleased with
his own gallantry, when suddenly the fair Franc-Comtoise assumed
an icy expression. One of her lovers had entered the doorway of the
café.

He came up to the counter, whistling and swaggering; he stared
at Julien. At once the imagination of the latter, always rushing to
extremes, was filled with ideas of a duel. He grew very pale, pushed
his cup aside, put on a confident expression, and stared steadily
back at his rival. As this rival looked aside for a moment to pour
himself a small glass of brandy at the bar, Amanda with a single
glance ordered Julien to lower his eyes. He obeyed, and for two
minutes sat motionless in his chair, pale, resolute, and thinking
only of what was going to happen. The rival had been astonished at
the look in Julien's eyes; having gulped down his brandy, he said a
few words to Amanda, stuffed his hands in his overcoat pockets,
and strode off to a billiard table, breathing heavily and staring at
Julien. The latter sprang to his feet in an access of rage; but he did
not know the procedures of insult. He put down his parcel, and in
the most strutting gait he could manage, marched toward the billiard table.

It was in vain that prudence reminded him: Fight a duel the day
you come to Besançon and your career in the church is over.

—What matter? no one will ever say I failed to resent an insult.

Amanda took note of his courage; it made a fine contrast with
the simplicity of his manners; in an instant she preferred him before the big young man in the overcoat. She rose, and even as she
seemed to be following with her eyes someone out in the street,
moved swiftly to place herself between him and the billiard table.

—I don't want you to stare at that gentleman, he's my brother-in-
law.

—What do I care? He stared at me.

—Do you want to get me in trouble? No doubt he looked at you,
perhaps he'll even come and talk to you. I told him you were related
to my mother, that you'd just come from Genlis. He's from the
Franche-Comté, and has never gone past Dôle on the Burgundy
road; you can tell him anything you want, he'll never know the difference.

6. *La Nouvelle Héloïse* (1761), Rousseau's passionate rhetorical novel, provided several
generations of Frenchmen with their sentimental rhetoric.

Julien still hesitated; she quickly added, as her barmaid's imagination furnished her with lies in abundance;

—All right, he stared at you; but that was when he was asking me who you were; he's a man who's rough with everybody; he didn't mean to insult you.

Julien's eye still followed the supposed brother-in-law; he watched him buy a number in the game getting under way at the farther of the two billiard tables. Julien heard his heavy voice blare out, in a threatening tone, "*All right, I'm in!*" He stepped swiftly around Mlle. Amanda and took a step toward the billiard table. Amanda caught him by the arm:

—Come and pay me first, she told him.

Quite right, thought Julien; she's afraid I'll go away without paying. Amanda was just as distressed as he, and very red; she returned his change as slowly as she could, meanwhile saying to him in an undertone:

—You must leave the café at once, otherwise I won't like you anymore; and yet I do like you very much.

So Julien left, but slowly. Isn't it my duty, he kept saying to himself, to go over to that crude type and stare and snuffle at him? This question kept him pacing the boulevard in front of the café for an hour, waiting to see if his man would come out. He didn't, so Julien left.

He had been in Besançon only a few hours and already he had an experience to regret. The old surgeon-major had once, in spite of his gout, given him a few lessons in fencing; that was the only science Julien could summon to the service of his anger. But this ignorance would have been nothing if he had only known how to pick a quarrel in some other way than by striking his man; if it had come to a fistfight, his rival, an enormous oaf, would have beaten him up and left him for dead.

For a poor devil like me, Julien said to himself, a man without protectors or money, there won't be much difference between a seminary and a prison; I'll have to leave my layman's dress in some inn where I'll change to my black suit. If ever I can get out of the seminary for a few hours, I might very well, if I had layman's clothing, see Mlle. Amanda again. This was fine reasoning; but though he walked by all the inns he didn't dare enter any of them.

Finally, as he was passing by the Ambassadors Hotel for the second time, his restless glance encountered the eyes of a fat woman, still fairly young and ruddy of complexion, who seemed to have a cheerful disposition. He went up to her and told his tale.

—Certainly, my fine young abbé, said the hostess of the Ambassadors, I'll keep your lay clothes for you, and even brush them now and then. You can't just leave a good suit hanging without touching it. She took a key and led him into a room, advising him to make an inventory of what he was leaving.

—Lord now, don't you look good that way, M. l'Abbé Sorel, said the fat woman, when he came down to the kitchen, I'm going to fix you a good dinner now, and what's more, she added in an undertone, it'll cost you only twenty sous instead of the fifty everyone else pays; you've got to be careful of your little *stockpile*.

—I have ten louis, Julien replied with a certain lofty air.

—Oh, good Lord, said the hostess in alarm, don't talk so loud; there are plenty of crooks in Besançon. They could get that money away from you in less than a minute. Above all, keep out of the cafés, they're full of crooks.

—Really! said Julien; this last sentence gave him something to think about.

—Never go anywhere except here. I'll have coffee for you. Remember, you'll always have a good friend here and a good dinner at twenty sous; I guess that won't hurt, eh? Go sit down at the table, I'll serve you myself.

—I won't be able to eat, Julien told her, I'm too upset. When I leave your house, I'll be going to the seminary.

The good woman let him go only after filling his pockets with food. Finally Julien set out for his fearful destination; from her doorstep the hostess pointed out the direction.

Chapter 25

THE SEMINARY

> Three hundred thirty-six dinners at 83 centimes, three hundred thirty-six suppers at 38 centimes, chocolate for those entitled; how much is there to make on the contract?
> —The Valenod of Besançon

From a distance he saw the gilded iron cross on the door; he walked slowly forward; his legs seemed to give way beneath him. So this is the hell on earth from which I can never escape! Finally he decided to ring. The sound of the bell echoed as if in an abandoned house. After a wait of ten minutes a pale man dressed in black came to open the door for him. Julien glanced at him and abruptly lowered his eyes. It seemed to him that this doorman had an extraordinary face. The prominent, green pupils of his eyes expanded and contracted like those of a cat; the unblinking eyelids announced the impossibility of all sympathy; his thin lips were stretched tight over protruding teeth. Yet the face was not that of a criminal; rather, it suggested that complete insensibility which for young people is even more terrifying than crime. The only emotion Julien's rapid glance could discover on that long, pious face was a perfect contempt for every subject one might bring up that did not serve the interests of heaven.

With a great effort Julien looked up, and speaking in a voice that the pounding of his heart caused to tremble, declared that he wanted to speak with M. Pirard, the director of the seminary. Without uttering a word, the black man signaled him to follow. They climbed two flights of a wide stairway with a wooden baluster; the stairs sagged noticeably on the side away from the wall and seemed on the point of collapsing. A little doorway, over which hung a big wooden cemetery cross painted black, was opened with difficulty, and the porter brought him into a low, dark room, the whitewashed walls of which were adorned with two big paintings grown black with age. There Julien was left alone; he was terrified, his heart was beating furiously; he would have been happy to summon up the courage for tears. A deathly silence reigned through the whole building.

After a quarter of an hour, which seemed a whole day to him, the sinister porter reappeared in a doorway at the other end of the room, and without deigning a word made a sign for him to come along. He entered a room much larger than the other and very badly lit. Here too the walls were whitewashed; but there was no furniture at all. Only in a corner near the door Julien saw as he passed a bed of white wood, a pair of wicker chairs, and a little armchair of pine planks without a cushion. At the other end of the room, by a little window with yellowed panes and some very dirty flowerpots, he saw a man in a ragged cassock seated before a work table; he seemed angry, and was picking up, one after the other, a number of little squares of paper which he arranged on his desk after writing a few words on each. He did not take notice of Julien's presence. The latter stood motionless in the middle of the room, where he had been left by the porter, who shut the door as he went out.

Ten minutes passed; the badly dressed man kept writing. Julien's terror and distress were such that he felt ready to faint. A philosopher would have said, perhaps wrongly: This is the violent impression made by the ugly on a soul formed to love the beautiful.

The man looked up in the middle of his writing; Julien noticed him only after a moment, and even after seeing him, he still stood motionless as if struck dead by the terrible glance that was turned on him. Julien's misty eyes could barely make out a long face covered with red spots except on the forehead, which was of a deathly pallor. Between the scarlet cheeks and the white forehead glittered two little black eyes, formed to strike terror in the bravest. The vast expanse of his brow was defined by a mass of thick, straight, jet-black hair.

—Will you come over here, yes or no? the man said at last, impatiently.

Julien stepped forward uncertainly, and at last, ready to collapse, and pale as he had never before been in his life, he stopped three paces from the little wooden table covered with paper squares.

—Closer, said the man.

Julien stepped forward, holding out his hand as if trying to steady himself on something.

—Your name?

—Julien Sorel.

—You're very late, he said, fixing him once more with a terrible glance.

This look Julien could not sustain; holding out his hand as if to catch himself, he fell full length to the floor.

The man rang his bell. Julien had lost only the power of sight and of motion; he heard footsteps approach.

They picked him up and set him in the little wooden armchair. He heard the terrible man say to the porter:

—He seems to be an epileptic; that's all we needed.

When Julien could open his eyes, he saw that the red-faced man had resumed his writing and the porter had gone. I must take heart, said our hero, and above all conceal what I feel: he felt a sharp pain at his heart; if I show weakness, God knows what they'll think of me. At last the man stopped writing, and looked askance at Julien:

—Are you well enough to answer my questions?

—Yes, sir, said Julien weakly.

—Well, that's lucky.

The man in black had half risen and was looking impatiently for a letter in the drawer of his pine table, which opened with a creak. He found it, sat slowly down, and looked Julien over again with a glance fit to wrench from him the little life still remaining:

—You are recommended to me by M. Chélan, the best priest in the diocese, a virtuous man if one ever lived, and my friend for the past thirty years.

—Ah, then it is M. Pirard himself whom I have the honor of addressing, said Julien in a dying voice.

—So it seems, replied the director of the seminary, casting a surly look at him.

The glitter in his little eyes brightened, and was followed by an involuntary motion of the muscles at the corners of his mouth. It was like the expression of a tiger anticipating the pleasure of devouring his prey.

—Chélan's letter is short, he said as if talking to himself. *Intelligenti pauca*,[7] as things go now a man can hardly write too little. He read aloud:

I am sending to you Julien Sorel, of this parish, whom I baptized going on twenty years ago; son of a rich carpenter, who will give him nothing. Julien will be a remarkable laborer in the vineyard of the Lord. Memory and intelligence aplenty; he can think. Will his calling last? Is it sincere?

—*Sincere!* repeated Abbé Pirard with an air of astonishment, looking again at Julien; but already the abbé's glance was less devoid of humanity; *sincere* he repeated, lowering his voice and resuming his reading:

I ask of you a scholarship for Julien; he will earn it by undergoing the necessary examinations. I have showed him a bit of theology, that good old theology of people like Bossuet, Arnault, Fleury. If this young man doesn't please you, send him back to me; the director of the poorhouse, whom you know well, offers him eight hundred francs to act as tutor to his children. —My conscience is at rest, thanks be to God. I am growing used to the terrible blow. *Vale et me ama*.

Abbé Pirard, slowing his speech as he read the signature, pronounced with a sigh the word *Chélan*.

—He is at rest, said he; well, a man of his virtue deserves that reward, anyhow. May God grant it to me under the same circumstances.

He glanced upward and made a sign of the cross. At the sight of this holy symbol Julien felt a slight easing of the profound horror that had frozen him since he entered this house.

—I have here three hundred and twenty-one aspirants to the holiest of positions, said Abbé Pirard at last, speaking sternly but not angrily; only seven or eight are recommended to me by men like Abbé Chélan; thus among the three hundred and twenty-one, you will be number nine. But my protection is neither favor nor weakness; it is redoubled attention and severity against vice. Go lock that door.

Julien struggled to his feet and succeeded in not falling. He noted that a little window near the entryway opened onto the countryside. He looked out at the trees; the sight comforted him, as if he had seen old friends.

—*Loquerisne linguam latinam?* (Do you speak Latin?) said Abbé Pirard as he returned.

---

7. "A word to the wise is sufficient."

—*Ita, pater optime* (Yes, most excellent father), replied Julien, regaining a bit of self-possession. Certainly no man in the world had ever seemed to him less excellent than M. Pirard during the last half hour.

The conversation continued in Latin. The abbé's eyes grew softer; Julien regained some poise. What a weakling I am, thought he, to let myself be impressed by these shows of virtue! This man is going to turn out to be simply another swindler like M. Maslon; and Julien congratulated himself on having hidden almost all his money in his shoes.

Abbé Pirard examined Julien in theology, and was surprised at the extent of his knowledge. His astonishment increased when he asked him some detailed questions on the Scriptures. But when he came to questions on the teachings of the Church Fathers, he saw that Julien knew nothing, hardly even the names, of Saints Jerome, Augustine, Bonaventura, Basil, etc., etc.

In fact, thought Abbé Pirard, here is that same fatal tendency to Protestantism which I've always rebuked in Chélan. A profound, a too profound, knowledge of the Scriptures.

(Julien had just been talking, and not in answer to a specific question, of the *actual date* when Genesis and the other books of the Pentateuch had been written.)

Where does it lead, this endless study of the Holy Scriptures, thought Abbé Pirard, if not to *personal questioning*, that is, to the most frightful Protestantism? And alongside this unwise erudition, no patristic learning at all to act as a balance.

But the astonishment of the director knew no bounds at all when he interrogated Julien on the authority of the pope, and the young man, instead of repeating the maxims of the ancient Gallican church, recited to him the entire book of M. de Maistre.

A strange man, this Chélan, thought Abbé Pirard; can he have taught the boy this book in order to make him mock it?

In vain did he question Julien further, trying to find out if he believed seriously in the doctrine of M. de Maistre. The young man replied only with his memory. From this point on, Julien was really in fine form, he felt master of himself. After a protracted examination it seemed to him that M. Pirard's severity toward him was no longer anything more than superficial. In fact, if it hadn't been for the principles of austere gravity which for fifteen years he had schooled himself to practice toward his pupils, the director of the seminary would have kissed Julien in the name of logic, such clarity, precision, and sharpness was manifest in his answers.

A bold, strong spirit, said he, but *corpus debile* (the body is feeble).

—Do you often collapse as you did? he asked Julien in French, pointing at the floor.

—That was the first time in my life; the porter's face paralyzed me, Julien said, blushing like a child.

Abbé Pirard came close to smiling.

—Such are the effect of the world's vanities; you seem to be used to laughing faces, theaters for the display of falsehood. Truth is austere, sir. But our task in this world is austere too, is it not? You must take care to guard your conscience carefully from this weakness: *Excess of feeling for vain exterior charms.*

—If you were not recommended to me, said Abbé Pirard, resuming the Latin tongue with obvious pleasure, if you were not recommended to me by a man like Abbé Chélan, I would address you in the vain language of the world, to which it appears you are all too well accustomed. The full scholarship you request is the hardest thing in the world to obtain. But Abbé Chélan has merited very little by his fifty-six years of apostolic devotion if he cannot command a scholarship at the seminary.

After this speech Abbé Pirard advised Julien not to join any group or secret congregation without his permission.

—I give you my word of honor, said Julien with the heartfelt impulse of an honest man.

For the first time the director of the seminary smiled.

—That expression has no meaning here, said he, it suggests too much the vain honor of worldly men which leads them into so many errors and often into crimes. You owe me sacred obedience by virtue of paragraph seventeen of the bull *Unam Ecclesiam* of St. Pius V.[8] I am your ecclesiastical superior. In this house, my very dear son, to hear is to obey. How much money have you?

Here we are at the point, said Julien to himself; this was the reason for the *very dear son.*

—Thirty-five francs, my father.

—Keep careful track of how you spend that money; you will have to account for it to me.

This painful interview had lasted three hours; Julien called the porter.

—Put Julien Sorel in cell number 103, Abbé Pirard told this man.

As a special mark of favor, Julien was given a room to himself.

—Take up his trunk, too, he added.

Julien looked down and noticed his trunk right in front of him; he had been looking straight at it for three hours and had not recognized it.

When he reached number 103, a little room eight feet square on the top story of the house, Julien saw that it looked out on the ram-

---

8. Pius V (1504–1572) was a rigorous, disciplinarian pope from 1566 to 1572, but the bull *Unam Ecclesiam* is a Stendhalian fiction.

parts, and beyond them on the fine fields that are separated by the Doubs from the town itself.

What a delightful view! Julien exclaimed; even as he said them, he did not feel anything of what the words expressed. The many violent sensations he had experienced during his short time at Besançon had completely exhausted his energies. He sat down by the window on the single wooden chair in the cell and promptly slipped into a deep slumber. He never heard the supper bell nor that for benediction; he had been forgotten.

When the first rays of the sun woke him the following morning he found himself stretched out on the floor.

Chapter 26

THE WORLD, OR WHAT A RICH MAN LACKS

I'm alone on the face of the earth, nobody bothers to think of me. All the men whom I see getting ahead have an outward boldness and an inward hardness of heart which is not in me. They hate me for my easy good will. Ah! before long I shall die, either of hunger or of unhappiness at seeing men so cruel.

—Young[9]

He hastened to brush off his clothes and go downstairs; he was late. An usher scolded him sharply; instead of trying to excuse himself, Julien crossed his arms over his chest:

—*Peccavi, pater optime* (I have sinned, I admit my fault, oh father), he said with a contrite expression.

This first step was a great success. The clever fellows among the seminarians saw they had to do with a man who didn't have to learn the rudiments of the game. When the recreation hour came, Julien was the object of general curiosity. But he replied only with reserve and silence. Following the maxims he had made for himself, he considered his three hundred and twenty-one comrades as so many enemies, and the most dangerous of all, in his eyes, was Abbé Pirard.

A few days later Julien had to select a confessor; they provided him with a list.

Well, good Lord, what do they take me for? said he; do they suppose I don't know what it's all about? and he chose Abbé Pirard.

Though he didn't suspect it, this step proved decisive. A little seminarian, almost a child, who came from Verrières and had declared himself a friend from the first day, told him that if he had

9. The tone of this quotation, in French in the original novel, is intended to suggest Edward Young (1683–1756), the author of *Night Thoughts*, but nothing in Young's magniloquent blank verse directly parallels Stendhal's pathetic prose.

chosen M. Castanède, deputy director of the seminary, he might well have acted with greater prudence.

—Abbé Castanède is opposed to M. Pirard, who is suspected of Jansenism, added the little seminarian, bending toward Julien's ear.

All the first actions of our hero, who considered himself such a politician, were, like his choice of a confessor, acts of folly. Misled by the presumption natural to an imaginative man, he mistook his inward intentions for outward acts and considered himself a consummate hypocrite. His folly reached the height of blaming himself for his supposed success in this art of the weak.

Alas, it's my only weapon! In another age, said he, it would have been eloquent actions in the face of the enemy that enabled me to *earn my bread*.

Satisfied with his own conduct, Julien looked about him and found everywhere the appearance of the most spotless virtue.

Eight or ten seminarians lived in the odor of sanctity and experienced visions like St. Theresa and St. Francis when he received the stigmata atop Mount Verna in the Apennines. But it was a great secret; their friends concealed it. These poor fellows with the visions were almost always in the infirmary. A hundred others managed to combine robust faith with unwearying industry. They worked themselves almost sick, but without learning much. Two or three were distinguished by a real talent, among them a man named Chazel, but Julien felt hostile to them and they to him.

The rest of the three hundred and twenty-one seminarians were gross creatures, never entirely sure they understood the Latin words they recited all day long. Almost all were the sons of peasants, who preferred to gain their daily bread by repeating a few Latin words instead of swinging a pickax. It was after surveying this field, during his first few days, that Julien promised himself quick success. In every line of work intelligent people are needed; after all, there's a job to be done, he told himself. Under Napoleon, I'd have been a sergeant; among these future priests, I can be grand vicar.

All these poor devils, he added, who were day laborers from birth, have lived until they came here on curds and black bread. In their native huts they ate meat maybe five or six times a year. Like Roman soldiers, who regarded warfare as a holiday from garrison duty, these cloddish peasants are enchanted with the pleasures of the seminary.

Julien never saw in their blank eyes anything but a sense of physical satisfaction after dinner and an expectation of physical pleasure before dinner. Such were the people among whom he must distinguish himself; but what Julien did not know, and what people took care not to tell him, was that gaining first place in the various

2nth - separation of church + state

courses given at the seminary in dogma, ecclesiastical history, etc., etc., was in their eyes nothing but a *sin of pride.* Since Voltaire's time, since government by two houses, which is nothing at bottom but *distrust of authority and personal examination,* which instills in the people the bad habit of *doubt,* the church in France seems to have understood that books themselves are its real enemy. In the eyes of the church, inward submission is all. Who can prevent the superior man from passing over to the other side like Sieyès or Gré- goire![1] The terrified church clings to the pope as to its only hope of salvation. Only the pope can attempt to put an end to personal ex- amination and, by the pious ceremonial pomp of his court, make an impression on the bored, sick spirits of modern worldlings.

Julien, half grasping these various truths, which nonetheless every word spoken in a seminary tends to deny, fell into a deep melancholy. He worked hard and rapidly succeeded in learning a number of things very useful to a priest, very false in his eyes, and which interested him not at all. He thought this was his only way out.

Am I then forgotten by the whole world? He asked himself. He did not know that M. Pirard had received, and flung into the fire, various letters postmarked from Dijon, in which, despite all the decorums of the most respectable style, the deepest ardor was ap- parent. Profound regret seemed to struggle, in these letters, against passion. So much the better, thought Abbé Pirard, at least it was not an impious woman with whom this young man was in love.

One day Abbé Pirard opened a letter that seemed half obliterated by tears; it was an eternal farewell. At last, the writer told Julien, it has been granted to me to hate, not the author of my fault, who will always be for me the dearest thing in the world, but my fault itself. The sacrifice is made, my darling. It was not made without tears, as you see. The welfare of those beings for whom I am wholly respon- sible and whom you loved so well has carried the day. No longer will a just but terrible God be able to revenge on them the crimes of their mother. Farewell, Julien, be just toward men.

The ending of this letter was almost entirely illegible. The writer gave an address at Dijon but hoped that Julien would never answer it or at least that he would use only words which a woman returned to virtue's path could read without blushing.

Julien's melancholy, helped along by the mediocre diet furnished to the seminary by a contractor at eighty-three centimes, was start- ing to have an influence on his health, when one morning Fouqué turned up abruptly in his room.

---

1. For Sieyès, see p. 60 note 2. Abbé Gregoire (1750–1831) became a liberal deputy for Grenoble and was regarded by the local ultras as a traitor.

—I finally got in. Five times I came to Besançon, it's not your fault, just to see you. Always old wooden face. I posted a watchman on the seminary gate; why the devil don't you ever go out?

—It's a test I've imposed on myself.

—You really have changed. Well, at last I'm here. Two fine six-franc crowns just taught me what a fool I was not to have offered them in the first place.

The conversation between the two friends was endless. Julien changed color when Fouqué said to him:

—By the way, have you heard? The mother of your pupils has turned religious.

And he talked on, in that offhand way that makes such a singular impression on the impassioned soul whose dearest interests are being, all unconsciously, tumbled about.

—Yes indeed, my friend, the highest strains of devotion. They say she's going on pilgrimages. But to the eternal disgrace of Abbé Maslon, who did all that spying on M. Chélan, Mme. de Rênal wants no part of him. She goes to confession at Dijon or Besançon.

—She comes to Besançon, said Julien, his brow suffused.

—Quite frequently, replied Fouqué in a questioning tone.

—Do you have any *Constitutionnels* about you?

—What's that you say? replied Fouqué.

—I asked if you have any *Constitutionnels*, Julien repeated in a tone of perfect tranquillity. They sell here at thirty sous an issue.

—Really! even in the seminary we find liberals! cried Fouqué. Ah, poor France! he added, assuming the hypocritical voice and dulcet accent of Abbé Maslon.

This visit would have made a profound impression on our hero if next day a word addressed to him by that little seminarian from Verrières, who seemed to him so childish, had not led to an important discovery. Since he had been at the seminary Julien's conduct had been nothing but one false step after another. He laughed scornfully at himself.

Actually, the important actions in his life had been skillfully managed; but he was not clever at the details, and in the seminary clever fellows pay attention only to the details. Thus, he was already considered by his fellows a *free thinker*. He had been betrayed by a host of little actions.

In their eyes he was already guilty of one enormous vice: *he thought, he judged for himself,* instead of following blindly *authority* and precedent. Abbé Pirard had been of no help to him; outside the confessional he had not said a single word to him, and even in the confessional he listened more than he talked. Things would certainly have been very different had he chosen Abbé Castanède.

The moment Julien became aware of his folly, his boredom disappeared. He wanted to know the full extent of the damage and to that end emerged slightly from the lofty, obstinate silence with which he had rebuffed his fellows. Then they got their own back. His advances were met with a scorn that reached the point of derision. He realized that since he entered the seminary there had not been a single hour, especially during the recess periods, which had not hurt or helped him, which had not augmented the number of his enemies or earned him the good will of some seminarian who was either sincerely virtuous or at least a little less gross than the others. The damage to be repaired was immense, the task difficult in the extreme. Henceforth Julien was constantly on the alert; his task was to create for himself a whole new character.

Managing his eyes, for example, gave him a great deal of trouble. It's not without good reason that in places of this sort they are always kept lowered. What presumption I showed at Verrières, Julien said to himself; I thought that was life; it was only a preparation for life; here I am at last, in the world as it is going to be for me until I play out my role, surrounded by real enemies. What immense difficulty, he added, in this minute-by-minute hypocrisy! It's worse than the labors of Hercules. The real Hercules of modern times is Sixtus V,[2] deceiving by his modesty for fifteen years on end forty cardinals who had seen him proud and vigorous in his youth.

So learning counts for nothing here! he said to himself with scorn; ability to learn dogma, sacred history, etc., counts only on the surface. Everything they say on this subject is only to make fools like me fall into their trap. Alas! my only merit was in my studies, my knack for reciting their humbug. Perhaps in their hearts they estimate that stuff at its true value? Perhaps they think of it just as I do? And I was fool enough to be proud of myself! All those first places I accumulated did nothing but accumulate mortal enemies for me. Chazel, who knows more than I do, always puts into his compositions some piece of idiocy which sets him down to fiftieth place; any time he's in first place, it's by mistake. Ah, how a word, just one word from M. Pirard, would have helped me!

As soon as the scales fell from Julien's eyes, the lengthy practices of ascetic piety, such as rosary drill five days a week, hymns to the Sacred Heart, etc., etc., all of which used to seem so mortally tedious, became occasions for his most interesting acting. Reflecting critically on his behavior, and striving above all not to exaggerate his methods, Julien did not aspire, like the seminarians who served as models for the others, to perform at every moment a *significant*

---

2. Stendhal's notions about Pope Sixtus V (1521–1590) came from an eighteenth-century biography published under the anagram Geltio Rogeri by a priest whose real name was Gregorio Leti Stendhal's picture of Sixtus's hypocrisy does not vary much from Leti's.

action, that is, one giving evidence of some Christian perfection.
Not all at once. In the seminary there's a way of eating a boiled
egg which declares how far one has progressed down the saintly
path.

The reader, who no doubt is smiling, will be kind enough to recall all the mistakes in eating an egg made by Abbé Delille when invited to lunch by a great lady in the court of Louis XVI.[3]

Julien sought as his first stage to reach the *non culpa,* that is, the
state of the young seminarian whose deportment, whose manner of
moving his arms and eyes, etc., reveals nothing of the worldly spirit,
it is true, but does not yet show the mind wholly absorbed in the
idea of the other world and the *absolute nullity* of this one.

Everywhere Julien saw, scribbled with charcoal on the corridor
walls, phrases like this: What are sixty years of trial compared with
an eternity of joy or an eternity of boiling oil in hell? He did not despise these slogans; he understood it was necessary to have them
constantly before one's eyes. What will I be doing all my life? he
asked himself; I'll be selling the faithful a seat in heaven. How will
that seat be made visible to them? by the difference between my exterior and that of a layman.

After several months of constant application, Julien still had the
look of a *thinker.* His way of moving his eyes and opening his
mouth did not declare a man of implicit faith, ready to believe
everything and endure everything, even martyrdom. With rage
Julien saw himself outdone in this respect by the most boorish of
peasants. They had good reason not to look like thinkers.

How he taxed himself to achieve that [blissful, narrow look, that]
expression of blind, fervent faith, ready to believe all and suffer all,
which is so often found in Italian convents, and of which Guercino
has left, for us laymen, such perfect examples in his ecclesiastical
paintings.[4]

On high festival days the seminarians were given sausages with
their cabbage. Julien's table companions had noted that he was indifferent to this delight; that was one of his first sins. His comrades
saw it as a trait of the most odious hypocrisy; nothing made him
more enemies. Look at that bourgeois, that snob, they said; look
how he pretends to despise our best grub, sausages with kraut.
What an ugly fellow! What an arrogant attitude! Damn him!

[He ought to have left part of it on his plate, sacrificed it, and

---

3. Jacques Delille (1738–1813), illegitimate as well as provincial by birth, and forced to
gain his livelihood by teaching elementary Latin, came to public attention with a translation of Virgil's *Georgics* in 1769; he was then taken up by Mme. Geoffrin and polished
to such effect that late in his life he wrote one of his best poems on the art of worldly
conversation.
4. See in the Louvre n. 1130, François Duc d'Aquitaine laying aside his armor and putting
on monastic robes [Stendhal's note].

then said to some friend, with a gesture at the kraut: What can man offer an all-powerful being if not *voluntary suffering?*

Julien did not have the experience which makes things of this sort so easy to see.]

It's my misfortune that the ignorance of these young peasants, who are my comrades, gives them an immense advantage over me, Julien exclaimed in his moments of discouragement. When they enter the seminary, the professor has no need to deliver them from the frightful quantity of worldly ideas which I bring with me, and which they can read in my face, no matter what I do.

Julien studied with an attention that approached envy the crudest of the young peasants who came to the seminary. At the moment when they were stripped of their nankeen jackets to put on the black habit their education was limited to an immense respect for *dry and liquid* money, as they say in the Franche-Comté.

It is their sacramental and heroic way of expressing the sublime idea of *cash on the line.*

Happiness for these seminarians, as for the heroes of Voltaire's stories, consisted primarily of a good dinner. Julien found that nearly all of them had an instinctive respect for the man who wore a suit of *good goods.* This sentiment of theirs values *distributive justice,* as our courts hand it down, at its proper price or even something less. What can be gained, they often asked one another, by pleading against a bigshot?

That's the expression used in the Jura valleys to describe a rich man. Imagine then what respect they have for the richest group of all: the government!

Not to smile respectfully at the very name of the prefect seems, to the peasants of the Franche-Comté, an act of folly; but folly on the part of poor people is quickly punished by loss of bread.

After having been almost suffocated at first by his sense of contempt, Julien ended by feeling some pity: it had often befallen the fathers of most of his comrades to come home on a winter night to their hovels and to find there neither bread nor chestnuts nor potatoes. So what's surprising, Julien asked himself, if they consider a happy man to be one who's just had a good dinner, and after that the man who has a good suit of clothes? My comrades have a sure vocation; that is, they see in their churchly functions a long spell of this happiness: having a good dinner and a warm suit of clothes in winter.

Julien happened to overhear a young seminarian endowed with imagination say to his companion:

—Why shouldn't I become Pope, like Sixtus V, who kept swine?

—Only Italians get made pope, replied his friend; but you can count on it, they'll draw lots among us for jobs as grand vicars, canons, and maybe even bishops. M. P_____, bishop of Châlons, is the son of a tub maker; now that's my father's job.

One day, in the middle of dogma class, Abbé Pirard summoned Julien. The poor young man was delighted to be withdrawn from the moral and physical atmosphere into which he had been plunged.

Julien received from the director the same welcome that had so terrified him the day he entered the seminary.

—Explain to me what you see written on this playing card, he said, looking at Julien in a manner to make him sink through the floor.

Julien read:

"Amanda Binet, Café of the Giraffe, before eight o'clock. Say you're from Genlis and my mother's cousin."

Julien saw the immensity of the peril; Abbé Castanède's agents had stolen this address from him.[5]

—The day I enrolled here, he said, looking at Abbé Pirard's forehead, for he could not endure his terrible glance, I was in terror: M. Chélan had told me this would be a place full of informers and all sorts of malice; spying and tale bearing are encouraged here. Heaven will have it so, to show young priests life as it is, and to fill them with disgust for the world and its empty displays.

—And you have the audacity to make phrases like that to me, cried Abbé Pirard in a rage. You young scoundrel!

—At Verrières, Julien replied cooly, my brothers used to beat me up when they had occasion to be jealous of me. . . .

—Come to the point! the point! cried M. Pirard, almost beside himself.

Without being in any way intimidated, Julien resumed his tale.

—The day of my arrival in Besançon, toward midday, I was hungry and entered a café. My heart was filled with detestation of a place so profane; but I bethought me that my lunch would cost less there than at a hotel. A lady, who seemed to be in charge of the place, took pity on my innocent air. Besançon is full of crooks, she told me; I fear for you, sir. If you get into any sort of trouble, call on me, send a message to my house before eight o'clock. If the porters at the seminary refuse to carry your message, say that you are my cousin, and come from Genlis. . . .

—All this fiddle-faddle will have to be investigated, cried Abbé Pirard, who was unable to sit still and had begun striding back and forth in the room.

—Back to your cell with you!

5. Abbé Castanède turns up in Part II as a full-fledged officer of the secret police.

The abbé followed Julien and locked him in. The latter at once began to look into his trunk, at the bottom of which the fatal card had been carefully hidden. Nothing was missing from the trunk, but several things were out of order, yet the key had never been out of his hands. What a good thing, thought Julien, that during the time of my blindness I never accepted that permission to leave the seminary offered me so assiduously by M. Castanède with a kindness I now understand. I might perhaps have been weak enough to change my garments and go to see the fair Amanda; I would be ruined. When they saw they couldn't use their information that way, rather than waste it, they made a direct charge out of it.

Two hours later the director sent for him.

—You didn't lie, he said to him with a less forbidding glance; but to keep such an address is an act of folly the gravity of which you cannot possibly conceive. Wretched boy! In ten years, perhaps, it may rise to harm your career.

Chapter 27

FIRST EXPERIENCE OF LIFE

> The present time, great God! is like the ark of the covenant. Unhappy the man who touches it!
>
> —Diderot[6]

The reader will kindly allow us to provide very few clear, precise facts on this period of Julien's life. It's not that we lack them, quite the contrary; but perhaps the life he lived at the seminary is too black for the middling colors we have tried to use in these pages. Modern men who suffer from certain things cannot recall them without a horror that freezes every other pleasure, even that of reading a story.

Julien had little success in his efforts at a hypocrisy of gestures; he fell into moments of disgust and even of complete discouragement. He was unsuccessful, and in a degrading career, at that. The least help from outside would have heartened him again; the difficulty to be overcome was not so great, but he was alone like a boat abandoned in the midst of the ocean. And suppose I succeed, he told himself; to pass one's whole life in such bad company! Gluttons who dream only of the ham omelet they are going to wolf down at dinner, or men like Abbé Castanède, for whom no crime is too repulsive! They'll rise to the seats of power, all right; but at what a price, good God!

Man's will is powerful, I read it everywhere; but is it strong

---

6. The quotation from Denis Diderot (1713–1784) is invented.

enough to surmount disgust like mine? The great men of history had it easy; however terrible their test, they thought it beautiful; and who but myself can understand the ugliness of everything that surrounds me?

This moment was the most trying in his whole life. It would have been so easy for him to enlist in one of the fine regiments garrisoned at Besançon! Or he could live by teaching Latin; he needed so little to live on! But then, no more career, no more future for his imagination: it was death to think of. Here is a detailed account of one of his bitter days.

How often I used to flatter myself on being different from other young peasants! Well, I've lived enough to see that *difference begets hatred*, he told himself one morning. This great truth had just been brought home to him by one of his most irksome failures. He had been working for a week to please a student who lived in the odor of sanctity. They were walking together in the courtyard listening submissively to some paralyzing drivel. Suddenly the weather turned stormy, the thunder grumbled, and the saintly student exclaimed, shoving Julien away with a rude gesture:

—Look here now, it's everyone for himself in this world; I don't want to be struck by lightning: God may blast you as an unbeliever, a Voltaire.

His teeth clenched in rage, his eyes glaring up at the lightning-streaked sky, Julien cried aloud:

—I'd deserve to be crushed if I went to sleep during the tempest. All right, I'll have to try working on some other bumpkin.

It was time for the course in sacred history given by Abbé Castanède.

The young peasants, terrified of their fathers' drudgery and poverty, learned from Abbé Castanède that the government which seemed so terrible to them, the government itself, had no real and legitimate power except as this was delegated to it by God's vicar on earth.

Render yourselves worthy of the Pope's bounty by the sanctity of your life, by your obedience, *be as a rod in his hands*, he added, and you will obtain a marvelous position where you will command from on high, free of all control; a post from which you cannot be dismissed, in which the government will pay one third of your salary, and the faithful, guided by your preachings, the other two thirds.

As he left the classroom, Abbé Castanède paused in the hallway [among his pupils, who that day were especially attentive].

—It's certainly true of priests what they say in general: a man gets what he earns. As he spoke, the students formed a circle around him.

—I myself have known, as sure as I'm speaking to you here, little mountain parishes where the perquisites came to more than many town priests get. There was just as much money, not to speak of the fat capons, the eggs, the fresh butter, the innumerable little delicacies here and there; and out in the country, the priest is number one and no rivals: never a good feast to which he's not invited, where he's not fussed over, etc.

Scarcely had M. Castanéde retired to his apartment when the students split into groups. Julien belonged to none; they drew away from him as from a sheep with the scab. In each group he saw one of the students tossing a coin in the air; his success in calling heads or tails was supposed to indicate to his fellows whether he would shortly have one of those fat livings.

Next came the anecdotes. Such and such a young priest, scarcely ordained for a year, gave a tame rabbit to the servant of an old curé, got made vicar by that means, and then a few months later, for the old priest died almost at once, succeeded him in a snug berth. Another fellow had succeeded in getting himself named successor to the priest of a wealthy country town by attending at all the meals of the old curé, who was paralyzed, and cutting up his chicken very dexterously indeed.

Seminarians, like young men in all professions, exaggerate the effect of these little tricks whenever they're out of the ordinary and strike the imagination.

I must take part in these conversations, Julien thought. When they weren't talking of sausages and good livings, their talk ran much to the worldly side of ecclesiastical politics; they talked of quarrels between bishops and prefects, between priests and mayors. Julien saw at the back of their minds the idea of a second God, a God much more powerful and more to be feared than the other; this second God was the Pope. It was actually murmured, but in an undertone and when M. Pirard could not possibly overhear, that if the Pope doesn't choose to name all the prefects and mayors of France himself, it's simply because he's entrusted this duty to the king of France, by naming him elder son of the church.

About this time Julien thought he might turn a profit on his knowledge of the book *The Pope*, by M. de Maistre.[7] As a matter of fact, he astounded his comrades; but even this was a misfortune. He irked them by expressing their own opinions better than they could themselves. M. Chélan had been a foolish counselor for Julien, as he had been for himself. After accustoming him to good logic and teaching him to avoid empty verbiage, he neglected to tell

7. Joseph de Maistre's book does not come far short of the seminarians' fantasies in proposing the power of the pope to appoint and dismiss heads of government.

him that in a person of low rank these customs are criminal; for all good reasoning is irksome.

Julien's fine speech was therefore a fresh offense. His comrades, having been compelled to notice him, succeeded in expressing all their horror of him in a single phrase; they nicknamed him *Martin Luther*; mainly, they said, because of that infernal logic of which he was so proud.

Several of the seminarians had fresher complexions and could be thought better looking than Julien, but his hands were white and he could not conceal certain habits of personal cleanliness. His advantage in this respect was not one in the gloomy quarters where fate had cast him. The dirty peasants among whom he lived declared that his morals were miserably lax. We are afraid of tiring the reader by describing the thousand misfortunes which befell our hero. For instance, the more muscular of his comrades tried to make a habit of beating him up; he was obliged to arm himself with an iron compass and to make plain, but by gestures, that he was ready to use it.[8] Gestures cannot be represented, in a spy's report, as conveniently as words.

Chapter 28

A PROCESSION

All hearts were stirred. The presence of God seemed to descend upon these narrow Gothic streets, stretching out in every direction and carefully sanded by the solicitude of the faithful.

—Young[9]

It was useless for Julien to make himself humble and stupid; he could not please, he was too different. And yet, he said to himself, all these professors are clever men, chosen from among thousands; how is it they aren't pleased with my humility? Only one of them all seemed ready to accept his complaisance in believing everything and seeming the dupe of everyone. This was Abbé Chas-Bernard, director of ceremonies in the cathedral, in which he had been hoping for the last fifteen years to receive a canonry; while waiting, he taught sacred eloquence in the seminary. During the period of his blindness, Julien had regularly found himself in first place in this class. Abbé Chas had taken this as grounds for showing him some

---

8. Another trait from Leti's biography of Sixtus V; Sixtus is said to have used a bundle of heavy keys, when he was in the monastery, to brain an inimical brother in Christ.
9. The original quotation is in French. It does not, by its content, suggest any particular Young (neither Edward nor Arthur, among the better-known Youngs) and is probably, like the previous epigraph, an invention of Stendhal's.

friendship, and after class would gladly take his arm for a stroll around the garden.

What's he getting at? Julien asked himself. He saw with astonishment that for hours on end Abbé Chas would talk to him about the ornaments the cathedral possessed. It had seventeen gold-braided chasubles, quite apart from the special trappings of mourning. They had high hopes of old President de Rubempré's widow; this lady, who was ninety years old, had been keeping for at least seventy of those years her wedding dress, of superb Lyon silk embroidered with gold. Just imagine, my friend, said Abbé Chas, stopping short and opening his eyes very wide, these dresses will stand up by themselves, that's how much gold there is in them. It's a very general opinion in Besançon that, under the old lady's will, the treasury of the cathedral will be enriched by more than ten chasubles, not to mention four or five capes for high holy days. Nay, I will go further, added Abbé Chas, lowering his voice. I have good reason to think the President's widow will leave us eight magnificent silver-gilt candlesticks, which are supposed to have been bought in Italy by the Duke of Burgundy, Charles the Bold, whose favorite minister was an ancestor of hers.

But what's this man getting at with all this flimflam? Julien thought. He's been a century building up to something, but nothing comes. He must really be afraid of me! He's cleverer than the rest; you can see to the bottom of them in a couple of weeks. But I understand, this fellow's ambition has been on the rack for fifteen years!

One evening in the midst of military drill,[1] Julien was summoned by Abbé Pirard, who told him:

—Tomorrow is the feast of Corpus Christi. Father Chas-Bernard needs you to help decorate the cathedral, go and obey him.

Abbé Pirard called him back, and added in a tone of compassion:

—It's up to you whether you want to take a ramble through the town.

—*Incedo per ignes*,[2] replied Julien—that is to say, I'll watch my step.

Next morning at sunrise Julien reported to the cathedral, walking with lowered eyes. The sight of the streets, and of the bustle just beginning in the town, was good for him. Everywhere the house fronts were being decorated for the procession. All the time he had spent in the seminary now seemed to him no more than an instant.

1. The idea that theological students were being drilled in their seminaries by Jesuit officers seems, at best, mildly paranoid; but it is in an old Voltairean tradition to represent the Jesuits as committed to using, in every way possible, the secular arm (see *Candide*, Chap. 14).
2. *Incedo per ignes*: from Horace's (65–8 B.C.E.) *Odes* II, i.

His thoughts were in Vergy, and with that pretty Amanda Binet whom he might just meet, as her café was not far off. In the distance he noted Abbé Chas-Bernard at the gate of his beloved cathedral; he was a bulky man with a jovial face and an open expression. On this particular day he was in his glory:

—I was expecting you, my dear son, he cried as soon as he saw Julien, you are welcome. The day's work will be long and hard; let us strengthen ourselves with a first breakfast; our second one will come at ten o'clock during high mass.

—Sir, said Julien gravely, I beg of you not to leave me alone for an instant; and will you be good enough to note, he added, pointing at the clock above their heads, that I came here at one minute before five.

—Ah, so you're afraid of those young imps at the seminary! You are too generous in giving them a thought, said Abbé Chas; is a road less beautiful because there are thorns in the hedges alongside it? Travelers push forward and leave the nasty thistles standing in their places. But now to work, my dear friend, to work.

Abbé Chas was right in saying the day's work would be hard. The day before there had been a great funeral service in the cathedral; nothing had been got ready; thus it was necessary, in one single morning, to cover all the Gothic columns lining the nave and the two aisles with a sort of red damask that was to be no less than thirty feet high. The bishop had imported four upholsterers from Paris by mail coach, but these gentlemen could not do the whole job themselves, and far from correcting the clumsiness of their helpers from Besançon, they increased it by making fun of them.

Julien saw that he must climb the ladder himself; his agility served him well. He took command of the local upholsterers. Abbé Chas watched in enchantment as he vaulted from ladder to ladder. When all the columns were draped in damask, the problem arose of placing five enormous bunches of feathers atop the huge canopy over the high altar. A rich crown of gilt wood was supported by eight big twisted columns of Italian marble. But to reach the center of the canopy, above the sanctuary, it would be necessary to walk across an old wooden cornice, probably worm-eaten and forty feet high.

The prospect of this dangerous climb extinguished the gaiety, hitherto so brilliant, of the Paris upholsterers; they looked up from below, discussed the matter at length, and did no climbing. Julien grasped the bunches of feathers and ran up the ladder. He placed them very suitably on the ornament, in the form of a crown at the center of the canopy. As he was climbing down the ladder, Abbé Chas-Bernard caught him in his arms:

—*Optime!* cried the good priest, I shall tell monsignor of that exploit.

Ten o'clock breakfast was very merry. Never had Abbé Chas seen his church look so well.

—My dear disciple, he told Julien, my mother used to rent out chairs in this venerable structure, so that in a way I was actually brought up here. Robespierre's terror ruined us; but at the age of eight, which I then was, I was already serving at private masses, and on mass day I got fed.[3] Nobody could outdo me at folding a chasuble; the braid was never broken. Since Napoleon restored the faith, I have been fortunate enough to manage everything in this ancient cathedral. Five times a year my eyes behold it decked in these splendid ornaments. But never has it been so splendid as today, never have the damask curtains been so well attached or clung so close to the columns.

—At last he's going to tell me his secret, thought Julien; he's got to talking about himself, there's a kind of warmth. But nothing in the least revealing was ever said by this man, though he was evidently in an exalted state. And yet he has worked hard, he is happy, said Julien to himself; and what's more, the good wine has not been spared. What a man! What an example for me! This takes the cake! (The latter was a low expression he recalled from the old surgeon.)

When the sanctus bell tolled during high mass, Julien made as if to put on a surplice in order to follow the bishop in the grand procession.

—And the robbers, my friend, the robbers! cried Abbé Chas, you've forgotten about them. The procession will go out; the church will be left empty; we'll watch over it, you and I. We'll be very lucky if we don't lose more than a few yards of that fine gold braid which runs around the foot of the columns. That's another gift from Mme. de Rubempré; it comes from the famous count her great grandfather; and it's pure gold, my friend, added the abbé, whispering into his ear with an air of great excitement, nothing imitation about it! I want you to take charge of inspecting the north aisle, don't leave it. I'll take on the south aisle and the nave. Keep an eye on the confessionals; that's where the robbers' girlfriends hang out to spy on us the moment our backs are turned.

As he finished his instructions the clock struck quarter of twelve, and shortly the big bell's tolling made itself heard. It was sounding at full volume; these rich, solemn tollings stirred Julien. His imagination rose from the earth.

Julien often compared to him

3. When the churches were closed under the Terror, private masses were said in houses. The youthful Stendhal in Grenoble had assisted at some of these.

The odor of incense and rose petals cast before the Blessed Sacrament by little children dressed as St. John completed his exaltation.

The solemn tolling of the bell should have caused Julien to think only of the work being done by twenty men at fifty centimes apiece and assisted perhaps by fifteen or twenty of the faithful. He should have calculated the wear and tear on the ropes or on the beams, should have considered the dangers from the bell itself, which falls every two centuries, and should have worked out ways to lower the pay of the ringers, or to pay them with an indulgence, or some other favor that can be drawn from the church's stockpile without depleting her purse.

Instead of these sensible calculations, Julien's soul, exalted by virile and capacious sounds, was wandering through imaginary space. Never will he make a good priest or a great administrator. Souls that can be so stirred are good, at most, to produce an artist. Here Julien's presumption makes itself fully apparent. Perhaps fifty of his comrades in the seminary, who had been awakened to life's realities by public hatred and the Jacobinism they had learned to suspect of lying in wait behind every hedge, would have though when they heard the great bell of the cathedral only of the money being given to the ringers. They would have estimated, with the genius of a Barême,[4] whether the degree of emotion aroused in the public was worth the money being expended for labor. If Julien had tried to think of the material interests of the church, his imagination, rushing far beyond its goal, would have thought of saving forty francs on the construction and lost a chance to get out of paying twenty-five centimes.

While the procession moved slowly through Besançon, under the most beautiful sky one could want, and halted at all the glittering stations raised by the various authorities in competition with one another, the church remained perfectly silent. In the half darkness an agreeable coolness prevailed; the church was still embalmed with the perfume of flowers and incense.

The silence, the perfect solitude, the coolness of the long nave rendered Julien's reverie all the sweeter. He had no fear of being disturbed by Abbé Chas, who was busy in another part of the edifice. His soul had almost escaped its mortal envelope, which continued to stroll slowly up the north aisle, over which it was to watch. He was all the more at ease because he had made sure there was nobody in the confessionals but a few pious women; his eye looked without seeing.

4. François Barême (1640–1703) was a mathematician, author of a little book on accounting that made his name a household word for an accurate calculator.

But his vacant mood was partly distracted by the sight of two well-dressed women on their knees, one in a confessional, the other, near the first, seated on a chair. He looked at them without seeing them; but, then, whether it was a vague sense of duty or admiration for the refined simplicity of the ladies' dress, he reflected that there was no priest in that confessional. It's curious, he thought, that these fine ladies aren't kneeling before an altar, if they're religious, or aren't sitting in the front row of a balcony if they're of the world. How well that dress suits her! What grace! He slowed his pace in an effort to see them.

The one who was kneeling in the confessional turned her head aside a bit when she heard the sound of Julien's footsteps in the midst of that great stillness. Suddenly she gave a little shriek and fainted.

As she lost consciousness this kneeling lady fell back; her friend, who was nearby, rushed forward to help. At the same moment Julien saw the shoulders of the stricken lady. A rope of large pearls, well known to him, caught his eye. What were his feelings when he recognized the hair of Mme. de Rênal; it was she. The lady who was holding her head, and trying to keep her from falling full length, was Mme. Derville. Julien, beside himself, sprang forward; Mme. de Rênal's collapse might have dragged down her friend if Julien had not held them up. He saw Mme. de Rênal's head, pale and absolutely unconscious, drooping on her shoulder. He helped Mme. Derville to prop that charming head on the back of a wicker chair; he was on his knees.

Mme. Derville looked back and recognized him:

—Leave us, sir, leave us! she said to him, in accents of the most passionate anger. She must not see you again, whatever happens. The sight of you ought to be horrible for her; she was so happy before you came! Your actions are atrocious. Leave us; go away, if you have any shame left in you.

This speech was delivered with such authority, and Julien was so weak at this moment, that he left. She has always hated me, said he, thinking of Mme. Derville.

At the same time the nasal chanting of the first priests in the procession resounded through the church; the procession was returning. Abbé Chas-Bernard called several times for Julien, who at first did not hear him; at last he came and plucked him by the arm from behind a pillar where Julien had taken refuge, nearly dead. He wanted to introduce him to the bishop.

—But you're not feeling well, my child, said the abbé when he saw him so pale and almost incapable of walking; you've overworked. The abbé lent him an arm. Come sit down here on this little sacristan's bench beside me; I won't let you be seen. They were then beside the main entry. Calm yourself; we still have twenty good minutes before the bishop appears. Try to get your strength back; when he passes, I'll give you a hand, for I'm still strong and vigorous, in spite of my age.

But when the bishop passed by, Julien was so shaky that Abbé Chas gave up on the idea of introducing him.

—Don't worry about it, said he, I'll find another occasion.

That evening he sent to the seminary chapel ten pounds of candles, saved, as he said, by Julien's industry and the promptness with which he had put them out. Nothing could have been less true. The poor boy was extinguished himself; he had not had a single idea since catching sight of Mme. de Rênal.

Chapter 29

A FIRST PROMOTION

He knew his century, he knew his district, and he is rich.
—The Precursor[5]

Julien had not yet emerged from the long reverie into which he had been plunged by events in the cathedral when one morning he was summoned by stern Abbé Pirard.

—Here is Abbé Chas-Bernard who writes me a letter in your favor. I'm pretty well pleased with your conduct as a whole. You are extremely rash and even scatterbrained, that's perfectly apparent; but so far your heart seems to be good, even generous; the mind is superior. All in all, I see in you a spark that must not be put out.

After fifteen years of labor, I am about to leave this establishment: my crime is having left the seminarians to their own free wills, to have neither protected nor harmed that secret society of which you told me in the confessional. Before I leave, I want to do something for you; I might have acted two months sooner, for you deserve it, had it not been for that denunciation based on the address of Amanda Binet found in your possession. I create you tutor in the Old and New Testaments.

Julien, overwhelmed with gratitude, had the notion of falling to his knees and thanking God; but he yielded to a truer impulse. He went up to Abbé Pirard, took his hand, and carried it to his lips.

—What's this? exclaimed the director, with an angry look; but Julien's eyes were even more eloquent than his action.

Abbé Pirard looked at him in astonishment, like a man who for many long years has been out of the way of delicate feelings. This moment of thought betrayed the director; his voice changed.

5. *The Precursor* was a Lyon newspaper.

—Well, yes, my child, it's true, I'm fond of you. Heaven knows, it's not of my impulse. I must be just and bear neither hate nor love toward anyone. Your career will be a hard one. I see in you a quality that offends the vulgar mob. Jealousy and calumny will dog you. Wherever providence leads you, your comrades will never be able to look upon you without hatred; if they pretend to love you, it will be only to betray you more securely. Against all this there is just one remedy; put your trust only in God, who bestowed upon you, as a punishment for your presumption, this quality of making enemies. Let your conduct be pure; I see no other safety for you. If you hold to the truth with unshakable strength, sooner or later your enemies will be confounded.

It had been so long since Julien heard a friendly voice that he must be pardoned for a weakness; he burst into tears. Abbé Pirard opened his arms; the moment was precious for them both.

Julien was mad with joy; this promotion was his first; it brought him immense advantages. To imagine them, one must have been condemned to pass months on end without an instant of solitude and in the immediate presence of comrades who were irksome at best and mostly unbearable. Their guffaws alone would have been enough to disorder a delicate system. The exuberant spirits of these well-fed, well-dressed peasants could find relief, could fulfill themselves completely, only when they were shouting at the top of their lungs.

Now, Julien ate alone, or almost so, an hour later than the other seminarians. He had a key to the garden and could walk there whenever it was empty.

To his great astonishment, Julien found himself less hated; he had expected a storm of spite. His secret wish not to be talked to, which was all too apparent and had earned him so many enemies, was no longer a token of ridiculous arrogance. In the opinion of the gross boors around him, it evinced a proper sense of his own dignity. The hatred ebbed perceptibly, above all among his younger fellow-students, who now became his pupils and whom he treated with great politeness. Gradually he even gained some supporters; it was ill-bred to call him Martin Luther.

But why enumerate his friends, his enemies? It's all ugly, and all the uglier because the picture is a true one. Yet these are the only teachers of morality that the populace has, and without them what would become of it? Can the daily newspaper ever replace the priest?

Since Julien's new dignity, the director of the seminary made a point of never talking to him except in the presence of a third party. This behavior showed prudence on the part of the master, as well as for the disciple; but, more than anything, it represented a *test*. The invariable principle of the severe Jansenist Pirard was this:

Does a man have merit in your eyes? then put obstacles in the way of everything he wants, everything he undertakes. If his merit is real, he'll be able to overturn or get around the obstacles.

Hunting season came, and Fouqué had the notion of sending to the seminary a buck and a boar, as from Julien's relatives. The dead animals were laid in the passageway between the kitchen and the refectory. There all the seminarians saw them as they came to dinner. They aroused much comment. The boar, dead as he was, terrified the younger seminarians; they fingered his tusks. Nothing else was talked of for a week.

This gift, which classed Julien's family in the section of society that must be respected, put an end for good to envy. His superiority had been consecrated by fortune. Chazel and the most distinguished of the seminarians made approaches to him, and almost reproached him openly for not having told them his family was rich, since he had thereby exposed them to the crime of showing disrespect for money.

There was a conscription call from which Julien, as a seminarian, was exempt. This incident moved him deeply. Well then, there goes the moment at which, if I'd lived twenty years ago, a life of heroic action would have begun for me!

He was walking alone in the seminary garden and overheard a talk between two masons working on the cloister wall.

—Well, we'd better clear out, here's a new conscription come along.

—In the *other man's* time, well, that was more like it! a mason got to be officer, got to be general; that happened once.[6]

But look at it now! Nobody goes but the beggars. Anyone who's *anybody* stays home.

—If you're born poor, you stay poor, that's how it is.

—Hey, tell me now, is it true what they say, asked a third mason, is the other man really dead?

—That's what the bigshots tell us, get it? They were scared of that other one.

—What a difference, the way things got done in his day! And they say he was betrayed by his marshals. There's always a traitor somewhere!

This conversation brought Julien some comfort; as he walked away, he repeated with a sigh:

The only king whose memory the people cherish![7]

---

6. Among Napoleon's senior staff, Joachim Murat was the son of an innkeeper, Massena of a wine merchant, and Ney (like the bishop of Châlons in Chapter 26) of a tub maker.
7. A verse that was originally applied to Henri IV and used to be written on the base of his statue on the Pont-Neuf.

Examination time came around. Julien answered brilliantly; he saw that even Chazel was doing his utmost.

On the first day, the examiners appointed by the famous grand vicar de Frilair were distressed at having always to rank first, or at worst second, on their lists that Julien Sorel who had been pointed out to them as the Benjamin of Abbé Pirard.[8] Bets were placed within the seminary that in the overall classification Julien would rank first, an eminence that carried with it the honor of dining with the bishop. But at the end of one session where the questions had dealt with the church fathers, a clever examiner, after questioning Julien on St. Jerome and his passion for Cicero, began to talk of Horace, Virgil, and other pagan writers. Working in secret, Julien had learned by heart a number of passages by these authors. Carried away by his own success, he forgot his circumstances, and under urgent questioning by the examiner repeated and paraphrased enthusiastically several odes of Horace. Having let him dig his own grave for twenty minutes, the examiner abruptly changed his expression and bitterly reproached him for wasting his time on these profane studies which could do nothing but fill his head with useless or criminal notions.

—I am a fool, sir, and you are absolutely right, said Julien modestly, recognizing the clever trick which had been played on him.

The examiner's trap was considered unfair, even in the seminary, but this opinion did not prevent Abbé de Frilair, that clever man who had woven so skillfully the network of the congregation in Besançon, whose dispatches to Paris struck terror into judges, prefects, and general officers of the garrison, it did not prevent him from placing the number 198 alongside the name of Julien Sorel. He was overjoyed to humiliate in this way his old enemy, Abbé Pirard.

For the last ten years the main business of his life had been to remove Pirard from administration of the seminary. The latter, following in his own life the policies he had outlined to Julien, was sincere, pious, free of intrigue, attached to his duty. But fate, for his sins, had given him a bilious temperament, prone to resent bitterly insults and hatred. Not one of the affronts offered to him was ever overlooked by this ardent spirit. He would have resigned a hundred times over, except that he thought himself useful in the post that providence had assigned him. I'm holding up the advances of Jesuitism and idolatry, he told himself.

At the time of the examinations, it was perhaps two months since he had addressed a word to Julien, and yet he was sick for a week when upon receiving the official letter announcing the results he saw the number 198 placed by the name of that student whom he

---

8. Benjamin: child of the right hand, favorite son.

considered the glory of his house. The only consolation open to this stern man was to concentrate on Julien all his methods of surveillance. He was overjoyed to discover in him neither resentment nor any project of revenge, nor discouragement.

Several weeks later Julien shuddered at receiving a letter; it bore a Paris postmark. At last, he thought, Mme. de Rênal has remembered her promises. Someone signing himself Paul Sorel and claiming to be his relative sent him a bill of exchange for five hundred francs. There was a further note that if Julien continued his successful study of good Latin authors, a similar sum would be sent him each year.

It is she, that's her goodness, Julien said to himself with feeling, she wants to comfort me; but why not a single word of affection?

He was mistaken about this letter. Mme. de Rênal, under the influence of her friend Mme. Derville, was wholly given over to her deep regrets. In spite of herself, she thought frequently of the strange being whose passage through her life had so convulsed it, but she never considered writing to him.

If we were talking seminary language, we might call this gift of five hundred francs a miracle, and say that heaven was making use of M. de Frilair himself in order to bestow this bounty on Julien.

Twelve years before, Abbé Frilair had arrived in Besançon with a very slender carpetbag, which, as the story went, contained his entire fortune. He now found himself one of the richest landowners in the district. In the course of making all this money, he had bought half a property, the other half of which passed by inheritance to M. de La Mole. Hence a great lawsuit between these two figures.

In spite of his brilliant life in Paris and appointments at court, the Marquis de La Mole sensed that it might be dangerous to make war in Besançon upon a grand vicar who was reputed to be a maker and unmaker of prefects. Instead of arranging a little fifty-thousand-franc tip for himself, disguised under some word or other that would pass in the budget, and then abandoning to Abbé de Frilair his grubby fifty-thousand-franc action, the marquis took umbrage. He thought his case was good; as if that were a proper legal consideration!

For, if one may presume to ask: Where is the judge who doesn't have a son, or at any rate a cousin, to push forward in the world?

As if to convince the blindest, a week after he won his first judgment, Abbé de Frilair took the bishop's own private carriage and went himself to bestow the cross of the Legion of Honor on his lawyer. M. de La Mole, taken aback by the boldness of his enemies and feeling his own lawyers weakening, took counsel with Abbé Chélan, who put him in touch with M. Pirard.

At the time of our story these relations had already lasted several years. Abbé Pirard brought to the business his naturally impulsive character. Consulting continually the lawyers of the marquis, he studied the whole case, found the marquis in the right, and openly became his partisan against the all-powerful grand vicar. The latter was infuriated by such insolence, and to have it coming from a little Jansenist was worse!

—You see what this court nobility amounts to, though it pretends to be so powerful, Abbé de Frilair used to say to his friends. M. de La Mole has not even sent one miserable cross to his agent at Besançon, and is going to let him be dismissed from his job without a murmur. And yet they tell me this noble peer never lets a week pass without going to display his blue ribbon in the drawing room of the keeper of the seals, for whatever that's worth.

In spite of Abbé Pirard's best efforts, and though M. de La Mole was on the best of terms with the minister of justice and particularly with his agents, the best he had been able to do after six years of effort was to keep from losing his case outright.

In continual correspondence with Abbé Pirard over matters both of them followed with passion, the marquis gradually came to appreciate the abbé's way of thinking. Little by little, despite the immense difference in their social positions, their correspondence took on the tones of friendship. Abbé Pirard told the marquis that he was being forced by repeated outrages to tender his resignation. Furious at the infamous stratagem he said had been employed against Julien, he described his pupil's story to the marquis.

Though extremely rich, this great lord was by no means miserly. He had never been able to prevail on Abbé Pirard to accept reimbursement even for the postal charges occasioned by the trial. He seized the occasion to send five hundred francs to his favorite pupil.

M. de La Mole took the trouble to write in his own hand the covering letter. This made him think of the abbé.

One day the latter received a little note requesting him to go at once, on a matter of urgent business, to an inn in the suburbs of Besançon. There he met M. de La Mole's steward.

—M. le Marquis has instructed me to bring you his carriage, said this man. He hopes that when you have read this letter it will suit your purposes to leave for Paris within four or five days. I will spend the time until you are ready in visiting the estates of M. le Marquis, here in the Franche-Comté. After which, on the day you see fit, we will leave for Paris.

The letter was brief:

—My dear sir, set aside all these provincial squabbles, come breathe a calmer air in Paris. I have sent you my carriage with orders to wait four days for your decision. I shall wait for you myself, in Paris, until Tuesday. All I need from you is one word, *yes*, to accept, in your name, one of the best livings in the neighborhood of Paris. The richest of your future parishioners has never laid eyes on you, but is more devoted to you than you can imagine; he is the Marquis de La Mole.

Without altogether realizing it, stern Abbé Pirard loved this seminary which was full of his enemies, and to which, for fifteen years on end, he had devoted all his thoughts. M. de La Mole's letter was for him the appearance of a surgeon charged with performing a painful and necessary operation. His dismissal was a certainty. He told the steward to return in three days.

For forty-eight hours he was in a fever of uncertainty. Then he wrote to M. de La Mole, and composed for the bishop a letter, a masterpiece of ecclesiastical style but a bit long. It would have been hard to find more impeccable expressions, or any which breathed a more sincere respect. And yet this letter, intended to give M. de Frilair an awkward hour with his patron, listed all the serious grounds of complaint and descended into all the little dirty tricks which now, after he had endured them with resignation for six years, had forced Abbé Pirard to leave the diocese.

They stole the wood out of his shed, they poisoned his dog, etc., etc.

His letter completed, he had Julien waked; at eight o'clock in the evening he was already asleep, like all the other seminarians.

—You know where the bishop's palace is? he asked him, speaking classical Latin. Take this letter to Monsignor. I shall not conceal from you that you are entering the wolf pit. Be all eyes and all ears. No lies in any of your answers; but remember, the man who is questioning you would perhaps be overjoyed to do you harm. I am glad, my child, to give you this experience before leaving you, for I shan't conceal it, this letter is my resignation.

Julien stood stock still; he loved Abbé Pirard. It was useless for prudence to remind him:

After this honest man leaves, the party of the Sacred Heart will dismiss me from my post and perhaps drive me out of the seminary altogether.

He could not think of himself. What troubled him was a sentence he wanted to cast in an elegant form, but for which his mind refused to serve him.

—Well, young man, aren't you going?

—Well, sir, you see, they say, Julien said timidly, that during your long administration here you have never put anything aside. I have six hundred francs.

Tears prevented him from continuing.

—*That too will be observed,* said the ex-director of the seminary, coldly. Go to the palace, it is getting late.

As luck would have it, Abbé de Frilair was on duty that evening in the bishop's drawing room; Monsignor was dining at the prefecture. It was therefore M. de Frilair himself to whom Julien delivered the letter, though he did not realize this.

Julien saw with amazement that this abbé boldly opened the letter addressed to the bishop. The handsome features of the grand vicar soon showed surprise mingled with lively pleasure, then an access of gravity. As he read, Julien, struck by his handsome features, took time to inspect him. The face would have had more weight if it were not for the extreme subtlety that appeared in several expressions, and which might even have indicated dishonesty if the owner of that fine face had ceased for a moment to compose it. The prominent nose formed a single absolutely straight line and unfortunately gave to a countenance, perfectly distinguished in every other respect, an unalterable resemblance to a fox. For the rest, this abbé who seemed so concerned with the resignation of M. Pirard was dressed with an elegance that delighted Julien, and that he had never seen in any other priest.

Only later did Julien discover the special talent of M. de Frilair. He knew how to entertain his bishop, a kindly old man intended by nature to live in Paris, who regarded Besançon as a place of exile. This bishop had weak eyes and was passionately fond of fish. Abbé de Frilair boned the fish that was served to the bishop.

Julien was watching silently as the abbé reread the letter of resignation, when suddenly the door opened with a crash. A lackey in full finery passed swiftly through the room. Julien had scarcely time to turn toward the door; he saw a little old man wearing a pectoral cross. He fell on his knees; the bishop cast him a kindly smile and passed on. The handsome abbé followed him out, and Julien remained alone in the drawing room to admire its sacred magnificence at leisure.

The bishop of Besançon, a man whose character had been tested but not crushed by long years of trouble as an *émigré,* was more than seventy-five years old and cared very little indeed what would be happening ten years from now.

—Who is that clever-looking seminarian whom I seemed to see as I came in? asked the bishop. Shouldn't they all be in bed, as my rule is, at this hour?

—This one is wide awake, I assure you, Monsignor, and he brings great news; it's the resignation of the last Jansenist left in your diocese. At last that terrible Abbé Pirard has taken the hint.

—All right, said the bishop with a laugh, but I defy you to replace

him with a man as good. And to show you the value of this man,
I'm going to invite him to dinner tomorrow.

The grand vicar wanted to slip in a few words on the choice of a
successor; but the bishop, feeling indisposed to talk business, said
to him:

—Before we bring in a new man, let's learn a little about the old
one. Bring in that seminarian; there's truth in the mouths of babes.

Julien was summoned: I'm going to be caught between two in-
quisitors, he thought. Never had he felt himself more courageous.

As he entered, two tall valets, better dressed than M. Valenod
himself, were disrobing Monsignor. The prelate, before getting
around to M. Pirard, thought it his duty to ask Julien about his
studies. He asked a few questions about dogma and was astonished. Soon he turned to humanistic studies, Virgil, Horace, Cicero. Those are the names, Julien thought, that earned me my rank
of 198. I have nothing to lose, I'll try to shine. He was successful;
the prelate, an excellent humanist himself, was delighted.

At dinner in the prefecture a girl whose fame was well deserved
had recited the poem "La Madeleine."[9] The bishop was in the vein
of literary talk and quickly forgot M. Pirard and all business matters in order to discuss with the seminarian an important question,
whether Horace was rich or poor. The prelate cited several odes,
but sometimes his memory failed him and Julien would recite the
whole poem with a modest air; what struck the bishop most was
that Julien never departed from the tone of good conversation; he
recited his twenty or thirty Latin verses as he would have described
events in the seminary. They talked for a long time of Virgil, of Cicero. At last the prelate could not refrain from paying the young
seminarian a compliment.

—It would be impossible to pursue one's studies more successfully.

—Monsignor, said Julien, your seminary can furnish you with a
hundred ninety-seven subjects far less unworthy of your esteemed
approbation.

—How's that? said the prelate, astounded at the figure.

—I can furnish official proof of what I have the honor of affirming before Monsignor.

At the annual examination of the seminary, when I answered precisely on the topics which at this moment earn me Monsignor's approbation, I received the rank of 198.

—Ah, it's the Abbé Pirard's Benjamin, cried the bishop with a

***

9. Delphine Gay (1804–1855), who in 1831 would become Mme. de Girardin, wrote "La
   Madeleine"; Stendhal admired her poetic talents but did not wholly appreciate her habit
   of giving frequent recitations of her poetry.

laugh and a glance at M. de Frilair; we ought to have expected this; but it's fair play. Tell me, young man, he added, turning to Julien, did they wake you up to send you here?

—Yes, Monsignor. I have left the seminary unaccompanied only once in my life, to help Abbé Chas-Bernard decorate the cathedral on the feast of Corpus Christi.

—*Optime*, said the bishop; then you were the one who showed so much courage in placing the bunches of feathers atop the canopy? Every year I'm terrified of that; I'm always afraid they'll cost the life of a man. My young friend, you will go far; but I don't want to cut short your brilliant career by making you die of hunger.

And, on the bishop's orders, servants brought in some biscuits and Malaga wine, to which Julien did justice, and the Abbé de Frilair did even more justice, since he knew his bishop liked to see people eat merrily and with good appetite.

The prelate, feeling more and more cheerful at the end of his evening, spoke a little on church history. He saw that Julien understood nothing of it. The prelate passed on to the moral condition of the Roman empire under the emperors of Constantine's age. The end of paganism was accompanied by a state of uneasiness and doubt such as brings desolation to gloomy and bored souls in the nineteenth century. Monsignor remarked that Julien seemed scarcely to know even the name of Tacitus.

Julien replied frankly, to the prelate's astonishment, that this author was not to be found in the seminary library.

—I'm happy to hear it, said the bishop cheerfully. You've relieved me of a difficulty: for the past ten minutes I've been thinking of a way to thank you for this pleasant evening you've provided for me, and in a most unexpected fashion. I didn't expect to find a man of learning in a student of my seminary. Though the gift may not be too canonical, I should like to present you with a complete Tacitus.

The prelate sent for the set of eight volumes, handsomely bound, and undertook to write himself, on the title page of the first, a compliment in Latin to Julien Sorel. The bishop prided himself on his Latinity; he ended by saying, in a serious tone quite different from that of the rest of the conversation:

—Young man, if you *behave yourself*, you shall one day have the best living in my diocese, and not a hundred leagues from the episcopal palace itself; but you must *behave*.

Weighed down by his volumes, Julien left the palace in a state of great astonishment, about midnight.

The bishop had not said a word to him about Abbé Pirard. Julien had been struck, above all else, by the bishop's extreme politeness. He had never before conceived of such urbanity in the social forms, combined with such natural dignity. Julien was particularly struck by the contrast when he saw somber Abbé Pirard, who was waiting for him in a state of high impatience.

—*Quid tibi dixerunt?* (What did they say to you?) he cried at the top of his voice, as soon as he caught sight of Julien.

Julien had a little trouble translating into Latin the conversation of the bishop:

—Speak French, and recite the bishop's actual words, without adding or omitting anything, said the ex-director in his harsh voice and inelegant manner.

—What a strange gift from a bishop to a young seminarian! said he, fingering through the superb Tacitus, the gilded spine of which seemed to fill him with horror.

Two o'clock had struck when, after a long and detailed report, he at last allowed his favorite pupil to return to his room.

—Leave with me the first volume of your Tacitus, in which the bishop's Latin compliment is inscribed, said he. That line of Latin will be your lightning rod in this house after I am gone.

Erit tibi, fili mi, successor meus tanquam leo quaerens quem devoret. (For to you, my son, the man who succeeds me will be like a hungry lion, seeking whom he may devour.)

Next morning Julien found something strange in the way his fellow-students spoke to him. This made him all the more withdrawn. Here now, said he, is an effect of M. Pirard's resignation. It's known throughout the house, and I'm considered his favorite. There must be an insult in these new manners; but he could not discover it. On the contrary, there seemed to be less hatred in the eyes of all those he met throughout the dormitories. What does this mean? A trap, no doubt; I'd better play it close. At last the little seminarian from Verrières said to him, laughingly: *Cornelli Taciti opera omnia* (Complete Works of Tacitus).

At this word, which was overheard, all the others vied with one another to compliment Julien, not only on the magnificent gift received from Monsignor but on the two-hour conversation with which he had been honored. They knew about it down to the smallest details. From that moment on there was no more envy; everyone paid court to him humbly: Abbé Castanède, who only the day before had behaved toward him with the utmost insolence, now came to take him by the arm and invite him to luncheon.

By a freak in Julien's character, the insolence of these boors had caused him great pain; their humility caused him disgust and no pleasure.

Toward midday Abbé Pirard left his pupils, not without addressing to them a severe lecture.

—Do you want the honors of the world, he asked them, social advantages, the pleasures of authority, the pleasure of deriding the laws and being insolent to all men with impunity? Or else do you want eternal salvation? The least brilliant among you have only to open their eyes to see the two paths.

Scarcely had he left the seminary when the devotees of the *Sacred Heart of Jesus* went off to intone a *Te Deum* in the chapel. No one in the seminary took seriously the ex-director's last lecture. He is bitterly angry at being dismissed, they said on all sides; not a single seminarian had the simplicity to believe he had voluntarily resigned a post that put him in touch with so many big contractors.

Abbé Pirard took a room in the finest inn of Besançon and, under pretext of some business, which really he did not have, proposed to spend a couple of days there.

The bishop had invited him to dinner and, by way of a joke on his grand vicar de Frilair, undertook to make him shine. They were in the midst of dessert when there arrived from Paris news that Abbé Pirard was named to the magnificent living of N——, just four leagues from the capital. The good prelate congratulated him sincerely. He saw in the whole business a well-played game which put him in good spirits and gave him the highest opinion of the abbé's talents. He presented him with a magnificent Latin certificate and imposed silence on Abbé de Frilair when he ventured to complain.

That evening Monsignor expressed his admiration in the drawing room of the Marquise de Rubempré. It was great news in the upper circles of Besançon society; people bewildered themselves with conjectures about this extraordinary shift in favor. They saw Abbé Pirard as a bishop already. The cleverest ones guessed that M. de La Mole was now a minister, and for this one day permitted themselves to smile at the imperious airs which Abbé de Frilair assumed in society.

Next morning Abbé Pirard was almost followed through the streets, and merchants came to the doorways of their shops when he went to confer with the judges in the marquis' case. For the first time he was politely received. The stern Jansenist, indignant at everything he saw, worked for a long time with the lawyers he had chosen for the Marquis de La Mole and then left for Paris. He was weak enough to tell two or three old friends, who accompanied him to the carriage and stood there admiring the coat of arms, that after administering the seminary for fifteen years he was leaving Besançon with savings of five hundred twenty francs. The friends bade him farewell with tears in their eyes, then said among themselves: really, the good abbé might have spared us that lie, it's much too ridiculous.

Vulgar men, blinded by cupidity, were unable to understand that his sincerity alone had given Abbé Pirard the strength to struggle singlehanded for six years against Marie Alacoque, the *Sacred Heart of Jesus*, the Jesuits, and his bishop.

Chapter 30

AMBITION

There's only one really noble rank left, that's the title of *duke*; marquis is ridiculous, at the word *duke* heads turn round.
—*Edinburgh Review*[1]

The abbé was surprised by the noble air and almost gay manners of the marquis. Yet this future minister received Abbé Pirard without any of those little lordly tricks so polite but so impertinent for a man who understands them. It would have been time wasted, and the marquis was deep enough in public business to have no time to waste.

For six months he had been scheming to make the king and the nation both accept a certain minister who, out of gratitude, would make him a duke.

The marquis had been vainly demanding from his Besançon lawyer for some years now a clear, exact accounting of his lawsuit in the Franche-Comté. How could the celebrated lawyer possibly have explained it, since he didn't understand it himself?

A little slip of paper which the abbé handed him explained everything.

—My dear abbé, said the marquis, having dispatched in less than five minutes all the polite formulas and personal questions, my dear abbé, in the midst of all my surface prosperity, I have no time to concern myself with two little matters which for all that are pretty important: my family and my business affairs. I concern myself in a broad way with the interests of my house, I may carry it far; I concern myself with my own pleasures, and that's what should come first, at least in my opinion, he went on, noting some surprise in the glance of Abbé Pirard. Though a person of sense, the abbé was amazed to see an old man talking so frankly of his pleasures.

No doubt work gets done in Paris, the nobleman continued, but only in the garrets, and as soon as I come to terms with a man, he moves down to the second floor and his wife starts a *day*;[2] and then, no more work, no effort for anything except being or seeming a man of the world. As soon as they have their daily bread, that's all they care for.

1. Another faked epigraph.
2. A social "day" appointed for callers, conversation, cards, scandal; a salon.

For my lawsuits, of course, and actually for each individual law-suit, I have lawyers who work themselves to death; one of them had a stroke just the other day. But as for my general business, would you believe it, my dear sir, for the last three years I've been without hope of finding a man who, while he's writing something for me, will condescend to think a little seriously of what he's doing? But this is all a preface.

I think well of you, and I will venture to add, though this is our first meeting, I'm going to like you. Will you serve as my secretary, with a salary of eight thousand francs, or, if you like, twice that much? I shall be the gainer, I assure you; and I shall make it my business to hold on to your fine living, against the day when we no longer get on with one another.

The abbé declined, but toward the end of the conversation he saw the marquis was in genuine difficulties, and this suggested an idea to him.

—I left, back in my seminary, a poor young man who, unless I'm much mistaken, is going to be brutally persecuted. If he were only a simple religious, he would already be *in pace.*[3]

So far this young man knows nothing but Latin and the Holy Scriptures; but it's not impossible that one day he will give proof of great talents, either for preaching or for the cure of souls. I don't know which way he will go; but he has the sacred fire, and may go far. I was counting on sending him to our bishop if ever we had one with a little of your way of looking at men and business.

—Where does your young man come from? asked the marquis.

—They say he's the son of a carpenter in our mountains, but I rather suspect he's the natural son of some rich man. I have seen him get an anonymous or pseudonymous letter containing a note of exchange for five hundred francs.

—Ah! it's Julien Sorel, said the marquis.

—How do you know his name? said the abbé in astonishment; and as he was blushing for that question:

—That is what I am not going to tell you, replied the marquis.

—Very well, said the abbé, you could try to make him your secretary; he has energy and good judgment; in a word, he's worth a try.

—Why not? said the marquis; but is he the sort of man to let his palm be greased by the prefect of police, or somebody else, to play the spy on me? That's my only objection.

Having received favorable assurances from Abbé Pirard, the marquis produced a thousand-franc note.

—Send this to Julien Sorel for traveling money; tell him to come.

—It's clear to see, Abbé Pirard told him, that you live in Paris.

---

3. *In pace:* in peace, that is, dead.

[Placed as you are in an elevated social position,] you don't appreciate the weight of tyranny that lies on us poor provincials, especially on priests who aren't friendly with the Jesuits. They won't want to let Julien Sorel go; they'll cover themselves with clever pretexts, they'll tell me he's sick, the post office will have mislaid letters, etc., etc.

—One of these days I shall carry a letter from the minister to that bishop of yours, said the marquis.

—I forgot one word of warning, added the abbé: this young man, though of low birth, has a high spirit; he will be of no use to you [in your business] if his pride is ruffled; you would only make him stupid.

—That rather pleases me, remarked the marquis, I shall make him my son's comrade; will that be good enough?

Shortly after, Julien received a letter written in an unknown hand and postmarked from Châlons; it contained a draft on a merchant in Besançon and instructions to proceed to Paris without delay. The letter was signed with an assumed name, but as he opened it, Julien trembled: a dried leaf had fallen at his feet; that was the sign he had arranged with Abbé Pirard.[4]

Less than an hour later Julien was called to the episcopal palace, where he was received with paternal warmth. Even as he cited verses of Horace, Monsignor referred to the lofty destinies awaiting him in Paris, making a series of extremely clever compliments which practically required, from the responder, some sort of explanation. Julien could say nothing, mainly because he knew nothing, and the bishop showed him many marks of high esteem. One of the little priests about the palace wrote to the mayor, who hastened to bring over, in his own person, a passport which had been signed but on which the name of the traveler had been left blank.

That night before twelve o'clock Julien was with Fouqué, whose wise judgment expressed more surprise than pleasure at the future that seemed to open before his friend.

—It'll all end for you, said this liberal voter, with a post in the government which will involve you in a deal for which you'll be libeled in all the papers. I'll get news of you when you're in disgrace. Remember, even in a financial sense, it's better to earn a hundred louis selling wood honestly, and owning your own business, than to get four thousand francs from a government, even King Solomon's.

Julien saw in this nothing but the petty spirit of a country bourgeois. At last he was going to make his appearance in the theater of

4. The Bucci copy reads: " . . . Julien trembled. A great blot of ink had fallen in the middle of the thirteenth word; that was the sign . . ." And Stendhal explained his change in a further note: "The spy who opened the letter might not replace the leaf."

the world. The happiness of going to Paris, which he supposed to be full of witty people, very devious, very hypocritical, but all as polite as the bishop of Besançon and the bishop of Agde, closed his eyes to every other consideration. To his friend he explained [in all humility] that he was practically deprived of his own free choice by Abbé Pirard's letter.

Next day about noon he arrived in Verrières, the happiest of men; he expected to see Mme. de Rênal again. He went first to his old protector, Abbé Chélan, where he found a gruff reception.

—Do you recognize any obligation at all to me? asked M. Chélan, without answering his greeting. Then you will have lunch with me; while you are eating, another horse will be rented for you, and you will leave Verrières *without seeing anybody else.*

—To hear is to obey, Julien replied with the meek mien of a seminarian; and they talked of nothing else but theology and good Latin.

He mounted his horse and rode a league, after which, seeing a wood and nobody around to spy on him, he hid himself within it. At sunset he sent back the horse. Later he went to the house of a peasant, who agreed to sell him a ladder and to help him carry it as far as the little grove which stands above LOYALTY SQUARE in Verrières.

—I'm helping out a poor draft dodger . . . or a smuggler of some sort, said the peasant as he bade him farewell; but why should I worry? my ladder has been well paid for, and I've had to get through some awkward moments in life myself.

The night was very dark. About one o'clock in the morning, Julien, burdened with his ladder, entered Verrières. As soon as he could, he climbed down into the bed of the stream which passes through M. de Rênal's magnificent gardens, in a gorge about ten feet deep between two walls. With the ladder Julien easily climbed to ground level. What sort of welcome will I get from the watchdogs? he thought, that's the whole question. The dogs barked and rushed at him; but he whistled softly and they came fawning toward him.

Climbing thus from terrace to terrace, though all the gates were shut, he found it easy to get just under the window of Mme. de Rênal's bedroom, which on the garden side is only eight or ten feet above ground level.

There was in the shutters a little opening in the shape of a heart, which Julien knew well. To his great distress, this little opening was not lit by the glow of a night light.

—Good Lord! said he to himself, Mme. de Rênal is not sleeping in this room tonight [otherwise there would be a light]. Where can she be? The family is in Verrières, since the dogs are out; but in this unlit room I may find M. de Rênal himself, or a stranger, and then what a scandal!

The wisest step was to withdraw; but the thought of such a step horrified Julien. If it's a stranger, I'll run away as fast as I can, leaving the ladder behind; but if it is she, how will she greet me? She has turned to remorse and profound piety, I can't doubt it; but anyhow, she still remembers me a little, since she just wrote to me. This reason determined him.

His heart trembled within him, but he was resolved to see her or perish; he threw some pebbles against the shutters, but there was no response. He leaned his ladder against the wall beside the window and knocked on the shutter, gently at first, then more sharply. In all this darkness they may go after me with a gun, Julien thought. This idea reduced the whole insane undertaking to a matter of physical bravery.

The room is empty tonight, he thought; if anyone were sleeping there, they'd be up by now. No need to worry about an occupant then; I just have to try not to be heard by people sleeping in other rooms.

He climbed down, set his ladder against one of the shutters, climbed up again, reached through the heart-shaped opening, and was lucky enough to find almost at once the metal wire attached to the latch that closed the shutter. He pulled at it, and felt, with indescribable joy, that the shutter was no longer locked, but yielded under his hand. I must open it gradually, and let my voice be recognized. He opened the shutter enough to get his head in, saying meanwhile in an undertone: *It is a friend.*

He made certain, by applying his ear, that the deep silence within the room was unbroken. But definitely there was no night light, not even a darkened one, on the mantelpiece; that was a bad sign indeed.

Keep an eye out for guns! He thought for a bit; then, with his finger, he ventured to rap on the windowpane: no answer; he tapped harder. Even if I break the glass, I have to get in. As he was knocking very loudly, he seemed to half see in the pitchy darkness a sort of white shadow crossing the room. Then he could no longer doubt; he saw a shadow that seemed to come toward him very slowly. Suddenly he saw a cheek pressed against the pane of glass to which he had applied his eye.

He shuddered and drew back. But the night was so dark that, even at that distance, he could not tell whether it was Mme. de Rênal. He feared lest there be a cry of alarm; he could hear the dogs prowling and growling around the foot of his ladder. It is I, he repeated quite loudly, a friend. No answer; the white phantom had disappeared. Please open up, I must talk with you, I am too wretched! and he knocked as if to smash the window.

A little dry noise was heard; the catch of the window opened; he pushed up the casement and leaped easily into the room.

The white phantom drew back; he grasped its arms; it was a woman. All his courageous ideas vanished in a flash. If it is she, what will she say? What were his feelings when he knew, by a little cry she gave, that it was Mme. de Rênal!

He strained her in his arms; she shuddered, and had scarcely strength to repel him.

—Wretch! What are you doing?

Her choked voice could scarcely articulate the words. Julien saw that she was genuinely angry.

—I have come to see you after fourteen months of cruel separation.

—Go away, leave me, this very instant. Ah, M. Chélan, why did you prevent me from writing to him? I might have prevented this horrible scene. She flung him away with a strength that was really extraordinary. I repent of my crime; God was good enough to enlighten me, she repeated in a muffled voice. Go away! Leave me!

—After fourteen months of misery, I certainly shan't leave without speaking to you. I want to know everything you've been doing. Ah, I have loved you well enough to deserve this confidence. . . . I want to know everything.

Despite Mme. de Rênal, this tone of authority had power over her heart.

Julien, who had been holding her passionately in his arms and resisting all her efforts to break loose, relaxed his grasp. This gesture reassured Mme. de Rênal somewhat.

—I am going to pull up the ladder, he said, so we shall not be discovered if some servant, roused by the noise, makes a tour of inspection.

—Ah, leave me, leave me instead, she said to him, in genuine rage. What do I care about men? It is God who sees the frightful situation you have created, and He will punish me for it. You are taking mean advantage of feelings I once had for you, but which I don't have any more. Do you understand that, Master Julien?

He drew up the ladder very slowly, in order to make no noise.

—Your husband is in town? he asked her, not out of impudence, but carried away by force of habit.

—Don't talk to me that way, if you please, or I'll call my husband. Already I'm all too guilty, I should have driven you away, whatever happened. I pity you, she told him, trying to wound his pride, which she knew to be sensitive.

Her refusal of intimacy, her brusque way of breaking a bond of tenderness on which he had still counted, raised Julien's transports of love to delirium.

—What now? Is it possible you no longer love me? he said to her, in those heartfelt tones which are so hard to hear unmoved.

She answered nothing; for his part, he was weeping bitterly [she heard the sound of his sobs.]

As a matter of fact, he no longer had strength to speak.

—So I'm completely forgotten by the only creature who ever loved me! What good to live now? All his courage had left him as soon as he no longer had to fear meeting a man; everything had left his heart except love.

For a long time he wept in silence. He took her hand, she tried to withdraw it; but after a few almost convulsive movements, she let him keep it. It was extremely dark; they found themselves seated side by side on Mme. de Rênal's bed.

What a difference from things as they were fourteen months ago! thought Julien; and his tears flowed more freely. Thus absence is sure to destroy all human feelings!

—Please tell me what has happened to you, Julien said at last, in a voice choked with sobs.

—Beyond any doubt, Mme. de Rênal began, in a sharp voice, the tone of which seemed to bear within it something dry and reproachful of Julien, my follies were known throughout the town at the time of your departure. You had been so imprudent in your behavior! Some time later, when I was in despair, that good man M. Chélan came to see me. For a long time he tried vainly to obtain a confession. One day he had the idea of taking me to that church in Dijon where I made my first communion. There he ventured to speak with me. . . . Mme. de Rênal was interrupted by her tears. What a shameful moment! I confessed everything. The good old man did not overwhelm me with the weight of his indignation; he sympathized with my sorrow. In those days I used to write you letters every day, which I didn't dare to post; I hid them away, and when I was too miserable, I used to shut myself in my room and reread my own letters.

Finally M. Chélan persuaded me to let him have them. . . . Some of them, written with a little more prudence than the rest, had been mailed to you; but you never answered.

—Never, I swear it, never did I receive a single letter from you at the seminary.

—Good God, who can have intercepted them?

—Imagine my wretchedness; until the day I saw you in the cathedral, I didn't know if you were alive or dead.

—God in his mercy gave me to understand how deeply I had

sinned toward Him, toward my children, toward my husband, Mme. de Rênal resumed. He has never loved me as I thought then that you loved me. . . .

Julien flung himself into her arms, acting blindly and instinctively. But Mme. de Rênal pushed him aside and continued with a certain firmness:

—My respectable friend M. Chélan showed me that in marrying M. de Rênal I had promised him all my affections, even those of which I was not yet aware, and which I had never experienced before a certain fatal affair. . . . Since the great sacrifice of those letters, which were so precious to me, my life has passed, if not happily, at least with a fair amount of calm. Don't disturb it; be a friend to me, the best of my friends. Julien covered her hand with kisses; she sensed that he was still weeping. Don't weep, you make me so unhappy. . . . Tell me now what you have been doing. Julien could not speak. I want to know how you lived in the seminary, she repeated, then you will go away.

Without thinking of what he was saying, Julien described the intrigues and innumerable jealousies he had met with at first, then of the quieter life he had led since being named tutor.

That was the period, he added, when after a long silence which was clearly intended to show me, as I can see only too clearly now, that you no longer loved me, and that I had become a figure of indifference to you. . . . Mme. de Rênal pressed his hands. That was the period when you sent me a gift of five hundred francs.

—Never, said Mme. de Rênal.

—It was a letter postmarked Paris, and signed Paul Sorel, in order to avoid suspicion.

A little discussion sprang up on the possible source of this letter. The moral position shifted. Without realizing it, Mme. de Rênal and Julien had dropped the tone of solemnity; they had returned to that of tender friendship. They could not see one another, the darkness was too thick, but the tone of voice told all. Julien passed his arm around his mistress' waist; it was a risky gesture. She tried to dislodge Julien's arm, but he rather cleverly distracted her attention for the moment with an interesting episode in his story. The arm was forgotten and remained where it lay.

After many speculations on the sender of the five-hundred-franc letter, Julien resumed his tale; he was gaining more control over himself as he talked on about his past life, which, actually, by comparison with what was happening at the moment, interested him very little. His thoughts were entirely concentrated on the way in which his visit would end. You must get out of here, she kept telling him from time to time, in a curt accent.

What a disgrace for me, if I'm given the gate! It will be a humiliation to poison my whole life, he thought to himself; and she will never write to me. God knows when I will ever return to this district! From that moment, whatever heavenly joy there was in Julien's position disappeared completely from his heart. Seated beside a woman whom he adored, holding her almost in his arms, in this room where he had been so happy, plunged in profound darkness, yet well aware that for the last minute she had been weeping, sensing from the motion of her breast that she was shaken with sobs, he unfortunately became a cold politician, almost as chilly and calculating as when in the seminary courtyard he saw himself the butt of some nasty trick played by a schoolfellow stronger than he. Julien spun out his story and talked of the unhappy life he had led since he left Verrières. That's how it is, said Mme. de Rênal to herself, after a year of absence during which he had no sign that anyone remembered him, he still thought only of the happy days at Vergy, while I was forgetting him. Her tears flowed more freely. Julien noted the success his story was having. He understood it was time to play his last card: he came abruptly to the letter he had just received from Paris.

—I have taken leave of Monsignor the bishop.

—What, you're not going back to Besançon! You're leaving us for good?

—Yes, Julien answered in a resolute tone; yes, I am leaving a land where I am forgotten even by the person I loved best in my life, and I'm leaving it never to return. I am going to Paris. . . .

—You're going to Paris! Mme. de Rênal cried aloud.

Her voice was almost choked with tears, and showed the violence of her grief. Julien had need of this encouragement; he was about to take a step that might decide everything against him; and before this exclamation, being unable to see anything, he had no notion of what effect he might produce. Now he hesitated no longer; fear of future regrets gave him complete command over himself; he added coldly as he rose to his feet:

—Yes, Madame, I am leaving you forever, be happy; farewell.

He took several steps toward the window; he was in the act of opening it. Mme. de Rênal ran to him and flung herself into his arms. [He felt her head on his shoulder, her cheek pressed against his.]

Thus, after three hours of discussion, Julien obtained what he had desired so passionately during the first two. Had they come a little sooner, the return to tender sentiments and the eclipsing of Mme. de Rênal's remorse might have been the occasion of heavenly joy; but obtained as they were with art, they yielded nothing more than gratification. Julien absolutely insisted, against the pleas of his mistress, on lighting the night light.

—Would you prefer, he asked her, that I not have a single memory of having seen you? Is the love which doubtless fills those charming eyes to be lost to me forever? Will I never be able to see the whiteness of that lovely hand? Think that I may be leaving you for a very long time.

[What a disgrace! said Mme. de Rênal to herself; but she] had no objection to raise against this idea which caused her to dissolve in tears. Dawn was starting to outline the shapes of the pine trees on the mountain to the east of Verrières. Instead of leaving, Julien, drunk with pleasure, begged Mme. de Rênal to let him spend the whole day hidden in her room, and to leave only the following night.

—Why not? she replied. This fatal relapse has destroyed all my self-respect and condemned me to lifelong misery, and she pressed him to her heart. My husband is no longer the same, he is getting suspicious; he thinks I managed him through this whole affair, and shows his resentment against me. If he hears the slightest noise, I am lost; he will drive me out of the house like the wretch I am.

—Ah, that's like a speech from M. Chélan, said Julien; you wouldn't have talked to me that way before I went to that cruel seminary; you used to love me then!

Julien was repaid for the coolness he put into this speech: he saw his mistress forget at once the danger she was running from her husband's presence in order to think of the much greater danger that Julien might doubt her love. Daylight came rapidly on, and lit up the whole room; Julien recaptured all the delights of pride when he saw in his arms and practically at his feet this charming woman, the only one he had ever loved, and who a few hours before had been wholly absorbed in her fear of a terrible God and in devotion to duty. Resolutions fortified by a year's constancy had not been able to withstand his courage.

Soon household stirrings began to be heard; a matter she had not previously considered arose to disturb Mme. de Rênal's mind.

—That nasty Elisa will be coming into the room; what shall we do with this enormous ladder? she asked her lover; where shall we hide it? I'll carry it up into the attic, she suddenly exclaimed, speaking almost playfully.

—But you have to go through the servant's room, said Julien in astonishment.

—I'll leave the ladder in the hallway, call for the servant, and send him on an errand.

—But you must have ready beforehand a word of explanation, in case the servant, when he passes by the ladder in the hallway, remarks upon it.

—Yes, my angel, said Mme. de Rênal, giving him a kiss. And for your part, get ready to hide yourself quickly under the bed in case Elisa comes in while I'm away.

Julien was amazed at this sudden gaiety. I see, thought he, physical danger when it approaches restores her gaiety instead of troubling her, because in it she can forget her remorse! What a wonderful woman! This is a heart in which it's glorious to reign! Julien was in ecstasies.

Mme. de Rênal took the ladder; it was obviously too heavy for her. Julien went to help her; he was admiring her elegant figure, which was far from giving evidence of physical strength, when suddenly she seized the ladder, lifted it without aid, and carried it off as she would have carried a chair. She took it swiftly down the third-floor hallway and laid it along the wall. Then she called the servant, and in order to give him time to dress, went up into the dovecote. Five minutes later, when she returned to the hall, the ladder was gone. What had become of it? If Julien had been out of the house, the problem would not have bothered her. But now, if her husband found the ladder here! there could be a nasty scene. Mme. de Rênal hunted everywhere. At last she discovered the ladder in the garret where the servant had carried it, and even concealed it. It was an odd circumstance; at another time it might have alarmed her.

Why should I worry, she thought, over what can happen twenty-four hours from now when Julien will be gone? Won't everything then be simply horror and remorse?

She had a vague sentiment that she would be able to live no longer, but what matter? After a separation she had supposed would last forever, he had returned to her, she could see him again, and what he had gone through to reach her showed so deep a love!

As she told Julien the story of the ladder:

—What shall I say to my husband, she asked him, if the servant tells him where that ladder was found? She thought for a moment; they will need at least twenty-four hours to find the peasant who sold it to you; and then, throwing herself into Julien's arms and clinging to him convulsively: Oh, to die, to die here and now! she cried, covering him with kisses; but we can't let you die of hunger, she said laughingly.

Come now; first I'll hide you in Mme. Derville's room, which is always locked. She stood guard at the end of the corridor, and Julien ran down it. Don't open even if someone knocks, she told him, as she turned the key on him; if it should happen, it will be only the children at one of their games.

—Bring them into the garden, under the window, said Julien, so that I can have the pleasure of seeing them; I want to hear their talk.

—Yes, oh yes, cried Mme. de Rênal, as she left him.

Soon she returned, carrying oranges, biscuits and a bottle of Malaga wine; she had found it impossible to steal any bread.

—What's your husband doing? Julien asked.

—He's writing up some market business with various peasants.

But eight o'clock had struck; the house was abustle. If Mme. de Rênal were not seen, people would come looking for her; she had to leave him. Soon she returned again, bringing him, against all prudence, a cup of coffee; she was afraid he would die of hunger. After lunch she succeeded in bringing her children under the window of Mme. Derville's room. He found them much taller, but they had picked up a common look, or else his ideas had changed.

Mme. de Rênal talked with them about Julien. The older one responded, expressing friendship and regret for his former tutor; but it seemed the younger ones had almost forgotten him.

M. de Rênal did not go out all morning long; he climbed up and down stairs, busy closing deals with peasants to whom he was selling his potato crop. Until dinnertime, Mme. de Rênal had not a free moment to devote to her prisoner. When dinner was served, the idea occurred to her of stealing a bowl of hot soup for him. As she was silently approaching the door of the room where he was hidden, carrying her bowl with great care, she found herself confronting the same servant who that morning had hidden the ladder. At the moment, he too was walking silently down the corridor, as if listening for something. Probably Julien had walked about too incautiously. The servant made off in some confusion. Mme. de Rênal entered boldly into Julien's room; her encounter made him shudder.

—You're afraid, she told him; as for me, I'll meet any trouble in the world without flinching. Only one thing terrifies me, the moment when I shall be left alone after you go; and she ran off again.

—Ah! said Julien to himself in a rapture, remorse is the only thing this sublime soul fears!

At last evening came. M. de Rênal went to the Casino.

His wife declared a frightful headache, withdrew to her room, sent Elisa away at once, and promptly got up to open the door for Julien.

In fact, he really was suffering from hunger. Mme. de Rênal went to the pantry to get him some bread. Julien heard a shriek. Mme. de Rênal returned and told him that as she entered the darkened pantry and approached a cupboard where there was bread she had reached out and touched a woman's arm. It was Elisa, who had uttered the shriek heard by Julien.

—What was she doing there?

—Either stealing sweets or else spying on us, said Mme. de Rênal with absolute indifference. Fortunately, I found a pie and a big
loaf of bread.

—And what's that? asked Julien, pointing to the pockets of her
apron.

Mme. de Rênal had forgotten that since dinner they had been
stuffed with bread.

Julien strained her in his arms with the most passionate feeling;
never before had she seemed to him so lovely. Even in Paris, he told
himself confusedly, I shall never find a more splendid character.
She had all the awkwardness of a woman little accustomed to this
sort of intrigue and at the same time the true courage of a person
who fears only dangers of a different, and far more terrible, order.

While Julien was eating avidly away, and his mistress was joking
about the simplicity of his meal, for she had a horror of serious
talk, the door of the room was suddenly shaken furiously. It was M.
de Rênal.

—Why have you shut yourself in? he shouted.

Julien had just time to slip under the sofa.

—What's this? You're fully dressed, said M. de Rênal as he came
in; you're eating and you've locked yourself in!

On ordinary days this question, put with the full crudity of a husband, would have upset Mme. de Rênal, but she realized that her
husband had only to lower his glance a bit in order to catch sight of
Julien; for M. de Rênal had flung himself down in the chair which
Julien had occupied a moment before, just opposite the sofa.

The headache served as an excuse for everything. While her husband told her at length all the episodes of a game he had won in
the billiard room of the Casino, a pot of nineteen francs, begad, he
added, she noticed on a chair, not three feet away, Julien's hat.
Cooler than ever, she began to disrobe, and at a certain moment,
passing swiftly behind her husband, threw a dress across the back
of the chair and on top of the hat.

At last M. de Rênal took his leave. She begged Julien to tell her
again the story of his life at the seminary; I wasn't listening to you
yesterday; all I could think of was where would I find the strength
to send you away.

She was boldness personified. They talked very loudly; it must
have been two o'clock in the morning when they were interrupted
by a violent banging at the door. It was M. de Rênal again.

—Open up at once; there are thieves in the house! he cried;
Saint-Jean found their ladder this morning.

—This is the end of everything, exclaimed Mme. de Rênal,
throwing herself into Julien's arms. He will kill us both; the thieves

are just a story; I shall die in your arms, happier in death than ever I was in life. She answered not a word to her husband, who grew furious; she was holding Julien in a passionate embrace.

—Save Stanislas's mother, he said to her, with a commanding glance. I shall jump down into the yard from the closet window and escape though the garden; the dogs know me. Make a bundle of my clothes and throw it into the garden as soon as you can. Meanwhile, let them break down the door. Above all, no confessions, I forbid them; it's better for him to be suspicious than certain.

—You will kill yourself with that jump! was her only reply and her only anxiety.

She went with him to the closet window; then she took time to hide his clothing. At last she opened the door to her husband, boiling with rage. He searched the room, searched the closet, without a word being said, and left. Julien's clothes were bundled out the window; he seized them and ran swiftly toward the lower end of the garden, beside the Doubs.

As he ran, he heard the whistle of a bullet and the report of a gun.

That's not M. de Rênal, he thought; he's not that good a shot. The dogs were running silently beside him; a second shot apparently struck one of them in the paw, for he began to emit yelps of pain, Julien leaped down the wall of one terrace, ran fifty feet under its shelter, then began to flee in another direction. He heard the voices of men shouting to one another and clearly saw the servant, his enemy, fire another shot; a farmer came, too, and shot at him from the other end of the garden, but Julien had already reached the bank of the Doubs, where he dressed himself.

An hour later he was a league away from Verrières, on the road to Geneva; if they have any suspicions, Julien thought, it's on the road to Paris that they'll look for me.

Book II

She isn't pretty, she wears no rouge.
—Sainte-Beuve[1]

Chapter 1

COUNTRY PLEASURES

O rus quando ego to aspiciam!
—Virgil[2]

—No doubt the gentleman has come to catch the mail coach for Paris? said the landlord of an inn where he stopped for breakfast.

—Today's or tomorrow's, it doesn't matter which, Julien replied.

The mail coach arrived as he was playing the indifferent. Two places were vacant.

—Well so that's you, my old friend Falcoz, said the traveler just coming from Geneva to the one who climbed into the coach along with Julien.

—I thought you had settled down near Lyon, said Falcoz, in that delightful valley near the Rhône.

—Settled down, indeed! I'm in flight.

—What's this? in flight? you, Saint-Giraud, with that virtuous expression of yours, you've been committing crimes? said Falcoz with a laugh.

—On my word, I might as well have. I'm in flight from the abominable sort of life one leads in the provinces. As you know, I'm fond of green trees and quiet fields; you've often accused me of being a romantic. But I never could stand political talk, and it's politics that have driven me out.

—Why, what's your party?

—I have no party, that's the root of my misfortune. Here's the sum of my political views: I love music and painting; a good book is a big event in my life; I shall soon be forty-four years old. What's left of my life? Fifteen, twenty, maybe thirty years at the most? All right. I submit that in thirty years the ministers will be a little more clever but exactly as honest as the ones we have today. English his-

---

1. Already used twice in Book I, as the epigraph to Chap. 14 and in the text of Chap. 15, this phrase about rouge is attributed here to Charles-Augustin Sainte-Beuve (1804–1869).
2. The alleged quotation from Virgil is really from Horace, *Satires*, II, iv, p. 60. Though often cited in perfect seriousness, it is attributed by Horace to a usurer who indulges in sentimental dreams of the simple life while grabbing at his *cent per cent*.

tory provides me with a mirror in which to see our future. There will always be a king anxious to enlarge his prerogative; always political ambition and the memory of Mirabeau[3] who gained glory along with several hundred thousand francs will keep our rich provincials awake nights: they will call it liberalism and love of the common people. Always our ultras will be eaten up by the passion to become peers or chamberlains. Aboard the ship of state everybody will want to stand at the helm, because the job pays well. But won't there ever be a meager little place for the ordinary passenger?

—Indeed, indeed, and it ought to be very amusing for a man of your quiet character. Is it these recent elections that are forcing you out of your district?

—My troubles date back before that. Four years ago I was forty years old and had five hundred thousand francs; today I'm four years older and probably fifty thousand francs poorer—that's about what I'll lose on the sale of my property at Monfleury, right by the Rhône in a magnificent location.

At Paris I was weary of that perpetual comedy in which nineteenth-century civilization, so-called, forces everyone to take a part. I yearned for friendship, for simplicity. So I bought a property among the mountains by the Rhône, nothing more beautiful under the sun.

For six months the vicar of the village and the local gentry paid court to me; I fed them dinners; I told them I had left Paris in order never again to hear, or be obliged to talk, about politics. You see, I told them, I don't subscribe to a newspaper; and the fewer letters the postman brings me, the better I like it.

But this wasn't the vicar's game; and before long I was subjected to a thousand different indiscreet requests and bits of chicanery. I want to give two or three hundred francs a year to the poor; they demand it of me for various pious associations, St. Joseph's, the Virgin's, and so forth.[4] I refuse; then they load me with insults. I'm stupid enough to be irked. I can no longer go out in the morning to rejoice in the beauty of our mountains without discovering some irritation which drags me down from my reverie and reminds me disagreeably of men and their mean dispositions. During the Rogation processions, for example, in which I'm very fond of the singing (it's probably a Greek melody), they refuse to bless my fields because, says the vicar, they belong to a blasphemer. The cow of a pious old peasant woman dies, she says it's because of a nearby pond belonging to me, the blasphemer, the philosopher from Paris, and a week

---

3. Mirabeau (1749–1791), an early, eloquent, and deeply corrupt leader of the Revolution, was buried with national honors in the Pantheon and removed from it a year and a half later when his secret correspondence with Louis XVI was uncovered.
4. Various pious associations: see pp. 81–82.

later I find all my fish floating belly up in the water, poisoned with lime. Intrigues surround me everywhere I turn. The justice of the peace, an honest man but afraid for his post, always rules against me. My rural peace becomes a hell. Once people see I've been abandoned by the vicar, head of the village congregation, and not taken up by the retired captain who's head of the liberals, they all fall on me, even the mason whom I've been supporting for a year, even the smith who tried to cheat me with the utmost impunity when I had my ploughs repaired there.

In order to get some support and win at least a few of my law cases, I turned liberal; but, as you were saying, these damned elections came along and they asked my support. . . .

—For an unknown?

—Not at all; for a fellow I know only too well. I refused: a frightful indiscretion! From that moment, I had the liberals on my hands, as well, and my position became intolerable. I think if it had occurred to the vicar to accuse me of having murdered my serving girl there would have been twenty witnesses, of both parties, to swear they had seen me commit the crime.

—You want to live in the country without flattering your neighbors' passions, without even listening to their chatter. What a mistake!

—I've corrected it now. Monfleury is for sale; I'll lose fifty thousand francs if necessary, but I'm overjoyed, I'll get out of this hell of hypocrisies and intrigues. I'm going to get my solitude and rural peace in the only place where they can be found in France, a fourth-floor apartment off the Champs-Elysées. And even there, I'm wondering whether I hadn't better begin my political career in the district of Roule[5] by presenting the blessed bread in the parish church.

—None of that would have happened under Bonaparte, said Falcoz, his eyes glittering with anger and regret.

—Doubtless, doubtless, but why couldn't he manage to hold onto his position, your Bonaparte? Everything I'm suffering today is really his fault.

Here Julien became especially attentive. He had grasped, from the first words spoken, that the Bonapartist Falcoz was the former childhood friend of M. de Rênal, repudiated by him in 1816; and that the philosopher Saint-Giraud must be the brother of that head of the prefecture of _____, who knew how to have town property granted to him on easy terms.

---

5. The district of Roule, formerly a little country village by this name, has for a long time now been a central district of Paris, between the Faubourg Saint-Honoré and the Champs-Elysées.

—And all that is what your Bonaparte did, Saint-Giraud continued. An honest man, harmless as a man can be, forty years old and
with five hundred thousand francs, cannot live in the country and
find peace there; Bonaparte's priests and nobles will drive him out.

—Ah! don't speak ill of him, cried Falcoz, never did France stand
so high among the nations as during the thirteen years of his rule.
Then there was a sort of grandeur in everything that men did.

another person
pro - Napoleon

—Your emperor, may the devil fly away with him, returned the
man of forty-four, was great only on the battlefield, and when he re-
organized the finances around 1802. What does his behavior since
then amount to? With his chamberlains, his ceremonies, his recep-
tions at the Tuileries, he simply offered a new version of all the old
imbecilities of the monarchy. It was a corrected version, it might
have got by for a century or two. The priests and nobles wanted to
go back to the old version, but they don't have the iron hand
needed to force public acceptance.

—There's the old printer talking now!

—Who drove me off my land? the printer went on, wrathfully.
The priests, whom Napoleon recalled with his concordat, instead of
treating them as the state treats doctors, lawyers, and astronomers,
instead of recognizing them simply as citizens, without inquiring
into the business by which they earn their bread. Would there be so
many arrogant gentry today if your Bonaparte hadn't created barons
and counts? No, that sort of thing was out of fashion. After the
priests, it is these little country noblemen who bothered me most
and forced me to turn liberal.

The discussion was endless; this subject will occupy France for
another half century. As Saint-Giraud kept repeating that it was impossible to live in the provinces, Julien timidly put forward the example of M. de Rênal.

—Gad, young man, that's a good one! cried Falcoz. He's made
himself into a hammer in order not to be an anvil, and a terrible
hammer he is. But all the same, I see he's been outdone by
Valenod. Do you know that rascal? He's the genuine article. What
will your M. de Rênal say when he finds himself kicked out of office, one of these fine days, and that Valenod set in his place?

—He will be left alone to reflect on his crimes, said Saint-
Giraud. So you know something about Verrières, then, young man?
All right. Bonaparte, confound him, he and his ragbag monarchy
made possible the rule of people like de Rênal and Chélan, which
led in turn to the rule of Valenod and Maslon.

This gloomy political conversation astonished Julien and distracted him from voluptuous reverie.

He paid little attention to his first sight of Paris as he saw it in
the distance. The castles in Spain which he was constructing on

the basis of his future career had to struggle with the still-vivid memory of the twenty-four hours he had just spent in Verrières. He swore never to abandon the children of his beloved, and to leave everything in order to protect them, if ever priestly excesses lead us back to a republic and provoke persecutions of the nobility.

What would have happened the night he came back to Verrières if, when he placed his ladder against Mme. de Rênal's window, he had found the room occupied by a stranger, or by M. de Rênal?

But also, what bliss in those first two hours, when his mistress really wanted to dismiss him, and he pleaded his case, seated beside her in the darkness! A soul like Julien's is haunted by such memories for an entire lifetime. The rest of their meeting had already mingled indistinguishably in his mind with the first period of their love, fourteen months before.

Julien was awakened from his deep meditation when the coach stopped. They had just entered the courtyard of the post office in Rue J.-J. Rousseau.—I want to go to Malmaison, he told a cabman who approached him.

—At this hour, sir, and what for?

—None of your business. Let's go.

True passion never thinks of anything but itself. This, it seems to me, is why the passions are so absurd in Paris, where your neighbor always pretends that people are thinking about him all the time. I shall not try to describe Julien's transports at Malmaison. He was in tears. What, you say? In spite of those ugly white walls, just put up that year, which cut the park into little pieces? Yes, sir: for Julien, as for posterity, there was no line to be drawn between Arcola, St. Helena, and Malmaison.[6]

That evening Julien hesitated a long time before going to the theater; he had strange ideas about this sink of iniquity.

A deep-seated suspicion prevented him from admiring the Paris of today; he was moved only by the monuments left behind by his hero.

Here I am now in the center of intrigue and hypocrisy! This is the kingdom of those men who protect Abbé de Frilair.

On the evening of the third day his curiosity prevailed over his plan to see the entire city before reporting to Abbé Pirard. The abbé explained to him in a chilly tone the manner of life that would be expected of him at M. de La Mole's.

—If at the end of several months you haven't proved useful, you will go back to the seminary, but by the front door. You will live with

---

6. Arcola, scene of one of Napoleon's greatest military triumphs (November 17, 1796); St. Helena, where he was exiled (1815–21); and Malmaison, the property near Paris furnished and enlivened by Josephine as a sort of rural artistic court for the First Consul.

the marquis, one of the most distinguished gentlemen in France. You will dress in black, but like a man in mourning, not an ecclesiastic. I insist that three times a week you continue your theological studies at a seminary where I shall introduce you. Every day at noon you will present yourself in the library of the marquis, who wants you to write letters for him, about his lawsuits and other business matters. The marquis will write in a couple of words, on the margin of each letter, the sort of answer it should get. I have undertaken that within three months you will be able to write replies such that, out of every dozen you present for his signature, he will be able to sign eight or nine. In the evening, at eight o'clock, you will get your desk in order, and at ten you will be free.

It may be, continued Abbé Pirard, that some old lady or some soft-voiced man will propose certain immense advantages to you, or quite crudely will offer you some money in exchange for your letting him see some of the letters received by the Marquis. . . .

—Oh, sir! cried Julien, blushing.

—It is curious, said the abbé with a bitter smile, that poor as you are, and after a year in the seminary, you still retain a bit of virtuous indignation. You must have been blind to a lot.

Can it be his blood that tells? said the abbé in an undertone, as if talking to himself. What is really curious, he added, glancing at Julien, is that the marquis knows you. . . . I don't know how. As a starting salary he will give you a hundred louis. He is a man who acts only on impulse; that is his weakness; his childishness will be equal even to yours. If he is pleased with you, your salary may be raised in time to eight thousand francs.

But you understand, the abbé added, with an edge in his voice, he is not giving you all this money just to look pretty. You've got to be useful. If I were in your position, I would talk very little indeed, and never about matters of which I was ignorant.

Ah! added the abbé, I have looked into some other matters for you; I was forgetting about the family. There are two children, a daughter and a son of nineteen, as elegant as can be, a kind of lunatic who never knows at noon what he will be doing at two o'clock. He has wit, he is brave; he served in the Spanish campaign.[7] The marquis hopes, for some reason I don't understand, that you will be friends with young Comte Norbert. I have told him that you are a great Latinist; perhaps he hopes you will teach his son some readymade opinions about Cicero and Virgil.

---

7. The efforts of Spanish liberals to establish a stable regime (1820–23) were crushed by a French invasion under the Duc d'Angoulême (1775–1844), and from then on the French did a good deal of intervening in Spanish political affairs.

In your place, I should never allow myself to be chaffed by this fine young man; and before answering his overtures, which will be perfectly polite but spoiled by a touch of irony, I should make him repeat them for me at least twice.

I shall not conceal from you that young Comte de La Mole is bound to despise you at first, because you are nothing but a little bourgeois. One of his own ancestors was at court, and had the honor of being beheaded in the Place de Grève, on the twenty-sixth of April, 1574, as a result of a political intrigue. As for you, you are the son of a Verrières carpenter, and what is more you are in the pay of his father. Weigh these differences properly, and study the history of this family in Moreri;[8] all the flatterers who come to dinner here make from time to time what they call delicate allusions to it.

Be careful how you reply to the jests of M. le Comte Norbert de La Mole, commander of a squadron of hussars and future peer of France, and do not come around to complain to me afterward.

—It seems to me, said Julien, blushing deeply, that I should not even answer a man who despises me.

—You have no notion of this form of contempt; it will find expression only in exaggerated compliments. If you were a fool, you might be taken in by them; if you want to make your fortune, you ought to let yourself be taken in by them.

—On the day when all this business no longer suits me, said Julien, will I be considered an ingrate if I return to my little cell, number 103?

—No doubt you will, said the abbé; all the fawners around the house will slander you, but then I will appear. *Adsum qui feci.* I will tell them that the decision stems from me.

Julien was dismayed by the bitter and almost malicious tone which he noted in M. Pirard; this tone altogether spoiled his last reply.

The fact is that the abbé felt a scruple of conscience over his fondness for Julien, and it was only with a sort of religious terror that he meddled so directly in the fate of another human being.

—You will also see, he added, with the same ill grace, and as if fulfilling a painful duty, you will see Mme. la Marquise de La Mole. She's a big blond woman, pious, proud, perfectly polite, and wholly insignificant. She is the daughter of the old Duc de Chaulnes, well known for his aristocratic prejudices. This great lady is a sort of epitome, in high relief, of everything that makes up the basic character of women of her rank. She herself makes no secret that hav-

---

8. Louis Moreri (1643–1680), author of a historical (actually biographical) dictionary.

ing had ancestors who went on the crusades is the only quality that interests her in a person. Money comes far behind that. Does that surprise you? We are no longer in the provinces, my friend.

In her salon you will find various fine gentlemen talking of our princes in a tone of singular levity. Mme. de La Mole herself lowers her voice out of respect every time she mentions a prince and above all a princess. I should not advise you to say in her presence that Philip II or Henry VIII were monsters. They were KINGS, and that gives them unquestionable right to respect from everyone, particularly creatures of no birth, like you and me. However, added M. Pirard, we are priests, for she will take you for such; on that basis, she considers us household servants necessary for her salvation.

—Sir, said Julien, it seems to me that I shan't be very long in Paris.

—Just as you say; but remember, there is no way to rise, for a man of our cloth, except through the fine lords. With that indefinable something, at least I can't define it, in your character, if you don't make your fortune, you will be persecuted; there is no middle state for you. Make no mistake. Men can see that they give you no pleasure by speaking to you; in a country as social as this one, you are doomed to misery if you don't earn peoples' respect.

What would have happened to you at Besançon, if it hadn't been for this whim of the Marquis de La Mole? One day you will understand what an extraordinary thing he did for you, and if you are not a monster, you will cherish an undying gratitude for him and his family. How many poverty-stricken abbés, more learned than you, have lived years and years in Paris on the fifteen sous for their masses and the ten sous for their classes in the Sorbonne! . . . Remember what I told you last winter about the first years of that wretched man, Cardinal Dubois.[9] Are you arrogant enough to suppose yourself more gifted, perhaps, than he was?

I myself, for example, though a placid and ungifted man, I was expecting to die in my seminary; I was childish enough to grow attached to it. All right. I was about to be fired when I submitted my resignation. Do you know what my fortune was? I had five hundred and twenty francs of capital, no more, no less; I had not a single friend, and scarcely two or three acquaintances. M. de La Mole, whom I had never seen, got me out of that jam; he had only to say a word, and I was given a post where all my parishioners are comfortable folk, far above the vulgar vices, and the income fills me

---

9. Cardinal Guillaume Dubois (1656–1723) is better known for his debauched and dissolute old age than for his penurious youth, but he certainly sprang from humble origins.

with shame, it is so disproportionate to my work. I have spoken at such length only to get a bit of ballast into your head.

One word more: it is my misfortune to have a bad temper; it is possible that you and I may cease to be on speaking terms.

If the arrogance of the marquise or the sarcasms of her son make this house unbearable for you, I advise you to finish your studies in a seminary within thirty leagues of Paris, and better to the north than to the south. There is more civilization in the north, and less injustice; and besides, he added, lowering his voice, I must admit that having the Paris newspapers near at hand makes the petty tyrants fearful.

If we continue to find pleasure in one another's company, but the house of the marquis doesn't suit you, I can offer you a post as my vicar, and will divide equally with you the income of my living. I owe you that and even more, he added, cutting off Julien's thanks, for the extraordinary offer you made me at Besançon. If instead of five hundred and twenty francs I had had nothing, you would have been my salvation.

The abbé had lost his harsh tone of voice. Much to his humiliation, Julien felt tears come to his eyes; he yearned to throw himself into the arms of his friend: he could not keep from saying, in the most manly voice he could assume:

—My father hated me ever since I was in the cradle; it was one of my greatest griefs; but I shall no longer complain of fortune, I have found another father in you, sir.

—Very well, very well, said the abbé in some embarrassment; then he recalled a timely expression from his days as director of the seminary: you must never speak of fortune, my boy, he told Julien, say providence instead.

The cab stopped; the driver raised a bronze knocker on an immense door: it was the HÔTEL DE LA MOLE; and, lest the passerby remain in any doubt, the same words were to be seen on a black marble slab over the door.

This affectation displeased Julien. They are so fearful of the Jacobins! They see a Robespierre and his cart behind every hedge; they're so worked up, it would make you die laughing, and they placard their house like this so the rabble will recognize it in a riot and be sure to sack it. He expressed his thoughts to Abbé Pirard.

—Ah, my poor boy, you'll be my vicar before long. What an appalling idea occurred to you there!

—I can think of nothing simpler, said Julien.

The solemnity of the porter and above all the cleanliness of the courtyard struck him with admiration. A bright sun was shining.

—What magnificent architecture! he said to his friend.

He was talking about one of those flat-faced façades in the

Faubourg Saint-Germain, built around the time of Voltaire's death. Never have the stylish and the beautiful been so distant from one another.

Chapter 2

ENTERING THE WORLD

Absurd and touching recollection: the first drawing room in which one appeared at the age of eighteen, alone and unsupported! the glance of a woman was enough to intimidate me. The harder I tried to please, the more awkward I became. I formed mistaken ideas about everything; either I surrendered without a reason, or I supposed a man was my enemy because he had looked gravely upon me. But then, amid the frightful torments of my timidity, a fine day could be *so* fine!

—Kant[1]

Julien stopped in the middle of the courtyard, struck with wonder.

—Try to look like a reasonable man, said Abbé Pirard; you get these horrible ideas, yet you're nothing but a child! Where is the *nil admirari* of Horace? (Never show any enthusiasm.) Keep in mind that this rabble of lackeys; when they see you in place here, will try to ridicule you; they will see in you an equal, unjustly promoted over their heads. Under the guise of good nature, good advice, attempts to help you along, they'll try to push you into some stupid blunder.

—I dare them to try it, said Julien, biting his lip; and he resumed all his earlier distrust.

The rooms through which these gentlemen of ours passed before reaching the study of the marquis on the first floor would have seemed to you, oh my reader, as melancholy as they were magnificent. If anyone made you a present of them, just as they were, you would have refused to live in them; they were the natural habitat of yawns and gloomy disputes. They completed Julien's enchantment. How could one possibly be unhappy, he thought, when one lives amid such splendid surroundings!

At last our gentlemen arrived at the ugliest of all the rooms in this splendid dwelling: it received hardly any daylight at all; there was a little lean man, quick of eye, and wearing a light periwig. The abbé turned to Julien and introduced him. It was the marquis. Julien could scarcely recognize him, he was so polite. This was no longer the fine gentleman, with such lofty expressions, whom he had seen at the abbey of Bray-le-Haut. It seemed to Julien that his

---

1. The writings of Kant do not yield any passage like this.

wig was much too hairy. Thanks to this impression, he was not in the least abashed. The descendant of the good friend of Henri III struck him as giving a rather mean impression. He was very spare of figure, and moved about a great deal. But he quickly remarked that the marquis had a style of politeness even more agreeable to his interlocutor than that of the bishop of Besançon himself. The conversation did not last three minutes. As they went out, the abbé said to Julien:

—You inspected the marquis as you would have done a painting. I am no authority on what these people call politeness, before long you will be better versed in it than I am, but the openness of your stare seemed to me hardly polite.

They returned to their cab; the driver stopped near the boulevard; the abbé brought Julien into an apartment of spacious rooms. Julien noted that they were largely unfurnished. He was looking at a magnificent gilt clock, representing a subject he considered indecent in the extreme, when a most elegant gentleman approached smilingly. Julien made him a slight bow.

The gentleman smiled back and placed his hand on his shoulder. Julien quivered and stepped back a pace. He was red with anger. In spite of his gravity, Abbé Pirard laughed until the tears came. The gentleman was a tailor.

—I grant you two days' leave, said the abbé as they went out; only after that time can you be presented to Mme. de La Mole. Anyone else would watch over you like a young girl in these first days of your stay in the new Babylon. Go ruin yourself at once if you're going to ruin yourself at all, and I shall be free to forget about you completely. On the day after tomorrow, in the morning, this tailor will bring you two suits; you may give five francs to the fitter. Otherwise, don't let these Parisians hear so much as the sound of your voice. If you say a single word, they will find a way of turning you to ridicule. That's their special talent. Day after tomorrow, come to my lodgings at noon. . . . Run along now, ruin yourself. . . . Oh, I was forgetting, go and order yourself boots, shirts, and a hat at the places listed here.

Julien noted the handwriting of the addresses.

—That's the marquis' hand, said the abbé; he is an active man, who foresees everything and who would rather do something himself than order it done. He is taking you into his household in order to save himself this sort of trouble. Will you be clever enough to carry out properly all the orders this quick-witted man will convey to you in half a word? That's what time will tell; meanwhile, take care of yourself!

Without uttering a single word, Julien made his way to the shops indicated on his list of addresses; he noted that he was received with great respect, and the bootmaker, when entering his name on the register, wrote M. Julien de Sorel.

At the cemetery of Père-Lachaise a gentleman who was extremely kind and particularly liberal in his opinions offered to show Julien the tomb of Marshal Ney, which a prudent administration has left without the honor of an epitaph.[2] But when he parted from this liberal, who with tears in his eyes almost hugged him, Julien no longer had a watch. It was with the riches of this experience in mind that he presented himself, two days later, to Abbé Pirard, who looked him over carefully.

—You are perhaps going to become a fop, the abbé told him with a severe expression. Julien had the look of a very young man in deep mourning; he did in fact look quite well dressed, but the good abbé was too provincial himself to note that Julien still had that swagger of the shoulders which in the provinces denotes elegance and importance. The marquis, when he saw Julien, saw his social graces in quite another light than the good abbé, to whom he said:

—Should you mind if M. Sorel took some dancing lessons?

The abbé was petrified.

—No, he said at last, I should not mind. Julien is not a priest.

The marquis, mounting two at a time the steps of a little hidden staircase, went in person to establish our hero in a neat attic room looking out on the immense garden behind the house. He asked how many shirts he had ordered of the haberdasher.

—Two, replied Julien, abashed to see so great a gentleman descend to such petty details.

—Very good, said the marquis, speaking seriously and with a certain imperious, curt tone to his voice which gave Julien to think; very good! Now order twenty-two more shirts. Here is your salary for the first quarter.

As they came down from the attic, the marquis called to an elderly man: Arsène, said he, you will take care of M. Sorel. A few minutes later, Julien found himself alone in a splendid library; it was a delicious moment. Lest he be observed in his emotion, he hid himself in a dark little corner, and from there he contemplated with delight the glittering backs of the books. I could read all that, he said to himself. And how could I be unhappy here? M. de Rênal would have thought himself dishonored forever if he had done for me a hundredth part of what the Marquis de La Mole has just done for me.

But let's see what letters there are to copy. When this work was

---

2. Marshal Ney (1769–1815), the "bravest of the brave," rejoined Napoleon for the Hundred Days, was executed by a firing squad at the instance of the Bourbons, and was buried in an unmarked grave.

done, Julien ventured to approach the books; he nearly went mad with joy on discovering an edition of Voltaire. He ran to open the door of the library, lest he be taken by surprise. Then he gave himself the pleasure of opening each one of the eighty volumes. They were magnificently bound; it was the masterpiece of the best bookbinder in London. Less would have served to raise Julien's admiration to a peak.

An hour later the marquis entered, glanced at the copies, and noted with amazement that Julien wrote *cela* with two l's, *cella*. Everything the abbé told me about his learning is simply a story, then! Much discouraged, the marquis said gently to him:

—You are not sure of your spelling?

—That's true, said Julien, wholly unaware of the harm he was doing himself; he had been softened by the consideration of the marquis, which made him think of M. de Rênal's harsh tone.

It's a waste of time, this whole experiment with a little priest from the Franche-Comté, thought the marquis; but I did have such need of a dependable man!

—*Cela* is written with just one *l*, the marquis told him; when you have finished your copying, you must look up in the dictionary any words of which you're not sure.

At six o'clock the marquis summoned him; he looked with obvious dismay at Julien's boots:—I am at fault, I should have told you that every day at five-thirty you must dress.

Julien looked at him, uncomprehendingly.

—I mean, put on stockings. Arsène will remind you; for today, I will make your apologies.

As he spoke, M. de La Mole showed Julien into a room glittering with gilt. On similar occasions, M. de Rênal never failed to push forward quickly so he might have the gratification of passing first through the door. His former patron's petty vanity was thus the reason that Julien trod on the heels of the marquis and caused him considerable pain because of his gout. Ah, he's even more of a lout than the average run, said the marquis to himself. He presented him to a tall woman of imposing appearance. It was the marquise. Julien decided she had a pretentious air, rather like Mme. de Maugiron, wife of the subprefect of the Verrières district, when she attended the dinner on St. Charles's day. Being slightly embarrassed by the extraordinary magnificence of the room, Julien did not understand quite what M. de La Mole was saying. The marquise barely deigned to glance at him. Several men were present, among whom Julien recognized with indescribable pleasure the young bishop of Agde, who had condescended to talk to him several months before at the ceremony of Bray-le-Haut. This young prelate was doubtless alarmed by the tender glances which Julien, in his timidity, cast toward him, and gave no sign of recognizing this provincial.

The men gathered together in this drawing room seemed to Julien to have about them something melancholy and constrained; people talk in undertones at Paris and don't exaggerate small circumstances.

A handsome young man, very pale and tall, came in at about six-thirty; he had an extremely small head.

—You always keep us waiting, said the marquise, as he kissed her hand.

Julien understood that this was Comte de La Mole; he found him charming at first glance.

Is it possible, he asked himself, that this is the man whose offensive joking is going to drive me out of the house?

Having studied Comte Norbert's person, Julien noted that he wore boots and spurs; and I should be wearing shoes, as a social inferior, evidently. They went in to dinner. Julien heard the marquise utter a sharp remark, raising her voice slightly. Almost at the same moment, he noticed a young lady, very blond and very shapely, who placed herself opposite him. She did not attract him at all, yet, on more careful inspection, he decided that he had never seen such beautiful eyes; but they expressed great coldness of spirit. Later, Julien thought they expressed a kind of watchful boredom which nonetheless always remembers the need to impress others. Mme. de Rênal had fine eyes, he told himself, people were always making compliments about them; but they had nothing in common with these. Julien did not have enough social experience to understand that it was the glitter of wit that shone from time to time in the eyes of Mlle. Mathilde, for so he heard her named. When Mme. de Rênal's eyes grew animated, it was with the fire of passion, or with generous indignation at the description of some wicked action. Toward the end of the meal Julien found a word to describe the sort of beauty he found in the eyes of Mlle. de La Mole: they scintillate, he told himself. In other respects she bore a cruel resemblance to her mother, whom he was disliking more and more, and he ceased to look at her. On the other hand, Comte Norbert seemed to him admirable in every respect. Julien was so carried away that the idea never occurred to him of feeling hatred and jealousy because this man was richer and better born than himself.

It seemed to Julien that the marquis was getting bored.

About the second course, he said to his son:

—Norbert, I must beg your good offices for M. Julien Sorel, whom I've just added to my staff, and propose to make a man of, if that (*cella*) can be done.

—It's my secretary, said the marquis to his neighbor, and he writes *cella* with two l's.

Everyone looked at Julien, who made a somewhat excessive bow in Norbert's direction; but in general, they were satisfied with his appearance.

The marquis must have said something about the sort of education Julien had received, for one of the diners tackled him on the topic of Horace: it was precisely by talking about Horace that I succeeded with the Bishop of Besançon, Julien said to himself; apparently this is the only author they know. From that moment on, he was perfectly in control of himself. This attitude was the easier for him to assume because he had just decided that Mlle. de La Mole would never be a woman in his eyes. Since his days in the seminary he expected the worst of men, and was not easily intimidated by them. He would have been perfectly at ease if the dining room had been less splendidly furnished. In fact, it was two enormous mirrors, each eight feet high, in which from time to time he caught sight of his interlocutor as he talked about Horace, which still daunted him. His sentences were not too long, for a provincial. His eyes were fine, and their timidity, either trembling or joyful when he had scored a good hit, enhanced his attractiveness. He was judged agreeable. This sort of trial added a bit of interest to an otherwise formal dinner. The marquis made a sign to Julien's adversary to push him harder. Can it be possible that he really does know something? was his thought.

Julien answered, and found new thoughts as he talked; he lost enough of his timidity to be able to display, not wit precisely, a thing impossible to anyone who does not know the special dialect of Paris, but new ideas, though presented without grace or ease of application; and it was clear that his Latinity was sound.

Julien's adversary was a member of the Academy of Inscriptions who, by accident, knew Latin himself; discovering in Julien an excellent humanist, he lost all fear of disgracing him, and really made an effort to test him. In the heat of combat, Julien finally forgot the splendid furnishings of the room and succeeded in expressing various ideas about the Latin poets which his opponent had never seen in print. As an honest man, he therefore gave credit for them to the young secretary. Fortunately, the discussion focused on the question whether Horace had been poor or rich; a pleasant, pleasure-loving careless man, making verses for his own amusement like Chapelle,[3] Molière's friend, and La Fontaine; or a poor devil of a

---

3. Chapelle (Claude-Emmanuel Luillier, illegitimate son of a great court functionary at the end of the seventeenth century) was very well-off indeed and made his verses, like his *bons mots*, for fun.

poet laureate, following the court around and making odes for the king's birthday, like Southey the calumniator of Lord Byron. They talked of the state of society under Augustus and under George IV: in both ages, the aristocracy was all-powerful, but in Rome it saw the power snatched from it by Maecenas, a mere knight; while in England, it had reduced George IV to a position scarcely more influential than that of a Venetian doge. This discussion seemed to draw the marquis out of the torpid state in which boredom had plunged him at the beginning of the dinner.

Julien understood nothing at all of the modern names, like Southey, Lord Byron, George IV, which he was just hearing for the first time. But no one could fail to see that when there was a question of incidents at Rome, of anything that could be learned from the works of Horace, Martial, Tacitus, etc., he held an unchallenged advantage. Julien made unscrupulous use of several ideas he had acquired from the bishop of Besançon in the course of his famous discussion with that prelate; and these were not the least acceptable.

When they were tired of talking about poets, the marquise, who made it a rule to admire everything that amused her husband, condescended to cast a glance upon Julien. The awkward manners of this young abbé may perhaps conceal a man of learning, said the academician to the marquise, who was sitting near him; and Julien partly overheard the words. Ready-made phrases were altogether pleasing to the lady of the house; she adopted this summary of Julien, and was pleased that she had asked the academician to dine. He amuses M. de La Mole, she thought.

Chapter 3

FIRST STEPS

> This immense valley filled with glittering lights and so many thousands of men dazzles my sight. Not one of them knows me, they are all my superiors. My thoughts fail me.
> —Poems of the advocate Reina[4]

Next morning very early Julien was copying letters in the library when Mlle. Mathilde entered by a little secret door carefully concealed as part of the shelving. While Julien was admiring this contrivance, Mlle. Mathilde seemed much astonished, and rather displeased, to find him there. Julien, seeing her in curl papers, decided she looked hard, arrogant, and almost masculine. Mlle. de La Mole had a little habit of taking books from her father's library

---

4. Francesco Reina (1772–1826), Milanese lawyer, critic, and minor poet.

without his knowledge. Julien's presence rendered this morning's visit fruitless, which irked her the more since she had come to get the second volume of Voltaire's *Princess of Babylon*, a book very suitable to complement an education that had been eminently monarchical and religious, an education that was the masterpiece of the Sacred Heart![5] The poor girl, at nineteen years of age, already required the spice of wit to be interested in a novel.

Comte Norbert appeared in the library about three o'clock; he came to study a newspaper in order to be able to talk politics that evening and was very pleased to find Julien, whose existence he had forgotten. He was perfectly charming; he offered to take him riding.

—My father leaves us free till dinnertime.

Julien understood that *us*, and was enchanted by it.

—Good Lord, Monsieur le comte, said Julien, if it were a matter of felling an eighty-foot tree, trimming it, and cutting it up into planks, I should do pretty well at it, I daresay; but getting on a horse is something I haven't done six times in my life.

—All right, this will be the seventh, said Norbert.

In the back of his mind, Julien recalled the entry of the king of * * * into Verrières, and thought himself an excellent horseman. But, as they were returning from the Bois de Boulogne, right in the middle of the rue du Bac, he fell, while trying to dodge a passing cab, and covered himself with mud. It was a good thing he had two suits. At dinner the marquis, trying to bring him into the conversation, asked about his ride; Norbert hastened to reply in general terms.

—Monsieur le comte is much too kind to me, said Julien; I thank him for it, and appreciate his generosity. He was good enough to give me the most docile and easy of his horses; but after all, he could not fasten me onto it, and, as a result, I fell off, right in the middle of that long street, near the bridge.

Mlle. Mathilde tried vainly to stifle a peal of laughter; then, carried away by her curiosity, demanded details. Julien carried it off with great simplicity; he had an unconscious air of grace.

—I look for good things from this little priest, said the marquis to the academician; a simple provincial in such a scrape! Such a thing was never seen before and never will be again; besides which, he tells about his disgrace before *ladies*!

Julien put his listeners so much at their ease over his mishap that after dinner, when the general conversation had taken another

---

5. Voltaire's *Princesse de Babylone*, a *conte* vaguely reputed to be scabrous; the Convent of the Sacred Heart was in 1830 as now a finishing school for daughters of the distinguished conservative social set.

turn, Mlle. Mathilde began to ask her brother about the details of the accident. As her questioning continued, and Julien met her glances several times, he ventured to reply directly, though the question had not been addressed to him, and all three ended by laughing together, like three young country folk of a village hidden deep in a forest.

Next day Julien attended two classes in theology and then returned to transcribe a score of letters. He found established next to him in the library a young man, very carefully dressed, but of a mean appearance and an envious expression.

The marquis appeared.

—What are you doing here, Monsieur Tanbeau? he asked the newcomer with a severe expression.

—I thought . . . the young man started to reply, with an obsequious smile.

—No, sir, *you did not think*. This is an experiment, but it has not worked.

Young Tanbeau rose in a rage and left the room. He was a nephew of the academician, Mme. de La Mole's friend, who hoped for a career in literature. The academician had arranged for the marquis to take him on as a secretary. Tanbeau, who worked in a separate room, had heard of the special favors bestowed on Julien, wanted to partake of them, and had arrived that morning to set up his desk in the library.

At four o'clock Julien ventured, after a moment's hesitation, to seek out Comte Norbert. The latter was about to go riding, and was embarrassed, for his manners were perfect.

—I expect, he said to Julien, that shortly you will go to riding school; and after a few weeks' time I shall be absolutely delighted to go riding with you.

—I wished to take the occasion to thank you for all your kindness toward me; believe me, sir, Julien added with great seriousness, I am quite conscious of how much I owe you. If your horse has not been hurt as a result of my clumsiness yesterday, and if it's not spoken for, I should very much like to ride it today.

—Gad, my dear Sorel, on your own head be it! Will you suppose that I have made every objection that prudence herself would have? The fact is, it's four o'clock, and we have no time to lose.

Once he was mounted:

—What must one do not to fall off? Julien asked the young count.

—Plenty of things, replied Norbert, with a burst of laughter; for example, sit further back in the saddle.

Julien set off at a full trot. They were in the square of Louis XVI.

—Ah! you young daredevil, said Norbert, there are too many carriages, and all with reckless drivers too! Once you're down, their tilburys will roll right over you; they're not going to risk spoiling their horses' mouths by pulling up short.

Twenty times Norbert saw Julien on the verge of falling; but finally, the ride finished without mishap. As they came back, the young count said to his sister:

—Let me introduce a real rough-rider.

At dinnertime, talking to his father from the full length of the table, he did full justice to Julien's boldness; it was the only thing one could praise in his horsemanship. During the morning the young count had heard the grooms in the yard make Julien's fall a pretext for deriding him outrageously.

Despite all this kindness, Julien soon felt himself completely isolated in the midst of this family. All their customs seemed strange to him, and he could not live up to them. His social blunders were the delight of the footmen.

Abbé Pirard had left for his parish. If Julien is a weak reed, let him snap; if he is a man of courage, let him make his way alone, thought he.

Chapter 4

THE HÔTEL DE LA MOLE

What's he doing here? pleasing himself?
trying to please himself?
—Ronsard[6]

If everything seemed strange to Julien in the well-bred drawing room of the Hôtel de La Mole, for his part this young man, pale of countenance and dressed in black, seemed quite remarkable to the people who deigned to notice him. Mme. de La Mole suggested to her husband that they might send him on errands whenever certain people came to dinner.

—I want to carry the experiment out to its end, replied the marquis. Abbé Pirard tells me we are wrong to destroy all the self-esteem of the people we take into our household. *You get no support except from what resists,* and so forth. This fellow is bothersome only because his face is unknown, for the rest he's a deaf mute.

In order to learn my way among these people, Julien told himself, I'll have to write down the names, and a word on the characters, of all the people I see appear in this drawing room.

He placed in the first rank five or six friends of the family, who

6. Pierre de Ronsard (1524–1585).

wooed him urgently, supposing him to be protected by a caprice of the marquis. They were sorry wretches, more or less drab; but it must be said on behalf of this class of men, as they turn up nowadays in the drawing rooms of the aristocracy, that they were not all equally servile to everybody. Some of them allowed themselves to be insulted by the marquis, though they would bitterly have resented a harsh word addressed to them by Mme. de La Mole.

Too much pride and too much boredom underlay the characters of the master and mistress of the house; they were too inclined to insult others for their own diversion to expect any genuine friendship. But, except for rainy days and moments of ferocious boredom, which were rare, they never failed to appear perfectly polite.

If the five or six trucklers who displayed such fatherly affection for Julien had abandoned the Hôtel de La Mole, the marquise would have been subjected to long periods of solitude; and women of this rank consider solitude a frightful affliction: it is the mark of *disgrace*.

The marquis was exactly suited to his wife; he made sure that her salon was properly filled; not, however, with peers, for he found his new colleagues were hardly noble enough to visit his house as friends, nor amusing enough to be invited as subordinates.

It was only later that Julien came to know these secrets. Questions of social policy, such as make up the main subject of conversation in bourgeois houses, are never mentioned by people of the marquis' class, except in moments of distress.

So powerful, even in this bored century, is the need for amusement that even on the days of dinner parties people fled from the room the instant the marquis left it himself. Provided one didn't joke about God, or the priests, or the king, or the men in power, or the artists protected by the court, or about any part of the establishment; provided one said nothing good about Béranger,[7] or the opposition newspapers, or Voltaire, or Rousseau, or of anything which involves the use of free speech; provided, above all, that one never talked politics, one could talk freely about anything whatever.

There is no income of a hundred thousand crowns, there is no blue ribbon, that can prevail against a salon so constituted. The smallest live idea seemed like a gross indiscretion. In spite of good breeding, perfect politeness, and a desire to please, boredom was written large on every countenance. The young people who attended out of duty were afraid to talk of anything which might arouse suspicion that they had been thinking, or reveal that they

---

7. Pierre-Jean Béranger (1780–1857) was a songwriter of immense fluency and popularity. He went to jail for three months in 1821 and for nine months in 1828 as a result of sarcasms and ironies against the Bourbons. His "Le Vieux Drapeau" ("The Old Flag") was a powerful and popular rallying cry in July 1830.

had read some prohibited book, so they fell silent after a few well-chosen words on Rossini and the weather.

Julien noted that the conversation was generally kept alive by two viscounts and five barons whom M. de La Mole had known during the emigration. These gentlemen rejoiced in incomes of eight to ten thousand florins; four of them were devoted to *La Quotidienne* and three to the *Gazette de France*. One of them was compelled to recite every day some new anecdote from the Castle,[8] in which the word *admirable* was used with some freedom. Julien took notice that he wore five crosses; the others generally had no more than three.

On the other hand, there were in the antechamber no fewer than ten liveried lackeys, and throughout the evening ices and tea were served every quarter of an hour, while at midnight there was a sort of supper with champagne.

That was the reason why Julien sometimes stayed to the end; otherwise, he failed to see how anyone could listen seriously to the ordinary conversation in this salon, with its magnificent gilded walls. Sometimes he looked curiously at the speakers to see if they themselves weren't aware of the absurdity of what they were saying. M. de Maistre whom I know by heart, thought he to himself, has said all this a hundred times better, and even he is a great bore.

Julien was not the only one to be aware of moral asphyxiation. Some of the guests consoled themselves by eating a great many ices, others by the pleasure of saying for the rest of the evening: I've just come from the Hôtel de La Mole, where I heard that Russia, etc.

Julien learned from one of the trucklers that less than six months ago Mme. de La Mole had rewarded more than twenty years of assiduous attendance by making a prefect out of poor Baron le Bourguignon, who had been a subprefect since the Restoration.

This great event had rekindled the zeal of all these gentry; before it, they would have been offended at any small slight; afterward they were offended at nothing. Rudeness here was rarely direct, but Julien had already overheard at the dinner table two or three curt dialogues between the marquis and his wife, painful to those who sat near them. These noble folk took no trouble to hide their sincere contempt for anyone not descended from people who *rode in the king's coaches*. Julien noted that the word *crusade* was the only one that brought to their faces a look of intent seriousness, mingled with respect. Their ordinary respect had always a shade of condescension.

Amid this splendor and this boredom, Julien took an interest only

8. The Castle is the court of Charles IX (1550–1574) at Saint-Cloud.

in M. de La Mole; he was pleased one day to hear him protest that he had had no hand in the promotion of poor le Bourguignon. It had been done out of regard for the marquise: Julien learned the truth from Abbé Pirard.

One morning while the abbé was working with Julien in the library of the marquis on that interminable lawsuit with de Frilair:

—Sir, said Julien abruptly, is dining every day with the marquise one of my duties, or are they doing me a favor?

—It's a great honor! said the abbé, scandalized. Why, M. N_____, the academician, who's been paying them court for fifteen years, has never been able to obtain such a favor for his nephew M. Tanbeau.

—For me, sir, it's the most painful part of my job. I was less bored in the seminary. Sometimes I see even Mlle. de La Mole yawning, though she ought to be used to these friends of the family and their nice manners. I'm afraid of falling asleep. For heaven's sake, get leave for me to go off and eat a forty-sou dinner in a second-class tavern.

The abbé, who was a real parvenu, had a great sense of the honor involved in dining with a member of the nobility. While he was trying to convey this thought to Julien, a slight noise made them turn their heads. Julien saw Mlle. de La Mole, who was listening. He blushed. She had come looking for a book, and had overheard everything; it gave her some respect for Julien. This fellow wasn't born on his knees, she thought, like that old abbé. Lord! isn't he ugly?

At dinner, Julien did not venture to glance toward Mlle. de La Mole, but she was good enough to talk to him. That day they were expecting a lot of company, and she begged him to stay for it. Girls in Paris are not very fond of persons of a certain age, particularly when they are carelessly dressed. Julien had not required much worldly wisdom to note that the colleagues of M. le Bourguignon who remained in the drawing room were generally the butts of Mlle. de La Mole's mockery. That day, whether from affectation or not, she was cruel in her treatment of the bores.

Mlle. de La Mole was the center of a little group that formed almost every evening behind the immense easy chair of the marquise. There one might find the Marquis de Croisenois, the Comte de Caylus, the Viscount de Luz, and two or three other young officers, friends of Norbert or of his sister. These gentlemen sat on a large blue sofa. At the other end of the sofa from that occupied by the brilliant Mathilde, Julien sat silently on a little low caned chair. This modest position was the envy of all the trucklers. Norbert gave countenance to his father's secretary in the possession of it by addressing him directly or mentioning his name every so often in the course of the evening. This particular day Mlle. de La Mole asked him how high was the hill on which the fortress of Besançon stands. Julien could not possibly have told whether this hill was higher or lower than Montmartre. He often laughed aloud at the things that were said in this little group; but he felt himself incapable of saying anything similar of his own. It was like a foreign language he could understand and appreciate, but which he could not talk.

Mathilde's friends were in a state of open warfare that evening against the guests who kept arriving to fill the magnificent drawing room. The friends of the family attracted first attention, being better known, and Julien paid strict attention. Everything interested him, both the things that were talked about and the way they were ridiculed.

—Ah! here is M. Descoulis, said Mathilde, he's left his wig at home. Perhaps he expects to get a prefecture through his genius and is showing off that bald brow which he says is filled with lofty thoughts.

—He's a man who knows the whole world, said the Marquis de Croisenois; he visits my uncle the cardinal, as well. He is capable of cultivating a special lie with each one of his friends for years on end, and he has two or three hundred friends. He knows how to cultivate friendship, that's his special gift. Just as you see him here, he sometimes appears in the mud of the roadway before the house of one of his friends at seven o'clock of a winter morning.

From time to time he has a quarrel and writes seven or eight letters to keep it going. Then he is reconciled, and has seven or eight letters for the transports of friendship. But it is the frank, sincere openness of an honest man who has nothing whatever to conceal that offers him the most brilliant part to play. That's his style when he has something to ask for. One of my uncle's grand vicars is really splendid when he describes the life of M. Descoulis since the Restoration. I shall bring him to see you.

—Bah! I shouldn't believe those tales, said the Comte de Caylus; it's nothing but the professional jealousy of little people.

—M. Descoulis will have a name in history, replied the marquis; he made the Restoration, along with Abbé de Pradt, M. Talleyrand, and Pozzo di Borgo.[9]

—This man has played with his millions, said Norbert, and I can't imagine why he comes here to swallow my father's insults, which are often abominable. How many times have you betrayed

9. At the Congress of Vienna (1814–15), Talleyrand, representing France, and Pozzo di Borgo, representing Russia, did play major roles in working out the restoration of the Bourbons; Abbé de Pradt, though associated with Talleyrand, was a relatively peripheral and uninfluential figure on this occasion.

your friends, my dear Descoulis? he shouted to him the other day, from one end of the table to the other.

—But is it true that he has betrayed people? said Mlle. de La Mole. After all, who hasn't?

—Who's this? said the Comte de Caylus to Norbert, you have here M. Sainclair, the great liberal; and what the devil is he doing here? I must go over, talk to him, and get him to talk; they say he's very witty.

—But how is your mother going to receive him? said M. de Croisenois. He has such extreme ideas, so generous, so independent. . . .

—Take a look, said Mlle. de La Mole, there's your independent man who's bowing to the floor before M. Descoulis and grasping his hand. I almost thought he was going to carry it to his lips.

—Descoulis must stand better with the powers that be than we thought, replied M. de Croisenois.

—Sainclair is here to get into the academy, said Norbert; look, Croisenois, at the way he greets Baron L_____.

—It would be less vulgar if he got down on his knees, said M. de Luz.

—My dear Sorel, said Norbert, you're a man of spirit though just come down from your mountains; try never to greet people the way that great poet does, not even God the Father.

—Ah! here comes a man of spirit, the real article, M. le Baron Bâton, said Mlle. de La Mole, parodying the voice of the lackey who had just announced him.

—I think even your servants are making fun of him. What a name, Baron Bâton! said M. de Caylus.

—What's in a name? as he said to us himself, only the other day, remarked Mathilde. Imagine the Duc de Bouillon announced for the first time; all the public needs, in any case, is a little time to get used to it. . . .

Julien left the company around the sofa. He was not yet particularly fond of the delicate touches of light raillery; if he was to laugh at a joke he required that it be founded on reason. In the chatter of the young people he saw nothing but the sneering tone, and he was shocked by it. His prudery, which was provincial or perhaps English, went so far as to suspect the speakers of envy, in which he was assuredly mistaken.

Comte Norbert, said he to himself, whom I've seen making three rough drafts of a twenty-line letter to his colonel, would be very glad indeed to have written one page in his whole life like those of M. Sainclair.

Passing unnoticed because of his unimportance, Julien wandered from group to group; he was following at a distance Baron Bâton, and wanted to hear him talk. This clever man wore a look of some disquiet, and Julien saw that he regained his composure only when he had enunciated three or four well-turned sentences. It seemed to Julien that this sort of with required open space.

The baron was incapable of epigrams; he needed at least four sentences of six lines each in order to shine.

—*That man lectures, he doesn't chat*, said someone behind Julien. He turned, and blushed with pleasure to hear the name of Comte Chalvet. This was the wittiest man of the day. Julien had often read his name in the *Mémorial de Sainte-Hélène* and the bits of history dictated by Napoleon. Comte Chalvet was curt in his speech; his phrases were flashes of light, accurate, swift, often penetrating. If he spoke on any topic, one immediately saw the conversation move forward to a new level. He had the facts at hand; it was a pleasure to listen to him. In politics, however, he was a shameless cynic.

—Personally, I'm an independent, he said to a man wearing three decorations, whom he was apparently mocking. Why should I try to have the same opinion today that I had six weeks ago? That would make me the slave of my own judgment.

Four solemn young men standing around him looked sour at this; such people never appreciate levity. The count saw he had overstepped himself. Fortunately he caught sight of honest M. Balland, the artist of honesty. The count began talking to him; a circle gathered, seeing that poor Balland was going to be flayed alive. By virtue of morals and morality, though he was horribly ugly and had got his start in life by some indescribable expedients, M. Balland had married an extremely rich woman, who died; then he married another woman, also very rich, who never appears in society. In all humility he now enjoys an income of sixty thousand florins and has his own toadies. Comte Chalvet discussed the whole business with him, mercilessly. They were soon surrounded by a circle of thirty persons. Everyone smiled, even those grave young men, the hope of the age.

Why does he call on M. de La Mole, where he's obviously a laughing stock? Julien thought. He crossed the room to ask Abbé Pirard.

M. Balland left the room.

—Good! said Norbert, there's one of my father's spies who's gone; there's nobody left now but little lame Napier.

—Is that the answer to the puzzle? thought Julien. But in that case, why does the marquis invite M. Balland at all?

Severe Abbé Pirard was making faces in a corner of the room every time he heard a new name called out by the footmen.

—Why, it's a den of thieves, he said, like Basilio,[1] I see nobody here but scoundrels.

The fact is that the stern abbé knew nothing about good society. But through his friends the Jansenists he did have very precise ideas about these men who worm their way into drawing rooms only through their extreme suppleness in the service of all parties or through an ill-gotten fortune. For several minutes that evening he answered Julien's eager questions out of the fullness of his heart, then stopped short, in despair at having nothing but evil to report about everyone, and charging it to himself as a sin. Being short of temper, a Jansenist, and a believer in Christian charity, his life in society was a perpetual struggle.

—What a frightful expression on that Abbé Pirard! said Mlle. de La Mole, as Julien returned toward the sofa.

Julien was irked, but she was perfectly right. M. Pirard was, beyond any doubt, the most honest man in the room, but his blotched face, distorted by the torturing of his conscience, rendered him perfectly hideous at the moment. Trust to appearances after this! thought Julien; it's precisely when Abbé Pirard in the delicacy of his conscience is reproaching himself for some peccadillo that he puts on an atrocious expression; while that little Napier, who is known to everyone as a spy, carries about an expression of perfect, tranquil happiness. Abbé Pirard had, however, made great concessions to the occasion; he had hired a servant and was quite well dressed.

Julien noted an unusual stir in the room; all eyes were turned toward the door, and an abrupt silence fell. Footmen announced the famous Baron de Tolly, who had come to public attention in the recent elections. Julien moved forward and got a good look at him. The baron was in charge of a certain constituency: he had had the luminous idea of abolishing the little slips of paper on which were recorded the votes of one of the parties. But, in order to keep things perfectly fair, he replaced them with other little slips of paper bearing a name that was altogether agreeable to him. This decisive maneuver was noted by several electors, who had hastened to present their kind regards to Baron de Tolly. The excellent fellow was still pale with the excitement of this great affair. Evil-minded people had even ventured to use the expression *the galleys*. M. de La Mole received him coolly. The poor baron made his escape.

—If he's off so quickly, it must be to go visit M. Comte,[2] said Comte Chalvet; there was laughter.

1. In Rossini's *Barber of Seville* (as, of course in Beaumarchais' original play), Basilio is a sour-faced music master and a hypocrite.
2. M. Comte was a famous magician of the day; Baron de Tolly is off for his lessons in prestidigitation.

Amid the crowd of great noblemen, mostly silent, and the swarm of intriguers, mostly disreputable but all clever fellows, who moved through M. de La Mole's drawing room that evening (there was talk of his getting a ministry), little Tanbeau was fighting his first battles. If he had not yet gained much delicacy of insight, he made up for it, as we shall see, by the energy of his talk.

—Why not send the man to jail for ten years? he was saying, as Julien approached his circle. Reptiles must be kept in the cellar; we must put them away where they'll die in the dark, otherwise their poison spreads and becomes more dangerous. Why condemn the fellow to a mere fine of a thousand crowns? He's poor, all right, so much the better; but his party will pay for him. Much better to give him a fine of five hundred francs and ten years in a dungeon cell.

Good Lord! who's this monster they're talking about? thought Julien, who was amazed at his colleague's vehement tone and jerky gestures. The meager, pinched face of the academician's favorite nephew was hideous at that instant. Julien soon learned that the man they were talking about was the greatest poet of the age.[3]

Ah, the monster! Julien exclaimed under his breath, and tears of sympathy came to his eyes. Ah, you little beggar, I'll get back at you for those words.

So these, he thought, are the lost souls of the party within which the marquis is one of the leaders. And that great man he was just slandering, how many decorations, how many sinecures couldn't he have had if he had sold himself, I don't say to the vulgar administration of M. de Nerval, but to any one of these passably honest ministers whom we've seen succeeding him.

From a distance Abbé Pirard beckoned to Julien; M. de La Mole had just said a word to him. But by the time Julien, who at that moment was listening with lowered eyes to the groanings of a bishop, could at last work free and join his friend, he found himself forestalled by that abominable little Tanbeau. This little monster loathed the abbé as the source of Julien's special favor, and had come to pay him court.

When will death deliver us from that ancient mass of corruption? It was in these terms, of biblical directness, that the little man of letters was talking at the moment of the respectable Lord Holland.[4] His claim to fame was a thorough acquaintance with the biographies of living persons, and he had just been running quickly

3. The "greatest poet of the age" (it is a generous judgment) was P. J. Béranger (1780–1857); see p. 208, n. 7.
4. Lord Holland (1778–1840) was staunch Whig in the House of Lords, indeed for a while almost the only Whig in the upper house. As such, he was an English "liberal," relatively friendly to Napoleon and the American cause.

through the various men who might aspire to some influence under the new king of England.[5]

Abbé Pirard stepped into a neighboring room; Julien followed:

—The marquis doesn't like scribblers, let me warn you; it is his only antipathy. Know Latin and Greek if you can, the history of the Egyptians, the Persians, and so on, he will honor you and protect you as a man of learning. But don't venture to write a single page in French, and above all on serious matters above your station in life, or he'll call you a scribbler and take a dislike to you. Can it be that you've lived in a nobleman's house without learning that phrase of the Duc de Castries about d'Alembert and Rousseau: that ruck want to have opinions about everything and don't even have a thousand crowns of income.[6]

Everything comes out, thought Julien, it's just like the seminary here! He had written eight or ten rather outspoken pages; it was a sort of historical eulogy of the old surgeon-major, who, he said, had made a man of him. And that little notebook, said Julien to himself, has always been kept under lock and key! He went up to his room, burned his manuscript, and returned to the drawing room. The clever rascals had gone; there was nobody left but men with decorations.

Around the table, which the servants had carried in fully set, were seven or eight women, very noble, very pious, very affected, between thirty and thirty-five years old. The brilliant widow of the Maréchal de Fervaques entered, with apologies for her lateness. It was past midnight; she went to sit beside the marquise. Julien was deeply moved; she had the eyes and the expression of Mme. de Rênal.

The group around Mlle. de La Mole still held together. She and her friends were engaged in jeering at the unfortunate Comte de Thaler. This was the only son of the famous Jew, known far and wide for the fortune he had made out of lending money to kings to make war on their people. The old man had just died, leaving his son an income of a hundred thousand crowns a month, and a name, alas! all too well known. Such an extraordinary position demanded either great simplicity of character or great power of will.

Unfortunately, the count was nothing but a good man encrusted with a multitude of affectations suggested to him by his parasites.

M. de Caylus declared that someone had convinced him he was determined to pay court to Mlle. de La Mole (she was in fact being courted by the Marquis de Croisenois, who stood to become a duke with an income of a hundred thousand florins).

---

5. George IV died on June 28, 1830, and was succeeded by William IV, third son of George III.
6. The phrase that Stendhal attributes here to the Duc de Castries he uses elsewhere and attributes to other people; it was more than likely his own.

—Don't accuse him of determination, Norbert said pityingly.

In fact, what poor Comte Thaler lacked most conspicuously was just this faculty of will. As far as this side of his character went, he could have been a very proper king. Continually taking advice from everyone, he did not have the courage to follow out any opinion to the end.

His face alone, Mlle. de La Mole used to say, would have been enough to keep her laughing for life. It was a curious mixture of anxiety and disappointment; but from time to time there passed across it visible gusts of self-importance combined with a sharp tone such as suits the richest man in France, especially when he is reasonably handsome and not yet thirty-six. He is timidly insolent, said M. de Croisenois. The Comte de Caylus, Norbert, and two or three other young men with moustaches bantered him to their hearts' content, without his ever suspecting it, and then sent him away as one o'clock struck:

—Are those your famous Arabian steeds that you keep waiting outside in this sort of weather? Norbert asked him.

—No, I have a new pair, much less expensive, replied M. de Thaler. The left horse cost me five thousand francs, the one on the right only a hundred louis; but I assure you, he's only harnessed up at night. The fact is, his trot is exactly like the other's.

Norbert's words made the count conscious that a man in his position ought to have a passion for horses, and that he should not allow his to get soaking wet. So he left, and the other gentlemen followed an instant after, still laughing at him.

That's it, thought Julien, as their laughter echoed up the stairwell, I've now seen the absolute opposite of my own position. I don't have an income of twenty louis a year, and I've been with a man whose income is twenty louis an hour, and people laughed at him. . . . It's a sight to cure one of envy.

Chapter 5

SENSIBILITY AND A GREAT LADY OF PIOUS DISPOSITION

> An idea of some vitality has the air of an indiscretion there, people are so used to flat language. Unhappy the man who makes it up as he goes along!
>
> —Faublas[7]

After several months of experiment, this is where Julien stood on the day when the steward of the house gave him his third quarter's wages. M. de La Mole had put him in charge of his properties in

---

7. Faublas is not an author but a character in a novel, *Les Amours du Chevalier de Faublas* (1787–1790), by Louvet de Couvray.

Brittany and Normandy. Julien made frequent trips to those districts. His main task was to carry on the correspondence pertaining to the famous lawsuit with the Abbé de Frilair. M. Pirard had given the case over to him.

From the brief notes the marquis scribbled on the margins of the many papers addressed to him, Julien composed letters, almost all of which were signed.

At the theological school, the professors complained that he did not apply himself, but considered him nonetheless one of their most distinguished pupils. These various tasks, accepted with all the energy of a repressed ambition, quickly robbed Julien of all the fresh coloring he had brought with him from the provinces. His pallor was a special merit in the eyes of the young seminarians his companions; he found them much less mean, much less likely to prostrate themselves before a coin, than the seminarians of Besançon; for their part, they thought him a consumptive. The marquis had given him a horse of his own.

Fearful of being recognized when he was out riding, Julien had told them that this exercise had been prescribed for him by doctors. The Abbé Pirard had taken him to visit various Jansenist societies. Julien was astonished; the idea of religion was indissolubly linked, in his mind, with that of hypocrisy and money making. He admired these pious, severe men who never gave a thought to the budget. Several of the Jansenists became friendly with him and gave him advice. A new world opened before him. He met among the Jansenists a Comte Altamira, a man six feet tall, condemned to death in his own country for liberalism, and pious. This strange mixture of piety and love of liberty impressed him.

Julien's friendship with the young count had cooled. Norbert had felt that he retorted too sharply to the jests of some of his friends. Julien, having committed a couple of social blunders, had sworn never to say another word to Mlle. Mathilde. People were always perfectly polite to him in the Hôtel de La Mole, but he felt himself in vague disgrace. His provincial common sense explained this change in the words of the proverb: *familiarity breeds contempt.*

Perhaps he saw a little more deeply into things than at first, or else the first enchantment produced by Parisian urbanity had passed.

As soon as work was finished, he fell prey to mortal boredom; this was the withering effect of that politeness, admirable in itself but so calculated, so carefully measured out according to one's social position, which is peculiar to high society. Any heart with a bit of feeling becomes aware of the artifice.

No doubt provincials are often guilty of a common or rough manner; but they show a little concern in their answers to you. In the

Hôtel de La Mole, Julien's self-esteem was never wounded; but often, at the end of the day, he was ready to weep. In the provinces, a waiter in a café will take an interest in you if some little incident occurs as you enter his café; but if this little incident involves anything painful to your self-esteem, even as he sympathizes with you, he will repeat ten times over the word that makes you wince. In Paris, they are considerate enough to turn aside in order to laugh at you, but you will always be a stranger.

We pass silently over a multitude of little episodes that would have subjected Julien to ridicule if he had not been in some sense beneath ridicule. An absurd sensitivity caused him to commit thousands of awkward errors. All his diversions were forms of precaution: he practiced with pistols every day, and he was one of the better students of the more famous fencing masters. As soon as he had a free moment, instead of spending it over a book as formerly, he ran to the stable and asked for the most vicious horses. When he went out with the riding master, he was almost always thrown.

The marquis found him convenient because of his hard work, his silence, and his intelligence; gradually he turned over to him for sorting out any business affair that was at all complicated. During the periods when his real ambitions left him some freedom, the marquis acted the part of a shrewd businessman; he was in a position to get inside information, and speculated boldly [on the market]. He bought houses and timber, but he was easily irked. He gave away hundreds of louis and went to court over hundreds of francs. Rich men with lofty ambitions treat business as a source of entertainment, not profit. The marquis needed a chief of staff who would reduce his financial affairs to a clear and easily intelligible order.

Mme. de La Mole, though of so dignified a character, sometimes made fun of Julien. The *unexpected*, deriving from personal sensitivity, is horrifying to great ladies; it's the absolute opposite of the conventional. Two or three times, the marquis took his part: If he is absurd in your drawing room, he is master in his own office. Julien, for his part, felt he had found the key to the character of the marquise. She condescended to be interested in everything as soon as the Baron de la Joumate was announced. He was a cold creature with a wooden face. He was short, thin, ugly, very well dressed, spent his life at the Castle, and as a general rule said absolutely nothing about anything. His mind was like that, too. Mme. de La Mole would have been overjoyed, for the first time in her life, if she could have got him as a husband for her daughter.

Chapter 6

LESSONS IN DICTION

> It is their lofty assignment to judge calmly of the little events
> which make up the daily lives of nations. Their wisdom must fore-
> stall the growth of great anger from tiny causes, or from events
> which the voice of rumor transfigures as it carries them abroad.
> —Gratius[8]

For a new arrival who, out of pride, never asked any questions,
Julien did not fall into too many gross errors. One day, when he had
been driven by a sudden shower into a café on the rue Saint-
Honoré, a big man in a beaver-trimmed overcoat was struck by his
gloomy gaze and began to stare back at him, exactly like Mlle.
Amanda's lover, long before, at Besançon.

Julien had too often blamed himself for letting that first insult
pass to endure this one. He demanded an explanation. The man in
the overcoat retorted with filthy insults: everyone in the café surrounded them, and passersby crowded the doorway. With provincial
caution, Julien carried a pair of little pistols; his hand clutched
them in his pocket with a convulsive gesture. But he thought better
of it, and confined himself to repeating steadily to his man: *Sir,
your address? I despise you.*

The steadiness with which he attached himself to these six words
ended by impressing the crowd.

Damn it, that fellow who goes on talking all by himself ought to
come out with his address. When the man in the overcoat heard
these words running through the crowd, he flung a half-dozen
cards at Julien. Luckily, none of them struck his face; he had sworn
to use his pistols only if he were touched. The man went off, not
without turning back from time to time to shake his fist and shout
insults.

Julien found himself bathed in sweat. So it's within the power of
the lowest of men to enrage me like this! he said furiously. How can
I get rid of this shameful excess of feeling?

He had to find a second, now; and he had no friend. Several acquaintances there had been; but all of them, regularly, after six
weeks of acquaintance, dropped him. I'm antisocial, and now I
must suffer for it, he thought. But at last he thought of looking up
a former lieutenant of the Ninety-sixth, a poor devil named Liévin,
with whom he often used to fence. Julien told him the full story.

—I'll be glad to act as your second, said Liévin, but on one con-

---

8. The quote from "Gratius" can scarcely be from Faliscus G., Roman author of a poem on
hunting, or Ortwinus G., a contributor to the *Epistolae Obscurorum Virorum* controversy. It is most likely an invention.

dition: if you don't wound your man, you will fight with me on the spot.

—Agreed, said Julien [with a hearty handshake], and they went to look up M. C. de Beauvoisis at the address indicated on the cards, in the heart of the Faubourg Saint-Germain.

It was seven in the morning. Only after he sent in his name did Julien think that this might very well be the young relative of Mme. de Rênal, who had given a letter of introduction to the singer Geronimo.

Julien had handed to a big footman one of the cards flung at him the day before and one of his own.

He was kept waiting, with his second, fully three quarters of an hour; at last they were ushered into a room of admirable elegance. They found there a tall young man dressed like a doll [in a white and rose dressing gown]; his features had the perfection and the vacancy of a Greek statue. His remarkably narrow head was crowned with a pyramid of fine blond hair. It had been dressed with immense care; not one hair was out of place. He had to finish his hairdo, thought the lieutenant of the Ninety-sixth, that was why this damned fop kept us waiting out there. His striped dressing gown, his morning trousers, everything down to his embroidered slippers was perfectly correct and marvelously sleek. His expression, nobly empty, announced a man of few and ordinary ideas: one whose ideal was to be agreeable, with a horror of the unexpected and of levity, with an abundance of solemnity.

Julien, to whom his lieutenant of the Ninety-sixth had explained that the man's making them wait so long after flinging those cards rudely in his face was a further insult, marched stiffly into M. de Beauvoisis' presence. He had planned to be insolent, but was also intent on showing good form.

He was so impressed with M. de Beauvoisis' gentle manners, with his affected, portentous, self-satisfied air, and with the wonderful elegance of his surroundings, that in an instant all thoughts of being insolent disappeared. It was not his man of the day before. His astonishment was so great at finding so distinguished a personage instead of the rude fellow he had met in the café that he could not say a word. He presented one of the cards that had been flung at him.

—That is my name, indeed, said the man of fashion, who was not very favorably impressed by Julien's black coat, worn at seven o'clock in the morning; but, upon my word, I don't understand the honor. . . .

His manner of pronouncing these words restored to Julien a bit of his ill humor.

—I have come to fight with you, sir, he said; and he quickly explained the whole affair.

M. Charles de Beauvoisis, having considered the matter more maturely, was reasonably content with the cut of Julien's black coat. It's by Staub, that's clear, he said, as he listened to the conversation; the vest is in good taste, the boots are all right; but, on the other hand, that black coat in the early-morning hours! . . . It will be to provide a poorer target for the bullet, said the chevalier de Beauvoisis to himself.

As soon as he had satisfied himself on this score, he resumed his perfect politeness, and spoke to Julien almost as an equal. The discussion was lengthy, the matter was of some delicacy; but in the end, Julien could not refuse the evidence. The well-bred young man before him bore no resemblance whatever to the rude personage who had insulted him the day before.

Julien felt immense reluctance to go away; he drew out the explanations. He was studying the complacency of the chevalier de Beauvoisis, for it was thus that the man referred to himself; he had been shocked that Julien called him simply Monsieur.

He admired his gravity, which sometimes mingled with a certain modest fatuity, but never adandoned him for an instant. He was astonished by a peculiar mannerism he had of moving his tongue about as he pronounced certain words. . . . But in none of that was there the slightest ground for picking a quarrel with him.

The youthful diplomat offered very gracefully to fight anyhow, but the ex-lieutenant of the Ninety-sixth, who had been sitting for an hour with his legs stretched out, his hands on his hips, and his arms akimbo, decided that his friend M. Sorel was not the man to pick a quarrel with someone simply because his visiting cards had been stolen.

Julien took his leave in the blackest of moods. The chevalier de Beauvoisis' carriage was waiting for him in the courtyard at the foot of the stairs; as he passed, Julien glanced up and recognized his man of the day before in the coachman.

To see him, drag him down from his high seat by the tails of his long coat, and set to lashing him with his own whip was the work of an instant. A pair of lackeys tried to defend their fellow-servant; Julien was struck several times: instantly, he drew one of his little pistols and fited at them; they fled. It was all the work of a minute.

The chevalier de Beauvoisis descended the stairs with the most amusing gravity, repeating in his lordly accent: What's this, what's this? He was obviously much intrigued, but his diplomatic dignity did not allow him to betray the slightest interest. When he learned what had happened, loftiness still disputed, in his features, with the mildly mocking coolness which should never be absent from a diplomatic countenance.

The lieutenant of the Ninety-sixth understood that M. de Beauvoisis really wanted to fight; being a diplomat himself, he also wanted to keep for his friend the advantage of the initiative.—This time, he cried, we certainly have grounds for a duel!—Indeed, I think so, replied the diplomat.

—That rascal has left my service, he told his servants; one of you must drive. The door of the carriage was opened, and the chevalier insisted that Julien and his second get in first. They went to look up a friend of M. de Beauvoisis, who knew of a secluded place. The conversation as they drove to it was first-rate. The only odd thing was the diplomat in his dressing gown.

Noble though they are, thought Julien, these gentlemen aren't such bores as the people who come to dinner at M. de La Mole's; and I see why, he added a moment later, they let themselves be indecent. They talked about various dancing girls whom the public had much appreciated in a ballet given the night before. The gentlemen made allusion to various spicy stories of which Julien and his second, the lieutenant of the Ninety-sixth, knew absolutely nothing. Julien was not such a fool as to pretend to be knowing in these matters; he frankly confessed ignorance. This frankness gratified the chevalier's friend; he repeated the stories in explicit detail, and told them very well.

One thing absolutely astounded Julien. A street altar which was being constructed in the middle of the road for the Corpus Christi procession held up the carriage for a moment. The gentlemen allowed themselves various pleasantries; as they told it, the priest in charge was the son of an archbishop. Never would anyone have dared to talk of such matters in the house of the Marquis de La Mole, who had hopes of becoming a duke.

The duel was over in a minute: Julien had a bullet in his arm, they bound it up for him with handkerchiefs soaked in brandy, and the chevalier de Beauvoisis asked Julien very politely to be allowed to return him to his residence, in the same carriage that had brought them. When Julien said he lived at the Hôtel de La Mole, glances passed between the diplomat and his friend. Julien had a cab waiting, but he found the conversation of the gentlemen far more amusing than that of the honest lieutenant of the Ninety-sixth.

Good Lord! is that all a duel amounts to Julien thought. What a piece of luck it was that I came across that coachman again! What a humiliation, if I had to swallow still another insult in a café! The amusing conversation had scarcely been interrupted. Julien now understood that diplomatic affectation is really good for something.

So boredom is not really inevitable, he said to himself, when people of good birth have a conversation! These people joke about the Corpus Christi procession, they venture to repeat scabrous stories, full of picturesque details. The only thing they lack completely is good political sense, and that deficiency is more than made up for by the charm of their style and the perfect correctness of their expressions. Julien felt a warm attraction for them. How happy I should be to see them often!

Scarcely had they separated when the chevalier de Beauvoisis hastened off in search of information; what he heard was not hopeful.

He was very curious to be acquainted with his man; could he, in decency, call on him? The little information he could glean was by no means encouraging.

—But this is really frightful said he to his second. It's unthinkable that I should confess I fought a duel with an ordinary secretary of M. de La Mole's, and just because my coachman stole my visiting cards.

—It's perfectly clear the whole story leaves one wide open to ridicule.

That evening the chevalier de Beauvoisis and his second spread everywhere the story that this M. Sorel, a most agreeable young man for that matter, was the illegitimate son of one of the Marquis de La Mole's intimate friends. The tale passed easily. Once it was well established, the young diplomat and his friend were kind enough to pay several calls on Julien during the fortnight he was confined to his room. Julien confessed to them that he had never in his life been to the opera.

—But this is shocking, they told him, it's the only place anyone ever goes. Your first visit must be when they put on *Le Comte Ory.*[9]

At the opera the chevalier de Beauvoisis introduced Julien to the famous singer Geronimo, who was having a tremendous vogue that year.

Julien fairly paid court to the chevalier; his mixture of self-esteem, mysterious importance, and youthful fatuity enchanted him. For example, the chevalier stammered a bit, because he had the honor to converse frequently with a great gentleman who had that mannerism. Never before had Julien seen in a single person both the absurdities that amuse one and the perfection of manners that a poor provincial is bound to imitate.

He was seen at the opera with the chevalier de Beauvoisis; their friendship caused his name to be mentioned.

—Well, indeed, M. de La Mole said to him one day, so now you're the illegitimate son of a rich gentleman in the Franche-Comté, who is my intimate friend?

9. Rossini's *Le Comte Ory* had its debut at the opera on August 20, 1828.

The marquis cut off Julien's protests; he wanted to say that he had done nothing to give this rumor currency.

—M. de Beauvoisis didn't want it thought that he had fought with a carpenter's son.

—I know, I know, said M. de La Mole; and now it's up to me to give the story some weight, as I'm perfectly willing to do. But I have a favor to ask of you, which will cost no more than a modest half hour of your time: every opera evening, about eleven-thirty, go and stand in the vestibule when the people of fashion come out. I still notice in you from time to time the mannerisms of the provinces; you really must get rid of them; besides, it's not a bad idea to know, at least by sight, important persons to whom I may have to send you someday on assignments. Call at the office to identify yourself; they have your name on the subscription list.

Chapter 7

AN ATTACK OF GOUT

> And so I was promoted, not on my merits, but because my master had the gout.
>
> —Bertolotti[1]

The reader is perhaps surprised at this free and almost friendly tone; we have neglected to note that for six weeks the marquis had been kept within doors by an attack of the gout.

Mlle. de La Mole and her mother had gone to Hyères to visit the mother of the marquise. Comte Norbert saw his father only for a few moments at a time; they were on perfectly good terms, but had nothing to say to one another. Reduced to Julien for companionship, M. de La Mole was astonished to find he had some ideas. He had him read newspapers aloud. Soon the young secretary was able to select the interesting passages. There was a new paper, which the marquis despised; he had sworn never to read it, and he talked about it, every day. Julien laughed, [and marveled at the feebleness of power before an idea. The marquis' pettiness restored him to the self-possession he might have lost after several evenings of private conversation with so great a gentleman.] The marquis, growing impatient with the present day, asked Julien to read him some Livy; the translation, improvised from the Latin text, entertained him.

One day the marquis said, with that tone of excessive politeness which Julien often found irksome:

—Allow me, my dear Sorel, to make you a present of a blue suit:

1. A. Bertolotti (1784–1860) was a Turinese poet mostly given to political themes.

when you feel disposed to put it on and pay me a call, you will be, in my eyes, the younger brother of the Comte de Retz, that is to say the son of my friend the old duke.

Julien was not too clear about this transaction; that same evening he ventured a visit in his blue coat. The marquis treated him as an equal. Julien had a heart capable of understanding simple politeness, but he had no notion of the finer shadings. He would have sworn, before the marquis took this whim, that one could not possibly be treated by him with more deference. What a remarkable gift! Julien said to himself; when he rose to take his leave, the marquis apologized for not being able to see him to the door because of his gout.

A curious idea took possession of Julien: Can he be making fun of me? he asked himself. He went to take counsel with the Abbé Pirard, who, less polite than the marquis, only whistled and changed the subject. Next morning, Julien appeared before the marquis dressed in black, with his portfolio and his letters to be signed. He was received in the old manner. That night, when he resumed the blue suit, he met with a completely different tone, and one just as polite as on the evening before.

—Since you aren't too bored by these visits which you are kind enough to make to a poor old invalid, said the marquis, you might as well describe to him all the little incidents of your life, but frankly, and with no other purpose than to tell the story clearly and amusingly. For people must be amused, continued the marquis; that's the only real thing in life. A man can't save my life in battle every day of the year, or present me every day with a fresh million; but if I had Rivarol[2] here by my couch, he would relieve me every day of an hour's suffering and boredom. I knew him well at Hamburg, during the emigration.

And the marquis told Julien stories of Rivarol among the Hamburgers, who used to form little societies in order to work out the point of his witticisms.

Limited to the company of this little abbé, M. de La Mole tried to liven him up. He challenged Julien's pride. Since he was asked for the truth, Julien determined to give it, but suppressed two things: his fanatical admiration for a name that enraged the marquis and his own perfect unbelief, which hardly suited a future clergyman. His little affair with the chevalier de Beauvoisis came in handy at this juncture. The marquis laughed until he cried at the scene in the café on the rue Saint-Honoré, with the foul-mouthed coachman. It was a period of perfect understanding between patron and protégé.

2. Antoine Rivarol (1753–1801), a witty and malicious writer and conversationalist of the *ancien régime*.

M. de La Mole grew interested in this singular character. At first, he cultivated Julien's absurdities for his own entertainment; soon he grew more interested in correcting gently the false conceptions of this young man. All the other provincials who come to Paris admire whatever they see, thought the marquis; this one hates whatever he sees. They have too much affectation; he has too little, and so fools consider him foolish.

The attack of gout was prolonged by cold winter weather and lasted several months.

One becomes fond of a fine spaniel, the marquis told himself, why should I be so ashamed of my fondness for this young abbé? He is an original. I treat him like a son; well, where's the harm in that? This notion, if it lasts, will cost me a diamond worth five hundred louis in my will.

Once the marquis was aware of his protégé's firm character, he gave him a fresh business assignment every day.

Julien was distressed to notice that his noble employer would sometimes give him contradictory instructions on the same subject.

This could compromise him seriously. Julien no longer acted for the marquis without a notebook, in which he wrote down all the decisions and gave them to the marquis for initialing. Julien had hired a clerk who transcribed all the decisions regarding each particular transaction into a special book. In this book were also filed copies of all the letters.

At first this scheme seemed ridiculous and tiresome in the extreme. But inside two months the marquis became aware of its advantages. Julien suggested hiring a clerk with banking experience, who should establish a set of double-entry books on all the receipts from and expenditures for properties of which Julien had charge.

These steps so enlightened the marquis on the conduct of his own business affairs that, to his delight, he was soon able to undertake two or three new speculations without the help of his broker, who had been swindling him.

—Take three thousand francs for yourself, he said one day to his young agent.

—But, sir, my conduct may be blamed.

—What do you want, then? said the marquis crossly.

—I want you to be good enough to make up a deed, and write it into the register with your own hand; it will grant me the sum of three thousand francs. As a matter of fact, it was the abbé Pirard who thought up this system of accounting. The marquis, looking as weary as the Marquis of Moncade when he listens to the accounts of his steward M. Poisson,[3] wrote out the deed.

---

3. The reference is to L. J. C. Soulas d'Allainval's comedy *L'École des bourgeois* (1728).

That evening, when Julien put in an appearance wearing the blue suit, there was no talk of business. The kind consideration of the marquis was so flattering to our hero's self-esteem, always on edge, that before long, in spite of himself, he felt a sort of affection for this genial old gentleman. Not that Julien was particularly sensitive, as the word is used in Paris; but he was no monster, and since the death of the old surgeon-major, nobody had spoken so kindly to him. He realized with astonishment that the marquis was more careful of his self-esteem than he had ever found the old surgeon to be. He understood at last that the surgeon had been more proud of his decoration than the marquis of his blue ribbon. The father of the marquis had been a great nobleman too.

One day, after a morning conversation during which the black suit was worn and business was discussed, Julien was chatting with the marquis, who kept him for several hours, and then insisted on giving him some bank notes which his broker had just brought in from the stock exchange.

—I hope, Monsieur le marquis, not to be lacking in the profound respect I owe, if I beg you to allow me a word.

—Speak, my friend.

—Will Monsieur le marquis be good enough to let me decline this gift? It is not offered to the man in the black suit, and it would immediately spoil the pleasant relation which you have been kind enough to establish with the man in the blue suit. He bowed most respectfully, and left the room without a backward glance.

This stroke of character amused the marquis. He spoke of it that evening to Abbé Pirard.

—And now I must make an admission to you, my dear abbé. I know about Julien's birth, and I authorize you not to keep secret this confidence of mine.

His behavior this morning was noble, thought the marquis, and now I am making him a member of the nobility.

Sometime later, the marquis was at last able to leave his room.

—Go spend a couple of months at London, he told Julien. Special couriers and some other messengers will bring you the letters I receive, along with my notes on them. You can write out the answers and send them back to me, enclosing each letter with its own response. I have figured that the delay will be no more than five days.

As he took the mail coach down the road to Calais, Julien thought with amazement of the triviality of the business on which he was being dispatched.

We shall not dwell on the sentiments of hatred and almost of horror which he felt as he touched English soil. We have made

clear his insane passion for Bonaparte. In every officer he saw a Sir
Hudson Lowe, in every grandee a Lord Bathurst,[4] giving orders for
the shameful treatment of St. Helena, and being rewarded for it
with ten years in a ministry.

At London he at last made the acquaintance of the higher fatuity.
He made friends with some young gentlemen from Russia, who initiated him.

—You're absolutely born for it, my dear Sorel, they all told him,
you have by nature that cool expression, *a thousand miles from the
sensation of the moment*, which we are all eager to acquire.

—You haven't understood our century, Prince Korasoff told him:
always do exactly the contrary of what people expect. Upon my word,
that's the only religion which is current nowadays. Don't be foolish,
don't be affected, for then people will expect of you follies and affectations, and the commandment will not be fulfilled.

Julien covered himself with glory one day in the drawing room of
the Duke of Fitz-Fulke,[7] who had invited him to dinner along with
Prince Korasoff. They were kept waiting for an hour. The way in
which Julien carried himself, amid the score of people who were
waiting, is still cited as a model to young secretaries in the London
embassies. His expression was inimitable.

In spite of [the jokes of] his friends the dandies, he wanted to
make the acquaintance of the celebrated Philip Vane, the only
philosopher in England since Locke. He found him just rounding
out his seventh year in prison. The aristocracy doesn't trifle with its
enemies in this country, thought Julien; in addition, Vane is disgraced, abused, etc.

Julien found him in a merry mood; the rage of the aristocracy
kept boredom at a distance. There, said Julien, as he left the prison,
there is the only cheerful man I've seen in England.

The most useful idea, for tyrants, is the idea of God, Vane had said
to him.

We pass in silence over the rest of the philosopher's system, as
being *cynical*.

When he returned:—What amusing notion have you brought me
back from England? M. de La Mole asked him. . . . There was a silence.—What notion did you pick up, amusing or not [, which
shows something about the people]? said the marquis sharply.

—Item one, said Julien, the wisest Englishman is crazy for an

4. Sir Hudson Lowe (1769–1844) was commanding officer of St. Helena during
Napoleon's confinement there, while Henry, third Earl of Bathurst, was secretary of war
during the same period. Both men were the objects of bitter hatred on the part of Las
Cases and the Napoleonic myth-makers.

hour every day; he is haunted by the demon of suicide, who is the national deity.

—Second, wit and genius are subject to a twenty-five-percent discount when they disembark in England.

—Third, there's nothing in the world so beautiful, so admirable, so heartwarming, as the English landscape.

—Now it's my turn, said the marquis:

—First, what made you say at the Russian ambassador's ball that there are in France three hundred thousand young men of twenty-five who are passionately eager for a war? Do you think that is altogether polite to the crowned heads?[5]

—One never knows how to make small talk with great diplomats, Julien replied. They have a mania for starting serious discussions. If one limits oneself to the usual newspaper commonplaces, they think one a fool. If one indulges in something a little true and new, they are stunned, they don't know what to say, and the next morning at seven o'clock they let one know through the first secretary of the embassy that one has been indiscreet.

—Not bad, said the marquis with a laugh. But apart from that, mister deep thinker, I'll wager you haven't discovered why you were sent to London.

—I beg your pardon, replied Julien; I was sent there to dine once a week with the royal ambassador, who is the most genteel of men.

—You went to earn the decoration which you see there, the marquis told him. I don't want you to give up your black suit, and I've grown accustomed to the more entertaining style I've adopted with the man in blue. Until further instructions, will you keep to this understanding: whenever I see this cross, you are the younger son of my friend the Duc de Retz, who, though he doesn't know it, has been pursuing a diplomatic career for the last six months. Please note, added the marquis, looking very serious, and cutting short all expressions of gratitude, note that I do not on any account want you to rise in the world. This is always a mistake, and a misfortune for the patron as well as for his favorite. When my lawsuits start to weary you, or you no longer suit me, I shall request a good living for you, like that of our friend Abbé Pirard, and *nothing else*, the marquis added drily.

The cross set Julien's pride at ease; he spoke up more freely. He was less apt to think himself insulted and made the butt of remarks, which though capable of rude interpretation, may unintentionally escape from anyone in the course of a vigorous conversation.

---

5. The crowned heads were the assembled monarchs of Europe, united against Napoleon and assembled after his downfall to divide Europe among themselves.

His cross was the occasion of an extraordinary visit; it was from M. le Baron de Valenod, who had come to Paris to thank the minister for his barony and to make his better acquaintance. He was going to be appointed mayor of Verrières after the dismissal of M. de Rênal.

Julien was shaken with silent laughter when M. de Valenod told him it had just been discovered that M. de Rênal was a Jacobin. As a matter of fact, in the new elections coming up, the new baron was to be the ministerial candidate, while in the district as a whole, which was naturally conservative, it was M. de Rênal who was being pushed by the liberals.

In vain did Julien try to learn something about Mme. de Rênal; the baron seemed to recall their former rivalry, and was impenetrable. He ended by asking Julien to help secure his father's vote in the next election. Julien promised to write.

—You really ought to introduce me, M. le chevalier, to the Marquis de La Mole.

I really *should*, thought Julien; but a rascal like this one! . . .

—To tell you the truth, he replied, I'm much too small a person around the Hôtel de La Mole to undertake introductions.

Julien told the whole story to the marquis; that evening, he told him not only of Valenod's pretensions but of his whole life and career since 1814.

—Not only, said M. de La Mole with great seriousness, not only will you introduce me tomorrow to the new baron, but I will invite him to dinner for the day after tomorrow. He will be one of our new prefects.

—In that case, Julien said coldly, I request the office of director of the poorhouse for my father.

—Absolutely, said the marquis, putting on his chaffing manner; I grant it, I was expecting a moral lecture. You are shaping up.

M. de Valenod informed Julien that the director of the lottery office at Verrières had just died: Julien found it a good joke to award his post to M. de Cholin, the ancient imbecile whose petition he had once picked up in the room occupied by M. de La Mole. The marquis laughed heartily at the petition which Julien repeated as he prepared for his signature the letter requesting this post from the minister of finance.

M. Cholin had barely been named when Julien learned that the post had been requested, by the deputies of the district, for M. Gros, the celebrated mathematician:[6] this large-spirited man, who himself had an income of only fourteen hundred francs, had been

---

6. Gros was the actual name of a man who tutored Stendahl in geometry.

lending six hundred of them every year to the late holder of the post, to help him raise his family.

Julien was stunned at what he had done. [What are the dead man's family to do now? The thought wrung his heart.] It's nothing important, he told himself, there are plenty of other injustices which I will have to commit if I'm to be successful; and what's more, I'll have to conceal them under lofty, sentimental words. Poor M. Gros! He deserved the cross; I have it, and I must play along with the government that gave it to me.

Conscious of his hypocrisy

Chapter 8

WHICH DECORATION CONFERS DISTINCTION?

> Your water does not refresh me, said the thirsty genie.—Yet it's the coolest well in the whole Diar Békir.
>
> —Pellico[7]

One day Julien was returning from the charming property of Villequier, along the banks of the Seine, an estate in which M. de La Mole took particular interest because, of all those he possessed, it was the only one that had belonged to the famous Boniface de La Mole. At the hotel Julien found the marquise and her daughter, just back from Hyères.

Julien was a dandy now and understood the art of living in Paris. He behaved with perfect coolness toward Mlle. de La Mole. He seemed to remember nothing at all of the period when she was asking so gaily for details on his technique of falling [gracefully] off a horse.

Mlle. de La Mole found him taller and paler. Neither his figure nor his dress betrayed any longer the mark of the provincial; not so, however, with his conversation: this was still too serious, too positive. But despite all these reasonable qualities, thanks to his pride, it conveyed no hint of servility; one was simply aware that he still considered too many things to be important. But it was clear that he was a man to maintain his opinion.

—He lacks the light touch, but not intelligence, said Mlle. de La Mole to her father; and she teased him about the cross he had given to Julien. My brother has been requesting it for these eighteen months, and he is a La Mole! . . .

—True; but Julien is capable of the unexpected, and that has never occurred to the La Mole you mention.

---

7. During the turbulent 1820s, Silvio Pellico (1788–1854), tragic poet and ardent liberal, suffered both a sentence of death and a long jail sentence for conspiracy—so that his name rightly stands at the head of this chapter.

The Duc de Retz was announced.

Mathilde was overcome with an irresistible urge to yawn; the sight of him somehow brought to mind all the antique gilt work and elderly visitors of her father's drawing room. She had a vision of the completely boring life she would be taking up again in Paris. At Hyères she had missed Paris.

And yet I'm nineteen years old! she thought; it's the age of happiness, at least according to all these gilt-edged idiots. She glanced at eight or ten volumes of new poetry that had piled up on the drawing-room table during her absence in Provence. She had the misfortune to be cleverer than MM de Croisenois, de Caylus, de Luz, and her other friends. She could foresee everything they would tell her about the beautiful sky of Provence, poetry, the south, etc., etc.

Her lovely eyes, in which there was an expression of profound boredom, and, worse still, of despair that she would ever find pleasure, paused a moment upon Julien. At least, he was not exactly like the next comer.

—M. Sorel, she said in that short, sharp, completely unfeminine voice which is customary among young women of the upper class, M. Sorel, are you coming this evening to the ball of M. de Retz?

—Mademoiselle, I have not had the honor of an introduction to M. le duc. (One would have said that these words and this title scorched the lips of the lofty provincial.)

—He has asked my brother to bring you along; and if you came, you could tell me something about the estate at Villequier; they're talking of moving out there this spring. I would like to know if the house is livable, and if the district is as pretty as I'm told. There are so many undeserved reputations!

Julien made no answer.

—Come to the ball with my brother, she added in a dry tone.

Julien bowed with respect. So even in the course of a dance I must render accounts to all the members of the family. Don't they pay me to be their businessman? His black humor added: God knows if what I tell the daughter won't cross in some way the plans of the father, the brother, or the mother! It's absolutely like the court of a reigning prince. One is expected to be a complete non-entity, but not to give anyone the slightest cause for complaint.

How disagreeable that big girl is! he thought, as he watched Mlle. de La Mole leave the room in response to a call from her mother, who wanted to introduce her to a number of women friends. She exaggerates all the styles, her dress is falling from her shoulders . . . she is even paler than she was before her trip . . . . What colorless hair, she overdoes even blondness! You would say the light was shining through it. What arrogance in her way of greeting you, in her glance! She has the gestures of a queen!

Mlle. de La Mole had just summoned her brother back as he was leaving the drawing room.

Comte Norbert came up to Julien:

—My dear Sorel, he said, where would you like me to pick you up, about midnight, for M. de Retz's ball? He told me specifically to bring you along.

—I know very well to whom I owe such kindness, Julien replied, bowing to the ground.

His ill humor, finding nothing to quarrel with in the tone of politeness, and even of interest, which Norbert had assumed with him, discharged itself on the reply which he, Julien, had made to this well-intentioned speech. He found in it a touch of obsequiousness.

That evening as he came to the ball he was struck by the magnificence of the Hôtel de Retz. The courtyard by which one entered was covered with an immense canvas awning painted scarlet and studded with gold stars: nothing could have been more elegant. Beneath this awning, the courtyard had been transformed into a grove of orange trees and of flowering laurel bushes. As pains had been taken to set the garden pots into the earth, the laurels and orange trees seemed to rise naturally from the ground. The carriage way had been sprinkled with sand.

The whole scene seemed extraordinary to our young man from the provinces. He had no idea of such magnificence; in an instant, his imagination caught fire and lifted him a thousand leagues from his ill humor. In the carriage as they came to the ball, Norbert had been gay, and he had been somber of mood; scarcely were they inside the courtyard when the roles were reversed.

Norbert was aware of nothing in all this magnificence but a few details that had not been seen to. He calculated the expense of everything, and since it added up to an impressive sum, Julien noted that he appeared jealous and promptly turned cross.

As for himself, he arrived in a state of enchanted admiration, and almost timid with emotion at the first of the rooms where they were dancing. There was a jam at the door of the second room, and the crowd was so dense that it was impossible to get through. The decoration of this second room represented the Alhambra of Granada.

—She's the belle of the ball, there's no doubt about it, said a moustached young man whose shoulder was firmly lodged in the middle of Julien's chest.

—Mlle. Fourmont, who has held the number-one spot all winter, said his neighbor, sees now that it's second place for her: look at her sulking.

—Actually, she's piling on canvas in an effort to attract. Look, look at that gracious smile when she moves into the central position in that quadrille. Upon my word, that's as good as a play.

—Mlle. de La Mole has the air of being superior to the pleasure she gets from her triumph, of which she is perfectly conscious. You would say she was afraid of pleasing anyone who speaks to her.

—Very good! That's the art of attraction.

Julien made vain efforts to catch sight of this seductive creature; seven or eight men taller than he prevented him from seeing her.

—There is plenty of coquetry in that lofty reserve, said the young man with the moustache.

—And those big blue eyes which lower so slowly just at the point when one would say they were about to give her away, added his neighbor. My word, she's a shrewd one.

—Look how, alongside her, the fair Fourmont seems common, said a third.

—That air of reserve seems to say: What delights I could unfold for you, if you were the man who is worthy of me!

—And who could be worthy of the sublime Mathilde? said the first: a reigning prince, perhaps, handsome, clever, manly, a hero in battle, and twenty years old at the most.

—A natural son of the Russian emperor . . . to whom, on the occasion of this marriage, a kingdom would be granted; or simply the Comte de Thaler, with his air of a peasant dressed up for a holiday. . . .

The door was now cleared, Julien could pass through.

Since these shop-window dummies consider her so remarkable, he thought, it's worth my while to study her. I can learn what constitutes perfection for this sort of creature.

As he was trying to catch her eye, Mathilde looked directly at him. Duty calls, said Julien to himself; but his ill humor was now only in his features. Curiosity drew him forward, with a pleasure that was quickly augmented by Mathilde's dress, cut very low off the shoulder, in a manner that did little for his self-possession. Her beauty is that of youth, he thought. Five or six young people, among whom Julien recognized those who had been talking around him in the doorway, were between them.

—You can tell me, sir, as you've been here all winter, she said to him, isn't this the finest ball of the season?

He made no answer.

—This Coulon quadrille is a wonderful dance, and the ladies all do it so well. The young men all turned to see who was the happy man from whom she was thus requiring an answer. She did not encourage their stares.

—You are a wise man, M. Sorel, she went on, with more pro-

nounced interest; you look upon all these balls and parties like a
philosopher, like Jean-Jacques Rousseau. These absurdities surprise
you without beguiling you.

A single word had just extinguished Julien's imagination and
driven the last illusion from his heart. His mouth assumed the expression of a somewhat exaggerated scorn.

—In my opinion, Jean-Jacques Rousseau was nothing but a fool
when he undertook to pass judgment on society; he understood it
not at all, and brought to it the feelings of a flunkey who has risen
above his station.

—He wrote the *Social Contract*, said Mathilde, in a tone of deep
respect.

—Even as he preaches republicanism and the overthrow of royal
titles, this upstart is drunk with delight if a duke changes the direction of his after-dinner walk in order to keep company with one of
his friends.

—Ah, yes, the Due de Luxembourg at Montmorency walks with
a M. Coindet in the direction of Paris . . . , replied Mlle. de La
Mole, with the joyous abandon of a first venture into pedantry. She
was delighted with her own erudition, much like the academician
who first discovers the existence of King Feretrius.[8] Julien's eye remained keen and severe. Mathilde had had an instant of enthusiasm; the coldness of her partner was profoundly disconcerting. She
was all the more struck by it, since generally it was she who produced this sort of effect on other people.

At that moment, the Marquis de Croisenois crossed the room
briskly toward Mlle. de La Mole. He paused for a moment within a
few feet of her, unable to reach her because of the crowd. He
looked at her, smiling across the obstacle. Beside him was the
young Marquise de Rouvray, who was a cousin of Mathilde's. She
was arm-in-arm with her husband; they had been married only a
fortnight. The Marquis de Rouvray, who was also youthful, displayed all that inane affection that enthralls a man who has made a
conventional marriage, arranged entirely by the family lawyers, and
then finds he has a perfectly beautiful bride. M. de Rouvray would
be a duke as soon as his aged uncle died.

While the Marquis de Croisenois, unable to penetrate the crowd,
stood smiling at Mathilde, she allowed her wide blue eyes to pass
slowly over him and his companions. What could be duller, she said
to herself, than that whole set! There's Croisenois, who wants to
marry me; he's kind, he's polite, he has manners just as good as M.

8. King Feretrius is a local joke, an allusion to an inspector of schools under the Restora-
    tion who invented a king of Rome named Feretrius and delivered a public lecture on
    him.

de Rouvray's. If it weren't for the boredom they create, these gentry would be very nice indeed. He too will follow me around at balls with that fatuous, complacent expression. A year after we marry, my carriage, my horses, my wardrobe, my country house twenty leagues from Paris, everything will be as fine as possible, exactly what's needed to make a vulgarian like the Comtesse de Roiville burst with envy; and after that? . . .

Mathilde was bored with expectations. The Marquis de Croisenois managed to get near her, and spoke, but she was dreaming without listening. The sound of his talk confused in her mind with the murmur and rustle of the ball. Her eye mechanically followed Julien, who had moved away with a respectful but haughty and discontented expression. She noted in a corner, far from the swirling crowd, Comte Altamira, who was under sentence of death in his own country, as the reader already knows. Under Louis XIV, one of his ancestors had married a prince of Conti; memories of this connection gave him some protection from the police of the congregation.

So far as I can see, nothing but the death sentence gives a man real distinction, Mathilde thought; it is the only thing that can't be bought.

Ah! there's a piece of wit I've wasted on myself! What a shame it didn't occur when I could get some credit for it! Mathilde was too well bred to bring a prearranged witticism into her conversation; but she had too much vanity not to be pleased with herself. A look of cheerfulness replaced the boredom on her face. The Marquis de Croisenois, who was still talking, thought he must be making an impression, and chattered away even more glibly.

What could a faultfinder say against my little joke? said Mathilde to herself. I could answer the critic like this: the title of baron, of viscount can be bought; a cross, a decoration is given away; my brother has one; what did he do for it? There are all sorts of ways to promotion. Ten years in a garrison, or a relative who's minister of war, and one is a squadron commander, like Norbert. Piles of money? . . . that's still the hardest thing to get, therefore the best proof of real merit. That's queer! All the books say exactly the opposite . . . Oh, well! to get money one simply marries Rothschild's daughter.

Seriously, my little joke has some truth in it. A death sentence is still the only thing that people haven't thought of asking for.

—Are you acquainted with Comte Altamira? she asked M. de Croisenois.

She had such an air of coming back to earth, and her question had so little relation to everything the poor marquis had been saying for the last five minutes, that his good humor was somewhat shaken. And yet he was a man of wit, and well known as such.

[handwritten margin note: More concerned w/ her wealth than her]

Mathilde is very strange, he thought; it's a disadvantage, but she'll give her husband such a distinguished social position! I can't imagine how the Marquis de La Mole manages it; he's on good terms with all the best people in every party; he can't possibly lose his position. And anyhow, this strangeness of Mathilde's may very well pass for genius. If one is well born and has plenty of money, genius is no cause for ridicule, and then, what distinction it brings! Besides, whenever she wants to, she brings into play such a mixture of wit and character and acuteness, which is the height of good breeding . . . As it's hard to do two things at once, the marquis replied to Mathilde with a vacant expression, like a man reciting a lesson:

—Ah, yes, poor Altamira, who doesn't know him? And he told her the story of his conspiracy and how it had failed ridiculously, absurdly.

—Absurd indeed! said Mathilde, as if talking to herself, but he *did* something. I should like to see a man; bring me to him, she said to the marquis, who was deeply shocked.

Comte Altamira was one of the declared admirers of Mlle. de La Mole's lofty and almost impudent manner; according to him, she was one of the loveliest women in Paris.

—How beautiful she would be on a throne! he said to M. Croisenois; and let himself be brought into her presence without difficulty.

Society includes plenty of people who are eager to establish that the most ill-bred thing in the world is a conspiracy; it smells of Jacobins. And what is more disagreeable than a failed Jacobin?

Mathilde's glance mocked the liberalism of Altamira with a glance at M. de Croisenois, but she listened to him with pleasure.

A conspirator at a ball makes a pretty contrast, she thought. She thought that this one, with his black moustaches, resembled the features of the lion in repose; but she quickly noted that his mind had but one consideration: *utility, admiration for the useful.*

Except for those things which might give his country a bicameral legislature, the young count found nothing worthy of his attention. He departed from Mathilde with pleasure, and she was the most attractive woman at the ball, because he had seen a Peruvian general come in.

Having given up all hope of Europe [as M. Metternich has arranged if], poor Altamira was reduced to hoping that when the states of South America became strong and stable, they might be able to return to Europe the liberty that Mirabeau sent them.

A storm cloud of young persons with moustaches drew near Mathilde. She had clearly seen that Altamira was not attracted and felt piqued at his departure; she saw his eye sparkle as he talked to the Peruvian general. Mlle. de La Mole surveyed the young French-men before her with that deep seriousness which none of her rivals was ever able to copy. Which one of them, she thought, could get himself sentenced to death, even if he were granted the most favor-able opportunities?

Her extraordinary gaze flattered those of little perception, but disturbed the others. They feared the explosion of a wit to which it would be hard to render an answer.

Being well born gives a man a hundred qualities the absence of which would offend me: that I can see in Julien's case, thought Mathilde; but it dries up those qualities in a man's soul which might get him condemned to death.

At that moment, someone nearby said: That Comte Altamira is the second son of the Prince of San Nazaro-Pimentel; it was a Pi-mentel who tried to rescue Conradin, beheaded in 1268. They are among the noblest families of Naples.[9]

There we are, said Mathilde to herself, that bears out my theory beautifully: Good birth destroys the strength of character without which a man can never get himself condemned to death! I am fated to think nothing but nonsense this evening. Well, since I'm just a woman like any other, I suppose I'd better dance. She yielded to the beseechings of the Marquis de Croisenois, who for the last hour had been imploring a dance. To forget her failures in philosophy, Mathilde chose to be perfectly alluring; M. de Croisenois was in ecstasy.

But neither the dance nor her wish to please one of the hand-somest men of the court, nothing could distract Mathilde. Nobody could have had a greater success. She was the queen of the ball; she realized it, but coldly.

What a wasted life I shall pass with a creature like Croisenois! she told herself, as he led her from the floor an hour later. . . . What can pleasure be for me, she added gloomily, if I can't find it, after a six months' absence, in a ball where I'm the envy of every woman in Paris? Here I am the center of admiration in a company that couldn't possibly be more elegant. There isn't a bourgeois in the assembly except perhaps for a couple of peers and one or two people like Julien. And so, she added with deepening melancholy, fate has given me all the advantages: rank, wealth, youth, every-thing, alas! except happiness.

My most dubious advantages are those that people have been telling me about all evening. Wit I suppose I have, for they're obvi-ously all afraid of me. If they dare to start a serious discussion, af-

9. The history is authentic: its purpose is to suggest that the tragedy of Boniface de La Mole has been many times enacted, throughout Europe, from remote antiquity onward.

ter five minutes' talk they arrive, puffing and breathless, as if they were making some great discovery, at something I've been saying for the last hour. I am beautiful, I have that advantage for which Mme. de Staël would have sacrificed all the others, and yet the fact is I'm dying of boredom. Is there any reason why I should be less bored when I have changed my name for that of the Marquis de Croisenois?

But, my God! she added, close to tears, isn't he the perfect man? He's the masterpiece of modern education; you can't so much as look at him without his finding something pleasant, and maybe even witty, to say; he is brave. . . . But that Sorel is an odd one, she said to herself, and her look of gloom was replaced by one of anger. I told him I had something to tell him, and he did not even bother to come back!

Chapter 9

THE BALL

The luxury of formal dresses, the glitter of candles, perfumes: so many pretty arms and lovely shoulders: bouquets, lively airs by Rossini, painting by Ciceri! My head's in a whirl!

—Uzeri's *Travels*[1]

—You are cross tonight, said the Marquise de La Mole; let me warn you, that's not the way to act at a ball.

—I just have a headache, replied Mathilde scornfully, it's too hot in here.

At that very moment, as if to confirm Mlle. de La Mole, old Baron de Tolly grew faint and slipped to the floor; he had to be carried out. There was talk of apoplexy; it was a disagreeable moment.

Mathilde paid no attention. It was one of her traits never to pay attention to old men or people who spoke on gloomy topics.

She danced to get away from the discussions of apoplexy, though indeed it wasn't really such, for a few days later the baron turned up again.

But M. Sorel is not coming back, she said to herself again when the dance was over. She was just casting about for him when she caught sight of him in another room. And what was astonishing, he seemed to have lost that tone of icy calm that was so natural to him; he no longer acted like an Englishman.

He's talking with Comte Altamira, my man with the death sen-

1. Perhaps Stendhal had in mind the *Schweizer-Reise*, a collection of songs of folk inspiration by the Zurich composer J. M. Usteri (1763–1827), but the sentiments of this epigraph are more Stendhal than Zurich.

tence, thought Mathilde. His glance is dark and angry; he acts like a prince in disguise; he looks more arrogant than ever.

Julien moved toward the place where she stood, still deep in talk with Altamira; she looked steadily at him, studying his features as if to discover somewhere among them those lofty qualities that can earn a man the honor of a death sentence.

As he was passing close to her:

—Yes, he said to Comte Altamira, Danton was really a man!

Good Lord, is he going to be another Danton, said Mathilde to herself; but he has a noble expression, and that Danton was to horribly ugly, I suppose he was a butcher.[2] Julien was still so close to her that she did not hesitate to call out to him; she was aware of, and proud of, asking an extraordinary question for a girl.

—Wasn't Danton a butcher? she asked him.

—Yes, certain people thought so, Julien replied with an expression of ill-concealed contempt, his eyes still ablaze from his conversation with Altamira; but, unhappily for these noble gentry, he was a lawyer at Méry-sur-Seine; which is to say, Mademoiselle, he added in a biting tone, he began life very much like several of the peers whom I see here. It is true that Danton had one immense disadvantage as far as the fair sex is concerned, he was extremely ugly.

These last words were said quickly, with an extraordinary air that was certainly far from courteous.

Julien waited a moment, his shoulders slightly forward, in an attitude of arrogant humility. He seemed to be saying: I am paid to answer your questions, and I live on my pay. He did not deign to look Mathilde in the eye. She, with her beautiful eyes opened extremely wide and fixed on his face, had the air of being his slave. At last, as the silence drew out, he looked toward her, as a servant looks toward his master to get orders from him. Although his eyes directly encountered those of Mathilde, still fixed on him with that strange expression, he turned away with a striking suddenness.

For him, who is really so handsome, to pay such tributes to ugliness! thought Mathilde, coming out of her reverie. And never a reflection on himself! He is not like Caylus or Croisenois. This Sorel has something of the look my father assumes when he acts out so impressively the role of Napoleon at a ball. She had quite forgotten Danton. No question about it, I'm bored this evening. She seized her brother's arm, and, much to his disgust, forced him to stroll with her through all the rooms. She wanted to follow that conver-

---

2. Georges-Jacques Danton (1759–1794) was the audacious and agile Jacobin chiefly responsible for the defense of the Revolution during its first years. He did indeed have heavy, almost brutal, features.

sation of Julien's with the man who had been condemned to death.

The crowd was immense. But she succeeded in overtaking them just as Altamira, standing a few feet away from her, had turned toward a tray to take an ice. He was talking to Julien and half turned toward him, when he noted an arm in a braided coat stretched forth beside his to take another ice. The gold braid seemed to attract his particular notice; he turned completely about to see whose arm it was. At once his dark eyes, lofty and direct, took on a veiled expression of disdain.

—You see that man, he said in an undertone to Julien; he is the Prince of Araceli, ambassador from_____.[3] This morning he made an application for my extradition to your French foreign minister, M. de Nerval. Look, there he is over there, playing whist. M. de Nerval is rather inclined to honor the request, since my country turned back to you two or three conspirators in 1816. If I am put in the power of my king, I'll be hanged within twenty-four hours. And it will be one of these pretty gentlemen with moustaches here who will *get his hands on me.*

—The villains! Julien exclaimed, in a low voice.

Mathilde did not miss a syllable of their talk. Her boredom had disappeared.

—Not such villains, replied Comte Altamira. I spoke of my own case only to make the picture clear. Watch the Prince of Araceli; every five minutes he glances down at his Order of the Golden Fleece; he's never really recovered from the pleasure of seeing that knicknack on his chest. At bottom the poor man is nothing but an anachronism. A hundred years ago the Fleece was a distinguished decoration, but at that time it would have been far out of his reach. Today, so far as well-bred people are concerned, you have to be an Araccli to be excited by it. He would have hanged a whole city to obtain it.

—Was that the price he paid for it? Julien asked anxiously.

—Not exactly, Altamira answered coolly; he perhaps had some thirty rich landowners of his district, who were alleged to be liberals, flung into the river.

—What a monster! said Julien again.

Mlle. de La Mole, leaning forward with the keenest concern, was so close to him that her beautiful hair almost fell across his shoulder.

—You are very young! replied Altamira. I told you that I had a married sister in Provence; she is still pretty, good, gentle, she is an excellent mother to her children, a person responsible in every way, pious but not bigoted.

---

3. Araceli is the name of the church to the Virgin that stands atop the Roman capitol, but the circumstances of Altamira's nationality are here left ambiguous.

What's this about? thought Mlle. de La Mole.

—She is happy, Comte Altamira went on, and she was happy in 1815. I was in hiding at that time, in her house near Antibes; well, when she learned of Marshal Ney's execution, she began to dance!

—Impossible! said Julien, horrified.

—It is the spirit of faction, replied Altamira. Genuine passion doesn't exist anymore in the nineteenth century; that's why everyone is so bored in France. People perform the cruelest actions but without cruelty.

—So much the worse! said Julien; the least one can do, when committing a crime, is to enjoy it; that's the only good thing about crimes, and the only thing that even partially justifies them.

Mlle. de La Mole, quite forgetful of her dignity, had placed herself almost directly between Altamira and Julien. Her brother, whose arm she still held, being accustomed to obey her, stood looking around the room, and to keep himself in countenance pretended that he had been held up by the press of the crowd.

—You are right, said Altamira; we do everything without pleasure and then we forget about it, even when it's criminal. I can show you at this very ball perhaps ten men who will be known as murderers. They have forgotten it, and so has everyone else.[4]

A good many of these people are moved to tears if their dog hurts his paw. At Père-Lachaise, when their tombs are being decked with flowers as you say so merrily in Paris, someone declares that they united in their persons all the virtues of all the knights of old, and we hear stories about the great things done by one of their ancestors who lived under Henri IV. If, despite the good offices of the Prince of Araceli, I don't go to the gallows, and if I ever come to the enjoyment of my fortune in Paris, I will invite you to dinner with eight or ten assassins, all in high public esteem, and all without remorse.

You and I will be the only ones at that dinner without blood on our hands, but I will be despised and almost hated, as a bloody Jacobin monster, and you will merely be despised as a plebeian who has pushed his way into good company.

—Nothing could be more true, said Mlle. de La Mole.

Altamira looked at her in amazement; Julien did not deign to look at her at all.

—You recall that the revolution I found myself heading up, Comte Altamira continued, failed simply because I refused to cut off three heads and distribute to our followers seven or eight millions which were kept in a safe to which I had the key. My king, who today is all eagerness to have me hanged, and who before the

_____

4. "It is a malcontent who says this": Molière's note to *Tartufe* [Stendhal's note].

revolution was my intimate friend, would have given me the grand cordon of his order if I had cut off those three heads and handed out the money in those safes; for I would have been half-successful anyhow, and my country would have had a constitution of sorts. . . . But that's how the world goes, it's like a game of chess.

—But at that time, Julien said, his eyes ablaze, you didn't know the game; nowadays. . . .

—I would cut off the heads, you mean to say, and I should not be a Girondin,[5] as you gave me to understand the other day? . . . I will give you an answer, said Altamira with a gloomy air, on the day when you've killed a man in a duel; and yet that's a good deal less ugly than having him butchered by an executioner.

—My word! said Julien, if you want the end you accept the means; if, instead of being an atom, I had a little power, I would have three men hanged to save the lives of four.

His eyes gave expression to the fire of an aroused conscience, and scorn for the vapid judgments of society; they met those of Mlle. de La Mole, by his side, and this scorn, far from altering to anything gracious and civil, seemed to grow fiercer.

She was profoundly shocked; but it was no longer in her power to forget Julien; she moved scornfully away, taking her brother with her.

I must take some punch and dance a lot, she told herself; I want to take the best there is, and create an effect at all costs. Good, here is that notorious insolent fellow, the Comte de Fervaques. She accepted his invitation; they danced together. What's to be settled now, she thought to herself, is which of us will be more insolent; but, in order to cut him down properly, I'll have to make him talk. Before long, what was left of the dance was a mere formality. Nobody wanted to miss any of Mathilde's stinging repartees. M. de Fervaques grew uneasy, and, being unable to find anything but elegant phrases instead of ideas, began to sulk; Mathilde, who was in an ill humor, dealt savagely with him, and made an enemy of him. She danced till dawn, and went home at last, in a horrible state of exhaustion. But in her carriage the little energy she retained was still devoted to making her gloomy and wretched. She had been despised by Julien, and could not scorn him in return.

Julien was supremely happy. Delighted, without being fully aware of it, by the music, the flowers, the beautiful women, the general elegance, and above all by his imagination, he dreamed of distinctions for himself and liberty for everyone.

---

5. The Girondins represented the liberal, theoretical, idealistic wing of the revolution—originally radical but later pushed into a conservative posture, and finally crushed by the "Montagne." They included heroic but relatively ineffectual figures like Buzot, Petiot, and the Rolands.

—What a fine ball! said he to the count, it lacks nothing.

—It lacks thought, said Altamira.

And his features expressed that contempt which is all the more stinging because one can see that politeness is making an effort to conceal it.

—You are here, Monsieur le comte. And what's more, your thoughts are on a conspiracy.

—I am here because of my name. But your drawing rooms hate thinking people. Thought should never get beyond the stage of a vaudeville joke: at that stage it's rewarded. But a man who thinks, if he has energy or originality in his remarks, is quickly called a *cynic*. Isn't that the name that one of your judges bestowed upon Courier?[6] You put him in prison, and Béranger as well. Anything of intellectual value, among you, is denounced by the congregation to the criminal division of the police bureau. And good society applauds.

The truth is, your senile society values conformity above everything else. . . . You will never get beyond the stage of military bravery; you'll have Murats but never any Washingtons.[7] I see nothing in France but vanity. A man who talks spontaneously as he thinks falls easily into a bold sally, and the master of the house feels disgraced.

At these words, the count's carriage, which was bringing Julien home, stopped before the Hôtel de La Mole. Julien was in love with his conspirator. Altamira had made him a fine compliment, evidently the fruit of deep conviction: You don't have the French frivolity, you understand the principle of *utility*. It happened that just two nights ago Julien had seen the tragedy of *Marino Faliero* by M. Casimir Delavigne.[8]

Isn't it true that Israel Bertuccio [, a mere carpenter in the arsenal,] had more character than all those Venetian noblemen? Our resentful plebeian asked himself; and yet those nobles could prove their pedigrees back to the year 700, a century before Charlemagne, while the most authentic aristocrats at M. de Retz's ball tonight can't trace their bloodlines back, by hook or by crook, any further than the thirteenth century. Well, among all those noblemen of Venice, whose greatness came only from their birth, [but

6. Paul-Louis Courier (1773–1825), a personal friend of Stendhal's, was a bitter opponent of the nobility and the reaction until his murder in 1825. Because he was a Hellenist, and rejoiced in the exercise of a mordant wit, a judge ventured to call him a *cynic* in Greek, in which the word "dog" is more apparent than in French or English; Courier responded ferociously.
7. The contrast between Murat and Washington is between a fierce soldier and a steady, thoughtful patriot.
8. Casimir Delavigne's *Marino Faliero* was first presented in 1829; it created a stir by disregarding classic rules. Israel Bertuccio was the major actor in a plot to murder the Venetian aristocracy and proclaim Faliero prince of Venice.

whose characters were so faded and washy,] it is only Israel Bertuccio who is remembered.

A conspiracy cancels all the titles given by society's caprice. There a man takes immediately the rank which he earns by his manner of facing death. Even intelligence loses its authority. . . .

What would Danton be today, in this century of Valenods and Rênals? Not even a second-string royal prosecutor. . . .

What am I saying? He would have sold out to the congregation; he would be a minister, for after all even the great Danton was a robber. Mirabeau sold out too. Napoleon stole his millions in Italy, without which he would have been cut short by poverty, like Pichegru.[9] Only Lafayette was never a thief. Do you have to steal, do you have to sell out? Julien wondered. This question drew him up short. He spent the rest of the night reading the history of the Revolution.

Next day, as he worked over his letters in the library, he thought of nothing but his conversation with Comte Altamira.

So, in fact, he concluded after a long reverie, if the Spanish liberals[1] had compromised the people by a few crimes, they would not have been wiped out so easily. They were high-minded, babbling children . . . like me! Julien suddenly exclaimed, as if waking from sleep with a start.

What difficult thing have I done which entitles me to pass judgment on some poor devils, who did, after all, for once in their lives, take action, and with daring? I'm like a man who rises from the table and exclaims: Tomorrow I shall eat no dinner; but that will not prevent me from being just as lively and vigorous as I am today. Who knows what people feel in the midst of a great action? [For after all, these things are not done in an instant, as one fires a pistol.] . . . These lofty thoughts were interrupted by the unexpected arrival of Mlle. de La Mole, who came into the library. He was so aroused by his admiration for the great qualities of Danton, Mirabeau, Carnot, who never knew when they were beaten, that though his glance rested on Mlle. de La Mole, it was without thinking of her, without greeting her, almost without seeing her. When at length his great staring eyes took note of her presence, the light died in them. Mlle. de La Mole noted the fact with bitterness.

In vain did she ask him for a volume of Vély's *History of France* which stood on the highest shelf and thus obliged Julien to fetch the

---

9. Charles Pichegru (1761–1804) was a magnificent general for the French revolutionary armies until he sold out to the Bourbons in 1795.
1. The Spanish liberals enjoyed a brief period of disorderly and divided power from 1820 to 1823; it is part of Stendhal's understated casualness about politics that Altamira (who is identified only casually and in afterthought as a Spaniard) is shown associating in a drawing room with Norbert de La Mole, whose service in the Spanish campaigns must have been devoted to crushing liberals of all persuasions.

longer of the two ladders. Julien carried in the ladder, sought out the book, and handed it to her, still without being able to think of her. As he carried the ladder away, in his haste he elbowed against one of the glass panes covering the shelves; a clatter of fragments on the floor finally awakened him. He hastened to make his apologies to Mlle. de La Mole; he tried to be polite, but he was polite and nothing more. Mathilde saw clearly that she had disturbed him, that rather than talk to her, he would have preferred to think of the topic which was occupying him when she came in. After a long, long look at him, she slowly walked away. Julien watched her as she went. He was pleased at the contrast between her present simple attire and the splendid luxuriance of the previous night. The difference in her expressions was almost as striking. This girl, who had been so haughty at the Duc de Retz's ball, had now almost the look of a suppliant. Really, Julien thought, that black dress shows off the beauty of her figure better than ever; but why is she in mourning?

If I ask anyone the reason for this mourning, it will turn out that I'm making a fool of myself again. Julien had quite recovered from his flights of enthusiasm. I must read over all the letters I've written this morning; Lord knows what sorts of blunders and oversights I'll find in them. As he was reading with fixed concentration the first of these letters, he heard close beside him the rustle of a silk dress; he looked up sharply; Mlle. de La Mole was two steps from his table and smiling. This second interruption angered Julien.

As for Mathilde, she had just been made to feel painfully that she counted for nothing in this young man's life; the smile was intended to mask her embarrassment, and it succeeded.

—Apparently you're thinking of something very interesting, M. Sorel. Isn't it some curious anecdote about the conspiracy which brought Comte Altamira here to Paris? Tell me what it's about; I'm dying to know; I can keep it quiet, I swear! She was astonished by this sentence, even as she heard herself say it. So now she was begging from a subordinate! As her embarrassment increased, she added, in an attempt at lightness:

—What could turn you, who are usually so chilly, into an inspired creature, a kind of Michelangelo prophet?

This direct and impertinent questioning cut Julien to the quick, and revived all his folly.

—Did Danton do right to steal? he said to her harshly, and in a manner that became more and more wild. The revolutionaries of Piedmont and in Spain, should they have compromised the people by committing crimes? Distributed, even to worthless people, all the posts in the army, all the decorations? Wouldn't the men who got these decorations have had a reason to fear the restoration of the king? Was it necessary to pillage the treasury at Turin? In short, mademoiselle, he said, approaching her with a terrible air, shouldn't a man who wants to drive ignorance and crime from the earth pass through it like a whirlwind and do evil blindly?

Mathilde was afraid; she could not sustain his gaze, and stepped back instinctively. For a moment she looked at him; then, ashamed of her fear, turned and left the library with a light step.

Chapter 10

QUEEN MARGUERITE

> Love! What act of folly is, there in which you cannot make us take pleasure?
>
> —*Letters of a Portuguese Nun*[2]

Julien read over his letters. When the bell sounded for dinner: What a fool I must have seemed in the eyes of that Paris doll he told himself; what idiocy to tell her what I was really thinking! And yet maybe not idiocy at all. On this occasion the truth was worthy of me.

Besides, why should she come around questioning me on my private beliefs? The questioning was rude on her side. It was a piece of ill breeding. My thoughts on Danton are no part of the service for which her father is paying me.

As he entered the dining room, Julien was distracted from his broody thoughts by the deep mourning worn by Mlle. de La Mole; it was the more striking since no other member of the family was in black.

After dinner he found himself quite relieved of the transports of enthusiasm that had obsessed him all day. By good fortune the academician who knew Latin was at the dinner party. There is the man who will sneer at me less than anyone else if, as I suppose, my question about Mlle. de La Mole's mourning is a piece of stupidity.

Mathilde was looking at him with an odd expression. That's playing the coquette as women in this part of the world do it, Julien thought; it's just as Mme. de Rênal described it for me. I wasn't agreeable to her this morning; I didn't indulge her little whim for conversation. So now she thinks better of me. And no doubt the devil keeps a finger in the pot. Later, her arrogance and pride will find a way to get back at me. Let her do her worst. What a difference from the woman I have lost! What natural charm there! What simplicity! I knew her thoughts before she did herself; I saw them forming in her mind; within her heart my only opponent was her fear that her children might die; it was a sensible and natural affec-

---

2. The title is that of an epistolary novel by Diderot, but the sentiment is a universal platitude.

tion, such that even I, who suffered from it, found it admirable. I've been a fool. My imaginings about Paris prevented me from appreciating that glorious woman.

What a difference, good God! And what do I find here? Vanity, dry and arrogant, every conceivable variety of self-approval, and nothing else.

They rose from the table. I can't let my academician get away, said Julien. As they strolled into the garden, he intercepted him, put on a meek, docile air, and sympathized with his fury against the success of *Hernani*.[3]

—If we still lived in the days when a *lettre de cachet*[4] was possible! . . . he said.

—Then, he would never have had the audacity! cried the academician, with a gesture worthy of Talma.[5]

While they were discussing a flower, Julien quoted several phrases from Virgil's *Georgics* and declared his opinion that Abbé Delille's poetry was unsurpassed.[6] In a word, he flattered the academician to the top of his bent. After which, putting on an air of complete indifference:

—I suppose, he said, that Mlle. de La Mole has received a legacy from some uncle and is in mourning for him.

—Good heavens! said the academician, you're in the household and you don't know about her mania? Really, it's very strange that her mother allows such goings on; but, just between us two, strength of character isn't their long suit around this house. Mlle. Mathilde has enough character for everyone, and manages them all. Today is April 30th! And the academician paused, looking at Julien with a knowing smile. In response, Julien put on the most intelligent smile he could manage.

What sort of connection can there be between managing the rest of the family, wearing a black dress, and the 30th of April? he asked himself. I must be even stupider than I thought.

—I must confess . . . he said to the academician, and his eye continued to question him.

—Let's take a turn around the garden, said the academician, delighted at seeing an opening for a long and elaborate lecture. Tell me now, is it really possible that you don't know what happened on the 30th of April, 1574?

3. Victor Hugo's *Hernani* was produced on February 25, 1830, amid stormy scenes of protest and counterprotest. It constituted a manifesto of the romantic party in France, to which the academician is, naturally, violently hostile.
4. *Lettre de cachet:* under the old regime, a letter that could be procured from the king ordering some particular person or persons to prison without trial.
5. F. J. Talma (1763–1826) was the foremost tragic actor of his day.
6. Abbé Delille: see p. 151, note 3. He was a most innocuous and insipid poetaster of the late eighteenth century, best known for a translation of Virgil's *Georgics*.

—Where? Julien asked in astonishment.

—On the Place de Grève.

Julien was so astonished that even now he failed to understand. His curiosity, and the expectation of a tragic tale, gave his eyes that brightness which a storyteller so much loves to see in his listener. The academician, overjoyed to discover a virgin ear, recounted at length to Julien the story of how, on the 30th of April, 1574, the handsomest young fellow of his day, Boniface de La Mole, and Annibal de Coconasso, a gentleman of the Piedmont who was his friend, had been beheaded on the Place de Grève.[7] La Mole was the adored lover of Queen Marguerite of Navarre; and you must note, added the academician, that Mlle. de La Mole is named *Mathilde-Marguerite*. La Mole was both the favorite of the Duc d'Alençon and the close friend of the King of Navarre, later Henri IV, his mistress's husband. It was on Shrove Tuesday of this year 1574; the court was at Saint-Germain around poor King Charles IX, who lay at the very point of death. La Mole wanted to rescue the princes his friends, whom Queen Catherine de Medici was keeping as prisoners at the court. He brought two hundred horsemen directly under the walls of Saint-Germain, the Duc d'Alençon took fright, and La Mole went to the block.

But what appeals to Mlle. Mathilde, as she told me herself seven or eight years ago when she was only twelve, for she has a head on her shoulders, such a head! . . . and the academician rolled his eyes to heaven. What really impressed her in this political tragedy was that Queen Marguerite of Navarre, who had concealed herself in a house on the Place de Grève, had the audacity to ask the executioner for her lover's head. And the following night, at the stroke of twelve, she took that head in her carriage and went to bury it with her own hands in a chapel standing at the foot of the hill of Montmartre.

—Is it possible? Julien exclaimed, enthralled.

—Mlle. Mathilde despises her brother because, as you can see, he pays no attention to any of this ancient history, and never wears mourning on April 30th. And ever since this famous execution, and in order to memorialize the close friendship of La Mole for Coconasso, and because Coconasso, like the Italian he was, had the name of Annibal, all the men in the family have that name. And what's more, added the academician, lowering his voice, this Coconasso was, on the say-so of Charles IX himself, one of the most

7. In fact, Joseph de Boniface (c. 1526–1574) seigneur de La Mole, and Annibal Coconasso did lead an insurrectionary movement and were executed in the Place de Grève on April 30, 1574. It is a curious element in Stendhal's intricate weaving of the sixteenth century with the nineteenth that the early history is generally factual, the nineteenth-century action largely imaginary.

brutal murderers of August 24, 1572.[8] But how can it be, my dear
Sorel, that you, who are a regular resident of the house, haven't
been told these things?

—Then that's the reason why Mlle. de La Mole, at dinner this
evening, twice addressed her brother as Annibal. I thought I hadn't
heard right.

—It was a reproach. Strange that the marquise puts up with
these follies. . . . That great girl's husband is going to have his
hands full!

This expression was followed by five or six satiric observations.
The malignant pleasure that glittered in the academician's eyes
shocked Julien. Here we are like a couple of servants busy slandering their masters, he thought. But nothing ought to surprise me
that comes from this academic gentleman.

One day Julien had surprised him on his knees before the Marquise de La Mole; he was begging a post in the tobacco monopoly
for a nephew he had somewhere in the provinces. That evening a
little maid of Mlle. de La Mole's, who was making advances to
Julien as Elisa had done before, reassured him that her mistress's
mourning was by no means a trick for attracting attention. She really loved this La Mole, adored lover of the wittiest queen of her
century, who had died in an effort to set his friends at liberty. And
what friends they were! The first prince of the blood, and Henri IV.

Accustomed as he was to the perfect naturalness that shone
through all the conduct of Mme. de Rênal, Julien saw nothing but
affectation in all the women of Paris, and when he was even slightly
touched with melancholy, he found nothing to say to them. Mlle.
de La Mole was an exception.

Gradually he ceased to assume that hardness of heart underlay
that sort of beauty which accompanies a noble demeanor. He had
long conversations with Mlle. de La Mole, who sometimes after
dinner used to stroll with him in the garden [when the spring
weather was fine,] past the open windows of the drawing room. She
told him one day that she was reading d'Aubigné's history, and
Brantôme.[9] Quite a reading list, thought Julien; and her mother
won't even allow her the novels of Walter Scott!

One day she told him, with that gleam of pleasure in her eyes
which betokens sincere admiration, about the behavior of a young
woman during Henri III's reign, about whom she had just been

8. On this date, St. Bartholomew's day, Catherine de Medici (1519–1589) instigated her
   son Charles IX to order the massacre of Huguenots throughout France.
9. D'Aubigné and Brantôme: The former (1550–1630) was a historian, the latter
   (1527–1614) a storyteller of the heroic age. Both are extraordinarily frank and outspoken and both serve as authorities for the story that Boniface de La Mole was the lover of
   Marguerite of Navarre.

reading in the *Mémoires* of l'Etoile:[1] finding that her husband was unfaithful, she stabbed him.

Julien's self-esteem was flattered. A person surrounded with so much deference, and who according to the academician ran the whole house, condescended to talk with him on terms that might well resemble those of friendship.

But then he thought, No, I was mistaken; this isn't friendship; I am only an audience for a tragedy she wants to recite, it all rises from her need to talk. I pass in this family as a man of learning. So I shall go read Brantôme, d'Aubigné, l'Etoile. Then I can match some of the stories Mlle. de La Mole tells me. For I've got to get out of this role of the passive listener.

Gradually his conversations with this girl whose bearing was so impressive and at the same time so casual became more interesting. He forgot to play the depressing part of a resentful plebeian. He found her to be learned and even rational. Her judgments in the garden were quite different from those she expressed in the drawing room. Sometimes she showed in his company an enthusiasm and a frankness that were completely at variance with her usual manner, so haughty and cold.

—The wars of the League[2] were the heroic days of France, she told him one day, her eyes sparkling with delighted enthusiasm. In those days a man fought to obtain something specific he wanted, in order to make his party victorious, not just to get a foolish decoration, as in the days of your emperor. You must agree, there was less self-glorification and pettiness then. I love that century.

—And Boniface de La Mole was the hero of the age, said he.

—At any rate he was loved as, very likely, it's a pleasure to be loved. What woman alive today would not be too horrified to touch the head of her decapitated lover?

Mme. de La Mole called her daughter. To be effective, hypocrisy must conceal itself; and Julien, as we have seen, had half-admitted to Mlle. de La Mole his admiration for Napoleon.

That's the main advantage they have over us, thought Julien, left alone in the garden. The history of their ancestors raises them far above vulgar feelings, and they aren't required to be always thinking about making a living! What wretchedness! he added bitterly; I'm not even in a position to think about the real interests of life. [I'd probably judge falsely of them, anyhow.] My life is nothing but a

---

1. Pierre de l'Etoile (1546–1611) was a Parisian bourgeois who kept an immensely detailed diary for many years not unlike Samuel Pepys's.
2. The League was a confederation of French Catholics toward the end of the sixteenth century. Henri IV had to fight and bargain with them to gain his throne and access to Paris.

long train of hypocrisies because I don't have a thousand francs' income to buy my bread.

—What are you thinking of, sir? Mathilde asked him. [There was a note of intimacy in her voice and she was out of breath from running to rejoin him.]

Julien was weary of his own self-contempt. Out of pride, he told her frankly what he was thinking. He blushed deeply at talking of his poverty to a person who was so rich. He tried to make very clear, by his proud tone, that he was not asking for anything. Never had he seemed to handsome to Mathilde; she saw in his face an expression of sensitivity and of frankness which he often lacked.

Less than a month later, Julien was strolling thoughtfully through the garden of the Hôtel de La Mole; but his face no longer had the hard, philosophical arrogance that had been printed on it by his continual sense of his own inferiority. He had just escorted back to the door of the drawing room Mlle. de La Mole, who pretended to have hurt her foot while running with her brother.

She hung on my arm in the strangest way! Julien thought. Am I a complete fool, or does she have some liking for me? She listens to me so gently, even when I talk to her of all the sufferings of my pride! She, who takes such a lofty tone with everybody else! They would be really surprised in the drawing room if they saw her put on that expression. It's perfectly clear, she takes this gentle, friendly way with nobody else.

Julien made some effort not to exaggerate this odd friendship. In his own mind he compared it to an armed truce. Every day when they saw one another, before resuming the old intimate tone of the day before, they almost asked one another: Well, shall we be friends or enemies today? [The first sentences they exchanged counted for nothing as far as content was concerned. On both sides they were concerned with nothing but the forms.] Julien had understood that to let himself be offended by this arrogant girl just once without retaliation was to forfeit everything. If I have to quarrel with her, isn't it better to do so from the first, in defense of my own legitimate pride, rather than in resenting the various marks of scorn that would certainly follow my first surrender of any part of my personal dignity?

Several times, when she was in a bad humor, Mathilde tried to assume with him the position of the great lady; she employed all her diplomacy in these ventures, but Julien repelled them coarsely.

One day he interrupted her suddenly: Has Mlle. de La Mole any instructions to give her father's secretary? he said to her. He is bound to hear her orders and carry them out respectfully; apart from that, he has not one single word to say to her. He is not paid to communicate his thoughts to her.

This state of affairs, and the singular doubts that Julien was fostering, dispelled the boredom which [during the first months] he had always felt in that grandiose drawing room where people were afraid of everything and where it was not respectable to joke about anything.

not really interested

~~It would be amusing if she fell in love with me~~. Whether she loves me or not, Julien went on, I have as my intimate confidant a girl of intelligence, before whom I can see that the whole household is afraid, and more than anybody else, the Marquis de Croisenois. That young man who is so polite, so gentle, so brave, and has all the advantages of birth and fortune, just one of which would quickly set my heart at ease! He's madly in love with her, [that is, so far as such a thing is possible for a Parisian,] and they're to be married. Think of all the letters M. de La Mole has had me write to the two lawyers who are drawing up the contract! And I, who every morning act out the part of a subordinate, with my pen in my hand, two hours later, here in the garden, I triumph over that exceedingly agreeable young man; for in fact her preference is striking, unmistakable. Perhaps she feels hatred for him as a future husband. She is arrogant enough for that. Then her kindness for me is on the basis of my being a confidential servant.

But no, either I am mad or she is making love to me; the more chilly and respectful I show myself toward her, the more she seeks me out. That might be a policy of hers, or an affectation; but I see her eyes light up when I appear unexpectedly. Are Paris women capable of that degree of deceit? Why should I care! Appearances are on my side; let's make what we can of appearances. My God, how beautiful she is! How fond I am of her big blue eyes, when they come close and look up at me as they often do! What a difference between this spring and last year's, when I was living in misery and keeping alive by sheer determination, in the midst of three hundred dirty, hateful hypocrites! I was almost as evil-minded as they were.

On days of black misgivings, Julien used to think: This girl is playing a game with me. She has a scheme with her brother to pull the wool over my eyes. But then she seems to despise her brother's lack of energy so heartily. He is brave, and that's it, she told me. [And even then, brave only when facing the swords of the Spaniards. In Paris everything frightens him, he sees everywhere a danger of being ridiculous.] He hasn't one thought that is bold enough to go against the fashion. It's always I who am obliged to come to his defense. A girl of nineteen! At that age can anyone devote every hour of the day to living up to the code of hypocrisy which one has laid down to follow?

On the other hand, when Mlle. de La Mole fixes her big blue

eyes on me with a certain strange expression, Comte Norbert always turns away. That's very suspicious; shouldn't he get angry that his sister gives special treatment to one of the *domestics* about the house? For that's the word I once heard the Duc de Chaulnes use about me. And as he remembered that, rage wiped out every other sentiment. Is it just a fondness for the old-fashioned terms in that idiotic duke?

In any case, she's pretty! Julien went on, with the glare of a tiger. I'll have her, then I'll leave, and woe to the man who tries to get in my way!

This idea became Julien's sole concern; he could no longer think of anything else. His days passed like hours.

Every time he tried to involve himself with some serious business, [his thoughts drifted off into a profound reverie,] he dropped everything, and came back to his sense only a quarter of an hour later, his heart throbbing [with ambition], his head in a whirl, and with this idea uppermost in his mind: Does she love me?

Chapter 11

A GIRL'S EMPIRE

I admire her beauty, but I fear her wit.
—*Mérimée*[3]

If Julien had spent as much time reflecting on events in the drawing room as he devoted to exaggerating Mathilde's beauty and waxing indignant against the natural arrogance of the family which she was forgetting for his sake, he might have understood the source of her power over everyone about her. As soon as anyone displeased Mlle. de La Mole, she was able to take her revenge with a sarcasm so deadly, so appropriate, so conventional in appearance, and so shrewdly aimed that the more one thought it over, the more deeply wounding it appeared. Over a period of time, such a phrase could become atrocious for the victim's self-esteem. As she valued not at all most of the things the rest of the family took seriously, they considered her cold and indifferent. Aristocratic drawing rooms are amusing to talk about in other social circles, but that's all. [Their complete vapidity, the interminable platitudes with which they encounter even hypocrisy, end by irking one with an excess of cloying sweetness.] Mere politeness counts for something only during the first days. That was Julien's experience; he was first

---

3. Prosper Mérimée (1803–1870), a French dramatist, historian, archaeologist, and short-story writer perhaps best known for his novella *Carmen*, the basis for Georges Bizet's opera of the same name.

enchanted, then appalled. Politeness, he told himself, is nothing but the absence of that anger which bad manners would create. Mathilde was often bored; perhaps she would have been bored anywhere. Then, sharpening an epigram became for her both a diversion and a real pleasure.

It was, no doubt, to have somewhat more amusing victims than her distinguished family, the academician, and the five or six other underlings who made up such a devoted following that she had encouraged the Marquis de Croisenois, the Comte de Caylus, and two or three other young men of the highest distinction. In her eyes they were nothing but new targets for epigrams.

With grief do we say it, for we are fond of Mathilde, but she had received letters from several of them, and had on occasion written replies. We hasten to declare that this character is a complete exception to the general rules and customs of the age. As a rule, lack of prudence is not a charge that can be leveled against the pupils of the noble Convent of the Sacred Heart.

One day the Marquis de Croisenois returned to Mathilde a moderately compromising letter she had written him the day before. He expected this token of supreme prudence would much advance his suit. But it was imprudence which Mathilde was aiming at in her letter writing. She loved to play with fire. For six weeks she refused to say a word to him.

She liked to get letters from young men; but in her opinion, they were all alike. It was always the same passion, as profound and melancholy as possible.

—They're always the same perfect gentle knights, ready to leave for Palestine, she told her cousin. Can you imagine anything more insipid? And this is the sort of letter I'm going to receive for the rest of my life! Letters like these must change about every twenty years, according to the trade that happens to be fashionable at the time. Maybe they were less colorless in the days of the Empire. Then all the young men in high society had done or seen actions in which there was something *really* great. My uncle, the Duc de N_____, was at Wagram.[4]

What brains do you need to hit somebody with a saber? And when anyone has done it, he always talks about it so much! said Mlle. de Sainte-Hérédité, Mathilde's cousin.

—Still, those stories are amusing. To have been in a *real* battle, a Napoleonic battle, where ten thousand soldiers were killed, that's proof of some courage. Exposure to danger livens the spirits, and

---

4. Near Vienna, Wagram was the scene of a smashing Napoleonic victory over the Austrians, July 5–6, 1809.

saves one from the bog of boredom in which all my poor admirers seem to be sunk; and their boredom is contagious. Which one of them has the wit to do anything out of the ordinary? They seek my hand in marriage—a big operation! I'm rich and my father will do something for his son-in-law. Ah, I only wish he could find me one who's a bit amusing!

Mathilde's way of seeing things, which was sharp, lively, and picturesque, had an unfortunate effect on her speech, as can be seen. Often an expression of hers seemed positively painful to her more polite friends. If she had been less the rage, they might even have admitted that her speech had about it something a little too highly colored for feminine delicacy.

She, on her part, was altogether unfair to the handsome horsemen who populate the Bois de Boulogne. She looked to the future, not with terror, that would be too strong a term, but with a disgust not often felt at her age.

What could she want? Fortune, noble birth, intelligence, beauty (as everyone kept telling her and as she believed herself) had been piled on her by the hand of fate.

Such were the thoughts of the most envied heiress of the Faubourg Saint-Germain when she began to take pleasure in strolling with Julien. She was astonished at his pride; she admired the cleverness of this young commoner. He'll know how to make himself a bishop like Abbé Maury,[5] she thought.

Before long the vigor, sincere and by no means feigned, with which our hero opposed various of her ideas intrigued her; she thought of him; she described to her friend the most minute details of their cnversations, and found that she could never succeed in representing them completely.

Suddenly an idea struck her: I must be in love, she said one day in a transport of incredible delight. I'm in love, I'm in love, it's clear! At my age, a girl who is young, beautiful, clever—where can she find sensations, if not in love? Whatever I do, I'll never feel anything like love for Croisenois, Caylus, or any of that lot. They're perfect, maybe too perfect; in a word, they bore me.

She reviewed in her mind all the descriptions of passion she had read in *Manon Lescaut*, the *Nouvelle Héloïse*, the *Letters of a Portuguese Nun*, and so on, and so forth. The only thing in question, naturally, was a grand passion; frivolous love was unworthy a girl of her age and station. She gave the name of love only to that heroic

---

5. Jean-Sifirein Maury (1746–1817) began life in a humble station, but through a combination of wit, bravery, eloquence, and ruthless ambition gained a cardinal's hat during the course of the Revolution.

sentiment that existed in France during the days of Henri III and
Bassompierre.[6] [Such a love as that never submitted basely before
obstacles, it was not life's diversion, but a force capable of changing
life altogether.] What a shame that I don't have a real court, like
that of Catherine de Medici or Louis XIII! I feel I could rise to the
heights of daring and nobility. What couldn't I accomplish with a
king who was also a man of feeling, like Louis XIII, at my feet! I
would lead him into the Vendée,[7] which is what Baron de Tolly is
always talking about, and from there he could regain his kingdom;
then, no need of a constitution . . . and Julien would be my agent.
In what way is he lacking? Only a reputation and a fortune. He
could make a name for himself and acquire a fortune.

Croisenois has everything, and for the rest of his life he will
never be anything but a duke, half-liberal, half-conservative, a creature of indecision, [of words not deeds,] always avoiding the extremes, and consequently *always falling into the second position*.

What splendid action can there be which is not *an extreme* at the
moment when one undertakes it? Only after it's accomplished does
it seem possible to people with ordinary minds. Yes, it's love with all
its wonders which must come to command my heart; I feel it in the
fire that stirs within me. Fate owed me this favor, lest all its gifts be
lavished on one person in vain. My new joys will be worthy of me.
Each of my days will not pass, a frigid imitation of the one before.
Already there is some splendor and boldness in my daring to love a
man placed so far beneath me on the social scale. Let's see: will he
continue to deserve me? At the first sign of weakness I find in him,
I'll leave him. A girl of my station, and with the chivalric temper
they say I have (it was her father's expression), shouldn't act the
fool.

Isn't that the role I'd play if I were in love with the Marquis de
Croisenois? I should have a new edition of my cousins' happiness,
which I despise so heartily. I already know in advance everything
that poor marquis is going to say to me, and everything I'll have to
say in reply. What sort of love is it that makes you yawn? I might as
well take up religion. I should have a contract to sign, like that of
my younger cousin, over which all the noble relatives would wax
sentimental, unless of course they should get angry over a clause
slipped into the contract at the last minute by the lawyer for the
other side.

6. François de Bassompierre (1579–1646) was a marshal and diplomat of France who confronted Richelieu and as a result spent a dozen years in jail. His *Mémoires* are of major
   historical and biographical interest.
7. The Vendée was the scene of a peasant counterrevolt (1793) against the Revolution and
   its accompanying wars. Centering in the west country and starting as a rural uprising,
   the revolt soon acquired enough aristocratic leadership and English support to require
   serious countermeasures.

Chapter 12

WILL HE BE A DANTON?

The need for excitement, that was the ruling passion of the
lovely Marguerite de Valois, my aunt, who shortly married the
king of Navarre, who reigns at present in France under the title of
Henri IV. The need to gamble was a fundamental impulse of this
pleasant princess; hence her quarrels and reconciliations with her
brothers, which continued from the age of sixteen. But what has a
girl got to gamble with? The most precious thing she owns: her
reputation, the thing she must think about all her life long.
—*Mémoires* of the Duc d'Angoulême, natural son of Charles IX

Between Julien and me there is no contract to be signed, no
lawyer [to arrange a settlement], everything is heroic, everything
is up to the free play of chance. Apart from nobility, which he
does not have, it is the love of Marguerite de Valois for young La
Mole, the most distinguished man of his day. Is it my fault if the
young people around the court today are so devoted to the *conventional*, and pale at the mere idea of a very minor adventure the
least bit out of the ordinary? A short trip to Greece or Africa is for
them the height of audacity, and even then they'll go only in a
crowd. As soon as they see they stand alone, they become afraid,
not of the Bedouin's lance, but of ridicule, and that fear drives
them wild.

My little Julien, on the other hand, much prefers to act alone.
Never, in this favored being, the slightest idea of seeking support
and help from other people! He despises other people, and that is
why I don't despise him.

If Julien, though still poor, happened to be noble, my love would
be nothing but a bit of vulgar stupidity, a fool's mistake; I should
not like that; it would have none of the qualities of a grand passion:
an immense difficulty to be surmounted, and the black uncertainty
of the outcome.

Mlle. de La Mole was so taken up with these fine reflections that
the next day, without being aware of what she was doing, she began
extolling Julien to the Marquis de Croisenois and to her brother.

—Better be careful of this young fellow who has so much energy,
exclaimed her brother; if the Revolution begins again, he'll have us
all guillotined.

She took care not to answer back, and began to tease her brother
and the Marquis de Croisenois about their fear of energy. At bottom, it was nothing but fear of the unexpected, fear of being caught
unprepared by something unforeseen. . . .

—Always and always, gentlemen, the same fear of ridicule, a
monster that, unfortunately, perished in 1816.

Nothing is ridiculous, M. de La Mole used to say, in a country where there are two parties.

His daughter had picked up this idea.

—And so, gentlemen, she told Julien's enemies, you will have been frightened all your lives, and later someone will tell you:

It wasn't a wolf at all, it was only his shadow.[8]

Mathilde soon left them. What her brother had said filled her with horror; she was much disturbed by it; but the next morning, she was ready to interpret it as the highest possible praise.

In this age when all energy seems dead, his energy terrifies them. I shall tell him what my brother said; I can watch the answer he makes. But I will choose one of those moments when his eyes are alight; then he cannot lie to me.

—Could he become another Danton? she added, after a long, vague reverie. All right, let us suppose the Revolution has begun again. What parts could Croisenois and my brother play? The script was prepared long ago: Sublime resignation. They would be heroic sheep, permitting their throats to be cut without a peep of protest. Their only fear even in the act of death would still be that of displaying poor taste. My little Julien would blow out the brains of the Jacobin who came to arrest him, as long as he had the least hope of escape. He has no fear of bad taste, not he.

The last phrase rendered her thoughtful; it raised painful memories, and robbed her of all her boldness. It recalled various jests of Messieurs de Caylus, de Croisenois, de Luz, and her brother. These gentlemen all charged Julien with having a *priestly* air: humble and hypocritical.

—But, she suddenly resumed, her eye sparkling with joy, by the bitterness and the frequency of their attacks they prove in spite of themselves that he is the most distinguished man we have seen this winter. What matter if he has faults, absurdities even? He has greatness, and they are shocked by it, though otherwise so gentle and indulgent. He knows very well that he is poor, and that he has studied to become a priest; they are squadron commanders, and have no need to study; it's the easier way.

Despite all the disadvantage of his perpetual black coat and that priestly face which he has to put on, poor boy, if he is not to die of hunger, his merit terrifies them, that's evident. And the priestly face, as soon as we've been alone together for a few moments, he no longer wears it. And when these gentlemen make a remark which they consider clever and unexpected, isn't it always Julien at whom they glance? I've often noted it. And yet they know very well

8. La Fontaine, "The Shepherd and his Flock," *Fables*, IX, 19.

that he never ventures to address them except in answer to a question. It is only with me that he ventures to talk freely. He thinks I have a lofty spirit. He never answers their objections except as politeness demands it. He immediately turns respectful. With me he will talk for hours on end; he is not sure of his ideas if I offer the slightest objection to them. And besides, we haven't heard any gunshots all winter; the only way to attract attention has been by talk. Well, my father, who is a great man and bound to raise high the fortunes of our house, respects Julien. Everyone else hates him, but no one despises him except my mother's devout friends.

The Comte de Caylus had, or pretended to have, a great passion for horses; he passed his life in the stable and often ate lunch there. This devouring passion, combined with the habit of never laughing, earned him much consideration among his friends: he was the leader of the little circle.

As soon as they had convened next day behind Mme. de La Mole's sofa, Julien not being present, M. de Caylus, supported by Croisenois and by Norbert, launched a sharp attack on Mathilde's good opinion of Julien, without any preliminaries, almost at the first instant he caught sight of Mlle. de La Mole. She saw through the strategy from a mile off, and was delighted by it.

Here they all are, she thought, banded together against a man of genius who has not ten louis of his own and can answer them back only when he's spoken to. They are afraid of him in his little black coat. What would they do if he wore epaulets?

Never had she been more brilliant. After the first attack, she raked Caylus and his allies with sarcasms. When the drumfire of jests from these brilliant officers was extinguished:

—Let some country squire from the Franche-Comté come tomorrow, she told M. de Caylus, suppose he discovers that Julien is his natural son, gives him a name and a few thousand francs; in six weeks he will have moustaches like you gentlemen; in six months he'll be an officer of the hussars like you gentlemen. And then the greatness of his character will no longer be a joke. I can see you reduced, Mr. Duke-in-the-future, to that old, bad argument about the superiority of court nobility to provincial nobility. But what will you have left if I push matters to the limit, if I am mean enough to assign Julien, as father, a Spanish duke, prisoner of war at Besançon in Napoleon's time, who, from a scruple of conscience, recognizes his son on his deathbed?

All these suppositions of illegitimate birth were considered most ill-bred by Messieurs de Caylus and Croisenois. But that was the only thing they saw in Mathilde's argument.

Though Norbert had been put down, his sister's meaning was so clear that he put on a grave look, which, it must be confessed, hardly suited his smiling, open features. He ventured to say a few words.

—Are you unwell, my dear? Mathilde replied with a small, serious expression. You must be really sick if you're answering jokes with moral lectures.

Moral lectures, from you! You must be getting ready to ask for a perfect's position.

Mathilde quickly dismissed from her mind the irritation of the Comte de Caylus, Norbert's ill humor, and the silent despair of M. de Croisenois. She had to reach a decision upon a fatal idea that had just taken possession of her.

Julien is quite open with me, she thought; at his age, in a position of inferiority, and miserable as he is by virtue of his terrible ambition, he needs a friend. I may perhaps be that friend; but I see no signs in him of love. Given the boldness of his character, he would certainly have told me of it.

This uncertainty, this inner dialogue, which from this moment on filled Mathilde's life, and within which she found new material for debate every time Julien spoke with her, completely banished those attacks of boredom to which previously she had been subject.

As the daughter of an intelligent man who might become a minister and return their estates to the clergy, Mlle. de La Mole had been subjected at the Convent of the Sacred Heart to the most outrageous flatteries. For such a misfortune as this there is no remedy. They had persuaded her that because of all her advantages of birth, fortune, etc., she ought to be happier than anybody else. This is the reason why princes are so bored and commit so many acts of folly.

Mathilde had never really escaped from the fatal influence of this notion. However intelligent one may be, there is no guarding at ten years old against the flattery of an entire convent, especially when it seems to be so well grounded.

From the moment of her decision that she loved Julien, she was no longer bored. Every day she congratulated herself on her decision to indulge in a great passion. It's a dangerous game, she thought; so much the better! A thousand times better!

Without a great passion, I was pining away from boredom during the best period of a girl's life, from sixteen to twenty. I had already wasted the best years of my life, with no other amusement than listening to the nonsense talked by my mother's friends—who, so I'm told, were by no means so strict in their behavior at Coblenz in 1792 as you would think to hear them talk today.

While Mathilde was still shaken by these immense uncertainties, Julien was unable to understand the long stares she kept directing at him. He found fresh coolness in the behavior of Comte Norbert and new arrogance in Messieurs de Caylus, de Luz, and de Croisenois. He was used to it. This sort of misfortune often befell him after an evening in which he had been more clever than befitted his social position. If it had not been for the special welcome which Mathilde granted him, and for the curiosity which the whole scene inspired in him, he would have found a way out of accompanying these brilliant young men with the moustaches when after dinner they escorted Mlle. de La Mole on a stroll around the garden.

It's true, I can't overlook it, Julien said to himself; Mlle. de La Mole keeps looking at me in a very odd way. But, even when her beautiful blue eyes seem to be gazing on me most openly and with the least restraint, I always feel that they are studying me, coldly and even with malice. Can that possibly be love? What a difference from the way Mme. de Rênal used to look!

One evening after dinner, Julien had accompanied M. de La Mole to his study and was returning unexpectedly to the garden. As he approached the group around Mathilde incautiously he overheard several words spoken loudly. She was provoking her brother. Julien distinctly heard his own name repeated twice. He appeared; a profound silence at once descended on the group, and only weak efforts were made to break it. Mlle. de La Mole and her brother were too aroused to venture on any other topic of conversation. Messieurs de Caylus, de Croisenois, de Luz, and another one of their friends behaved toward Julien with icy coldness. He left.

Chapter 13

A PLOT

> Random words, accidental encounters turn into conclusive evidence in the mind of an imaginative man, if he has a bit of fire in his heart.
>
> —Schiller[9]

Next day he again surprised Norbert and his sister deep in conversation about him. Just as the night before, a deathly silence followed his appearance. His suspicions knew no limits. Are these nice young people trying to make a fool of me? That would be much more probable, much more natural, than any pretended passion on Mlle. de La Mole's part for a poor devil of a secretary. Who knows if these people even have passions? Misleading other people

---

9. Friedrich von Schiller (1759–1805), German poet, philosopher, historian, and dramatist.

is their long suit. They're jealous of my miserable little superiority of language. Jealousy, that's another one of their weaknesses. That explains everything. Mlle. de La Mole wants to convince me that I'm her special favorite, simply so she can make a spectacle of me for her intended.

This bitter suspicion completely altered Julien's moral posture. The notion of a plot found in his heart the first seed of a love it had no difficulty in exterminating. This love was founded on nothing but Mathilde's rare beauty, or rather on her queenly manners and admirable style of dress. In this respect, Julien was still an upstart. A pretty woman of high fashion is, we are told, the thing that most impresses a clever man of low birth when he first finds his way into the upper ranks of society. Certainly it was not Mathilde's character that had inspired Julien's dreaming for several days past. He had enough sense to realize that he knew nothing at all about her character. Whatever he had seen of it might be just a pretense.

For example, Mathilde would not have missed Sunday mass for anything in the world; in fact, she went to mass with her mother nearly every day. If some foolish fellow forgot himself in the drawing room of the Hôtel de La Mole so far as to make a remote allusion to some joke against the real or supposed interests of either the throne or the altar, Mathilde would freeze on the instant into icy seriousness. Her glance, which had been so sparkling, would take on all the lofty impassivity of an old family portrait.

But Julien knew very well that she always kept in her room one or two of the most philosophical writings of Voltaire. He himself often borrowed several volumes of the handsomely printed and beautifully bound edition. By slightly separating each of the remaining volumes from its neighbor, he concealed the absence of the one he had borrowed, but before long he noticed that somebody else was reading Voltaire. He had recourse to a seminary trick; he placed snippets of horsehair across the volumes he thought might interest Mlle. de La Mole. They disappeared for weeks on end.

M. de La Mole, becoming irked with his bookseller who kept sending him all the mock *Mémoires*,[1] instructed Julien to buy anything new that seemed likely to have some life in it. But to keep the venom from spreading through the household, the secretary was told to place these books on some shelves in the marquis' own bedroom. Before long he was quite certain that these new books, whenever they were hostile to the interests of throne or altar, disap-

---

1. A man named Soulavie was particularly ingenious and prolific in fabricating memoirs pretending to be the work of Revolutionary figures; the Napoleonic wars and Empire produced many more.

peared immediately. Certainly, it was not Norbert who was reading them.

Julien, exaggerating the incident, attributed to Mlle. de La Mole the duplicity of Machiavelli. Her pretense to criminality was a charm in his eyes, almost the only moral charm she had for him. Boredom with hypocrisy and virtuous conversation drove him to this excess.

He excited his own imagination more than he was carried away by his love.

It was after he had lost himself in dreams about the grace of Mlle. de La Mole's figure, the excellence of her taste in dress, the whiteness of her hand, the beauty of her arms, the ease of all her movements that he found he was in love. Then, to complete the spell, he imagined her a Catherine de Medici.[2] Nothing was too subtle or too wicked for the character he attributed to her. It was the ideal of the people like Maslon, Frilair, and Castanède, whom he had admired in his youth. In a word, it was for him the ideal of Paris.

Was even before a man so ridiculous as to attribute profundity and criminality to the Parisian character?

It is possible that this trio has undertaken to make a fool of me, thought Julien. The reader has little sense of his character if he has not already envisaged the gloomy, cold expression which his features assumed in response to the glances of Mathilde. A bitter irony repelled, to her great astonishment, the friendly assurances on which Mlle. de La Mole ventured two or three times.

Stung by this sudden whim, the heart of this girl who was naturally cold, bored, and responsive to wit became as much aroused as it was in her nature to be. But there was a great deal of pride in Mathilde's character, and the birth of a sentiment that left all her happiness dependent on someone else was accompanied by a dark melancholy.

Julien had learned enough since his arrival in Paris to perceive that this was not the dusty melancholy of boredom. Instead of being eager, as she used to be, for parties, shows, and distractions of every sort, she avoided them.

Music performed by French singers bored Mathilde to death, and yet Julien, who made it his responsibility to appear every night at the end of the opera, noted that she had herself escorted there as often as possible. He thought he could discern that she had lost a little of that perfect control which used to be evident in all her ac-

---

2. Catherine de Medici was the wife of Henri II but became more famous as the mother of Henri III, whom she incited to the St. Bartholomew's Day massacre of the Huguenots.

tions. She sometimes answered her friends with sarcasms that outraged them, so pointed and forceful were they. It seemed to him that she had taken umbrage at the Marquis de Croisenois. That young man must be furiously in love with money, Julien thought, if he doesn't drop that girl cold, however rich she is! And for his own part, furious at her insults to masculine dignity, he grew colder than ever toward her. Often he went so far as to answer her back impolitely.

Though determined not to be duped by Mathilde's marks of interest, Julien found them so apparent on certain days, and now that his eyes had begun to see so much more clearly, he thought her so pretty that sometimes he was embarrassed.

These young people with their experience of high society, he told himself, are so subtle and tenacious that in the end they will overcome my inexperience; I must go away and put an end to all this. The marquis had just made him responsible for a number of small properties and houses which he owned in lower Languedoc.[3] A visit became necessary: M. de La Mole authorized it reluctantly. Except in matters of lofty ambition, Julien had become his second self.

The game is over and they still haven't caught me, Julien said to himself as he prepared to leave. Whether Mlle. de La Mole's sarcasms against these gentlemen are sincere or just designed to entrap me, I've had my fun with them.

If there is no conspiracy against the carpenter's son, Mlle. de La Mole is a riddle, but she is so for the Marquis de Croisenois at least as much as for me. Yesterday, for example, her ill humor was perfectly genuine, and I had the pleasure of seeing her snub in my favor a young man who is as noble and rich as I am plebeian and poor. That was the finest of my victories; the thought of it will keep me amused in my mail coach as it rolls across the plains of Languedoc.

He had kept his departure a secret, but Mathilde knew even better than he that he would be leaving Paris the next day, and for a long time. She resorted to a wretched headache, which was intensified by the stuffy atmosphere of the drawing room. For a long time she walked about in the garden and plied her morbid shafts of wit so vigorously in tormenting Norbert, the Marquis de Croisenois, Caylus, de Luz, and several other young men who had dined at the Hôtel de La Mole that at last she drove them from the field. She was watching Julien in a strange way.

The look may be a piece of make-believe, Julien thought, but that quick breathing, that troubled expression! Bah! he told himself, who am I to judge of things like this? This is the most superb and subtle example of Parisian women. That quick breathing, which al-

3. Languedoc: the south of France, the Midi.

most convinced me, she has doubtless copied from Léontine Fay,[4] whom she admires so much.

They had been left alone; the conversation languished. No! Julien has no feeling for me, Mathilde told herself in a moment of genuine unhappiness.

As he was taking his leave, she grasped his arm forcefully:

—You will receive a letter from me tonight, she said to him, in a voice so altered that it was scarcely recognizable.

Her altered speech had an immediate effect on Julien.

—My father, she went on, fully appreciates all the things you do for him. You *must* not leave tomorrow; find an excuse. And she ran from the garden.

Her figure was charming. No woman ever had a prettier foot; she ran with a grace that enchanted Julien; but would you ever guess what was his second thought after she was gone? He was offended at the imperious way she had pronounced that word *must*. Louis XV, too, lying on his deathbed, was deeply distressed by that word *must*, foolishly used by his chief physician, and yet Louis XV was no upstart.[5]

An hour later a footman delivered a letter to Julien; it was, quite simply, a declaration of love.

There's not too much affectation about the style, Julien thought, trying by means of literary observations to suppress the joy that was distorting his features and forcing him to laugh in spite of himself.

So it's happened, he suddenly exclaimed, the passion having proved too strong to be bottled up; I, poor peasant that I am, I have a declaration of love from a great lady!

As for my performance, it's not been too bad, he added, controlling his delight as much as possible. I've been able to sustain the dignity of my character. I never said I loved her. He began to study the shaping of the various letters; Mlle. de La Mole wrote a delicate little English script. He required some physical activity to distract him from a joy that had begun to verge on delirium.

"Your departure forces me to speak out. . . . It would be more than I could stand not to see you again."

A thought struck Julien like a sudden discovery, interrupting his careful examination of Mathilde's letter, and redoubling his joy. I am carrying the day over the Marquis de Croisenois, he exclaimed; I, who never talk except about serious things! And he is so handsome! He has moustaches, an impressive uniform; and he's always

---

4. Léontine Fay was the stage name of the light comic actress Léontine Volny at the Gymnase. She first took part in various frivolous plays of Scribe and later graduated to more solemn exercises of the tragic muse.

5. Louis XV, who was five years old when Louis XIV died, attained his legal majority at thirteen, and reigned until his death at the age of sixty-four, had every reason to feel insulted at a command, even from his doctor.

able, at the proper moment, to come up with some observation which is witty and acute.

Julien had a moment of supreme pleasure; he was wandering at random through the garden, mad with happiness.

Later he went up to his office and asked to see the Marquis de La Mole, who, by good fortune, had not gone out. He easily demonstrated, by showing him various marked papers coming from Normandy, that business in connection with the Norman properties made it necessary to put off his departure for Languedoc.

—I'm glad you're not going, the marquis told him when they had finished their business talk, *I like to see you.* Julien took his leave; the expression upset him.

And now I am going to seduce his daughter! perhaps render impossible that marriage with the Marquis de Croisenois which makes his future rosy; if he isn't a duke himself, at least his daughter will have a *tabouret*.[6] The idea occurred to Julien that he might leave for Languedoc in spite of Mathilde's letter, in spite of all his explanations to the marquis. This ray of virtuous resolution disappeared almost at once.

I'm really a good one! he told himself; I'm a plebeian, but I must feel pity for a family of this rank! I'm the man whom the Duc de Chaulnes calls a domestic servant! How does the marquis add to his immense fortune? By selling securities when he hears around the court that there's likely to be some show of revolutionary opposition next day. And I, whom wretched fate placed in the lowest rank of society, I, who have been cursed with a noble heart and not a thousand francs of income, which is to say, not enough for my daily bread, *literally speaking not enough for my daily bread*; am I to turn down a pleasure that offers itself? A cooling spring which comes along to quench my thirst in the burning desert of mediocrity through which I have to struggle! My word, I'll be no such fool; every man for himself in this desert of selfishness they call life.

And he recalled various looks of disdain cast in his direction by Mme. de La Mole, and above all by *the ladies*, her friends.

The pleasure of triumphing over the Marquis de Croisenois occurred to him at this point, and completed the rout of lingering virtue.

How pleased I should be at his rage! Julien thought; how confidently, now, I could cross swords with him. And he sketched in the air a gesture of riposte. Before this, I would have been a bumpkin, taking vulgar advantage of a bit of courage. After this letter, I am his equal.

---

6. Literally, *a tabouret* is a footstool; metaphorically it is the rank of duchess, since only duchesses had the right to take these seats around the queen's circle.

Yes, he said to himself with infinite pleasure, rolling the words slowly in his mind, our merits have been weighed, the marquis' and mine, and the poor carpenter from the Jura takes the prize.

Good! he cried, that's the way in which I shall sign my reply. Never imagine, Mlle. de La Mole, that I am going to forget my social position. I will make you understand and feel that it is for the son of a carpenter that you are betraying a descendant of the famous Guy de Croisenois, who accompanied Saint-Louis on his crusade.

Julien could not contain his joy. He was obliged to go down to the garden again. His room, into which he had locked himself, seemed too narrow for him to breathe there.

I, a poor peasant from the Jura, he kept repeating to himself over and over, I who am condemned to wear forever this gloomy black costume! Alas! twenty years ago I would have worn a uniform, as they do! In those days a man like me was either killed or a *general at thirty-six!* The letter, which he was still clutching in his hand, gave him the bearing and gestures of a hero. Nowadays, it is true, by using that black coat, a man can have a hundred thousand francs in salary, and a blue ribbon, like the bishop of Beauvais.[7]

All right! said he to himself, laughing like Mephistopheles, I've got more brains than they do; I know how to choose the uniform of my century. And he felt his ambition redoubled, as well as his attachment to the ecclesiastical garb. How many cardinals born lower than I was have risen to power in the government! my countryman Granvelle, for example.[8]

Gradually Julien's agitation subsided; prudence came to the surface. He told himself, like his master Tartufe, whose role he knew by heart:

> I'll trust these words, an honest artifice.
> . . . .
> But not believe in such beguiling speeches
> Unless I have some proof from her I love
> To validate what she's been talking of.
> *Tartuffe*, Act IV, scene v

Tartufe too was ruined by a woman, and he was just as good a man as the next one. . . . My answer may be shown about . . . for

---

7. Jean-Hyacinthe Feutrier (1785–1830), who became Bishop of Beauvais in 1825 at the age of forty, was responsible for several orders limiting the power of the Jesuits; when the ministry changed, August 8, 1829, he retired to Beauvais, having recently been made count, peer of France, and a pensionnaire to the tune of twelve thousand francs. But he did not enjoy his good fortune for long, as he died in 1830.

8. Antoine Perrenot de Granvelle (1517–1586) was a cleric, born in Besançon, whose learning and capacity for business made him one of the most trusted ministers of the Roman Emperor Charles V and of Philip II of Spain. He was made cardinal in 1561.

which we'll find this remedy, he added, pronouncing his words very slowly and with an expression of contained ferocity; we will begin the reply by repeating the most striking expressions in the letter of the sublime Mathilde.

All right, but then four of M. de Croisenois' lackeys may jump on me and tear away the original.

No, for I go well armed, and they know very well that I have some practice in firing on lackeys.

Well, let's suppose one of them has a bit of spunk and attacks me. He's been promised a hundred napoleons. I kill him or wound him; that's just great, I've played right into their hands. They throw me into jail, with all the law on their side; I appear in police court, and they send me with all the forms of judicial correctness to keep company in Poissy with Fontan and Magalon.[9] There I'm thrown into a dungeon with four hundred other beggars higgledy-piggledy. . . . And I would take pity on these people! he cried, jumping furiously to his feet. Do they ever have any for the common people when they have us in their clutches? This outburst was the dying gasp of his gratitude toward M. de La Mole, which in spite of him had been tormenting him until then.

Let's go easy now, my fine gentlemen, I understand this little trick out of Machiavelli; Abbé Maslon or M. Castanède in the seminary couldn't have planned it better. You rob me of the letter which *incited* me, and then I become volume two in the story of Colonel Caron at Colmar.[1]

Just a moment, gentlemen, I'm going to send this all-important letter in a sealed parcel for Abbé Pirard to keep. He's an honest man, a Jansenist, and as such beyond the temptations of a budget. Yes, but he opens letters. . . . I'll have to send this one to Fouqué.

It must be admitted that Julien's expression was atrocious, his features hideous; it was the look of a criminal outlaw. It was an unhappy man at war with his whole society.

To arms! Julien cried. And he rushed at one bound, down the steps and out of the house. Around the corner was a letter writer's booth; Julien entered, alarming the man. Copy this, he said, handing him Mlle. de La Mole's letter.

While the copyist was at work, he himself wrote to Fouqué, asking him to receive and keep a precious item in trust. But, he said, stopping in the middle, the secret-service agents in the post office will open my letter and return to you the one you're looking for; no, gentlemen. Off he went to buy an enormous Bible at a Protestant

9. Fontan and Magalon had edited a little satiric periodical, *The Album,* and were sent to jail by the Restoration government as a result of their attacks on it.
1. Colonel Caron, Augustin-Joseph Caron (1774–1822), was executed by firing squad at Colmar as a conspirator against the restored Bourbons.

bookstore, cleverly concealed Mathilde's letter under the binding, had it wrapped, and sent off the package by the stagecoach, addressed to one of Fouqué's workmen whose name was completely unknown in Paris.

That done, he returned joyous and free to the Hôtel de La Mole. *And now it's our turn!* he exclaimed, locking himself into his room and throwing off his jacket:

"Can it be, mademoiselle," he wrote to Mathilde, "is it Mlle. de La Mole who had Arsène, her father's servant, bring a much too alluring letter to a poor carpenter from the Jura, no doubt in order to take advantage of his simplicity. . . ." And he proceeded to transcribe the most outspoken sentences from the letter he had received.

His own letter would have been a credit to the diplomatic prudence of the chevalier de Beauvoisis. It was still only ten o'clock; Julien, drunk with joy and the sense of his own power, completely new sensations for a poor devil like him, went off to the Italian opera. He heard his friend Geronimo sing. Never had music so exalted him. He was a god.[2]

Chapter 14

REFLECTIONS OF A GIRL

What perplexities! How many sleepless nights! Good God! Will I expose myself to contempt? He will despise me himself. But he is leaving, he is going away.

—Alfred de Musset

Mathilde had not written without an inner struggle. Whatever the source of her original interest in Julien, it soon overrode the pride that, so long as she had been aware of her own character, had been her dominant trait. For the first time that cold and arrogant spirit was swept away by a feeling of passion. But though passion dominated pride, it was still true to the habits pride had formed. Two months of inner strife and novel sensations had, so to speak, reconstituted her whole moral nature.

Mathilde felt that happiness lay before her. This prospect, irresistible to courageous spirits when linked with superior intelligence, struggled for a long time against her sense of dignity and of

---

2. *Esprit per. pré. gui II. A. 30* [Stendhal's note]. This mysterious footnote of Stendhal's has nothing to do with the novel, but relates to an incident that occurred while he was correcting the proofs. The message seems to expand into "Esprit perd préfecture Guizot 11 August 1830." The minister Guizot denied Stendhal an administrative appointment after the July revolution because he did not trust men of wit; a few weeks later, however, Stendhal was named consul at Trieste.

simple obligation. One day she entered her mother's room at seven in the morning, begging to be allowed to take refuge at Villequier. The marquise did not even deign to give her an answer, and told her to go back to bed. That was her last effort at vulgar prudence and at deference to conventional ideas.

The fear of doing "wrong" and violating the values held sacred by people like Caylus, de Luz, and Croisenois disturbed her not at all; such creatures didn't seem to be constructed to understand her; she might have asked their opinion if it had been a matter of buying a carriage or a property. Her real terror was that Julien might be displeased with her.

Perhaps he too has only the outer show of a superior man?

She abhorred want of character; it was her only objection to the handsome young men who flocked around her. The more graceful jokes they made about people who disregarded fashion, or followed it clumsily though obediently, the more they lost her consideration.

They were brave, and that was all. And even then, how were they brave? she asked herself: in duels, but duels nowadays are mere formalities. Everything is known beforehand, even the victim's dying words. Stretched out on the turf, with a hand on one's heart, one breathes a generous pardon for the adversary and a word for the fair creature, often imaginary—or else she goes dancing the day of your death, to ward off suspicion.

Men may face danger bravely at the head of a squadron all aglitter with steel; but danger that is solitary, strange, unexpected, and actually ugly?

Alas! thought Mathilde, it was in the court of Henri III that men showed themselves great by character as well as by birth! Ah, if Julien had seen action at Jarnac or at Moncontour,[3] I should have no doubts of him. In those days of power and prowess, Frenchmen were not mere puppets. The day of battle was almost the simplest of all.

Their life was not wrapped up like an Egyptian mummy in a coating always the same for everyone, always identical. Yes, she added, there was more real courage in walking home alone at eleven o'clock at night from the Hôtel de Soissons, where Catherine de Medici lived, than there is nowadays in a trip to Algiers.[4] A man's life was one continual train of dangers. Nowadays civilization [and policemen have] eliminated danger, and the unexpected never hap-

---

3. Jarnac and Moncontour were two military victories won for Henri III by the Maréchale de Tavannes (1569).
4. The Hôtel de Soissons, originally the Hôtel de Nesle, was an immense, intricate structure, long since destroyed, but thronged in Catherine de Medici's time (the sixteenth century) with men-at-arms, courtiers, and assorted quick-tempered ruffians. Algiers had just been captured by the French, July 4, 1830.

pens. If by chance it appears among our ideas, there are not epigrams enough to drive it away; if it appears in the form of action,
no act of cowardice can properly express our terror. Whatever idiocy we do out of fear is excused. What a dull, degenerate century!
What would Boniface de La Mole have said, if, raising his severed
head from the tomb, he had seen seventeen of his descendants
taken captive in 1793 like so many sheep, in order to be guillotined
two days later? Death was certain but it would have been bad form
to defend themselves and take a Jacobin or two with them. Ah, in
the heroic days of France, in the age of Boniface de La Mole, Julien
would have been the squadron commander, and my brother the
young priest of conventional manners, with wisdom in his eyes and
reason on his lips.

A few months before, Mathilde had been in despair that she
would never meet anyone the least out of the common run. She
had found some amusement in allowing herself to write to various
young men of rank. This act of boldness, so unconventional and
improper in a young girl, might well have dishonored her in the
eyes of M. de Croisenois, her grandfather the Duc de Chaulnes,
and the whole household, who, when they saw the proposed marriage broken off, would have wanted to know why. In those days,
when she had written one of her letters, Mathilde could not sleep
at night. But those letters were only answers.

Now she had had the audacity to confess herself in love. She was
writing, and writing *first* (what a terrible word!) to a man in the lowest ranks of society.

This circumstance guaranteed, in case she were discovered, eternal disgrace. Which of the women who visited with her mother
would have dared take her part? What polite formula could be
handed to them which would soften the shock of society's fearful
contempt?

And then talking was frightful, but writing was worse! *There are
some things one doesn't put on paper,* Napoleon shouted when he
heard of the surrender of Bailén.[5] And it was Julien himself who
had told her of this expression, as if teaching her a lesson in advance!

But all this was still nothing; Mathilde's anguish had other
sources. Forgetting the terrible effect on society, the ineffaceable
blot of shame as a result of betraying her class, Mathilde was writing to a being entirely different from people like Croisenois, de
Luz, and Caylus.

---

5. General Dupont surrendered Bailén to the Spanish on July 23, 1809; when Napoleon
learned of the terms, which he thought humiliating since they involved an admission of
various misdeeds, he was furious.

The depth, the *unknown* quality of Julien's character would have frightened her, even if she had been forming an ordinary relation with him. And she was going to take him for her lover, perhaps her master!

What won't he pretend to, if ever he is in a position of power over me? No matter! I can say like Medea: *Amid so many perils, still I have MYSELF.*[6]

Julien, she understood, had no veneration for blue blood. Worse still, it was possible that he felt no love for her!

In these last moments of fearful doubts, ideas of feminine pride rose to afflict her. Everything must be strange in the destiny of a girl like me, Mathilde cried with impatience. Thus the pride that had been taught her from the cradle became an adversary to her virtue. And at this moment, Julien's announced departure precipitated everything.

(Such characters are fortunately very rare indeed.)

That night, very late, Julien was spiteful enough to have an extremely heavy trunk carried down to the porter's room; to carry it, he summoned the footman who was paying court to Mlle. de La Mole's maid. This little device may be pointless, he thought, but if it succeeds, she will think I've left. He went to sleep much pleased with this bit of cleverness. Mathilde never closed an eye.

Next morning very early Julien left the house without being seen by anyone, but he came back before eight.

Hardly was he in the library when Mlle. de La Mole appeared in the doorway. He handed his answer to her. He thought it might be his duty to say a few words to her; nothing would have been easier, but Mlle. de La Mole refused to listen and disappeared. Julien was delighted at this turn; he had not known what to say.

If this whole thing isn't just a game worked out with Comte Norbert, it's clear that my cold looks have sparked the extraordinary affection that this high-born girl has persuaded herself she feels for me. I should be a good deal more stupid than the situation calls for if ever I let myself be attracted into some feeling for this big blond doll. This bit of logic left him more cold and calculating than he had ever been before in his life.

In the battle that is shaping up, he added, pride of birth will be like a high hill, forming a point of military vantage between us. That's where we have to maneuver. I made a mistake to stay in Paris; putting off my departure cheapens me and leaves me wide open if this is nothing but a game. What danger was there in going? I would have fooled them, if they had been trying to fool me. And if

6. Corneille, *Médée*, I, 5; inaccurate, as usual.

there's anything to her interest in me, I would have strengthened it a hundredfold.

Mlle. de La Mole's letter had so roused Julien's vanity that he had forgotten, in his joy at what was happening, to think seriously of all the advantages of going away.

It was a fixed feature of his character to be very conscious of his own faults. This particular one annoyed him extremely, so that he almost forgot the incredible victory that had preceded this slight oversight. Then, about nine o'clock, Mlle. de La Mole appeared on the threshold of the library door, tossed him a letter, and fled.

It looks as if this is going to be an epistolary novel, he said, as he picked up this missive. The enemy makes a false move; I reply with coolness and virtue.

The letter demanded a decisive answer with a haughtiness that increased his inner glee. He gave himself the pleasure of mystifying for two pages the people who were trying to make a fool of him, and by way of another pleasantry he ended his reply by announcing that he had decided to leave next morning.

When his letter was finished, he thought: The garden can serve me as a way of delivering it, and went there. He looked up at the window of Mlle. de La Mole's room.

It was on the second floor, beside her mother's bedchamber, but there was a rather high mezzanine.

The second floor, in fact, was so high that Julien as he walked under the row of linden trees with his letter in his hand could not be seen from Mlle. de La Mole's window. The vault formed by the lindens, which had been carefully pruned to shape, screened him from view. But what have I done now! Julien told himself angrily. Another piece of folly! If they're trying to make a fool of me, I'm just playing the enemy's game if I let myself be seen walking around with a letter in my hand.

Norbert's room was directly above his sister's, and if Julien came out from under the vault formed by the trimmed lindens, the count and his friends would have been able to follow his every move.

Mlle. de La Mole appeared behind her window; he half-showed her the letter; she bowed her head. Julien promptly returned to his own room at a run, and just happened to meet on the main staircase the fair Mathilde, who grasped his letter with perfect assurance and gay eyes.

What passion there was in the eyes of poor Mme. de Rênal, thought Julien, when even after six months of intimate relations she ventured to accept a letter from me! In her whole life, I daresay, she never once looked at me with a laugh in her eyes.

He did not formulate so clearly the rest of his judgment; was he ashamed of the futility of his present motives? But also, what a difference, his thought added, in the elegance of her morning dress, of her whole appearance! Looking at Mlle. de La Mole from a distance of thirty feet, a man of taste would be able to recognize at a glance her social rank. That's what one could call an explicit advantage.

Even as he jested, Julien avoided giving full expression to his thought; Mme. de Rênal had had no Marquis de Croisenois to sacrifice to him. As a rival he had had only that ignoble subprefect M. Charcot, who had himself called de Maugiron because there are no more real de Maugirons.

At five o'clock Julien received a third letter; it was tossed to him through the library door. Once more Mlle. de La Mole ran away. What a craze for writing she has! said he, with a laugh, when it would be so easy for us to talk! The enemy wants to have my letters, that is clear, and lots of them! He was in no hurry to open this one. More elegant phrases, he thought; but as he read it, he paled. It was only eight lines long.

"I must speak with you: I must speak with you tonight; be in the garden when one o'clock strikes. Take the gardener's long ladder from beside the well; place it next to my window and come up. There will be a full moon: no matter."

Chapter 15

IS IT A PLOT?

> Ah! what a painful interval between the first thoughts of a project and its execution! So many vain terrors! So many doubts! Life is at stake. Or rather, much more than life—honor!
>
> —Schiller

This is becoming serious, Julien thought . . . and altogether too obvious, he added, after a bit of thought. What! This fine young lady can talk to me in the library just as freely, God be praised, as she wants; to keep from being bothered with accounts, the marquis never comes there. What the deuce! M. de La Mole and Comte Norbert, the only people who ever come here, are out almost all day; nothing is easier than to see when they return to the house, and the sublime Mathilde, for whose hand a reigning prince would not be too noble, begs me to commit an act of abominable rashness!

It's perfectly clear, they're out to ruin me, or turn me to ridicule at least. First they tried to ruin me with the letters, but I was too shrewd for them; well, now they need an action as open as daylight. These pretty little gentlemen either think I'm dumb or think I'm conceited. What the devil! Under the brightest moonlight in the world, they want me to climb a ladder to a second-story window twenty-five feet from the ground! People will have time to see me even from the houses down the street. I'll be a fine sight on my ladder! Julien went up to his room and began to pack his trunk, whistling as he went. He had decided to leave without even answering the note.

But this sensible decision gave him no peace of mind. If by chance, he suddenly thought as his trunk snapped shut, if Mathilde were sincere! Then I will have acted, in her eyes, the role of an accomplished coward. I have no distinction of birth, so I need great qualities, to be produced on demand without flattering promises, qualities thoroughly backed by eloquent actions . . . .

He was a quarter hour [striding up and down his room.] Why deny it? he said at last; I shall be a coward in her eyes. I shall lose not only the most brilliant woman in high society, as everyone kept telling me at the Duc de Retz's ball, but also the heavenly pleasure of seeing her sacrifice for me the Marquis de Croisenois, who is the son of a duke and will be a duke himself. A charming young man, who has all the qualities I lack: wit on demand, birth, fortune . . . .

The missed opportunity will haunt me all my life, not for her sake, there's no lack of mistresses!

But there's only one honor!

as old Don Diego says,[7] and here, clearly and explicitly, I draw back from the first danger I encounter; for that duel with M. de Beauvoisis turned out to be a mere joke. Here everything is different. I may be shot dead by a concealed servant, but that's the least of it; I may be dishonored.

This is getting serious, my lad, he added, putting on a Gascon accent and a Gascon gaiety. It's a *pint of honnur*. A poor devil like me, dropped by fate in the lowest rank of society, will never get a chance like this again; adventures I may have, but not on this scale . . . .

For a long time he thought it over, now striding hastily up and down the room, now stopping short for a while. There stood in his room a splendid marble bust of Cardinal Richelieu,[8] toward which his eye involuntarily strayed. [Under the lamplight,] the bust seemed to look at him with a severe expression, as if reproaching him for lacking that audacity which ought to be so instinctive in the French character. In your day, O great man, would I have hesitated?

---

7. Corneille, *Le Cid*, III, 6.
8. Cardinal Richelieu, who was diverted from a military career into the church by a mere accident, became during the early seventeenth century what Julien aspires to become in the early nineteenth: a figure of immense political and social power.

At the worst, Julien told himself at last, let's suppose the whole thing is a trap; it's a very ugly one, and very compromising for a young girl. They know I'm not the man to keep my mouth shut. So they will have to kill me. That was all right in 1574, in the days of Boniface de La Mole, but today's La Mole would never dare. These people are not what they used to be. Mlle. de La Mole is so much envied! Four hundred drawing rooms would echo to her shame the next day, and what pleasure would be found in it!

The servants joke together about the marked preference she shows for me, I know it, I've overheard them.

On the other hand, her letters! . . . They may suppose that I'll have them on me. When they catch me in her room, they'll take them. I'll have to deal with two, three, four men, how can I tell? But where can they find men for this job? Where in Paris can they find discreet agents for a job like this? They're afraid of the law . . . . By God, it will be Caylus, Croisenois, and de Luz themselves. That moment when they've caught me, and the idiotic figure I'll cut in their midst, will be the last reward of their plot. Beware the fate of Abelard,[9] master secretary!

By God, though, gentlemen! You'll carry away a few scratches from me; I'll strike at the face, like Caesar's soldiers at Pharsalia. . . .[1] As for the letters, I can get them into a safe place.

Julien made copies of the two last letters, hid them in a volume of the fine Voltaire in the library, and with his own hand carried the originals to the post office.

When he returned to the house: What sort of idiocy am I jumping into? he asked himself, in surprise and terror. He had been a quarter of an hour without looking squarely at the evening's proposed action.

But if I turn back, I'll despise myself forever! All my life long this action will be a matter of doubt for me, and in my case this sort of doubt is the most terrible of pains. Didn't I feel the same way about Amanda's lover? I believe I'd pardon myself more readily for an open crime; once I had confessed it, I should never think of it again.

How's this? I find myself, by some stroke of luck, in rivalry with a man bearing one of the finest names in France, and now I propose in all cheerfulness to declare myself his inferior! At bottom, it's cowardice not to go. That word decides it, Julien exclaimed, rising to his feet . . . and besides, she is really pretty.

---

9. Abelard was castrated by the father of Héloïse, the canon Fulbert.
1. Plutarch (*Life of Caesar*) tells how, at the battle of Pharsalia, Caesar, seeing that many of Pompey's troops were vain, good-looking Roman blades, ordered his own grim veterans to strike chiefly at their faces.

If it isn't all a trap, what madness she's undertaking for my sake!
. . . If it is a trap, by God, gentlemen, I can turn jest to earnest, and
that's just what I'll do.

But if they pinion my arms as I enter the room; or they may have
some clever contraption there, ready to catch me!

It's like a duel, said he, with a laugh, there's a parry for every
thrust, so my fencing master says, but the good Lord, who wants to
get it over with, manages things so that one of the two forgets to
parry. And for that matter, I have here an answer for them: he drew
his pocket pistols, and though they were already loaded, renewed
the primings.

There were still many hours to wait; in order to be doing something, Julien wrote to Fouqué: "My friend, you must not open the
enclosed letter except in case of accident, that is, if you hear that
something strange has happened to me. Then, erase all the proper
names from the manuscript I am sending you, and make eight
copies of it, which you will send to the newspapers of Marseille,
Bordeaux, Lyon, Brussels, and so forth; ten days later, have the
manuscript printed, and send the first copy to the Marquis de La
Mole; then, two weeks after that, scatter the remaining copies at
night through the streets of Verrières."

This brief apologetic memoir, arranged in the form of a story, was
only to be opened by Fouqué in case of accident; Julien tried to
phrase things in a fashion as little compromising as possible for
Mlle. de La Mole, but he described his position very explicitly indeed.

Julien finished making up his package just as the dinner bell
sounded; it made his heart beat rapidly. His imagination, caught up
in the story he had just finished writing, was full of gloomy forebod-
ings. He had pictures of himself seized by servants, throttled, carried down into a dungeon with a gag in his mouth. There a flunkey
stood guard over him, and if the honor of the noble family demanded a tragic end to the story, nothing was easier than to finish
it off with one of those poisons which leave no trace; then they
would say he had died of an unfortunate illness and would carry his
corpse back to his room.

Stirred by his own story like a playwright by his play, Julien was
in real physical fear when he entered the dining room. He looked at
all the servants in their full livery. He studied their faces. Which of
them have been selected for tonight's expedition? he asked himself.
In this family, memories of the court of Henri III are so strong, so
often recalled, that if they think themselves insulted, they will react
more decisively than other people of their rank. He looked at Mlle.
de La Mole to read in her eyes her family's plans; she was pale, and

he thought she had a thoroughly medieval appearance. Never had he seen such an air of grandeur about her; she was truly beautiful and impressive. He almost fell in love with her. *Pallida morte futura* (Her pallor presages a great action)[2] he said to himself.

In vain, after dinner, did he walk ostentatiously for a long time in the garden. Mlle. de La Mole did not appear. Being able to talk with her would have relieved his heart, at that moment, of a great burden.

Why not admit it? he was afraid. As he had resolved to take action, he abandoned himself to this emotion without shame. Provided I find the necessary courage when action is needed, he told himself, who cares what I feel now? He went over to survey the situation and discover the weight of the ladder.

It's an implement, he told himself with a laugh, of which I'm destined to make use! here, as at Verrières. What a difference! There, he added with a sigh, I didn't have to mistrust the person for whose sake I was running risks. What a difference, too, in the danger!

I might have been killed in M. de Rênal's gardens, but without any risk of dishonor. It would have been easy enough to make my death inexplicable. Here, what abominable stories they'll tell in the drawing rooms of the Hôtel de Chaulnes, the Hôtel de Caylus, the Hôtel de Retz, and so on, all over Paris. I shall be a monster to all posterity.

That is, for two or three years, he laughed, catching himself up. But the thought depressed him. And as for me, who will take my part? Supposing Fouqué prints my posthumous pamphlet; it will be only one more disgraceful act. What a picture! I'm taken into a house, and as a reward for the hospitality I receive there, for the kindness that is lavished on me, I publish a pamphlet on the things that happen there! I attack the honor of the women! Ah, better a thousand times to be duped!

It was an awful evening.

---

2. The phrase is Virgil's, describing Dido: *Aeneid*, IV, 644.

Chapter 16

ONE O'CLOCK IN THE MORNING

It was a big garden, laid out only a few years ago, in perfect
taste. But the trees had stood in the famous Pré-aux-Clercs, so
renowned in the days of Henri III, and were more than a hundred
years old: There was something pastoral about it.

—Massinger[3]

He was about to countermand his instructions to Fouqué when
the clock struck eleven. He rattled the key in the lock of his door
loudly, as if he were locking himself in. Then he prowled like a wolf
through the rest of the house to see what was happening, especially
in the attic rooms on the fourth floor, where the servants slept.
Nothing unusual was to be seen. One of Mme. de La Mole's maids
was having a party, and the servants were drinking punch very merrily. People who laugh like that, Julien thought, will not be taking
part in any expeditions tonight; they would be more serious.

At last he stationed himself in a dark corner of the garden. If
their plan is to keep the house servants out of it, they will get in
the mercenaries who are going to attack me by way of the garden
wall.

If M. de Croisenois keeps cool about all this, he is bound to find
it less compromising for the young person he wants to marry if he
has me caught before I get into her room.

He carried out a reconaissance patrol, after the military fashion,
and very detailed. It's a matter of my own honor, he thought; if I fall
into some ambush, it will be no excuse in my own eyes to say: I
never thought of that.

The sky was infuriatingly clear. The moon had risen about
eleven, and by twelve-thirty it shone full on the façade of the house
facing the garden.

She is crazy, Julien said; as one o'clock struck, there was still
light in the windows of Comte Norbert's room. In all his life Julien
had never been so terrified; he saw nothing but the dangers of the
undertaking, and felt not the slightest enthusiasm.

He went to take up the vast ladder, waited five minutes to give
time for a counterorder, and at five minutes past the hour placed
the ladder against Mathilde's casement. He climbed quietly, pistol
in hand, astonished at not being assailed. As he rose to the level of
the window, she opened it noiselessly:

3. Since Stendhal corrected various phrases of this epigraph in the Bucci copy, he evidently
felt free to exercise an author's right over it. Massinger (whom he probably never read)
was a wicked and hard-minded author.

—So here you are, sir, said Mathilde with deep emotion; I've been following your movements for the last hour.

Julien was much embarrassed; he did not know how to behave; he felt no love whatever. In his embarrassment he decided he must make a bold gesture; he tried to kiss Mathilde.

—Oh, come now! she said, and thrust him away.

Much relieved at this repulse, he proceeded to look around the room: the moon was so bright that the shadows it cast in Mlle. de La Mole's room were black. There could well be men hidden in those shadows without my seeing them, he thought.

—What's that you have in your coat pocket? Mathilde asked him, delighted at finding a subject of conversation. She was strangely distressed; all the sentiments of reserve and timidity, so natural to a girl of good family, had taken command again and were putting her to the torture.

—I have all sorts of weapons and pistols, Julien replied, no less happy at having something to say.

—We must lower that ladder, said Mathilde.

—It's enormous, and may break a pane of glass in the living room or the mezzanine.

—Mustn't break the glass, said Mathilde, trying to catch the tone of ordinary conversation; you ought to be able to get it down, I should think, by tying a rope to the top rung. I always keep plenty of ropes in my room.

And this is a woman in love! thought Julien, a woman bold enough to declare her love! Such coolness, such wariness in the arrangements, makes plain that I'm not victorious over M. de Croisenois, as I was fool enough to suppose; I'm merely his successor. But after all, what does it matter? It's not as if I loved her. I triumph over the marquis in this sense, that he'll be furious to have a successor, and particularly to have me for a successor. How arrogantly he looked at me last night in the café Tortoni,[4] when he pretended not to recognize me! And then what a sulky face he put on it when he couldn't avoid greeting me!

Julien had tied the rope to the top rung of the ladder and lowered it gently, leaning far out over the balcony to make sure it did not touch the windows. A good time to kill me, he thought, if there's anyone hidden in Mathilde's room; but perfect silence reigned everywhere.

The ladder touched the ground; Julien succeeded in burying it in a bed of exotic flowers which ran along the wall.

—What will my mother say, Mathilde remarked, when she sees

---

4. Tortoni opened his café in Paris on the Boulevard des Italiens in 1804 and grew rich selling there his delectable *biscuits* and varieties of ice cream.

her beautiful flowers all trampled down! . . . You must throw down the rope, she added, very coolly. If anyone saw it running up to the balcony, that might be a hard thing to explain.

—And how me gwine get way? said Julien, speaking playfully and assuming a Creole dialect. (One of the household maids had been born in Santo Domingo.)

—You, you go way by the door, said Mathilde, delighted with this notion.

—Ah! but this man is really worthy of all my love! she thought.

Julien had just dropped the rope into the garden; Mathilde clutched his arm. He thought he was being seized by an enemy, and turned sharply about, drawing a dagger. She thought she had heard a window being opened. They remained motionless, not even breathing. The moon shone full upon them. As there was no further sound, their anxiety faded.

Then embarrassment set in again, as thick as ever on both sides. Julien made sure the door was locked with all its bolts; he thought of looking under the bed, but was ashamed of doing so; they might have been able to slip a servant or two underneath it. Finally the fear of future reproaches from his common sense overcame him, and he looked.

Mathilde had fallen into all the distress of extreme timidity. She felt a horror of her present position.

—What did you do with my letters? she finally asked.

What a good way to baffle those gentlemen, if they're spying around, and so avoid fighting with them! Julien thought.

—The first is hidden in a big Protestant Bible which yesterday's mail coach has carried far from here.

He spoke very distinctly as he explained these details, and in such a manner as to be heard clearly by anyone who might be hidden in the two great mahogany wardrobes he had not dared to inspect.

—The two others are at the post office and going the same way as the first.

—Good Lord! Why all these precautions? said Mathilde in amazement.

Why should I lie? thought Julien, and told her of all his suspicions.

—So that's the reason your letters were so cold! Mathilde exclaimed, with an expression more of madness than of affection.

Julien paid no attention to this subtlety; she had used the grammatical form of intimacy, and this singular pronoun made him lose his head—[at any rate, he rose in his own esteem,] and his suspicions evaporated. He ventured to embrace this girl who was so beautiful and whom he respected so much. Her rebuff was only half-hearted.

He called upon his memory, as formerly at Besançon with Amanda Binet, and recited several of the finest passages from the *Nouvelle Héloïse*.

—You have a manly heart, she told him, without listening too carefully to his phrases; I wanted to prove your bravery, I must admit. Your first suspicions and then your determination prove you're even braver than I thought.

Throughout this speech Mathilde made a conscious effort to use the intimate form; she was obviously paying more attention to this novel grammatical form than to what she was saying. This use of endearments stripped of every sort of affectionate expression soon ceased to give Julien any pleasure at all; he was surprised at not feeling the least happiness; finally, in order to feel some, he had recourse to his reason. He saw himself much admired by this girl who was so proud and who never bestowed her praises unreservedly; and this line of reasoning led him finally to a happiness founded on self-approval.

True enough, this was not that spiritual delight he had sometimes found in the company of Mme. de Rênal. [My God, what a difference!] There was absolutely nothing tender in his sentiments at this first moment. He was happy over his gratified ambition, and Julien was nothing if not ambitious. He spoke further of the men whom he had suspected, and of the precautions he had contrived. As he talked, he was thinking of various ways to profit by his victory.

Mathilde was still much embarrassed, and had the air of one appalled at her own conduct; she seemed enchanted to find a new topic of conversation. They talked of ways to meet again. Julien reveled in the display of wit and bravery which this discussion made possible. They had to deal with extremely sharpsighted people: little Tanbeau was certainly a spy, but Mathilde and he were not wholly unskilled either.

What could be easier than to meet in the library, and there arrange everything?

—Without arousing suspicion, Julien said, I can appear anywhere in the house, practically in Mme. de La Mole's bedchamber. In fact, that room had to be passed through in order to reach her daughter's. If Mathilde thought he should always come by ladder, he would be overjoyed to expose himself to that little danger.

As she listened to him talk, Mathilde was shocked by his triumphant air. He is now my master! she told herself. Already she was assailed by remorse. Her reason stood in horror of the extraordinary folly she had just committed. Given the power, she would have wiped herself and Julien from the face of the earth. When the force of her will momentarily suppressed the voice of remorse, feelings of timidity and outraged modesty rendered her wretched in the extreme. She had never anticipated the frightful condition in which she found herself.

But I must talk to him, she told herself, that's in the rules, one talks to one's lover. And then, to fulfill her duty, and with a tenderness that expressed itself much more in the words she selected than in the tone with which she pronounced them, she described the various decisions she had reached regarding him in the last few days.

She had decided that if he ventured to climb up to her room with the gardener's ladder, as she had asked him to do, she would give herself to him. But never were such tender things said in a colder, more formal way. So far, their assignation had been ice-cold. It was enough to render the very idea of love hateful. What a lesson in morality for a rash young woman! Is it worthwhile for her to ruin her future for a moment like this?

After prolonged uncertainties, which a superficial observer might have supposed to spring from implacable hatred—so hard is it for the feeling of respect which a woman bears toward herself to give way even before a powerful will—Mathilde ended by becoming his loving mistress.

To tell the truth, their transports were a bit *conscious*. Passionate love was still more a model for them to imitate than a reality.

Mlle. de La Mole supposed she was fulfilling a duty to herself and to her lover. The poor boy, she thought to herself, he's shown perfect bravery, he ought to be happy or else the fault lies in my want of character. But she would have been glad to ransom herself, at the cost of eternal misery, from the cruel necessity imposed upon her.

[margin note: Similar feeling of duty]

In spite of the frightful violence with which she repressed her feelings, she was in perfect command of her speech.

No regret, no reproach came from her lips to spoil this night, which seemed strange to Julien, rather than happy. What a difference, good God! from his last stay of twenty-four hours at Verrières! These fancy Paris fashions have found a way to spoil everything, even love, he said to himself, in an excess of injustice.

He was indulging in these reflections as he stood in one of the great mahogany wardrobes into which he had slipped at the first sounds coming from the next room, which was that of Mme. de La Mole. Mathilde went off with her mother to mass; the maids quickly left the room, and Julien easily escaped before they came back to finish their tasks.

He took a horse and sought out the loneliest parts of the forest of Meudon near Paris. He was far more surprised than happy. The happiness that came from time to time like a gleam of light in his

soul was like that of a young second lieutenant who after some astounding action has just been promoted full colonel by the commanding general; he felt himself raised to an immense height.
Everything that had been far above him yesterday was now at his
level or even beneath him. Gradually Julien's happiness increased
as it became more remote.

If there was nothing tender in his soul, the reason, however
strange it may seem, was that Mathilde in all her dealings with him
had been doing nothing but her duty. There was nothing unexpected for her in all the events of the night, except the misery and
shame she had discovered instead of those divine raptures that novels talk about.

Was I mistaken, don't I love him at all? she asked herself.

Chapter 17

AN OLD SWORD

> I now mean to be serious;—it is time,
> Since laughter now-a-days is deem'd too serious;
> A jest at vice by virtue's called a crime.
> —*Don Juan*, canto XIII, stanza 1

At dinner she did not appear. That evening she came for an instant to the drawing room but never looked at Julien. This behavior
seemed strange to him; but, he thought, I don't know the ways of
these fine folk [except from their everyday behavior, which I've
watched many times;] no doubt she'll give me some good reason for
all this. Still, as he was tormented by the most unbearable curiosity,
he studied Mathilde's features; and he could not deny that she had
a dry, sharp expression. Evidently, it was not the same woman who,
the night before, had or feigned to have transports of delight too extravagant to be true.

The next day, the day after, the same coldness on her part; she
never looked at him, she never noticed his existence. Julien, victim
to the keenest uneasiness, was far removed from the sense of triumph which had been all that stirred him on the first day. Could
this by any chance, he asked himself, be a return to virtue? But that
was a word too plebeian for the lofty Mathilde.

In the ordinary course of life, she hardly believes in religion at
all, Julien thought; she likes it because it's useful to the interests of
her caste.

But out of simple womanly delicacy, may she not be reproaching
herself bitterly for the irreparable mistake she has committed?
Julien thought he was her first lover.

But, he told himself at other moments, it must be admitted that

there is nothing innocent, simple, or tender in any part of her being; [I've never seen her look more like a queen just stepped down
from her throne.] Maybe she despises me? It would be just like her
to reproach herself for what she's done for me, simply because of
my humble birth.

While Julien, filled with ideas he had drawn from books and
memories of Verrières, was pursuing the phantom of a mistress who
should be naturally tender and give not a thought to her own existence as soon as she had made her lover happy, Mathilde's vanity
was furiously inflamed against him.

As she had not been bored for two months now, she had lost her
fear of boredom; thus without suspecting it in any way, Julien had
lost his greatest advantage.

I have given myself a master! said Mlle. de La Mole, [walking
about her room in great agitation.] She was suffering from black remorse. He's the soul of honor, well, maybe so; but if I strain his
vanity, he'll take his revenge by making our relations known. [This
is the malady of our century; not even the strangest follies are proof
against boredom.] Julien was Mathilde's first lover, and in this relationship, which generally affords a few tender illusions even to the
most withered souls, she was racked by thoughts of the utmost ferocity.

He holds immense power over me, since he reigns by terror and
can punish me atrociously if I drive him to it. This idea alone was
enough to make Mlle. de La Mole insult him, since courage was
the first trait of her character. Nothing could provide her with any
distraction and cure her of the boredom that was continually building up inside her, except the idea that she was playing, double or
nothing, with her entire existence.

The third day, as Mlle. de La Mole persisted in not glancing at
him, Julien followed her after dinner into the billiard room, obviously against her wishes.

—Well, sir, I suppose you think you have some special rights over
me, she broke out with ill-concealed rage, since in opposition to my
clearly declared desires, you keep trying to talk to me? [What sort
of cruelty and treachery is this?] Do you realize that nobody else in
the world would take such liberties?

Nothing could have been more amusing than the dialogue of
these two young lovers; without fully realizing it, they felt for one
another nothing but the keenest hatred. As neither one of them had
a patient disposition, and as they were both trained in the manners
of good society, they were not long in reaching the blunt conclusion
that they were enemies for life.

—I swear to you eternal secrecy, said Julien; I should even add
that I will never address another word to you, if it weren't that your

reputation might suffer from too marked a change. He bowed coldly and left her.

Without too many pains he accomplished what he regarded as a duty; for he was far from realizing that he was deeply in love with Mlle. de La Mole. No doubt he hadn't been in love three days before when he was hiding in the mahogany wardrobe. But things changed quickly in his spirit as soon as he saw that he had quarreled with her forever.

His cruel memory set itself the task of retracing every slight detail of that night which in reality had left him so cold.

On the [second] night after their declaration of perpetual hatred, Julien nearly went mad when he found himself forced to confess that he was in love with Mlle. de La Mole.

Frightful struggles followed this discovery: all his feelings were uprooted.

A week later, instead of being arrogant with M. de Croisenois, he felt like falling on his neck and bursting into tears.

As he became accustomed to his misery, a gleam of common sense made itself felt, he decided to leave for the Languedoc, packed his trunk, and went to the post house.

He almost fainted when they told him at the booking office that by the merest chance there was a seat in the mail coach for Toulouse tomorrow. He took it and returned to the Hôtel de La Mole to tell the marquis he was leaving.

M. de La Mole was out. More dead than alive, Julien went to wait for him in the library. What were his feelings when he found Mlle. de La Mole there!

When she saw him come in, she assumed an air of malignant hatred which it was impossible to misconstrue.

Carried away by his misery, stunned by surprise, Julien had the weakness to say, in the most tender and heartfelt tones: Then you don't love me any more?

—I am horrified at having given myself to the first comer, said Mathilde, weeping with fury at herself.

—*To the first comer!* cried Julien, and snatched from the wall an old sword of the Middle Ages which was kept in the library as a curiosity.

His grief, which he thought at its peak when he first spoke to Mlle. de La Mole, had been increased a hundredfold by the tears of shame which she shed. He would have been the happiest of men had it been in his power to kill her.

Just as he was drawing the sword, with some difficulty, from its ancient sheath, Mathilde, delighted at such a new sensation, advanced proudly toward him; her tears had dried.

A thought of the Marquis de La Mole, his benefactor, rose vividly in Julien's mind. I would be killing his daughter! he thought, what a horrible thing! He made a gesture as if to throw away the sword. Certainly, he thought, she will start laughing now at this melodramatic scene: this idea was responsible for restoring all his self-control. He looked carefully over the blade of the old sword, as carefully as if he were inspecting it for rust spots, then thrust it back in the sheath, and with the greatest tranquillity hung it on the gilt bronze nail where it usually rested.

This whole performance, very deliberate toward the end, lasted for a full minute; Mlle. de La Mole watched it in amazement. So I have been on the verge of being killed by my lover! she thought to herself.

The idea carried her back to the finest years of the age of Charles IX and Henri III.

She stood motionless before Julien [erect and taller than usual]; as he replaced the sword, she looked on him with eyes from which hatred no longer shone. It must be admitted that she was very desirable at that moment; certainly no woman ever looked less like a Paris doll (and this phrase summed up Julien's objections to the women of that part of the world).

I'm going to relapse into a certain fondness for him, Mathilde thought, and then right away he'll be sure he's my lord and master, especially if I give in right after speaking so sharply to him. She took flight.

My God! but she's beautiful, Julien said as he watched her run off: that's the creature who flung herself into my arms so frantically not a fortnight ago. . . . And those moments will never return! And it's all my fault! And at the time of such an extraordinary action, which concerned me so deeply, I was only half awake to it! I can't deny it, I was born with a terribly dull, uninteresting nature.

The marquis made his appearance; Julien hastened to tell him he was leaving.

—Where to? asked M. de La Mole.

—To Languedoc.

—No, indeed, if you'll be so kind, you are reserved for higher destinies; if you leave at all, it will be for the north . . . in fact, to put it in military terms, I confine you to barracks. You will oblige me by not being gone for more than two or three hours at a time; I may need you at any minute.

Julien bowed and retired without saying another word, leaving the marquis in a state of great astonishment; he was in no condition to speak, and locked himself into his room. There he was free to expatiate on the awful misery of his fate.

And so, he thought, I can't even go away! God knows how long the marquis will keep me here in Paris; good God! what's going to become of me? And not a friend to whom I can talk: Abbé Pirard wouldn't let me finish the first sentence, and Comte Altamira [to distract my mind] would try to involve me in some conspiracy.

And meanwhile, I am going mad, I can feel it, I'm going mad! Who can guide me, what's to become of me?

Chapter 18

BITTER MOMENTS

And she tells me all about it! She gives me all the details down
to the most trifling! Her lovely eye, fixed on mine, reveals the love
she feels for someone else!

—Schiller

In her delight, Mlle. de La Mole could think of nothing but the joy of having come within an inch of losing her life. She went so far as to say: he is worthy to be my master, since he came so close to killing me. How many pretty young gentlemen of good society would you have to melt down to get one such moment of passion?

I must admit, he did look handsome just then when he climbed on the chair to replace the sword in precisely the same position the interior decorator had found for it! After all, I was not so crazy to be in love with him.

At that moment if some suitable way of making up had presented itself, she would have seized it with pleasure. Julien, locked in his room, was prey to the most violent despair. In his madness, he thought of flinging himself at her feet. If, instead of hiding away in a hole in the wall, he had wandered out into the garden and the house, in such a way as to be ready for any opportunity, he might in a single instant have changed all his awful misery into the keenest happiness.

But the social poise which we reproach him for not having would have rendered impossible the sublime gesture of snatching the sword, which for that single moment made him appear so fine in Mlle. de La Mole's eyes. This caprice of looking favorably on Julien lasted for the rest of the day; Mathilde made for herself a charming picture of the brief instants during which she had loved him, and she recalled them regretfully.

In fact, she said, my passion for this poor boy only lasted, as he sees the matter, from one o'clock in the morning, when I saw him climb the ladder with all his pistols in his coat pockets, until nine o'clock of the same morning. It was a quarter hour later, while I was hearing mass at Sainte-Valère, that I began to think of how he would be my master, and that he might try to terrify me into obeying him.

After dinner, Mlle. de La Mole, far from avoiding Julien, talked to him and practically obliged him to accompany her to the garden; he obeyed. There was a new test for him to pass. Mathilde was yielding, without too many misgivings, to a love that was once more gaining ascendancy over her. She found it very pleasant to walk beside him, looking with curiosity at those hands which only this morning had seized a sword to kill her.

But after such an action, after everything that had passed between them, there was no longer any question of their picking up old conversational threads.

Gradually, Mathilde began to talk to him, confidentially and intimately, of the state of her heart. She found a particular delight in this sort of conversation; she proceeded to tell him of the various fleeting impulses she had felt first for M. de Croisenois, then for M. de Caylus. . . .

—What! for M. de Caylus too! exclaimed Julien; and in this expression was made manifest all the bitterness of a cast lover. Mathilde took it this way, and was by no means displeased.

She continued to torture Julien by describing to him in full detail all her former feelings, using the most vivid and particular language and speaking in tones of absolute, intimate sincerity. He saw that she was describing something immediately present to her. He was further stricken to see that as she talked she made new discoveries among her own feelings.

The misery of jealousy can go no further.

To suspect that one's rival is preferred is a bitter blow, already; but to hear in detail about the love that rival inspires in the woman one adores is beyond any doubt the peak of misfortune.

Oh what a punishment descended on Julien at that moment for his many gestures of pride at the expense of people like Caylus and Croisenois! With what an intense and intimate misery did he now dwell on their most trifling advantages! With what ardent and artless sincerity did he despise himself!

Mathilde seemed to him [a superhuman creature]; words are too weak to express the excess of his admiration. As he walked beside her, he kept glancing furtively at her hands, her arms, her queenly carriage. He was on the point of falling at her feet, crushed with love and misery, and crying: Mercy!

And this woman who is so beautiful, so superior to everything, who once loved me, doubtless will be in love with M. de Caylus before long!

Julien could not question Mlle. de La Mole's sincerity; the accents of truth were too apparent in everything she said. Lest anything whatever be lacking to his grief, there were moments when, as a result of dwelling on the sentiments she had once felt for M.

de Croisenois, Mathilde began to talk of him as if she were in love with him still. Certainly, love spoke in her accent, Julien could sense it clearly.

Had his chest been poured full of molten lead, he would have suffered less pain. How could the poor boy guess, stretched as he was on this rack of torment, that it was precisely because she was talking to him that Mlle. de La Mole took such pleasure in running over the faded recollections of that love she had felt in the past for M. de Caylus or M. de Croisenois?

Words cannot express Julien's torments. He was listening to detailed accounts of the love she felt for others in the shade of those very lindens where, a few days before, he had been waiting for one o'clock to strike before going to her room. A human being cannot sustain pain of higher intensity than this. [Mathilde left the garden and dismissed Julien after nine-thirty only when she had been called three times by her mother. . . . The man I love now, how much better he is than those I was on the point of loving before! she thought, without being fully aware of what she meant.]

This type of savage intimacy lasted for a whole long week. Sometimes Mathilde seemed to seek him out, other times she did not avoid occasions for talking to him; and the subject of these conversations, to which they both returned with a kind of cruel delight, was always what she had felt for someone else; she told him about the letters she had written, she recollected the very expressions she had used, and repeated for his benefit entire sentences. As time passed, she seemed to be contemplating Julien with a kind of malignant joy. His misery was a source of keen enjoyment to her. [She saw in them her tyrant's weakness and so could permit herself to love him. The future tyrant's grief was a source of delight for her.]

It's clear that Julien had no experience of life; he had not even read novels; if he had been a bit less awkward, and merely said with some coolness to this girl whom he adored and who made such strange confessions to him: You agree, of course, that though I'm not the equal of any of these gentlemen, I am the one you love. . . .

She might have been happy to be found out; at least, the outcome would have depended on the grace with which Julien expressed this idea and his choice of an opportune moment. In any case, he might have emerged successfully and with advantage for himself, from a position which was threatening to become monotonous for Mathilde.

—So you no longer love me, and I adore you! Julien told her one day, in an access of love and grief. This was perhaps the most foolish thing he could possibly have said.

His speech destroyed instantly all the pleasure which Mlle. de La Mole found in talking to him about the state of her heart. She was beginning to feel some astonishment that after everything that had happened he did not take offense at her confessions; when he made this stupid speech, she had almost gone so far as to imagine that he no longer loved her. His natural pride has no doubt killed all love, she told herself. He is not the man to watch meekly while preference is given to people like Caylus, de Luz, and Croisenois, even though he admits they are so superior to himself. No, I shall never again see him at my feet.

In earlier days, in the simplicity of his grief, Julien often made eloquent panegyrics describing the brilliant qualities of these gentlemen; he went so far as to exaggerate. This subtlety had not escaped Mlle. de La Mole; she was surprised at it but could not guess the reason. In the depths of his frantic spirit, Julien, when he praised a rival whom he thought happy, was sympathizing with his joy.

His perfectly frank, but perfectly stupid, expression changed everything in an instant: Mathilde, confident of his love, despised him completely.

She was strolling with him at the moment of his unlucky expression; she left him at once, and her last glance expressed the most murderous contempt. Back in the drawing room, she never gave him another look for the rest of the evening. Next day this scorn was in full command of her heart; there was no further question of the impulse that, for the last week, had made her find so much pleasure in treating Julien as her most intimate friend; the very sight of him was odious to her. Before long, Mathilde's feeling reached the point of disgust; nothing could express the extraordinary contempt she felt when her eyes happened to fall on him.

Julien had understood nothing at all of what had been going on in Mathilde's heart for the past week, but contempt he understood. He had the good sense to appear in her presence as rarely as possible, and he never looked at her.

But it was not without mortal pangs that he deprived himself almost entirely of her company. He thought his misery was actually increased thereby. The courage of a man's heart can go no farther, he told himself. His life was spent at a little window in the attic of the house; the shutters were carefully closed, but through them he could at least see Mlle. de La Mole during the brief moments when she was in the garden.

What were his feelings when he saw her strolling after dinner with M. de Caylus, M. de Luz, or some other man for whom she admitted having formerly felt some erotic inclination?

Julien had no notion of such intense misery; he was on the point of screaming aloud; this hypocritical soul, to whom hypocrisy was almost second nature, was completely overwhelmed.

Every idea that did not pertain to Mlle. de La Mole became hateful to him; he was incapable of writing the simplest letters.

—You must be mad, the marquis told him one morning.

Julien, fearful of being found out, talked of being sick and managed to carry some conviction. Luckily for him, the marquis joked with him at dinner about his next trip: Mathilde grasped that it might well be a long one. For several days now, Julien had been avoiding her, and the brilliant young people, who had everything this pale, gloomy creature once loved by her did not, were incapable of drawing her out of her reverie.

An ordinary girl, she thought, would have selected the man of her choice from among these young men who attract every eye in a drawing room; but one of the traits of genius is not to drag its thought through the rut worn by vulgar minds.

As the companion of a man like Julien, who lacks only the fortune I possess, I shall continually attract attention, I'll never pass through life unperceived. Far from living in continual dread of a revolution, like my cousins, who for fear of popular dislike don't even dare to scold a position who drives them badly, I shall be sure of playing a role, and a great role, for the man I have chosen has character and boundless ambition. What does he lack? friends, money? I can provide them. But in her secret thoughts she considered Julien an inferior being, whose fortune one makes when and how one chooses and whose devotion is never even to be questioned.

Chapter 19

THE OPERA BUFFA

O how this spring of love resembleth
The uncertain glory of a summer day;
Which now shows all the beauty of the sun,
And by and by a cloud takes all away.
                                        —Shakespeare[5]

Occupied with thoughts of the future and the singular role she hoped to play in it, Mathilde soon began to miss the dry metaphysical discussions she used to have with Julien. Wearied too by such lofty ideas, she missed the moments of happiness she had known with him; these last memories were not untouched by remorse; at times she was overcome by it.

But if one has a weakness, she told herself, it is very much up to a girl like me never to neglect her duties except for a man of merit.

5. See Book I, epigraph to Chapter 17.

Never let it be said that his handsome moustaches or the graceful way he mounts a horse seduced me, but rather his profound thoughts on the future which awaits France, his ideas about a possible parallel between the events soon to burst upon us and the revolution of 1688 in England.[6] I have been seduced, she answered boldly back to her own remorse, I am nothing but a weak woman, but at least I wasn't deceived like a stuffed doll by exterior advantages. [What I loved in him was the breaking out of a great soul.]

If there should be a revolution, why shouldn't Julien play the part of Roland, and I that of Mme. Roland?[7] I much prefer that to the part of Mme. de Staël:[8] immoral behavior is going to be a great impediment in our century. Certainly no one will ever be able to reproach me with a second weakness; I should die of shame.

Not all Mathilde's meditations were so solemn, it must be admitted, as the thoughts we have just transcribed.

She watched Julien furtively, and found a delightful grace in his least actions.

No doubt, she told herself, I have succeeded in destroying every notion that he might have certain rights.

The air of grief and deep passion in which the poor boy spoke to me of his love, [spoke so naïvely in the garden about a week ago,] is proof of it. I must admit, it was very strange of me to be provoked by words in which there shone so much respect, so much passion. Am I not his wife? What he said was perfectly natural, and, I must admit, it pleased me. Julien still loved me after those endless conversations in which I talked to him, and pretty cruelly I must admit, of nothing but the feelings of love which my boredom had encouraged toward those young fellows of whom he's now so jealous. Ah, if he only knew how little he has to fear from them! How faded and pale they seem to me, as if each one had been copied from the other!

As these thoughts strayed through her mind, Mathilde, [to keep herself in countenance with her watching mother,] began to trace at random a few lines in her album. One of the profiles as she finished it struck her with delight: it looked remarkably like Julien. It's the voice of heaven, one of the miracles of love, she cried in a transport, unconsciously I draw his portrait!

She fled to her room, locked herself in, [took some pastels] and

---

6. The English revolution of 1688 sent into permanent exile the House of Stuart, which Stendhal clearly identified with the Bourbons, and fully vindicated the democratic rights of English property owners.

7. Calm and noble as a queen, Mme. Roland was, with her husband, an intellectual leader of the Girondin party until 1793, when she was guillotined and he committed suicide.

8. Mme. de Staël, whose latest biography titles her, rather fulsomely, *Mistress to an Age*, had in prose, as in love, an enthusiastic, undiscriminating style that was to Stendhal an abomination.

with a great deal of effort undertook seriously to make a portrait of Julien, but it was a failure; the profile penciled at random was a far better likeness; Mathilde was delighted with it; she saw in it conclusive evidence of a great passion.

She did not lay down her album until late, when the marquise summoned her to go to the Italian opera. She had only one idea, to catch sight of Julien and ask her mother to have him escort them.

But he was not to be seen; the ladies had only commonplace beings in their box. During the entire first act of the opera, Mathilde dreamed of the man she loved now with the keenest transports of passion; but during the second act a phrase about love, sung to a melody that was really worthy of Cimarosa, struck her to the heart. The heroine of the opera sang: You must punish me for the excessive adoration I feel for him, I love him far too much!

From the moment when she heard this sublime aria, everything in the world faded into nothingness for Mathilde. People talked to her; she made no answer; her mother scolded, she could barely bring herself to look at her. Her ecstasy rose to a point of exalted passion comparable to the most violent sentiments that Julien had felt for her over the past several days. The aria, a divinely graceful melody over which played the phrase that seemed to bear so strikingly on her position, occupied every instant in which she was not thinking directly of Julien. Thanks to her love of music, she was for that one evening what Mme. de Rênal always was when she thought of Julien. Doubtless the love born in the head is more witty than real love, but it experiences only instants of enthusiasm; it knows itself too well; it is always standing in judgment over itself; far from baffling thought, it is built only on a frame of thought.

When they were back home, Mathilde pretended, in spite of everything Mme. de La Mole could say, that she had a fever, and spent a part of the night playing over the aria on her piano. She sang the words of the celebrated tune which had enchanted her:

> *Devo punirmi, devo punirmi,*
> *Se troppo amai,* etc.

The outcome of this night of madness was that she supposed she had triumphed over her love. (This page will damage the unfortunate author in more than one way. Ice-cold souls will accuse him of indecency. It does no harm to the young ladies who glitter in the drawing rooms of Paris to suppose that one of them is capable of such mad impulses as degrade the character of Mathilde. Her character is entirely imaginary, and indeed imagined at a great distance from those social customs that, among all the ages of history, will assure such a distinguished rank for the civilization of the nineteenth century.

It is by no means prudence that is lacking in the young ladies who have been the ornaments of this winter's balls.

I don't think, either, that anyone can accuse them of undervaluing a brilliant fortune, horses, fine properties, and everything that ensures an agreeable position in the world. Far from seeing nothing but boredom in these advantages, they generally desire them most constantly, and whatever passion their hearts hold is for these things.

Nor is love generally the path by which young men endowed with some talent like Julien hope to gain their fortune; they attach themselves immovably to a certain "crowd," and when the crowd arrives, all the good things of society pour down on them. Woe to the man of education who belongs to no "crowd", even his uncertain little successes will be held against him, and the higher virtue will condemn him even as it robs him. Look here, sit, a novel is a mirror moving along a highway. One minute you see it reflect the azure skies, next minute the mud and puddles of the road. And the man who carries the mirror in his pack will be accused by you of immorality! His mirror shows the mud and you accuse the mirror! Rather you should accuse the road in which the puddle lies, or, even better, the inspector of roads who lets the water collect and the puddle form.

Now that it's fully understood that a character like Mathilde's is impossible in our age, no less prudent than virtuous, I am less afraid of distressing the reader by describing further the follies of this attractive girl.)

All the following day she sought for occasions to prove that she had overcome her insane passion. Her great aim was to displease Julien in everything; but none of his actions escaped her notice.

Julien was too wretched and above all too agitated to see completely through such a complicated strategem of passion; still less could he see in it the element making for his advantage: he fell victim to it. Never, perhaps, had his misery been so extreme. His actions were so little under conscious control that if some gloomy philosopher had told him: "Think of making good use of circumstances favorable to you; in this sort of love-in-the-head which prevails at Paris, a single disposition can never last more than two days," he would not have understood it. But throughout his distractions Julien retained a sense of honor. His first duty was to be discreet; and so he understood it. To ask advice or tell the tale of his sufferings to the first comer would have been a happiness equal to that of the man who, while crossing a scorching desert, receives from heaven a glass of ice water. He recognized his danger; he was afraid if any curious person questioned him, he would reply only with a torrent of tears; he shut himself in his room.

He saw Mathilde walk for a long time in the garden; when finally she went in, he came down and went to a rose bush from which she had plucked a blossom.

The night was dark. He could give himself up to his griefs without fear of being seen. It was perfectly plain to him that Mlle. de La Mole was in love with one of those young officers with whom she had just been chatting so gaily. Once she had loved him, but she had recognized his unworthiness.

And in fact, I am not worth much! Julien said to himself, with full conviction; take me for what I am, I'm a dull fellow, very common, a great bore to other people, completely unbearable to myself. He was sick to death of all his good qualities, of all the things he had once loved with enthusiasm; and in this state of *inverse imagination* he undertook to criticize life imaginatively. It was the error of a superior man.

Several times the idea of suicide rose up before him; it was an idea full of charm, like a delicious resting place; it was the glass of ice water offered to the wretch wandering in the desert and dying of thirst and heat.

My death will even increase her contempt for me! he exclaimed. What a memory I'll leave behind!

Fallen into the absolute pit of misery, a human being has no recourse except courage. Julien had not the inspiration to say: Be bold; but as he watched Mathilde's window, he saw through the shutters that she put out her light. He recalled that charming room, which he had seen, alas! just once in his life. His imagination went no further.

One o'clock tolled. To hear the bell and say to himself: I shall climb the ladder, was the work of an instant.

It was the flash of genius; supporting reasons flooded in on him. I can't possibly be more miserable, he told himself. He ran to the ladder; the gardener had chained it down. With the hammer of one of his little pistols, which he broke in the process, Julien, whose strength at that moment was superhuman, twisted open one of the links of the chain holding the ladder; in a few instants it was free, and he placed it against Mathilde's window.

She will be furious; she will heap contempt on me, what matter? I will give her a kiss, one last kiss, go up to my room, and kill myself . . .; my lips will touch her cheek before I die.

He flew up the ladder and rapped at the shutter; after a few moments Mathilde heard him; she wanted to open the shutter but the ladder was in the way. Julien clung to the iron latch used to hold the shutter open, risking a fall at every instant, gave a violent push at the ladder, and moved it over a bit. Mathilde was able to open the shutter.

He flung himself into the room, more dead than alive.

—It is you, my dear, she said, as she threw herself into his arms. . . .

Who could describe the extravagance of Julien's joy? Mathilde's was almost as great.

She talked against herself, she denounced herself to him.

—Punish me for my atrocious pride, she told him, straining him in her arms as if to throttle him; you are my master, I am your slave, I must beg your pardon on bended knees for having tried to revolt. She slipped out of his arms to fall at his feet. Yes, you are my master, she told him, still drunk with love and happiness; reign forever over me, punish savagely your slave whenever she tries to rebel.

At another moment, she leaped from his arms, lit a candle, and Julien had all he could do to prevent her from cutting off one whole side of her hair.

—I want to remind myself, she told him, that I am your servant: if ever I'm misled again by that horrible pride, show me this lock of hair and tell me: it's not a matter of love, it's not a matter of the sentiment your heart happens to hold at this instant, you have sworn to obey, now obey, on your honor.

But it is wiser to suppress the description of such wild felicity.

Julien's virtue was equal to his good fortune; I must go back down the ladder, he told Mathilde, when he saw daylight touching the distant chimneys on the far side of the garden. The sacrifice I am undertaking is worthy of you; I am depriving myself of a few more hours of the most astounding delight a human being can enjoy; it's a sacrifice I make to your reputation. If you know what I feel, you will understand the violence I am inflicting on myself. Will you always be for me what at this moment you are? Honor speaks, and that's enough. But you must know that since our first meeting, there has been suspicion, and not only of robbers. M. de La Mole has ordered a watch kept on the garden. M. de Croisenois is dogged by spies; they report what he does every night. . . .

—The poor fellow, cried Mathilde, with a burst of laughter. Her mother and a serving girl were awakened by it; suddenly they began calling to her through the door. Julien glanced at her, she turned pale as she scolded the maid and avoided saying a word to her mother.

—But if they open the window they can see the ladder! Julien said to her.

He clasped her once more in his arms, leaped onto the ladder, and slid rather than clambered down it; in an instant he was on the ground.

Three seconds later the ladder was under the linden trees, and Mathilde's honor was safe. Julien, returning to consciousness, found that he was bleeding and almost naked: he had cut himself in his wild descent.

An immense joy had restored the full energy of his character: had twenty men confronted him at that moment, to attack them single-handed would have been only a pleasure the more. By good fortune, his military ardor was not put to the test. He replaced the ladder in its usual place; he put back the chain which fastened it; nor did he forget to come back and rub out the marks which the ladder had left in the border of exotic flowers under Mathilde's window.

As he was passing his hand, in the darkness, over the soft earth, to make sure that the prints were entirely obliterated, he felt something fall on his hands; it was one whole side of Mathilde's hair which she had cut off and was now throwing to him.

She was at the window.

—This is what your servant sends to you, she told him, speaking quite loudly, it is the mark of an eternal obedience. I surrender the right to exercise my own reason; you must be my master.

Julien, overcome, was on the point of picking up the ladder again and climbing back up to her. Reason finally prevailed.

To get back into the house from the garden was not easy. He succeeded in forcing the door of a cellar; then, once inside the house, he was obliged to force, with the utmost silence, the door of his own room. In his agitation, he had left behind in the little room he had just quitted so hurriedly everything, including the key which was in his coat pocket. Let's hope, he thought, that she remembers to hide all that fatal evidence!

At last, weariness won out over happiness, and as the sun rose he sank into a deep sleep.

The luncheon bell barely succeeded in waking him; he descended to the dining room. Shortly after, Mathilde appeared. Julien's pride had a moment of joy when he saw the love glowing in the eyes of this girl who was so beautiful and surrounded by so much deference; but soon his prudence had reason to feel affrighted.

Under pretext of inadequate time to prepare her coiffure, Mathilde had arranged her hair in such a way that Julien could see at a glance the extent of the sacrifice she had made for him when she cut it off the night before. If such lovely features could be spoiled in any way, Mathilde might seem to have done it; one whole side of her beautiful head of ash-blonde hair had been clipped to within half an inch of the scalp.

At lunch, Mathilde's whole behavior bore out this original act of rashness. It seemed she was trying to make everyone aware of her insane passion for Julien. Fortunately, on that day, M. de La Mole and his wife were much exercised over a list of promotions to the order of the blue ribbon, in which M. de Chaulnes had somehow not been included. Toward the end of the meal, it happened that Mathilde, in the course of talking to Julien, addressed him as *my master*. He blushed to the whites of his eyes.

Whether it was accidental, or part of a plan by Mme. de La Mole, Mathilde was not alone for an instant all day. But that evening, as they were passing from the dining room to the drawing room, she found a moment to tell Julien:

—[All my plans are upset.] Will you think this is only a pretext on my part? My mother has just decided that one of her maids will spend the night in my room.

The day passed in a flash. Julien was at the peak of happiness. Next day at seven A.M. he was at his post in the library; he hoped that Mlle. de La Mole would appear there; he had written her an interminable letter.

He did not see her until a good many hours later, at lunch. And this time her hair was done up with the greatest care; a marvelous art had been invoked to hide the place where the hair had been clipped. She glanced once or twice at Julien, but with a courteous and calm expression; there was no question now of calling him *my master*.

Julien gasped in astonishment. . . . Mathilde was blaming herself for practically everything she had done for him.

When she reflected on the matter at leisure, she decided that this was a being, if not altogether common, at least not sufficiently out of the ordinary to deserve all the strange follies she had ventured to commit for him. On the whole, she did not want to think of love; that day, she was tired of loving.

As for Julien, the reactions of his heart were those of a sixteen-year-old. He was assailed alternately by frightful doubt, amazement, and despair throughout that luncheon which seemed to last forever.

As soon as he could decently leave the table, he dashed rather than ran to the stable, saddled his horse for himself, and was off at a gallop; he was afraid of disgracing himself by some show of weakness. I must kill my feelings by physical exhaustion, he told himself, as he galloped through the woods of Meudon. What did I do, what did I say, to deserve such disgrace?

I must do nothing, I must say nothing today, he thought, as he came back to the house; I must be dead in the body as I am in the soul. Julien is no longer alive, it is his corpse that is still writhing.

Chapter 20

THE JAPANESE VASE

> At first his heart does not realize the full extent of his misery; he is more bothered than distressed. But as reason returns, he feels the depth of his misfortune. All the pleasures of life are ruined for him, he can feel nothing but the keen edges of despair tearing at him. But what good is it to talk of physical pain? What pain felt by the body alone is comparable to this one?
>
> —Jean Paul

The bell rang for dinner; Julien had just time to dress. He found in the drawing room Mathilde, who was imploring her brother and M. de Croisenois not to go and spend the evening with Mme. la Maréchale de Fervaques.

She could scarcely have been more alluring and attractive with them. After dinner MM de Luz, de Caylus, and several of their friends put in an appearance. It seemed that Mlle. de La Mole had resumed, along with friendship for her brother, a cult of strict conventionality. Although the weather was delightful that evening, she insisted they must not go into the garden; she refused to leave the armchair where Mme. de La Mole was seated. The blue sofa was the center of the group, as in winter.

Mathilde was angry with the garden, or at least it seemed to her completely boring: it was linked with the memory of Julien.

Misery weakens the judgment. Our hero was fool enough to return to that little cane-bottom chair which formerly had been the scene of his brightest triumphs. Today nobody said a word to him; his presence passed as if unperceived, or even worse. Those of Mlle. de La Mole's friends who sat near him, at the end of the sofa, seemed to make a point of turning their backs on him, or at least so he thought.

It's like the fall of a favorite in a court, he thought. He wanted to study for a while the people who pretended thus to crush him with their disdain.

The uncle of M. de Luz had an important post in the king's service, from which it followed that this spruce young officer began his conversation with each successive arrival by bringing forth the following fascinating detail: his uncle had left about seven o'clock for Saint-Cloud and expected to spend the night there. This detail was introduced with many formulas of good fellowship, but it never failed to turn up.

Observing M. de Croisenois with the acid eye of the unhappy, Julien noted what an extraordinary consequence this decent and

agreeable young man ascribed to occult influences. He carried it so
far as to grow gloomy and sulky if he saw an event of any importance at all explained by a simple and natural cause. There's a
touch of madness here, Julien thought. His character corresponds
remarkably with that of the Emperor Alexander as it was described
to me by Prince Korasoff. During the first year of his stay in Paris,
poor Julien, who came straight from the seminary, was so dazzled
by the graces of all these attractive young men, which were quite
new to him, that he could only admire them. Only now was their
real character starting to unfold before his eyes.

I am playing an undignified part here, he thought suddenly. The
problem was how to leave his little cane chair in not too clumsy a
manner. He wanted to invent; he demanded something new of an
imagination fully engaged elsewhere. He was obliged to have recourse to memory, and his was, admittedly, not very fertile in resources of this sort; the poor fellow still had very little polish, so
that when he rose to leave the drawing room, his clumsiness was
complete and everyone noticed it. Misery was all too evident in his
whole deportment. For three quarters of an hour he had been playing the role of a bothersome underling from whom people don't
bother to conceal their opinion of him.

The critical attention he had been paying his rivals, however, prevented him from taking his misery too tragically; and, to sustain his
pride, he had the memory of what had occurred the night before
last. However many advantages they may have over me, he thought,
as he wandered into the garden by himself, Mathilde has never
been for any of them what twice in my life she deigned to be for
me.

His wisdom went no further than that. He understood not at all
the character of the singular person whom chance had rendered
absolute mistress of all his happiness.

The following day he undertook to kill both his horse and himself
with exhaustion. That evening he made no effort to approach the
blue sofa to which Mathilde remained faithful. He noted that
Comte Norbert did not even condescend to look at him when they
met around the house. He must be doing some violence to his feelings, Julien thought, since by nature he is so polite.

For Julien, sleep would have been perfect happiness. Despite
physical fatigue, memories that were all too seductive began to occupy his entire imagination. He did not have the wit to see that
when he took those long horseback rides through the woods around
Paris, acting only on himself and not at all on Mathilde's mind or
heart, he was leaving up to chance the disposition of his own destiny.

It seemed to him that only one thing could bring perfect solace to his grief: that would be to talk to Mathilde. But then what would he dare to say to her?

This is what he was brooding over one morning about seven o'-clock when suddenly he saw her enter the library.

—I know, sir, that you want to talk to me.

—Great God! Who told you that?

—I know it, what more do you want? If you are devoid of honor, you can ruin me, or at least try it; but this danger, which I don't think is real, will certainly not stop me from speaking my mind. I no longer love you, sir, my foolish imagination misled me. . . .

Under this terrible blow, frantic with love and misery, Julien tried to excuse himself. Nothing more ridiculous. Is there any excuse for failing to please? But reason was no longer in control of his be-havior. A blind instinct drove him to put off the decision of his fate. It seemed to him that as long as he was talking all was not over. Mathilde did not hear his words; their very sound angered her; she could not imagine anyone having the audacity to interrupt her.

This morning she was being tormented equally by remorse springing from virtue and remorse springing from pride. She was practically crushed at the thought of having given rights over her person to a little abbé, the son of a peasant. It is very nearly, she told herself when exaggerating her grief, as if [, after dreaming of the lofty qualities and distinction of the man I loved,] I had to be ashamed of a weakness for one of the footmen.

With these bold, proud people, it is always just one step from self-hatred to fury against other people; when this step is taken, transports of rage give them keen pleasure.

In an instant, Mlle. de La Mole reached the stage of overwhelm-ing Julien with marks of the most withering contempt. She was fearfully clever, and her cleverness was at its best in the art of tor-turing peoples' self-esteem and inflicting savage wounds.

For the first time in his life Julien found himself subjected to the working of a superior mind, aroused against him to the most violent hatred. Far from having the slightest idea of defending himself at this moment, his [agile imagination] turned at once to self-contempt. When he heard himself covered with a scorn so bitter and so skillfully directed to the destruction of every last good opin-ion he might have of himself, he thought that Mathilde must be right, and that she wasn't going far enough.

For her part, she felt a delicious pleasure in thus punishing her-self and him for the adoration she had felt several days before.

She had no need to invent or to cultivate originality when she be-gan heaping bitter words upon him with so much self-satisfaction.

She had merely to repeat the things that had been said in her heart for the last week by the spokesman of the anti-love party.

Every word increased Julien's fearful misery a hundredfold. He tried to escape; Mlle. de La Mole gripped him imperiously by the arm.

—Be good enough to observe, he told her, that you are talking very loud; people can hear you in the next room.

—What do I care? replied Mlle. de La Mole arrogantly, who will ever dare to tell me he listened? I want to purge your puny little self-esteem forever of certain conceptions it may have formed on my account.

When Julien could leave the library, he was so stunned that he actually felt his grief less keenly. All right! so she doesn't love me anymore, he kept saying to himself, speaking aloud as though explaining his position to himself. It seems she loved me for eight or ten days, and I shall love her all my life long.

Is it possible that she meant nothing to me, nothing at all, only a few days ago!

The pleasures of pride flooded through Mathilde's heart; so she had managed to break off forever! To triumph absolutely over so pronounced an inclination would surely render her perfectly happy. And so this little gentleman will understand, once and for all, that he doesn't have and will never have any power of command over me. She was so happy that at this moment she was really quite drained of love.

After so atrocious and humiliating a scene, anyone less impassioned than Julien would have found love impossible. Without abandoning for an instant her dignity, Mlle. de La Mole had flung at him certain of those disagreeable remarks that are so subtly calculated that they seem to be true even when one recollects them in a moment of calm.

The first conclusion that Julien drew on the spot from this amazing scene was that Mathilde's pride was limitless. He firmly believed that all was over between them, and yet, next day at luncheon, he was awkward and timid in her presence. That was a fault that could not have been found with him before. In little as in great things, he had usually known exactly what he should do, and wanted to do, then carried it out.

That day, after lunch, Mme. de La Mole requested a seditious and rather rare pamphlet that her parish priest had given her secretly that morning; as he picked it up from a side table, Julien knocked over an old vase of blue porcelain, the most hideous thing there could be.

Mme. de La Mole rose with a cry of distress and came over to inspect the shattered ruins of her favorite vase. It was an antique

from Japan, she said; it came from my great aunt the Abbess of
Chelles; it was a present given by the Dutch to the regent Duke of
Orleans, who gave it to his daughter . . . .

Mathilde had followed her mother, rejoicing in the ruin of this
blue vase, which had always seemed to her horribly ugly. Julien was
silent and by no means overly disturbed; he glanced at Mlle. de La
Mole, standing beside him.

—The vase, he said, is destroyed forever, and so it is with a feeling that once ruled in my heart; I beg you to accept my apologies
for all the follies into which it led me; and he went out.

—Really! said Mme. de La Mole as he left, one would think this
M. Sorel was proud and pleased at what he has just done.

The phrase struck Mathilde to the heart. It is true, she told herself, my mother guessed right, that is exactly how he feels. Only
then did her joy in the scene she had played with him the day before come to an end. All right, everything is over, she told herself
with apparent calm; what I have left is a great example; this sort of
mistake is frightful, humiliating! It will guarantee my wisdom for
the rest of my life.

Wasn't I telling the truth, Julien thought; why does the love I felt
for that madwoman keep on tormenting me?

That love, far from dying away, as he had hoped, was making
rapid strides. She is crazy, it's true, he told himself, but is she any
less adorable for that? Is it possible for a girl to be more beautiful?
Everything that the most elegant civilization can offer in the way of
brilliant delight, isn't it all perfectly present in Mlle. de La Mole?
Memories of bygone happiness took possession of Julien and rapidly undermined all the fortifications of reason.

Reason strives in vain against memories of this sort; its sternest
efforts succeed only in augmenting the charm.

Twenty-four hours after breaking the antique Japanese vase,
Julien was decidedly one of the unhappiest of mortals.

Chapter 21

THE SECRET NOTE

> For everything I describe I've seen; and though I may have seen
> incorrectly, I am certainly not deceiving you in my descriptions.
> —From a letter to the author

The marquis summoned him; M. de La Mole seemed younger,
his eye was sparkling.

—Let's have a word about your memory, he said to Julien, I hear
that it's prodigious. Could you get four pages by heart and go and
recite them in London? But without changing a word! . . .

The marquis was thumbing crossly through the pages of that morning's *Quotidienne* and trying vainly to conceal an air of great seriousness which Julien had never seen him assume, not even when they were talking about the lawsuit with Frilair.

Julien had enough social grace to feel that he ought to go along with the casual manner that was being displayed.

—Very likely this issue of the *Quotidienne* is not particularly amusing; but, if Monsieur le marquis will allow me, tomorrow morning I shall have the honor to recite the whole thing to him.

—What! even the ads?

—Precisely, and word for word.

—You give me your word? replied the marquis, looking suddenly grave.

—Indeed, sir, only the fear of not keeping it might disturb my memory.

—The fact is, I should have asked that question yesterday: I am not going to ask you for a vow never to repeat what you are about to hear; I know you too well to insult you that way. I have vouched for you, I am going to bring you into a room where some dozen people will be gathered; you will keep notes of what each one says.

Don't be upset, it won't be confused conversation, each one will speak in turn; I don't mean to say formally, the marquis added, resuming that light, clever tone that was his natural manner. While we talk, you will write down twenty pages or so; we will come back here and reduce those twenty pages to four. Those four pages are what you will repeat to me tomorrow morning instead of this whole issue of the *Quotidienne*. You will then leave at once; you will have to travel post like a young man traveling for pleasure. Your chief purpose will be to pass unnoticed by anyone. You will come into the presence of a great personage. There you will need more subtlety. It will be a matter of deceiving his whole retinue; for among his secretaries, among his servants, there are men in the pay of our enemies, who are on the lookout for our agents to intercept them.

You will have a meaningless letter of introduction.

When His Excellency first looks at you, you will pull out my watch, which I have here and will lend you for your trip. Take it now, while we think of it, and give me yours.

The duke himself will condescend to copy, from your dictation, the four pages you have learned by heart.

When that is done, but, mark my words, not a moment sooner, you may, if His Excellency questions you, tell him about the meeting you are going to attend.

It may keep you from feeling bored on your trip to know that between Paris and the minister's residence there are people who would like nothing better than to put a bullet into Abbé Sorel. Then his mission is over, and I foresee a long delay in our business; for, my dear fellow, how will we learn of your death? Your zeal will scarcely suffice to bring us the word.

Run along now, and buy yourself a complete outfit, the marquis resumed, speaking seriously. Dress after the fashion of a couple of years back. Tonight you must have a slightly scruffy look. When you travel, however, you will look as usual. That surprises you; you are suspicious enough to guess why? Yes, my friend, one of the venerable persons who will be delivering his opinion tonight is quite capable of sending dispatches, as a result of which you would be given opium at least one evening in some fine inn where you had asked for supper.

—It might be better, said Julien, to do another thirty leagues and not take the direct road. I am heading toward Rome, I suppose. . . .

The marquis assumed an air of lofty discontent which Julien had not seen in so marked a form since Bray-le-Haut.

—That's a matter of which you will learn, sir, when I think it appropriate to tell you. I don't like questions.

—This wasn't a question, Julien replied effusively; I swear, sir, I was just thinking out loud, I was trying to imagine the safest road.

—Yes, it's apparent your mind was wandering far away. Never forget that an ambassador, especially when he is of your age, must not seem to be forcing confidences.

Julien was greatly mortified; he was in the wrong. His self-esteem cast about for an excuse, and found none.

—You should understand, too, M. de La Mole went on, that people always appeal to their sincerity when they have done something foolish.

An hour later, Julien was in the marquis' waiting room, dressed as an underling in a castoff suit with a neckcloth of dubious whiteness, and something definitely menial about his whole appearance.

When he saw him, the marquis burst out laughing, and only then was Julien really returned to favor.

If this young man betrays me, thought M. de La Mole, whom can I trust? And yet when action is called for, one must trust somebody. My son and his brilliant friends of that ilk have honesty and loyalty enough for a hundred thousand; if it came to a battle, they would perish on the steps of the throne, they know everything . . . except what we need at this moment. Devil take me if I can think of one of them who could learn four pages by heart and cover a hundred leagues without being tracked down. Norbert might get himself killed like his ancestors, and that's what a conscript can do too. . . .

The marquis sank into a deep meditation: And even at getting himself killed, he reflected with a sigh, perhaps this Sorel could do it just as well as he. . . .

—Let's take the carriage, said the marquis, as if to banish an un-welcome thought.

—Sir, said Julien, while they were getting this costume ready for me, I learned by heart the first page of today's *Quotidienne*.

The marquis took up the paper; Julien recited without missing a single word. Good, thought the marquis, very much the diplomat that evening; during all this time the young man is paying no atten-tion to the streets through which we are driving.

They entered a large room of rather gloomy aspect, partly pan-eled and partly hung in green velvet. In the middle of the room a hard-faced footman had just finished setting up a big dinner table, which he then converted to a work table by spreading over it an im-mense green cloth spattered with ink blots, discarded from some-one's office.

The master of the house was an enormous man whose name was never mentioned; Julien thought he had the features and the elo-quence of a man preoccupied with his own digestion.

At a gesture from the marquis, Julien had taken his position at the foot of the table. To give himself countenance, he began to trim his pens. Out of the corner of his eye, he counted seven speakers, but he could see nothing of them but their backs. Two of them seemed to address M. de La Mole on a footing of equality, the oth-ers seemed more or less deferential.

Another person arrived unannounced. This is odd, Julien thought, they don't announce people in this house. Have they taken this precaution in my honor? Everyone rose to welcome the newcomer. He wore the same extremely distinguished decoration as three other people already in the room. They talked in undertones. To judge the newcomer, Julien was forced to rely on what he could learn from his features and his dress. He was short and thick-set, ruddy in coloring, with a keen eye and no other expression on his face than the ferocity of a wild boar.

Julien's attention was distracted abruptly by the arrival of a quite different person. It was a tall man, very lean, wearing three or four waistcoats. His expression was soothing, his comportment suave.

That's just the expression of the old bishop of Besançon, Julien thought. This man plainly belongs to the church; he doesn't look more than fifty or fifty-five, and no one could have a more paternal expression.

The young bishop of Agde appeared, looking very much aston-ished; as he glanced over those in attendance, his eye fell on Julien. He had not addressed a word to him since the ceremony of Bray-le-Haut. His look of surprise embarrassed and irked Julien. What the deuce! he said to himself, is knowing a man always going to be held against me? All these great gentlemen whom I've never laid eyes on before disturb me not at all, and a look from this young bishop turns me to ice! It can't be doubted, I'm a strange, unlucky fellow.

A small black-haired man entered noisily and began to talk as he crossed the threshold; he had a sallow complexion and a slightly distracted expression. As soon as this pitiless talker arrived, little groups began to shape up, apparently to escape the boredom of listening to him.

As the group around the fireplace broke up, they came closer to the foot of the table where Julien was placed. His expression became more and more embarrassed; for, in fact, whatever efforts he made, he could not help overhearing them, and however little experience he had, he could not help understanding the full importance of what was being openly discussed. And he understood too how important it was for the distinguished people around him to keep these matters secret.

Already, working as slowly as he could, Julien had sharpened a score of pens; before long this resource would fail him. He looked vainly for instructions from the eyes of M. de La Mole; the marquis had forgotten him.

What I am doing is silly, Julien thought, as he trimmed his pens; but these people who look so mediocre and are charged, either by others or by themselves, with such great interests must be extremely touchy. My unhappy expression has about it something questioning and disrespectful, which will surely irk them. And if I lower my eyes too far, it will look as if I am trying to keep account of their words.

His embarrassment was extreme; he was hearing some extraordinary things.

Chapter 22

THE DISCUSSION

> The republic—there is not one person today who would sacrifice his all to the public good; there are thousands and millions who know nothing but their pleasures, their vanity. A man is esteemed in Paris because of his carriage, not because of his conscience.
> —Napoleon, *Mémorial*

The footman burst in, saying: His Excellency, the Duke of _____.

—Hold your tongue, you fool, said the duke as he entered. He said it so well, and with so much dignity, that in spite of himself Julien thought that the sum of this great man's knowledge must be his talent for getting angry with footmen. Julien raised his eyes, then lowered them at once. He had estimated so exactly the capacity of the new arrival that he was afraid his glance might be thought an indiscretion.

The duke was a man of fifty, dressed like a dandy, and moving as if he had been wound up. He had a narrow head with a big nose, and a face that seemed to curve forward as if to come to a point; it would have been hard to appear more noble or more insignificant. His coming marked the start of the discussion.

Julien was startled out of his study of physiognomies by the voice of M. de La Mole.—Let me introduce to you Abbé Sorel, said the marquis; he is possessed of an astounding memory. Barely an hour after I told him of the mission that might be entrusted to him, he gave proof of his memory by learning verbatim the first page of the *Quotidienne*.

—Ah, the strange news about poor N_____, said the master of the house. He snatched up the paper, and, looking at Julien with a mocking eye, in an effort to look important, said to him: Well, begin, sir.

Silence fell; every eye was fixed on Julien; he recited so well that after twenty lines the duke said:—All right, that will do. The little man who looked like a boar sat down. He was to preside over the meeting, for as soon as he had sat down, he showed Julien a card table and gestured for him to place it alongside his seat. Julien established himself there with all his writing materials. He counted twelve persons seated around the green cloth.

—M. Sorel, said the duke, withdraw into the next room, we will send for you.

The master of the house grew uneasy: the shutters aren't locked, he said half-audibly to his neighbor.—There's no good your trying to look out the window, he called foolishly to Julien. —Well, thought the latter, here I am caught up in a conspiracy, or maybe something worse. Fortunately, it's not one of the sort that lead to the Place de Grève. Even if there is a bit of danger, I owe this and a lot more to the marquis. I should be happy if I could atone in this way for all the distress my follies may some day cause him.

Even as he was thinking of his follies and his griefs, he was studying his surroundings to be sure of never forgetting them. Only then did he recall that he had never heard the marquis tell his footman the name of the street to which he was going, and that the marquis had called a public cab, as he never used to do.

Julien was left long to his own reflections. He was in a room hung in red velvet with wide gold fringe. On the side table stood a big ivory crucifix, and on the mantlepiece lay M. de Maistre's book *On the Pope*, with gilt edges and a magnificent binding. Julien opened it in order not to seem to be eavesdropping. From time to time loud voices were heard from the neighboring room. At last the door opened and he was summoned.

—Remember, gentlemen, said the chairman, from this moment on, we speak as in the presence of the Duc de _____. This gentleman, he added with a nod at Julien, is a young levite, devoted to our holy cause, who, thanks to his astonishing memory, will be able to repeat to the duke every last word we say.

The gentleman has the floor, he said, indicating the fatherly-looking man who wore extra waistcoats. Julien felt it would have been more natural to call the man with the waistcoats by his name. He took paper and wrote copiously.

(Here the author would have liked to place a page full of dots. That'll be rather clumsy, says the publisher, and for a book as frivolous as this one, clumsiness is fatal.

—Politics, replies the author, is a millstone hung on the neck of literature: within six months it will drag it to the bottom. Politics in the midst of imaginative activity is like a pistol shot in the middle of a concert. The noise is shattering without being forceful. It doesn't harmonize with any of the other instruments. Half the readers will be mortally offended at this politics, and the other half, who have already found more exciting and immediate politics in their morning paper, will be bored. . . .

—If your characters don't talk politics, says the publisher, then they are no longer Frenchmen of 1830, and your book is no longer a mirror, as you claim. . . .)

Julien's transcript ran to twenty-six pages; here is a pallid extract of it; for it was necessary, as usual, to suppress absurdities, which otherwise would be so many and tedious as to be quite improbable (see the *Gazette des Tribunaux*).[9]

The man with waistcoats and a fatherly expression (perhaps he was a bishop) smiled frequently, and then his eyes, between their quivering lids, took on a singular brilliance and an expression less indecisive than usual. This personage, who was asked to speak first in the presence of the duke (but what duke? Julien asked himself), and who seemed to take the role of attorney general, fell prey in Julien's opinion to the uncertainty and indecisiveness which is the common failing of such officials. In the course of the discussion, the duke went so far as to rebuke him for this.

After a few phrases of morality and indulgent philosophy, the man in waistcoats said:

—Noble England, guided by a great man, the immortal Pitt, has spent forty billion francs to destroy the Revolution. If this gathering

[handwritten margin note: emphasis on politics]

---

9. The *Gazette des Tribunaux* was a Paris journal, established during the 1820s, reporting law cases from all over France; here Stendhal first encountered the story of Antoine Berthet, the germ of the *Rouge*. But he did not much admire its ordinary style.

will permit me to express frankly an unhappy truth, England never really understood that with a man like Bonaparte, especially when one had nothing to put up against him but a collection of good intentions, the only decisive thing was personal measures. . . .[1]

—Ah! now we're back to praises of assassination! said the master of the house, looking uneasy.

—Spare us your sentimental homilies, cried the chairman angrily; his boar's eye glittered with a ferocious gleam. Go on, he said to the man in waistcoats. The cheeks and brow of the chairman were turning purple.

—Noble England, the speaker began again, is prostrate today because every Englishman, before buying his daily bread, is obliged to pay interest on the forty billion francs spent in defeating the Jacobins. She no longer has a Pitt. . . .

—She has the Duke of Wellington,[2] said a military personage, assuming a most imposing air.

—Silence, gentlemen, please, shouted the chairman; if we keep on arguing, there will be no point in our having sent for M. Sorel.

—We all know the gentleman has plenty of ideas, said the duke, looking angrily at the interrupter, who was a former general of Napoleon's. Julien saw this expression alluded to something personal and extremely offensive. Everyone smiled; the turncoat general seemed beside himself with fury.

—Pitt is no more, gentlemen, the speaker resumed, with the discouraged look of one who despairs of making his listeners hear reason. Even if a new Pitt should arise in England, it's impossible to diddle a nation twice with the same tricks. . . .

—That's exactly why a victorious general, a Bonaparte, will never be seen again in France, shouted the military heckler.

Neither the chairman nor the duke ventured to show their anger at this juncture, though Julien thought he could see in their eyes that they would very much have liked to. They lowered their eyes, and the duke contented himself with sighing loudly enough to be heard by everyone.

But the speaker had taken umbrage.

—You're very anxious to see me finish, he said heatedly, dropping completely all that smiling politeness and oily language that Julien

1. "Personal measures" is a polite term for assassination. The conspiracy represented in these chapters of the *Rouge* undoubtedly corresponds largely to the reality of ultraconservative political circles during the years between Waterloo and 1830. There were conspiracies to bring in foreign aid against reviving French radicalism. But though Stendhal built on fact, and many of the conspirators have traits reminiscent of actual figures of the ultra party, the conspiracy itself is a matter of fantasy.

2. The Duke of Wellington (1769–1852) was, after Waterloo, a sort of unofficial guardian of the peace of Europe; reactionaries everywhere kept in touch with him.

had thought was his natural way of expressing himself: you're anxious to see me finish; you don't appreciate the efforts I'm making not to offend anyone's ears, however long they happen to be. All right, gentlemen, I shall be brief.

And I will tell you in plain blunt words: England has not a penny left for the service of the good cause. Even if Pitt himself came back, with all his genius he would never succeed in deluding the petty English landlords, because they know that short campaign at Waterloo cost them, all by itself, a billion francs. Since you want plain words, added the speaker, growing more and more excited, I will give you one: *Help yourselves*, because England has not a guinea to give you, and when England doesn't pay, then Austria, Russia, and Prussia, which have only courage and no money, can fight no more than one or two campaigns against France.

It's possible to hope that the raw recruits raised by Jacobins will be beaten in the first campaign, maybe even in the second; but in the third, though to your partial eyes I may seem like a revolutionary, in the third, you'll have the soldiers of 1794, who were no longer the untrained peasants of 1792.[3]

Here interruptions broke out from three or four speakers at once.

—Sir, said the chairman to Julien, go into the next room and correct the first part of the transcript you've made. Julien left, much to his regret. The speaker had touched on a set of speculations that formed the usual topic of his own thinking.

They're afraid that I'll laugh at them, he thought. When they called him back, M. de La Mole was saying with a seriousness that, for Julien who knew him, seemed extremely droll:

. . . Yes, gentlemen, this is the unhappy nation of which, more than any other, it can be said:

Shall it be a god, a table, or a pot?

Let it be a god! was the poet's cry.[4] And you, gentlemen, are the ones to whom this word, so noble and profound, should most appeal. Act on your own, and a noble France will reappear, much as our ancestors formed her, and as we ourselves saw her before the death of Louis XVI.

The English, or at least their noble lords, loathe as much as we do the shameful Jacobin: without English financing, Austria, Russia, and Prussia can hardly fight more than two or three battles. Will that serve to bring about a successful occupation, such as

---

3. Remembering the wars in which enthusiastic French Jacobins defended their revolution against all Europe during the early 1790s, the speaker assumes that royalist Europe will once more be united against revolutionary France.
4. "Shall it be a god, a table, or a pot?" La Fontaine, "The Sculptor and the Statue of Jupiter." *Fables*, IX, 6.

M. de Richelieu[5] frittered away so stupidly in 1817? I don't think so.

Here there was an interruption, but it was repressed by a general murmur for silence. Its source once again was the former imperial general, who wanted the blue ribbon decoration and so was eager to be included among the writers of the secret note.

—I do not think so, M. de La Mole resumed, when the stir had subsided. He emphasized the "I" with an insolence that charmed Julien. That was a fine stroke, he told himself, even as his pen flew over the paper almost as fast as the marquis' words. With a single well-placed emphasis, M. de La Mole wiped from the slate all the turncoat's twenty campaigns.

—We cannot depend on foreigners alone, the marquis continued, in the most judicial of tones, for a new military occupation. All these young people who are now writing incendiary articles in the *Globe* will give you three or four thousand young captains, among whom there may be found a Kléber, a Hoche, a Jourdan, a Pichegru,[6] but less well intentioned.

—We didn't know how to give him his proper glory, said the chairman, we ought to have made him immortal.

There must, in a word, be two parties in France, M. de La Mole resumed, two parties, not merely in name, but two clear, sharply divided parties. Let us know who has to be crushed. On the one hand, the journalists, the electors, public opinion; in a word, youth, and everyone who admires it. While these people stupefy themselves with empty words, we on our side have the definite advantage of eating off the budget.

At this point, more interruptions.

—You, sir, said M. de La Mole, addressing the interrupter with an admirable indolent ease, you don't eat off the budget, since that word seems to shock you, no, you devour forty thousand francs carried on the state budget and eighty thousand that you get from the civil list.

All right, sir, since you force me to it, I'll take you boldly as an example. Like your noble ancestors who followed Saint Louis on the crusade, in return for these hundred and twenty thousand francs,

---

5. M. de Richelieu is not, of course, the cardinal but his namesake the duke (1766–1822), who at the congress of Aix-la-Chapelle obtained in 1818 the departure of foreign troops from French soil.

6. Kléber was an architect, Hoche a private soldier, Jourdan a silk merchant, and Pichegru the son of a day laborer when the Revolution uncovered their military talents and made them generals and marshals of France. (But Pichegru sold out to the Bourbons—hence the chairman's melancholy reflection.) The *Globe* was a journal, liberal in its politics and romantic in its literary tastes (and one of the first French journals to combine those stances, thereby giving French romanticism a decisive turn away from the conservative "Throne and Altar" views of German romanticism); Stendhal contributed to the *Globe*, and it was widely influential in the July revolution of 1830.

you ought to show us at least a regiment, a company, or if that's too much, just a half company, just fifty men, ready to fight and devoted to the good cause, come life, come death. You have nothing but footmen, who in case of a revolt would be a threat only to yourself.

The throne, the altar, and the nobility may perish tomorrow, gentlemen, unless you can create in each district a force of five hundred *dedicated* men; dedicated, I mean, not only with the gallantry of the French but also with the tenacity of the Spanish.

Half of this troop should be composed of our sons, our nephews, in a word, of true gentlemen. Each one of them will have by his side not a cheeky little ribbon clerk who will show his true colors in a minute if ever 1815 recurs but an honest peasant, simple and straight as Cathelineau;[7] our gentleman will have indoctrinated him, will be his foster brother if possible. Let each one of us sacrifice a *fifth part* of his income to form this little troop of five hundred dedicated men to a district. Then you can count on a foreign occupation. Foreign soldiery will never enter our country even as far as Dijon unless they are certain of finding five hundred friendly soldiers in each district.

The crowned heads will never listen to you until you can report twenty thousand gentlemen ready to take up arms to open for them the gates of France. The service is hard, you say; gentlemen, this is the price of our heads. Between a free press and our existence as gentlemen it is war to the knife. Either you become businessmen, peasants, or you take up your guns. Be weak, if you want, but don't be stupid; open your eyes.

Form up your battalions, I say to you, in the words of the Jacobin song; then there will appear some noble Gustavus-Adolphus, who, seeing the principle of monarchy in imminent danger, will march three hundred leagues beyond his own boundaries and do for you what Gustavus did for the Protestant princes. Will you always go on talking instead of acting? In fifty years nothing will be left in Europe but presidents of republics, not a single king. And with those four letters, K-I-N-G, away go the priests and the gentlemen. I see in the future nothing but *candidates* making up to slimy *majorities*.

There's no point in my reminding you that France does not have today a trusted general, known and loved by all; that the army is organized only in the interests of the throne and the altar; that it has lost all its old troopers while each one of the Prussian and Austrian regiments counts fifty noncoms who have been under fire.

---

7. Jacques Cathelineau (1759–1793) was a peasant leader of the Vendée revolt, killed at the siege of Nantes.

Two hundred thousand young men of the middle class are passionately eager for war. . . .[8]

—No more of these unpleasant truths! The words came decisively from a grave personage, apparently a lofty ecclesiastic, for M. de La Mole smiled graciously instead of losing his temper—a point not lost upon Julien.

No more of these unpleasant truths. Let us sum up, gentlemen. The man who is about to have a gangrenous leg amputated has no business telling his surgeon: This diseased leg is perfectly sound. If you'll forgive the expression, gentlemen, the noble duke of —— is our surgeon.

There's the key word at last, thought Julien; so I shall be posting toward the —— tonight.

Chapter 23

THE CLERGY, LAND, AND LIBERTY

The first law of every creature is self-preservation, to keep alive. You sow hemlock and expect to reap corn!
—Machiavelli

The grave personage went on; it was clear that he was in the know; he expounded, with a gentle and moderate eloquence, wonderfully pleasing to Julien, the following grand truths:

1. England has not a guinea to give us; economy and Hume are in fashion there. Not even the *Saints* will contribute money, and Mr. Brougham will laugh in our faces.[9]
2. Impossible to obtain more than two campaigns from the crowned heads of Europe without English gold; and against the middle classes two campaigns will not be enough.
3. Necessity of forming an armed party in France, failing which the monarchical principle in Europe cannot be roused even to venture those two campaigns.

The fourth point I venture to propose to you as evident is this:

Impossibility of forming an armed party in France without the clergy. I say this boldly because I am going to prove it to you, gentlemen. The clergy must have everything.

1. Because, going about their business day and night, under the guidance of highly able men established far from the

8. Julien's phrase (p. 230) is picked up here by M. de La Mole as a cry of warning to the reaction.
9. The *Saints* and Mr. Brougham are, in the ultra accounting, the nonconformists and a leading independent of liberal leanings.

center of the storm, three hundred leagues from your frontiers. . . .

—Ah, Rome! Rome! cried the master of the house.

—Yes, sir, *Rome*, the cardinal replied proudly. Whatever jokes,
more or less clever, may have been customary when you were
young, I will say flatly that in 1830, the clergy, guided by Rome, is
the only body that speaks to the little man.

Fifty thousand priests repeat the same words on the exact day appointed by their leaders and the common people, who, after all,
furnish the soldiers, will be more stirred by the voice of their priests
than by all the little worms in the world. . . . (The directness of this
remark aroused some murmurs.)

The clergy have a spirit superior to yours, resumed the cardinal,
raising his voice; every step you have taken in the direction of this
capital point, *having an armed party in France*, has been taken by
us. Here various facts were cited. Who sent eighty thousand guns
into the Vendée? . . . etc., etc.

As long as the clergy do not have their lands, their wooded lands,
they have nothing.[1] The minute war breaks out, the minister of finance writes to his agents, there's no more money except for parish
priests. At heart, the French have no religious faith, and they love
war. So whoever gives them a war will be doubly popular, for making war is starving Jesuits, to use a vulgar expression; making war is
delivering the French people, those monsters of pride, from the
threat of foreign occupation.

The cardinal was heard with favor. . . . It is imperative, he said,
that M. de Nerval resign from the ministry; his name angers people
to no purpose.

At this, they all rose to their feet and began talking at once.
They'll send me out again, Julien thought; but even the prudent
chairman had forgotten Julien's presence and existence.

All eyes were turned on a man whom Julien recognized. It was
M. de Nerval, the first minister, whom he had seen before at the
Duc de Retz's ball.

The disorder was at its height, as newspapers say when they talk
about the Chamber of Deputies. After a long quarter hour, a measure of quiet was established.

Then M. de Nerval got up and put on an apostolic manner:

—I shall not for a moment pretend, said he in an unnatural
voice, that I do not want to remain in the ministry.

It has been demonstrated, gentlemen, that my name multiplies

---

1. After the Restoration a concerted move to restore to the clergy their ancient domains of
forest land was defeated, but the issue remained alive, particularly in the minds of the
clergy.

the influence of the Jacobins by turning many of the moderates against us. I should, therefore, be happy to resign; for the Lord's ways are visible to only a few; but, he added, looking directly at the cardinal, I have a mission; heaven has said to me: Either you will forfeit your head on a scaffold or you will reestablish monarchy in France and reduce the chambers to what they were in the parliament of Louis XV, and that, gentlemen, *that I will do.*

He stopped, sat down, and a great silence followed.

There's a good actor, thought Julien. As usual, he made the mistake of crediting people with too much intelligence. Agitated by the evening's lively controversy, and above all by the sincerity of the discussion, M. de Nerval for the moment actually believed in his mission. With a great deal of courage, he had little common sense.

Midnight struck during the silence that followed the fine phrase, *that I will do.* Julien felt that the clock's striking had something funereal and imposing about it. He was much moved.

Soon the discussion resumed, with increasing energy and above all with an incredible simplicity of mind. These people will have to have me poisoned, Julien thought at certain moments. How can they say such things in front of a plebeian?

Two o'clock struck, and they were still talking. The master of the house had long been asleep; M. de La Mole was obliged to ring for fresh candles. M. de Nerval the minister had left at quarter of two, but not until he had carefully studied Julien's features in a pocket mirror which the minister had with him. His departure seemed to leave everyone more at ease.

While the candles were being replaced,—God knows what that man is going to say to the king, the man in waistcoats whispered to his neighbor. He can make us all look foolish and spoil our game for the future.

But you must admit he shows plenty of assurance, or you might even call it effrontery, in turning up here. Before he became a minister, he used to be one of the regulars; but the portfolio changes all that; it buries a man's private concerns; he ought to have realized that.

No sooner had the minister left than Bonaparte's general closed his eyes. Now he murmured something about his health, his wounds, glanced at his watch, and took his leave.

—I'll bet, said the man in waistcoats, that the general is running after the minister; he is going to make his excuses for being found here, and pretend that he is our leader.

When the heavy-eyed servants had finished replacing the candles:

—Let's reach some decisions now, gentlemen, said the chairman, let's not try to persuade one another any more. Let us try to decide the tenor of the note that in less than forty-eight hours will be reaching our friends abroad. There has been talk of ministers. Now that M. de Nerval is gone, we can say openly, What do we care for ministers? They will want what we want.

The cardinal indicated his approval with a thin smile.

—Nothing easier, it seems to me, than to summarize our position, said the young bishop of Agde, with the concentrated, collected passion of the most exalted fanaticism. He had been silent until now; after the first hour of discussion, his expression had changed, as Julien watched it, from an original gentle calm to fiery energy. Now he poured forth his soul like lava from Vesuvius.

—Between 1806 and 1814, England made only one mistake, said he, and that was not to act directly and personally against Napoleon. As soon as that man began creating dukes and chamberlains, as soon as he reestablished the throne, the mission that God gave him was over; the only thing to do was to destroy him. The Holy Scriptures teach us in more than one passage how to get rid of tyrants. (Here there were several citations in Latin.)

Today, gentlemen, it is not just a single man who must be destroyed, it is Paris. All France takes Paris as its model. What good will it do to arm your five hundred men per district? A dangerous project, and an endless one. Why involve all France in a matter that pertains only to Paris? Paris alone with its newspapers and its drawing rooms has done the harm; let the new Babylon perish.

Between the altar and Paris there is war to the death. This catastrophe is even to the worldly advantage of the throne. Why didn't Paris dare to breathe under Bonaparte? Ask the artillerymen of Saint-Roch. . . .[2]

It was not until three in the morning that Julien left with M. de La Mole.

The marquis was tired and disheartened. For the first time in his conversations with Julien there was a tone of appeal in his voice. He begged him on his word not to reveal the excesses of zeal, that was his expression, which he had just chanced to observe. Don't speak of it to our friend abroad unless he really insists on it in order to know something about our young hotheads. What do they care if the state is overthrown? They will be cardinals, and will take refuge in Rome, while we, in our country houses, are being massacred by the peasants.

The secret note the marquis drew up on the basis of Julien's big twenty-six page transcript was not ready until quarter of five.

—I am dead tired, said the marquis, and that's perfectly plain

---

2. Near the church of St. Roch by the Tuileries, Napoleon's artillerymen fired the "whiff of grapeshot" (October 5, 1795).

from the note itself, which is rather short on clarity toward the end; I'm more dissatisfied with it than with anything I ever did in my life. And now, my friend, he added, go get a few hours' rest, and just to keep anyone from kidnapping you, I'm going to lock you in your room.

The next day the marquis brought Julien to an isolated country house at some distance from Paris. His hosts there were some remarkable people, whom Julien supposed to be priests. They gave him a passport bearing a false name, but did at last reveal the destination of his journey, of which he had always pretended to be ignorant. He drove off alone in an open carriage.

The marquis had no misgivings about his memory since Julien had recited the secret note several times, but he was much afraid of his being waylaid.

—Be sure at all costs to look like a fop traveling to kill time, was his last friendly warning as he left the room. There may have been more than one false friend at our meeting last night.

The trip was rapid and very monotonous. Julien was scarcely out of the marquis' sight when he forgot the secret note and the mission and began to think of nothing but Mathilde's contempt.

At a village several leagues beyond Metz the master of the posting station came to inform him that no horses were to be had. It was ten o'clock at night; Julien, much put out, ordered supper. He strolled about before the door, and gradually, without seeming to do so, wandered toward the stable yard. No horses were to be seen.

Just the same, that man had a funny look about him, Julien said to himself; his ox-eye kept staring at me.

The reader will note that he was starting not to believe exactly everything that was told him. He thought about getting away after supper, and to learn something about the lie of the land, he left his room to go down and warm himself by the kitchen fire. He was overjoyed to find there Signor Geronimo, the celebrated singer.

Firmly planted in an armchair he had had shoved close to the fire, the Neapolitan was groaning aloud and talking more, all by himself, than the twenty gaping German peasants who stood around him.

—These people are going to ruin me, he called to Julien. I've promised to sing tomorrow at Mainz. Seven sovereign princes have gathered there to hear me. But let's go out for a breath of air, he added in a significant tone.

When he was a hundred feet down the road and out of earshot:

—Do you know what's going on? he asked Julien; this postmaster is a scoundrel. While strolling about, I gave twenty sous to a little blackguard who told me everything. There are more than a dozen horses in a stable at the other end of town. They're trying to hold up some courier.

—Oh, really? said Julien with an innocent air.

It wasn't enough to uncover the cheat, they had to get on with their journey; and this Geronimo and his friend were unable to do.—Let's wait for daylight, said the singer at last, these people suspect us. Perhaps it's you or me that they're looking for. Tomorrow morning we'll order a good breakfast; while it's preparing, we'll go for a stroll, make our escape, hire some horses, and use them to get to the next post station.

—And how about your luggage? said Julien, who was thinking that perhaps Geronimo himself might be an agent sent to intercept him. There was nothing to do but eat supper and go to bed. Julien was still in his first sleep when he was awakened with a start by the voices of two men talking in his room without any effort at concealment.

He recognized the master of the post, who was carrying a dark lantern. The light shone on the trunk of Julien's carriage, which had been carried up to his room. Beside the postmaster was a man who was coolly ransacking the open trunk. Julien could make out only the cuffs of his coat, which were black and very close fitting.

It's a cassock, he said to himself, and reached quietly for the little pistols he had put under his pillow.

—Don't worry about his waking up, your reverence, said the postmaster. The wine they were served was some of that you prepared yourself.

—I find no trace of papers, replied the priest. Plenty of clean linen, perfumes, ointments, fripperics; it's a young fellow of good society, interested in his own pleasures. The messenger is probably the other fellow, who pretends to speak with an Italian accent.

The men turned toward Julien to rummage in the pockets of his traveling coat. He was greatly minded to kill them as thieves. His moral position would have been unassailable. He was sorely tempted. I'd be no better than a fool, he thought, I would be endangering my mission. The priest finished searching through his coat, and said: This is no diplomat. He turned away, and it was a good thing he did.

If he touches me in my bed, so much the worse for him, Julien was thinking; it's perfectly possible he'll be trying to stab me, and that I can't have.

The priest turned his head; Julien half opened his eyes; and what was his amazement to see Abbé Castanède! Actually, though the two men had lowered their voices a little, he had felt from the first that he recognized the speech of one, Julien was seized with a sudden impulse to purge the earth of one of its lowest scoundrels. . . .

—But my mission! he reminded himself.

The priest and his acolyte went out. After a quarter of an hour

Julien pretended to wake up. He shouted and woke the entire house.

—I've been poisoned! he cried. I'm in agonies! He needed a pretext for going to the aid of Geronimo. He found him half overcome by the dose of laudanum that had been in his wine.

Julien, fearing some trick of this sort, had eaten nothing but some chocolate brought from Paris. He could not succeed in rousing Geronimo enough to get him on the road.

—You could offer me the whole kingdom of Naples, said the singer, I still wouldn't give up the pleasure of going back to bed.

—But the seven sovereign princes!

—Let them wait.

Julien left by himself and arrived without further adventures at the residence of the great personage. He wasted a whole morning asking vainly for a hearing. Luckily, about four o'clock the duke decided to go out for a stroll. Julien saw him leave the house on foot and had no hesitation about going up to him and begging for charity. When only a few feet away from the great personage, he drew forth the Marquis de La Mole's watch and ostentatiously consulted it. *Follow me at a distance*, he was told without so much as a second glance.

A quarter of a league further on the duke turned abruptly into a little *Kaffeehaus*. It was in a room of this very inferior inn that Julien had the honor of reciting his four pages to the duke. When he had finished, he was told: *Begin again and go more slowly.*

The prince took notes. *Go on foot to the next post. Leave your luggage and your carriage here. Go to Strasbourg any way you can, and on the twenty-second of this month* (it was now the tenth) *be in this Kaffeehaus at half past twelve noon. Wait half an hour before you leave here. Silence!*

These were the only words that Julien heard. They sufficed to raise him to a pitch of admiration. Now this, he thought, this is the way to handle great affairs; what would this great statesman say if he had heard those passionate babblers three days ago?

Julien put two days into reaching Strasbourg, where he supposed he would have nothing to do. He took the long way around. If that devil Abbé Castanède recognized me, he is not a man to be easily thrown off the scent. . . . And what pleasure it would be for him to make a fool of me and bring my whole mission to naught!

Fortunately, Abbé Castanède, chief of the congregation police along the northern frontier, had not recognized him. And the Jesuits of Strasbourg, though thoroughly zealous, never dreamed of setting a watch on Julien, who, with his cross and his blue greatcoat, had the look of a youthful soldier much attached to his own personal appearance.

Chapter 24

STRASBOURG

Fascination! you have all the energy of love, all its power to endure suffering. Only its enchanting pleasures, its sweet delights,
are beyond your sphere. I could not say, when I saw her lying
asleep: she is all mine, with her angelic beauty and her sweet frailties! There she is delivered into my power, just as heaven created
her in its compassion to enchant the heart of man.

—Ode of Schiller

Compelled to spend a week in Strasbourg, Julien tried to divert
himself with thoughts of military glory and patriotic devotion. Was
he really in love? He could not tell; he knew only that within his
tortured spirit Mathilde remained in full command of his happiness
as of his imagination. He required the full energy of his character
to maintain himself above the level of despair. To think of something unrelated to Mme. de La Mole was beyond his power. In earlier days ambition and the simple triumphs of vanity had distracted
him from the feelings that Mme. de Rênal aroused in him.
Mathilde had absorbed everything; he found her everywhere in his
future.

Wherever he looked, Julien saw in this future nothing but failure. The man who appeared at Verrières so bloated with presumption and pride had now fallen into a ridiculous extreme of modesty.

Three days before, he would joyfully have killed Abbé Castanède,
and now at Strasbourg, if a child had picked a quarrel with him, he
would have knuckled under. When he numbered over the adversaries and enemies he had had during his life, Julien found that invariably he himself had been in the wrong.

The fact was that he now had as an implacable enemy that brilliant imagination of his, which previously had been busy all the
time painting the future with his splendid successes.

The absolute solitude of a traveler's life further reinforced the
power of this somber imagination. What a treasure a friend would
have been! But, Julien asked himself, is there a heart anywhere that
beats for me? And even if I had a friend, doesn't honor impose perpetual silence on me?

He took horse and rode gloomily in the suburbs of Kehl; it is a
town on the banks of the Rhine rendered immortal by Desaix and
Gouvion Saint-Cyr.[3] A German peasant pointed out to him the little
streams, the roads, and the islands in the Rhine which the courage

---

3. Desaix and Gouvion St. Cyr won a brilliant victory at Kehl in 1796 by an audacious
crossing of the Rhine against heavy opposition.

of those great generals made known. Julien, as he held the reins with his left hand, unfolded with his right the superb map that adorns the *Mémoires* of Marshal Saint-Cyr. A merry hail caused him to lift his head.

It was Prince Korasoff, that London acquaintance, from whom Julien had acquired some months before the first principles of the higher fatuity. Faithful to this great art, Korasoff, who had been at Strasbourg since yesterday and at Kehl for an hour, who had never in his life read a line about the siege of 1796, set about explaining the whole thing to Julien. The German peasant looked at him in amazement; he knew just enough French to recognize the enormous blunders the prince was making. Julien's ideas were a thousand miles from those of the peasant; he was looking with astonishment at this handsome young man and admiring his poise in the saddle.

What a happy disposition! he said to himself. How well his trousers fit, how elegantly his hair is cut! Alas! if I had been like that, perhaps after loving me for three days she might not have taken such a dislike to me.

When the prince had finished his siege of Kehl: —You look like a Trappist monk, he told Julien, you're overdoing the principle of gravity I laid down for you in London. A gloomy air can never be good form; what you need is the air of boredom. If you're gloomy, there must be something you lack, something at which you haven't succeeded.

It is admitting your inferiority. But if you're bored, on the other hand, it's the person who has tried unsuccessfully to please you who is inferior. You must understand, my dear fellow, what a grave mistake you are making.

Julien flung a crown to the peasant who was listening to them, open-mouthed.

—Well done, said the prince, there was grace in that gesture, a noble disdain! Very good indeed! And he put his horse to the gallop. Julien followed him, full of stunned admiration.

Ah! if I had been like that she would not have preferred Croisenois before me! The more his reason was shocked by the prince's absurdities, the more he despised himself for not admiring them, and thought himself unfortunate not to have them in his own person. [That's the way to be, he told himself.] Self-loathing cannot be carried any further.

The prince, finding him decidedly gloomy: —Come along, now, my dear fellow, he told him as they rode back to Strasbourg, [you're very poor company,] have you lost all your money or are you in love with some little actress?

The Russians copy French customs, but always at a distance of fifty years. They are just now coming into the age of Louis XV.

These jests about love brought tears to Julien's eyes: Why not seek the advice of this friendly man? he asked himself suddenly.

—Very well, my dear fellow, he told the prince, as a matter of fact you're right; here I am at Strasbourg, head over heels in love, but unhappily. A charming woman who lives in one of the towns nearby has turned me out after three days of passion, and this change will be the death of me.

Using fictitious names, he described to the prince the actions and character of Mathilde.

—Say no more, said Korasoff; to give you confidence in your doctor, I cut short your confession. Either this young lady's husband is enormously rich or else she belongs to the most distinguished nobility. She must have something to be proud of.

Julien inclined his head; he no longer had strength to speak.

—Very well, said the prince, here are three medicines, all rather bitter, for you to take without delay:

1. See every day Mme . . . what's her name?

—Mme. de Dubois.

—What a name! said the prince, with a shout of laughter; but I beg your pardon, for you it is sublime. Well, you must see Mme. de Dubois every day; and make a point of never seeming cold or out of sorts in her presence. Remember the great principle of your century: always be the contrary of what people expect. Show yourself as the exact same person you were a week before you were honored with her favors.

—Ah, I was at peace then, Julien cried in despair, I wanted to arouse her pity. . . .

—The moth burned up in the candle, said the prince, the oldest story in the world.

1. You will see her every day;

2. You will court another woman whom she knows, but without the slightest appearance of passion, do you understand? I won't conceal from you, your role is a hard one; you are acting a comedy, and if anyone suspects you of acting, there's no hope for you.

—She is so clever, and I am so dull, Julien said sadly; there's no hope for me.

—No, you're just more in love than I thought. Mme. de Dubois is deeply devoted to herself, like all women who have been granted either too much nobility or too much money. She has her eye on herself instead of on you, hence she does not know you. During the two or three periods when she felt impulses of love toward you, she made a great effort of imagination, seeing you as her dream hero, but not yourself as you really are . . .

But what the devil, these are the mere rudiments, my dear Sorel, are you just a schoolboy?

Damn it, look at this shop window; there's a perfectly charming black cravat, it might have been made by John Anderson of Burlington Street; do me the great favor of accepting it and throwing away that ignoble bit of black string you have around your neck.

Now then, continued the prince, as they left the shop of the best haberdasher in Strasbourg, what sort of friends has your Mme. de Dubois? Good God! what a name! Don't get angry, my dear Sorel, it's too much for me. . . . Where are you going to do your courting?

—To the most prudish prude in the world, daughter of a stocking merchant who has become immensely rich. She has lovely eyes, they please me no end; there's no doubt she's of the very highest rank in the district; but in the middle of all this splendor, she blushes and loses all her poise if anyone happens to talk of commerce and shops. And unhappily, her father was one of the best-known tradesmen in Strasbourg.

—So if one mentions *industry*, said the prince with a laugh, one can be quite sure the dear creature is thinking of herself and not of you. A divine weakness and extremely useful; it will prevent you from ever seeming foolish in her fair eyes. Success is assured.

Julien was thinking of Mme. de Fervaques, the maréchale's widow, who often visited the Hôtel de La Mole. She was a beautiful foreigner who had married the maréchal the year before he died. Her whole life seemed to have no other aim than to make people forget she was the daughter of *a man in trade*, and in order to be something in Paris she had appointed herself leader of the party of virtue.

Julien admired the prince with all his heart; what wouldn't he have given to be possessed of his absurdities! The conversation between the two friends was interminable; Korasoff was in ecstasies: never had a Frenchman listened to him for such a long time. I've finally succeeded, the prince said to himself joyously. I've made my presence felt, and given lessons to my own teachers!

—We're agreed, then, he repeated to Julien for the tenth time, not a shadow of passion when you talk to this young beauty, the daughter of a Strasbourg stocking merchant, in the presence of your Mme. de Dubois. On the other hand, burning passion every time you write her. Reading a well-written love letter is the greatest pleasure in life for a prude; it is a moment of relaxation. She isn't playing the comedy; she summons up the courage to listen to her heart; so give her two letters a day.

—Never, never, said Julien, desponding; I'd sooner let myself be pounded up in a mortar than compose three sentences; I'm a corpse, my dear fellow, you can't expect anything of me. Let me die in a ditch.

—And who said anything about composing sentences? I have in

my traveling case six volumes of manuscript love letters. There are some for every different sort of woman; I have a set for the loftiest virtue. Don't you remember that Kalisky made love, at Richmond Terrace—you know, a few leagues from London—to the prettiest Quakeress in all England?

Julien was less wretched when he left his friend at two o'clock in the morning.

Next day the prince summoned a copyist, and two days later Julien had fifty-three love letters, carefully numbered, and designed to cope with the noblest and gloomiest case of virtue.

—The reason there aren't fifty-four, said the prince, is that Kalisky was given the boot; but what do you care if you're ill treated by the stocking man's daughter, since your only intent is to play on the heart of Mme. de Dubois?

Every day they went out riding: The prince was madly devoted to Julien. Not knowing how else to give proof of his sudden affection, he ended by offering him the hand of one of his cousins, a rich heiress in Moscow. Once married, he added, my influence and the decoration you have there will make you a colonel in two years.

—But this decoration was not given by Napoleon, far from it.

—What matter? said the prince. Didn't he invent it? It is still the most distinguished, by a long shot, in all Europe.[4]

Julien was on the point of accepting; but his duty called him back to the great personage; as he parted from Korasoff, he promised to write. He picked up the answer to the secret note he had delivered and posted toward Paris; but he had hardly been alone for two days on end when the thought of leaving France and Mathilde seemed to him a torture far worse than death. I shan't marry the millions Korasoff offered me, he said, but I will take his advice. After all, the art of seduction is his main business; he has thought about nothing else for more than fifteen years, since he is now thirty. You can't say he's lacking in brains; he's clever and shrewd; enthusiasm and poetry are impossibilities, given his character; he's a conniver; all the more reason why he probably is not wrong.

It's a necessity; I will pay court to Mme. de Fervaques.

She will bore me a good deal, no doubt, but I can gaze into those lovely eyes that resemble so much another pair which loved me more than anything in the world.

She's a foreigner; that's a new sort of character to study.

I am mad, I am drowning, I must follow the advice of my friend and not trust my own instincts.

---

4. The order instituted by Napoleon is the Legion of Honor, which he established in 1802.

Chapter 25

THE MINISTRY OF VIRTUE

> But if I sample this pleasure with so much prudence and cir-
> cumspection, it will no longer be a pleasure for me.
> —Lope de Vega

Scarcely was he back in Paris, no sooner had he left the study of
the Marquis de La Mole, who seemed much disconcerted by the
messages delivered to him, than our hero hastened to visit Comte
Altamira. Besides his special quality of carrying a death sentence,
this handsome foreigner rejoiced in a grave demeanor and was naturally devout; these two merits, and, above all, the count's lofty
birth, were most agreeable to Mme. de Fervaques, and she saw him
frequently.

Julien solemnly assured him that he was passionately in love.

—She is pure and lofty virtue incarnate, replied Altamira, she is
only a little Jesuitical and emphatic. There are days when I understand every individual word she uses but make no sense out of what
she is saying. She often gives me the impression that I don't know
French as well as people say. This acquaintance will make your
name known; it will give you standing in the world. But let's go and
see Bustos, said Comte Altamira, who had a strong sense of order;
he has paid court to Mme. la Maréchale.

Don Diego Bustos required a full-length explanation of the matter; meanwhile, he said not a word, like a lawyer in his office. He
had a fat monkish face with black moustaches and an unmatchable
solemnity; for the rest, a good revolutionary.[5]

—I understand, he told Julien at last. Has the Maréchale de Fervaques had lovers or hasn't she? Have you, thus, some hope of success or don't you? There is the question. I must confess that for my
own part I failed. Now that I am no longer nettled at it, I reason
this way: the lady is often out of sorts, and, as I shall explain to you
shortly, has a certain talent for spite.

I do not recognize in her that bilious temperament that is often a
mark of genius, and which casts over all one's actions, as it were, a
veneer of passion. On the contrary, it is because she is calm and
phlegmatic like a Dutchwoman that she preserves her rare beauty
and fresh complexion.

Julien was waxing impatient with the slow pace and unruffled
calm of the Spaniard; from time to time, in spite of himself, he gave
vent to various monosyllables.

---

5. The original reads, for "revolutionary," *carbonaro*, that is, an Italian republican conspirator.

—Do you want to hear what I have to say? Don Diego Bustos
said to him solemnly.

—Please excuse the *furia francese*,[6] Julien replied; I'm all ears.

—The Maréchale de Fervaques is, then, much addicted to hate;
she pursues implacably people whom she has never seen, lawyers,
poor devils of writers who have composed songs like Collé—[7] do
you know it?

> I have the woeful folly
> To be in love with Polly, etc.

And Julien had to listen to the whole thing. The Spaniard was
much gratified to be singing in French.

Never was that divine song listened to with greater impatience.
When it was over: —The maréchale, said Don Diego Bustos,
brought ruin upon the author of that song:

> One day the lover at the inn . . .

Julien shuddered lest he sing the whole thing. But he contented
himself with a critical analysis. As a matter of fact, it was an impious and almost indecent song.

When the maréchale grew angry with that song, said Don Diego,
I took occasion to remark that a lady of her station should not read
all the trash that people publish. However widespread piety and
gravity become, France will always have its tavern literature, I said.
When Mme. de Fervaques had deprived the author, a poor devil on
half pay, of a post worth eighteen hundred francs, I told her: Watch
out, you have attacked his rhymester with your weapons; he may
come back at you with his own: he'll make a song about virtue. No
doubt the gilded drawing rooms will be on your side, but the people
who like to laugh will repeat his epigrams. Do you know, my dear
sir, what the maréchale replied to me? —In the service of the Lord,
all Paris could turn out to see me tread the martyr's path; it would
be a new spectacle in France. The vulgar would learn to respect the
quality. It would be the most beautiful day of my life. And her eyes
had never been more enchanting.

—She has lovely eyes, Julien exclaimed.

—I can see that you're in love. . . . Well, then, said Don Diego
Bustos with great solemnity, she does not have the bilious constitution that conducts a woman to vengeance. If, nonetheless, she likes

---

6. Renaissance Italians, astonished at the French audacity in a charge, by contrast with the
   decorous mercenaries to whom they were accustomed, coined the term *furia francese*,
   that is French madness.
7. Charles Collé (1709–1783) wrote a great number of popular songs while employed as a
   government clerk.

to hurt people, it must be because she is unhappy; I suspect an *inward grief*. May she not be a prude grown tired of her trade?

The Spaniard stared at him silently for a full minute.

—This, then, is the basic question, he added gravely, and from this consideration you may draw some hope. I thought about it a good deal during the two years that I professed myself her humble obedient servant. Your entire future as a man in love depends on this great problem: Is she a prude grown tired of her trade and malicious because she is miserable?

—Or else, said Altamira, starting at last from his profound silence, would it be what I have told you twenty times over? simply French vanity. It's the recollection of her father, the famous haberdasher, which brings such grief to her naturally gloomy, dry character. There could be only one happiness for her, to live in Toledo and be tormented by a confessor who would describe to her every day the gaping mouth of hell.

As Julien was taking his leave: —Altamira tells me you are one of us, Don Diego told him, more gravely than ever. One day you will help us regain our liberty, so I should like to be of help to you in this little diversion. It would be a good idea for you to know the maréchale's style; here are four letters of her writing.

—I shall have them copied, said Julien, and bring them back to you.

—And no one will ever hear from you a word of what we've been saying?

—Never, on my honor! cried Julien.

—Then, God be with you! added the Spaniard; and without another word he ushered out to the staircase Julien and Altamira.

This scene restored our hero's spirits somewhat; he was on the verge of smiling. And here's the devout Altamira, he said to himself, helping me in an adulterous enterprise.

During all of Don Diego Bustos's weighty conversation, Julien had been listening to the hours as they were sounded by the clock of the Hôtel d'Aligre.

Dinnertime was at hand; he was about to see Mathilde again! He went home and dressed with great care.

First piece of foolishness, he told himself, as he was going downstairs; I must follow the prince's instructions to the letter.

He went back to his room and changed to a traveling costume of extreme simplicity.

Now, he said to himself, it's a matter of how to look at her. It was only five-thirty and they sat down to dinner at six. He had the notion of going down to the drawing room, which he found empty. [At the sight of the blue sofa, he fell to his knees and kissed the spot

where Mathilde placed her arm, tears flowed, his cheeks were
afire.] I must work off this absurd sensitivity, he told himself angrily; it will betray me. He picked up a newspaper to give himself
countenance, and strolled three or four times from the drawing
room into the garden and back.

It was only with great trepidation, and from the concealment af-
forded by a great oak, that he dared to raise his eyes to Mlle. de La
Mole's window. It was shut tight; he was on the point of collapse,
and stood for a long time, leaning against the oak; then, with wa-
vering steps, he went over to look at the gardener's ladder.

The link of chain, which he had twisted open under circumstances very different, alas, from the present, had not been repaired. Carried away by an impulse of madness, Julien pressed it to
his lips.

After straying back and forth for a long time between the drawing
room and the garden, Julien found himself horribly tired; it was a
first success which gave him great pleasure. My glances will be dull
and won't give me away! Gradually the guests gathered in the drawing room; the door never opened without striking mortal anguish to
Julien's heart.

They sat down to table. At last Mlle. de La Mole appeared, faithful to her rule of making people wait for her. She blushed deeply at
the sight of Julien; she had not been told of his return. Following
Prince Korasoff's advice, Julien looked at her hands; they were
trembling. Though indescribably disturbed by this discovery, he was
lucky enough to appear merely tired.

M. de La Mole sang his praises. The marquise spoke to him a
moment later and was kind enough to observe his air of weariness.
Julien kept saying to himself at every instant: I must not look too
often at Mlle. de La Mole, but neither must my eyes seem to avoid
her. I must seem to be exactly what I was in reality a week before
my misfortune. . . . He had reason to be satisfied with his performance, and remained in the drawing room after dinner. Attentive,
for the first time, to the lady of the house, he bent all his efforts toward making the men of her group talk and keeping the conversation alive.

His politeness was rewarded: promptly at eight Mme. la Maréchale de Fervaques was announced. Julien left the room and reappeared shortly, dressed with the most meticulous care. Mme. de La
Mole was infinitely obliged to him for this mark of respect, and undertook to show her pleasure by talking to Mme. de Fervaques of
his journey. Julien placed himself beside the maréchale in such a
way that his eyes could not be seen by Mathilde. So stationed, and
taking care to follow all the rules of the art, he focused upon Mme.
de Fervaques his most openmouthed admiration. The first of the

fifty-three letters given him by Prince Korasoff began with a tirade on this sentiment.

The maréchale declared she was going to the Opera Buffa. Julien hastened there too; he found the chevalier de Beauvoisis, who took him to a box occupied by gentlemen of the chamber, right alongside that of Mme. de Fervaques. Julien gazed at her continually. As he returned to the house, he told himself: I must keep a journal of the siege, otherwise I'll forget my various attacks. He forced himself to write two or three pages on this tedious topic, and thus succeeded, miracle of miracles! in hardly thinking of Mlle. de La Mole at all.

Mathilde had almost forgotten him while he was away. After all, he is only a common creature; his name will always remind me of the blackest blot on my life. I shall have to go back to those vulgar ideas of prudence and honor, when she forgets them, a woman has everything to lose. She showed herself disposed to allow the final steps to be taken in her arrangement with the Marquis de Croisenois, which had been so long in preparation. He was mad with joy; and he would have been amazed to learn that resignation was at the root of Mathilde's new attitude which was making him so proud.

All Mlle. de La Mole's ideas changed when she saw Julien. Actually, that man is my husband, she told herself; if I'm really sincere about returning to the paths of prudence, he is the man I ought to marry.

She was looking for importunities, an air of grieving on Julien's part; she was preparing her responses: for no doubt, when dinner was over, he would try to say a few words to her. Far from doing so, he remained planted in the drawing room; his glances never even turned toward the garden, Lord knows at what cost to his feelings! It's best to get the whole scene over with, thought Mlle. de La Mole; she strolled alone into the garden; Julien did not go. Mathilde walked past the drawing room windows; she saw him fully engaged in describing to Mme. de Fervaques those ancient ruined castles which crown the hilltops along the Rhine and give that landscape so much character. He was starting to draw with some fluency on that vein of sentimental and picturesque diction which, in certain quarters, is known as *wit*.

Prince Korasoff would have been proud indeed had he been at Paris: the evening took exactly the form he had predicted.

He would have approved, too, of Julien's conduct during the following days.

An intrigue within the backstairs cabinet was about to make available various blue-ribbon decorations; Mme. la Maréchale de Fervaques insisted that her uncle must be made a knight of the order. The Marquis de La Mole was putting forward for the same honor his father-in-law; they joined forces, and the maréchale came almost every day to the Hôtel de La Mole. It was from her that Julien learned that the marquis was to be a minister: he had offered the ruling clique an extremely clever scheme for destroying the charter, without any protest, in three years' time.

Julien might hope for a bishopric if M. de La Mole got into the ministry; but in his eyes all these great projects were hidden as behind a veil. His imagination grasped them now only hazily and, so to speak, from a distance. The frightful misery that was making a maniac of him converted all the interests of life into ways of being with Mlle. de La Mole. He calculated that after five or six years of constant effort he might make her love him again.

This head, usually so cool, had, as we see, sunk into a state of complete irrationality. Of all the qualities that had once distinguished him, nothing remained but a little firmness. Mechanically faithful to the plan of conduct dictated by Prince Korasoff, every evening he placed himself beside the armchair of Mme. de Fervaques, but he found it impossible to scrape up a word to say to her.

The effort he was making to appear healed in the eyes of Mathilde absorbed all the energy of his soul; he sat beside the maréchale like an almost lifeless being; even his eyes, as happens to men under the most extreme suffering, had lost all their light.

As Mme. de La Mole's way of seeing things was always a feeble imitation of the opinions of her husband, who might make her a duchess, she spent several days praising Julien to the skies.

Chapter 26

MORAL LOVE

> There also was of course in Adeline
>   That calm patrician polish in the address,
> Which ne'er can pass the equinoctial line
>   Of any thing which Nature would express:
> Just as a Mandarin finds nothing fine,
>   At least his manner suffers not to guess
> That anything he views can greatly please.
>   —*Don Juan*, canto XIII, stanza 84

This whole family has a rather crazy way of looking at things, thought the maréchale; they are all mad for their little abbé, who does nothing but sit still and listen, though it's true, his eyes are not bad-looking.

Julien, for his part, found in the manners of the maréchale an almost perfect specimen of that *patrician calm* which breathes an air of perfect politeness and especially the total impossibility of any keen emotion. Any spontaneous gesture, any lapse of complete self-control, would have scandalized Mme. de Fervaques almost as much as a failure of dignified condescension toward one's inferiors. The slightest sign of sensitivity would have been in her eyes a sort of *moral intoxication* of which one ought to be ashamed, since it undermines everything that a person of lofty rank owes to herself. Her greatest happiness was to talk about the king's latest hunting party; her favorite book was the *Mémoires du duc de Saint-Simon*,[8] especially the genealogical part.

Julien knew just what position in the drawing room, as the lights were arranged, was most suitable for Mme. de Fervaques' variety of beauty. He was always there waiting for her, but took great pains to adjust his chair so as not to notice Mathilde. Astonished at his persistence in avoiding her, she left the blue sofa one day and came to do her needlework at a little table near the maréchale's armchair. Julien saw her nearby from under the brim of Mme. de Fervaques' hat. Seeing [so near to him] those eyes in which his destiny was to be read, he was first terrified, then flung violently out of his ordinary apathy; he talked, and very well.

All his words were addressed to the maréchale, but his only end was to work on the mind of Mathilde. He grew so animated that Mme. de Fervaques found herself unable to understand what he was talking about.

That was a first merit. If Julien had had the notion of piling on a few sentences of German mysticity, lofty religiosity, and Jesuitism, the maréchale would immediately have placed him in the ranks of the superior men called to redeem the century.

Since he displays such bad taste, Mlle. de La Mole told herself, as to talk so long and so animatedly to Mme. de Fervaques, I shall pay no further attention to him. And for the rest of the evening she kept her word, though only with an effort.

That night, after Mathilde picked up her mother's candlestick to accompany her to her bedroom, Mme. de La Mole stopped short on the stairway to deliver an absolute eulogy of Julien. Mathilde at this finally lost her temper; she was unable to fall asleep. Only one idea soothed her: the man I despise still seems like a person of great merit to the maréchale.

As for Julien, he had taken an action, he was less miserable; his eyes fell by accident on the Russia-leather briefcase in which

---

8. The *Mémoires* of Saint-Simon (1675-1755) is a standard authority for the first half of the eighteenth century and a work of great literary merit; but the genealogies are not the liveliest part of it.

Prince Korasoff had placed the fifty-three love letters that were his gift to Julien. At the foot of the first letter was a note: *Send number one a week after the first meeting.*

I'm already behind schedule, Julien exclaimed, for I've been seeing Mme. de Fervaques a long time now. At once he sat down to transcribe this first love letter; it was a homily on virtue and deadly dull; Julien was lucky enough to fall asleep over the second page of it.

Some hours later the rising sun came upon him with his head resting on the table. One of the most painful moments of his life was that in which each morning as he awoke he *returned* to the sense of his misery. On this day, he finished copying his letter almost with a laugh. Is it possible, he asked himself, that anywhere in the world there's a young man who writes this way? He counted a number of sentences that were nine lines long. Under the original he found a penciled note.

> These letters are delivered by hand: on horseback, black necktie, blue greatcoat. Hand the letter to the porter with an air of contrition; deep melancholy in the gaze. If one catches sight of a chambermaid, wipe the eyes furtively. Say a few words to the maid.

All these instructions were faithfully carried out.

What I am doing is very bold, thought Julien, as he left the Hôtel de Fervaques; but so much the worse for Korasoff. Venturing to write to a woman so notorious for virtue! I shall meet with the fiercest scorn from her, and nothing could amuse me more. At bottom, it's the only sort of comedy I can enjoy. Yes, it will be fun to cover with ridicule that odious creature whom I call *me*. If I trusted my own feelings, I would commit some crime simply to divert myself.

For the last month, the happiest moment in Julien's life had been that in which he returned his horse to the stable. Korasoff had expressly forbidden him to look, on any pretext whatever, at the mistress who had left him. But the gait of that horse which she recognized so well, the way in which Julien knocked with his whip at the stable door in order to summon a man, these things sometimes attracted Mathilde behind the curtain of her window. The muslin was so filmy that Julien could see through. By looking in a certain way from under the brim of his hat he could see Mathilde's figure without seeing her eyes. Consequently, he told himself, she cannot see my eyes, and this does not amount, in any way, to looking at her.

That night Mme. de Fervaques behaved toward him exactly as if she had never received that philosophical-mystical-religious dissertation he had passed to her porter that morning with such a melancholy expression. The night before, accident had revealed to Julien the path to eloquence; he placed himself in such a way as to catch sight of Mathilde's eyes. She, for her part, left the blue sofa an instant after the maréchale arrived. To do this was to desert her regular set. M. de Croisenois seemed thunderstruck at this new caprice; his evident distress relieved Julien of the most atrocious part of his own suffering.

This unforeseen episode made him talk like an angel; and as complacency sometimes slips even into those hearts that act as temples to the most austere virtue: Mme. de La Mole is right, said the maréchale to herself as she stepped into her carriage, this young priest is really distinguished. It must have been that during the first days my presence intimidated him. Indeed, the general tone of this house is tinged with a good deal of levity; such virtue as I see needs help from old age and requires assistance from the cool hand of maturity. This young man must have made good note of the difference; he writes very well; but I greatly fear that request he made in his letter, that I should enlighten him with my counsels, is at bottom nothing better than a sentiment unaware of itself.

And yet, how many conversions have begun in this way! The thing that makes me augur well for this one is the difference between his style and that of the other young people whose letters I have had occasion to see. It is impossible not to be aware of the unction, the deep seriousness, and an abundant conviction in the prose of this young levite; surely he will inherit the soothing virtue of Massillon.[9]

Chapter 27

THE BEST JOBS IN THE CHURCH

Services! talents! merit! bah! join a clique.
—*Télémaque*[1]

Thus the concept *bishop* was for the first time joined to the image of Julien in the mind of a woman who sooner or later would be handing out the best jobs in the church of France. To have gained this ground would have meant little to Julien; at the moment his mind was incapable of any idea apart from his immediate grief: everything augmented it; for example, the very sight of his room had become intolerable. When he returned at night with his candle, every stick of furniture, every little ornament, seemed to have a voice in which to announce fresh details of his misery.

9. J. B. Massillon (1663–1742); his doctrinal liberality and persuasive eloquence made him popular with the philosophic skeptics of the later eighteenth century as a model of what a preacher in the pathetic strain should be.
1. *Télémaque* is Fénelon's treatise on education and government, written for the guidance of the Duke of Burgundy and published in 1699.

But on this particular day it was with more vivacity than he had felt in a long time that he urged himself: Back to our slave labor; let's hope the second letter is as boring as the first.

It was more so. What he was copying seemed so ridiculous that he began to copy it line for line without giving a thought to the sense.

It's even more emphatic, he told himself, than the official phrases in the treaty of Munster which my instructor in diplomacy made me copy out in London.

Only then did he recall the letters from Mme. de Fervaques, the originals of which he had forgotten to return to the solemn Spaniard, Don Diego Bustos. He pulled them out; and really, they were almost as wishy-washy as those of the young gentleman from Russia. Vagueness could go no further. The letters said everything and nothing. It's the Aeolian harp of style, Julien thought. Amid the loftiest reflections on the void, death, the infinite, and so forth, I see nothing solid except an abominable fear of ridicule.

The monologue we have just abridged was repeated for two weeks on end. Dozing off while copying a sort of commentary on the Apocalypse, carrying a letter the next day with a melancholy air, returning the horse to the stable while hoping to catch a glimpse of Mathilde's dress, working, putting in an appearance at the opera when Mme. de Fervaques did not visit the Hôtel de La Mole—such were the monotonous incidents of Julien's life. It was a little more interesting when Mme. de Fervaques did come visiting; for then he could catch a glimpse of Mathilde's eyes from under the brim of the maréchale's hat, and wax eloquent. His picturesque sentimental phrases began to take on more striking and at the same time more elegant contours.

He knew very well that what he was saying was absurd in the eyes of Mathilde, but he wanted to impress her with his elegance of diction. The more I say what is false, the more I'm bound to please her, Julien thought; and so, with abominable boldness, he began to exaggerate certain aspects of nature. He very quickly sensed that, to avoid seeming vulgar in the eyes of the maréchale, the most essential thing was to shun completely any simple or reasonable ideas. He continued to work on these principles, or cut short his amplifications, as he read success or indifference in the eyes of the two great ladies whom he was trying to please.

On the whole, his life was less frightful than when his days were passed in inaction.

But, he told himself one evening, here I am transcribing the fifteenth of these abominable disquisitions; the first fourteen have been faithfully delivered to the maréchale's doorman. Before long I shall have had the honor of filling every pigeonhole in her desk.

And yet she treats me exactly as if I were not writing at all! Where will this whole thing wind up? Will my constancy finish by boring her as much as it does me? It's perfectly clear, that Russian, Korasoff's friend, who was in love with the fair Quakeress of Richmond, must have been a terrible fellow; they don't come any more deadly than that one.

Like all mediocre creatures who become involved by accident in the maneuvers of a great general, Julien understood nothing of the strategic assault launched by the young Russian against the heart of his severe Englishwoman. The first forty letters were intended merely to beg her pardon for his boldness in writing. It was necessary to induce this sweet creature, who perhaps was bored to tears, to form the habit of receiving letters perhaps a little bit less insipid than her everyday life.

One day Julien received a letter; he recognized the crest of Mme. de Fervaques and broke the seal with more eagerness than he would have supposed possible a few days before: it was nothing but an invitation to dinner.

He hastened to consult Prince Korasoff's instructions. Unfortunately, the young Russian had tried to cultivate a light tone, like Dorat,[2] just where he should have been simple and intelligible; Julien could not make out what moral position he should occupy at the maréchale's dinner party.

The drawing room was of the utmost magnificence, gilded like Diana's gallery at the Tuileries, with oil paintings in the panels. There were various white spots on the surface of the paintings. Julien learned later that the subjects had seemed improper to the lady of the house, who had therefore had the paintings corrected. A *moral age!* was his thought.

In this drawing room he caught sight of three of the persons who had taken part in preparing the secret note. One of them, the Right Reverend Bishop of _____, the maréchale's uncle, was in charge of giving out benefices, and, as people said, could refuse his niece nothing. What giant steps I've taken, Julien thought with a melancholy smile, and how little difference it makes to me! Here I am dining with the famous Bishop of _____.

The dinner was mediocre and the conversation irksome. It's like the table of contents in a bad book, Julien thought. All the greatest topics of human thought are paraded proudly before you. Listen for three minutes, and you'll be asking which is worse, the emphasis of the speaker or his abominable ignorance.

The reader has no doubt forgotten that little man of letters

2. Claude Dorat (1734–1780) was a French man of letters 'legendary for his awkwardness in handling peoples' feelings; he managed to provoke *all* the factions.

named Tanbeau, the nephew of the academician and a future professor himself, who seemed employed expressly to poison with his snide slanders the drawing room of the Hôtel de La Mole.

It was from this little man that Julien got the first notion that Mme. de Fervaques, while not replying to his letters, might well view with indulgence the sentiment that gave rise to them. M. Tanbeau's black spirit was torn to shreds when he thought of Julien's success; but since, on the other hand, a man of merit cannot be in two places at once any better than a fool, if Sorel becomes the sublime maréchale's lover, the future professor told himself, she'll put him in some snug berth in the church, and I'll be rid of him at the Hôtel de La Mole.

Abbé Pirard also directed at Julien various long sermons on the topic of his success at the Hôtel de Fervaques. There was a bit of *sectarian jealousy* between the austere Jansenist and the Jesuitical drawing room, reactionary[3] and monarchical, of the virtuous maréchale.

Chapter 28

MANON LESCAUT

> But once he was thoroughly convinced of the stupidity of that ass of a prior, he got along with him rather well by calling black anything that was white and white what was black.
> —Lichtenberg[4]

The Russian instructions prescribed imperiously that one must never contradict to her face the person to whom one was writing. One must never abandon, under any pretext whatever, the role of the ecstatic admirer; all the letters took this as their point of departure.

One evening at the opera, in Mme. de Fervaques' box, Julien praised to the skies the ballet of *Manon Lescaut*.[5] His only reason for talking this way was that he considered it contemptible.

The maréchale declared that this ballet was much inferior to Abbé Prévost's novel.

How's this! thought Julien, amazed and amused, a lady of such extraordinary virtue praising a novel! Mme. de Fervaques gave vent,

---

3. The French original is *régénérateur*—that is, revivalist, or reconstitutive, intent on regenerating the French Roman Catholic Church.
4. Georg Christoph Lichtenberg (1742–1799), primarily a physicist, was also a satiric writer of considerable acerbity and acuteness.
5. With music by Halévy and a scenario by Scribe, the ballet of *Manon Lescaut* had its first presentation at the opera on May 3, 1830.

two or three times a week, to her deepest scorn for those scribblers who make use of their shabby writings to corrupt a younger generation already all too prone, alas! to the errors of the senses.

Amid this class of immoral and dangerous works, continued the maréchale, *Manon Lescaut* occupies, as people tell me, one of the first places. The frailties and well-deserved sufferings of a profoundly criminal heart are depicted there, so people tell me, with a veracity that has some depth; yet this did not prevent your Bonaparte from remarking, at St. Helena, that it was a novel written for lackeys.

This expression restored to Julien all his spiritual energy. People have been trying to traduce me to the maréchale; they have told her of my enthusiasm for Napoleon. This story has irked her to the point where she has yielded to the temptation of talking about it. The discovery amused him all evening long, and rendered him amusing. As he was taking leave of the maréchale in the lobby of the opera: —Remember, sir, she told him, people may not love Bonaparte when they love me; at best, one may accept him as a fatal necessity imposed by providence. In any case, the man had not a soul flexible enough to appreciate masterworks in the arts.

When they love me! Julien repeated silently; either that means nothing or it means everything. These are some of the secrets of language that will be forever hidden from us poor provincials. And he thought a great deal about Mme. de Rênal as he copied out an immense letter destined for the maréchale.

—How does it happen, she asked him next day with an air of indifference that he thought rather forced, that you speak to me of *London* and of *Richmond* in a letter you apparently wrote yesterday evening after leaving the opera?

Julien was much embarrassed; he had been copying line by line without thinking of what he was writing, and evidently had forgotten to substitute for the names *London* and *Richmond* in the original those of *Paris* and *Saint-Cloud*. He began two or three phrases, but was unable to finish any of them; he felt himself on the verge of bursting into peals of helpless laughter. Finally, as he cast about for words, he fell upon this idea: —Exalted by the discussion of the most sublime, the most lofty ideas of which the human soul is capable, my own spirit, as I wrote to you, must have suffered a momentary oblivion.

I am producing an impression, he told himself, so I can spare myself the boredom of the rest of the evening. He left the Hôtel de Fervaques at a run. That evening, as he looked over the original of the letter he had copied the night before, he quickly found the fatal passage in which the young Russian spoke of London and Richmond. Julien was quite amazed to find that this letter was nearly tender.

It was the contrast between the apparent levity of his talk and the sublime profundity and almost apocalyptic spirit of his letters that had distinguished him. Above all, the length of his sentences pleased the maréchale; none of that swift, dashing style brought into favor by Voltaire, that immoral man! Although our hero made every effort conceivable to banish every sort of good sense from his conversation, it still retained an antimonarchical and irreligious flavor which Mme. de Fervaques had observed. Surrounded by persons of impeccable morality but who often didn't have an idea in an evening, this lady was profoundly impressed by anything resembling a novelty; but at the same time she thought it incumbent on her to be shocked by it. She called the failing, *retaining the imprint of the age's frivolity.* . . .

But such drawing rooms are worth observing only when one has a favor to solicit. No doubt the reader shares all Julien's boredom at this life without interest that he was forced to lead. These are the flatlands of our journey.

During the entire period occupied in Julien's life by the Fervaques episode, Mlle. de La Mole had to make constant efforts not to think of him. Her soul was the scene of a violent struggle; sometimes she was pleased to think she despised that gloomy young man; but in spite of herself, she was enchanted by his conversation. What amazed her more than anything was his perfect insincerity; he never said a single word to the maréchale that was not a lie or at least an abominable distortion of his point of view, which Mathilde knew perfectly well on practically all topics. This Machiavellianism impressed her. What subtlety! she said to herself; what a difference from those emphatic fools or the common cheats, like M. Tanbeau, who make use of the same language!

All the same, Julien had some frightful days. It was by way of fulfilling the most painful of his duties that he showed up every evening in the drawing room of the maréchale. His efforts to play a role ended by draining all his spiritual vitality. Very often as he crossed the immense courtyard of the Hôtel de Fervaques at night, it was only by force of character and by dint of logic that he kept himself from sinking into abject despair.

I overcame despair in the seminary, he kept telling himself: and yet what a horrible future faced me then! Whether I made my fortune or failed of it, in either case I would be obliged to pass my whole life in intimate companionship with the most contemptible and disgusting creatures under heaven. Yet the following spring, just eleven short months later, I was probably the happiest young man of my age in the whole world.

But very often these fine reasonings proved ineffectual against hideous reality. Every day he saw Mathilde at lunch and dinner. From the numerous letters dictated by M. de La Mole, he gathered that she was on the point of marrying M. de Croisenois. Already that pleasant young man had begun to appear twice a day at the Hôtel de La Mole: the jealous eye of a cast lover did not overlook one of his actions.

When he thought he noted that Mlle. de La Mole was treating her fiancé well, Julien as he returned to his room could not keep from looking lovingly toward his pistols.

Ah! how much wiser I would be, he said to himself, to remove the marks from my linen and go off into some lonely forest twenty leagues from Paris to put an end to this execrable life! As a stranger in that part of the world, my death would go unremarked for a fortnight, and who would think of me after a fortnight!

This was very good thinking. But next day a glimpse of Mathilde's arm, seen for an instant between her sleeve and her glove, was enough to plunge our young philosopher into some bitter memories which nonetheless renewed his attachment to life. All right, then, he told himself at that point, I'll follow out this Russian politics to the bitter end. How will it finish?

As far as the maréchale is concerned, when I've finished transcribing these fifty-three letters, I will never write any others.

As for Mathilde, either these six weeks of painful play acting will do nothing to alter her anger or they'll earn me an instant of reconciliation. Great God! I should die of joy! and he was unable to complete his thought.

When, after a long reverie, he succeeded in resuming the use of his reason: Well, then, said he, I might have a single day of happiness, after which she would resume her rigors—which are quite justified, alas, by my meager powers to please her; and then I should have no further resources; I should be ruined, lost forever. . . .

Given her character, what guarantee can she give me? My inadequate abilities, alas, are responsible for everything. My manners will have no distinction, my way of talking will be heavy and monotonous. Good God! why am I myself?

Chapter 29

BOREDOM

To sacrifice oneself to one's passions, well, maybe; but to passions one does not feel! Oh, the sad nineteenth century!
                                                    —Girodet[6]

Having begun by reading Julien's long letters without any pleasure, Mme. de Fervaques was beginning to be concerned with them;
but one thought reduced her to despair: What a shame that
M. Sorel was not really a priest! One might then admit him to a
sort of intimacy; but with that decoration and that thoroughly
middle-class jacket, one is exposed to ugly questions, and how to
answer them? She did not complete her thought: some malicious
friend may suppose, and even spread the story, that this is a little
cousin from the provinces, a relative of my father's, a button salesman decorated by the National Guard.

Until the day she met Julien, the greatest pleasure in Mme. de
Fervaques' life had been to write the title *maréchale* alongside her
name. Afterward, her upstart's vanity, uneasy and quick to take offense, had to struggle with a new interest.

It would be so easy, said the maréchale, for me to have him created a grand vicar in some diocese near Paris! But just plain
M. Sorel, and what's worse a mere secretary to M. de La Mole! It is
very distressing.

For the first time this soul *which was afraid of everything* was
stirred by an interest alien to its social pretentions and claims of superiority. Her ancient porter remarked that when he brought a letter from that handsome young man who always looked so sad, that
distracted, discontented air which the marquise was always careful
to assume when one of her servants was present, was sure to disappear.

Boredom with a way of life wholly devoted to creating a public
impression, and which did not have at the heart of it even any real
enjoyment of this sort of success, had become intolerable since she
began to think of Julien; the chambermaids were often exempt
from ill treatment for a whole day because she had passed an hour,
the evening before, in the company of this extraordinary young
man. His growing credit withstood the assaults of several anonymous letters, extremely well composed. In vain did little Tanbeau
supply de Luz, Croisenois, and Caylus with two or three truly ingenious calumnies, which these gentlemen took pleasure in spreading about without taking too much care to find out if they were

6. Girodet (1767–1824) was primarily a painter, one of mediocre merits.

true or not. The maréchale, whose spirit was not made to stand up against such vulgar tactics, talked over her misgivings with Mathilde, and was always consoled.

One day when she had asked three times if there were any letters, Mme. de Fervaques decided abruptly to write an answer to Julien. It was a triumph for boredom. With the second letter, the maréchale was almost brought up short by the disagreeableness of writing, with her own hand, such a plebeian address as: *To M. Sorel, at the Marquis de La Mole's.*

That evening she told Julien in the driest of tones: —You must bring me some envelopes on which your address is written.

So now I'm formally established as lover-flunkey, thought Julien, and as he made his bow he amused himself by grimacing like Arsène, the marquis' elderly valet.

That evening he brought the envelopes, and next day very early he received a third letter: he read five or six lines of it at the beginning and two or three toward the end. It amounted to four pages in a tiny, cramped script.

Gradually she fell into the gratifying habit of writing nearly every day. Julien replied with faithful transcripts of the Russian letters, and such is the advantage of the emphatic style that Mme. de Fervaques was in no way surprised at the lack of connection between letters and answers.

How deeply her pride would have been wounded if little Tanbeau, who had appointed himself spy in ordinary upon Julien's daily activities, could have reported to her that all these letters, with their seals unbroken, were flung pell-mell into Julien's desk drawer.

One morning the porter brought up to the library a letter for him from the maréchale; Mathilde encountered the man, and saw the address in Julien's handwriting. She entered the library as the porter left; the letter was still on the edge of the table; Julien, deeply involved with his writing, had not stuffed it into the drawer.

—This is something I will not endure, cried Mathilde, snatching up the letter; you have forgotten me completely, yes, me, and I am your wife. Your behavior is appalling, sir!

At these words her pride, overwhelmed by the frightful unconventionality of her behavior, choked her; she burst into tears and for an instant seemed to Julien to be struggling for breath.

Amazed and bewildered, Julien could not clearly sort out all the admirable and joyful elements of the scene. He helped Mathilde to a chair; she practically abandoned herself in his arms.

The first instant in which he became aware of this gesture was one of extreme joy. His second thought was for Korasoff: a single word and I lose everything.

His arms stiffened, so painful was the effort demanded of him by

his political strategy. I must not even allow myself to embrace this
yielding and delicate body or she will despise me and mistreat me.
What a horrible character!

And even as he cursed Mathilde's character, he loved her for it a
hundred times more than before; he felt that he was holding in his
arms a queen.

Julien's impenetrable coolness multiplied the miseries of
wounded pride that were flaying Mlle. de La Mole's spirit. She was
far from having enough self-possession to read in his eyes what he
was really feeling for her at that moment. She could not bring herself even to look at him; she was afraid of encountering an expression of scorn.

Seated on the library sofa, motionless and with her head turned
away from Julien, she was a victim of the keenest anguish that love
and pride can inflict upon a human soul. What a ghastly step she
had just taken!

It was left for me, wretch that I am, to make the most indelicate
advances and then have them repulsed! And repulsed by whom?
she added, her pride inflamed by suffering, repulsed by one of my
father's servants!

—This is something I will not endure, she cried aloud.

And, leaping furiously to her feet, she flung open the drawer of
Julien's desk which stood a few feet away. She stopped as if frozen
in horror when she saw there eight or ten unopened letters, similar
in every way to the one the porter had just brought up. In all the addresses she recognized Julien's handwriting, more or less disguised.

—And so, she cried, beside herself with fury, not only are you intimate with her but you despise her. You, a man of no position at
all, despising the Maréchale de Fervaques!

—Oh, forgive me, my dear, she added, flinging herself at his feet,
despise me if you will, but love me, I can no longer live without
your love. And she fell in a dead faint.

So there she is, that proud beauty, at my feet! thought Julien.

Chapter 30

A BOX AT THE ITALIAN OPERA

As the blackest sky
Foretells the heaviest tempest.
—*Don Juan*, Canto 1, stanza 73

Amidst all these emotional upheavals, Julien was more astonished than happy. Mathilde's insults clearly showed him how wise
the Russian policy had been. *Say little, do little*, that's my only salvation.

He raised Mathilde and without a word set her on the sofa again. Gradually she gave way to tears.

To give herself countenance, she picked up the letters of Mme. de Fervaques and slowly unsealed them. She started perceptibly on recognizing the maréchale's hand. She turned over the pages of these letters without reading them; most of them were six pages long.

—Tell me this at least, said Mathilde slowly, in the most supplicating manner but without even daring to look at Julien. You know very well that I am proud; it's the misfortune of my position in life, and, I'll admit it, of my character. So Mme. de Fervaques has taken your heart from me. . . . Has she made for you all the sacrifices into which passion betrayed me?

A gloomy silence was Julien's only response. By what right, he was thinking, does she think she can ask me for confidences unworthy of an honest man?

Mathilde tried to read the letters, but her eyes filled with tears and she could not.

She had been wretched for the past month, but her lofty spirit was far from admitting any such feeling. Only accident had brought about this outburst. For an instant, love and jealousy had overcome pride. She was seated on the sofa close beside him. Her hair and her alabaster throat were before his eyes. For a moment he forgot everything he owed himself; he passed his arm around her waist and strained her to him.

She turned her head slowly toward him: he was staggered at the extremity of grief he read in her eyes; he could scarcely recognize them as belonging to her.

Julien felt his powers slipping away, so deadly painful was the act of courage he required of himself.

In a minute those eyes will express nothing but icy disdain, Julien told himself, if I let myself be carried away by the joy of loving her. Meanwhile, in a strangled voice and with words she had barely the strength to form, she kept repeating to him her repentance for a line of conduct that she said had been dictated by her excessive pride.

—I have some pride myself, Julien said to her in a hardly distinguishable voice; his face gave evidence of complete physical exhaustion.

Mathilde turned sharply toward him. To hear his voice was a joy she had almost given up hoping for. At that moment she was aware of her own pride only as a quality to be cursed; she craved to find some extraordinary, incredible form of behavior to show how much she adored him and detested herself.

—It is probably because of this pride of mine, Julien went on,

[margin, handwritten:] Is it love or just jealousy and possessiveness?

[margin, handwritten:] jealousy shows you care, but not love necessarily

that you granted me for a moment your favor; it is certainly because of this firm and manly courage that you respect me now. I
may be in love with the maréchale. . . .

Mathilde shuddered; her eyes assumed a strange look. She was
about to hear her fate pronounced. This gesture did not escape
Julien; he felt his courage weakening.

Ah! he thought, listening to the sound of the empty words being
pronounced by his own mouth as he might have listened to an alien
noise; if only I could cover those pale cheeks with kisses, without
your knowing it!

—I may be in love with the maréchale, he went on, his voice
growing weaker at each word; but certainly her interest in me has
given no conclusive proof of itself. . . .

Mathilde looked directly at him: he met her gaze, at least he
hoped his expression had not betrayed him. He felt himself suffused with love down to the inmost recesses of his being. Never had
he adored her to this point; he was almost as mad as Mathilde. If
she could have found in her own character enough coolness and
courage to maneuver, he would have fallen at her feet, renouncing
all idle play acting. He had just enough strength to keep on talking.
Ah, Korasoff! his inner mind cried out, why aren't you here! How I
need a word from you to control my conduct! And meanwhile his
voice went on saying:

—Even in the absence of any other sentiment, gratitude would
amply suffice to attach me to the maréchale; she has shown me
great indulgence; she consoled me when I was in disgrace. . . . I
may, perchance, not place unconditional confidence in certain
signs that are extremely flattering, no doubt about it, but which
may also prove of brief duration.

—Ah! Great God! cried Mathilde.

—Very well, then! What guarantee will you give me? Julien
replied, in a quick, firm tone that seemed to cast aside in an instant
the prudent forms of diplomacy. What guarantee, what god will assure me that the position you now seem inclined to restore me to
will last more than two days?

—The excess of my love and of my misery if you don't love me
anymore, she said to him, seizing his hands and turning toward
him.

Her sudden turning threw slightly aside her scarf; Julien had a
glimpse of her delicate shoulders. Her hair, in some disorder, recalled to him an exquisite memory. . . .

He was about to break down. A single ill-timed word, he told
himself, and I shall have to start again down that long track of
despair-filled days. Mme. de Rênal always found reasons to do what

her heart dictated; this high-society girl lets her heart be moved only when she has found proofs based upon good logic that it ought to be moved.

He grasped this truth in the flicker of an eyelash, and in the same instant regained his courage.

He freed his hands, which Mathilde had been pressing in her own, and with a deep bow stepped away from her. Human courage can do no more. He then busied himself gathering up the letters from Mme. de Fervaques which were scattered about the sofa, and it was with an air of almost excessive politeness, particularly cruel at that moment, that he added:

—Mlle. de La Mole will be kind enough to allow me to think things over. He turned swiftly away and left the library; she heard him closing all the doors, one after one, behind him.

The monster, he's not upset at all, she said to herself. . . .

But what am I saying, monster! He is sensible, careful, kind; I am the one who has done more wrong than can be imagined.

This outlook on things persisted. Mathilde was almost happy that day, for she was completely in love; you would have said her heart had never been lashed by pride—and such pride!

She shuddered with horror that evening in the drawing room when a footman announced Mme. de Fervaques; the man's voice seemed full of menace. She could not stand to look at the maréchale, and shortly left the room. Julien, not much emboldened by the day's painful victory and fearful of betraying himself through his glances, had not dined at the Hôtel de La Mole.

His love and his happiness increased rapidly as the battle itself receded into the distance; he was now at the stage of finding fault with his own conduct. How could I have resisted her? he asked himself. Suppose she never loves me again! An instant can completely alter that disdainful spirit, and I confess I've treated her wretchedly.

That evening he felt it was absolutely necessary for him to be present at the Italian opera, in the box of Mme. de Fervaques. She had invited him directly; Mathilde would not fail to take note either of his presence or of an absence which would be rude. Though fully convinced by this logic, he simply did not have the strength at the beginning of the evening to plunge into society. By talking he would destroy half his happiness.

Ten o'clock struck; it was absolutely necessary that he make an appearance.

Fortunately he found the maréchale's box filled with women, and was relegated to a seat near the door where he was quite concealed by their hats. As a result of this position, he was spared an absurdity; the divine accents of Caroline's despair in the *Matrimonio segreto*[7] caused him to burst into tears. Mme. de Fervaques noticed these tears; they provided such a contrast with the masculine firmness of his ordinary expression that even the spirit of this great lady, long immersed in the most corrosive acids of upstart ambition, was touched by it. The little that was left in her of a woman's heart stirred her to speak. She wanted to hear the sound of his voice at that moment.

—Have you seen the de La Mole ladies? she asked him. They are in the third tier. Immediately Julien rose to lean forward, supporting himself rudely enough on the railing of the box: he saw Mathilde; her eyes were bright with tears.

And yet it is not their day at the opera, Julien thought; what a rush they must have had!

Mathilde had persuaded her mother to come to the Italian opera, in spite of the inconvenient location of the box which a friend of the family had hastened to offer them. She wanted to see if Julien would be spending the evening with the maréchale.

Chapter 31

MAKING HER AFRAID

And so that's the supreme achievement of your civilization! You have converted love into an ordinary concern.

—Barnave[8]

Julien hurried to Mme. de La Mole's box. His glance fell at once on the tear-drenched eyes of Mathilde; she was weeping uncontrollably; there was nobody present of any particular importance, only the lady who had lent the box and some men of her acquaintance. Mathilde placed her hand on Julien's; she seemed to have forgotten to be afraid of her mother. Almost choked by her sobs, she could say nothing but the single word: *Guarantees!*

I must be sure not to say anything to her, Julien thought; he was deeply stirred himself, and tried to cover his eyes as well as he could with his hand, on the pretext of avoiding the glare from the lusters that lit the third tier of boxes. If I say anything, she can no longer be in doubt about the intensity of my feeling; my voice will betray me, and the whole struggle will be lost again.

His inner conflict was far more painful than it had been that morning; his spirit had had time to mobilize itself. He was afraid of

---

7. Cimarosa's *Matrimonio segreto* was for Stendhal the archetypal opera, the voice of true passion set to music.
8. On Barnave, see p. 10, note 9.

seeing Mathilde relapse into wounded vanity. Drunk with love and pleasure, he took an oath not to speak to her.

In my opinion, this was one of the finest traits of his character; a man capable of imposing such restraint on his own impulses may go far, *si fata sinant*.[9]

Mlle. de La Mole insisted on their taking Julien home. Fortunately, it was raining heavily. But the marquise had him seated opposite her, talked to him constantly, and prevented his saying a word to her daughter. One might have thought the marquise was standing guard over Julien's happiness. No longer afraid of destroying everything by the excess of his emotion, he yielded himself up to it with delight.

Dare I report that when he returned to his room Julien fell on his knees and covered with kisses the love letters given him by Prince Korasoff?

Oh, great man that you are! he cried in his madness; what don't I owe to you?

Gradually some coolness returned to him. He compared himself to a general who has just half-won a great battle. The advantage is positive, it is immense, he told himself; but what will happen tomorrow? An instant can ruin everything.

On a passionate impulse, he opened the *Mémoires dictated at Saint Helena* by Napoleon[1] and for two long hours forced himself to read them; nothing in fact was reading except his eyes, but, no matter, he held himself to the task. During this singular exercise, his head and heart, rising to the level of everything great and grand, were unconsciously at work. This heart is very different from Mme. de Rênal's, he told himself, but he went no further.

Make her afraid, he cried suddenly, flinging the book away. The enemy will obey me only if I make him afraid, then he won't dare to despise me.

He strode about his little room, delirious with joy. In point of fact, this happiness derived from pride more than from love.

Make her afraid! he repeated proudly, and he had reason to be proud. Even in her happiest moments, Mme. de Rênal was always uncertain whether my love was equal to hers. Here, it is a demon with which I am wrestling, and it must be *beaten*.

He knew perfectly well that Mathilde would be in the library next morning at eight o'clock; he did not make his appearance until nine, aflame with love, but with his head in strict control of his heart. Probably not a single minute passed without his repeating to

9. If the fates allow.
1. Napoleon's *Mémoires dictated at Saint Helena* are probably those dictated to the Marquis de Montholon and published by him in 1821, 1823, and so on.

himself: Keep her always occupied with this one great doubt: Does he love me? Her brilliant position, the flatteries of all her friends, incline her *a little too much* to self-assurance.

He found her calm, pale, sitting on the sofa but apparently quite incapable of making a single movement. She held forth her hand:

—My dear, I have offended you, it is true; perhaps you are angry with me? . . .

Julien had not expected such a simple tone. He was on the point of giving way.

—You ask for guarantees, my dear, she added, after a silence she had hoped he would break; that's only fair. Elope with me then, we'll go to London. . . . I shall be ruined forever, disgraced. . . . She had the courage to withdraw her hand from Julien's in order to cover her eyes. All the sentiments of reserve and female virtue had returned to her mind. . . . All right, then; disgrace me, she said with a sigh, it is *a guarantee.*

Yesterday I was happy because I was strong enough to be strict with myself, Julien thought. After a short period of silence, he had gained enough control over his heart to say, in an icy tone:

—Once we're on the road to London, once you're disgraced (to use your own expression), who can promise that you will still love me? that my presence in the mail coach will not seem irksome to you? I'm not a monster; the fact that I disgraced you in public opinion will be only one more misery for me. It's not your position in the world that stands in my way; it is, unhappily, your character. Can you answer for yourself that after a week you will still love me?

(Ah! let her love me for a week, just one week, said Julien silently to himself, and I shall die of joy. What do I care about the future, or about my life? And this divine happiness may begin this very minute if I choose; it depends only on me!)

Mathilde saw him deep in thought.

—So I am completely unworthy of you, she said to him, taking his hand.

Julien kissed her, but at that very moment the iron hand of duty clutched his heart. If she sees how much I adore her, I have lost her. And as he stepped back, he resumed all the dignity that befits a man.

On that day and on those that followed, he was able to conceal the immensity of his joy; there were moments in which he refused himself even the pleasure of holding her in his arms.

At other times, the delirium of happiness swept away all counsels of prudence.

It was beside a trellis of honeysuckle, which served to hide the ladder in the garden, that he used to post himself in order to watch the distant shutters of Mathilde's window, and deplore her fickle disposition. An immense oak grew nearby, and its trunk prevented his being seen by the curious.

As he strolled with Mathilde past this very spot which reminded him so vividly of his terrible sorrows, the contrast between past despair and present felicity was too much for his character; tears flooded his eyes, and as he lifted to his lips the hand of his mistress, he exclaimed:—Here I used to live with thoughts of you; from here I watched that shutter; I waited hours on end for the happy moment when I would see this hand open it. . . .

His weakness was abject. He described to her, in those true colors which it is impossible to invent, the extremities of his former despair. Short bursts of passionate emotion made plain the present bliss that had replaced that fearful suffering. . . .

Good God! what am I doing? Julien thought, returning to his senses abruptly. I am destroying the whole thing.

In the extremity of his alarm, he thought he could already read in Mlle. de La Mole's eyes the signs of diminishing love. It was an illusion; but Julien's face underwent a sudden change, and was overcome by deathly pallor. His eyes darkened in an instant, and an expression of arrogance tinged with malice succeeded that of the most sincere and unrestrained love.

—What's the matter, my dear? Mathilde asked him with tender concern.

—I am lying, Julien said, and I am lying to you. I blame myself for doing it, and God knows I respect you enough not to lie to you. You love me, you are devoted to me, and I have no need to make fancy phrases in order to please you.

—Good God! Then they were only fancy phrases, all those wonderful things you've just been saying to me?

—And I blame myself bitterly for them, my dear. I made them up long ago for a woman who was in love with me and a bore. . . . It's a defect in my character, I confess it to you, forgive me.

Bitter tears poured down Mathilde's cheeks.

—As soon as some trifle upsets me, Julien went on, and I am compelled to think of things for a moment, my wretched memory, which I could curse at this instant, offers me a way out, and I abuse it.

—Then I must have done something, without knowing it, which displeased you? said Mathilde, with charming simplicity.

—One day I recall, when you were passing by this honeysuckle, you plucked a flower, M. de Luz took it from you, and you let him have it. I was standing close by.

—M. de Luz? impossible! said Mathilde, with the lofty expression so natural to her: I never do things like that.

—I am quite sure of it, Julien replied quickly.

—All right! It is true, my dear, said Mathilde, lowering her eyes sadly. She was absolutely positive that it was many months since she had allowed M. de Luz any such liberty.

Julien glanced at her with indescribable tenderness: No, he told himself, her love for me has not grown *less*.

She playfully reproached him that evening with his love for Mme. de Fervaques: a *bourgeois* in love with a *parvenue*! Hearts of that sort are perhaps the only ones that my Julien cannot intoxicate. She had turned you into a real dandy, she said, as she played with his hair.

During the time when he thought himself in disgrace with Mathilde, Julien had become one of the best-dressed men in Paris. But he had one extra advantage over most men of this sort; once he was dressed, he never gave his appearance another thought.

One thing irked Mathilde; Julien continued to copy out the Russian letters and send them to the maréchale.

Chapter 32

THE TIGER

Alas! Why these things and not others?
—Beaumarchais

An English traveler tells how he lived on intimate terms with a tiger; he had reared it and used to pet it, but he always kept a loaded pistol on the table.

Julien never abandoned himself to the full sense of his joy except at times when Mathilde could not read the expression of it in his eyes. He carried out with exactitude the duty of every so often saying to her something disagreeable.

When Mathilde's sweetness, which he noted with amazement, and the full measure of her devotion were on the point of depriving him of all self-control, he found the courage to leave her abruptly.

For the first time, Mathilde was in love.

Life, which for her had always struggled past at a snail's pace, now flew by.

But as, all the same, her pride required some outlet, she wanted to expose herself boldly to all the dangers which her love might entail. It was Julien who showed prudence; and it was only when some danger was involved that she stood out against his will; but, though submissive and almost humble with him, she showed herself all the more haughty toward anyone in the household who came near her, whether relatives or servants.

At night in the drawing room, she singled out Julien from among sixty guests and held long, private conversations with him.

One day little Tanbeau sat down alongside them; she asked him to go to the library and get her the volume of Smollett describing the revolution of 1688; and as he hesitated: —You needn't hurry back, she added with an expression of insulting arrogance which brought balm to Julien's soul.

—Did you see how that little monster looked at us? she asked him.

—His uncle has done ten or twelve years' service in this drawing room, otherwise I should have had him thrown out this minute.

Her conduct toward Messieurs de Croisenois, de Luz, etc., though perfectly polite as far as formalities went, was in reality scarcely less provoking. Mathilde bitterly regretted all the confessions she had formerly made to Julien, and all the more since she did not dare admit to him that she had much exaggerated the almost wholly innocent marks of interest she had shown in these gentlemen.

Despite her best resolutions, feminine pride prevented her every day from saying to Julien: It was because I was talking to *you* that I took such pleasure in describing my weakness when I didn't withdraw my hand after M. de Croisenois, placing his hand beside mine on a marble table, managed to stroke it a trifle.

Nowadays hardly any of these gentlemen spoke to her for a moment without her finding some question on which to consult Julien; this was a pretext for keeping him by her side.

She found that she was pregnant, and told Julien joyously.

—Now do you have any doubts of me? Isn't this a guarantee? I am your wife forever.

This announcement struck Julien with profound astonishment. He was on the point of forgetting the first principles of his conduct. How to be deliberately cold and disagreeable to this poor girl who is ruining herself for my sake? If she looked in the least unwell, even though on that day reason was making heard its terrible voice, he no longer had the courage to address to her one of those brutal remarks that were so indispensable, as experience had shown him, to the continuance of their love.

—I want to write a note to my father, Mathilde told him one day; he has been more than a father to me, he has been a friend: as such, I should think it unworthy of you and me to try to deceive him, even for a moment.

—Good God! What are you going to do? Julien asked, in disquiet.

—My duty, she replied, her eyes glittering with joy.

She sensed that she was being more magnanimous than her lover.

—But he will dismiss me from the house in disgrace!

—That's his privilege, we must respect it. I shall give you my arm, and we will go out the front door together, in the full light of day.

Julien, staggered by this turn, begged her to wait a week.

—I cannot, she told him; honor calls, I have seen my duty, I must do it, and right away.

—Very well! I order you to wait. Your honor is safe; I am your husband. Both our conditions are going to be changed by this drastic step. I too have my rights. Today is Tuesday; next Tuesday is the Duc de Retz's party; that evening, when M. de La Mole comes home, the porter will hand him the fatal letter. . . . He has been thinking of nothing but making you a duchess, I'm sure of that; imagine how angry he will be!

—Do you mean: imagine what revenge he'll take?

—I may feel sorrow for my benefactor, and distress at harming him; but I am not, and never will be, afraid of any man.

Mathilde submitted. Since she announced her new state to Julien, this was the first time that he had spoken to her with authority; never had he been so much in love with her. The tender part of his soul seized gladly on this pretext of Mathilde's condition to free him of the obligation of addressing brutal words to her. The idea of confession to M. de La Mole distressed him greatly. Would he be separated from Mathilde? And, however sad she felt to see him go, once he had been gone a month, would she ever think of him again?

He felt almost as much horror at the prospect of the blame the marquis would heap on him, and with justice.

That night he admitted to Mathilde the latter cause of distress, and then, quite carried away by his love, he admitted also to the first.

She changed color.

—Is that really true, she asked him, that six months away from me would make you unhappy?

—Immensely so, he replied; it's the only prospect in the world I view with terror.

Mathilde was overjoyed. Julien had played his part so carefully that he had actually succeeded in making her think she was more in love than he.

The fatal Tuesday soon came around. When he returned home at midnight, the marquis found a letter addressed to him personally and confidentially, to be opened only when he was alone and unobserved.

My Father,

Every social bond between us is broken, all that is left is the bond of nature. After my husband, you are and always will be the dearest person in my life. My eyes fill with tears as I think of the pain I am causing you, but to prevent my shame from becoming public, to give you time to think and act, I could delay no longer the confession I owe you. If your generosity, which has always been excessive in my regard, can bring itself to grant me a small pension, I will go and settle wherever you say, in Switzerland, for example, with my husband. His name is so obscure that nobody will recognize your daughter in Mme. Sorel, daughter-in-law of a carpenter in Verrières. There is the name which I have found it so hard to write. I fear your anger against Julien, which seems so justified. I shall never be a duchess, dear father; but I knew it when I fell in love with him; for it was I who fell in love with him first, I who seduced him. From you and from our ancestors I inherit a spirit too proud to be attracted to anything that is or seems vulgar. I tried in vain, hoping to please you, to be interested in M. de Croisenois. Why had you placed genuine merit before my eyes? You told me yourself, when I came back from Hyères, This young Sorel is the only person who amuses me. The poor boy is as much distressed as I, if that be possible, to think of the grief this letter will cause you. I cannot prevent your being angry, as a father; but love me still as a friend.

Julien respected me. If he talked to me, sometimes, it was simply out of his profound gratitude to you: for the natural pride of his character leads him to reply only officially to people placed so far above him in rank. He has a strong inner sense of the differences of social position. I was the one, I must admit it with a blush to my dearest friend and will never admit it to anyone else, I was the one who one day in the garden took him by the arm.

After twenty-four hours, what reason will you have to be angry with him? My fault cannot be undone. If you insist, you will receive through me his assurances of profound respect for you and of grief at being the object of your displeasure. You will never see him again; but I shall go and join him wherever he chooses. It is his right, it is my duty, he is the father of my child. If your kindness will grant us six thousand francs on which to live, I will accept them with gratitude: if not, Julien plans to set up at Besançon as a teacher of Latin and literature. However low the rank at which he begins, I am sure he will rise. With him, I have no fear of obscurity. If there is a revolution, I am sure he will have a leading role in it. Could you say as much for any of the others who have sought my hand? They have fine estates! That doesn't seem to me sufficient grounds for admiration. Even under the present regime, my Julien would hold a lofty position if he had a million and were protected by my father. . . .

Mathilde, who knew that the marquis was a man of immediate impulses, had written eight pages.

—What's to be done? Julien said to himself, [as he paced the garden at midnight,] while M. de La Mole read the letter; where do (1) my duty and (2) my interest lie? My debt to him is immense: without his help, I should have been a subordinate rascal, and not even enough of a rascal to keep from being hated and persecuted by the others. He made me a man of the world. From now on my *necessary* rascalities will be (1) fewer, (2) less ignoble. That's better than if he had given me a million. I am in his debt for this decoration and the semblance of diplomatic services, which lift me out of the ruck.

If he were to take pen in hand to prescribe my conduct, what would he write?

Julien was suddenly interrupted by M. de La Mole's elderly valet.

—The marquis wants to see you this minute, whether you're dressed or not.

As he walked beside Julien, the valet added in an undertone:

—Be careful, the marquis is in a rage.

Chapter 33

THE HELL OF WEAKNESS

> By cutting this diamond a clumsy jeweler deprived it of several of its brightest lusters. In the Middle Ages—what am I saying?— even under Richelieu, the Frenchman had *strength of desire*.
>   —Mirabeau

Julien found the marquis furious: perhaps for the first time in his life this great gentleman was in bad taste; he covered Julien with every insult that came to his tongue. Our hero was astonished, angered, but his feeling of gratitude was not altered. How many fine projects, long cherished in the back of his mind, must be collapsing within the poor man at this moment! But I owe him at least an answer; my silence will increase his anger. The response was furnished by the role of Tartufe.

—*I am no angel*. . . . I have served you well, you have paid me generously. . . . I was grateful, but I am twenty-two years old. . . . In this household there was nobody to understand my thoughts except you and that attractive person. . . .

—Monster! shouted the marquis. Attractive! attractive! The day you found her attractive you should have left.

—I tried to; that was the time I asked if I might go to the Languedoc.

Tired of pacing the room in a rage, the marquis, subdued by grief, flung himself into a chair; Julien overheard him saying, under his breath: —This is not really a vicious man.

—No, toward you I am not, Julien cried, and fell to his knees. But he was much ashamed of this gesture and quickly arose.

The marquis was quite out of his mind. When he saw this gesture, he again began to pour on Julien atrocious insults, worthy of a hackney coachman. The novelty of his oaths was perhaps a distraction.

—What! My daughter will be called Mme. Sorel! The devil! My daughter will not be a duchess! Whenever these two ideas appeared distinctly before him, the marquis was in agony, and the impulses of his mind were altogether beyond his control. Julien began to fear a beating.

In his lucid intervals, as the marquis began to get used to his distress, he reproached Julien in perfectly reasonable terms:

—You should have left, sir, he told him. . . . It was your duty to go away. . . . You are the meanest of men . . .

Julien went to the table and wrote:

> For a long time my life has been unbearable; I am putting an end to it. I beg Monsieur le marquis to accept, with the expression of my boundless gratitude, my apologies for the embarrassment that my death within his house may cause.

—Will Monsieur le marquis be good enough to peruse this note. . . . Kill me, said Julien, or have me killed by your valet. It is one o'clock; I am going to walk in the garden by the wall at the far end.

—Go to the devil, the marquis shouted after him as he left.

I understand, Julien thought; he would not be sorry to see me spare his valet responsibility for my death. . . . Let him kill me, fair enough, it's a satisfaction I can offer him. . . . But, deuce take it, I am fond of life. . . . I have a duty to my son.

This idea, which was just forming clearly for the first time in his imagination, took full possession of him after the first few minutes of his stroll, which were devoted to the sense of danger.

His new concern made of him a prudent man. I need some advice on how to behave with this fiery man. He is beyond reason, he is capable of anything. Fouqué is too far away; besides he would never understand the impulses of a heart like the marquis'.

Comte Altamira. . . . Can I be sure he will keep it quiet forever? My request for advice must not be an outward action, or do anything to complicate my position. Alas! There's nobody left for me

but that gloomy Abbé Pirard. . . . His spirit has been shriveled up by
Jansenism. . . . A rascally Jesuit would know more of the world and
suit my need better. . . . M. Pirard is capable of beating me the
minute I tell what I've done.

The genius of Tartufe came to Julien's rescue: All right, I will go
and make confession to him. That was the last decision he took in
the garden, after walking about there for two long hours. He no
longer thought he might be surprised by a gunshot; sleep was overtaking him.

Next day very early Julien was several leagues from Paris, knocking at the door of the stern Jansenist. He found, to his surprise,
that his confession met with no great astonishment.

—Perhaps I too am to blame in part, said the abbé, more in sorrow than anger. I thought I could detect something of this affair.
My affection for you, you little rascal, kept me from warning the father. . . .

—What will he do? Julien asked directly.

(At this moment he loved the abbé, and a quarrel would have
been very painful to him.)

I see three possibilities, Julien went on: first, M. de La Mole may
have me put to death; and he described the suicide note he had left
in the marquis' possession; second, he may have me shot by Comte
Norbert, who would challenge me to a duel.

—You would accept? said the abbé, leaping furiously to his feet.

—You aren't letting me finish. Certainly I should never fire on
the son of my benefactor.

Third, he may send me away. If he told me: Go to Edinburgh, or
Go to New York, I would obey. Then they can conceal the position
of Mlle. de La Mole; but I shall never allow them to destroy my
son.

—That's the first expedient, never fear, that that corrupt man will
think of. . . .

At Paris, Mathilde was in despair. She had seen her father about
seven o'clock. He had showed her Julien's letter, and she was fearful that he might have thought it the noble thing to end his own
life: And without my permission! she said to herself with an anguish that rose out of anger.

—If he is dead, I shall die, she told her father. You will have been
the cause of his death. . . . Perhaps you will be glad of it. . . . But I
swear by his ghost, the first thing I shall do is to put on mourning,
and declare myself publicly *Mme. veuve Sorel*; I shall send out the
usual cards, you may be sure of that. . . . You will not find me weak
or cowardly.

Her love reached the point of madness. For his part, M. de La
Mole was dumbfounded.

He began to look upon events a little more rationally. At lunch Mathilde did not appear. The marquis was delivered of an immense burden, and flattered too, when he saw that she had said nothing to her mother.

[Toward midday Julien returned. The clatter of his horse's hoofs resounded through the court.] Julien dismounted. Mathilde had him summoned and flung herself into his arms, almost under the eyes of her maid. Julien was not too grateful for these transports; he had emerged very diplomatic and calculating from his long talk with Abbé Pirard. His imagination was depressed by the calculation of possibilities. Mathilde, with tears in her eyes, told him that she had seen his suicide note.

—My father may reconsider; you must do me a favor and leave right away for Villequier. Take the horse again and leave the house before they have finished eating.

As Julien never altered his look of chilly surprise, she burst into tears.

—Let me manage our affairs, she cried passionately, clasping him in her arms. You know very well that it's not my decision to separate us. You must write as to my maid, disguising your hand in the address; as for me, I shall write volumes. Farewell! Be off!

Her last words wounded Julien's feelings, but he left nonetheless. It's in the stars, he thought, even in their best moments these people can find the trick of hurting me.

M. de La Mole did not have enough determination to play the usual heavy father. Mathilde maintained a solid defense against all her father's *prudent* plans. She would undertake negotiations on no other basis than this: She would be Mme. Sorel, and would live in poverty with her husband in Switzerland, or with her father in Paris. The idea of a clandestine confinement she dismissed altogether.

—That would be the beginning for me of possible calumny and disgrace. Two months after our marriage, I shall take a trip with my husband, and it will be easy for us to pretend that my child was born at the proper time.

Though he met it at first with transports of rage, her firmness ended by shaking the position of the marquis.

In a moment of tenderness:—Look, he said to his daughter, here is a paper conveying ten thousand florins a year; send it to your Julien and tell him to put it immediately where I can never call it back.

To *obey* Mathilde, whose love for giving orders was well known to him, Julien had made a useless journey of forty leagues: he was at Villequier, going over the tenants' accounts; this generous act of the marquis occasioned his return. He went to beg asylum with Abbé

Pirard, who during his absence had become Mathilde's most useful ally. Every time he was questioned by the marquis, he demonstrated that any step other than open marriage would be a sin in the eyes of God.

—And, by good fortune, added the abbé, worldly wisdom is here in agreement with religion. Given the fiery character of Mlle. de La Mole, could one count for a moment on her keeping any secret she had not imposed on herself? If you don't consent to the open course of a public marriage, society will concern itself much longer with this strange misalliance. Everything must be declared openly at one time, without the slightest mystery either in appearance or reality.

—It is true, said the marquis thoughtfully. If we follow your plan, talk of this marriage three days after it has taken place will be considered the chatter of a man who has no ideas. We might well profit by some great move of the government against Jacobins to slip unnoticed into the aftermath.

Two or three friends of M. de La Mole agreed with Abbé Pirard. The great obstacle, as they saw it, was Mathilde's obstinate nature. But after all these fine arguments, the spirit of the marquis could not bring itself to abandon hope of a *tabouret*[2] for his daughter.

His memory and his imagination were filled with tricks and devices of all sorts which had still been possible in his youth. Yielding to necessity and respecting the law seemed to him absurd and dishonorable recourses for a man of his rank. He was paying dearly now for those enchanting dreams in which, for the past ten years, he had been indulging concerning the future of his beloved daughter.

Who could have guessed? he asked himself. A girl of such lofty character, of so distinguished a mind, and prouder even than I am of the name she bears! Whose hand had been sought of me, previously, by all the most illustrious blood in France!

We must give up prudence! The age was created to bring everything into confusion! We are on the march toward chaos!

---

2. On *tabouret*, see p. 268, note 6.

Chapter 34

A MAN OF SPIRIT

The prefect riding down the road on his horse said to himself:
Why shouldn't I be a minister, president of the council, duke?
This is how I would carry on the war. . . . And so we'll throw all
these radicals into irons. . . .

—*The Globe*

No argument is strong enough to destroy the empire built up by
ten years of agreeable reverie. The marquis realized it was unrea-
sonable to be angry, but could not bring himself to grant a pardon.
If that Julien would only meet with a fatal accident, he sometimes
said to himself. . . . Thus it was that this wounded imagination
found some relief in pursuing absurd phantasms. They paralyzed all
Abbé Pirard's sensible thoughts. A month passed in this way without a step being taken in the negotiations.

In this family affair, as in political affairs, the marquis had some
brilliant insights over which he grew enthusiastic for three days.
Then a course of conduct no longer pleased him because it was
supported by good reasons; rather, the reasons pleased him insofar as they supported his favorite plan. During those three days
he worked with all the fervent enthusiasm of a poet to bring matters to a certain stage; the next day he no longer gave them a
thought.

At first Julien was disconcerted by the marquis' delays; but after
several weeks he began to see that M. de La Mole had no fixed plan
at all for managing this affair.

Mme. de La Mole and the whole household supposed that Julien
was traveling in the provinces to look after the marquis' estates; he
was actually hiding in Abbé Pirard's parsonage and saw Mathilde
almost every day; she went every morning to spend an hour with
her father, but they were often weeks on end without talking of the
topic that occupied both their thoughts.

—I don't want to know where that man is, the marquis said to
her one day; send him this letter. Mathilde read:

The estates in Languedoc bring in 20,600 francs. I give 10,600
francs to my daughter and 10,000 francs to M. Julien Sorel.
That is, I give the estates themselves. Tell the notary to draw
up two separate deeds of gift and to bring them tomorrow; after which, no further relations between us. Ah, sir, is this what
I should have expected?

The Marquis de La Mole.

—Thank you very much, said Mathilde gaily. We shall settle at the Chateau d'Aiguillon, between Agen and Marmande.[3] They say it's a district as beautiful as Italy.

This gift was a great surprise to Julien. He was no longer the cold, severe man we have come to know. The destiny of his son was already absorbing all his thoughts. This unexpected fortune, which seemed very substantial to so poor a man, made him ambitious. He now saw himself possessed, between his wife's income and his own, of 36,000 florins per year. As for Mathilde, all her feelings were wrapped up in admiration for her husband, for that was the title her pride bestowed on Julien. Her great, her only, ambition was to have her marriage recognized. She passed her days in exaggerating the immense prudence she had displayed in joining her fate with that of a superior man. Personal merit was all the rage in her brain.

Their almost constant separation, the multiplicity of their business concerns, and the little time they had to talk of love put the crowning touches on the good effects wrought by Julien's wise policies in the past.

Mathilde at last grew impatient at seeing so little of the man with whom she had succeeded in really falling in love.

In a moment of anger she wrote to her father, and began her letter like Othello:[4]

"That I have preferred Julien above any of the pleasures that society offered to the daughter of the Marquis de La Mole, my choice of him shows clearly enough. The pleasures of status and of petty vanity are meaningless to me. It is now six weeks that I have been living in separation from my husband. That is enough to serve as evidence of my respect for you. Before next Thursday I shall leave my father's house. Your generosity has made us rich. Nobody knows my secret but the respectable Abbé Pirard. I shall go to him; he will marry us, and an hour after the ceremony we shall be off for Languedoc, never to reappear in Paris except on your orders. But what hurts me most is that all this will give rise to nasty stories at my expense and at yours. It is possible that the epigrams of a silly public may oblige our good Norbert to pick a quarrel with Julien. Under these circumstances, I know him, I can have no control of him. We should rouse in his character the rebellious plebeian. I beg you on bended knee, my dear father! Come and be present at my marriage in M. Pirard's church next Thursday. The point of the ugly

---

3. The chateau of Aiguillon, which actually stood halfway between Agen and Marmande at the junction of the Lot and Garonne rivers, was an enormous eighteenth-century structure, begun by Armand-Désiré, the last duke of Aiguillon, but never completed because of the Revolution, and standing stripped and desolate after the expropriation.
4. Like Othello: actually, like Desdemona (1, 3).

stories will be blunted, the life of your only son, and the life of my husband will be made safe," etc., etc.

This letter cast the marquis into a strange predicament. Finally he had now to *make up his mind*. All his little habits, all his old friends, had lost their influence.

Under these strange circumstances his fundamental character, which had been established by the events of his youth, resumed its sway. The miseries of the emigration had formed him into a man of imagination. After he had enjoyed for two years an immense fortune and the highest distinction at court, 1790 had flung him into all the miseries of exile. This hard school had quite transformed the mind of a man who was just twenty-two. At heart, he was far from being dominated by his present possessions; he merely camped out in the midst of them. But this very imagination, which had preserved his mind from the gangrene of gold, had left him prey to an insane passion for seeing his daughter possessed of a fancy title.

During the six weeks just passed, the marquis, as if driven by a momentary caprice, had undertaken to make Julien rich; poverty seemed to him ignoble, shameful to himself, M. de La Mole, impossible for his daughter's husband; he flung down the money. Next day, his imagination taking another tack, it seemed to him that Julien must hear the mute language of this financial generosity, change his name, disappear to America, write to Mathilde that he was dead to her. M. de La Mole imagined this letter already written; he was tracing in his mind's eye its effect on his daughter's character. . . .

The day on which he was roused from these youthful dreams by Mathilde's *real* letter, after having thought for a long time of killing Julien or bringing about his disappearance, he was dreaming of making him a brilliant fortune. He was conferring on him the name of one of his properties; and why should he not pass on to him his own position in the peerage? The Duc de Chaulnes, his father-in-law, had spoken several times, since his only son had been killed in Spain, of wanting to pass on his title to Norbert. . . .

There's no denying Julien has a singular aptitude for business, boldness, perhaps even *brilliance*, thought the marquis. . . . But at the root of his character is something terrifying. It's the impression he produces on everyone, so there must be something real in it (the harder this real point was to grasp, the more it terrified the imaginative spirit of the old marquis).

My daughter expressed it very shrewdly the other day (in a letter we have suppressed): "Julien has no connections with any set or any coterie." He has not built up any support against me, he hasn't the slightest resource if I abandon him. . . . But is that ignorance of the present state of society? . . . Two or three times I told him: There is no real, no profitable campaign, except that waged in the drawing rooms. . . .

No, he doesn't have the wily, cautious spirit of a conniver who never wastes a minute or misses a main chance. . . . He is not a character after the style of Louis XI.[5] On the other hand, I see in him the most ungenerous maxims. . . . And at that point I lose him. . . . Does he repeat those maxims to himself in order to use them as a *dike* against his passions?

In any case, one consideration prevails: he cannot stand contempt, and I have him there.

He has not the religion of high birth; it is perfectly true, he does not respect us on instinct. . . . That's a fault; but after all, the usual seminarian is impatient only when he lacks pleasure and money. He is very different; he cannot endure contempt at any price.

Under pressure from his daughter's letter, M. de La Mole saw the necessity of making up his mind: —Well, this is the great question: Did Julien have the audacity to make love to my daughter simply because he knows I love her better than all the world, and that I have an income of a hundred thousand crowns?

Mathilde protests to the contrary. . . . No, Julien, my boy, that's one point on which I don't want to be under any illusions.

Was it authentic, spontaneous love? Or just a vulgar greed to raise himself to a good position? Mathilde saw very clearly from the first that this suspicion could ruin him in my good opinion, that was why she made that confession: that it was she who first thought of love. . . .

A girl of such lofty character forgetting herself so far as to make physical advances! . . . Catching him by the arm in the garden one evening, what a horror! As if she didn't have a hundred less indecent ways of letting him know that she favored him.

Excusing yourself is accusing yourself; I don't trust Mathilde. . . . On that day, the reflections of the marquis were more conclusive than usual. But habit carried the day. He resolved to gain time and write to his daughter. For they were writing letters, during this period, from one part of the house to the other. M. de La Mole was afraid of entering into a discussion with Mathilde in which he would have to stand up against her. He was afraid of ending everything by a too-sudden concession.

Letter

Take care to commit no new follies; here is a commission as lieutenant of hussars for M. le chevalier Julien Sorel de La

---

5. Unscrupulous, suspicious, cunning, cruel, and dishonest are some of the adjectives that have been applied to Louis XI (1423–1483).

Vernaye. You see what I am doing for him. Don't contradict me, don't ask any questions. Let him leave in twenty-four hours and report to Strasbourg where his regiment is quartered. Here is a draft on my banker; I expect to be obeyed.

Mathilde's love and joy knew no bounds; she sought to profit by her victory, and replied at once:

M. de La Vernaye would be at your feet, overcome with gratitude, if he knew everything you have been kind enough to do for him. But in the midst of this generosity, my father has forgotten me; the honor of your daughter is in danger. One indiscretion may create a blot that would last forever: an income of twenty thousand crowns would not efface it. I shall send the commission to M. de La Vernaye only if you give me your word that in the course of the next month my marriage will be celebrated in public at Villequier. Soon after that period, which I implore you not to exceed, your daughter will not be able to appear in public except with the name of Mme. de La Vernaye. Let me thank you, dearest papa, for having saved me from that name of Sorel, etc., etc.

The reply was unexpected:

Obey, or I withdraw everything. Take care, foolish girl. I do not yet know what your Julien is, and you know even less than I do. Let him be off to Strasbourg, and walk the straight and narrow path. I shall make known my will in two weeks.

The firmness of this reply astounded Mathilde. *I do not know Julien*; that expression threw her into a reverie that presently led to the most enchanting suppositions; but she thought they were true. My Julien's mind has not donned the mean little *uniform* of the drawing rooms, and my father doesn't believe in his superiority precisely because of the quality that proves it. . . .

Still, if I don't give way to this whim of his, we may well come to a public scene; a scandal will lower my position in the world and perhaps render me less attractive to Julien. After the scandal . . . poverty for ten years; and the madness of choosing a husband on the score of merit can be rescued from ridicule only by the most brilliant opulence. If I live at a distance from my father, at his age he may forget me. . . . Norbert will marry a woman who is agreeable and clever: Louis XIV was beguiled in his old age by the Duchess of Burgundy. . . .

She decided to obey, but was careful not to show her father's letter to Julien; his wild nature might rush him into some act of folly.

That evening, when she told Julien he was a lieutenant of hussars, his joy knew no bounds. It can be estimated from the ambition of his whole life, and from the passion he was now feeling for his new son. The change of name struck him with wonder.

Now at last, he thought, the novel of my career is over, and the credit is all mine. I was able to make myself loved by that monster of pride, he thought, glancing at Mathilde; her father cannot live without her nor she without me.

Chapter 35

WHIRLWIND

My God, give me mediocrity!
—Mirabeau

He was absorbed in thought; he only half-responded to the lively tenderness she showed him. He remained silent and somber. Never had he seemed so great, so adorable in the eyes of Mathilde. She was afraid of some subtle quirk of his pride that might turn up to overthrow the whole situation.

Nearly every morning she saw Abbé Pirard entering the house. Through his intervention might not Julien have learned something about her father's intentions? Might not the marquis himself, in a momentary whim, have written to him? After so great a happiness, how to account for Julien's severe air? She did not dare ask him.

She *did not dare!* she, Mathilde! From that moment, her feeling for Julien contained something vague, unaccountable, almost terrifying. That arid soul felt everything in passion that is possible for a person raised amid the excess of civilization which Paris admires.

Next morning very early Julien was at Abbé Pirard's parsonage. Post horses arrived in the court drawing a tattered chaise rented from the nearest stage house.

—This sort of rig is no longer suitable, said the stern abbé crossly. Here are twenty thousand francs which M. de La Mole bestows upon you; he requires you to spend them within the year, but with as few absurdities as possible. (In such an immense sum given to such a young man the priest saw nothing but an occasion for sin.)

The marquis adds: M. Julien de la Vernaye will have received this money from his father, whom it is useless to identify in any other way. M. de La Vernaye will perhaps find it appropriate to make a gift to M. Sorel, a carpenter at Verrières, who took care of him as an infant . . . . I myself will take care of this part of the business, added the abbé; I have finally convinced M. de La Mole to compromise with that Abbé de Frilair who is such a Jesuit. His position is definitely too strong for us. Implicit recognition of your high birth

by that man who governs Besançon will be one of the tacit conditions of the compromise.

Julien could no longer master his transports; he embraced the
abbé; he saw himself recognized.

—Pshaw! said M. Pirard, thrusting him away; what means all
this worldly vanity? . . . As for Sorel and his sons, I shall offer them,
in my name, an annual pension of five hundred francs apiece,
which will be paid to them during my good pleasure.

Julien was already cool and correct again. He expressed his
thanks, but in very vague terms which committed him to nothing.
Is it actually possible, he asked himself, that I might be the natural
son of some aristocrat exiled among our mountains by the terrible
Napoleon? At every instant this idea appeared less improbable to
him. . . . My hate for my father would be a proof. . . . I would no
longer be a monster!

A few days after this monologue, the fifteenth regiment of hussars, one of the most distinguished in the army, was drawn up on
parade in the public square of Strasbourg. M. le chevalier de La
Vernaye bestrode the finest horse in Alsace, which had cost him six
thousand francs. He had been accepted as lieutenant, without ever
having been sublieutenant except on the rosters of a regiment he
had never heard of.

His impassive air, his stern and almost savage glance, his pallor,
his unruffled coolness earned him a reputation from the day he arrived. Before long, his perfectly measured courtesy, and his skill
with pistol and sword, which he made known without too much affectation, tempered any tendency to make public jokes at his expense. After five or six days of hesitation, public opinion in the
regiment declared in his favor. This young man has everything, said
the older officers chaffingly, except youth.

From Strasbourg, Julien wrote to M. Chélan, former priest of
Verrières, who was now verging on the last stages of old age:

> You will have learned with a joy of which I make no question
> about the events which have persuaded my family to make me
> rich. Here are five hundred francs, which I should like you to
> distribute quietly, without any mention of my name, to those
> poor folk who are in need, as I once was myself, and whom you
> are doubtless helping now as you once helped me.

Julien was wild with ambition, not vanity; still, he devoted a great
deal of attention to his outward appearance. His horses, his uniforms, the liveries of his servants were maintained with a smartness
that would have done credit to the style of an English gentleman.
Though only a lieutenant, promoted by favor and with just two
days' service, he was already calculating that to be a commander in

chief by thirty at the latest, like all the other great generals, he would have to be more than a lieutenant at twenty-three. He thought of nothing but glory and his son.

It was in the midst of these transports of unbridled ambition that he was surprised by a young servant from the Hôtel de La Mole, who arrived bearing a letter.

All is lost, (Mathilde wrote him); come as quickly as possible, give up everything, desert if need be. As soon as you get here, wait for me in a cab by the little garden gate, Number _____, rue de _____. I will come out and talk with you; perhaps I will be able to get you into the garden. All is lost, and I fear beyond redemption; you may count on me, you will find me steadfast and devoted in adversity. I love you.

Within a few minutes Julien obtained leave of the colonel and left Strasbourg at a gallop; but the frightful doubts gnawing at him did not allow him to continue this mode of travel any further than Metz. He leaped into a chaise, and with almost unbelievable rapidity reached the meeting place near the little garden gate of the Hôtel de La Mole. The door opened and at once Mathilde, forgetting all restraint, flung herself into his arms. By good fortune it was five o'clock in the morning and the street was still empty.

—All is lost; my father, fearing my tears, left Thursday night. Where did he go? Nobody knows. Here is his letter; read it. And she got into the cab with Julien.

I could forgive everything except the plan of seducing you because you are rich. That, you unhappy child, is the awful truth. I give you my word of honor that I will never consent to your marriage with that man. I grant him ten thousand florins income if he will live abroad, outside the frontiers of France, or better still in America. Read the letter I received in reply to a request for information about him. The rascal told me himself to write to Mme. de Rênal. Never will I read a line from you about that man. I am horrified at Paris, at you. I implore you to cloak what must shortly happen in the greatest secrecy. Give up *honestly* this vile fellow and you will regain a father.

—Where is the letter from Mme. de Rênal? Julien asked coldly.
—I have it here. I didn't want to show it to you until you were prepared.

Letter
The obligations I feel toward the sacred cause of religion and morality oblige me, sir, to take the painful step of addressing myself to you; an unfailing rule requires me at this point to do harm to my neighbor, but only to avoid a greater scandal.

The grief I feel must yield to a sense of duty. It is only too true, sir, the conduct of the person you ask about may have seemed inexplicable to you or even honorable. It may have seemed appropriate to conceal or disguise part of the truth, worldly wisdom as well as religion would require it. But this conduct, about which you wish to know the whole truth, has actually been extremely blameworthy, and more so than I can tell you. Born poor and greedy, this man has tried by means of the most consummate hypocrisy, and by the seduction of a weak and wretched woman, to find himself a position and rise in the world. It is part of my painful duty to add that I am forced to believe M. J_____ has no religious principles. In all conscience I am obliged to think that his way to rise in a household is to try to seduce the woman who is most influential there. Cloaking himself under the guise of disinterestedness and phrases from novels, he makes it his great and only end to gain control over the master of the house and his fortune. He leaves behind him a trail of misery and eternal regrets, etc., etc., etc.

This letter, which was extremely long and half-blurred by tears, was indeed in the hand of Mme. de Rênal; it was even written with more than her usual care.

—I cannot blame M. de La Mole, Julien said, when he had finished it; he is perfectly right and proper. What father would want to give his beloved daughter to such a man! Farewell!

Julien leaped out of the cab and ran to his chaise, which was waiting for him at the end of the street. Mathilde, whom he seemed to have forgotten, took a few steps after him; but the stares of the shopkeepers who were looking out their doors and to whom she was known, forced her to return hastily into the garden.

Julien had left for Verrières. On this swift journey he was unable to write to Mathilde, as he had intended to do; his hand formed nothing on the paper but illegible scrawls.

He reached Verrières Sunday morning. He went to the shop of a gunsmith, who overwhelmed him with compliments on his new fortune. It was the talk of the town.

Julien had great difficulty in making him understand he wanted a pair of pistols. At his request the gunsmith loaded the pistols.

Three bells sounded; this is a signal well known in the villages of France; following the various peals of the particular day, it announces the immediate beginning of the mass.

Julien entered the new church of Verrières. All the lofty windows of the church were draped in crimson curtains. Julien found himself standing a few paces behind Mme. de Rênal's bench. It seemed to him that she was praying fervently. The sight of this woman whom he had loved deeply made Julien's arm tremble so violently that at first he could not carry out his plan. I cannot do it, he told himself; physically, I cannot do it.

At that moment the young cleric who was serving the mass rang the bell for the *elevation*. Mme. de Rênal bowed her head, which for a moment was almost entirely hidden in the folds of her shawl. Julien no longer recognized her so clearly; he fired his first pistol at her and missed; he fired again, she fell.

Chapter 36

PAINFUL PARTICULARS

> Look for no weakness on my part, I took my revenge. I have merited death, and here I am. Pray for my soul.
>
> —Schiller

Julien stood motionless, unseeing. When he returned to himself a little, he saw the crowd of worshippers rushing out of the church; the priest had left the altar. Julien began to follow, at a walk, various women who were shrieking as they ran. One woman who wanted to get away faster than the others gave him a rude shove; he fell. His feet were tangled in a chair overturned by the mob; as he got up, he felt himself clutched by the collar; it was a policeman in full uniform, who was arresting him. Mechanically Julien reached for his little pistols, but a second policeman pinioned his arms.

He was led to jail. They took him to a room, handcuffed him, and left him alone; the door was closed on him and double-locked; the whole thing was done very quickly, and he was quite unaware of it.

—Well, that finishes it, he said aloud as he returned to himself. . . . Yes, in a couple of weeks, the guillotine . . . or else kill myself between now and then.

His reasoning went no further; he felt a pain in his head as if it were being violently compressed. He looked around to see if somebody was holding onto him. After a few minutes he sank into a deep sleep.

Mme. de Rênal was not fatally wounded. The first bullet had passed through her hat; the second was fired just as she turned around. The bullet struck her in the shoulder, glanced off her shoulder blade and fractured it, and then, rather surprisingly, went on to strike a Gothic pillar from which it broke off a big splinter of stone.

When, after a long and painful dressing of the wound, the solemn-faced surgeon told Mme. de Rênal: I will answer for your life as for my own, she was deeply afflicted.

For a long time she had sincerely wanted to be dead. The letter that had been required of her by her present confessor, and which she had written to M. de La Mole, was a final blow to the poor woman, weakened already by excessive grief. Her grief was in fact the absence of Julien; she called it *remorse*. Her spiritual director, a young ecclesiastic newly arrived from Dijon, full of virtue and fervor, made no mistake about that.

To die in this way, but not by my own hand, cannot be a sin, thought Mme. de Rênal. God will perhaps pardon me for rejoicing in my own death. She did not dare to add. And to die by Julien's hand is the height of bliss.

Hardly was she rid of the surgeon and of the crowd of her friends who had come to see her than she sent for Elisa, her maid.

—The jailer, she said, blushing deeply, is a cruel man. No doubt he will mistreat him, thinking thereby to do something pleasing to me. . . . The idea is unbearable to me. Can't you go, as if on your own account, and give the jailer this little package containing a few louis? You must tell him that religion forbids his mistreating him. . . . It's particularly important that he shouldn't mention this gift of money.

It was to the circumstances we have just described that Julien owed the unusual humanity of the Verrières jail keeper; he was still that M. Noiroud, the perfect government man, whom we saw thrown into such a spasm of fright by the sight of M. Appert.

An examining magistrate appeared at the prison.

—I have taken life in a premeditated act, Julien told him; I bought the pistols and had them loaded at the shop of So-and-So, the gunsmith. Article 1342 of the penal code is perfectly clear, I deserve to die and I'm expecting to.[6]

The judge, amazed at this frank response, tried to multiply questions in order to make the accused *contradict himself* in his answers.

—But don't you see, said Julien with a smile, I am making myself out just as guilty as you could want? Be off with you, sir, you are not going to lose the prey you're hunting after. You will have the pleasure of condemning me. And now spare me your presence.

I have one more tiresome job to do, thought Julien; I must write Mlle. de La Mole.

> I have my revenge, (he told her). Unfortunately, my name will appear in the newspapers, I cannot escape from this world *incognito* [and for this I beg your pardon.] In two months I shall be dead. My vengeance was savage, like my grief at being separated from you. From this moment on, I forbid myself to

6. Article 1342 of the penal code is an impressive particularity; but the code of 1810 had only 484 articles.

write or speak your name. Never speak of me, not even to my son: silence is the only way to do me honor. For the ordinary run of men I shall be a vulgar murderer. . . . Allow me to speak truth at this supreme moment of my life: you will forget me. This great catastrophe, about which I advise you never to say a word to a human being, will have exhausted for several years everything I recognize as romantic and overadventurous in your character. You were made to live with the heroes of the Middle Ages; summon up for this occasion their firmness of character. Let what is going to happen happen, in secret and without compromising you. You will assume a pseudonym and have no confidant. If you absolutely require the help of a friend, I bequeath you Abbé Pirard.

Do not talk to anyone else, particularly not to people of your own class like de Luz, Caylus.

A year after my death, marry M. de Croisenois; I beg you to do this, I order you as your husband; I will have no argument on the point. Don't write to me at all, I shall not reply. Though far less malicious than Iago, as it seems to me, I am going to say like him: *From this time forth I never will speak word.*[7]

No one will see me write or speak; you will have had my last words along with my last devotions.

J.S.

For the first time after he had sent off this letter, Julien, returning slightly to himself, became extremely unhappy. Each of ambition's promises had to be ripped in turn from his heart by this great thought: *I am going to die. [I must die.]* Death in itself was not *horrible* in his eyes. All his life had been nothing but one long preparation for misfortune, and he had certainly not overlooked that which passes for one of the greatest of them all.

What the deuce! he told himself, if in sixty days I had to fight a duel with a man who was an expert fencer, would I be weak enough to think of it continually, would I carry terror about in my soul?

He passed more than an hour trying to understand himself from this angle.

When he had seen straight into his soul, and the truth stood before his eyes as sharply outlined as one of the pillars of his prison, he thought of remorse.

Why should I feel any? I have been insulted in atrocious fashion; I have killed, I have deserved death myself, but that's all. I die after settling my score with humanity. I leave behind no unfulfilled obligation, I owe nothing to anybody; the only thing shameful about my death is the instrument of it: that alone, to be sure, is ample cause

---

7. *Othello,* V, 2.

of shame in the eyes of the Verrières middle class; but, intellectually considered, what could be more contemptible? I still have one
way to acquire distinction in their eyes: that would be to scatter
gold pieces among the people on my way to the scaffold. My memory, linked with the idea of gold, will glitter forever in their minds.

After this chain of thought, which when he had contemplated it
for a moment seemed perfectly clear: I have nothing more to do on
this earth, said Julien, and fell fast asleep.

About nine that evening, the jailer waked him to bring him some
soup.

—What are they saying in Verrières?

—Monsieur Julien, the oath I swore on the crucifix in the king's
court the day I took office obliges me to silence.

He was silent, but stayed in the room. The sight of this vulgar
hypocrisy amused Julien. Let's keep him waiting a long time, he
thought, for the five francs he wants as the price of selling his conscience to me.

When the jailer saw the meal finishing without any effort at
bribery:

—The friendship I bear you, Monsieur Julien, he said with an air
of false sweetness, obliges me to speak; although they do say that
this is against the interests of justice because it may help you to set
up your defense. . . . Monsieur Julien, who is a good fellow, will be
happy to learn that Mme. de Rênal is feeling better.

—What! She isn't dead! Julien exclaimed, [jumping up from the
table] in his excitement.

—What! you didn't know about that! said the jailer, with a stupid
expression that quickly changed to one of joyful greed. It would
only be right if Monsieur made a contribution to the surgeon, who,
in all law and justice, shouldn't have talked. But to give Monsieur
pleasure, I went to his house and he told me everything. . . .

—In a word, the wound isn't fatal, Julien said, turning upon him
impatiently; will you answer for that with your life?

The jailer, a giant six feet tall, was afraid, and backed toward the
door. Julien saw he was on the wrong tack, sat down again, and
tossed a napoleon to M. Noiroud.

As this man's story proved to Julien that Mme. de Rênal's wound
was not fatal, he felt the impulse to weep gaining on him.

—Go now, he said sharply.

The jailer obeyed. Hardly was the door closed: —Great God! She
is not dead! Julien cried out; and he fell to his knees, weeping passionately.

At this supreme moment he was a believer. What matter the
priestly hypocrisies? Can they do anything to diminish the truth
and sublimity of the idea of God?

Only then did Julien begin to repent of the crime he had committed. By a coincidence that saved him from despair, only at that moment was he relieved of the state of physical irritation and half madness in which he had been sunk since he left Paris for Verrières.

His tears sprang from a generous feeling; he had not the slightest doubt about the sentence that awaited him.

And so she will live! he thought. . . . She will live to forgive me and to love me. . . .

It was late the next morning when the jailer waked him.

—You must have a first-rate heart, Monsieur Julien, the fellow said to him. Twice I came and didn't want to wake you. Here are two bottles of excellent wine sent by M. Maslon, our priest.

—How's that? Is that rascal still here? Julien asked.

—Yes, sir, replied the jailer, lowering his voice, but you mustn't talk so loud; that could harm your case.

Julien laughed heartily.

—At the point I've reached, my friend, you are the only one who can harm me if you stop being gentle and humane. . . . You will be well paid, said Julien, interrupting himself and resuming his imperious air. This air was immediately reinforced by the gift of a small coin.

M. Noiroud told all over again and in the greatest detail everything he had learned about Mme. de Rênal, but he said not a word about the visit of Mlle. Elisa.

The man was as humble and submissive as possible. An idea flashed through Julien's head: This species of misshapen giant may earn as much as three or four hundred francs, for his jail is not much occupied; I can guarantee him ten thousand francs if he wants to escape into Switzerland with me. . . . The hard thing will be to persuade him of my good faith. The idea of a long colloquy to be held with such a vile creature filled Julien with disgust; he thought of something else.

That evening there was no longer time. A mail coach came to take him away at midnight. He was much pleased with the policemen who were his traveling companions. Next morning, when he reached the prison at Besançon, they were kind enough to give him a room on the upper story of a Gothic tower. He estimated the architecture to date from the beginning of the fourteenth century; he admired its grace and sharp delicacy. Through a narrow interval between two walls on the far side of a deep courtyard there was a glimpse of a magnificent view.

Next day there was an interrogation, after which for several days they left him alone. His spirit was calm. He found nothing in his case that was not perfectly simple: I tried to kill, I ought to be killed.

His thought never moved beyond this logic. The trial, the bother of appearing in public, the defense, he considered all those matters trivial nuisances, boring ceremonies which there would be plenty of time to think about on the day itself. The moment of death hardly concerned him anymore: I'll think of that after the trial. Life was by no means boring to him; he was considering everything under a new aspect. Ambition was dead in him. He rarely thought of Mlle. de La Mole. Remorse agitated him a good deal and often brought before him the image of Mme. de Rênal, especially during the silence of the nights, broken in this lofty tower only by the cry of the screech-owl![8]

He thanked heaven that he had not wounded her mortally. Astonishing thing! he said to himself; I thought that by her letter to M. de La Mole she had destroyed forever my future happiness; now, less than two weeks from the date of that letter, I never give a thought to the things that used to occupy me completely. . . . Two or three thousand florins a year to live peacefully in a little mountain town like Vergy. . . . I was happy then. . . . I didn't know how happy I was!

At other moments he leaped from his seat. If I had wounded Mme. de Rênal fatally, I should have killed myself. . . . I must be sure of that to keep from feeling horrified at myself.

Kill myself! There's the big question, he thought. These judges with their formalities who are so avid for the blood of the poor accused, who would hang the best citizen in the town to get a decoration for themselves. . . . I should be out of their power, free from their insults in bad French, which the district newspapers will describe as eloquence. . . .

I may still live five or six weeks, more or less. . . . Kill myself! My word, no, he told himself, a few days later, Napoleon went on living. . . .

Besides, life is pleasant for me here; I'm getting a good rest; I have nothing to bother about, he added with a laugh, and began to make a list of the books he wanted to have sent from Paris.

8. The bird in Julien's tower is actually called an *orfraie* or "osprey." The ornithologically oriented reader may wonder what the large fish-hawk he knows under the name of "osprey" is doing nesting in the prison-tower at Besançon. French *orfraie*, however, is often confused with "effraie" or screech-owl, the cry of which is supposed to terrify (*effrayer*) people because it is a premonition of death. Julien's bird has to be a screech-owl.

Chapter 37

A DUNGEON

The tomb of a friend.
—Sterne

He heard a great racket in the corridor; it was not the usual hour for visiting his cell; the owl flew away screaming, the door opened, and the venerable priest M. Chélan, trembling and leaning on a cane, flung himself into Julien's arms.

—Ah! Great God! Is it possible, my child. . . . Monster! I should say.

And the good old man could not add another word. Julien was afraid he would collapse; he was obliged to lead him to a seat. Time's hand had born heavily on this man, once so energetic. To Julien he seemed only the ghost of his former self.

When he had caught his breath: —Only the day before yesterday I got your letter from Strasbourg, with your five hundred francs for the poor of Verrières; it was delivered to me in the mountains at Liveru, where I have gone to live with my nephew Jean. Yesterday, I learned of the catastrophe . . . . Oh God! Is it possible! And the old man wept no more; he seemed to be stunned beyond all thought, and added mechanically: You will need your five hundred francs, I have brought them to you.

—I need to see you, Father! Julien cried with emotion. I have more money than I need.

But he could not get a coherent answer. From time to time M. Chélan shed a few tears, which trickled silently down his cheeks; then he looked at Julien, and was stunned to see him take his hands and raise them to his lips. His features which had once been so lively and expressed with such energy the loftiest sentiments were sunk in a kind of apathy. Before long a sort of peasant came to look up the old man. —He must not tire himself out by talking too much, he said to Julien, who understood that this was the nephew. The visit left Julien plunged in deep unhappiness, too deep for tears. Everything seemed to him sad beyond consolation; he felt his heart turn to ice in his bosom.

This moment was the bitterest he had experienced since his crime. He had just seen death, and in all its ugliness. All his illusions about spiritual grandeur and generosity had been dissipated like a cloud before a windstorm.

His frightful situation lasted several hours. A case of moral poisoning requires physical remedies, specifically a bottle of champagne. Julien would have thought himself a coward if he had sought comfort there. Toward the end of a horrible day which he had spent entirely in pacing up and down his narrow cell: What a fool I am! he exclaimed. If I expected to die like everyone else, the sight of that poor old man might well have made me completely miserable; but a quick death in the flower of my youth is just what will save me from that wretched decrepitude.

Whatever his reasonings, Julien found himself softened, like any other fainthearted fellow, and consequently despondent as a result of this visit.

There was nothing left in him of the rough and grandiose, nothing of Roman virtue; death seemed to him a more elevated matter, less easy to undergo.

Let this be my thermometer, he said. Tonight I am ten degrees below the courage which will lead me to the level of the guillotine. This morning I was brave. And for all that, what does it matter? provided I have it at the crucial moment. The notion of a thermometer amused him and ended by distracting his thoughts.

Next day when he woke up he was ashamed of his conduct the day before. My happiness, my peace of mind are at stake. He almost decided to write the district attorney and ask that nobody be allowed to visit him. And Fouqué? he thought. Suppose he undertakes a trip to Besançon, how upset he would be!

It was perhaps two months since he had given a thought to Fouqué. I was a great fool at Strasbourg; my thoughts never reached beyond my coat collar. The memory of Fouqué preoccupied his mind and left him in a more tender mood. He paced up and down agitatedly. Here I am a full twenty degrees below the death temperature . . . . If this weakness gets any worse, it will be better to kill myself. What a pleasure for the Abbé Maslons and Valenods if I die like a cur!

Fouqué came; this simple, honest fellow was haggard with grief. His only idea, if he had any at all, was to sell everything he owned in order to bribe the jailer and get Julien away. He talked to him for a long time of the escape of M. de Lavalette.[9]

—You're upsetting me, my dear fellow, Julien told him; M. de Lavalette was innocent, I am guilty. Without meaning to, you are making me think of the difference. . . .

But, is it true! The devil! Would you really sell everything you own? said Julien, returning to his old role of the suspicious observer.

Fouqué, overjoyed to see his friend at last responsive to his ruling

9. After Waterloo, Comte Antoine de Lavalette was condemned to the guillotine. The day before the execution his wife made her way into the prison, changed clothes with her husband, and enabled him to escape (December 20, 1815).

passion, described to him in great detail, practically down to the last hundred francs, what he could realize on each one of his properties.

What a superb gesture on the part of a little provincial landowner, Julien thought. How many savings, how many petty economies which would make me blush if I saw them being practiced, he is ready to sacrifice for me! One of those handsome young men I used to see about the Hôtel de La Mole reading *René*[1] might not have had any of these absurdities; but, except for a few who are very young, who have inherited their money and so have no idea of its value, which one of those fine Parisians would be capable of such a sacrifice?

All of Fouqué's mispronunciations, all his vulgar manners disappeared; Julien flung himself into his arms. Never did the provinces, when compared with Paris, receive a more handsome tribute. Fouqué, overjoyed at the momentary enthusiasm he read in his friend's eyes, mistook it for agreement to the escape.

This glimpse of the *sublime* restored to Julien all the energy that the specter of M. Chélan had dissipated. He was still very young; but in my opinion, he was a fine plant. Instead of treading the common path from softness to cunning, like most men, advancing years would have given him easy access to a fund of generous feeling; he would have overcome his morbid mistrust. . . . But what is the point of these vain suppositions?

The interrogations became more frequent despite the best efforts of Julien, whose answers all tended to cut the business short: —I have killed, or at least tried to kill, and with premeditation, he repeated every day. But the judge was a stickler for the formalities. Julien's statements in no way cut short the interrogations; they punctured the judge's self-importance. Julien did not know they wanted to move him into a frightful dungeon, and that it was thanks only to the efforts of Fouqué that they left him in his pleasant room a hundred and eighty steps above the ground.

Abbé de Frilair was one of several influential men who dealt with Fouqué for their firewood. The honest merchant managed to get himself in touch with the all-powerful grand vicar. To his inexpressible delight, M. de Frilair told him that, impressed by Julien's good qualities and by the services he had formerly rendered at the seminary, he intended to intervene with the judges. Fouqué glimpsed a half-hope of saving his friend, and as he left the presence, bowing

---

1. Stendhal held a particular grudge against Chateaubriand, whose style was too flowery for his taste; the reference here mocks romantic young men who cultivate generous and pathetic sentiments in novels (*René*) but nowhere else.

to the ground, he begged the grand vicar to expend on masses for the acquittal of the accused the sum of ten louis.

Fouqué was strangely in error here. M. de Frilair was by no means a Valenod. He refused, and even undertook to make the honest peasant see he would do much better to keep his money in his own pocket. Seeing that it was impossible to be clear without indiscretion, he advised him to give the sum in charities for the poor prisoners, who in fact lacked everything.

This Julien is a strange bird, his behavior is inexplicable, thought M. de Frilair, and for me nothing should be inexplicable. . . . Perhaps we can make a martyr out of him. . . . In any event, I shall get the *inside story* of this matter, and may even find a way to put some fear into that Mme. de Rênal, who has no respect for us, and really loathes me. . . . Perhaps I can even find in this business a way of producing a spectacular reconciliation with M. de La Mole, who has a weakness for this little seminarian.

The compromise in the matter of the suit had been signed some weeks before, and Abbé Pirard had left Besançon, where he dropped a few words about the mystery surrounding Julien's birth, on the very day when the unfortunate young man was firing on Mme. de Rênal in the church of Verrières.

Julien saw only one more disagreeable episode standing between him and death: that was the visit of his father. He talked with Fouqué about writing to the attorney general for permission to be spared this visit. His horror at the thought of seeing his father, and at such a moment, profoundly shocked the honest middle-class mind of the wood seller.

He thought he could see why so many people hated his friend so violently. Out of respect for the unfortunate, he concealed his feelings.

—In any case, he said coldly, an order for solitary confinement would not apply to your father.

Chapter 38

AN INFLUENTIAL MAN

> But there are so many mysteries in her deportment, and such elegance in her appearance! Who can she be?
> —Schiller

The cell doors swung open very early next day. Julien woke with a start.

—Oh, Good Lord! he thought, here comes my father. What a disagreeable scene!

At the same instant a woman dressed as a peasant flung herself into his arms [and clung convulsively to him]. It was Mlle. de La Mole.

—Wretch, it was only from your letter that I learned where you were. What you call your crime, and which was only a noble act of vengeance that shows me the full loftiness of your spirit, this I learned of only in Verrières. . . .

Despite his prejudices against Mlle. de La Mole, to which in any case he had not yet admitted distinctly, Julien found her very beautiful. How could he not recognize in this style of speech and action a noble, disinterested sentiment, far beyond any of which a petty, vulgar soul would have been capable? He felt he was still the lover of a queen, [he yielded to the spell,] and after a few moments it was with a rare nobility of speech and thought that he said to her:

—The future was very clearly before my eyes. After my death, I married you off to M. de Croisenois, who would be marrying a widow. The noble if somewhat romantic soul of this lovely widow, frighted and turned back to the values of common prudence by an episode of singular tragic moment for her life, would easily have appreciated the genuine merits of the young marquis. You would soon have resigned yourself to what constitutes happiness for everyone else in the world: esteem, money, social position. . . . But, my dear Mathilde, your coming to Besançon, if ever it gets out, will be a mortal blow to M. de La Mole, and for that I should never forgive myself. I've already caused him so much sorrow! The academician will say he nourished a viper in his bosom.

—I confess, I didn't expect from you quite so much cold reason or quite so much concern for the future, said Mlle. de La Mole, half-angry. My maid, who is quite as prudent as you, took a passport under her name, and it was as Mme. Michelet that I traveled here.

—And Mme. Michelet found it easy to gain access to me?

—Ah! You are still the superior man, the man of my choice! First I offered a hundred francs to a secretary of the judge, who had declared it was quite impossible for me to be admitted to the jail. But once he had the money, this honest fellow made me wait, raised objections, I thought he was out to rob me. . . . She paused.

—Well? said Julien.

—Don't be angry, my little Julien, she said, kissing him, I was obliged to give my real name to this secretary; he had thought I was a little Paris shop girl in love with the handsome Julien. . . . Those were actually his words. I swore to him that I was your wife and I have permission now to visit you every day.

Her folly is now complete, Julien thought; there was nothing I could do to prevent it. After all, M. de La Mole is such a great man that public opinion will be able to find excuses for the young colonel who marries this charming widow. My death, which is close at hand, will cover everything; and he yielded with delight to Mathilde's love; it was madness, grandeur of spirit, everything that was most strange. She seriously proposed to kill herself with him.

After these first transports, and when she had fully savored the pleasure of seeing Julien again, a lively curiosity invaded her spirit. She examined her lover carefully, and found him far above what she had imagined. Boniface de La Mole seemed reborn in him, but in an even more heroic mold.

Mathilde visited the leading lawyers of the district and offended them by offering money too crudely; but in the end they took the case.

She speedily reached the conclusion that in any controversial business of high importance everything at Besançon depended on Abbé de Frilair.

Under the unknown name of Mme. Michelet, she at first found insurmountable difficulties in reaching the all-powerful head of the congregation. But rumors of a beautiful young dressmaker who was madly in love and had come from Paris to Besançon to bring comfort to young Abbé Julien Sorel began to spread through the town.

Alone and on foot, Mathilde passed through the streets of Besançon; she hoped to escape recognition. In any event, she calculated it might not harm her cause to produce a strong impression on the people. Her madness even envisaged fomenting a revolt in order to save Julien as he walked to the scaffold. Mlle. de La Mole thought she was dressed simply and suitably for a woman in mourning; in fact, her dress made her the center of all eyes.

Everyone in Besançon took note of it when, after a week of pleading, she obtained an audience with M. de Frilair.

Courageous though she was, the notion of an influential leader of the congregation and the concept of profound, prudent rascality were so linked in her mind that she trembled as she rang the doorbell of the bishop's palace. She could scarcely walk when she had to climb the staircase leading to the apartment of the first grand vicar. The emptiness of the episcopal palace chilled her spirit. I may sit in an armchair, it will clutch my arms, I will be gone. Where can my maid ask after me? The police chief will take great care to do nothing. . . . I am all alone in this big town!

Her first glance around the apartment set Mlle. de La Mole's mind at rest. First, it was a footman in really elegant livery who showed her in. The room in which she was asked to wait displayed a sensitive and delicate luxury, quite different from crude magnificence, and such as one finds only in the best houses of Paris. As soon as she saw M. de Frilair approaching her with a fatherly air all ideas of foul play disappeared. She did not even find on his handsome features the imprint of a virtue, energetic and perhaps a bit savage, which is so antipathetic to good company in Paris. The half smile on the face of the priest who controlled everything in Besançon announced a man of good society, a knowing prelate, a clever administrator. Mathilde thought she was in Paris.

M. de Frilair needed only a few minutes to get Mathilde to admit that she was the daughter of his powerful adversary, the Marquis de La Mole.

—In fact, I am not Mme. Michelet at all, she said, resuming her usual lofty demeanor, and this admission does not much distress me, for I've come to consult you, sir, concerning the possibility of bringing about the escape of M. de La Vernaye. In the first place, he is guilty of nothing worse than a stupid blunder; the woman at whom he shot is perfectly well. In the second place, to corrupt the subordinates, I can put down, on the spot, fifty thousand francs and promise twice as much. Finally, my gratitude and that of my family will consider nothing impossible for the person who saves M. de La Vernaye.

M. de Frilair seemed surprised at that name. Mathilde showed him letters from the minister of war addressed to M. Julien Sorel de La Vernaye.

—You see, sir, my father had undertaken to make his fortune. [It is perfectly simple.] I married him in secret; my father wanted him to be a senior officer before making known this marriage, which is a little out of the way for a La Mole.

Mathilde noted that the expression of kindness and gentle gaiety vanished at once as soon as M. de Frilair began to learn something of importance. Subtlety mingled with profound duplicity began to appear on his face.

The abbé was doubtful; he reread the official documents slowly.

What can I get for myself from these odd confidences? he asked himself. Here I am, all of a sudden, in close relations with a friend of the celebrated Maréchale de Fervaques, all-powerful niece of my lord the Bishop of ＿＿＿, through whom one becomes a bishop in France.

Things that I regarded as hidden in the future now turn up unexpectedly to hand. This may lead me to the great goal of all my ambition.

At first Mathilde was terrified by the sudden changes of expression on the part of this influential man with whom she found herself alone in a lonely chamber. But, what the deuce! she told herself shortly, wouldn't the worst thing have been to make no impression at all on the icy egotism of a priest already glutted on power and pleasure?

Dazzled by this rapid road to the episcopacy that had opened unexpectedly before his eyes, M. de Frilair dropped his guard for a moment. Mlle. de La Mole saw him almost at her feet, avid with ambition to the point of a nervous tremor.

It's getting clearer, she thought; nothing will be impossible here for a friend of Mme. de Fervaques. In spite of a twinge of still-painful jealousy, she had the courage to explain that Julien was the good friend of the maréchale, and at her house met nearly every day with my lord the Bishop of _____.

—If you were to draw by lot four or five times in a row a list of thirty-six jurors selected from the notable residents of this district, said the grand vicar, with the sour gaze of an ambitious man and giving great weight to each of his words, I should think myself very unfortunate if in each list I did not have eight or ten friends, and the most intelligent of the lot. Almost always I will have the majority, more than the majority needed to condemn; you see, mademoiselle, with what ease I can get an acquittal. . . .

The abbé stopped suddenly, as if astounded by the sound of his own words; he was admitting to things that are never uttered before the profane.

But he in turn dumbfounded Mathilde when he told her that what astonished and interested Besançon society more than anything else in the strange history of Julien was that he had once inspired a great passion in Mme. de Rênal, and that he had long returned it. M. de Frilair could not fail to note the extreme distress that his story produced.

I have my revenge! thought he. At last, here is a way of managing this very decided young person; I thought I would never find one. Her distinguished and independent air added in his eyes to the charm of the rare beauty which he now saw almost suppliant before him. He regained all his self-possession, and did not hesitate to twist the knife in the wound.

—I should not be surprised after all, he told her in a jesting way, if we should learn that jealousy impelled M. Sorel to fire a pistol twice at this woman whom once he loved so dearly. She cannot have lived without her diversions, and for some time now she had been seeing a good deal of a certain Abbé Marquinot in Dijon, some sort of Jansenist without any morals like the rest of that lot.

With great pleasure M. de Frilair tortured at his leisure the heart of this pretty girl, whose weakness he had discovered.

—I ask you, he said, fixing his burning eyes on Mathilde, why should M. Sorel have selected the church, if it was not because, precisely at that moment, his rival was celebrating mass there? Everyone concedes immense resources of wit and even more of prudence to the lucky man you have favored with your interest.

What would have been simpler than to conceal himself in the gardens of M. de Rénal's house, with which he is so familiar? There, with the almost perfect assurance of being neither seen, nor captured, nor suspected, he could have killed the woman of whom he was jealous.

This reasoning, so just on the surface, succeeded in driving Mathilde out of her mind. Her soul was lofty, but saturated with that dry prudence which passes in the great world as the essence of the human heart; she was not made to understand the pleasure that lies in defying all prudence, and which can be so keen for an impassioned spirit. In the upper classes of Parisian society, where Mathilde had lived, passion only rarely dispenses with prudence, and it is only the people who live on the fifth story who jump out of the window.

At last Abbé de Frilair was sure of his conquest. He gave Mathilde to understand (doubtless he was lying) that he could influence any way he chose the district attorney, who would present the case against Julien.

After the names of the thirty-six jurors had been chosen by lot, he would make a direct and personal intervention with at least thirty of them.

If Mathilde had not seemed so pretty to M. de Frilair, he would not have been so clear and explicit until the fifth or sixth interview.

Chapter 39

SCHEMING

> Castres, 1676 (March 31)—He that endeavored to kill his sister in our house had before killed a man, and it had cost his father five hundred *écus* to get him off; by their secret distributions gaining the favor of the counselors.
>
> —Locke, *Journey through France*[2]

As she left the episcopal palace, Mathilde, without a moment's hesitation, dispatched a messenger to Mme. de Fervaques; fear of compromising herself did not restrain her an instant. She implored her rival to obtain a letter to M. de Frilair written entirely in the hand of my lord the Bishop of _____. She went so far as to beg her to come to Besançon herself. This was a heroic step on the part of a spirit both jealous and proud.

Following Fouqué's advice, she was prudent enough not to mention her actions to Julien. Her presence troubled him enough with-

---

2. From Peter King's *Life of John Locke, with extracts from his Correspondence, Journals, and Commonplace Books*, dated March 31, 1676.

out that. A more honest man as death approached than he had ever been in life, he was experiencing remorse not only for M. de La Mole but also for Mathilde.

How can this be! he said to himself, I find there are times when, in her presence, I am absent-minded, or even bored. She is ruining herself for me, and that is how I repay her! Am I really an evil person? This question would not have concerned him much when he was ambitious; at that time, to fail in life was the only cause of shame he recognized.

His moral disquiet in the presence of Mathilde was the more striking because at that moment he was inspiring her to the most extraordinary and insane passions. She talked of nothing but the extravagant sacrifices she wanted to make in order to save him.

Exalted by a sentiment of which she was proud, and which trampled all her pride underfoot, she wanted to let not a moment of her life pass without filling it with some amazing action. The strangest projects, the most perilous for herself, occupied her long conversations with Julien. The jailers, well paid, let her have her own way in the prison. Mathilde's ideas were not confined to sacrificing her reputation; little did she care about making her condition known to the whole of society. Falling to her knees before the king's careening carriage to beg a pardon for Julien, attracting the prince's attention at the risk of being crushed a thousand times over, these were the least of the dreams in which this exalted and courageous imagination indulged. Through her friends at court, she knew she could gain access to the reserved portions of the park at Saint-Cloud.[3]

Julien found himself scarcely worthy of all this devotion; to tell the truth, he was getting tired of heroics. He would have been responsive to a simple, a naïve and almost timid approach, whereas Mathilde's lofty soul always had to be conscious of a public and of *other people*.

Amid all her anguish, all her fears for the life of this lover whom she did not want to outlive, Julien sensed in her a secret need to amaze the public with the splendor of her love and the sublimity of her projects.

Julien was irked to find that he was not touched at all by this excess of heroism. What would he have thought if he had known of all the follies with which Mathilde overwhelmed the devoted, but essentially, reasonable and limited mind of the good Fouqué?

The latter was not too sure what to find fault with in Mathilde's devotion; for he too would have sacrificed his fortune and exposed his life to the greatest dangers to save Julien. He was dumbfounded

3. The park at Saint-Cloud: see p. 209, n. 8.

at the quantity of money that Mathilde threw about. During the first days the sums disposed of in this way awed Fouqué, who had a provincial's reverence for money.

At last he discovered that Mlle. de La Mole's projects altered from day to day, and discovered, to his great relief, a word to describe this character that exhausted him: she was *changeable*. From this epithet to that of *wrongheaded*, the worst thing they can call you in the provinces, it's only a short step.

It is very strange, thought Julien one day, as Mathilde was leaving the prison, that such passionate feelings, of which I am the object, should leave me so unmoved! And only two months ago I adored her! I have read somewhere that the approach of death makes us lose interest in everything; but it is frightful to feel oneself ungrateful and to be unable to change. Am I an egotist, then? On this score he addressed to himself the bitterest reproaches.

Ambition was dead within his heart; another passion rose from its ashes; he called it remorse for having tried to kill Mme. de Rênal.

As a matter of fact, he was madly in love with her. He found an extraordinary happiness when, in absolute solitude and without any fear of interruption, he could devote himself entirely to memories of the happy days he had once spent at Verrières or Vergy. The slightest incidents of that time that had slipped so rapidly from him retained an irresistible freshness and charm. He never thought of his success at Paris; he was bored by it.

These feelings, which grew in intensity from day to day, did not pass altogether unperceived by the jealous Mathilde. She saw very clearly that she must struggle against his love of solitude. Sometimes she spoke the name of Mme. de Rênal out of sheer terror. She saw Julien shudder. From then on her passion knew no measure or bounds.

If he dies, I shall die after him, she said with all the sincerity conceivable. What would the drawing rooms of Paris say upon seeing a girl of my rank adore to that point a lover condemned to death? To find feelings like that you must go back to the heroic days; it was love of this sort that animated hearts in the days of Charles IX and Henri III.

Amid the wildest transports, when she held Julien's head against her heart: Can it be! she said to herself with horror, is this precious head doomed to fall! Very well, she added, inflamed with heroic feelings that were not altogether unpleasant, my lips which are now pressed against his dear hair will be ice-cold no more than twenty-four hours later.

Thoughts of these moments of heroism and of their fearful pleasures locked her in overpowering constraint. The idea of suicide, so potent in itself and hitherto so remote from her lofty spirit, made headway and soon came to reign over her with absolute sway. No, the blood of my ancestors has not grown tepid in its descent to me, Mathilde told herself proudly.

—I have a favor to ask of you, her lover told her one day: put your child out to nurse at Verrières; Mme. de Rênal will keep an eye on the nurse.

—What you said to me just then was really cruel. . . . And Mathilde grew pale.

—You are right, I beg your pardon a thousand times over, cried Julien, roused from his reverie, and clasping her in his arms.

Having dried her tears, he returned to his train of thought, but more subtly. He had given the conversation a tone of philosophic melancholy. He spoke of that future which would so soon be closed off for him.

—You must agree, my darling, that the passions are only an accident in life, but this accident happens only when superior people meet. . . . The death of my son would gratify the pride of your family, and that's what the flunkies will guess about it. Neglect will be the lot of this child of misery and shame. . . . I hope someday, at a time I don't want to determine, but which nonetheless I am bold enough to foresee, you will heed my dying wish: You will marry M. le Marquis de Croisenois.

—How can that be, a woman in disgrace!

—Disgrace has no power over a name like yours. You will be a widow and the widow of a madman, that's all. I will go further: since my crime did not have money for a motive, it will not be thought dishonorable. Perhaps by that time some philosophic legislator will have extracted from his prejudiced contemporaries abolition of the death penalty. Then some friendly voice will bring up an example: Look, Mlle. de La Mole's first husband was a madman, but not a really evil man, not a villain. It was absurd to cut off his head. . . . Then my memory will by no means be odious; at least after a certain period of time. . . . Your position in the world, your fortune, and, allow me to say, your genius will entitle M. de Croisenois, if he becomes your husband, to a role in society he could never attain on his own. He has nothing but birth and bravery, and these qualities all by themselves, which made a man of accomplishments in 1729, are an anachronism a century later, and only breed pretensions. Other things are needed to place a man at the head of the youth of France.

You will bring the support of a firm and enterprising character to any political party you direct your husband into. You could become a successor to the Chevreuses and Longuevilles of the Fronde. . . .[4] But by then, my darling, the celestial fire that glows in you at this minute will have cooled a little.

Allow me to say, he added, after a great many other preparatory phrases, that in fifteen years you will regard the love you have borne me as an excusable folly, perhaps, but still a folly. . . .

He stopped suddenly and sank into deep thought. He found himself once more face-to-face with that idea which so distressed Mathilde: in fifteen years, Mme. de Rênal will adore my son, and you will have forgotten him.

Chapter 40

TRANQUILITY

It is because I was foolish then that I am wise today. O philosopher who sees nothing but the fleeting moment, how short is your vision! Your eye was not made to follow the underground working of the passions.

—W. Goethe

This discussion was cut short by an interrogation, followed by a conference with the lawyer for the defense. These were the only completely disagreeable moments in an existence marked by perfect resignation and tender reflections.

—It is a case of murder and premeditated murder, Julien said to the judge and to the lawyer as well. I am sorry, gentlemen, he added with a smile; but this reduces your task to a very trivial matter.

After all, Julien said when he had succeeded in escaping from these two creatures, I must be brave, and braver, it seems, than these two men. They regard as the supreme misfortune, as the monarch of terrors, this duel with a built-in unhappy ending, which I shall only have to think about seriously on the day itself.

The fact is, I have known worse misfortune, continued Julien, playing the philosopher for his own amusement. I suffered far more on my first journey to Strasbourg when I thought I had been abandoned by Mathilde. . . . And to think that I yearned then so passionately for this perfect intimacy which today leaves me absolutely cold! . . . Actually, I am more happy alone than when I have that lovely girl to share my solitude. . . .

The lawyer, a man of rules and formalities, thought he was crazy and supposed, like the general public, that it was jealousy that had

---

4. The Fronde was a civil war fomented in France by factions of disgruntled landlords from 1648 to 1652; it centered about the great Prince of Condé and his family, among whom two of the most passionate and influential figures were his sister the Duchess of Longueville and Mme. de Chevreuse.

put the pistol in his hand. One day he ventured to intimate to Julien that this allegation, whether true or false, would make an excellent line of defense. But the accused became on the instant a man of incisive passion.

—As you value your life, sir, cried Julien, beside himself, take care never to put forward that abominable lie. For a moment the prudent lawyer feared for his life.

He was preparing his brief because the decisive moment was rapidly approaching. Besançon and the whole district around had talked of nothing but this notorious trial. Julien was wholly ignorant of this circumstance; he had asked never to be told this sort of thing.

On that day, when Mathilde and Fouqué tried to tell him of certain public rumors very suitable in their opinion, to raise his hopes, Julien stopped them at the first word.

—Leave me my ideal life. Your little tricks and details from real life, all more or less irritating to me, would drag me out of heaven. One dies as one can; I want to think about death only in my own personal way. What do *other people* matter? My relations with *other people* are going to be severed abruptly. For heaven's sake, don't talk to me of those people anymore: it's quite enough if I have to play the swine before the judge and the lawyer.

As a matter of fact, he told himself, it seems that my fate is to die in a dream. An obscure creature like myself, who is sure to be forgotten in two weeks' time, would be a complete fool to play out the comedy. . . .

Still, it is strange that I have learned the art of enjoying life only since I have seen the end of it so close to me.

He passed these last days walking about the narrow terrace atop his tower, smoking some excellent cigars Mathilde had had brought from Holland by a courier; he never suspected that his appearance was awaited each day by every telescope in town. His thoughts were at Vergy. He never talked about Mme. de Rênal with Fouqué, but two or three times his friend told him that she was recovering rapidly, and the phrase reverberated in his heart.

While Julien's soul was almost always wandering through the world of ideas, Mathilde, still occupied with real things, as befits an aristocratic spirit, had been able to advance the direct correspondence between Mme. de Fervaques and M. de Frilair to such a point that already the glorious word *bishopric* had been pronounced.

The venerable prelate whose care was the distribution of benefices added in a postscript to a letter to his niece: *That poor Sorel is merely a thoughtless fellow; I hope they will soon restore him to us.*

At the sight of these words, M. de Frilair was almost beside himself. He had no doubt of being able to save Julien.

—Without that Jacobin law that requires the drawing up of an immense list of jurors, and which has no other real purpose than to take away all influence from well-born people, he told Mathilde the night before the drawing of lots for the thirty-six jurors of the assize, I would have answered for the verdict. I was responsible, after all, for the acquittal of Curé N _____.

It was a great pleasure for M. de Frilair to discover next day, among the names drawn from the urn, those of five members of the congregation from Besançon, and among the people from outside the town the names of MM Valenod, de Moirod, de Cholin. —To start with, I'll answer for those eight jurors, he told Mathilde. The five first are merely *machines*. Valenod is my creature, Moirod owes his whole existence to me, de Cholin is an imbecile who's afraid of everything.

The newspaper spread throughout the district the names of the jurors, and Mme. de Rênal, to the indescribable horror of her husband, expressed a desire to go to Besançon. The only thing M. de Rênal could obtain of her was a promise not to leave her bed, lest she have to undergo the annoyance of appearing as a witness.

—You don't understand my position, said the former mayor of Verrières, I am now a liberal of the *défection*,[5] as people say; no doubt that scoundrel Valenod and M. de Frilair will easily get the attorney general and the judges to do anything that can be disagreeable to me.

Mme. de Rênal yielded without protest to the orders of her husband. If I appeared at the assize court, she told herself, it would seem that I was asking for vengeance.

In spite of all the promises of prudence she had made to her confessor and her husband, she had scarcely arrived in Besançon before she wrote, in her own hand, to each one of the thirty-six jurors.

"I shall not be present the day of the trial, sir, because my appearance might cast an unfavorable light on the case of M. Sorel. I desire only one thing in the world, and that passionately, his acquittal. You must have no doubt on this score, the frightful idea that because of me an innocent man has gone to his death will poison the rest of my life, and no doubt shorten it. How could you sentence him to death while I am still alive? No, there can be no doubt, society has no right to take life, above all from a man like Julien Sorel. Everyone at Verrières has seen him suffer short periods of distraction. This poor young man has influential enemies; but even among his enemies (and how numerous they are!) who is there who will

---

5. A liberal of the *défection* was one created during the 1827 elections by the defection of certain groups from the rightist coalition. M. de Rênal wants it understood that he is the most wishy-washy liberal that can possibly be.

call into question his admirable talents, his deep learning? It is not just an ordinary person whom you are called upon to judge, sir. During almost eighteen months we knew him to be pious, well behaved, dutiful; but two or three times every year he suffered attacks of melancholy which verged on distraction. The whole town of Verrières, all our neighbors at Vergy where we pass the summer months, my whole family, even the sub-prefect himself, will bear witness to his exemplary piety; he knows by heart the entire Holy Bible. Would an impious person ever have applied himself whole years on end to learn the sacred scriptures? My sons will have the honor to bring this letter to you; they are mere children. Be good enough to question them, sir, they will tell you everything about this poor young man that is needed to convince you of the barbarity of condemning him. Far from revenging me, you would be dealing me a death stroke.

"What can his enemies advance in answer to the following fact? The wound resulting from one of those seizures which my children themselves remarked in their tutor is so far from dangerous that less than two months later it has allowed me to come post from Verrières to Besançon. If I learn, sir, that you hesitate ever so little to rescue from the barbarity of our laws a person whose guilt is so slight, I shall rise from my bed, where only the orders of my husband have kept me, to throw myself at your feet.

"Remember, sir, that premeditation has not been charged, and you will have no occasion to reproach yourself with the blood of an innocent being," etc., etc.

Chapter 41

THE JUDGMENT

The country will long recall that celebrated trial. Interest in the accused reached the point of agitation; it was because his crime was astonishing, though not atrocious. Even if it had been, the young man was so handsome! His lofty destiny, so quickly come to grief, increased the general sentiment of tenderness. Will they condemn him? was what women asked the men of their acquaintance, and they grew visibly pale as they waited for the reply.
—Sainte-Beuve

At last the day dawned so dreaded by Mme. de Rênal and by Mathilde.

The strange look of the town multiplied their terror, and distressed even the solid soul of Fouqué. The whole province had flocked to Besançon to watch the outcome of this romantic trial.

For the last several days there had been no room at the inns. The president of the assize court had been besieged with requests for tickets; all the ladies in town wanted to be present at the trial; Julien's portrait was peddled in the streets, etc., etc.

Mathilde had been holding in reserve for this supreme moment a letter written from beginning to end in the hand of my lord the Bishop of ———. This prelate, who directed the destinies of the church of France and who created bishops, deigned to request Julien's acquittal. The night before the trial, Mathilde brought this letter to the all-powerful grand vicar.

At the end of the interview, as she left the room in a flood of tears:
—I can answer for the verdict of the jury, M. de Frilair told her, emerging at last from his diplomatic reserve and seeming almost moved himself. Among the twelve persons charged with deciding if your protégé's guilt is proved, and particularly if there was premeditation, I count six devoted friends of my fortune, and I have given them to understand that it all depends on them to raise me to the episcopate. Baron Valenod, whom I made mayor of Verrières, carries in his pocket two of his subordinates, MM de Moirod and de Cholin. Actually, the drawing of lots has given us two quite wrongheaded jurors; but though ultraliberals, they are faithful to my commands on big issues, and I have asked them to vote with M. Valenod. I have learned that a sixth juror, a manufacturer who is immensely rich and always talks the liberal line, has secret hopes of getting a contract from the ministry of war, and no doubt he will not want to displease me. He has been told that M. Valenod has my last word.

—And who is this M. Valenod? Mathilde asked uneasily.

—If you knew him, you would have no doubt of the outcome. He is a loud talker, impudent, gross, made to be a captain among fools. The year 1814 saw him in the pit of misery, and I am going to make a prefect out of him. He is capable of beating the other jurors if they don't vote as he would have them.

Mathilde was somewhat comforted.

Another discussion awaited her that evening. Not to prolong a disagreeable scene which he felt could lead to only one conclusion, Julien had resolved to stand mute.

—My lawyer will talk, that's quite enough, he told Mathilde. I am going to be exposed long enough as a spectacle before all my enemies. These provincials were shocked by that rapid rise to fortune which I owe to you, and, believe me, there is not one of them that does not crave my conviction, though of course he'll blubber like a fool when I'm led to my death.

—They want to see you humiliated, it's perfectly true, replied Mathilde, but I don't believe they are all that cruel. My coming to Besançon and the spectacle of my grief have won the sympathy of the women; your handsome face will do the rest. If you say a word to the judges, the whole audience will be yours, etc., etc.

Next day at nine when Julien came down from his cell to enter the great hall of the district courthouse, the police had great difficulty holding back the immense crowd that had gathered in the yard. Julien had slept well, he was very calm, and had no feeling other than philosophic pity for this crowd of envious folk who, without any cruel intent, were about to applaud his sentencing to death. He was quite surprised when, having been held back for more than a quarter of an hour amid the crowd, he saw that his presence aroused in the public only warmth and compassion. He heard not a single disagreeable word. These provincials are less nasty than I thought, he told himself.

As they entered the trial room, he was struck by the elegant architecture. It was in pure Gothic style, with clusters of pretty little columns cut from stone with the most perfect workmanship. He might have been in England.

But soon his attention was caught by twelve or fifteen pretty women who were seated directly opposite the bench for the accused and filled three galleries above the judges and the jury. As he turned toward the public, he saw that the circular gallery which overhung the ground floor was filled with women: most were young and seemed to him quite pretty; their eyes were shining and filled with interest. Throughout the rest of the room, the crowd was immense; people were beating at the doors to get in, and the guards could not keep them quiet.

When all the eyes that were searching for Julien became aware of his presence as he sat down on the slightly raised bench reserved for the accused, he was met with a murmur of surprise and tender interest.

On that day you would have said he was not yet twenty; he was dressed very simply, but with perfect grace; his hair and brow were charming; Mathilde had insisted on presiding in person at his toilet. Julien's pallor was extreme. Scarcely was he seated on his bench than he heard from all sides: God! How young he is! . . . But he's only a boy. . . . He's much better-looking than his portrait.

—Prisoner, said the policeman seated on his right, do you see those six ladies in the balcony up there? The policeman pointed to a little box jutting out above the amphitheater in which the jury were placed. That is the wife of the prefect, continued the policeman, alongside her is Mme. la Marquise de M____. She is much attracted to you; I heard her talking to the examining judge. And there is Mme. Derville. . . .

—Mme. Derville! Julien exclaimed, and a deep blush rose to his face. When she leaves, he thought, she will write to Mme de Rênal. He did not know that Mme. de Rênal herself was in Besançon.

The witnesses were heard. [That took several hours.] At the first words of the indictment pronounced by the district attorney, two of the ladies in the little balcony opposite Julien burst into tears. Mme. Derville is not so soft, Julien thought. But he noted that she was very flushed.

The district attorney waxed pathetic in bad French on the barbarity of the crime committed; Julien noted that Mme. Derville's neighbors seemed most disapproving. Several jurors, apparently acquainted with these ladies, spoke to them and seemed to reassure them. That's very likely a good sign, Julien thought.

Until then he had felt within himself nothing but the purest contempt for all the people present at the trial. The district attorney's tepid eloquence increased his sense of disgust. But gradually Julien's frozen soul thawed a little under the marks of interest directed toward him.

He was satisfied with his lawyer's firm expression. No fine phrases, he whispered to him, as he was about to begin.

—All that emphasis cribbed out of Bossuet which they piled up against you has helped your cause, said the lawyer. And in fact, he had hardly been talking five minutes when all the women had their handkerchiefs out. The lawyer, taking fresh courage, addressed some extremely strong remarks to the jury. Julien shuddered; he felt he was on the point of shedding tears himself. Good God! What will my enemies say?

He was about to yield to the tender sentiment that was gaining on him when fortunately his eye met an insolent glance from the Baron de Valenod.

The eyes of that hound are all aglitter, he said to himself; what a triumph for that low beast! If my crime led to nothing but this, I would have to hate it. God knows what he will say about me to Mme. de Rênal [during the long winter evenings]!

This idea replaced all others. Soon after, Julien was brought back to himself by marks of public approval. The lawyer had finished his speech for the defense. Julien remembered it was the customary thing to shake his hand. The time had passed quickly.

Refreshments were furnished for the lawyer and the prisoner. Only then was Julien struck by an odd circumstance: none of the women had left the room for dinner.

—Upon my word, I'm starving, said the lawyer; how about you?

—Me too, said Julien.

—Look, there's the prefect's wife having her lunch too, said the lawyer, pointing up at the little balcony. Keep your chin up, it's going all right. The trial resumed.

As the presiding judge was summing up, midnight struck. The judge was obliged to stop; amid the silence of universal anxiety, the resonance of the great bell filled the whole room.

And so I begin the last day of my life, Julien thought. Soon he felt himself filled with the idea of duty. Hitherto he had dominated his own softer sentiments and preserved his determination not to speak; but when the presiding judge asked if he had anything to say, he rose. He saw before him the eyes of Mme. Derville, which under the lights seemed particularly brilliant. Has she been weeping, by any chance? he thought.

—Gentlemen of the jury: My horror of contempt, which I thought I could stand until the hour of my death, compels me to break silence. Gentlemen, I have not the honor to belong to your social class, you see in me a peasant in open revolt against his humble station.

—I ask no favors of you, Julien went on, his voice hardening. I have no illusions, death awaits me: I have deserved it. I have attempted to cut short the life of a woman most worthy of respect, most worthy of devotion. Mme. de Rênal had been like a mother to me. My crime is atrocious, and it was *premeditated*. I have therefore deserved the death sentence, gentlemen of the jury. But even if I were less guilty than I am, I see before me men who, without ever considering whether my youth merits some pity, are determined to punish in me and discourage forever a certain class of young men—those who, born to a lower social order, and buried by poverty, are lucky enough to get a good education and bold enough to mingle with what the arrogant rich call good society.

—There is my crime, gentlemen, and it will be punished all the more severely because, in reality, I am not being judged by my peers. I do not see in the seats of the jury a single rich peasant, only outraged *bourgeois*. . . .

For twenty minutes Julien talked in this vein; he said everything that was in his heart; the district attorney, who hoped to win the favor of the aristocracy, kept squirming on his seat; but in spite of the somewhat abstract turn Julien had imposed on the discussion, all the women were dissolved in tears. Mme. Derville herself had her handkerchief at her eyes. Before he finished, Julien returned to the matter of premeditation, to his regret, his respect, and to the unbounded filial adoration which in happier days he had felt for Mme. de Rênal. . . . Mme. Derville gave a little cry and fainted.

One o'clock was tolling as the jurors retired to their room. No woman had left her seat; several men had tears in their eyes. At first the spectators talked animatedly; but gradually, as the jury's decision was delayed, fatigue began to impose a measure of calm on the assembly. It was a solemn moment; the lamps were growing dim. Julien, though exhausted, heard various discussions going on around him as to whether the delay was a good sign or a bad one. He noted with pleasure that people's wishes were generally favorable to him; still the jury did not come back and still not a single woman left the hall.

As two o'clock sounded, a great commotion was heard. The little door of the jury room opened. M. le Baron de Valenod marched in, solemn and theatrical, followed by the other jurors. He coughed, then declared that on their souls and consciences the jury declared unanimously that Julien Sorel was guilty of murder, and murder with premeditation: this finding carried with it the death penalty, and it was pronounced a moment later. Julien glanced at his watch, with a thought for M. de Lavalette;[6] it was just two-fifteen. Today is Friday, he thought.

Yes, but this is a happy day for Valenod, who is pronouncing sentence on me. . . . I am too closely watched for Mathilde to be able to save me, as Mme. de Lavalette did. . . . And so, in three days at this same time, I shall know what to think about *the great perhaps*.

At that moment, he heard a cry and was recalled to things of this world. The women around him began to sob; he saw that all eyes were turned toward a little box hidden behind the capital of a Gothic pillar. He learned later that Mathilde had been hidden there. As the cry was not renewed, everyone turned back to stare at Julien, whom the police were trying to shoulder through the crowd.

Let's try to give no occasion for laughter to that villain Valenod, Julien thought. What a wheedling, oily look he had when he pronounced a sentence that carries with it the death penalty! whereas that poor presiding judge, even though he's a judge and has been one for many years, had a tear in his eye when he sentenced me. What a pleasure for Valenod to get his revenge here for our old rivalry over Mme. de Rênal! . . . So I shall never see her again! It's all over. . . . A last farewell is impossible between us, I sense it. . . . How happy I would have been to tell her what horror I feel of my crime!

Only these words: I feel I have been rightly convicted.

Chapter 42

When they returned Julien to jail, they put him in the death cell. Though ordinarily aware of the slightest circumstances, he did not even notice that they had not returned him to his former room. He was thinking of what he would say to Mme. de Rênal if he were happy enough to see her before the final moment. He thought that

6. See p. 379, n. 9.

she might interrupt him, and was trying to show in his very first words the depth of his repentance. After such an action, how ever to persuade her that she is the only one I love? After all, I did try to kill her, out of ambition or out of love of Mathilde.

As he went to bed, he found his sheets were of coarse linen. His eyes were opened. Ah! I'm in the death house, he thought, sentence has been passed on me. Quite right.

Comte Altamira told me that the night before he died, Danton said in his great voice: It's a funny thing, the verb *guillotine* can't be conjugated in all its tenses. One can very well say, I will be guillotined, you will be guillotined, but it's impossible to say: I have been guillotined.

Why not, Julien thought, if there is an afterlife? . . . My word, if I find the God of the Christians, it's all up with me: he's a despot and, as such, full of vengeful ideas; his Bible talks of nothing but frightful punishments. I never liked him; I never could believe that anyone sincerely loved him. He is merciless (and he recalled several scriptural passages). He will punish me in some abominable way. . . .

But if I should find the God of Fénelon![7] He is capable of saying to me: much will be pardoned you, my child, because you have felt much love. . . .

Have I felt much love? Ah! I loved Mme. de Rênal, but I behaved terribly toward her. There, as everywhere else, I left simple, modest merit in the lurch to run after what was flashy. . . .

But then, what a prospect! . . . Colonel in the hussars, if we had a war; secretary of a legation in peacetime; afterward, ambassador . . . for I would have picked up the business quickly . . . and, as long as I'm not a mere fool, the son-in-law of M. de La Mole surely need fear no rival. All my blunders would have been forgiven or rather imputed to me as merits. A man of merit, and enjoying the good life to the full in Vienna or London. . . .

—No, not exactly, sir, guillotining in three days' time.

Julien laughed aloud at this sally of his wit. It's really true, he thought, man does have two spirits within him. Who the devil thought up that malicious expression?

—All right, yes, my friend, guillotining within three days, he answered his interrupter. M. de Cholin will rent a window, splitting the price with Abbé Maslon. Well, when they fall to haggling over the price of the window, which one of these worthy gentlemen will cheat the other?

---

7. Fénelon, like Massillon, was a priest of the late seventeenth and early eighteenth century whose invocation of sincere feeling and relative doctrinal toleration appealed to the *philosophes* of the later eighteenth century (and to Stendhal) as a model of Christian piety.

This passage from Rotrou's *Wenceslas*[8] came suddenly to mind.

Ladislas: . . . My soul is all prepared.
The King, *father of Ladislas:* So is the scaffold; just bring your head to it.

A fine answer! he thought, and fell asleep. Someone woke him up in the morning by shaking him violently.

—What, already? said Julien, opening a haggard eye. He thought he was in the hands of the executioner.

It was Mathilde. Fortunately, she did not understand. His awareness of this fact brought back all his self-possession. He found Mathilde altered as by a six-months' illness: she was actually unrecognizable.

—That unspeakable Frilair betrayed me, she told him, wringing her hands; she could hardly speak for rage.

—Wasn't I fine yesterday when I began to talk? Julien replied. I was improvising, and for the first time in my life! It's true, there's also reason to fear it was the last.

At this point Julien was playing on the character of Mathilde with all the self-possession of a skilled pianist at the keyboard. . . . I lack the advantage of distinguished birth, it's true, he added, but the glorious soul of Mathilde has raised her lover to her own level. Do you suppose that Boniface de La Mole behaved any better before his judges?

Mathilde on this day was unaffectedly tender, like any poor shop girl in a garret; but she was unable to extract from him any simpler speech. Without knowing what he was doing, he was paying her back for the torments she had often inflicted on him.

No man knows the sources of the Nile, Julien thought to himself; man's eye has not been privileged to see the king of rivers in the state of a simple brooklet: similarly, no human eye will ever see Julien weak, primarily because he isn't. But my heart is easily touched; the most ordinary word, if spoken with a genuine accent, can soften my voice and cause my tears to flow. How often the hard-hearted people have despised me for this failing! They thought I was begging pardon: that is what I will not endure.

They say the thought of his wife distressed Danton at the foot of the scaffold; but Danton had infused strength into a nation of coxcombs, and prevented the enemy from getting into Paris. . . . I alone know what I might have done. . . . For the others, I am at most nothing but a PERHAPS.

If Mme. de Rênal were here in my cell instead of Mathilde,

---

8. *Wenceslas*, acted in 1647 and printed the year following, is considered the best of Rotrou's many plays.

could I answer for my own behavior? The excess of my despair and repentance might have been interpreted by the Valenods and the aristocrats of the district as ignoble terror of death; they are so proud, those feeble spirits whom their financial position places out of the reach of temptation! When they had just condemned me to death, Mm de Moirod and de Cholin might well have said: See what it means to be born a carpenter's son! You may become learned, you may become shrewd, but the heart! . . . the heart can't be trained. Even with this poor Mathilde, who is weeping now, or rather who can weep no more, he thought, looking at her red eyes . . . and he took her in his arms: the sight of authentic grief made him forget his syllogism. . . . Probably she has wept all night long, he thought; but one day, how ashamed she will be to think of this! She will picture herself as having been led astray in her early youth by the vulgar judgments of a plebeian. . . . Croisenois is weak enough to marry her, and, good Lord, for him that's the right thing to do. She'll make him play a role,

> by that right
> That a strong spirit, fixed in its designs,
> Holds over fools and their ignoble minds.[9]

Now there's an oddity: since I was condemned to death, all the poetry I ever knew in my life comes back in my memory. It must be a mark of decadence. . . .

Mathilde was saying to him, in a dying tone: He's there in the next room. He finally paid attention to what she was saying. Her voice is weak, he thought, but all her imperious character is still to be heard. She is lowering her voice to keep from losing her temper.

—And who is it, out there? he asked her gently.

—The lawyer, with an appeal for you to sign.

—I shall not appeal.

—What's that! You're not going to appeal, she cried, leaping to her feet, her eyes blazing with rage, and why is that, if you please?

—Because, at this moment, I feel I have the courage to die without provoking too much laughter at my expense. And who knows if after two months spent in this soggy hole I'll be as well prepared? I can foresee interviews with priests, conversations with my father. . . . Nothing in the world could be more unpleasant. Let me die.

This unexpected perversity roused all the haughty part of Mathilde's character. She had been unable to see Abbé de Frilair before the visiting hours of the Besançon prison; her full fury fell

9. The verses are cited approximately, as is customary with Stendhal, from Voltaire's *Mahomet* (II, 5).

on Julien. She adored him, and for a long quarter of an hour she raged against his character, and expressed her bitter regret at ever having loved him, while he reflected that this was indeed the proud spirit which had heaped such coals of burning fire on his head in the library of the Hôtel de La Mole.

—For the honor of your family, he told her, providence should have formed you a man.

But as for me, he thought, I'd be a pretty fool to live two months longer in this disgusting hole, the butt of every disgraceful, humiliating tale the patricians can think up,[1] and having as my only consolation the diatribes of this crazy woman. . . . All right, day after tomorrow I fight a duel with a man known far and wide for his composure and his remarkable skill. . . . It's a most remarkable thing, whispered his Mephistopheles side, that man never misses his thrust.

All right, so be it, enough (Mathilde continued to wax eloquent). No, by God, he said to himself, I shall never appeal.

This resolution taken, he returned to his thoughts. . . . The courier, making his rounds, will bring the newspaper at six, as he usually does; at eight, after M. de Rênal has read it, Elisa, walking on tiptoe, will come and leave it on her bed. Later, she will wake up: suddenly, as she reads it, she will grow disturbed; her delicate hand will tremble; she will read as far as these words. . . . *At five minutes past ten he had ceased to live.*

She will shed bitter tears, I know her; it does not matter that I tried to kill her, all will be forgotten. And the person whose life I tried to take will be the only one to weep sincerely for my death.

Ah! there is an antithesis! he thought, and for the full quarter of an hour during which Mathilde continued to play out her scene, he thought only of Mme. de Rênal. In spite of himself, and though he made frequent answers to what Mathilde was saying, he could not distract his thoughts from memories of the bedroom at Verrières. He saw the Besançon newspaper lying on the orange taffeta counterpane. He saw a white hand clutch at it with a convulsive gesture; he saw Mme. de Rênal weeping. . . . He followed the course of each tear down that charming face.

Mlle. de La Mole, unable to get anything out of Julien, summoned the lawyer. By good fortune it was a former captain of the army of Italy of 1796, where he had been a comrade of Manuel.[2]

For form's sake, he opposed the condemned man's resolution. Julien, wanting to treat him with respect, laid out all his reasons.

---

1. It is a Jacobin speaking [Stendhal's note].
2. Jacques-Antoine Manuel (1775–1827) was first a soldier of the Revolution, then a brilliant liberal orator whose inflexible courage under the Restoration roused Stendhal's warm admiration.

—My word, one may think as you do, M. Félix Vaneau concluded; that was the lawyer's name. But you have three free days in
which to appeal, and it is my duty to come back every day. If sometime in the next two months a volcano opened up under the prison,
you would be saved. You may even die of a sickness, he said with a
glance at Julien.

Julien shook his hand. —I'm grateful to you, you are a good man.
I'll think it over.

And when Mathilde finally took herself off with the lawyer, he
felt much more affection for the lawyer than for her.

Chapter 43

An hour later when he was in a deep sleep, he was awakened by
tears which he felt trickling on his hand.

Ah! it's Mathilde again, he thought, still half asleep. Here she
comes, true to her theory, attacking my decision with her tender
sentiments. Bored by the prospect of another scene in the pathetic
vein, he did not open his eyes. The verses about Belphégor in flight
from his wife came into his mind.[3]

He heard an unusual sob; he opened his eyes, it was Mme. de
Rênal.

—Ah! So I can see you again before I die, or is it an illusion? he
cried, flinging himself at her feet.

But forgive me, madame, I am nothing but a murderer in your
eyes, he said at once, returning to himself.

—Sir. . . . I have come to beg you to appeal; I know you don't
want to. . . . Her tears choked her; she could say no more.

—Only if you forgive me.

—If you want me to forgive you, she told him, rising to her feet
and throwing herself into his arms, appeal immediately against your
death sentence.

Julien covered her with kisses.

—Will you come to see me every day during those two months?

—I swear it. Every day, unless my husband forbids me.

—I'll sign! cried Julien. What! You forgive me! Is it possible!

He seized her in his arms; he was out of his mind. She gave a little cry.

—It's nothing, she told him, you hurt me.

—Your shoulder, Julien cried, and burst into tears. He stepped
back slightly and covered her hand with burning kisses. Who would
ever have thought it the last time I saw you in your room at Verrières?

3. "Belphégor" is a story by La Fontaine imitated from one by Machiavelli, with the irk-
someness of marriage as its central theme.

—Who would ever have thought I would write that terrible letter to M. de La Mole?

—You must know that I've always loved you, I never loved anyone but you.

—Is it possible! cried Mme. de Rênal, in equal ecstasy. She bent over Julien, who was at her knees, and for a long time they wept in silence.

Such a moment Julien had never known at any other period of his life.

Long afterward, when they could talk again:

—And this young Mme. Michelet, said Mme. de Rênal, or rather this Mlle. de La Mole; for I am starting actually to believe this strange story!

—It's true only superficially, Julien replied. She is my wife but she is not my mistress.

And, interrupting one another a hundred times over, they succeeded with great difficulty in telling each other the things they had not known. The letter written to M. de La Mole had been the work of the young priest who was Mme. de Rênal's confessor, and she had copied it out.

—What a horrible thing religion made me do, she told him; and even so, I softened the most frightful passages of that letter. . . .

Julien's transports of joy proved how fully he forgave her. Never had he been so delirious with love.

—And yet I think myself a religious woman, Mme. de Rênal told him in the course of their conversation. I believe sincerely in God; I believe just as sincerely, and indeed it has been proved to me, that the crime I am committing is frightful, and as soon as I see you, even after you have fired a pistol twice at me. . . . And here, despite her protests, Julien covered her with kisses.

—Let me alone, she went on, I want to make this clear to you, before I forget. . . . As soon as I see you, all my duties fade from sight, I am nothing except love for you, or rather the word "love" is too feeble. I feel for you what I should feel only for God: a mixture of respect, love, devotion. . . . In fact, I don't really know what I feel for you. You could tell me to cut the jailer's throat, and the crime would be done before I leave you, I want to see clearly into my heart; for in two months we must be separated. Or, by the way, need we be separated? she asked him with a smile.

—I withdraw my word, Julien cried, springing to his feet; I shall not appeal against the death sentence if by poison, knife, pistol, gas,[4] or any other manner you try to end your life or put it in danger.

---

4. The original French was *charbon*, "charcoal," where I have translated "gas"; the principle is asphyxiation [Translator's note].

Mme. de Rênal's features altered abruptly; passionate affection gave way to a dreamy expression.

—Suppose we should die right way? she said at last.

—Who knows what's to be found in the other world? Julien replied; perhaps tortures, perhaps nothing at all. Can't we pass two months together in a delectable way? Two months, that's a good many days. I shall never have been so happy before!

—You will never have been so happy!

—Never, Julien repeated, and I am speaking to you as I do to myself. May God keep me from exaggeration.

—To speak that way is to command me, she said with a sad, timid smile.

—Very well. You swear, by the love you bear me, to make no attempt on your own life, by any means, whether direct or indirect. . . . You must suppose, he added, that you are required to live for my son, whom Mathilde will abandon to the care of lackeys as soon as she is Marquise de Croisenois.

—I swear, she replied coldly, but I must take away with me your appeal, written and signed in your own hand. I shall go myself to the district attorney.

—Be careful, you will compromise yourself.

—After my act in coming publicly to visit your prison cell, she said with an air of deep affliction, I shall be the subject of stories forever, in Besançon and throughout the Franche-Comté. I am beyond the pale of prudence, of modesty. . . . I am a woman lost to honor; it is true, I did it for you. . . .

Her voice was so sad that Julien kissed her with a pleasure that was quite new to him. It was no longer the intoxication of love, but rather a profound gratitude. He had just perceived, for the first time, the full extent of the sacrifice she was making for him.

Some charitable soul evidently informed M. de Rênal of the long visits his wife was making to Julien's prison cell; for, at the end of three days, he sent his carriage for her with explicit orders to return immediately to Verrières.

This bitter separation began the day badly for Julien. Two or three hours later, they told him that a certain priest, much given to intrigue but for all that incapable of getting along with the Besançon Jesuits, had set up in the street outside the prison gate since early morning. It was raining heavily, and there the man was, playing the martyr. Julien was already touchy; this piece of idiocy disturbed him deeply.

Already this morning he had once refused a visit from this priest, but the man had it in his head to confess Julien and make a name for himself among the girls of Besançon by retailing all the confidences he would pretend to have received.

He declared loudly that he would pass day and night before the prison gate; —God has sent me to touch the heart of this new apostate. . . . And the mob, always eager for a scene, began to gather.

—Yes, my brothers, he told them, I shall pass the day here, the night, every single day, and every single night from now on. The Holy Ghost has communed with me, I have a mission from on high; I am he who is chosen to save the soul of young Sorel. Join with me in prayer, etc., etc.

Julien had a horror of scandal and of anything that could draw public attention to him. He thought for a moment of seizing this occasion to get out of the world incognito; but he had some hope of seeing Mme. de Rênal again, and he was frantically in love.

The prison gate opened onto one of the busiest streets. The idea of this filthy priest gathering a crowd and making a scandal tortured his soul.—And, no doubt, every minute of the day he is repeating my name! This moment was more painful than death.

He called two or three times, at one-hour intervals, a turnkey who was his friend, asking him to go see if the priest was still at the prison gate.

—Sir, he's kneeling in the mud, was always the turnkey's answer; he's praying aloud, and reciting litanies for your soul. . . . What gall! Julien thought. And at that moment he actually heard a distant grumble; it was the crowd responding to the litany. To complete his frustration, he saw the turnkey himself begin to move his lips as he repeated the Latin words. —They're beginning to say, added the turnkey, that you must have a pretty hard heart if you refuse the help of this holy man.

—Oh, my native land! how barbarous you still are! Julien exclaimed, overcome by rage. And he continued his thought, without being aware of the turnkey's presence.

—What this man wants is an article in the newspapers, and he's bound to get it.

Oh, cursed provincials! At Paris I wouldn't have to put up with all these vexations. The frauds they have there aren't so crude.

—Let the saintly priest come in, he said at last to the turnkey, and the sweat stood out on his forehead. The turnkey made the sign of the cross and went off joyfully.

The saintly priest turned out to be horribly ugly, and even more dirty. The cold rain outside increased the darkness and dampness of the cell. The priest tried to kiss Julien, and began to wax pathetic as he talked to him. The basest hypocrisy was all too apparent; in all his life Julien had never been so enraged.

A quarter hour after the priest came Julien found himself a complete coward. For the first time death seemed horrible to him. He thought of the state of putrefaction in which his body would be two days after the execution, etc., etc.

He was about to give himself away by some sign of weakness, or else fling himself on the priest and strangle him with his chain, when he got the idea of asking the holy man to go say a good forty-franc mass for him that very day.

As it was nearly noon, the priest took himself off.

Chapter 44

As soon as he had left, Julien began to weep, and he wept at the thought of dying. After a while he realized that if Mme. de Rênal had been at Besançon he could have admitted his weakness to her. . . .

Just as he was feeling most regret at the absence of this woman whom he adored, he heard Mathilde's footstep.

The worst thing about a prison, he thought, is that you can't shut your door. Everything Mathilde said rubbed him the wrong way.

She told him that on the day of the trial, M. Valenod, having in pocket his appointment as prefect, had ventured to defy M. de Frilair and indulge himself in the pleasure of condemning Julien to death.

—What came over your friend, M. de Frilair said to me just now, to whip up and then attack the petty vanity of that *bourgeois aristocracy?* Why did he have to talk of *caste?* He pointed out to them what they ought to do in their own political interests: those boobies could never think it out for themselves, they were ready to weep. The interest of their caste came along and clouded their eyes to the real horror of condemning a man to death. It's very clear that M. Sorel is a novice in business matters. If we don't succeed in saving him through an appeal for mercy, his death will be a kind of *suicide.* . . .

Mathilde, of course, did not mention to Julien something she herself did not yet suspect: that Abbé de Frilair, seeing Julien was doomed, thought it might serve his ambition to put himself in the way of becoming his successor.

Almost beside himself with repressed anger and frustration:
—Go have a mass said for me, he told Mathilde, and let me have a minute's peace. Mathilde, who was already very jealous over Mme. de Rênal's visits, and who had just heard of her departure, understood the cause of Julien's anger, and burst into tears.

Her grief was genuine; Julien saw that it was, and was all the more angered by it. He was in absolute need of solitude, and how was he to get any?

Finally, Mathilde, after trying all the arguments she knew to soften him, left him alone, but just at that moment Fouqué appeared.

—I really must be alone, he said to that faithful friend. . . . And as he saw him hesitate: I am writing a paper in support of my appeal . . . and besides . . . do me a favor, and never talk to me about death. If I need any special services on the day itself, let me be the one to raise the subject.

When Julien had finally got himself some solitude, he found he was more crushed and cowardly than before. The little strength left to his enfeebled spirit had gone into concealing his condition from Mlle. de La Mole and from Fouqué.

Toward evening a consoling idea occurred to him:

If this morning, at the moment when death seemed so horrible to me, I had been called to execution, *the public eye would have been my spur to glory*; perhaps my step might have been a trifle heavy, like that of a timid fop entering a drawing room. And a few clairvoyant people, if there are any such in the provinces, might have been able to guess my weakness . . . but nobody *would have seen it.*

He felt himself delivered from a part of his grief. He made a tune and hummed it to himself: I am a coward this very minute, but nobody will ever know it.

An even more disagreeable event lay in wait for him next day. For a long time his father had been threatening to visit; next morning, before Julien was awake, the white-haired carpenter appeared in his cell.

Julien felt weak; he was expecting the most disagreeable tirades. To complete his sense of dread, he was prey that morning to remorse for not loving his father.

Chance has placed us near one another on the earth, he told himself, while the turnkey was setting the cell a bit to rights, and we've done one another almost all the harm we could. Here he's come at the moment of my death to give me the final kick.

As soon as they were alone together the old man's vituperation began.

Julien could not hold back his tears. What shameful weakness! he said to himself, in a rage. He will go all around the town talking about my lack of courage; what a triumph for the Valenods and all those stupid hypocrites who hold power in Verrières. They are the big men in France, they have in their fists all the social advantages. But until now I could always tell myself: they're piling up the honors, it's true, but I have nobility in my heart.

And now here's a witness they will all believe, and who will assure all Verrières, even exaggerating the facts, that I was fearful in the face of death! I shall be showed up as a coward in this test that everyone can understand!

Julien was close to despair. He did not know how to get rid of his father. And to feign well enough to deceive this shrewd old man was at this point quite beyond his power.

His mind ran quickly over the possible expedients.

—*I have some money saved up!* he exclaimed suddenly.

This inspired phrase immediately changed the expression on the old man's face, and Julien's position.

—What do you suppose I should do with it? Julien continued more calmly: the effect he had produced had freed him of all sense of inferiority.

The old carpenter was aflame with impatience to lay his hands on this money, a part of which it seemed that Julien wanted to bequeath to his brothers. He talked for a long time and with much animation. Julien was in a position to tease him.

—Well, the Lord has inspired me to make my will. I will give a thousand francs to each of my brothers, and the remainder to you.

—All right, said, the old man, that remainder is my due; but since the Lord has touched your heart, if you want to die like a good Christian, you ought to pay your debts. There is still the whole expense of your feeding and your education which I laid down, and which you never think of. . . .

That's paternal affection for you! thought Julien, with desolation in his heart, when at last he was alone. Shortly the jailer appeared.

—Sir, after a visit from the family, I always bring my guests a bottle of good champagne. It's a bit dear, six francs a bottle, but it does the heart good.

—Bring three glasses, Julien said to him with boyish enthusiasm, and bring in two of the prisoners I hear walking about the corridor.

The jailer brought him two galley slaves condemned as second offenders and preparing for another term in the hulks. They were a pair of merry scoundrels, really quite remarkable for their cunning, courage, and self-possession.

—If you give me twenty francs, one of them told Julien, I'll tell you my whole life story. It's a real hairy tale.

—But you'll lie to me? said Julien.

—Not me, said he; here's my pal, would like to have my twenty francs; he'll peach on me if I lie to you.

His story was abominable. It showed a bold heart in which only one passion survived, that for money.

After they had left, Julien was no longer the same man. All his wrath against himself had evaporated. The savage grief, embittered by a sense of pusillanimity, to which he had been prey since Mme. de Rênal's departure, had turned into melancholy.

Had I been a little less the dupe of circumstance, he told himself, I would have seen that the drawing rooms of Paris are filled with honest folk like my father, or else clever rascals like these jailbirds. They are right, the men in the drawing room never wake up in the morning with this thought gnawing into their minds: How am I going to eat today? And yet they boast of how honest they are! And when they're called for jury duty, they are proud to condemn a man who stole a silver spoon because he felt he was dying of hunger.

But if there's a court, if it's a question of getting or losing a portfolio, then my honest men in the drawing room fall into crimes exactly like those my two jailbirds committed for lack of bread. . . .

There is no *law of nature:* the phrase is nothing but a bit of antiquated nonsense worthy of the district attorney who hunted me down the other day, and whose ancestor grew rich on one of Louis XIV's confiscations. There is no *right* except when there's a law to prevent one's doing such and such a thing on pain of punishment. Before the law, there's nothing *natural* except the strength of the lion, or the need of the creature that is hungry or cold, *need* in a word. . . . *No*, the people who stand well with the world are simply sneak thieves lucky enough not to have been caught in the act. The prosecutor whom society unleashes against me grew rich on disgraceful practices. . . . I attempted a murder, I am rightly condemned, but except for this one action, the Valenod who condemned me is a hundred times more harmful to society.

All right, Julien added sadly but without anger, my father for all his avarice is better than that lot. He never loved me. I have just filled his measure to overflowing, and disgraced him by coming to a shameful end. That fear of being left penniless, that exaggerated view of human wickedness which we call *avarice*, makes him see an immense source of consolation and security in a sum of three or four hundred louis, which I may actually leave him. One Sunday after dinner he will show off his wealth to all the envious spirits of Verrières. And his glance will be saying to them, At this price, which one of you would not be delighted to have a son guillotined?

This philosophy might be true, but it was of a nature to make a man eager for death. Thus passed five long days. Toward Mathilde he was polite and gentle; he saw she was prey to the most furious jealousy. One evening Julien thought seriously of committing suicide. His soul was exhausted by the long misery into which Mme. de Rênal's departure had plunged it. Nothing gave him any pleasure, either in real life or in his imagination. Lack of exercise was starting to affect his health and give him the exalted, feeble temper

of a young German student. He was losing that masculine haughtiness which rejects with a vigorous oath certain unconventional notions by which the souls of men in misery are assailed.

I have loved truth. . . . Where is it? Everywhere hypocrisy, or at
least charlatanism, even among the most virtuous, even among the
greatest; and his looks twisted to an expression of disgust. . . . No,
a man cannot have any faith in men.

Mme. de _____, making a collection for her poor orphans, told
me that some prince or other had just given ten louis; it was a lie.
But what am I saying? Napoleon on St. Helena! . . . Pure charlatanism, a proclamation in favor of the King of Rome.[5]

Good God! if a man like that can sink to charlatanism, and just
at the time when his troubles should be holding him strictly to duty,
what can you expect from the rest of the species? . . .

Where is truth? In religion. . . . Yes, he added, with the bitter
smile of the most intense scorn, in the mouths of the Maslons,
Frílairs, Castanèdes. . . . Perhaps under real Christianity, when the
priests would not be paid any more than the apostles were? . . . But
St. Paul was paid with the pleasure of giving orders, of talking, of
making himself talked about. . . .

Ah! if there were a true religion. . . . Fool that I am! I see a
Gothic cathedral, ancient stained glass; my heart in its weakness
forms from those windows a picture of the priest. . . . My soul
would understand him, my soul has need of him. . . . I find nothing
but a fop with greasy hair . . . a chevalier de Beauvoisis without the
pleasing exterior.

But a real priest, a Massillon, a Fénelon . . . Massillon consecrated Dubois.[6] The *Mémoires* of Saint-Simon have spoiled Fénelon
for me;[7] but still, a real priest. . . . Then the sensitive souls would
have a meeting place in the world. . . . We would not be so isolated.
. . . The good priest would tell us about God. But what God? Not
that in the Bible, a petty despot, cruel and thirsting for revenge . . .
but the God of Voltaire, just, kind, infinite. . . .

He was agitated by recollections of that Bible which he knew by
heart. . . . But how, whenever *two or three are gathered together*, can
we believe in that great name of *God*, after the fearful abuse our
priests have imposed on it?

---

5. When Napoleon abdicated the second time (June 22, 1815), he did so in favor of his
   son, Napoleon François-Joseph Charles (1841–1832), known generally as the King of
   Rome. But this son, just four years old at the time, was never allowed to advance beyond
   the rank of a minor Bavarian dukedom and died at the age of twenty-one.
6. Saint-Simon has a good many sharp things to say about Massillon's part in the consecra-
   tion of Abbé (later Cardinal) Guillaume Dubois, a slippery fellow whose ecclesiastical
   careerism occasioned much scandal.
7. Saint-Simon's *Mémoires* portray Fénelon as an unctuous, insinuating man with a great
   passion for making himself well liked.

To live alone, in isolation! . . . What torture! . . .

I am becoming silly and unfair, Julien told himself, striking his brow. I am isolated here in this dungeon; but I have not *lived in isolation* on the earth; I had the powerful idea of *duty*. The duty I assigned myself, whether wrong or right . . . has been like the trunk of a solid tree, on which I supported myself during the storm; I wavered, I was shaken. After all, I was only a man. . . . But I was not carried away.

It is the damp air of this dungeon that makes me think of isolation. . . .

And why be hypocritical still, even as I curse hypocrisy? It's neither death, nor the dungeon, nor the damp air, it's the absence of Mme. de Rênal that is crushing me. If I were at Verrières, and in order to see her had to spend weeks on end hidden in the cellar of her house, should I complain of that?

The influence of my contemporaries is stronger than I am, he said aloud, and with a bitter laugh. Talking in solitude to myself, only two steps away from death, I am still a hypocrite. . . . O nineteenth century!

. . . A hunter fires his gun in a forest, his victim falls, he rushes forward to seize it. His boot strikes an anthill two feet high, destroys the ant house, and scatters ants and ant eggs all around. . . . The most philosophical of the ants will never be able to understand that black, enormous, terrifying body: the hunter's boot that burst into their house with unbelievable rapidity, preceded by a terrifying blast and a flare of reddish flame. . . .

. . . And so death, life, and eternity, things perfectly simple for anyone who has organs vast enough to form a conception of them. . . .

A momentary little fly is born at nine o'clock one morning of a long summer's day, he dies at five that evening; how could he possibly understand the word *night*?

Give him five hours of existence more, he will see and understand what night is.

So with me; I shall be dead at twenty-three. Give me five years more of life, to be spent with Mme. de Rênal.

And he began to laugh like Mephistopheles. What lunacy to be thinking about these great problems!

First, I am a hypocrite, just as if there were someone here to hear me.

Second, I am forgetting to live and love, when I have so few days left to live. . . . Alas! Mme. de Rênal is not here; perhaps her husband won't let her come back to Besançon and disgrace herself any further.

That is what isolates me, and not the absence of a God who is

just, good, all-powerful, who is not malignant, not hungry for
vengeance.

Ah! if He existed. . . . Alas! I should fall at His feet. I have deserved death, I should tell him; but, great God, good God, kind
God, give me back the woman I love!

It was very late by now. After an hour or two of peaceful sleep,
Fouqué came.

Julien felt himself strong and resolute, like a man who has seen
clearly into his own soul.

Chapter 45

—I cannot play such a mean trick on poor Abbé Chas-Bernard as
to summon him, he told Fouqué; he would not be able to eat his
dinner for three days afterward. But try to find me a Jansenist,
friendly to M. Pirard, and beyond the reach of intrigue.

Fouqué had been waiting impatiently for this overture. Julien
carried out respectably all the observances required by public opinion in the provinces. Thanks to Abbé de Frilair, and in spite of his
bad choice of a confessor, Julien in his cell was under the protection of the congregation; with more suppleness of spirit, he might
have escaped altogether. But the bad air of the dungeon was producing its effect; his reason was fading. He was all the happier
when Mme. de Rênal came back.

—My first duty is to you, she said, kissing him; I have fled from
Verrières. . . .

In her presence, Julien was not subject to petty pride; he described all his weaknesses. She was kind and gracious toward him.

That evening as soon as she had left the prison, she summoned
to her aunt's house that priest who had attached himself to Julien
as to a victim; since he wanted nothing more than to make himself
a name among the young ladies of the better classes in Besançon,
Mme. de Rênal easily persuaded him to go off and offer a novena at
the abbey of Bray-le-Haut.

Words cannot describe the excess and madness of Julien's devotion.

Through bribery, and the use or abuse of her aunt's reputation, a
woman famous for her piety and her wealth, Mme. de Rênal gained
permission to see him twice a day.

When she heard of this, Mathilde's jealousy rose to the level of
insanity. M. de Frilair had admitted to her that all his power would
not avail to overturn the decorums and get her permission to see
her lover more than once a day. Mathilde had Mme. de Rênal followed, so as to be informed of her slightest actions. M. de Frilair

exhausted all the resources of a most ingenious mind trying to prove that Julien was unworthy of her.

Amidst all these torments, she only loved him the more, and almost every day she made a horrible scene in his cell.

Julien wanted at all costs to behave honorably until the end toward this poor girl whom he had so strangely compromised; but at every moment the boundless love he felt for Mme. de Rênal carried him away. When he could not succeed in persuading Mathilde, by various bad reasons, that her rival's visits were quite innocent:

—Well, the end of the drama is very close now, he told himself; that must be my excuse if I cannot put up a better front.

Mlle. de La Mole learned that the Marquis de Croisenois was dead. M. de Thaler, that man who was so rich, had indulged himself in various disagreeable remarks on the disappearance of Mathilde; M. de Croisenois paid a call to ask him to withdraw them: M. de Thaler showed him various anonymous letters addressed to him, and full of details so skillfully woven together that the poor marquis could not possibly fail to see the truth.

M. de Thaler then permitted himself some jests that were quite devoid of subtlety; M. de Croisenois insisted on such sweeping apologies that the millionaire preferred a duel. Stupidity was triumphant; and one of the men most deserving of love in all Paris was dead at the age of twenty-four.

This death produced a strange and morbid effect on Julien's weakened spirit.

—Poor Croisenois, he told Mathilde, he acted the part of a perfectly reasonable, perfectly honest man, in our regard; he should really have hated me ever since you behaved so imprudently in your mother's drawing room, and should have picked a quarrel with me; for the hatred that grows out of scorn is generally insatiable. . . .

The death of M. de Croisenois changed all Julien's ideas about the future of Mathilde; he devoted several days to proving to her that she ought to accept the hand of M. de Luz. He's a timid man, not too Jesuitical, he told her, and no doubt he intends to get onto the ladder. His ambition is more limited and more steady than that of poor Croisenois, and there's no dukedom in the family, thus he will raise no objections to marrying the widow of Julien Sorel.

—And a widow who despises great passions, Mathilde replied coldly; for she will have lived long enough to see her lover prefer, after only six months, another woman, and what's more, a woman who was the source of all their troubles.

—That's not fair; Mme. de Rênal's visits will provide some remarkable arguments for the Paris lawyer who presents my appeal for clemency; he will describe the murderer being honored by the special care of his victim. That may make an effect, you may see me become the subject of some melodrama, etc., etc.

A raging jealousy, quite helpless to take vengeful action, a long-standing hopeless grief (for even supposing Julien freed, how could she hope to regain his heart?), the shame and sorrow of loving this faithless lover more than ever, all had cast Mlle. de La Mole into a gloomy silence from which neither the eager concern of M. de Frilair nor the rude frankness of Fouqué could rouse her.

As for Julien, except for the moments usurped by Mathilde's presence, he was living on love and almost without a thought for the future. By a strange effect of this passion when it is at its height and perfectly sincere, Mme. de Rênal almost shared in his indifference and gentle gaiety.

—In the old days, Julien told her, when I could have been so happy during our walks through the forest at Vergy, smoldering ambition dragged my soul away into imaginary lands. When I should have been pressing to my heart this lovely form that was so close to my lips, I was stolen away from you by the future, my mind was on the endless struggles I would have to endure in order to build a colossal fortune. . . . No, I should have died without ever knowing happiness if you had not come to see me in this prison.

Two incidents arose to disturb this peaceful existence. Julien's confessor, Jansenist though he was, was not beyond reach of a Jesuit intrigue, and without knowing it became their agent.

One day he turned up saying that unless Julien wished to fall into the frightful sin of suicide, he would have to take all the steps necessary to gain clemency. Since, now, the clergy had a great deal of influence in the ministry of justice at Paris, an easy means of enlisting their support appeared: he would have to undergo a sensational conversation. . . .

—Sensational! Julien repeated. Ah! so I've caught you at it too, Father, you want to act in a play like any missionary. . . .

—Your age, the Jansenist resumed solemnly, the interesting features providence has bestowed on you, the motive of your crime which still remains inexplicable, the heroic struggles that Mlle. de La Mole has undertaken on your behalf, in a word, everything, including the astounding friendship your victim continues to show for you, everything has conspired to make you the hero of all the young ladies in Besançon. They have forgotten everything for you, even politics. . . .

Your conversion would strike them to the heart and leave a profound impression there. You can be of the greatest service to the cause of religion, and am I to palter over the frivolous objection that on a similar occasion the Jesuits would follow the same policy?

In that case, they would be able to do harm even in this particular situation which is beyond reach of their rapacity! Perish the thought. . . . The tears shed over your conversion will wash away the corrosive effect of ten editions of the impious works of Voltaire.

—And what will be left for me, Julien asked coldly, if I despise myself? I have been ambitious, but I have no intention of blaming myself for that; I was acting in those days according to the code of the times. Now I am living from day to day. But it seems to me that I should make myself very miserable indeed if I took part in some cowardly scheme. . . .

The other incident that affected Julien far differently arose from Mme. de Rênal. Some intriguing friend or other had succeeded in persuading this naïve, timid soul that it was her duty to rush off to Saint-Cloud and fall on her knees before the king, Charles X.[8]

She had resigned herself to a separation from Julien, and after that effort, the unpleasantness of making a public spectacle of herself, which at other times would have seemed worse than death, was nothing to her eyes.

—I shall go to the king, I shall tell him frankly that you are my lover: the life of a man, especially a man such as Julien, overrides all other considerations. I shall say that it was jealousy that led you to attempt my life. There are many instances of poor young men rescued under these circumstances by the humanity of the jury, or that of the king. . . .

—I will refuse to see you, I will ask that you be barred from the prison, Julien cried, and I vow that the next day I will kill myself in despair if you do not swear that you will do nothing to make us both a public spectacle. This idea of going to Paris isn't your own. Tell me the name of that conniving female who suggested it to you. . . .

Let us be happy during the few days remaining to us of this short life. Let us conceal our existence; my crime is only too apparent. Mlle. de La Mole has immense influence at Paris; you must believe she is doing everything that is humanly possible. Here in the provinces I have against me all the rich and influential people. Your action would embitter even further those rich and particularly moderate men for whom life is such an easy affair. . . . Let us give no cause for laughter to the Maslons, Valenods, and a thousand people who are worth more than they are.

The bad air of the prison cell was becoming insupportable to

---

8. For the first time in the book Stendhal mentions the monarch who reigned over France until his abdication on July 30, 1830. And yet, according to the chronology of the novel, the July revolution has already taken place by this point in the text. Mme. de Rênal would therefore be throwing herself at the feet of Louis-Philippe; but the change in regime, the entire July revolution, is conspicuously absent from this chronicle of 1830.

Julien. Fortunately on the day set for his execution a bright sun was shining upon the earth, and Julien was in the vein of courage. To walk in the open air was for him a delicious experience, as treading the solid ground is for a sailor who has been long at sea. There now, things are going very well, he told himself, I shall have no lack of courage.

Never had that head been so poetic as at the moment when it was about to fall. The sweetest moments he had ever known in the woods at Vergy came crowding back into his mind, and with immense vividness.

Everything proceeded simply, decently, and without the slightest affectation on his part.

Two days before he had told Fouqué:

—As for emotion, I can't quite answer; this dungeon is so ugly and damp it gives me feverish moments in which I don't recognize myself; but fear is another matter, I shall never be seen to grow pale.

He had made arrangements in advance that on the last day Fouqué should take away Mathilde and Mme. de Rênal.

—Put them in the same coach, he told him. Keep the post horses at a steady gallop. Either they will fall in one another's arms or they will fall into mortal hatred. In either case, the poor women will be somewhat distracted from their terrible grief.

Julien had forced from Mme. de Rênal an oath that she would live to look after Mathilde's son.

—Who knows? Perhaps we retain some consciousness after death, he said one day to Fouqué. I should like to rest, since rest is the word, in that little cave atop the big mountain that overlooks Verrières. I've told how several times when I spent the night in that cave and looked out over the richest provinces of France, my heart was afire with ambition: that was my passion in those days. . . . Well, that cave is precious to me, and nobody can deny that it's located in a spot that a philosopher's heart might envy. . . . You know these good congregationists in Besançon can coin money out of anything; go about it the right way, and they'll sell you my mortal remains. . . .

Fouqué was successful in this morbid transaction. He was spending the night alone in his room beside the body of his friend, when, to his great surprise, he saw Mathilde enter. Only a few hours before he had left her ten leagues from Besançon. Her eyes were wild.

—I want to see him, she said.

Fouqué was afraid to speak or rise. He pointed at a blue greatcoat on the floor; it covered everything that remained of Julien.

She fell to her knees. The memory of Boniface de La Mole and Marguerite of Navarre no doubt gave her superhuman courage.

Her trembling fingers opened the coat. Fouqué turned his eyes away.

He heard Mathilde stride swiftly about the room. She was lighting a number of candles. When Fouqué had the strength to look, she had placed in front of her, on a little marble table, the head of Julien, and was kissing its brow. . . .

Mathilde followed her lover to the tomb he had selected. A great number of priests accompanied the bier, and, unknown to all, alone in her draped carriage, she carried on her knees the head of the man she had loved so much.

Arriving thus near the peak of one of the highest mountains in the Jura in the middle of the night, in that little cave magnificently lighted by innumerable candles, twenty priests celebrated the service for the dead. All the inhabitants of the little mountain villages through which the procession had passed followed it, drawn by the oddity of this strange ceremony.

Mathilde appeared among them, swathed in black, and after the service ordered several thousand five-franc coins to be distributed among them.

Left alone with Fouqué, she insisted on burying with her own hands the head of her lover. Fouqué almost went mad with grief at the sight.

By Mathilde's orders, this savage grotto was adorned with marbles sculptured at great expense in Italy.

Mme. de Rênal was true to her word. She never tried in any way to take her own life; but three days after Julien, she died in the act of embracing her children.

THE END

The great disadvantage to the reign of public opinion, which does indeed <u>achieve freedom</u>, is that it meddles in matters where it does not belong, for example: private life. <u>Hence the gloom of America and England.</u> To avoid laying a finger on private life, the author has invented a little town, *Verrières*, and when he had need of a bishop, a jury, a court of assizes, put the whole thing in Besançon, where he has never been.

anti-democracy

says none of the characters are real and he's never been to Besançon

BACKGROUNDS
AND CONTEXTS

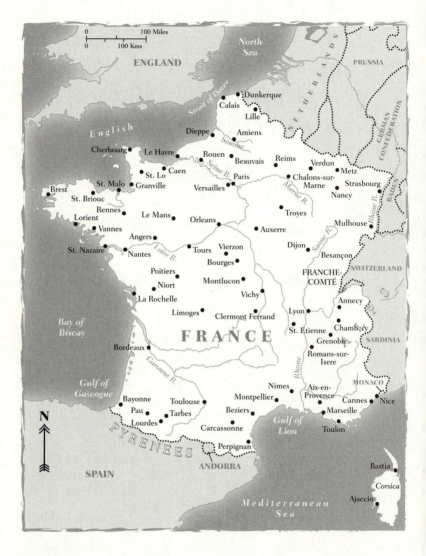

Map of France

Political Chronology of France, 1774–1830

1774	Louis XVI becomes king.
1778–83	The kingdom supports the American Revolution.
1789	French Revolution, storming of La Bastille.
	Declaration of Rights of Man and the Citizen written by the Marquis de Lafayette.
	Church property nationalized.
1790	Noble titles abolished. Monastic vows forbidden.
1792	Louis XVI tried for treason and convicted; monarchy abolished.
	First Republic (of five) proclaimed.
1793	Louis XVI and Queen Marie Antoinette are guillotined in Paris.
	Revolutionary calendar introduced.
	Start of Reign of Terror.
1794	Robespierre overthrown; end of Reign of Terror.
1795	Death of Louis XVII, son of Louis XVI.
1796	Napoleon marries Rose de Beauharnais (the future Empress Joséphine).
	Napoleon invades Italy.
1799	Napoleon overthrows directory government and seizes power in France.
	Austria declares war on France.
1801	Concordat signed by Napoleon, revoking the Civil Constitution of the Clergy, agreeing to a restoration of Catholicism in France.
1803–15	Napoleonic Wars expand the Empire.
1804	Bonaparte crowns himself Emperor Napoleon I, thus ending the First Republic.
	Napoleonic, or Civil, Code synthesizes different laws and standards into a single legal system.
1805	Battles of Ulm and Austerlitz: Napoleonic victories over the Austrians.
1808	Napoleonic Commercial Code goes into effect, standardizing commercial practices throughout the French Empire.

1812   Napoleon invades Russia: a debacle.
1814   Napoleon abdicates and is exiled to Elba.
1814–24   Reign of Louis XVIII, brother of Louis XVI.
              Start of the Bourbon Restoration.
1815   Napoleon returns to France at Elba, thus beginning the
              "100 Days" (March 20–June 22)
              Napoleon defeated at Waterloo on June 18.
              Napoleon deported to St. Helena, an island off the
              coast of Africa.
              Louis XVIII reclaims power.
1821   Death of Napoleon at St. Helena.
1824   Death of Louis XVIII.
1824–30   Reign of Charles X, brother of Louis XVIII and
              Louis XVI. Charles X will be more severe and reac-
              tionary than his brothers, introducing repressive mea-
              sures that ultimately lead to the revolution.
1825   Charles X passes Anti-Sacrilege Act.
1827   Resignation of reactionary chief minister Villèle, under
              liberal pressure.
1829   Appointment of Polignac, an ultrareactionary, as chief
              minister.
1830   Introduction, in early July, of several repressive decrees:
              dissolution of the Chamber of Deputies, restrictions on
              freedom of the press, restrictions on voting eligibility,
              and demand for new elections based on the newly cir-
              cumscribed electorate.
              The July Revolution: a combination of urban mobs an-
              gered by several years of economic downturn and lib-
              eral forces angered by the king's despotism.
1830–48   The "July Monarchy," or reign of Louis-Philippe. Louis-
              Philippe is an Orléan, not a Bourbon; so, though royal,
              he represented a departure from the Bourbon monar-
              chy.

Selected Chronology of French Literature, 1800–1850

1800	Mme. de Staël, *De la Littérature*
1801	Chateaubriand, *Atala*
1802	Chateaubriand, *René, Génie du christianisme*
1809	Chateaubriand, *Les Martyrs*
1810–13	Mme. de Staël, *De l'Allemagne*
1816	Constant, *Adolphe*
1819	Lamartine, *Méditations poétiques*
1822	Stendhal, *De l'Amour*
1827	Stendhal, *Armance*
1830	Stendhal, *Le Rouge et le noir*
	Lamartine, *Harmonies*
	Hugo, *Hernani*
1831	Hugo, *Notre-Dame de Paris*
	Balzac, *La Peau de chagrin*
1832	Sand, *Indiana*
1833	Balzac, *Eugénie Grandet*
1833–44	Michelet, *Histoire de France* (I à VI)
1835	Balzac, *Le Père Goriot*
	De Vigny, *Chatterton*
	Hugo, *Les Chants du crépuscule*
	Musset, *Lorenzaccio*
1836	Musset, *La Confession d'un enfant du siècle*
	Lamartine, *Jocelyn*
1837	Balzac, *Les Illusions perdues*
1838	Hugo, *Ruy Blas*
1839	Stendhal, *La Chartreuse de Parme*
	Balzac, *Splendeur et misères des courtisanes*
1840	Hugo, *Les Rayons et les ombres*
1843	Hugo, *Les Burgraves*
1845	Mérimée, *Carmen*
1848–50	Chateaubriand, *Mémoires d'Outre-Tombe*

From André Lagarde and Laurent Michard, *XIXe Siècle: les grands auteurs français* (Paris: Bordas, 1985), and Pierre Brunel, *Histoire de la littérature française* (Paris: Bordas, 1972).

The Trial of Antoine Berthet†

Criminal Proceedings

SESSION OF THE CRIMINAL COURT OF ISÈRE (GRENOBLE)
(SPECIAL REPORT)
PROSECUTION OF MURDER COMMITTED BY A SEMINARIAN IN
A CHURCH

It was on December 15th that the arguments in this extraordinary case began. The lengthy preparation necessarily entailed in giving a complete account of these arguments as it will appear in the *Gazette des Tribunaux* will explain and justify a delay of several days. The depositions of witnesses, the replies of the accused, his explanations of the motives of his crime, of the passions by which his soul was consumed, will offer to the speculations of the moralist a multitude of very interesting details, which are still unknown and which we ought not to sacrifice to unwarranted haste.

Never had the entrances to the Criminal Court been beset by a greater multitude. They jammed the doors of the chamber, access to which was allowed only to people provided with tickets. Love and jealousy were to be discussed there, and the most splendid of ladies had hastened to be present.

The accused is presented and immediately all eyes turn on him with eager curiosity.

There appears a young man of less than average height, slender, and of delicate complexion; a white handkerchief tied beneath his chin and knotted above his head recalls the shot which was intended to take his life, and which had the cruel effect of leaving two bullets, only one of which could be extracted, between the lower jawbone and the neck. Yet his dress and hair are meticulous; his face is expressive; his pallor contrasts with the great dark eyes

---

† From *La Gazette des Tribunaux*, December 28 and 31, 1827, and February 29, 1828. When Stendhal experienced the "idea of Julien" during the night of October 25–26, 1829, and set about writing a first draft of *Le Rouge et le noir*, he had before him two models for a provincial crime of passion. In the little village of Bagnéres in the Pyrenees, a woodworker named Lafargue had recently murdered his mistress and had been condemned (March 21, 1829) to five years in jail. Stendhal was very interested in this story and drew upon it for an essay, inserted bodily in the *Promenades dans Rome*, going directly to the printer, the point of which was that vital passion was still to be found in France. M. Claude Liprandi has written an extended account of this crime and trial, as they worked on Stendhal's imagination; and there seems no doubt that he was most taken by the criminal's capacity for heroic energy. But there are also striking parallels between *RB* and another crime of passion which took place just a year or two before in Stendhal's native town. Antoine Berthet, a seminarian from the little town of Brangues near Grenoble, was perhaps a less colorful character than Lafargue, but the pattern of his career, the nature of his crime, and his final fate come very close to Julien Sorel's. Stendhal read about the matter in the recently founded *Gazette des Tribunaux*, a journal reporting notable trials at law from all corners of France; we excerpt from the *Gazette's* somewhat puffy journalese the narrative of Antoine Berthet's trial.

which bear the marks of fatigue and sickness. He lets them wander over the business going forward around him; some bewilderment is apparent in his gaze.

During the reading of the charges and the presentation of the case by the District Attorney, M. Guernon-Ranville, Berthet remains immobile. The following facts are learned:

Antoine Berthet, present age twenty-five, was born of poor but honest artisans; his father is a blacksmith in the village of Brangues. A delicate constitution hardly fit for physical toil, an intelligence superior to his position, a precociously evident taste for higher studies attracted the favorable interest of several persons; their benevolence, more enthusiastic than enlightened, proposed to remove young Berthet from the modest condition in which the accident of birth had placed him and make him a member of the clergy. The pastor of Brangues adopted him as a favorite child, taught him his first lessons, and thanks to his kindness, Berthet entered the junior seminary at Grenoble in 1818. In 1822 a serious illness forced him to discontinue his studies. He was taken in by the pastor, whose solicitude successfully made up for the poverty of his parents. At the urgent solicitation of this sponsor, he was taken into the home of M. M____, who entrusted to him the education of his children; thus grim fate paved the way for him to become the scourge of that family. Did Mme. M____, a pleasant and intelligent woman, then aged thirty-six and of an impeccable reputation, think that she could without risk lavish tokens of kindness on a young man of twenty whose delicate health required special attentions? Did a precocious depravity in Berthet cause him to mistake the nature of these attentions? Whatever the case, before the year was out M. M____ had to think of terminating the stay of the young seminarian in his house.

Berthet entered the junior seminary at Belley to continue his studies there. He remained there two years, and returned to Brangues to spend the holiday of 1825.

He was unable to return to that institution. He then managed to be admitted to the advanced seminary in Grenoble; but after remaining there a month, having been judged by his superiors unworthy of the office to which he aspired, he was dismissed without hope of returning. His father, angered, banished him from his presence. In the end he could find shelter only with his married sister in Brangues.

Were these rejections the consequence of the discovery of weak principles and serious faults in his conduct? Did Berthet consider himself the victim of a secret persecution by M. M____, whom he had offended? Some letters which he wrote at that time to Mme. M____ contain virulent reproaches and calumnies. In spite of

that, M. M——— made some efforts on behalf of the former tutor
of his children.

Berthet succeeded in placing himself as a tutor again with M. de
C———. He had then given up the church; but after a year M. de
C——— dismissed him for reasons which are not clear and which
appear to involve another intrigue.

He again considered the career which had been the aim of all his
efforts, the priesthood. But his appeals and the appeals that he had
others make to the officials of the seminaries at Belley, Lyons, and
Grenoble were futile. He was accepted nowhere. Then he was
seized with despair.

While these efforts were in process, he attributed their failure to
the M——— family. The pleas and reproaches which filled the letters that he continued to send to Mme. M——— became terrifying
threats. Sinister remarks are found there: *I want to kill her*, he said
in a fit of sullen melancholy. He wrote to the pastor at Brangues,
his first benefactor's successor: *When I appear beneath the steeple
of the parish church, they will know why.* These bizarre methods
produced a partial effect. M. M——— actively set about reopening
the door of some seminary for him; but he failed at Grenoble; he
likewise failed at Belley, where he travelled expressly with the pastor of Brangues. All he could manage was to find a place for
Berthet with M. Trolliet, a notary in Morestel connected with the
M——— family, by concealing the reasons for his dissatisfaction.
But Berthet, in his frustrated ambition, was disgusted, according to
his disdainful remark, at the thought of being forever nothing more
than *a village schoolmaster with a two-hundred-franc salary.* He did
not cease sending a stream of threatening letters; he declared to
several persons his intention to kill Mme. M——— and then take
his own life. Unfortunately, its very heinousness made the atrocious
project seem improbable; yet it was on the point of fulfillment!

It was during the month of June just past that Berthet entered
the Trolliet household. About July 15 he goes to Lyons to purchase
some pistols; from there he writes to Mme. M——— a letter full of
new threats; it concludes with these words: *Your triumph will be
like Haman's, short-lived.* Back in Morestel, he practices with the
pistols; one of his two weapons is misfiring; after considering having it repaired, he replaces it with another pistol, which he takes
from the room of M. Trolliet, who is away at the time.

On Sunday, July 22, very early in the morning, Berthet loads his
two pistols with a double charge, puts them beneath his coat, and
leaves for Brangues. He arrives at the home of his sister, who
makes him eat a light meal. At the hour for the parish mass, he
goes to the church and places himself about three paces from
Mme. M———'s pew. He soon sees her arrive accompanied by her

two children, one of whom had been his pupil. There he waits, un-
moving . . . until the moment when the priest is distributing communion. "Neither the countenance of his benefactress," said the
District Attorney, "nor the sanctity of the place, nor the celebration
of the most sublime mystery of a religion to whose service Berthet
was to have dedicated himself, nothing can move that soul devoted
to the demon of destruction. His eye fixed on his victim, a stranger
to the religious feeling being expressed all around him, he awaits
with diabolic patience the moment when the elevation of the host
will give him the chance to fire two safe shots. This moment arrives, and when all hearts rise up to God present on the altar, when
Mme. M_____, bowed low, is perhaps mingling with her fervent
prayers the name of the ingrate who had made himself her cruelest
enemy, two shots in rapid succession ring out. The horrified congregation see Berthet and Mme. M_____ fall almost simultaneously; the latter's first impulse, anticipating a further crime, is to
protect her two terrified children with her own body. The mingled
blood of the murderer and of his victim gush as far as the sanctuary
steps."

"Such," continues the District Attorney, "is the crime that leads
Berthet into these precincts. We could have foregone calling witnesses, gentlemen of the jury, and built our case upon facts which
have been admitted by the accused himself; but we have acted in
deference to that philanthropic maxim that a man cannot be condemned on the strength of his own admissions alone. Your task, like
ours, will be confined to the primary matter of confirming the admissions of the accused through these testimonies.

"But another matter of high importance will arouse all our solicitude, will invite your consideration. A crime so atrocious as this
would only be the result of a dreadful madness, if it had not been
explained by one of those violent passions whose fatal power you
have daily had opportunity to study. We ought therefore to consider
in what moral perspective it was conceived and executed; if in the
actions which preceded and prepared for the crime, if, in the very
act, the accused did not perhaps cease to enjoy the full use of his
reason, as much, at least, as can exist in a man disturbed by a violent passion.

"An adulterous love affair, the scorn growing out of it, the conviction that Mme. M_____ was by no means unconnected with his
humiliations and the obstacles excluding him from the career to
which he had dared to aspire, and a thirst for vengeance—such
were, in the pattern of indictment, the causes of this fierce hatred,
this frantic despair, resulting in murder, sacrilege, suicide.

"The quite extraordinary horror of the crime would suffice to
capture your attention; but your concern, gentlemen of the jury,

will be more strongly exercised by the need not to pronounce a sentence of death except insofar as you have become overwhelmingly convinced that the act was voluntary, and the result of lengthy premeditation."

The court next hears the witnesses.

Four persons are summoned to verify the material circumstances, so to speak, of the event of July 22; three of them state that Berthet remained standing, without kneeling, during the whole mass up to the communion; his bearing and the expression on his face were calm; suddenly he was seen drawing a pistol from under his clothing and firing it at Mme. M_____.

M. Morin, surgeon and deputy-mayor of Brangues, rushed down from the gallery at the sound of the explosion, and immediately another report was heard. In the midst of the terrible confusion which reigned in the church; he saw only Berthet, his face horribly stained by the blood which gushed from his wound and ran from his mouth. He hastened to lead him away and apply an emergency dressing; but soon he was sought to return to attend a second victim; it was Mme. M_____, mortally wounded; she had been taken home, unconscious and completely paralyzed. Revived with the greatest difficulty, she was very reluctant to consent to the extraction of the bullet; but after that painful operation, the surgeon noticed that there remained a second bullet which had penetrated the epigastrium and which also had to be removed.

Berthet identifies the pistols shown him. With a total absence of emotion he indicates the larger as the one he used against Mme. M_____.

His Honor, the judge: What motive can have driven you to to this crime?

Berthet: Two passions which have tormented me for four years, love and jealousy.

The District Attorney concentrates, in making the case for premeditation, on fixing the period of the crime's conception: "Accused," he says, "I warn you that your answers to the questionings you have undergone up to the present are not recognized; you could have been mistaken, or wanted to be mistaken; it does not matter: your defense has remained uncommitted; therefore I ask you when you conceived the plan of killing Mme. M_____?"

Berthet, after hesitating, traces his decision back to the trip that he made to Lyon to purchase the pistols; "But," he adds, "up until the last moment I was not sure that I would do it; I wavered constantly between the idea of killing myself alone and that of including Mme. M_____ in my destruction." He acknowledges that he had loaded the pistols in Morestel just before leaving for Brangues.

District Attorney: What thoughts, what moral considerations passed through your mind during the trip from Morestel to Brangues; and up to the moment when you fired on Mme. M_____? Prisoner, we do not want to trick you; I am going to tell you the purpose of the question that I ask you: might you not have been somewhat deranged during the period of time I have mentioned?

Berthet: I was so beside myself that I could scarcely recognize a route which I had taken many times; I nearly missed finding a bridge along the way, my vision was so confused! As I stood behind Mme. M_____'s pew, so close to her, my thoughts were wild and full of incoherencies; I did not know where I was; I confused the past and the present; my very existence seemed an illusion to me; at certain moments I thought of nothing but suicide; but finally, I saw in my imagination Mme. M_____ giving herself to another; then I was seized by a jealous rage, I was no longer in control of myself and I aimed my pistol at Mme. M_____; but until then I had been so indisposed to act on my fatal resolution that, when I saw Mme. M_____ enter the church with another lady and whisper to her after having noticed me, as if she were thinking of withdrawing, I felt quite clearly that if she had taken this course. I would have turned the two pistols on myself alone, if necessary; but her evil destiny and mine determined that she should remain. . . .

District Attorney: Did you feel remorse for what you had done?

Berthet: My first thought was to demand urgent news of Mme. M_____'s condition. I would gladly have given what remained of my life to be certain that she was not mortally wounded.

M. Morin states that in fact Berthet manifested some regret for his action; nevertheless, he enjoyed full use of his reason and remained quite calm.

Criminal Court of Isère (Grenoble)

(SPECIAL REPORT)

PROSECUTION OF MURDER COMMITTED BY A SEMINARIAN IN
A CHURCH
(CONCLUSION)

Mme. Marigny, friend of Mme. M_____ since childhood, had come to the church with her on the fatal day. She fainted at the moment of the explosion; recovering consciousness, her first impulse was to run to the aid of Mme. M_____; she found her completely paralyzed; when she undressed her, the blood spurted from the wound with such force that she was completely covered by it.

"A month before," said Mme. Marigny, "I received a letter from M. Berthet; knowing that I took an interest in him as I did in many others, he begged me to do something on his behalf. He complained of *the fatality which was intent on pursuing him*, and ended with vague remarks through which he seemed to warn of a homicide and a suicide. I had the occasion to tell Mme. M_____ of this letter; she told me that she was all too sure that it was she that M. Berthet meant. Mme. M_____ told me of the threats to which she had been long subjected by that young man."

"Four or five days afterwards, M. Berthet came to my home and told me that he was going to Lyon; I asked him if he had hopes of finding a job in that city. 'No', he replied, 'I am going there to buy some pistols to kill Mme. M_____ and kill myself after. I had intended to kill her last Sunday, on Corpus Christi day, with a piece of iron that I had sharpened; but now I am determined.' This horrifying admission upset me terribly. —What, do you mean to kill her, I cried out! —Yes, he said, she has done me nothing but harm. —But, M. Berthet, instead of committing two tragic wrongs, as you seem to have decided to do, you ought at least to commit only one and kill yourself alone."

District Attorney: The advice was bad.

Mme. Marigny: I was in such a state of confusion, sir, that I was visibly exhausted by it; for M. Berthet, in leaving me, apologized for having come to tell me such a thing, he asked me not to mention it to Mme. M_____; but I hastened to inform her of it.

Berthet confirms all these facts and adds that if he did not carry out the plan he had conceived on Corpus Christi day, it was because he had meanwhile learned that they were doing something for him.

District Attorney, in a forceful tone: That explanation is an overwhelming indictment against you. Thus it was a position that was the object of all your threats; it was a position that you were demanding with pistol and dagger! You consented to let Mme. M_____ live after Corpus Christi only because you had been given hopes that they would find a job for you! That is cowardly, cruel behavior.

The hearing of the witnesses concluded, the session is recessed, to be resumed with the pleas of counsel.

The District Attorney speaks in support of the charge. The material fact is admitted; as for the free and considered will which directed the crime, the speaker bases it on Berthet's calm, unruffled patience in the church at Brangues. The premeditation seems to him obvious from the threats made in advance, the confidences imparted to Mme. Marigny by the accused, the preparations for the murder. As for Berthet's excuses, he refutes them one after another. "Before ordinary judges," says this officer of the court, "we would successfully maintain that one can not accept any extenuations except those recognized as such by the law; before you, gentlemen of the jury, we must use another kind of language. You need account only to God for the influences on your decision; you will have to decide if the accused is guilty, and this word applies to the morality as much as to the material fact; we have therefore had to resist everything that might qualify the morality of the act in your eyes."

The defense's turn having arrived, Berthet rises and reads a long account written in an elegant, natural style, in which, going into minute details and excusing himself for portraying Mme. M____ as the corrupter of his youth on the grounds of his dangerous situation, he tells how through a series of caresses and insinuations she apparently lost her own innocence and guided all too skillfully his long-blind, ignorant simplicity toward a goal which he should have foreseen. This account, painful to those who had taken an interest in Berthet, and read coldly, gave proof that if it was necessary to admit the jealousy of love as one of the inciting motives of the crime, a second, no less powerful motive existed in the soul of the accused, the frustrated pride of ambition and egotism. This young man, endowed by nature with physical advantages and an excellent mind, made too much of by those around him, misled by his very successes, had in imagination created for himself a brilliant future all the more glorious in that it would not be based on his own talents. The son of the Brangues blacksmith saw in the distance a horizon which was perhaps limitless. Then, suddenly, one and the same cause betrays and annihilates his hopes; everything goes wrong at once; humiliating rebuffs everywhere replace benevolence and favors. Then, weary of life, despair makes him resolve to end it and impels him at the same time to include in his destruction the woman who was the first to launch him on his fatal course. Such a story could not help but inspire general interest.

"What a picture we have before us," said M. Massonnet, his defender: "in Berthet's heart was innocence; he outstripped his rivals through his talents; from the bosom of the school a great citizen might perhaps have risen; and now you see him as good as destroyed before you. . . . He seems lost to society."

"Perhaps if I could have obeyed his wishes, I would not have come to defend him at all. Life is not at all what he desires; what does life without honor mean to him? Life . . . he has half lost it; a fatal bullet is there, awaiting his last sigh. Berthet himself condemned himself to death. . . . Your condemnation would only aid his futile efforts to destroy an unbearable life. But no, Berthet, I must defend you; your wish to die serves as proof in the eyes of men that you still deserve to live; in the eyes of heaven that you are not ready to die."

"This case, gentlemen of the jury, is of a kind rare in the annals of the Criminal Courts; it is not by means of the cold words of the law, *all who are guilty of murder shall be punished by death*, that one ought to evaluate an action which can have no judges except conscience, humanity, a heart which feels. I intend to prove that love caused the death; that love is often a madness, that the will of the accused was not his own when he became simultaneously a suicide and a homicide."

"Of course, it will be necessary to reveal details which will make my task painful, as they will make yours painful, gentlemen of the jury; but it is quite necessary to show you how the storm gathered, the tempest which dragged this luckless young man into the abyss. Why should we not portray for the judges, as a true defense requires, the spectacle of love, when every day unnecessary and even incestuous loves fill our tragic dramas with horror for the vain pleasure of audiences? Will what is permitted in order to arouse the frivolous curiosity of men be forbidden when it is intended to save them from the scaffold?"

The able defender portrays Berthet at the mercy of his fatal passion; he describes all the periods up to the moment when, a prey to the delirium of jealousy, he goes to seek out and slay his victim even in the temple of that God which she herself had chosen as judge and witness when she swore before his image never to be forsworn.

M. Massonnet then maintains the proposition that the murder was committed without real intent: "There are two kinds of madness," he says, "the madness of those whose faculties are forever impaired, the madness of those whose faculties are only momentarily overshadowed by a great passion. These madness differ only in duration. The lawmaker cannot impose any penal responsibility on men who are afflicted by one or the other; like blind men without guides on an unknown road, the misfortunes that they cause are *accidents*, and never *crimes*. . . . The luckless Berthet is a distressing example of those overwhelming aberrations of love. Ah, gentlemen of the jury, if at this moment I should question those members of the tender sex who have entered these precincts to lament the misfortunes of the passion which they know so well how to inspire; if I appealed to their emotions, they would join their voice with ours to recommend to you the doctrines that love justifies, that human law could not condemn."

After M. Massonnet's speech and the judge's summary, the jurors begin their deliberations. Some time later, they reappear, and from the grave expressions which can be seen on their faces, the terrible sentence of death is foreseen. Berthet is declared guilty of wilful murder with premeditation. The accused is presented and the

Court pronounces the fatal decision, which he hears without the slightest show of emotion.

The day after next, Berthet has the presiding judge of the criminal court come to his place of imprisonment and makes some important revelations. There, he puts in his hand a written declaration in which he expresses his regret for the scheme of defamation into which the exigencies of his defense drew him during the trial. He declares that the jealousy which consumed him had made him think that Mme. M_____ had been at fault; he concludes by begging *pardon for a young man who was misled by a passion and by emotions which she had never shared. It is*, he adds, *without hope of leniency that I speak.*

Actually, he had as yet made no appeal against his sentence; but since that time he has appealed for a reversal of the decision and sent a request for pardon to the king. "He asks to live," he says, "only in order not to dishonor a humble but honest family by dying on the scaffold."

Execution of the Seminarian Berthet

It was at 11 A.M. on February 23 that Berthet suffered his punishment in the Place d'Armes in Grenoble. An immense throng, composed chiefly of women of all ages, crowded the street through which he was to pass. The sympathy which his infamous defense had alienated revived at that supreme moment; one could see in this unfortunate young man, who had escaped the death of despair only to achieve death at the scaffold, neither an ordinary murderer nor a villain; it was rather a victim of his passions, dragged to his ruin by a fatal conjunction of circumstances, who evoked wonder and pity rather than terror. The space of time which had elapsed since his condemnation had given rise to a general belief that his petition for pardon would be followed by a commutation of the sentence; and that clemency, sought by the District Attorney, would have satisfied the public's expectations. M. Appert, member of the society for the improvement of prisons, visiting, some time ago, the prison in Grenoble, saw Berthet, and promised to take up his cause. On his return to Paris, he made some efforts which remained fruitless; he finally wrote him a letter which, as far as anyone knows, must have left him little hope. Thus, the evening before, Berthet said to one of those prison women who constantly turned up at his side: *I have a premonition that tomorrow will be my last day!* The answer could only be silence, it was known that his petition for pardon had just been rejected. All the consolations of religion were lavished on him; he had asked for them, and received them calmly; the exhortations of the priest at one moment brought tears to his eyes.

He was seen leaving the prison, attended by two priests, one of whom supported him with one hand and with the other held out a crucifix to him. Extremely emaciated, pale, his beard long, and his face wan, he bent over the crucifix and appeared to recite prayers in an undertone, but with a movement of the lips so rapid that one might have attributed it to the convulsive agitation of delirium as much as to fervor. Thus he reached the foot of the scaffold. There, however, he seemed to regard the terrible apparatus without fear. He turned back toward the two priests who had rendered him a sad last duty, and embraced them; then, recovering his steadfastness, he climbed up alone; the executioner had preceded him. On the scaffold, he genuflected and seemed to collect himself and pray. A moment later he rose and assumed the position himself. . . . A kind of involuntary cry, wrung from the emotion of the throng, announced that all was finished.

Stendhal on Stendhal

STENDHAL

From Love†

Chapter 2. Concering the Birth of Love

Here is what happens in the soul:

1. Admiration.

2. You think, 'How delightful it would be to kiss her, to be kissed by her,' and so on . . .

3. Hope. You observe her perfections, and it is at this moment that a woman really ought to surrender, for the utmost physical pleasure. Even the most reserved women blush to the whites of their eyes at this moment of hope. The passion is so strong, and the pleasure so sharp, that they betray themselves unmistakably.

4. Love is born. To love is to enjoy seeing, touching, and sensing with all the senses, as closely as possible, a lovable object which loves in return.

5. The first crystallization begins. If you are sure that a woman loves you, it is a pleasure to endow her with a thousand perfections and to count your blessings with infinite satisfaction. In the end you overrate wildly, and regard her as something fallen from Heaven, unknown as yet, but certain to be yours.

Leave a lover with his thoughts for twenty-four hours, and this is what will happen:

At the salt mines of Salzburg, they throw a leafless wintry bough into one of the abandoned workings. Two or three months later they haul it out covered with a shining deposit of crystals. The smallest twig, no bigger than a torn-tit's claw, is studded with a galaxy of scintillating diamonds. The original branch is no longer recognizable.

What I have called crystallization is a mental process which

† From *De L'Amour*. Translated by Gilbert and Suzanne Sale (Monmouth: Merlin Press, 1957), pp. 45–52. Reprinted by permission of the publisher.

draws from everything that happens new proofs of the perfection of the loved one.

You hear a traveller speaking of the cool orange groves beside the sea at Genoa in the summer heat: Oh, if you could only share that coolness with *her*!

One of your friends goes hunting, and breaks his arm: wouldn't it be wonderful to be looked after by the woman you love! To be with her all the time and to see her loving you . . . a broken arm would be heaven . . . and so your friend's injury provides you with conclusive proof of the angelic kindness of your mistress. In short, no sooner do you think of a virtue than you detect it in your beloved.

The phenomenon that I have called crystallization springs from Nature, which ordains that we shall feel pleasure and sends the blood to our heads. It also evolves from the feeling that the degree of pleasure is related to the perfections of the loved one, and from the idea that 'She is mine.' The savage has no time to go beyond the first step. He feels pleasure, but his brain is fully occupied in chasing deer through the forest, so that he can eat, keep up his strength, and avoid his enemy's axe.

At the other end of the scale of civilization, I have no doubt that a sensitive woman can feel physical pleasure only with the man she loves.[1] This is the direct opposite of the savage's condition. But then, in civilized countries, the woman has leisure, while the savage is so taken up with his occupation that he cannot help treating his female as a beast of burden. If the mates of many animals are happier, it is only because the male has less difficulty in obtaining his food.

But let us leave the forest and return to Paris. A man in love sees every perfection in the object of his love, but his attention is still liable to wander after a time because one gets tired of anything uniform, even perfect happiness.[2]

This is what happens next to fix the attention:

6. Doubt creeps in. First a dozen or so glances, or some other sequence of actions, raise and confirm the lover's hopes. Then, as he recovers from the initial shock, he grows accustomed to his good fortune, or acts on a theory drawn from the common multitude of easily-won women. He asks for more positive proofs of affection and tries to press his suit further.

He is met with indifference,[3] coldness, or even anger if he ap-

---

1. If men do not display this peculiarity, it is because they have no modesty to sacrifice.
2. Which means that the same subtlety of existence can offer only one moment of perfect happiness; but the passionate man's *manner of being* changes ten times a day.
3. What the seventeenth-century novelists called the *coup de foudre* (or thunderbolt), which determines the destiny of the hero and his mistress, is a movement of the soul which, for all its debasement by a thousand scribblers, is nonetheless a fact of nature. It comes from the impossibility of performing this defensive maneuver. A woman in love

pears too confident. In France there is even a shade of irony which seems to say 'You think you're farther ahead than you really are.' A woman may behave like this either because she is recovering from a moment of intoxication and obeying the dictates of modesty, which she may fear she has offended; or simply for the sake of prudence or coquetry.

The lover begins to be less sure of the good fortune he was anticipating and subjects his grounds for hope to a critical examination.

He tries to recoup by indulging in other pleasures but finds them inane. He is seized by the dread of a frightful calamity and now concentrates fully. Thus begins:

7. The second crystallization, which deposits diamond layers of proof that 'she loves me.'

Every few minutes throughout the night which follows the birth of doubt, the lover has a moment of dreadful misgiving, and then reassures himself, 'she loves me'; and crystallization begins to reveal new charms. Then once again the haggard eye of doubt pierces him and he stops transfixed. He forgets to draw breath and mutters, 'But does she love me?' Torn between doubt and delight, the poor lover convinces himself that she could give him such pleasure as he could find nowhere else on earth.

It is the pre-eminence of this truth, and the road to it, with a fearsome precipice on one hand and a view of perfect happiness on the other, which set the second crystallization so far above the first.

The lover's mind vacillates between three ideas:

1. She is perfect.
2. She loves me.
3. How can I get the strongest possible proofs of her love?

The most hearttrending moment of love in its infancy is the realization that you have been mistaken about something, and that a whole framework of crystals has to be destroyed. You begin to feel doubtful about the entire process of crystallization.

Chapter 3. Concerning Hope

It only needs a very small quantity of hope to beget love. Even when hope gives way to despair after a day or two, love will persist.

In a decisive, bold, and impetuous person, with an imagination whetted by misfortune, the degree of hope can be even smaller and more fleeting, without endangering the love.

If the lover has suffered; if he is sensitive and thoughtful; if he turns from other women in keen admiration of the lady in question,

---

finds so much happiness in the feelings she is experiencing that she is unable to pretend; tired of being prudent, she throws caution to the wind and flings herself blindly into the happiness of loving. Where there is mistrust there can be no *coup de foudre*.

no ordinary pleasure will lure him away from the second crystallization. He will prefer to dream of the slenderest chance of pleasing her, rather than to receive all the favours of any ordinary woman.

It is at this stage, and no later, mark you, that a woman who wishes to crush her lover's hopes should do so cruelly, and heap on his head, in public, insults which will make it quite impossible for him ever to see her again.

Even when the periods between all these stages are prolonged, love can still result.

Cold, prudent, phlegmatic people must hope longer and more deeply before they fall in love, and the same is true of elderly people.

The second crystallization ensures that love will last; for you feel that the only alternatives are to win her love or to die. The very idea of ceasing to love is absurd when your convictions are confirmed moment by moment, until the passing months make love a habit. The stronger your character, the slighter the impulse to inconstancy.

This second crystallization is almost entirely lacking when love is inspired by a woman who yields too soon.

When the two crystallization processes have taken place, and particularly the second, which is far the stronger, the original naked branch is no longer recognizable by indifferent eyes, because it now sparkles with perfections, or diamonds, which they do not see or which they simply do not consider to be perfections.

Del Rosso was talking to a former admirer of his mistress, who described her charms in some detail. Del Rosso saw a particular twinkle in the teller's eye, which at once provided another diamond for his crystalline branch.[1] An idea like this, conceived in the evening, would keep him dreaming the whole night through.

---

1. I have called this essay a book of ideology. I intended to convey that although it was about *love*, it was not a novel, and was not entertaining in the way that a novel is. I beg the forgiveness of the philosophers for having chosen the word *ideology*; I certainly had no intention of stealing a title that by rights should belong to someone else. If ideology be a detailed description of ideas and of all the parts into which those ideas can be analysed, this book is a detailed and painstaking description of all the feelings which make up the passion called *love*. I then draw certain conclusions from this description; for instance, the way in which love can be cured. I know of no word derived from Greek that would indicate discourse upon feelings, as ideology indicates discourse upon ideas. I might have had a word invented for me by one of my scholarly friends, but I am already quite annoyed enough at having had to adopt the new word *crystallization*, and it may well be that if this essay wins any readers, they will not forgive me the neologism. I agree that literary talent would have avoided it and I tried to do so, but without any success. In my opinion this word does express the principal process of the madness known as love, a madness which nevertheless provides man with the greatest pleasure the species can know on earth. If I had not used the word *crystallization* I should have had to replace it repeatedly by an awkward periphrasis, and my description of what happens in the head and in the heart of a man in love would have become obscure, heavy, and wearisome even to me, the author. I hesitate to guess what the reader would have thought of it.

I therefore urge anyone who is shocked by the word *crystallization* to shut the book forthwith. It is no part of my desire, fortunately, to have a great number of readers. It would make me very happy to please about thirty or forty people in Paris, whom I shall never see but nevertheless love devotedly without ever having met them: some young

An impromptu remark gives *me*[2] dreams enough to last a whole night through. I see a sensitive, generous, burning spirit—*romantic*[3] as it is commonly called—who sets above the happiness of kings the simple pleasure of walking alone with her lover at midnight in a secluded wood.

Del Rosso would say that my mistress is a prude; I think his a harlot.

Chapter 4

In the unattached heart of a girl who is living in a secluded château in the depths of the country the least touch of surprise can lead to a mild admiration. When this is followed by even the slenderest hope, admiration leads to love and crystallization.

This kind of love is rather fun at first.

Surprise and hope are powerfully supported by the need for love and the melancholy which characterize the sixteen-year-old. It is a commonplace that sixteen is an age which thirsts for love and is not excessively particular about what beverage chance may provide.

The seven stages of love, then, are as follows:

1. Admiration.
2. How delightful . . . etc.
3. Hope.
4. The birth of love.
5. First crystallization.
6. Doubt creeps in . . .
7. Second crystallization.

The interval between 1 and 2 may be a year. Between 2 and 3 it may be a month; unless hope follows closely stage 2 is imperceptibly given up, as causing unhappiness; 3 leads to 4 in a twinkling.

Madame Roland, for instance, surreptitiously reading a volume which she thrusts into a drawer at the slightest noise, by the workbench in the back of her father's watch-engraving shop. Someone like Madame Roland will, I hope, forgive me not only the word *crystallization*, which I use to express the impulse of folly that makes us see all beauties and perfections in the woman we are beginning to love, but also many bolder ellipses. The only thing to do is to take a pencil and write in the few missing words between the lines.

2. It is for the sake of *brevity*, and in order to depict experience from the inside, that the author, by using the first person singular, brings together a number of feelings quite alien to him. He has had none of his own which are worth mentioning.

3. At first all these actions seemed to me to have the sublimity that immediately sets a man apart and differentiates him from all others. I thought I saw in his eyes that thirst for more sublime happiness, that unavowed melancholy which aspires to something better than we can know here below, and which, for a romantic soul, however placed by chance or revolution,

> . . . *Still prompts the celestial sight,*
> *For which we wish to live, or dare to die.*
> (*Ultima lettera di Bianca a sua madre*. Forli, 1817.)

There is no interval between 4 and 5; only intimacy could possibly come between them.

Depending on the impetuousness and habitual boldness of the individual, several days may elapse between 5 and 6. There is no interval between 6 and 7.

Chapter 5

Man is not free to avoid doing what gives him greater pleasure than any other action.[1]

Love is like a fever which comes and goes quite independently of the will. It is chiefly in this that mannered love differs from passionate love. The charms of your beloved are not a matter of self-congratulation, except as a stroke of luck.

Finally, there are no age limits for love. Look at Madame du Deffand's infatuation with the churlish Horace Walpole, or the more recent and certainly pleasanter example in Paris itself.

The embarrassing consequences of grand passion are the only proofs I will admit in evidence of its existence. Shyness, for instance, is a proof of love; I do *not* mean the awkward shame of a boy leaving school.

Chapter 6. The Salzburg Bough

Crystallization goes on throughout love almost without a break. The process is something like this: whenever all is not well between you and your beloved, you crystallize out an *imaginary solution.* Only through imagination can you be sure that your beloved is perfect in any given way. After intimacy, ever-resurgent fears are lulled by more real solutions. Thus happiness never stays the same, except in its origin; every day brings forth a new blossom.

If your beloved gives way to her passion and commits the cardinal error of removing your fear by the intensity of her response,[2] then crystallization stops for a moment, but what love loses in intensity—its fears, that is—it makes up for by the charm of complete abandon and infinite trust, becoming a gentle habit which softens the hardships of life and gives a new interest to its enjoyment.

If she leaves you, crystallization begins again, and every act of admiration, the sight of every happiness she could give you, and whose existence you had forgotten, ends in the searing reflection: 'I shall never know that joy again, and it is through my fault that I

---

1. Where crime is concerned, a good education instils remorse; and foreseen remorse acts as a deterrent.
2. Diane de Poitiers, in the *Princesse de Clèves.*

have lost it!' It is no use seeking consolation in pleasures of another sort; they turn to dust and ashes. Your imagination can paint a physical picture for you, and take you a-hunting on a swift horse through Devon woods;[1] but you are aware at the same time that you could find no pleasure in it. This is the optical illusion which leads to the fatal pistol shot.

Gambling also has its crystallization process, concerned with the use you will make of the money you hope to win.

The intrigues at court, so much mourned by the nobles under the cloak of Legitimism, were only fascinating because of the crystallization they bred. Not a courtier but envied Luynes and Lauzun their swift ascent to affluence; not an attractive woman but saw herself with a duchy as great as that of Mme. de Polignac. No rational form of government can possibly recapture that crystallization. There is nothing quite so anti-imagination as the government of the United States of America. We have already seen that among their neighbours the savages crystallization is almost unknown. The Romans had but a bare idea of it, and then only about physical love.

Hatred, too, has its crystallization; as soon as you see a hope of revenge, your hatred breaks out afresh.

If belief in the absurd or unproven tends to bring the most incongruous people to the top, that is another effect of crystallization. It even exists in mathematics (see the Newtonians in 1740), in minds which could not at any given moment grasp simultaneously all the stages of proof in evidence of their beliefs.

Think of the fate of the great German philosophers, whose immortality, so widely proclaimed, never managed to last more than thirty or forty years.

It is because we can never understand the whys and wherefores of our feelings that even the wisest men are fanatical about such things as music.

It is impossible to justify oneself at will against someone who holds an opposite view.

---

1. Because, if you could imagine happiness there, crystallization would have claimed for your mistress the exclusive right to give you that happiness.

STENDHAL

From The Life of Henri Brulard†

Chapter II

My fall coincided with Nap[oleon's] in April 1814. I traveled to
Italy to live as I had at rue d'Angivilliers. In 1821, I left Milan in
despair because of Métilde and seriously considered blowing my
brains out. Everything about Paris bored me at first; later on, I took
up writing to give myself something to do; Métilde died, so there
was no sense in returning to Milan. By 1830, I had become quite
happy—no, that's going too far, but I had become reasonably
happy—when I was writing *Le Rouge et le noir*.

The July Days delighted me; I saw the bullets fly beneath the
columns of the Théâtre-Français, not exactly risking my neck as I
did so. Never will I forget the beautiful sun that greeted me, along
with my first glimpse of the *tricolore*, on the 29th or 30th at around
eight in the morning, having spent the night with Commander Pinto
and his frightened niece. On September 25th, I was appointed Consul in Trieste by Mr. Molé, whom I had never met before. In 1831 I
moved from Trieste to Civita-Vecchia and Rome, where I still reside
and continue to die of boredom for no other reason than my own
narrow-mindedness. I occasionally need an evening's conversation
in witty company; I feel suffocated without it.

So the major chapters of my story are these: born in 1783, dragoon
in 1800, student from 1803 to 1806. In 1806, Deputy War Commissar, Intendant in Brunswick. In 1809, collected the wounded at
Essling or at Wagram, carrying out missions along the snowy banks
of the Danube; in Linz and Passau, fell in love with Countess Petit;
to see her again, I asked to be sent to Spain. On August 3rd 1810,
appointed—by her, more or less—Auditor of the Council of State.
This privileged, costly lifestyle led me to Moscow, as Intendant at
Sagan in Silesia, ending at last in April 1815. Who could have believed it! Speaking for myself, my downfall gladdened me.

After the fall, a student, madly in love, published *Histoire de la
P[einture] en Italie* [*History of Italian Painting*] in 1817; my father,
who had become an *ultra*,[1] went bankrupt and died in 1819, I be-

---

† From *Vie de Henry Brulard*. Translated by Margaret Flynn for this Norton Critical Edition (Geneva: Edito-Service, 1968), pp. 17–28, 35–49. Reprinted by permission of the
translator.

1. Short for *ultraroyaliste*; the term refers to a reactionary political faction known for being
"more royalist than the king." The *ultras* enjoyed political dominance during the Bourbon Restoration (1815–1830) [*Translator*].

lieve; I returned to Paris in June 1821. Métilde was driving me to despair; she died; I loved her better dead than unfaithful; I write, I console myself, I am happy. In 1830, in September, I return to the administrative minefield where I remain today, mourning my writer's life on the fourth floor of the Hôtel de Valois, rue de Richelieu, no. 71.

I've been an *homme d'esprit*, indulging my wit in writing, since the winter of 1826. Before then, I held my tongue out of sheer laziness. I give the impression, I believe, of being a most lighthearted, callous fellow; the truth is, I've never spoken a word about any of the women I've loved. In this regard, I unquestionably exhibit all of the symptoms of the melancholy temperament described by Cabanis. I was never much of a ladies' man.

The other day, however, pondering my life as I walked alone above Lake Albano, I realized that my life could be summed up by the names that appear below, and whose initials I wrote in the dust, like Zadig, with my cane, as I sat on the little bench behind the *Minori Osservanti* Stations of the Cross built by the brother of Urban VIII, Barberini, near two fine trees enclosed by a small circular wall:

Virginie (Kubly),
Angela (Pietragrua),
Adèle (Rebuffel),
Mélanie (Guilbert),
Mina (de Griesheim),
Alexandrine (Petit),
Angéline, whom I never loved (Bereyter),
Angela (Pietragrua),
Métilde (Dembowski),
Clémentine (. . .),
Giulia,

And, lastly, for a month at most, Madame Azur, whose Christian name escapes me,
And, most unwisely, yesterday, Amalia (B[ettini]).

Most of these charming creatures did not honor me with their favors; nevertheless, they occupied literally every moment of my life. My work came second to them. In reality, I have never had great ambitions, but in 1811 I thought I did.

The habitual condition of my life was that of a man unlucky in love who loved music and painting; that is, who loved appreciating the products of these arts rather than practicing them badly himself. With finely honed sensitivity, I sought out lovely landscapes to view; it's the only reason I traveled at all. These landscapes were like a violin bow playing over the strings of my soul, and vistas that had gone unmentioned by others (the line of boulders along the approach to Arbois, I believe, coming from Dole via the main road was, for me, a tangible and clear image of Métilde's soul). I see now that I preferred reverie to all else, even to passing for an *homme d'esprit*. It was only in 1826 that I took the trouble to do the latter, adopting the habit of improvising dialogues for the amusement of the company I kept, fighting the despair that assailed me during the early months of this calamitous year.

I recently learned—reading it in a book (the letters of Victor Jacquemont, the Indian)—that someone apparently found me quite brilliant. Some years ago, I read more or less the same thing in a book, very much in fashion at the time, by Lady Morgan. I had forgotten this fine quality that earned me so many enemies. This quality may only have been apparent rather than real, and one's enemies are of too common a stripe to judge what is brilliant or not; for example, how can someone like the comte d'Argout judge what is *brilliant*? A man who, on a daily basis, reads two or three volumes of in-12-format novels for chambermaids! How would Monsieur de Lamartine be any judge of wit? First of all, he has none himself; second, he, too, devours a couple of volumes a day of the dullest works imaginable (seen in Florence in 1824 or 1826).

The major drawback of being a writer is that you have to keep a sharp eye on the dullards all around you and *take in their dull sensations*. A flaw of mine is that I grow attached to individuals whose imaginations are the least impotent and become unintelligible to everyone else, which may suit them just fine.

Since I've been in Rome, the impulse to write only visits me once a week, for no more than five minutes at a stretch; I'd rather daydream. The people here do not understand the intricacies of the French language well enough to grasp the subtlety of my observations; they only respond to the broad wit of the traveling salesman, such as that of Melodrama, which they adore (example: M[ichel]-Ange Caetani) and which is well and truly their daily bread. The prospect of such a success makes my blood run cold; I no longer deign to speak to people who have applauded Melodrama. In it I see all of the emptiness of vanity.

So two months ago, in September 1835, as I was thinking about writing these *Mémoires* while sitting on the shore of Lake Albano (two hundred feet away from the lake itself), I wrote these initials in the dust, Zadig-like:

I reflected on these names at length, along with the unbelievably stupid, idiotic things they made me do (I say "unbelievably" for myself, not for the reader; nevertheless, I don't regret having done them).

The truth is that I only slept with six of these women I loved.

As for who the object of my greatest passion was, it's debatable whether it was Mélanie 2, Alexandrine, Métilde, or Clémentine 4.

Clémentine is the one who hurt me the most when she left me. But is this pain comparable to that brought on by Métilde, who didn't want to tell me she loved me?

With all of these women, and a number of others, I was always a child; as a result, I rarely got anywhere with them in an amorous sense. On the other hand, however, they greatly preoccupied me, and passionately so, leaving me with memories that still enchant me (some of them go back twenty-four years, such as the memory of the Madonna del Monte in Varese in 1811). I was not at all *galant*, or not enough so; only the woman I was in love with at the time occupied me, and when I wasn't in love I pondered the spectacle of human things or savored my reading of Montesquieu or Walter Scott.

So now, as children might say, I am so far from being inured to their ruses and little charms that at my age, fifty-two, and as I write this, I am still under the spell of a lengthy chat that Amalia had with me yesterday evening at the Théâtre Valle.

In order to consider them as philosophically as possible and to try, in doing so, to remove the blindingly bright haloes they wear, which bedazzle me and keep me from seeing clearly, I will *put these ladies in order* (in the mathematical sense) based on their various qualities. So to begin with their usual passion, vanity, I will say that two of them were countesses and one was a baroness.

Alexandrine was the richest; she and her husband easily burned through 80,000 francs a year. The poorest was Mina de Griesheim, the youngest daughter of a general with no fortune, the ex-favorite of a fallen prince, whose family lived on his salary alone, or Mademoiselle Bereyter, an actress at the Opéra Buffa.

I'm trying to destroy the charm, the dazzlingness of events, by viewing them with such military strictness. Doing so is my only resource for reaching the truth within a topic that I can't speak to anyone about. Due to the modesty that is part of my melancholy temperament (Cabanis), I have always been the soul of discretion, even absurdly so. As for who had the greatest wit, Clémentine by far outshone the rest. Métilde's distinction was her noble Spanish sense of feeling; Giulia's was, I believe, her strength of character, even though she appeared the weakest at first; Angela P[ietragrua] was a sublime wench in the Italian style, à la Lucretia Borgia, and Madame Azur was an unsublime wench, à la Madame du Barry.

Want of money only afflicted me twice: at the end of 1805, and in 1806 up to August; my father had stopped sending me money and *didn't tell me*; there was the rub. Once he went five months without paying my pension of 150 francs. Hence our ongoing troubles with the viscount, who would receive his pension without fail but regularly gambled it away on the day he received it.

In 1829 and 1830, my money troubles were more a matter of inattention and carelessness than any real lack of means, since from 1821 to 1830 I made three or four trips to Italy, England, and Barcelona, and by the end of this period owed only 400 francs.

My greatest lack of money led me to take the unpleasant step of borrowing 100 francs, or sometimes 200, from Monsieur Besançon. I paid him back in a month or two; and lastly, in September 1830, I owed 400 francs to my tailor Michel. Those familiar with the lifestyle of my generation in its youth will find this quite moderate. From 1800 to 1830 I never owed a penny to my tailor Léger or to his successor, Michel (22, rue Vivienne).

My friends during that period, 1830, Mm de Mareste and Colomb, were friends of all odd type indeed; they would doubtless have gone to great lengths to get me out of great danger, but whenever I appeared in a new set of clothes, they (especially the former) would have given twenty francs to anyone who would toss a glass of dirty water at me. (Except for the vicomte de Barral and Bigillion [from Saint-Ismier], I have nearly always had, throughout my life, friends of this type.)

They were fine, exceedingly prudent people who had saved 12,000 or 15,000 francs' worth of salary or private income through tremendously hard work or skill and who couldn't bear to see me free as a bird, devil-may-care, happy with a notebook of white paper and a pen and living on no more than 4,000 or 5,000 francs. They would have loved me a hundred times more if they had seen me downcast and unhappy at having only a half or a third of their income; I, who may have shocked them a bit in the days when I had a coachman, two horses, a barouche, and a cabriolet, for my *luxe* had reached this level during the Emperor's day. So I was, or believed myself to be, a young man in a hurry; but what bothered me about this notion was that I didn't know what to want. I was ashamed to be in love with Countess Alexandrine Petit; I kept Mademoiselle A. Bereyter, actress at the Opéra Buffa, as my mistress; I dined at the Café Hardy; I was a whirlwind of activity. I returned from Saint-Cloud to Paris expressly to attend one act of the *Matrimonio segreto* at the Odéon (Madame Barilli, Barilli, Tachinardi, Madame Festa, Mademoiselle Bereyter). My cabriolet awaited me at the door to the Café Hardy: this is what my brother-in-law could never forgive me for.

All of this could be taken for mere conceit, but it wasn't. I wanted to enjoy life and to play an active part in it, but in no way did I want to have it appear that my life had more instances of en-

joyment or action than it actually did. Monsieur Prunelle, a physician and writer, whose habits of mind greatly appealed to me and
who was dreadfully ugly, later to become known as a corrupt
Deputy and Mayor of Lyon around 1833, and whom I knew somewhat during that period, said about me:

—He's a self-satisfied fool.

My acquaintances echoed this opinion. Perhaps they were right.

* * *

Chapter III

My earliest memory is biting Pison du Galland—my cousin and
wife to the writer and Deputy to the Constituent Assembly—on the
cheek or forehead. I can still see her, a stout woman of twenty-five
who wore a lot of rouge. It was apparently the rouge that set me
off. Sitting in the middle of the field called the *glacis de la porte de
Bonne*, her cheek was right at my height.

—Give me a kiss, Henri, she said.

I didn't want to. She got angry. I gave her a hearty bite. I can still
see the scene, but this is probably because the incident was made
much of and everyone kept talking to me about it. This *glacis de la
porte de Bonne* was covered in daisies. It's a pretty little flower and
I was gathering a bouquet of them. What was a field in 1786 is
probably in the middle of town today, south of the secondary
school's church. My aunt Séraphie declared that I was a monster
and had an appalling character. This aunt Séraphie displayed all of
the sourness of a God-fearing young woman who never managed to
get married. What had happened to her? I never found out—we
never hear do the full story about our relatives' scandalous pasts—
and I left the town for good at sixteen, following three years of most
intense passion that had relegated me to utter solitude.

My second character trait was of a far darker cast.

I had collected some rushes, again at the *glacis de la porte de
Bonne (Bonne de Lesdiguières)*. Ask for the rush's botanical name;
it's a type of grass, cylindrical in shape like a chicken feather and
about a foot long.

I had been brought back to the house; one of its second-story
windows gave onto the Grande-Rue at the corner with Place
Grenette. I was making a garden by cutting these rushes into small,
two-inch pieces and placing them inside the gap between the balcony and casement downspout. The kitchen knife I was using
slipped out of my hand and fell into the street; that is, about twelve
feet down, either near or directly onto a Madame Chenevaz. She
was the meanest woman in the entire city (mother of Candide
Chenevaz who, in his youth, adored Richardson's *Clarissa Harlowe*;

thereafter, he became one of Monsieur de Villèle's three hundred and was compensated by being given the position of first president at the *cour royale de Grenoble*; he died in Lyon a social outcast).

My aunt Séraphie said that I had tried to kill Madame Chenevaz; I was declared to have a dreadful personality, scolded by my beloved grandfather, Monsieur Gagnon (who was afraid of his daughter Séraphie, the most influential *dévote* in the city), and was even scolded by my Grand-aunt Mademoiselle Élisabeth Gagnon, who was of a lofty Spanish disposition.

I protested mightily; I suppose I was all of four years old; my horror of religion dates back to this period, a horror that my mind was eventually able, with great difficulty, to reduce to reasonable dimensions; the latter is quite a recent event, occurring no more than six years ago. Almost at the same time was born my instinctive filial love, impassioned during that period, for the republic.

I was no more than five years old.

This aunt Séraphie was my evil genius throughout my childhood; people in the family hated her but her opinion carried a lot of weight. I presume that at some time thereafter my father fell in love with her; at the least, they took long walks in the Granges, in a marsh beneath the city walls, during which I was very much the *fifth wheel* and bored to death. I would hide when it was time to take these walks. This marked the end of what little warm feeling I felt for my father.

As it happened, I was raised exclusively by my grandfather, Monsieur Henri Gagnon. This fine man had gone on a pilgrimage to Ferney in order to see Voltaire and was received there with distinction. He had a small bust of Voltaire, about as tall as one's fist, that sat atop an ebony base six inches high. (It was in somewhat odd taste, but the arts were never a strong point for Voltaire or my grandfather.)

This bust was placed opposite the desk where he would write; his study was buried within an enormous apartment that opened onto an elegant, flower-bedecked terrace. It was a rare treat for me to be allowed inside, and a still-rarer treat to see and touch the bust of Voltaire.

And yet, as far back as I can remember, I have always tremendously disliked Voltaire's writings; they seemed childish to me. I can honestly say that I never liked anything about this great man. At the time, I couldn't understand that he was France's legislator and apostle, its Martin Luther.

Monsieur Henri Gagnon wore a round, powdered wig with three rows of curls because he was a doctor of medicine, and a doctor much in fashion among the ladies; he was even accused of having been the lover of many of them, including one named Teysseire, one of the prettiest women in town, whom I don't recall ever seeing because at that time we were not on good terms, but who later informed me of this in a most odd way. My grandfather always looked eighty years old to me because of his wig. He had vapors (as do I, wretch that I am), rheumatism, and walked with difficulty, but on principle never rode in a carriage and never wore his hat: a small triangular hat to be tucked under one's arm; it was a source of joy for me when I managed to steal it away from him and put it on my head, which was considered by the entire family as wanting in respect; finally, out of respect, I stopped bothering about the triangular hat and his small walking stick, a stick with a boxwood-root handle decorated with shell inlay. My grandfather adored Hippocrates' apocryphal correspondence, which he would read in Latin (although he knew a little Greek), and the Johannes Bond edition of Horace, printed in horribly tiny characters. He passed on these two passions to me and, in fact, almost all of the things he liked, as I will explain a bit later.

If I ever return to Grenoble, I'll have to get someone to look up the birth and death certificates for this great man who so loved me and did not in the least love his own son, Monsieur [Romain] Gagnon, father of Monsieur Oronce Gagnon, a dragoon squadron leader who killed his opponent in a duel three years ago; I am grateful to him for doing so; it means he's probably not a complete fool. It's been thirty-three years since I last saw him; he's probably thirty-five years old or so.

I lost my grandfather while I was in Germany. Was it in 1807 or 1813? I can't recall exactly. I remember that I traveled to Grenoble to see him again; I found him in a most sorrowful state; this lovable man, once the center of the all-night revels he would frequent, had nearly stopped speaking altogether. He said to me:

—*C'est une visite d'adieu.*

Then he went on to speak of other things; he loathed foolish family displays of emotion.

One memory comes to mind. Around 1807, I had my portrait painted so that Madame Alexandrine Petit would have hers painted too, and because she objected to the number of sittings required, I took her to see a painter opposite the Diorama fountain who did oil paintings in a single sitting for 120 francs. My fine grandfather saw this portrait, which I had sent to my sister, I believe, to get rid of it; he had already lost much of his mental acuity; he said, as he looked at the portrait:

—That's the real one.

And then he fell back into his dejection and sadness. He died not long afterward, I seem to recall, at the age of eighty-two, I believe. If this date is accurate, he must have been sixty-one in 1789 and thus born around 1728. Sometimes he would tell the story of the battle of Assiette, a doomed assault in the Alps led by the chevalier de Belle-Isle in 1742, I think. His father, a strong-minded man, full of energy and honor, had sent him there as an army surgeon to put some backbone in him. My grandfather was starting his medical studies and was somewhere around eighteen or twenty years old, which also points to 1724 as being the year he was born.

He had an old house located in the finest site in the city, at Place Grenette, at the corner of the Grande-Rue; it was a sunny spot and looked out onto the loveliest square in the city, which, with its two rival cafés, was the center of its social life. There, on the second story, which was a very low-ceilinged but wonderfully cheerful place, my grandfather lived until 1789.

He must have been rich at that time, because he bought a superb house, located behind his own, that had belonged to the female members of the Marnais family. He occupied the third story of his house, on Place Grenette, along with the entire corresponding story of the Marnais house, and fashioned for himself the most impressive lodgings in the city. There was a staircase magnificent for its time and a salon that measured roughly thirty-five by twenty-eight feet.

The two bedrooms of this apartment, which looked out onto Place Grenette, were renovated and, among other things, a *gippe* was added (an interior wall made of plaster and bricks set edge-to-edge atop each other), in order to separate the bedroom of formidable Aunt Séraphie, Monsieur Gagnon's daughter, from that of my great-aunt Élisabeth, her sister. Iron dogs were placed into this *gippe* and on the plaster of each of these dogs I wrote: "Henri Beyle 1789." I can still see these beautiful inscriptions that won my grandfather's admiration.

—Since you have such fine handwriting, he said to me, you're ready to start learning Latin.

This word struck a kind of terror into me, and a pedant who was horrid for the sake of being horrid, Monsieur Joubert, tall, pale, quite thin, leaning on a blackthorn walking stick, came to show me, teach me the word *mura*, mulberry. We went to buy a primer from Monsieur Giroud, the bookseller, inside the courtyard that led onto the Place aux Herbes. At the time, I had no idea what an instrument of harm was being purchased for me there.

Here my troubles began.

But I've long put off telling a necessary story, one of the two or three, perhaps, that will make me throw these *Mémoires* into the fire.

My mother, Madame Henriette Gagnon, was a charming woman, and I was in love with my mother.

I hasten to add that I lost her when I was seven years old.

When I loved her at the age of six perhaps, in 1789, I had absolutely the same personality as in 1828 when I was madly in love with Alberthe de Rubempré. My approach to the pursuit of happiness had basically not changed in the slightest, with only one exception: as regards my physical constitution for the act of love, I was as Caesar would be if he were to come back to life to learn how to use cannon and small arms. I would have been a quick learner and that wouldn't have changed my tactics in any significant way.

I wanted to cover my mother with kisses and with no clothes to get in our way. She loved me passionately and would often kiss me; I returned her kisses with such intensity that she often had to leave the room. I despised my father when he turned up to interrupt our kisses. I always wanted to rub his nose in them. Kindly remember that I lost her in childbirth when I was barely seven years old.

She was plump, with a perfect complexion; she was very pretty, and I think that her only physical fault was that she wasn't tall enough. Her features displayed nobility and untroubled serenity; she was very high-spirited, preferring to see to her own needs rather than ordering around her three servants; and lastly, she would often read from Dante's *Divine Comedy* in the original; much later, I found five or six copies of various editions in her apartment, which had remained closed since her death.

She was lost in the full bloom of her youth and beauty in 1790; she must have been twenty-eight or thirty years old.

Here began my moral life. My aunt Séraphie had the gall to scold me for not crying enough. Imagine my pain and what I was feeling! But I thought that I'd be seeing her again the next day, I didn't understand what death was. So forty-five years have passed since I lost what I loved most in the world.

She can't take offense at the liberty I'm taking with her by revealing that I loved her; if I were ever to see her again, I'd tell her the same thing. Moreover, she never in any way took part in this love. She didn't engage in any Venetian intrigue over it, the way Madame Benzoni did with the author of *Nella*. As for myself, I was as guilty as it as possible to be; I was beside myself with love for her charms.

One evening, as if by chance, I had been put to bed on a mattress on the floor in her bedroom; this lively woman, as lightfooted as a doe, leapt over my mattress to reach her bed faster.

Her bedroom remained closed for ten years after she died. With difficulty, my father allowed me to place a waxed-canvas tablet there and to sketch out its mathematics in 1789. But no servants ever came in; they would have been roundly scolded if they had; I alone had the key. This fine feeling exhibited by my father makes me feel very proud of him, now that I think about it.

So she died in her bedroom, rue des Vieux-Jésuites, the fifth or sixth house on the left as you come from the Grande-Rue, opposite Monsieur Teysseire's house. I was born there; this house belonged to my father, who sold it when he started to build his new road, getting in over his head. This road, which led him to financial ruin, was named rue *Dauphin* (my father was extremely *ultra*, and a partisan of priests and nobles); I believe that it is now called *rue Lafayette*.

I spent my life at my grandfather's house, which was no more than a hundred feet away from ours.

Writers Read Stendhal

PAUL VALÉRY

Stendhal†

Fortunately, Beyle inherited from the century into which he was born the inestimable gift of liveliness.[1] The heavy-handed pundits and the bores never had an adversary quicker on the draw. Classics and romantics alike, in whose midst be moved and glittered, provoked his ready wit. He would have been amused (but decidedly flattered) if someone had shown him in a magic bowl his future swamped with doctoral theses. In the enchanted water he would have seen his sallies transformed into dogmas, his fancies turned into precepts, his quips developed into theories, doctrines extracted from his works, his brief maxims expanded into interminable homilies. His favorite subjects, *Napoleon, love, energy, happiness*, have produced volumes of exegesis. Philosophers have joined in the game. Scholarship has turned its magnifying glass on the least events of his life, on his scribbled notes, on his tradesmen's bills. The iconoclast's name and relics are venerated with a sort of naïve and mysterious idolatry. In accordance with custom his eccentricities have encouraged imitators. All that is most contrary to the man, to his freedom, his whims, and his love of opposition has come out of him. There is a good deal that is unexpected in the growth of a reputation. A *mystique* attaches to fame, even the fame of atheists.

"To hell with this Stendhal!" the spirit of Stendhal must sometimes cry out in some nonconformist reader.

He had to put up with a great deal from his father and from the worthy, serious-minded people who kept him under their thumb, or who bored him; he was the slave—in whom there was so little of the slave—of those pompous individuals who worked in the Coun-

---

† From *Master and Friends: The Collected Works of Paul Valéry*. Translated by Martin Turnell (Princeton: Princeton University Press, 1968), pp. 179–82, 192–203, 210–12. Reprinted by permission of Gallimard.
1. Henri Beyle was the real name of Stendhal [*Editor*].

cil of State, pillars of the Empire, counselors and consultants who were compelled unendingly to provide the hotheaded master of France, a France vastly expanded and in a continual state of crisis, with the required answers, the correct details, the figures, the decisions and specifications needed; he had seen at close quarters, noted, penetrated, and mocked the follies and virtues of people in official positions; had observed their occasional corruption, their invariable thirst for promotion, their profound and puerile schemes, their meticulous pettiness, their love of high-sounding language, their self-importance; the trouble they made for themselves and others; their incredible courage when confronted with mountains of files, columns of figures which crush the spirit without enriching the mind, the unending memoranda which give those in power the illusion of being alive, of knowing, foreseeing, and taking action. . . . Beyle always pits a pure young man, or a man of wit, against such gluttons for work, those monsters of silliness, greed, aridity, hypocrisy, or envy whose features, characters, and actions he portrayed on so many occasions. He learned from his own disgust, and knew in himself that true value may be divorced from vanity, from mountains of paper, lies, solemnity, and automatism. He had observed that those self-important personages so inevitably associated with the smooth working of the State are speechless nonentities the moment they are faced with the unexpected. A State that fails to keep a few improvisers on hand is a State without sinews. Anything that moves quickly becomes a threat. Anything out of the blue annihilates it.

It is easy to see from his writings that Beyle would have loved to handle great affairs as though they were a game. He creates with loving care men of clear, quick judgment, whose reactions are *as sudden as events*, as brisk and breath-taking as a surprise—ministers or bankers who direct, settle, or cut their way through circumstances, who combine charm and profundity, finesse and good sense, in whose skins we are aware of the presence of Beyle himself; we feel that he is plotting or impertinently ruling under their masks, and besides, that by creating them he is taking his revenge for not being the sort of person they are. Every writer compensates himself as best he can for the injustices of fate.

What is valuable in many men of value depends on the variety of roles they feel capable of playing. Henri Beyle, who would have made a good prefect by the standards of 1810, was nonetheless a devil of a man, always on the warpath against respectability. A skeptic who believed in love. This unruly character was a patriot. This man always noting down abstract ideas was interested in painting (or strove or pretended to be interested). He claimed to be a positivist, and worked out a *mystique* of passion.

Perhaps the growth of self-awareness, constant self-scrutiny tend to make us discover or create our diversity? The mind multiplies among its own possibilities, changes at every moment from what it was the moment before, listens to what it has just said, flies to the opposite, replies to itself, and watches the effect. I find in Stendhal the mobility and the fire, the rapid reflexes, the lightning retort, and the frank cynicism of that admirable pair of actors, Diderot and Beaumarchais. To know yourself is simply to predict yourself; to predict yourself ends in playing a part. Beyle's consciousness is a theater, and there is a good deal of the actor in the author. His work is full of sallies aimed at the audience. His prefaces stand down front and speak to it, wink at the reader, making signs of complicity, to convince him that he is the least foolish of the lot, that he is "in the know," that he alone gets the real subtlety. "No one but you and I," is what they say.

The effect on Stendhal's posthumous fame has been stupendous. He makes the reader proud to be his reader.

* * *

On one of his birthdays, Henri Brulard unbuttons his trousers and writes inside the belt: "I have just passed my fiftieth birthday."

Every admirer of Brulard must have spent a few minutes puzzling over this disclosure. What on earth can have prompted it? What was the point of this uncommon act? And what is the sense of the act that followed—that of writing it down? Did Beyle really record it on so personal a fly-leaf? If it was a piece of sheer invention, what was the object of such a curious fabrication? What future reader did he think would be impressed by it? Was he hoping to make himself appear a "living and singular figure," or to emphasize the sincerity of his diary by the almost indecent intimacy of this detail? *Hypotheses non fingo.* . . .

But apart from this, what was the point of his linguistic fantasies, the numerous notes in which he uses English or Italian words that have nothing particularly mysterious about them?

Why write: "Lettre *of the author of the** Cenci"? Or "C'est à *forthy* (sic) *seven* que Dominique," etc.?

On other occasions he indulges in unusual permutations of syllables: the *trespres*, the *ligionre*. . . .

I hope with all my heart that he did not flatter himself that this would put inquisitive people off the scent.

These habits seem to me to be nothing but a piece of cryptographic comedy. He pretends to write in code, in much the same

---

*English in the French text.

way that an actor pretends to eat or drink; and perhaps he does so in order to create the illusion that he is in league with himself, *that he is on rather more intimate terms with himself than the common run of Egos.*

Did he imagine vaguely that his native language—the language of the inner word—might secretly suggest to him, by being written down, some manner of feeling which was absolutely his own and independent of his country? The liberated Ego lives in Cosmopolis and thinks in all languages.

It is true that everyone who is jealously and strongly individual works out a secret language. What takes place in a family, or in a very tiny secret society like a couple of friends or lovers, also takes place in a single head. The immediate invention of a special vocabulary sets the seal on every form of complicity. Every form of private understanding is created at the expense of public conventions. Stendhal conspires with Stendhal under a variety of names— (Léautaud counted 129 pseudonyms)—conspires sometimes against Stendhal, always against fools, the self-important, the insensitive.

Stendhal, the inventor of the *happy few,* had such a marked taste for secrecy in matters of opinion, and for cliques who share the same likes and dislikes, that he makes me think of the spontaneous generation of those very small, very ardent, and vigorously uncompromising groups which have been responsible for all the innovations and ideas that on two or three occasions during the past fifty or sixty years have transformed our literature and our art. He is in a sense the forerunner of the "esotericism" which was the source of Naturalism, the Parnassians, and Symbolism. Experience has shown that coteries have their virtues. The "general public" is entitled to the normal and well-tried products of the industry. But the reconditioning of the industry itself calls for many tests, daring experiments that can only take place in laboratories, and only in laboratories is it possible to obtain the very high temperatures, the exceptionally rare reactions, the degrees of enthusiasm and the extremes of analysis without which science and art would follow an all too beaten track.

The characteristics of Beyle that I have just recalled are interesting because they are not easy to explain. They are no doubt the result of his theories and eccentricities: I think I detect in them an element of calculation, a tendency to gamble on the reader of the future, a marked determination to attract by carelessness and apparent improvisation—which imply and suggest a "just between you and me" relationship between the author and the unknown reader who is to be won over. . . .

Stendhal was an "ideologist" in his way, and liked precepts and principles. He formulated rules of conduct and aesthetics for his own guidance; he claimed to be a reasoner. It is not impossible that he did a good deal of reasoning where reason scarcely applies.

As for his eccentricities, they are plainly visible. But what is an eccentricity?

What is most striking about a page of Stendhal—what gives him away at once and attracts or irritates the reader—is the *tone*. He possesses, and for that matter affects, the most individual tone to be found in literature. This tone is so pronounced, it makes us so strongly aware of the man as a presence, that in the eyes of Stendhalians it excuses (1) his carelessness, his willful carelessness, and his contempt for all the formal qualities of style; (2) a good deal of pillaging and a great many plagiarisms. In all criminal cases the essential thing for the accussed is to make himself appear infinitely more interesting than his victims. What do we care about Beyle's victims? He transforms their sorry goods into books that are readable because he has introduced a certain *tone*.

What does the tone consist of? I may perhaps already have given the answer: be lively at all costs; write as you speak when you are a man of wit, with plenty of allusions even if they happen to be obscure, with gaps and leaps and lots of parentheses; write almost as though you were talking to yourself; keep up the pace of free and lively conversation; push it occasionally to the point where it becomes pure monologue; avoid the poetic style like the plague, and let the reader know that you are avoiding it, that you are breaking up the sentence per se which, because of its rhythm and length, would sound too pure and grand, would turn into the sustained style which Stendhal ridiculed and detested and in which he saw nothing but affectation, attitudinizing, and ulterior motives not in the least disinterested.

But it is a law of nature that you can only protect yourself against one form of affectation by using another.

The plans and prohibitions he prescribes for himself have one aim, to make us hear a real voice; his own pretension leads him to cram into a book all the symptoms most expressive of *sincerity*. His originality, so far as style is concerned, was to be bold enough to write in accordance with his own *character*, which he knew—and could even *imitate* to perfection.

I do not dislike the tone he created. There are times when I find it enchanting, and it never fails to entertain me; but contrary to the intention of the author, it does so by the comic effect that so much sincerity coupled with a little too much *life* invariably has on me. I confess to finding his accent three or four times too sincere; I sense a determination to be himself, to be genuine to the point of falsity. The genuineness he strives to promote changes imperceptibly under his pen into a tone designed to appear genuine. Truth and the will to truth together form an unstable mixture in which there is a ferment of contradiction and from which, without fail, a falsified product emerges.

How can we avoid selecting what is best out of the *true* we are working on? How we can avoid underlining, rounding off, touching up, adding color, trying to make it clearer, stronger, more disturbing, more intimate, more brutal than the model? *In literature the true is inconceivable.* Sometimes by simplicity, sometimes by oddity, sometimes by an exactness carried too far, sometimes by carelessness, sometimes by the confession of things that are more or less shameful, but always *selected*—as carefully selected as possible—always and by every means in the author's power, whether he is Pascal, Diderot, Rousseau, or Beyle, and whether the nakedness exhibited is that of a sinner, a cynic, a moralist, or a libertine, it is inevitably lighted, painted, and made up according to all the rules of the mind's theater. We know very well that people only expose themselves for an effect. A great saint who undressed in the market place knew it too. Everything that is contrary to custom is contrary to nature; it implies an effort, a conscious effort, an intention and therefore artifice. A woman undresses as though she were about to go onto the stage.

It follows therefore that there are two methods of falsification: the first is by *embellishment*, the second by the effort to *appear true*.

The second case is perhaps the one that reveals the most urgent pretensions. It is also a sign of despair of arousing public interest by purely literary means. Eroticism is never far from the minds of the utterly frank.

Moreover, the authors of confessions or memoirs or private diaries are invariably taken in by their own desire to shock; and we ourselves are the dupes of such dupes. It is never one's self that anyone wants to present; we know perfectly well that a real person has very little to tell us about what he is. He therefore writes the confessions of somebody else who is more impressive, purer, blacker, livelier, more sensitive, and even more himself than is permissible, for the self has its degrees. Anyone who confesses is a liar and is running away from what is really true, which is something null or shapeless and, in general, blurred. But every confession has an ulterior motive: fame, scandal, an excuse, or propaganda.

Beyle plays a dozen parts in his private theater—the dandy, the coolly rational man, the connoisseur of the fine arts, the soldier of 1812, the man in love with love, the politician, the historian. He gives himself a hundred pseudonyms, less as a disguise than to have the sensation of living a number of different lives. Like an actor on tour with his wigs, beards, and costumes, he carries round in his suitcase his Bombets, his Brulards, his Dominiques, his ironmongers. . . . In the *Mémoires d'un touriste*, made up as a prosperous traveling salesman, he talks as people do in a public conveyance, plays the economist, gives his views on administration, criticizes and suggests improvements in the plans for the layout of the railways of the future. He enjoys frightening himself about the espionage system of the police, is suspicious of the postal service, uses codes and signs so transparent that they would be comic if his fears were not fictitious and if he didn't want to be frightened. He populated his own life as best he could; and the pretense of being afraid helped him to feel that he was alive. Sometimes his exaggerated taste for mystification and the parade of secrecy reminds us vaguely of Punch. . . .

His temperament, which transformed his life into a perpetual scenario, made him in turn treat all human affairs as comedy. He was supremely sensitive to hypocrisy, and could smell a hundred miles off any suggestion of pretense or deceit in the social sphere. His belief in universal falsehood was unshakable and almost constitutional. He went so far as to seek out and to define the things it is impossible for a man to simulate (personal courage and absolute pleasure).

This highly "conscious" being attached immense value to the "natural." This painter of the double life was always creating types delicious in their simplicity—the Fabrices and the Luciens, people still pure, brave, young, and fresh, caught at the moment when they enter the world and begin acting in all innocence in the midst of a conspiratorial charade.

He himself acted his own person, and put on his own sincerity. What does being sincere mean? There is practically no difficulty when you are dealing with the relations between individuals; but what about one's relations with oneself? As I have said and repeated here, as soon as the "will" comes into the matter, the *will to be sincere with oneself* is inevitably a principle of falsification.

External sincerity is a pact between the two faces of man, one visible, the other a deduction or a probability. But to give a meaning to the idea of inner sincerity, there must be some sort of operation, some sort of division of the subject in order to introduce an absolute observer of our recent states of mind almost at the moment of their formation. . . . Now the function of this observer is to inform *us* whether the thought we have just had is in conformity or not with the persistent idea that we have, or should have, of ourselves. This crude analysis is sufficient to make explicit some of the conventions at work in the illusion of sincerity. Nor is that all. These very conventions are necessarily borrowed from the external world—for example, from acquired morality (to judge or blame oneself is play-acting).

Comedy and convention consist in substituting *what one knows* for *what one is*—and one does not know what one is.

In short, Stendhal's own sincerity—like all forms of willed sincerity, without exception—was part of the comedy of sincerity he played for himself. To be sincere means ignoring the observer who is the judge in the case, or imagining that he is *off duty*. In this way and in accordance with the promptings of his heart, Stendhal assessed the pretenses of others and felt that he was somehow infinitely *sensitized* to this kind of "truth" at one remove which can be attributed to anyone; and which anyone would reveal to a witness sufficiently withdrawn into his own reflective consciousness.

Almost every word he heard sounded like a lie in his ears. He could read people like an open book, or imagined he could.

The period was eminently suited to this form of intellectual activity.

Never were circumstances more propitious to every form of social masquerade. Ten different regimes in fifty years. People had lived as best they could under governments whose life was short and rough, all anxious to probe people's hearts and none of them inimical to fraud. People were used to the extraordinary suddenness with which the gravest personalities molted and renewed their plumage, to the abruptness with which badges changed, to the phantasmagoria of power, to the exits and re-entrances of legitimacy, freedom, eagles—of God Himself; to the astonishing spectacle of men reduced to distraction by the different oaths they had taken, divided between their memories, their emotions, their interests, their rancors, and their prognostications. . . . Some of them brought confusion on their heads by wearing a whole scaffolding of different hats and hair styles: wigs, skullcaps, red caps, hats with tricolor plumes, cocked hats, bourgeois hats. They were sometimes surprised, sometimes justified by events; now by the restoration of the fleur-de-lis, now by the backlash of 1815, now by the trickery of 1830, they were kept hanging on the moment, all set to change overnight from proscribers into proscribed, from suspects into magistrates, from ministers into fugitives; they lived through a more or less dangerous farce, and most of them, of all parties and under all sorts of masks, finished up by no longer believing in anything but money. This *positive* attitude emerged under Louis-Philippe, when finally the acquisition of wealth was put forward shamelessly and nakedly as the supreme moral lesson, the ultimate truth, the defin-

itive ethic of half a century of political and social experiment.
Stendhal saw the new world established on the ruins of the different regimes. He was in a position to observe the beginning of the
reign of talk and business. The parliamentary system was being
given a trial—a system which is by nature dramatic, rigorously sub-
ordinated to the laws of the theater, entirely made up of harangues
and retorts, sudden reversals of opinion; a system based on words,
on the emotional approach to events, on the outcome of meetings,
and on stage idols. The parties were in the process of formation. It
was the moment of the monstrous advent of statistical values, *public opinion*, averages, confused and fluctuating majorities; and the
rigging of majorities led to the immediate creation of the art of viti-
ating and poisoning the sources of power, already far from pure,
and of interpreting their unconscious utterances; the reign of abstract myths and their battles, the apparition and antics of black
specters and red specters, conjured up, exhibited, and controlled by
skillful showmen. . . .

The same period witnessed the loudly trumpeted entry into the
political sphere of the twin forces of finance and publicity. The era
of big business had dawned. The hour had struck for the vast in-
dustrial transformation of the world. But not all the sciences together could have succeeded without the power of the spoken
word. On all sides commercial eloquence created the vocation of
"gulls" in innumerable varieties. As the campaigns for the issue of
shares, prospectuses, and the irresistible publicity multiplied their
crude blandishments, wealth of all sorts was mobilized at the appeal of the jobbers and the joint-stock companies. Public credulity
exceeded the wildest expectations.

Even in literature there was a sort of revolution which initiated
the Muses into the behavior, violence, and charlatanism of elec-
toral campaigns. Among the poets, factions came into being which
adopted the rough and ruthless methods of the political parties.
Manifestoes were drawn up. The first night of *Hernani* was a real
"public meeting," with partisans and their adversaries well organized, their stations and roles worked out in advance.

This sort of thing did not encourage general frankness. Everyone
who counted lied, exaggerated, pretended. How could it have been
otherwise?

It was a time when all the highest posts were filled with "turn-
coats"; decorated with handsome "weathercocks."

The most august tongues had been heard to lie on the most sacred occasions. Swearing either by their swords, on the Gospels, or
by the Charter, everybody in turn found themselves compelled to
sacrifice solemnly to falsehood. The promises of peace, freedom,

and pardon—the pledges of the Allies—allies. The dispatches of the
Grand Army, the proclamations of a succession of authorities, the
newspapers of all political shades had lied, were lying, and were to
go on lying. People lied on the rostrum, in the pulpit, on the stock
exchange, at the Institute; even philosophy lied, even the arts, even
style! Chateaubriand and the poetic style lied. Monsieur Victor
Hugo and his friends disfigured and inflated the truth every time
they opened their mouths.

This brief review of the functions of lying between 1800 and
1840 could be duplicated by any reader with a little patience simply
by choosing sentences from the books, letters, and notes of
"Dominique."

* * *

This Beyle was a highly entertaining person, possessed by a great
desire to scandalize, along with more refined ambitions. He seldom
failed to point out that his reader ought to take offense at what he
said. He was by no means without the desired effect. He provoked
artists by his style, the powers that be by his disrespect, women by
his cynicism and his strategy. The loquacity, the opinions, the
"cheek" of this man of so much wit sometimes remind us of those
prehistoric commercial travelers who dazzled and exasperated their
corner of the inn table in the days of the last stagecoaches and the
first railways. But this Gaudissart who puts up at the *Grand Hôtel
de l'Europe et de l'Amour* is an *original* of the first order. What he
deals out is alive; it will live and he will live. His stock of singular
and glittering goods will excite many a philosophical mind. Serious
men will do their utmost to make themselves brisk and sharp like
him.

In my view, Henri Beyle is much more a type of mind than a man
of letters. He is too radically himself to be reducible to a writer.
That is why he rouses strong likes and dislikes, and why I like him.

I have seen Pierre Louÿs heap insults on his intolerable prose,
fling *Le Rouge et le Noir* on the floor and stamp on it with a strange
and perhaps justifiable fury. . . .

But Stendhal, such as he is and whatever he is, has become, in
spite of the Muses, in spite of his pen and almost in spite of himself, one of the demigods of our literature, a master of that ardent
and abstract style which is drier and lighter than any other, and
characteristic of the French. His work is of a kind that deals only in
actions and ideas, disdains ornament, laughs at harmony and formal balance. It is concentrated in the flash, the phrase, the tone,
the sting; it multiplies the short cuts and the lightning reactions of
the mind. It is always fast-moving, quick to be insolent; it seems
ageless and in a sense without substance; it is personal to the extreme, directly *centered* in the author, as disconcerting as a retort,

avoiding both the dogmatic and the poetic, which it finds about equally detestable.

We should never have done with Stendhal. I can think of no higher praise.

JULES JANIN

On *The Red and the Black*†

Never have I witnessed more anti-Jesuit, anti-bourgeois rage than in M. de Stendhal's book. Under his pen everything withers away, never to bloom again; the finest day, the loveliest scenery, the most joyous sentiments. With admirable sangfroid he steers his hero, his monster, through a thousand depravities, a thousand acts of folly worse than depravities; it's a strange pleasure indeed that our writer indulges in, bringing together a comprehensive assembly of all of the tedious complaints, all of the posturing, all of the lies, all of the superstitions, all of the ruthlessness of our social condition; and it's with a strange relentlessness that he establishes the France from before our July Revolution as being inferior to the France of barbarousness and pedantry we know today. Heavens! Could that *really* be what provincial France is like? And further on, when the hero is in Paris, could that *really* be what Paris is like? To which we reply: *perhaps*; for the book is well written.

* * *

The remarkable part of this novel is Julien's schooling at the seminary. Here the author's rage and horror are redoubled. This hideous tableau is beyond description; it impressed me as much as the first ghost story I heard at my nurse's knee. Here is what it depicts: The seminary at Besançon, similar to the way Verrières is represented as a typical city, is offered as an illustration of seminaries in general, made up of loutish brutes, yokels, loathsome peasants, and other aspirants to the priesthood, delighted to have a cassock and a bowl of soup to themselves; greedily wolfing down their bread and *choucroute*; dimwitted wretches, hypocritical underlings, gnarly-handed, red-nosed moralizers. In this seminary, as in Verrières, there are Jansenists and Jesuits. The Jansenist is a very fine man whom the Jesuit sends packing. The Jesuit is a scoundrel forever laying traps for Julien. This seminary is the counterpart of Verrières: Life there is appalling, hopeless, a combination of abject

† From *Revue des Temps Modernes*, 1830. Translated by Margaret Flynn for this Norton Critical Edition.

vice and hypocritical folly. It's Tartuffe in his shirtsleeves, Tartuffe in a dirty monk's habit, standing on the street corner, acting on his seamiest impulses. There is food for thought here. If seminaries long ago—"long ago" meaning "last week"—were really like this, M. de Stendhal has done us a favor; because he takes responsibility for being so vile, I'll forgive him this time.

* * *

So Mademoiselle de La Mole is mad. She calls Julien back to her bedchamber, cuts off a hank of her beautiful blond hair for Julien and tosses it out into the garden for him. For Julien's sake, she rejects the marquis de Croisenois' offer of marriage; she becomes pregnant by Julien, declaring to her father that she loves Julien; her love is a fever, a kind of madness. This Mathilde is insane, she cries, she laughs, she calls on death to take her, she is as high-strung as a heroine; the likes of this girl have never before been imagined. I find it impossible to believe that there is a social scene in Paris resembling the one that Mr. de Stendhal paints for us. For a *bourgeois* coming from a narrow social sphere, these kinds of depictions always appear improbable. I ask those who have a broad knowledge of worldly society at its highest level—the society populated by lords, high-ranking Jesuits, men with legendary names and vast fortunes—to be so kind as to tell me what they think of Mademoiselle de La Mole. And if, by chance, her behavior is true to life, God save me from women of the court, women at court whom no-one wants to court, and fathers who go to court!

* * *

It occurs to me that I have spoken at great length about this chronicle; I would have been much wiser to speak about its author. While Mr. de Stendhal's latest novel is, despite its many serious (and seriously immoral) improbabilities, a remarkable, lively, finely hued work, full of issues and emotions, it is worth reading, even though contemporary literature has largely fallen into oblivion. Mr. de Stendhal is one of these three-faced writers who sport multiple names, ever serious-minded; you can't be too careful around them. He is a cold-eyed observer, a merciless mocker, a spiteful skeptic who is happy to believe in nothing, because having no beliefs entitles him to have no respect for anything and to sully whatever he touches. An author whose body and soul are thus constituted goes on his merry way, untroubled by worry or regret, spewing his venom onto everything he comes across: youth, beauty, grace, life's illusions; even the fields, forests, and flowers are laid waste and blighted. This stripe of *philosophe* is like an evil genie from the Orient who compels you to follow him, leading you on in spite of yourself; you are unable to break free of him; he threatens you endlessly, making you stop at delightful sites only to lead you to fearsome precipices. I have no doubt that a book so richly imagined can be a successful one, but never, never will you love the author who has shattered your illusions, who has shown the world to be too ugly a place for you to live in it without blanching in horror.

Along with his unconquerable need to paint everything in the colors of ugliness and to raise his voice the better to frighten you, we must add that Mr. de Stendhal is a maker of paradoxes. In the most true-to-life moment of his fiction, at the very instant he sees that you are engaged and interested, he suspends his narrative, breaks off in mid-sentence, stops abruptly, and coldly fires an unexpected paradox at you. Yes, he even exploits paradox. He has managed to make paradox, this powerful aide to artists and historians, into an odious thing. Paradox, worthy helper of speakers and writers, tireless companion who gives rest to his master when he is tired, who reassures him when he trembles, who renews his strength when he is weary. Well! Mr. de Stendhal couldn't care less about this benevolent servant: He has enslaved it, denied it all honor, and treated it like a thug, tossed it into the fire, and calmly watched it burn. To it, he has done the same thing he has done to friendship, love, vengeance, all of the human heart's passions, as if it were something over and done with, unwanted and cast aside. How sad it is to see a man brought so low. How sorry we should feel for him, the writer who bids farewell to his last remaining writerly resources! How pathetic I find him for not believing in anything, not even in the fiction he invents, not even in the virtues he seeks to depict, nay, not even in the paradox that he creates and should respect as his final resource, as the sole genie who can still inspire anyone who has seen it all, written it all, thought it all, and who has nothing left to learn, nothing new to feel.

CRITICISM

ERICH AUERBACH

In the Hôtel de La Mole†

Julien Sorel, the hero of Stendhal's novel *Le Rouge et le Noir* (1830), an ambitious and passionate young man, son of an uneducated petty bourgeois from the Franche-Comté, is conducted by a series of circumstances from the seminary at Besançon, where he has been studying theology, to Paris and the position of secretary to a gentleman of rank, the Marquis de La Mole, whose confidence he gains. Mathilde, the marquis's daughter, is a girl of nineteen, witty, spoiled, imaginative, and so arrogant that her own position and circle begin to bore her. The dawning of her passion for her father's *domestique* is one of Stendhal's masterpieces and has been greatly admired. One of the preparatory scenes, in which her interest in Julien begins to awaken, is the following, from Book II, chapter 4:

> Un matin que l'abbé travaillait avec Julien, dans la biblio-
> thèque du marquis, à l'éternel procès de Frilair:
> —Monsieur, dit Julien tout à coup, dîner tous les jours avec
> madame la marquise, est-ce un de mes devoirs, ou est-ce une
> bonté que l'on a pour moi?
> —C'est un honneur insigne! reprit l'abbé, scandalisé. Jamais
> M. N. . . . l'académicien, qui, depuis quinze ans, fait une cour
> assidue, n'a pu l'obtenir pour son neveu M. Tanbeau.
> —C'est pour moi, monsieur, la partie la plus pénible de mon
> emploi. Je m'ennuyais moins au séminaire. Je vois bâiller
> quelquefois jusqu'à mademoiselle de La Mole, qui pourtant
> doit être accoutumée à l'amabilité des amis de la maison.
> J'ai peur de m'endormir. De grâce, obtenez-moi la permission
> d'aller dîner à quarante sous dans quelque auberge obscure.
> L'abbé, véritable parvenu, était fort sensible à l'honneur de

† From *Mimesis: the Representation of Reality in Western Literature*. Translated by Willard R. Trask. (Princeton: Princeton UP, 1953) pp. 454–66. Reprinted by permission of Princeton University Press.

Professor Auerbach's epochal *Mimesis* uses a series of texts selected over a period of three thousand years, studying them closely to reveal the differing conceptions of reality they represent through such elements as the syntactic linking of generals and particulars, abstractions and specifics. A crucial instance of a new and apparently random realism, which wholly fractures the old idea of arbitrarily divided levels of style, is provided by the chapter on Stendhal and Balzac. This is a major crux in Auerbach's book; in his terms, Stendhal and Balzac represent a turning point in the representation of reality, a turn that his book exemplifies as well as defines. His instances seem to be chosen at random; yet they illustrate fundamental principles of conflict and growth, even as Stendhal, with a woman, an abbé, and a young man in a library, suggests an entire complex of social forces in post-Napoleonic Europe.

dîner avec un grand seigneur. Pendant qu'il s'efforçait de faire comprendre ce sentiment par Julien, un bruit léger leur fit tourner la tête. Julien vit mademoiselle de La Mole qui écoutait. Il rougit. Elle était venue chercher un livre et avait tout entendu; elle prit quelque considération pour Julien. Celui-là n'est pas né à genoux, pensa-t-elle, comme ce vieil abbé. Dieu! qu'il est laid.

A dîner, Julien n'osait pas regarder mademoiselle de La Mole, mais elle eut la bonté de lui adresser la parole. Ce jour-là, on attendait beaucoup de monde, elle l'engagea à rester. . . .

(One morning while the Abbé was with Julien in the Marquis's library, working on the interminable Frilair suit:

"Monsieur," said Julien suddenly, "is dining with Madame la Marquise every day one of my duties, or is it a favor to me?"

"It is an extraordinary honor!" the Abbé corrected him, scandalized. "Monsieur N., the academician, who has been paying court here assiduously for fifteen years, was never able to manage it for his nephew, Monsieur Tanbeau."

"For me, Monsieur, it is the most painful part of my position. Nothing at the seminary bored me so much. I even see Mademoiselle de la Mole yawning sometimes, yet she must be well inured to the amiabilities of the guests of this house. I am in dread of falling asleep. Do me the favor of getting me permission to eat a forty-sou dinner at some inn."

The Abbé, a true parvenu, was extremely conscious of the honor of dining with a noble lord. While he was trying to inculcate this sentiment into Julien, a slight sound made them turn. Julien saw Mademoiselle de la Mole listening. He blushed. She had come for a book and had heard everything; she began to feel a certain esteem for Julien. He was not born on his knees, like that old Abbé, she thought. God, how ugly he is!

At dinner Julien did not dare to look at Mademoiselle de la Mole, but she condescended to speak to him. A number of guests were expected that day, she asked him to stay. . . .)

The scene, as I said, is designed to prepare for a passionate and extremely tragic love intrigue. Its function and its psychological value we shall not here discuss; they lie outside of our subject. What interests us in the scene is this: it would be almost incomprehensible without a most accurate and detailed knowledge of the political situation, the social stratification, and the economic circumstances of a perfectly definite historical moment, namely, that in which France found itself just before the July Revolution; accordingly, the novel bears the subtitle, *Chronique de 1830*. Even the boredom which reigns in the dining room and salon of this no-

ble house is no ordinary boredom. It does not arise from the fortuitous personal dullness of the people who are brought together
there; among them there are highly educated, witty, and sometimes
important people, and the master of the house is intelligent and
amiable. Rather, we are confronted, in their boredom, by a phenomenon politically and ideologically characteristic of the Restoration period. In the seventeenth century, and even more in the
eighteenth, the corresponding salons were anything but boring. But
the inadequately implemented attempt which the Bourbon regime
made to restore conditions long since made obsolete by events, creates, among its adherents in the official and ruling classes, an atmosphere of pure convention, of limitation, of constraint and lack of
freedom, against which the intelligence and good will of the persons
involved are powerless. In these salons the things which interest
everyone—the political and religious problems of the present, and
consequently most of the subjects of its literature or of that of the
very recent past—could not be discussed, or at best could be discussed only in official phrases so mendacious that a man of taste
and tact would rather avoid them. How different from the intellectual daring of the famous eighteenth-century salons, which, to be
sure, did not dream of the dangers to their own existence which they
were unleashing! Now the dangers are known, and life is governed
by the fear that the catastrophe of 1793 might be repeated. As these
people are conscious that they no longer themselves believe in the
thing they represent, and that they are bound to be defeated in any
public argument, they choose to talk of nothing but the weather,
music, and court gossip. In addition, they are obliged to accept as
allies snobbish and corrupt people from among the newly rich bourgeoisie, who, with the unashamed baseness of their ambition and
with their fear for their ill-gotten wealth, completely vitiate the atmosphere of society. So much for the pervading boredom.

But Julien's reaction, too, and the very fact that he and the former director of his seminary, the Abbé Pirard, are present at all in
the house of the Marquis de la Mole, are only to be understood in
terms of the actual historical moment. Julien's passionate and
imaginative nature has from his earliest youth been filled with enthusiasm for the great ideas of the Revolution and of Rousseau, for
the great events of the Napoleonic period; from his earliest youth
he has felt nothing but loathing and scorn for the piddling
hypocrisy and the petty lying corruption of the classes in power
since Napoleon's fall. He is too imaginative, too ambitious, and too
fond of power to be satisfied with a mediocre life within the bourgeoisie, such as his friend Fouqué proposes to him. Having observed that a man of petty-bourgeois origin can attain to a situation
of command only through the all-powerful Church, he has con-

sciously and deliberately become a hypocrite; and his great talents would assure him a brilliant intellectual career, were not his real personal and political feelings, the direct passionateness of his nature, prone to burst forth at decisive moments. One such moment of self-betrayal we have in the passage before us, when Julien confides his feelings in the Marquise's salon to the Abbé Pirard, his former teacher and protector; for the intellectual freedom to which it testifies is unthinkable without an admixture of intellectual arrogance and a sense of inner superiority hardly becoming in a young ecclesiastic and protégé of the house. (In this particular instance his frankness does him no harm; the Abbé Pirard is his friend, and upon Mathilde, who happens to overhear him, his words make an entirely different impression from that which he must expect and fear.) The Abbé is here described as a true parvenu, who knows how highly the honor of sitting at a great man's table should be esteemed and hence disapproves of Julien's remarks; as another motive for the Abbé's disapproval Stendhal could have cited the fact that uncritical submission to the evil of this world, in full consciousness that it is evil, is a typical attitude for strict Jansenists; and the Abbé Pirard is a Jansenist. We know from the previous part of the novel that as director of the seminary at Besançon he had had to endure much persecution and much chicanery on account of his Jansenism and his strict piety which no intrigues could touch; for the clergy of the province were under the influence of the Jesuits. When the Marquis de La Mole's most powerful opponent, the Abbé de Frilair, a vicar-general to the bishop, had brought a suit against him, the Marquis had made the Abbé Pirard his confidant and had thus learned to value his intelligence and uprightness; so that finally, to free him from his untenable position at Besançon, the Marquis had procured him a benefice in Paris and somewhat later had taken the Abbé's favorite pupil, Julien Sorel, into his household as private secretary.

The characters, attitudes, and relationships of the dramatis personae, then, are very closely connected with contemporary historical circumstances; contemporary political and social conditions are woven into the action in a manner more detailed and more real than had been exhibited in any earlier novel, and indeed in any works of literary art except those expressly purporting to be politico-satirical tracts. So logically and systematically to situate the tragically conceived life of a man of low social position (as here that of Julien Sorel) within the most concrete kind of contemporary history and to develop it therefrom—this is an entirely new and highly significant phenomenon. The other circles in which Julien Sorel moves—his father's family, the house of the mayor of Verrières, M. de Rênal, the seminary at Besançon—are sociologically defined in conformity with the historical moment with the same penetration as is the La Mole household; and not one of the minor characters—the old priest Chélan, for example, or the director of the *dépôt de mendicité* [poorhouse], Valenod—would be conceivable outside the particular historical situation of the Restoration period, in the manner in which they are set before us. The same laying of a contemporary foundation for events is to be found in Stendhal's other novels—still incomplete and too narrowly circumscribed in *Armance*, but fully developed in the later works: in the *Chartreuse de Parme* (which, however, since its setting is a place not yet greatly affected by modern development, sometimes gives the effect of being a historical novel), as also in *Lucien Leuwen*, a novel of the Louis-Philippe period, which Stendhal left unfinished. In the latter, indeed, in the form in which it has come down to us, the element of current history and politics is too heavily emphasized: it is not always wholly integrated into the course of the action and is set forth in far too great detail in proportion to the principal theme; but perhaps in a final revision Stendhal would have achieved an organic articulation of the whole. Finally, his autobiographical works, despite the capricious and erratic "egotism" of their style and manner, are likewise far more closely, essentially, and concretely connected with the politics, sociology, and economics of the period than are, for example, the corresponding works of Rousseau or Goethe; one feels that the great events of contemporary history affected Stendhal much more directly than they did the other two; Rousseau did not live to see them, and Goethe had managed to keep aloof from them.

To have stated this is also to have stated what circumstance it was which, at that particular moment and in a man of that particular period, gave rise to modern tragic realism based on the contemporary; it was the first of the great movements of modern times in which large masses of men consciously took part—the French Revolution with all the consequent convulsions which spread from it over Europe. From the Reformation movement, which was no less powerful and which aroused the masses no less, it is distinguished by the much faster tempo of its spread, its mass effects, and the changes which it produced in practical daily life within a comparatively extensive territory; for the progress then achieved in transportation and communication, together with the spread of elementary education resulting from the trends of the Revolution itself, made it possible to mobilize the people far more rapidly and in a far more unified direction; everyone was reached by the same ideas and events far more quickly, more consciously, and more uniformly. For Europe there began that process of temporal concentration, both of historical events themselves and of everyone's knowledge of them, which has since made tremendous progress and which not only permits us to prophesy a unification of human life throughout the world but has in a certain sense already achieved it. Such a development abrogates or renders powerless the entire social structure of orders and categories previously held valid; the tempo of the changes demands a perpetual and extremely difficult effort toward inner adaptation and produces intense concomitant crises. He who would account to himself for his real life and his place in human society is obliged to do so upon a far wider practical foundation and in a far larger context than before, and to be continually conscious that the social base upon which he lives is not constant for a moment but is perpetually changing through convulsions of the most various kinds.

We may ask ourselves how it came about that modern consciousness of reality began to find literary form for the first time precisely in Henri Beyle of Grenoble. Beyle-Stendhal was a man of keen intelligence, quick and alive, mentally independent and courageous, but not quite a great figure. His ideas are often forceful and inspired, but they are erratic, arbitrarily advanced, and, despite all their show of boldness, lacking in inward certainty and continuity. There is something unsettled about his whole nature: his fluctuation between realistic candor in general and silly mystification in particulars, between cold self-control, rapturous abandonment to sensual pleasures, and insecure and sometimes sentimental vaingloriousness, is not always easy to put up with; his literary style is very impressive and unmistakably original, but it is short-winded, not uniformly successful, and only seldom wholly takes possession of and fixes the subject. But, such as he was, he offered himself to the moment; circumstances seized him, tossed him about, and laid upon him a unique and unexpected destiny; they formed him so that he was compelled to come to terms with reality in a way which no one had done before him.

When the Revolution broke out Stendhal was a boy of six; when he left his native city of Grenoble and his reactionary, solidly bourgeois family, who though glumly sulking at the new situation were still very wealthy, and went to Paris, he was sixteen. He arrived there immediately after Napoleon's *coup d'état*; one of his relatives, Pierre Daru, was an influential adherent of the First Consul; after some hesitations and interruptions, Stendhal made a brilliant career in the Napoleonic administration. He saw Europe on Napoleon's expeditions; he grew to be a man, and indeed an extremely elegant man of the world; he also became, it appears, a useful administrative official and a reliable, cold-blooded organizer who did not lose his calm even in danger. When Napoleon's fall threw

Stendhal out of the saddle, he was in his thirty-second year. The first, active, successful, and brilliant part of his career was over. Thenceforth he has no profession and no place claims him. He can go where he pleases, so long as he has money enough and so long as the suspicious officials of the post-Napoleonic period have no objection to his sojourns. But his financial circumstances gradually become worse; in 1821 he is exiled from Milan, where he had first settled down, by Metternich's police; he goes to Paris, and there he lives for another nine years, without a profession, alone, and with very slender means. After the July Revolution his friends get him a post in the diplomatic service; since the Austrians refuse him an exequatur for Trieste, he has to go as consul to the little port of Città Vecchia; it is a dreary place to live, and there are those who try to get him into trouble if he prolongs his visits to Rome unduly; to be sure, he is allowed to spend a few years in Paris on leave—so long, that is, as one of his protectors is Minister of Foreign Affairs. Finally he falls seriously ill in Città Vecchia and is given another leave in Paris; he dies there in 1842, smitten by apoplexy in the street, not yet sixty. This is the second half of his life; during this period, he acquires the reputation of being a witty, eccentric, politically and morally unreliable man; during this period, he begins to write. He writes first on music, on Italy and Italian art, on love; it is not until he is forty-three and is in Paris during the first flowering of the Romantic movement (to which he contributed in his way) that he publishes his first novel.

From this sketch of his life it should appear that he first reached the point of accounting for himself, and the point of realistic writing, when he was seeking a haven in his "storm-tossed boat," and discovered that, for his boat, there was no fit and safe haven; when, though in no sense weary or discouraged, yet already a man of forty, whose early and successful career lay far behind him, alone and comparatively poor, he became aware, with all the sting of that knowledge, that he belonged nowhere. For the first time, the social world around him became a problem; his feeling that he was different from other men, until now borne easily and proudly, doubtless now first became the predominant concern of his consciousness and finally the recurring theme of his literary activity. Stendhal's realistic writing grew out of his discomfort in the post-Napoleonic world and his consciousness that he did not belong to it and had no place in it. Discomfort in the given world and inability to become part of it is, to be sure, characteristic of Rousseauvian romanticism, and it is probable that Stendhal had something of that even in his youth; there is something of it in his congenital disposition, and the course of his youth can only have strengthened such tendencies,

which, so to speak, harmonized with the tenor of life of his generation; on the other hand, he did not write his recollections of his
youth, the *Vie de Henry Brulard*, until he was in his thirties [actu-
ally, his fifties: R.M.A.], and we must allow for the possibility that,
from the viewpoint of his later development, from the viewpoint of
1832, he overstressed such motifs of individualistic isolation. It is,
in any case, certain that the motifs and expressions of his isolation
and his problematic relation to society are wholly different from the
corresponding phenomena in Rousseau and his early romantic dis-
ciples.

Stendhal, in contrast to Rousseau, had a bent for practical affairs
and the requisite ability; he aspired to sensual enjoyment of life as
given; he did not withdraw from practical reality from the outset,
did not entirely condemn it from the outset—instead he attempted,
and successfully at first, to master it. Material success and material
enjoyments were desirable to him; he admires energy and the ability to master life, and even his cherished dreams (the silence of
happiness) are more sensual, more concrete, more dependent upon
human society and human creations (Cimarosa, Mozart, Shakespeare, Italian art) than those of the *Promeneur Solitaire*. Not until
success and pleasure began to slip away from him, not until practical circumstances threatened to cut the ground from under his
feet, did the society of his time become a problem and a subject to
him. Rousseau did not find himself at home in the social world he
encountered, which did not appreciably change during his lifetime;
he rose in it without thereby becoming happier or more reconciled
to it, while it appeared to remain unchanged. Stendhal lived while
one earthquake after another shook the foundations of society;
one of the earthquakes jarred him out of the everyday course of life
prescribed for men of his station, flung him, like many of his contemporaries, into previously inconceivable adventures, events, responsibilities, tests of himself, and experiences of freedom and
power; another flung him back into a new everyday which he
thought more boring, more stupid, and less attractive than the old;
the most interesting thing about it was that it too gave no promise
of enduring; new upheavals were in the air, and indeed broke out
here and there even though not with the power of the first.

Because Stendhal's interest arose out of the experiences of his
own life, it was held not by the structure of a possible society but
by the changes in the society actually given. Temporal perspective
is a factor of which he never loses sight, the concept of incessantly
changing forms and manners of life dominates his thoughts—the
more so as it holds a hope for him: In 1880 or 1930 I shall find
readers who understand me! I will cite a few examples. When he
speaks of La Bruyère's wit (*Henry Brulard*, chapter 30), it is appar-

ent to him that this type of formative endeavor of the intellect has lost in validity since 1789:

> "Wit, so delicious for one who relishes it, does not last long. As a peach goes bad in a few days, so wit goes bad in a couple of centuries, even quicker if there is a revolution in the mutual relations of the different social classes."

The *Souvenirs d'égotisme* contain an abundance of observations (for the most part truly prophetic) based on temporal perspective. He foresees (chapter 7, near the end) that "at the time when this chatter is read" it will have become a commonplace to make the ruling classes responsible for the crimes of thieves and murderers; he fears, at the beginning of chapter 9, that all his bold utterances, which he dares put forth only with fear and trembling, will have become platitudes ten years after his death, if heaven grants him a decent allowance of life, say eighty or ninety years; in the next chapter he speaks of one of his friends who pays an unusually high price for the favors of an "honest working-class woman," and adds in explanation: "five hundred francs in 1832, that amounts to a thousand in 1872"—that is, forty years after the time at which he is writing and thirty after his death.

It would be possible to quote many more passages of the same general import. But it is unnecessary, for the element of time-perspective is apparent everywhere in the presentation itself. In his realistic writings, Stendhal everywhere deals with the reality which presents itself to him: "I take at random whatever turns up in my path," he says not far from the passage just quoted: in his effort to understand men, he does not pick and choose among them; this method, as Montaigne knew, is the best for eliminating the arbitrariness of one's own constructions, and for surrendering oneself to reality as given. But the reality which he encountered was so constituted that, without permanent reference to the immense changes of the immediate past and without a premonitory searching after the imminent changes of the future, one could not represent it; all the human figures and all the human events in his work appear upon a ground politically and socially disturbed. To bring the significance of this graphically before us, we have but to compare him with the best-known realistic writers of the pre-Revolutionary eighteenth century: with Lesage or the Abbé Prévost, with the preeminent Henry Fielding or with Goldsmith; we have but to consider how much more accurately and profoundly he enters into given contemporary reality than Voltaire, Rousseau, and the youthful realistic work of Schiller, and upon how much broader a basis than Saint-Simon, whom, though in the very incomplete edition then available, he read assiduously. Insofar as the serious

realism of modern times cannot represent man otherwise than as
embedded in a total reality, political, social, and economic, which is
concrete and constantly evolving—as is the case today in any novel
or film—Stendhal is its founder.

However, the attitude from which Stendhal apprehends the
world of events and attempts to reproduce it with all its intercon-
nections is as yet hardly influenced by Historism—which, though it
penetrated into France in his time, had little effect upon him. For
that very reason we have referred in the last few pages to time-
perspective and to a constant consciousness of changes and cata-
clysms, but not to a comprehension of evolutions. It is not too easy
to describe Stendhal's inner attitude toward social phenomena. It is
his aim to seize their every nuance; he most accurately represents
the particular structure of any given milieu, he has no preconceived
rationalistic system concerning the general factors which determine social life, nor any pattern-concept of how the ideal society
ought to look; but in particulars his representation of events is oriented, wholly in the spirit of classic ethical psychology, upon an
"analysis of the human heart," not upon discovery or premonitions
of historical forces; we find rationalistic, empirical, sensual motifs
in him, but hardly those of romantic Historism. Absolutism, religion and the Church, the privileges of rank, he regards very much
as would an average protagonist of the Enlightenment, that is, as a
web of superstition, deceit, and intrigue; in general, artfully contrived intrigue (together with passion) plays a decisive role in his
plot construction, while the historical forces which are the basis of
it hardly appear. Naturally all this can be explained by his political
viewpoint, which was democratic-republican; this alone sufficed to
render him immune to romantic Historism; besides which the emphatic manner of such writers as Chateaubriand displeased him in
the extreme. On the other hand, he treats even the classes of society which, according to his views, should be closest to him, extremely critically and without a trace of the emotional values which
romanticism attached to the word *people.* The practically active
bourgeoisie, with its respectable money-making, inspires him with
unconquerable boredom; he shudders at the "republican virtue" of
the United States, and despite his ostensible lack of sentimentality
he regrets the fall of the social culture of the *ancien régime.* "My
word, there's no more wit," he writes in chapter 30 of *Henri Brulard,* "everyone is saving all his energy for a job which will give him
standing in the world." No longer is birth or intelligence or the self-
cultivation of the *honnête homme* the deciding factor—it is ability
in some profession. This is no world in which Stendhal-Dominique
can live and breathe. Of course, like his heroes, he too can work
and work efficiently, when that is what is called for. But how can

one take anything like practical professional work seriously in the long run! Love, music, passion, intrigue, heroism—these are the things that make life worthwhile. . . .

Stendhal is an aristocratic son of the big bourgeoisie of the old regime, he will and can be no nineteenth-century bourgeois. He says so himself time and again: "My views were Republican even in my youth but my family handed down their aristocratic instincts to me" (*Brulard*, ch. 14); "since the Revolution theater audiences have become stupid" (*Brulard*, ch. 22); "I was a liberal myself (in 1821), and yet I found the liberals outrageously stupid" (*Souvenirs d'égotisme*, ch. 6); "to converse with a fat provincial tradesman makes me dull and unhappy all day" (*Égotisme*, ch. 7 and *passim*)— these and similar remarks, which sometimes also refer to his physical constitution ("Nature gave me the delicate nerves and sensitive skin of a woman," *Brulard*, ch. 32), occur plentifully. Sometimes he has pronounced accesses of socialism: in 1811, he writes, "energy was to be found only in the class which is struggling to satisfy real needs" (*Brulard*, ch. 2). But he finds the smell and the noise of the masses unendurable, and in his books, outspokenly realistic though they are in other respects, we find no "people," either in the romantic "folk" sense or in the socialist sense—only petty bourgeois, and occasional accessory figures such as soldiers, domestic servants, and coffee-house mademoiselles. Finally, he sees the individual man far less as the product of his historical situation and as taking part in it, than as an atom within it; a man seems to have been thrown almost by chance into the milieu in which he lives; it is a resistance with which he can deal more or less successfully, not really a culture-medium with which he is organically connected. In addition, Stendhal's conception of mankind is on the whole preponderantly materialistic and sensualistic; an excellent illustration of this occurs in *Henry Brulard* (ch. 26): "What I call the character of a man is his habitual manner of undertaking the pursuit of happiness, or to put it in clearer but less definite terms, *the sum of his moral habits*." But in Stendhal, happiness, even though highly organized human beings can find it only in the mind, in art, passion, or fame, always has a far more sensory and earthy coloring than in the romanticists. His aversion to philistine efficiency, to the type of bourgeois that was coming into existence, could be romantic too. But a romantic would hardly conclude a passage on his distaste for money-making with the words: "I have had the rare pleasure of doing throughout my life pretty much what it pleased me to do" (*Brulard*; ch. 32). His conception of wit and of freedom is still entirely that of the pre-Revolutionary eighteenth century, although it is only with effort and a little spasmodically that he succeeds in realizing it in his own person. For freedom he has to pay the price of poverty and loneliness and his wit easily becomes paradox, bitter and wounding: "a gaiety which terrifies" (*Brulard*, ch. 6). His wit no longer has the self-assurance of the Voltaire period; he manages neither his social life nor that particularly important part of it, his sexual relations, with the easy mastery of a gentleman of rank of the old regime; he even goes so far as to say that he cultivated wit only to conceal his passion for a woman whom he did not possess— "that fear, a thousand times repeated, was actually the controlling principle of my life for ten years" (*Égotisme*, ch. 1). Such traits make him appear a man born too late who tries in vain to realize the form of life of a past period; other elements of his character, the merciless objectivity of his realistic power, his courageous assertion of his personality against the triviality of the rising middle-of-the-roads, and much more, show him as the forerunner of certain later intellectual modes and forms of life; but he always feels and experiences the reality of his period as a resistance. That very thing makes his realism (though it proceeded, if at all, to only a very slight degree from a loving genetic comprehension of evolutions—that is, from the historistic attitude) so energetic and so closely connected with his own existence: the realism of this "fractious horse" is a product of his fight for self-assertion. And this explains the fact that the stylistic level of his great realistic novels is much closer to the old great and heroic concept of tragedy than is that of most later realists—Julien Sorel is much more a "hero" than the characters of Balzac, to say nothing of Flaubert.

RENÉ GIRARD

The Red and the Black†

According to literary historians Stendhal inherited most of his ideas from the *philosophes* or the *idéologues*.

If this were true, this novelist whom we consider so great would not have a thought of his own; for his whole life he would remain

---

† From *Mensonge romantique et vérité romanesque*, translated by Yvonne Freccero as *Deceit, Desire, and the Novel* (Baltimore: The Johns Hopkins Press, 1965), pp. 113–38. Copyright © 1966 by René Girard. Reprinted with the permission of The Johns Hopkins University Press.

Girard's analysis of romantic lies and novelistic truths traces a political as well as a psychological and literary pattern through various romantic and postromantic novelists. It is, essentially, the pattern of triangular desire, best illustrated by the mechanism of jealousy in which A supposes he desires something because he imagines B also desires it. B thus becomes a "mediator" of A's desire. When his autonomous impulses are so contaminated by the thought of B that the rival need not even be present to inflame A's appetitive fantasies, we are confronted with what Girard calls "inner mediation." It is his argument that Stendhal, like Dostoevsky and Proust, is an acute analyst of this unhealthy condition in the body politic as well as within the psyche of his protagonists.

faithful to the thought of others. It is a hard legend to kill. It is popular both with those who would deny intelligence in the novel and with those who are trying to find a complete Stendhalian system and think they have found it in his early writing, that is, in the only more or less didactic texts ever written by Stendhal.

Their thoughts dwell longingly on a huge key which would open all the gates of his work. A whole trousseau can be gathered effortlessly from the childish *Letters to Pauline*, from the *Journal*, and from his *New Philosophy*. There is a loud rattle in the lock but the gates remain closed. No page of *The Red and the Black* will ever be explained by means of Cabanis or Destutt de Tracy. Except for occasional borrowings from the system of temperaments, there is no trace of the theories of his youth in the novels of his maturity. Stendhal is one of the few thinkers of his time who won his independence from the giants of the preceding epoch. For this reason he can render homage as an equal to the gods of his youth. Most of his romantic contemporaries are incapable of doing as much; they look on the rationalist Pantheon with great condescension, but should it enter their head to reason we find ourselves back in the century of the Enlightenment. Their opinions are different and even antithetical but the intellectual frameworks have not changed.

Stendhal does not give up thinking the day he stops copying the thought of others; he begins to think for himself. If the writer had never changed his opinion on the great political and social problems, why did he declare, at the beginning of the *Life of Henry Brulard*, that he had at last decided on his point of view regarding the nobility? Nothing in the Stendhalian vision is more important than the nobility, yet this definitive point of view is never systematically set down. The real Stendhal had an aversion to didacticism. His original thought *is* the novel and only the novel, for the moment Stendhal escapes from his characters the ghost of the Other begins to haunt him again. Therefore everything has to be gathered from his novels. The non novelistic texts sometimes contribute details but they should be handled with care.

Far from blindly trusting the past, Stendhal, even as early as *De l'Amour*, considers the problem of the *error* in Montesquieu and other great minds of the eighteenth century. The alleged disciple wonders why such keen observers as the *philosophes* should have been so completely wrong in their visions of the future. At the end of *Memoirs of a Tourist* the theme of philosophical error is resumed and studied further. Stendhal finds nothing in Montesquieu to justify the condemnation of Louis-Philippe. The bourgeois king gave the French greater liberty and prosperity than ever before. The progress is real but it does not accord the people who benefit from it the increase of happiness foreseen by the theoreticians.

Stendhal's own duty is indicated to him by the mistakes of the *philosophes*. He must amend the conclusions of abstract intelligence by contact with experience. The intact Bastilles limited the vision of prerevolutionary thinkers. The Bastilles have fallen and the world is changing at a dizzying pace. Stendhal finds he is straddling several universes. He is observing the constitutional monarchy but he has not forgotten the *ancien régime*; he has visited England; and he keeps up with the constant stream of books dealing with the United States.

All the nations Stendhal is concerned with have embarked on the same adventure but they are moving at different speeds. The novelist is living in a veritable laboratory of historical and sociological observation. His novels are, in a sense, merely this same laboratory carried to the second degree. In them Stendhal brings together various elements which would remain isolated from each other even in the modern world. He confronts the provinces and Paris, aristocrats and bourgeois, France and Italy, and even the present and the past. Various experiments are carried out and they all have the same aim—they are all meant to answer the same fundamental question: "Why are men not happy in the modern world?"

This question is not original. Everybody, or almost everybody, was asking it in Stendhal's day. But few ask it sincerely, without having already decided a priori that one more or one less revolution is required. In his nonnovelistic writings Stendhal often seems to request both at the same time. But these secondary texts should not be allowed to worry us too much. Stendhal's real answer is blended into his novels, scattered through them; it is diffuse, full of hesitations and modifications. Stendhal is as prudent in the novels as he can be assertive, when he is expressing his own "personal" opinion in the face of the opinion of others.

Why are men not happy in the modern world? Stendhal's answer cannot be expressed in the language of political parties or of the various "social sciences." It is nonsense to both bourgeois common sense and romantic "idealism." We are not happy, says Stendhal, because we are *vaniteux*.

Morality and psychology are not the only sources of this answer. Stendhalian vanity has a historical component which is essential and which we must now clarify. In order to do this, we must first set forth Stendhal's idea of nobility, which, he tells us in the *Life of Henry Brulard*, took a solid form rather late in his development.

In Stendhal's eyes, nobility belongs to the man whose desires come from within himself and who exerts every ounce of his energy to satisfy them. Nobility, in the spiritual sense of the term, is therefore exactly synonymous with passion. The noble being rises above others by the strength of his desire. There must originally be nobility in the spiritual sense for there to be nobility in the social sense. At a certain point in history both senses of the word "noble" coincided, at least theoretically. This coincidence is illustrated in *The Italian Chronicles*. In fourteenth- and fifteenth-century Italy the greatest passions were born and developed in the elite of society.

This relative accord between the social organization and natural hierarchy of men cannot last. The nobleman's becoming aware of it is, in a sense, sufficient to precipitate its dissolution. A comparison is necessary to discover that one is superior to others: comparison means bringing closer together, putting on the same level, and, to a certain extent, treating the things compared in the same way. The equality of man cannot be denied unless it is first posited, however briefly. The oscillation between pride and shame which defines metaphysical desire can already be found in this first comparison. The nobleman who makes the comparison becomes a little more noble in the social sense but a little less noble in the spiritual sense. He begins the reflection that will gradually cut him off from his own nobility and transform it into a mere possession mediated by the *look* of the commoner. The nobleman as an individual is thus the passionate being *par excellence*, but nobility as a class is devoted to vanity. The more nobility is transformed into a caste and becomes hereditary, the more it closes its ranks to the passionate being who might rise from the lower classes and the more serious the ontological sickness becomes. Henceforth the nobility will be leading constantly toward vanity the other classes dedicated to its imitation and will precede them along the fatal road of metaphysical desire.

Thus the nobility is the first class to become decadent, and the history of this decadence is identical with the inevitable evolution of metaphysical desire. The nobility is already eaten up with vanity when it rushes to Versailles, drawn by the lure of vain rewards. Louis XIV is not the demigod worshipped by the royalists, nor is he the oriental tyrant loathed by the Jacobins. He is a clever politician who distrusts the aristocracy and uses its vanity as a means of government, thereby hastening the decomposition of the noble soul. The aristocracy lets itself be drawn into sterile rivalries by the monarchy which reserves the right of arbitration. The Duc de Saint-Simon, perceptive but fascinated by the king, observes with quenchless rage this emasculation of the nobility. Saint-Simon, the historian of "impotent hatred," is one of Stendhal's and Proust's great teachers.

The absolute monarchy is one stage on the road to revolution and to the most modern forms of vanity. But it is only a stage. The vanity of the court presents a strong contrast with true nobility but it makes an equally strong contrast with the vanity of the bourgeois.

At Versailles the slightest desires must be approved and permitted by a whim of the king. Existence at the court is a perpetual imitation of Louis XIV. The Sun King is the mediator for all who surround him, and this mediator remains separated from his faithful followers by an immense spiritual distance. The king cannot become the rival of his own subjects. M. de Montespan would suffer much more were his wife being unfaithful to him with an ordinary mortal. The theory of "divine right" provides a perfect definition of the particular type of *external mediation* which flourishes at Versailles and in the whole of France during the last two centuries of the monarchy.

What was the state of mind of a courtier of the *ancien régime*, or rather what was Stendhal's impression of it? Several secondary characters in his novels and the brief but suggestive remarks scattered through some twenty works provide us with a fairly precise answer to that question. The pain caused by vanity exists in the eighteenth century but it is not unbearable. It is still possible to enjoy oneself in the protective shade of the monarchy somewhat like children at the feet of their parents. Indeed a delicate pleasure is found in mocking the futile and rigorous rules of a perpetually idle existence. The great lord has a perfect ease and grace by knowing that he is nearer the sun than other human beings and thus a little less human than they, that he is illuminated by the divine rays. He always knows exactly what to say and what not to say, what to do and what not to do. He is not afraid of being ridiculed and he gladly laughs in ridicule of others. Anything which is the slightest bit different from the latest fashion at court is ridiculous in his eyes, thus everything outside Versailles and Paris is ridiculous. It is impossible to imagine a more favorable setting for the growth of a comic theater than this universe of courtiers. Not a single allusion is lost on this public which is not many but *one*. Diderot would have been astonished to discover that laughter in the theater disappears with the "tyrant"!

The revolution destroys only one thing—but that one thing is the most important of all though it seems trivial to barren minds—the divine right of kings. After the Restoration Louis, Charles, and Philippe ascend the throne; they cling to it and descend from it more or less precipitously; only fools pay any attention to these monotonous gymnastics. The monarchy no longer exists. Stendhal insists on this fact at some length in the last part of *Lucien Leuwen*. The ceremonies at Versailles cannot turn the head of a positive-minded banker. The real power is elsewhere. And this false king, Louis-Philippe, plays the stock exchange, making himself—the ultimate downfall!—the *rival* of his own subjects!

This last touch gives us the key to the situation. The courtier's external mediation is replaced by a system of internal mediation in which the pseudo-king himself takes part. The revolutionaries thought they would be destroying vanity when they destroyed the privileges of the noble. But vanity is like a virulent cancer that spreads in a more serious form throughout the body just when one thinks it has been removed. Who is there left to imitate after the "tyrant"? Henceforth men shall copy each other; idolatry of one person is replaced by hatred of a hundred thousand rivals. In Balzac's opinion, too, there is no other god but envy for the modern crowd whose greed is no longer stemmed and held within acceptable limits by the monarch. *Men will become gods for each other.* Young men of the nobility and of the middle class come to Paris to seek their fortune, as courtiers once came to Versailles. They crowd into the garrets of the Latin Quarter as once they used to pile into the attics of Versailles. Democracy is one vast middle-class court where the courtiers are everywhere and the king is nowhere. Balzac, whose observations in all these matters frequently corroborate Stendhal's, has also described this phenomenon: "In the monarchy you have either courtiers or servants, whereas under a Charter you are served, flattered, and fawned on by free men." When speaking of the United States, Tocqueville too mentions the "esprit de cour" which reigns in the democracies. The sociologist's reflection throws a vivid light on the transition from external to internal mediation:

> When all the privileges of birth and fortune have been destroyed so that all professions are open to everyone and it is possible to climb to the top by oneself, an immense and easy career seems available to men's ambitions, and they gladly imagine a great destiny for themselves. But they are mistaken, as daily experience proves to them. The very equality which enables each citizen to sustain great hopes makes all citizens equally weak. It limits their strength on all sides at the same time as it allows their desires to spread.
>
> The have destroyed the annoying privileges of some of their fellow-men; they encounter the competition of everyone. The boundary has changed its shape rather than its position.
>
> The constant opposition on the one hand of instincts which give birth to equality and on the other of the means provided to satisfy them, torments and tires souls. . . . However democratic the social state and political constitution of a nation may be, yet inevitably . . . each of its citizens will behold around him several aspects which dominate him, and it can be anticipated that he will obstinately fix his eyes in this one direction.

We find in Stendhal this "uneasiness" which Tocqueville attributes to democratic regimes. The vanity of the *ancien régime* was gay, unconcerned, and frivolous; the vanity of the nineteenth century is sad and suspicious; it has a terrible fear of ridicule. "Envy, jealousy, and impotent hatred" are the accompaniment of internal mediation. Stendhal declares that everything has changed in a country when even fools—always the most stable element—have changed. The fool of 1780 wanted to be witty; to make people laugh was his only ambition. The fool of 1825 wants to be serious and formal. He is set on appearing profound and easily succeeds, the novelist adds, because he is truly unhappy. Stendhal never tires of describing the effects of *la vanité triste* on the customs and psychology of the French. The aristocrats are most hard hit.

> When one stops considering the serious results of the revolution, one of the first sights that strikes one's imagination is the present state of French society. I spent my youth among great lords who were very pleasant; today they are old, disagreeable reactionaries. At first I thought their peevish humor was an unfortunate effect of age, so I made the acquaintance of their children who will inherit great wealth and noble titles, in fact most of the privileges that men drawn together in society can confer on some among them; I found them sunk even deeper in despondency than their parents.

The transition from external to internal mediation constitutes the supreme phase in the decline of the nobility. Revolution and emigration completed what reflection had begun; the nobleman, physically separated from his privileges, is henceforth forced to see them for what they really are—*arbitrary*. Stendhal clearly understood that the revolution could not destroy the nobility by taking away its privileges. But the nobility could destroy itself by desiring that of which it had been deprived by the bourgeoisie, and by devoting itself to the ignoble sentiments of internal mediation. To realize that the privilege is arbitrary and to desire it anyhow is obviously the height of vanity. The noble thinks he is defending his nobility by fighting for its privileges against the other classes of a nation but he only succeeds in ruining it. He desires to recuperate his wealth as a bourgeois might and the envy of the bourgeoisie stimulates his desire and endows the pettiest of honorary trifles with immense value. Mediated by each other, henceforth the two classes will desire the same things in the same way. The Restoration duke who regains his titles and fortune, thanks to the millions granted to the *émigrés*, is little more than a bourgeois "who won in the lottery." The nobleman constantly grows nearer the bourgeois, even in the hatred he feels for him. They are all ignoble, Stendhal writes somewhat strongly in his letter to Balzac, *because they prize nobility*. . . .

Only their elegant manners and politeness, the results of long training, give the nobles a little distinction over the bourgeoisie, and even this will soon disappear. Double mediation is a melting-pot in which differences among classes and individuals gradually dissolve. It functions all the more efficiently because it does not even appear to affect diversity. In fact, the latter is even given a fresh though deceptive brilliance: the opposition of the Same to the Same, which flourishes everywhere, will hide itself for a long time to come behind traditional diversity, sheltering new conflicts behind the shadow of old ones and nourishing belief in the integral survival of the past.

Under the Restoration the nobility seems more alive than ever. Never have its privileges been more desired, nor its ancient families so eager to emphasize the barriers between themselves and the common people. Superficial observers are not aware that internal mediation is at work; they can only conceive uniformity as that of marbles in a bag or sheep in a meadow. They do not recognize the modern tendency to identity in passionate divisions, their own divisions. But the clash of cymbals is loudest when they fit each other exactly.

Because it is no longer distinct the aristocracy tries to distinguish itself, and it succeeds marvelously—but that does not make it any more noble. It is a fact, for instance, that under the constitutional monarchy the aristocracy is the stuffiest and most virtuous class in the nation. The frivolous and seductive nobleman of the Louis XV era has been replaced by the scowling and morose gentleman of the Restoration. This depressing character lives on his property, he works hard, goes to bed early, and worst of all, even manages to economize. What is the significance of such austere morals? Is it really a return to the "ancestral virtues"? This is what we are told constantly in the *bien-pensant* journals but there is no need to believe it. This gloomy, sour-tempered, and totally negative kind of wisdom is typically bourgeois. The aristocracy is trying to prove to the Others that it has "earned" its privileges; that is why it borrows its code of ethics from the class which is competing for those same privileges. Mediated by its bourgeois audience, the nobility copies the bourgeoisie without even realizing it. In *Memoirs of a Tourist* Stendhal remarks sardonically that the revolution has bequeathed to the French aristocracy the customs of democratic, protestant Geneva.

Thus their very hatred of the bourgeoisie makes them middle-class. And, since mediation is reciprocal, we must expect to find a bourgeois-gentleman to match the gentleman-bourgeois, we must anticipate a bourgeois comedy which is symmetrical and inverse to to aristocratic comedy. The courtiers may copy Rousseau's *vicaire savoyard* in order to capture the good opinion of the bourgeois, but the bourgeois will also play at being great lords to impress the aristocrats. The type of the bourgeois imitator reaches the height of comic perfection in the character of Baron Nerwinde in *Lamiel*. Nerwinde, the son of a general of the Empire, slavishly and laboriously copies a synthetic model, made up in equal parts of a *roué* of the *ancien régime* and a dandy from across the Channel. Nerwinde leads a tedious and boring existence, but its very disorder he has organized methodically. He goes bankrupt conscientiously while keeping very exact accounts. He does it all to make people forget— and to make himself forget—that he is the grandson of a hatter from Périgueux.

Double mediation flourishes everywhere; there is a "set to partners" in every figure of Stendhal's social ballet. Everything is reversed from its previous state. Stendhal's wit amuses us but it seems a little too geometric to be true. It is important to note that Tocqueville, who is a completely humorless observer, makes assertions parallel to Stendhal's. In *The Ancient Regime and the Revolution*, for instance, we find the paradox of an aristocracy that by its opposition to the middle class begins to resemble it, and that adopts all the virtues of which the middle class is trying to rid itself. He writes: "The most anti-democratic classes of the nation reveal most clearly to us the kind of morality it is reasonable to expect from a democracy."

When the aristocracy seems most alive is precisely when it is most dead. In an early edition of *Lamiel*, Nerwinde is called D'Aubigné; this imitative dandy belonged to the aristocracy, not to the parvenu middle class: he was a descendant of Mme. de Maintenon. Otherwise his conduct was exactly the same as in the last version of the novel. No doubt Stendhal chose the parvenu bourgeois—the commoner—to play the comedy of the nobility because he felt that the comic effect would be more apparent and reliable, but this does not mean he was mistaken in the first version; it illustrates an essential aspect of the Stendhalian truth. In that case it was a nobleman by blood who played the comedy of nobility. With or without a coat-of-arms, one can "desire" nobility under Louis-Philippe only in the manner of Molière's *bourgeois gentilhomme*. One can only mime it, as passionately as M. Jourdain but less naïvely. It is this kind of mimicry which Stendhal is trying to reveal to us. The complexity of the task and the fragmentation of the public—which are, ultimately, one and the same phenomenon—make the theater unsuited to carrying out this literary function. Comic theater died with the monarchy and "gay vanity." A more flexible genre is needed to describe the infinite metamorphoses of *vanité triste* and reveal how void are its oppositions. This genre is the novel. Stendhal finally understood this; after long years of effort and failure, which transformed his soul, he gave up the theater. But he never renounced his ambition of becoming a great comic writer. All novelistic works have a tendency to the comic and Stendhal's are no exception. Flaubert excels himself in *Bouvard et Pécuchet*; Proust reaches his peak in the comic figure of the Baron Charlus; Stendhal sums up and completes his work in the great comic scenes of *Lamiel*.

The paradox of an aristocracy that becomes democratic through its very hatred of democracy is nowhere more striking than in political life. The tendency of the nobility to become bourgeois is clearly seen in its sympathy for the *ultra* party, a party devoted entirely to the defense of privilege; this party's conflict with Louis XVIII showed clearly that the monarchy was no longer the polar star of the nobility but a political instrument in the hands of the noble party. This noble party is oriented not toward the king but toward the rival bourgeoisie. The *ultra* ideology is merely the pure and simple reversal of revolutionary ideology. The theme throughout is *reaction* and reveals the negative slavery of internal mediation. Party rule is the natural political expression of this mediation; party platforms do not bring about political opposition—opposition brings about party platforms.

To understand how ignoble ultraism is, it must be compared with a form of thought which was anterior to the revolution and which, in its time, convinced a whole section of the nobility: the philosophy of the Enlightenment. Stendhal believes that this philosophy is the only one possible for nobility that intends to remain noble in the exercise of its thought. When a genuine aristocrat—and there were still a few during the last century of the monarchy—enters the territory of thought, he does not abandon his native virtues. He remains spontaneous even in his reflection. Unlike the ultras he does not expect the ideas he adopts to serve the interests of his class, any more than he would ask a challenger, in a truly heroic era, to present proof of nobility; the challenge alone would prove the nobility of the challenger, in the eyes of someone with self-respect. In the realm of thought rational evidence takes the place of the challenge. The nobleman accepts the challenge and judges everything in universal terms. He goes straight to the most general truths and applies them to all mankind. He does not acknowledge any exceptions, especially those from which he would profit. In Montesquieu, and in the best of the enlightened nobles of the eighteenth century, there is no distinction between the aristocratic and the liberal mind. Eighteenth-century rationalism is noble even in its illusions; it puts its trust in "human nature." It does not allow for the irrational in human relations, nor does it recognize meta-physical imitation, which frustrates the calculations of sound re-flection. Montesquieu would have been less likeable had he foreseen the *vanité triste* of the nineteenth century.

Moreover, we soon realize that rationalism means the death of privilege. Truly noble reflection resigns itself to that death, just as the truly noble warrior is prepared to die on the battlefield. The no-bility cannot reflect on itself and remain noble without destroying itself as a caste; and since the revolution forced the nobility to think about itself, its own extinction is the only choice left to it. The nobility can die nobly by the one and only political gesture worthy of it, the destruction of its own privileged existence—the night of August 4, 1789.[1] It dies meanly, in a bourgeois fashion, on the benches of some House of Lords, confronted by Valenods whom it ends up resembling through fighting with them over the spoils. This was the solution of the ultras.

First came the nobility; then followed the noble class; finally only a noble party is left. After the period when the two coincided, spir-itual and social nobility now tend to exclude each other; henceforth the incompatibility of privilege with greatness of soul is so radical that it is patent even in the attempts to conceal it. Take for example the justification of privilege given by Dr. Du Périer, the intellectual jack-of-all-trades of the Nancy nobility:

> A man is born a duke, a millionaire and a peer of France, it is not for him to consider whether his position conforms with virtue, or with the general good or with other fine ideas. His position is good; so he should do everything to maintain and improve it, or be despised generally as a coward and a fool.

Du Périer would like to convince us that the nineteenth-century nobleman is still living in a happy era, not yet affected by the "look" of the Other, still enjoying his privileges spontaneously. Yet the lie is so flagrant that Du Périer does not phrase it directly; he uses a neg-ative periphrasis that suggests without affirming: "It is not for him to consider," etc. Despite this oratorical precaution, the "look" of the Other is too obsessive and Du Périer is forced to acknowledge it in the following sentence. But then he imagines a cynical point of honor to which this "look" forces the aristocrat to submit. If the privileged person does not hang on to his privilege, "he will be de-spised as a coward or a fool." Du Périer is once again lying. Aristo-crats are neither innocent nor cynical: they are merely *vaniteux*; they want privilege merely as parvenus. This is the horrible truth

---

1. During that night the deputies of the aristocracy at the revolutionary *Assemblée constitu-ante* voted the abolition of most feudal privileges.

which must be hidden at all cost. They are ignoble *because they prize nobility.*

Since the Revolution no one can be privileged without knowing it. Stendhal's kind of hero is impossible in France. Stendhal likes to believe that he is still just possible in Italy. In that happy country, scarcely touched by the Revolution, reflection and concern with the Other have not yet completely poisoned enjoyment of the world and of oneself. A truly heroic soul is still compatible with the privileged circumstances which allow him free play. Fabrice del Dongo can be spontaneous and generous in the midst of an injustice from which he benefits.

First we see Fabrice flying to the aid of an emperor who embodies the spirit of the Revolution; a little later we find our hero, haughty, devout, and aristocratic, in the Italy of his childhood. Fabrice does not think for a minute he is "demeaning" himself when he challenges a simple soldier of the glorious imperial army to a duel. Yet he speaks harshly to the servant who risks his life for him. Still later, despite his devotion, he does not hesitate to join in the simoniac intrigues which will make him an archbishop of Parma. Fabrice is not a hypocrite, nor does he lack intelligence; he is merely lacking the historical foundations for the ability to reflect. The comparisons which a privileged young Frenchman would be forced to make never even enter his mind.

The French will never recover the innocence of a Fabrice for *it is not possible to move backward in the order of the passions.* Historic and psychic evolution are irreversible. Stendhal finds the Restoration revolting but not because he sees in it naïvely a "return to the *ancien régime.*" Such a return is unthinkable; moreover, Louis XVIII's Charter marks the first concrete step toward democracy "since 1792." The current interpretation of *The Red and the Black* therefore is inadmissible. The Jacobin novel described in the handbooks of literature does not exist. If Stendhal were writing for all those bourgeois who are temporarily cut off from lucrative careers by the temporary triumph of an absolutist and feudal party, his would be a very clumsy work. Traditional interpretations go counter to the most basic tenets of the author and disregard the *facts* of the novel, among which is the brilliant career of Julien. One might object that this career is broken by the reactionary and clerical *Congrégation.*[2] True, yet this same *Congrégation* a little later makes every effort to save the protégé of the Marquis de la Mole. Julien is not so much the victim of the ultras as of the wealthy and jealous bourgeois who will triumph in July 1830. Moreover, we should not look for any partisan lesson in Stendhal's masterpieces—to under-

2. A secret Catholic organization with great political influence.

stand this novelist who is always talking politics we must free ourselves of political ways of thinking.

Julien has a brilliant career which he owes to M. de la Mole. In
his article on *The Red and the Black*, Stendhal describes the latter
in these words: "His character as nobleman was not formed by the
revolution of 1794." In other words, M. de la Mole retains some
genuine nobility; he has not become middle-class through hatred of
the middle class. His freedom of thought has not made him a demo-
crat but it prevents him from being a reactionary in the worst sense
of the word. M. de la Mole does not depend exclusively on excom-
munications, negations, and refusals; ultraism and the nobleman's
reaction have not smothered all other sentiments in him. His wife
and his friends judge men only by their birth, their fortune, and
their political orthodoxy, and so would a Valenod in their place; but
M. de la Mole is still capable of approving the rise of a talented
commoner. He proves it with Julien Sorel. Only once does Stendhal
find his character vulgar—when he loses his temper at the thought
that his daughter, by marrying Julien, will never be a duchess.

Julien owes his success to that element under the new regime
which has most truly survived from the *ancien régime*. This is a
strange way for Stendhal to campaign against a return to the past;
even if the novelist had shown the failure of the numerous young
people who did not have the good fortune to meet their Marquis de
la Mole, his novel would still not have proved anything against the
ancien régime. In fact it is the Revolution which has increased the
obstacles, since most people with status owe "their character of nobleman"—i.e., their implacable ultraism—to the Revolution.

Must then the obstacle in the way of these young people be
called democratic? Is not this an empty subtlety, and even an untenable paradox? Surely it is only fair that the bourgeoisie should
take over the controls since it is "the most energetic and active
class in the nation." Is it not true that a little more "democracy"
would smooth the way for the ambitious?

It is true; in any case, the stupidity of the ultras makes their
downfall inevitable. But Stendhal looks further. The political elimi-
nation of the noble party cannot reestablish harmony and satisfy
the desires that have been awakened. The political conflict which
rages under the constitutional monarchy is considered the sequel
of a great historic drama, the last thunderclaps of a storm that is
moving away. The revolutionaries suppose they must clear the
ground and make a fresh start; Stendhal is telling them that they
have already started. Ancient historic appearances hide a new
structure of human relations. The party struggle is rooted not in
past inequality but in the present equality, no matter how imperfect
it may be.

The historical justification of the internal struggles is scarcely more than a pretext now. Put aside the pretext and the true cause will appear. Ultraism will disappear like liberalism, but internal mediation remains; and internal mediation will never be lacking in excuses for maintaining the division into rival camps. Following religious society, civic society has become schismatic. To look forward optimistically to the democratic future under the pretext that the ultras, or their successors, are destined to disappear from the political scene is once again to put the object before the mediator and desire before envy. This error can be compared to that of the chronic sufferer from jealousy who always thinks his illness will be cured when the current rival is eliminated.

The last century of French history has proved Stendhal right. The party struggle is the only stable element in contemporary instability. Principles no longer cause rivalry; it is a metaphysical rivalry, which slips into contrary principles like mollusks that nature has not provided with shells and that install themselves in the first ones to come along, no matter what kind.

Proof of this can be furnished by the pair Rênal–Valenod. M. de Rênal abandons ultraism before the 1827 elections. He has himself entered as a candidate on the liberal ticket. Jean Prévost discovers in this sudden conversion proof that even Stendhal's secondary characters are capable of "surprising" the reader.[3] Prévost, usually so perspicacious, in this point has fallen victim to the pernicious myths of the "true to life" and "spontaneity" which plague literary criticism.

Julien smiles when he learns of the political about-face of his former patron—he knows very well that nothing has changed. Once more it is a question of playing a role opposite Valenod. The latter has gotten in the good graces of the *Congrégation*; he will therefore be the ultras' candidate. For M. de Rênal there is nothing left to do but turn toward those liberals who seemed so formidable to him a few years before. We meet the mayor of Verrières again in the last pages of the novel. He introduces himself pompously as a "liberal of the defection," but from his second sentence on he merely echoes Valenod. Submission to the Other is no less absolute when it assumes negative forms—a puppet is no less a puppet when the strings are crossed. With regard to the virtues of opposition Stendhal does not share in the optimism of a Hegel or of our contemporary "rebels."

The figure cut by the two businessmen of Verrières was not perfect so long as they both belonged to the same political party. Double mediation demanded M. de Rênal's conversion to liberalism.

3. *La Création chez Stendhal* (Paris, 1955).

There was a need for symmetry which had not yet been fulfilled. And that final *entrechat* was needed to bring to a proper end the ballet of Rênal–Valenod, which was being performed in a corner of the stage all through *The Red and the Black*.

Julien savors the "conversion" of M. de Rênal like a music lover who sees a melodic theme reappear under a new orchestral disguise. Most men are taken in by the disguises. Stendhal places a smile on Julien's lips so that his readers should not be deceived. He does not want us to be fooled: he wants to turn our attention away from the objects and fix it on the mediator; he wishes to reveal to us the genesis of desire, to teach us to distinguish true freedom from the negative slavery which caricatures it. If we take M. de Rênal's liberalism seriously we are destroying the very essence of *The Red and the Black* and reducing a work of genius to the proportions of a Victor Cousin or a Saint-Marc Girardin.

M. de Rênal's conversion is the first act of a political tragicomedy which excites the enthusiasm of naïve spectators throughout the nineteenth century. First the actors exchange threats, then they exchange roles. They leave the stage and return in a new costume. Behind this perpetually similar but different spectacle the same opposition continues to exist, becoming ever more empty and yet more ferocious. And internal mediation continues its underground work.

The political thinkers of our time are always seeking in Stendhal an echo of their own thoughts. They recreate a revolutionary Stendhal or a reactionary Stendhal according to their own passions. But the shroud is never large enough to cover the corpse. Aragon's Stendhal is no more satisfactory than that of Maurice Barrès or Charles Maurras. One line of the writer's own suffices to bring the weak ideological scaffoldings tumbling down into the void: "As regards extreme parties," we read in the preface to *Lucien Leuwen*, "it is always those we have seen most recently which seem the most ridiculous."

The youthful Stendhal most certainly leaned toward the republicans. The mature Stendhal is not lacking in sympathy for the incorruptible Catos who, deaf to Louis-Philippe's objurgations, refuse to grow rich and are preparing in the shadows a new revolution. But we must not confuse with political affiliation this very particular feeling of sympathy. The problem is discussed at length in *Lucien Leuwen* and the position of the later Stendhal—the Stendhal who carries most weight—is in no way ambiguous.

We must seek among the austere republicans whatever is left of nobility in the political arena. Only these republicans still hope for the destruction of all forms of vanity. They retain the eighteenth-century illusion concerning the excellence of human nature. They have understood neither the revolution nor *vanité triste*. They do not realize that the most beautiful fruits of ideological thought will always be spoiled by the worm of irrationality. These men of integrity do not have the *philosophes'* excuse of living *before* the Revolution; thus they are much less intelligent than Montesquieu, and they are much less amusing. If their hands were free, they would create a regime identical with that which flourishes under republican, protestant puritanism in the state of New York. Individual rights would be respected; prosperity would be assured, but the last refinements of aristocratic existence would disappear; vanity would take an even baser form than under the constitutional monarchy. Stendhal concludes that it is less distressing to flatter a Talleyrand or even a minister of Louis-Philippe's than to pay court "to one's shoemaker."

Stendhal is an atheist in politics, a fact hard to believe either in his day or in ours. Despite the levity of its manifestations this atheism is not a frivolous skepticism but a profound conviction. Stendhal does not evade problems; his point of view is the outcome of a whole life of meditation. But it is a point of view which will never be understood by party-minded people nor by many other people who unconsciously are influenced by the party spirit. An ambiguous homage is paid to the novelist's thought, which secretly denies its coherence. It is considered "impulsive" and "disconcerting." It is full of "whims" and "paradoxes." The unfortunate writer is lucky if "a double heritage, both aristocratic and popular" is not invoked which would tear him apart. Let us leave to Ménimée the image of a Stendhal dominated by the spirit of contradiction and we shall understand perhaps that Stendhal is accusing *us* and our time of self-contradictions.

As usual, if we are to have a better understanding of the novelist's thought, we should compare it with a later work which will amply justify its perspectives and will make even its more daring aspects seem banal, merely by revealing a more advanced stage of metaphysical desire. In Stendhal's case, we must ask Flaubert to provide us with a key. Although Emma Bovary's desire still belongs to the area of external mediation, Flaubert's universe as a whole, and especially the urban life of *The Sentimental Education*, are the result of an internal mediation which is even more extreme than that of Stendhal. Flaubert's mediation exaggerates the characteristics of Stendhalian mediation and draws a caricature of it that is much easier for us to figure out than the original.

The environment of *The Sentimental Education* is the same as that of *The Red and the Black*. Again the provinces and Paris are opposed to one another, but it is clear that the center of gravity has moved toward Paris, the capital of desire, which increasingly polarizes the vital forces of the nation. Relationships between people remain the same and enable us to measure the progress of internal mediation. M. de La Mole has been replaced by M. Dambreuse, a "liberal" who owes his character of rapacious big banker as much to 1830 as to 1794. Mathilde is succeeded by the venal Mme. Dambreuse. Julien Sorel is followed by a whole crowd of young men who come, like him, to "conquer" the capital. They are less talented but more greedy. Chances of success are not wanting but everybody wants the most "conspicuous" position, and the front row can never be stretched far since it owes its position purely to the inevitably limited attention of the crowd. The number of those who are called increases constantly but the number of the elect does not. Flaubert's ambitious man never attains the object of his desires. He knows neither the real misery nor the real despair caused by possession and disillusionment. His horizon never grows wider. He is doomed to bitterness, malice, and petty rivalries. Flaubert's novel confirms Stendhal's dire predictions on the future of the bourgeois.

The opposition between the ambitious younger men and those who are successful grows ever more bitter although there are no more ultras. The intellectual basis of the oppositions is even more ridiculous and unstable than in Stendhal. If there is a victor in this bourgeois *cursus honorum* described in *The Sentimental Education* then it is Martinon, the most insipid of the characters and the biggest schemer, who corresponds, though he is even duller-witted, to little Tanbeau of *The Red and the Black*. The democratic court which has replaced that of the monarchy grows larger, more anonymous, and more unjust. Unfit for true freedom, Flaubert's characters are always attracted by what attracts their fellow men. They can desire only what the Others desire. The priority of rivalry over desire inevitably increases the amount of suffering caused by vanity.

Flaubert too is an atheist in politics. If we make allowance for the differences of time and temperament, his attitude is amazingly similar to that of Stendhal. This spiritual relationship becomes more apparent on reading Tocqueville: the sociologist, too, is immunized against partisan positions, and the best of his work almost succeeds in providing the systematic expression of an historical and political truth which often remains implicit in the great works of the two novelists.

The increasing equality—the approach of the mediator in our terms—does not give rise to harmony but to an even keener rivalry. Although this rivalry is the source of considerable material benefits, it also leads to even more considerable spiritual sufferings, for nothing material can appease it. Equality which alleviates poverty is in itself good but it cannot satisfy even those who are keenest in demanding it; it only exasperates their desire. When he emphasizes the vicious circle in which the passion for equality is trapped, Tocqueville reveals an essential aspect of triangular desire. The ontological sickness, we know, always leads its victims toward the "solutions" that are most likely to aggravate it. The passion for equality is a madness uequalled except by the contrary and symmetrical passion for inequality, which is even more abstract and contributes even more directly to the unhappiness caused by freedom in those who are incapable of accepting it in a manly fashion. Rival ideologies merely reflect both the unhappiness and the incapability; thus they result from internal mediation—rival ideologies owe their power of persuasion only to the secret support the opposing factions lend each other. Fruits of the ontological scission, their duality reflects its unhuman geometry and in return they provide food for the devouring rivalry.

Stendhal, Flaubert, Tocqueville describe as "republican" or "democratic" an evolution which we today would call *totalitarian*. As the mediator comes nearer and the concrete differences between men grow smaller, abstract opposition plays an ever larger part in individual and collective existence. All the forces of being are gradually organized into twin structures whose opposition grows ever more exact. Thus every human force is braced in a struggle that is as relentless as it is senseless, since no concrete difference or positive value is involved. Totalitarianism is precisely this. The social and political aspects of this phenomenon cannot be distinguished from its personal and private aspects. Totalitarianism exists when all desires have been organized one by one into a general and permanent mobilization of being in the service of nothingness.

Balzac often treats very seriously the oppositions he sees around him; Stendhal and Flaubert, on the other hand, always point out their futility. In the work of these two authors, this double structure is embodied in "cerebral love," political struggles, petty rivalries among businessmen and the notables of the provinces. Starting from these particular areas, it is the truly schismatic tendency of romantic and modern society which in each case is demonstrated. But Stendhal and Flaubert did not foresee, and no doubt could not foresee where this tendency would lead humanity. Double mediation has invaded the growing domain of collective existence and wormed its way into the more intimate depths of the individual soul, until finally it stretches beyond national boundaries and annexes countries, races, and continents, in the heart of a universe where technical progress is wiping away one by one the differences between men. Stendhal and Flaubert underestimated the extent to which triangular desire might expand, perhaps because they lived too early, or perhaps because they did not see clearly its metaphysical nature. Whatever the reason, they did not foresee the at once cataclysmic yet insignificant conflicts of the twentieth century. They perceived the grotesque element of the era which was about to begin but they did not suspect its tragedy.

VICTOR BROMBERT

Le Rouge et le Noir: The Ambiguities of Freedom†

Approaches

Stendhal himself guides us into the novel: we enter the provincial town of Verrières together with a Parisian traveler-narrator. This tourist beginning, with its description of white houses, red tiles, and opulent chestnut trees, is not gratuitous. Through the eyes of the sophisticated Parisian itinerant, we survey, with apparent detachment, a setting to which we are not invited to belong. The transient nature of the arrival suggests mental mobility and ironic distance. The presence of the foreign observer introduces, from the very start, an intermediary voice between the events of the book and the reader. The specific perspective is that of the outsider. But the device also establishes, proleptically, the two geographic and moral poles of the novel: Paris and the Provinces. Indeed, the Parisian tourist is more involved than he might at first appear to be. The irony is two-edged, and ultimately cancels itself out. Already in the first pages of the novel, savoir-faire and worldly experience discredit themselves. As the amused and hypothetical "Parisian" glimpses Madame de Rênal, the connoisseur in him immediately conjures up libertine visions. Yet Madame de Rênal's "naïve grace" and total lack of coquetry would be quite inconceivable in the unspontaneous, unnatural, and devitalized world of Paris.

The antithesis of city and nature is at first developed within the provincial context. Verrières, with its constricting walls and petty commercial concerns, is surrounded by splendid mountains. Upon entering the town, one immediately hears the horrible din of a nail factory. The machine "of terrifying aspect" with twenty heavy hammers is serviced by pretty young girls who appear like slaves of the voracious monster of industry. The contrast between the strident

---

† From *Stendhal: Fiction and the Themes of Freedom* (New York: Random House, 1968), pp. 61–99. Reprinted by permission of the author.

mechanism and the delicate human figures conveys the notion of an inhuman ceremony. Nature is being brutalized and profaned by the ogre of mercantilism. The image of these frail young hands exposed to the blows of the hammers serves as an initial commentary on social values that in Stendhal's view have dehumanized modern man. But it also serves to introduce the owner of the factory, the mayor of Verrières, M. de Rênal. His vulgar materialism, as well as the plight of a woman forced by marriage to tolerate his loud, obtrusive presence, is symbolized by the image of the deafening factory.

The casual, ambling beginning is studded with symbolic details. The gardens in Verrières are locked in by jealous and possessive walls. Trees are cut, clipped, and pruned in a barbaric manner. What is suggested is not merely a utilitarian spirit of conformity, but the steady repression of nature. Stendhal explicitly compares these amputated plants to the "splendid shapes" of English plane trees left to grow unhampered. What adds significance to these arboreal observations is Stendhal's habit of comparing a vigorous humanity (for instance, the dynamic men of the Renaissance) to a powerful and exuberant vegetation. To clip trees is to deprive them of their individuality; it is in fact a form of emasculation. This reduction to humiliating conformity symbolizes the pervasive tyranny of inhibitions and servile social conventions.

The theme of freedom introduced in the second paragraph by the *topos* of the mountain is developed by other images of verticality. When we first see Julien Sorel in the shed of the sawmill, which he is supposed to supervise, he is sitting five or six feet high, astride one of the rafters of the roof. His position "à cheval" is of course in harmony with the book he is reading, his beloved *Mémorial de Sainte-Hélène*. The altitude is physical, to be sure, but intellectual (his reading of books infuriates his illiterate father) and emotional as well. His imagination carries him high above the concerns of his axe-wielding brothers to the epic and mythic realm of Napoleon's exploits. The translation of spiritual exaltation into ascensional images occurs again, at the end of Chapter 10, in almost Rousseauistic terms, when Julien, to "see clearly in his own soul," climbs the rocky mountain and feels a lofty separation from ordinary humanity. Stendhal is quite explicit: the sense of height corresponds symbolically to the "position he was burning to attain in the moral sphere." The expressions "pure air," "serenity," and "joy" indicate the spirit in which the episode must be read. The immense panorama, the hawk describing large circles over his head, the inebriating silence and isolation—all contribute to the theme of victorious elevation above the choking realities of Verrières.

The novel clearly offers from the start a complex thematic structure. Point of view and images suggest a mobile perspective and a multiplicity of topics. Specific approaches-by-subject are of course tempting. Viewed in an autobiographic light, this fictional transposition of a criminal case covered by the *Gazette des Tribunaux* reveals Stendhal's father-hatred, his need for liberation from the constrictions symbolized by his home town, his particular compensation dreams, and his concept of seduction as a state of tension and hostility. From a psychological point of view, *Le Rouge et le Noir* provides a refined analysis of cerebral love—a delicate study of the early stages of passion—as well as ironic insights into the self-inflicted torments of an insecure but ambitious adolescent. Pride and timidity are at war in the psyche of this young plebeian, who is subjected but not resigned to the social and political pressures of his time.

The story of Julien Sorel thus presents itself, in part, as a social document. The climate of opportunism in the wake of the Revolution and the Empire, the attraction of talented young men to the increasingly centralized capital, the fluidity of social classes, the spread of bourgeois values—Stendhal diagnoses all these in his novel, often satirically. The worlds of Verrières, of the theological seminary in Besançon, of *ultra* society in Paris are presented in terms reminiscent of the most caustic pages in the *Courrier anglais*. The political and historical concern is all-pervasive in *Le Rouge et le Noir*, though it most often takes the form of caricature. The intellectual and spiritual divorce of different generations, the nefarious reactionary aims of a frightened Church and a devitalized nobility, the suffocating effect of a conformist and servile public, the very despotism of history—these are matters which Stendhal takes very seriously indeed. For beyond their immediate threat, these social and political factors raise moral questions: how is one to protect one's precious individuality? how is one to remain sincere in a world of hypocrisy? how can one use the weapons of one's enemies without submitting to their values? In other words, what are the possible strategies of self-defense in a social context that denies the priority of private values?

Finally, *Le Rouge et le Noir* could be approached in terms of literary history, as a self-conscious product of a writer exploiting a literary tradition, as a novel where Laclos' Valmont, Beaumarchais' Chérubin and Countess Almaviva, Rousseau's Saint-Preux, and Molière's Tartuffe all seem to meet, but whose combined and heterogeneous presence, far from inhibiting the author, allows him to elaborate, in devious ways, his personal myth of energy, spirituality, and freedom. The novel raises the problem of literary realism, in particular the relationship between a given historical-social situation and its artistic reflection and elaboration.

All these questions deserve closer investigation. Yet the topical approach when focused on a single theme or problem has its dangers—especially in the case of Stendhal. Few works indeed lend themselves as readily to misreading as *Le Rouge et le Noir*. Stendhal's taste for contrast and nuance, his technique of ironic disclaimers and inversion of values, the oscillating movements of his narration, his ellipses and understatements, but above all his habit of denigrating his hero at the very moment he enjoys him most, and his subversive delight in thus becoming the mouthpiece of a point of view he cannot possibly espouse—all this makes for a fictional development that betrays values in order to protect them better. Such an interplay of meanings can easily disconcert even the most qualified minds. Mérimée, who was not exactly a sentimentalist, blamed Stendhal for having revealed in Julien some "atrocious" sides of human nature. Balzac complained of the book's "sinister and cold philosophy," of Stendhal's poignant mockeries, of his "demonic laughter." As for T. S. Eliot, he felt that Stendhal was a master at debunking human illusion.

The tone and rhythm of *Le Rouge et le Noir* are more immediately important than plot and character analysis. Even a seemingly insignificant detail like the use of epigraphs at the beginning of chapters—a much exploited convention at the time—can help the reader attune himself to the characteristic voice of Stendhal. For these epigraphs, at times completely invented (as the one attributed to Hobbes at the beginning of the book) are irrelevant and yet deeply pertinent allusive devices that help establish a sense of intellectual complicity between the teasing author and the alert reader. Similarly, the portraits, which are often mere silhouettes, invite the reader to react and collaborate in the process of creation. The first impression of Madame de Rênal, conveyed by means of two hypothetical sentences, remains properly speculative: "This naïve grace, with its innocence and vivacity, might have recalled to the mind of a Parisian images of tender sensuality. If she had realized this type of success, Madame de Rênal would have been quite ashamed of it." The allusive and conditional method of presentation protects the very intimacy it reveals. The observation of a "real" character by an imaginary one serves here to delicately nuance the suggestion of eroticism, while stressing the authenticity of Madame de Rênal's modesty. The *might have been* contributes to a fictional elaboration. Ellipsis prepares for future actions and future self-discoveries. But the effectiveness of such a portrait depends entirely on the reader's rapidity of mind.

Ellipsis is indeed one of Stendhal's most characteristic modes. Sly, subversive, and intellectually flattering, it denounces a given reality at the same time as it camouflages its own intentions. The building of a splendid church in Verrières when Julien was a boy or the unjust sentences of the Justice of the Peace, who is the father of a large family, may appear to be gratuitous details (I, 5).* A page later, we learn that the construction of the church and the inequitable sentences suddenly enlighten Julien ("l'éclairèrent tout à coup"). A brisk stylistic pace corresponds to this sudden insight. There is danger that the reader may not immediately make the necessary connection. Already the next idea—this is typical of Stendhal's staccato of glimpses and suggestions—presses itself forward. Yet the church and the unethical sentences on the one hand, and the illumination of Julien on the other, are not only decisive in the adolescent's development and ambition but also symbolize the entire ethos of a reactionary period, when the Church thirsts for worldly power, when notions of individual dignity become dim, when the very people whose vocation it is to stand up for justice are cowed into servility.

To the ellipses of thought correspond ellipses in the articulation of the narrative. Rapid shifts of point of view, calling for several layers of simultaneous interpretation, almost totally abolish explicatory transitions. The following passage is typical:

> "Monsieur Julien, restrain yourself, I beg of you. Remember that we all have our moments of anger," said Madame Derville rapidly.
>
> Julien looked at her coldly with eyes expressing the most extreme contempt.
>
> This look astonished Madame Derville, and it would have surprised her even more if she had guessed its real meaning; she would have read in it a vague hope of the most frightful vengeance. It is, no doubt, such moments of humiliation which have created men like Robespierre.
>
> "Your Julien is quite violent; he frightens me," said Madame Derville to her friend, in a whisper. (I, 9)

At first glance, hardly anything in this passage seems to interrupt the flow of the narration. The little "scene" begins and ends with a dialogue. But the author immediately draws us away from the interlocutress, and we see Julien from the outside, objectively. Soon again, the point of view shifts; by means of a conditional construction we are taken into the author's confidence. We learn what no outside observer, not even Julien himself, could possibly know. This is the moment when, having progressively invaded his fictional substance, Stendhal strikes. It is a swift blow. The sally on the revolu-

---

* The numbers in parentheses refer to part (roman) and chapter number (arabic) in *Le Rouge et le Noir*.

tionary dynamics of humiliation has barely made its imprint, when we are again carried along. Already Madame Derville has continued speaking, or rather nothing seems to have happened except her speech. The Stendhalian commentary is submerged in the very movement which had drawn us to the author. The reader is plunged once again into the flux of the narrative development.

Reading Stendhal is an exercise in agility. The capers and somersaults of irony, the juggling of contents, and inversions of meaning sustain a climate of ambiguity. Nothing can be more unsettling to the unprepared reader than the constant instability of the Stendhalian vocabulary, its shifts and reversals of signification. For "sot," "sottise," "ridicule," "faiblesse" are not derogatory terms at all when applied to the hero. They usually point to his charming clumsiness, to his inability to live up to his own calculating schemes, to his fundamental spontaneity. When Julien is "sot à mourir toute la journée," when he makes a shocking fool of himself with Madame de Rênal (I, 14), we must understand that he is distressingly and delightfully timid in the author's eyes. His silliness is the very proof of his touching inexperience and emotional vulnerability. "He had a ludicrous idea in the evening . . ." (I, 15) The "idée ridicule" is the announcement to Madame de Rênal that he will come to her room at ten o'clock that night. But the adjective "ridicule" is far from pejorative in context. Stendhal applauds his hero's awkward courage. In fact, the terms of blame, in the case of Julien, must almost automatically be translated to mean "lively," "natural," "authentic," "spontaneous," "endearing," "generous." Conversely, the conventional vocabulary of approbation must often be read as insincere and self-debunking compliments. Words such as "sang-froid" and "prudence" are simply damning. They are synonymous with "sec," "triste," "glacé"—in short, with everything that is stiff, frigid, and devitalized. This manipulation of meanings introduces a whole strategy of subversion into the novel, extending beyond the character of Julien to the social and political spheres. The reader learns to react and to think in a context where "no" often means "yes," where, in fact, "yes" can survive only because "no" is there to shield it. This fictional technique corresponds, within the rhetorical texture of the novel, to the larger issue of the protection of values. This precisely is one of the principal problems raised in *Le Rouge et le Noir*: how does one maintain one's freedom of spirit, how does one victoriously camouflage one's "heretical" views? Lip service to the infidel in power may be the only way to defend one's inner freedom.

Ambiguity extends, of course, to all aspects of Julien's character, specifically to those that involve tensions between individual and social values. At every point, the author introduces elements that destroy the mental picture the reader might be forming. This is particularly true of the early pages of the novel, where the hero's character begins to take shape. Julien's frenetic ambition seems to be summed up by his plebeian expression of horror at the thought of eating with the servants. "Je ne veux pas être domestique." (I, 5) But no sooner has he made this proud and categorical statement than Stendhal informs us that this abhorrence of sharing meals with the servants was "not natural" to Julien, that it was bookish, that he in fact derived this repugnance from Rousseau's *Confessions*. Similarly, we learn in the same chapter of Julien's hypocritical visit to the church; but the very turn of phrase is tersely ambiguous. Julien considers that appearing in church for a quick prayer on his way to the Rênals' would be "useful for his hypocrisy" ("utile à son hypocrisie"). But the need to perfect a role suggests that the role is not a congenital one. Only a fundamentally non-hypocritical person could thus decide, from the outside, to espouse the role of hypocrite, as though hypocrisy itself were a mask. The very nature of Julien's ambition is allied to lyric fervor rather than to materialistic calculations. On the one hand Stendhal informs us that Julien is determined to risk a thousand deaths rather than fail to make his fortune, but on the other, this impression of ruthless appetite for success is immediately corrected by the statement that success means getting out of his abhorred Verrières, where everything freezes his imagination. The notion of success turns out to be synonymous not with Machiavelian schemes, but with enthusiasm and dreams of escape.

These underlying suggestions of spontaneity and extreme sensibility, incompatibly blended with the superficial impressions of cold and ruthless ambition, are confirmed by two episodes. At a priest's dinner, to which the promising student of theology has been invited, he cannot refrain from praising Napoleon. (He immediately punishes himself for this grave lapse.) The second episode is more revealing: the tears he sheds and his crisis of overwhelming timidity ("invincible timidité") as he is about to enter the house of the mayor. Madame de Rênal's first impression of Julien is that he is a young girl in disguise. The impression echoes Cherubino's aria from *Nozze di Figaro* evoked in the epigraph at the beginning of the chapter. (1, 6) Tears flow quite generously from Julien's fiery eyes. He weeps "with delight" when made aware of the paternal love of the abbé Chélan. At every point, Stendhal stresses the repressed and self-conscious candor of Julien's adolescent emotions.

Conflict is at the heart of Stendhal's presentation, and it is of course at the heart of Julien's character. The tension is not merely between what Julien really is and what he would like to be; it involves dynamics that propel him to become what he is not and that lead to the discovery of what he becomes (and also remains) despite his self-imposed ambition. Timidity and resoluteness are constantly at war. The famous scene in the garden of Vergy, when Julien orders himself, in almost military style, to take Madame de Rênal's hand, describes the "awful battle raging between duty and timidity." (I, 9) There is comedy here too, for Julien is so taken with himself and with his tactical problems that he fails to notice his victory: Madame de Rênal, who has to get up for a moment, spontaneously returns her hand to him. This blindness is almost more significant than the battle between intrepidity and timorousness. It prefigures other states of hypnotic surrender to violent emotions and *idées fixes*, as in the abbé Pirard's study or on his way back to Verrières to shoot Madame de Rênal. This blindness in the face of felicity—this inability to assess and possess the privileged moment—is one of the profound themes of the book. Only through the perspective of time past is Julien's happiness rescued from the obsessive contingencies of the present.

Other comic details stress this combination of timidity and blinding compulsions. On his way to Madame de Rênal's bedroom at 2 A.M., Julien is most unhappy to hear snoring coming from her husband's room. Now he has no excuse left for not carrying out his mission! But more ironical than his fear of success ("Rien cependant ne l'eût plus embarrassé que le succès"—I, 15) is his inability to attribute his victory to the real cause. For it is Madame de Rênal's love, not his own clumsy tactics, that leads him to her intimacy. The ultimate irony of this passage is that concentration on his role as a new Valmont prevents him from enjoying himself in her arms. The puzzled question, "Have I played my part well?" thus logically corresponds to his momentary disenchantment with love and happiness: ". . . n'est-ce que ça?"

But there is also honesty in this struggle with one's self, in this refusal to take anything for granted. The scepticism is in large part self-directed. Julien not only imposes obligations but passes judgment and inflicts castigation on himself as well. After the emotional tirade about Napoleon at the priest's dinner, he binds his right arm over his breast (a symbolic pose) and carries it in his painful position for two entire months. What emerges early in the book is a morality of multiple standards, in which the only standard that really counts is the privately established one, imposed with arbitrary self-discipline. Such ascetic demands made upon the self, without the comfort of objective, external guidance other than historical myths and literary images, are clearly related to a steady self-depreciation, which is another form of blindness. Julien both needs and fears the judgment of an external conscience. He would love nothing better, we are told, than to find someone who could prove

to him that he is simply a fool. (I, 8) Yet he does everything to camouflage his real feelings and to disguise his acts. He thus has only
himself to rely on for criticism and reprimands. But he is persistently wrong about his feelings and, above all, charmingly unaware
of his real qualities. When he says silly things, which happens not
infrequently, he despises himself thoroughly and even exaggerates
the extent of his own absurdity. But he fails to see the only thing
that counts: the expression of his eyes, which "were so beautiful
and proclaimed so ardent a soul." In other words, his own spontaneity utterly escapes him. (I, 7)

How to present characters who are self-conscious and yet totally
spontaneous, that is the chief narrative problem for Stendhal. And
it is in a sense his own personal problem: lucidity and enthusiasm,
as Jean-Pierre Richard suggests, are the two poles of Stendhal's
sensibility. It would be easy to show how, throughout *Le Rouge et le
Noir*, the protagonists' spontaneity is protected by their blindness to
themselves. Madame de Rênal gives her husband a totally dishonest answer to conceal her pleasure at the hiring of Julien. But this
instinctive impulse—the author explains—she certainly did not
own to herself. (I, 6) She gradually becomes coquettish, but—insists Stendhal—"sans intention directe." (I, 8) Similarly, she falls in
love without fully realizing it, becomes jealous without admitting it,
and altogether fails to read her own heart accurately. Stendhal
plays subtle variations on this counterpoint of impulsiveness and
unawareness. The author's numerous interventions, often ironic
and self-protective, thus assume a poetic function. The omniscience of the novelist protects the inner life of his protagonists, allowing them the necessary freedom to pursue their own dreams.

But the novelist's intrusions also establish a complex of tensions
within the structure of the book. Disguising his enthusiasm
through disclaimers and perfidious excuses, freeing himself from
apparent commitment to his characters by means of disloyal asides,
Stendhal exploits the resources of a protean irony for self-
protective and camouflaging purposes. His characters' actions elicit
from him patronizing advice, urbane maxims, discursive comments,
and surprised exclamations. These interventions do not, however,
arrest the imaginative development. Toying with the actualities of a
given situation, the author constantly fabricates gratuitous hypo-
thetic projections, thus creating fiction within fiction, as well as the
illusion that the characters are free to chart their own courses.

This creative duplicity, so useful for the motifs of freedom, extends to the author's own temperament and vision. The game of intervention is often in the service of a cruel reenactment of his
own past defeats, of a self-punishing exploration of his own poorly
healed wounds. Julien's clumsy tactics hurt Stendhal more than

Julien, but they also provide him with opportunities for self-compensation. The author stresses, and relives, the most vexing mortifications, at the same time as he grants himself imaginary victories. He contrives situations of embarrassment and frustration, but he also knows, and can hint at, what his hero cannot possibly guess: the proximity of victory. Only this promised land of bliss, glimpsed by the author, remains outside the reach of his hero.

The author's interventions not only guarantee the characters' lack of awareness of their success and of their qualities ("le vrai héros fait sa belle action sans se douter qu'elle est belle"), but also give expression to Stendhal's fundamental *instability* vis-à-vis his own literary creation. Caught between the desire to move and yet not to uncover what moves him, he transfers his sensibility to his fictional creatures, and grants himself the privilege of reliving, but also of transcending, his private predicament. The real action of the novel is thus indistinguishably associated with the very process of writing the novel. It is a plot in which the author-subject, present to himself as though he were his own protagonist, has neither defined nor confined himself. His intrusive presence, his proclaimed lack of solidarity with his own fictional creatures, paradoxically ensures not only their autonomy, but his own. This stance, which allows for freedom, corresponds to the interplay of past and present in Stendhal's autobiographic writings.

Levels of Tension

Although the very title of the novel suggests antithesis (red or black, army or clergy, physical exploit or mental energy, priest or hangman, fiery Jacobinism or somber reaction), too much emphasis should not be placed on its symbolism. Color symbolism appealed to Stendhal. A few years later, when he was writing *Lucien Leuwen*, he again considered other color combinations as possible titles: *L'Amarante ou le Noir* or *Le Rouge et le Blanc*. The title *Le Rouge et le Noir* was, moreover, an afterthought; the idea of it came to Stendhal in May 1830, when the novel was already at the printer's.

Yet the principle of contrasts holds. It is illustrated rhetorically, throughout the novel, by a mania for making distinctions and comparisons. Julien cannot admire anything without first formulating a disparity. "Quelle différence!" is one of his favorite phrases. "What a difference with what was fourteen months ago."—"What a difference with what I have lost."—"What a difference with Madame de Rênal's eyes." The refrain echoes through Julien's interior monologues. It is as though he needed these contrasts both to provoke and to justify his most valued reactions. The habit of defining by means of such tensions can be traced back to Stendhal's own need

to experience everything in terms of opposites. The world of Stendhal—whether that of Grenoble or of a fictional Verrières or
Parma—is sharply divided into irreconcilable camps. His enthusiasm feeds on his capacity for scorn. Aversion and even contempt
are for him propelling forces. Repugnance, for him and for his heroes, is the very condition of tenderness. Thus, in order to evoke
lovingly the image of Madame de Rênal, Julien must first take stock
of the coarseness and bad taste of Mme. Valenod. The affective
importance of contrasts is explicitly stated: "His distrustful nature
made him rarely responsive to any memories save those which are
evoked by contrasts, but such memories moved him to tears . . ."
(I, 22)

Love, more specifically, is served by the dynamics of contempt. It
is her husband's "coarse laughter" that makes Madame de Rênal
aware of Julien's "magnanimity" and of his beautiful, well-arched
black eyebrows. (I, 7) Admiration is here directly dependent on relief from distaste. It is around this very principle of opposites that
the key scene in the library of the Hôtel de La Mole is built. When
Mathilde de La Mole overhears the conversation between Julien
and the abbé Pirard, she is struck by the contrast between the free
spirit of Julien and the servile or "parvenu" mentality of Pirard.
"This one was not born on his knees, she thought, like that old
abbé. Heavens, how ugly he is!" (II, 4) Her love—if that word ade-
quately describes Mathilde's emotions—can perhaps be dated from
that moment of illumination. Aversion and sympathy are locked in
a permanent relationship.

No scene better illustrates this interrelationship, this function of
disdain than the ball at the Hôtel de Retz. (II, 8) The episode,
largely experienced through the eyes of Mathilde, has at the center
two "heroic" figures: Altamira, the Italian patriot who has been condemned to death, and Julien. But this admiring perspective is possible only because of the negative experience of boredom and
general disdain. Mathilde haughtily surveys the platitude of good
manners, the smugness of the "gilt-edged ninnies" who make up
the bulk of her aristocratic relatives and friends. Stendhal stresses
her mental yawns. But ennui, in the Stendhalian context, does not,
as in the world of Flaubert or Baudelaire, imply an oppressive and
ironically self-destructive paralysis of the will or even the yearning
for nothingness. With Stendhal, ennui is eminently curable, indeed
calls for a prompt remedy, and thus indirectly serves as a principle
of enthusiasm. Boredom, much like execration, galvanizes the
Stendhalian characters; it is almost the prime condition of fervor.
This spirited potential of boredom is admirably summed up by the
elliptic sentence: "Mathilde s'ennuyait en espoir." Symbolically, she
makes a point of never looking at old men. She holds herself in re-

serve for the opportunity to admire. "Je veux voir un homme . . ." is her regal request.

This imperious nostalgia for enthusiasm does not feed solely on scorn for mediocrity. It is rendered more acute by the fear of being, in turn, held in contempt. Mathilde, who is disconcerted by Julien's almost insolent coldness, begins to attribute to him a fabulous origin. His haughtiness makes him appear "like a prince in disguise." (II, 9) His beauty forces itself on her imagination in direct proportion to a growing sense of humiliation. "She had been despised by Julien, and she could not despise him." This mechanism of contempt remains a permanent reality; it is related to the themes of self-consciousness and almost assumes the value of an irrefutable principle. "He despises others; that is why I do not despise him." (II, 12)

The primary tension is evidently internal. The awesome contempt is first of all self-contempt. It is characteristic that Julien overcomes his reluctance to climb to Mathilde's room (he thinks her invitation is part of a plot) when he considers the lifelong self-accusation of cowardice with which he would have to live. "But if I refuse, I am sure to despise myself afterwards." (II, 15) The real difficulty of living is cohabitation with one's own anxious self-questioning and reproaches. Love itself becomes a pretext for a study in strife and apprehension. As for jealousy, it provides the best illustration of that state of *"imagination renversée,"* which is, so to speak, the chronic condition of private suffering of the Stendhalian protagonists. Stendhal even suggests that anger toward oneself, "colère contre soi-même," precedes the clash with others. (II, 20) Ultimately, the tortured lover becomes the accomplice of his torturer. The *imagination renversée* is in fact what Stendhal describes in *De l'Amour* (II, 41) as the profound unhappiness of seeing oneself inferior and vulnerable—"voir *soi inférieur."* But this vulnerability, this "dégoût de soi-même" is also a principle of fecund emotions and a mainspring for dramatic action. As a good disciple of the Idéologues, Stendhal always sees passion as a dynamic force.

Stendhal complicates tensions within the novel by repeatedly stressing a state of disseverance between the author's voice and those of his characters. Mathilde de La Mole, who writes wild letters and yearns for heroic deeds, is so unlike the typical "Parisian doll" that the author feels compelled to apologize for this unlikely type, slyly commenting that a description of a character such as hers is bound to be prejudicial, in more than one way, to the "unfortunate author." (II, 17, 19) The author's lack of solidarity with his own fictional projections produces a double ambiguity: it conveys a devious admiration for such characters, who are "happily very rare," but it also conveys the underhanded critique of a society that criticizes a character like Mathilde. The other type of disparity between author and protagonists, neater though no less complex as a functional value within the novel, includes all the occasions when the author chooses to enter into open conflict with his own favorite creatures. Thus, when Julien expresses his admiration for the architectural style of the Hôtel de La Mole, the author intervenes to observe dryly that never had passion and beauty been so far removed from each other. (II, 1)

Stendhal is, however, at his crafty best in combining these two modes of intervention: apparent lack of solidarity with his own affective mood and lack of solidarity with his fictional projections are typically blended and transmuted into a positive poetic value. The conditional approach—at once critical, contingent, and conjectural—is particularly conducive to inventive suspense. When Julien fails to see through Mathilde's malicious joy in torturing him, when he fails above all to come up with the proper tactics, the author jumps onto the stage:

> One sees that Julien was totally lacking in experience—he had not even read any novels. Had he been slightly less awkward and cooly said to this young girl, whom he adored and who made him the strangest avowals: "Admit that even though I am less worthy than these gentlemen it is nonetheless me you love," she might have been happy at having her mind thus read. At least Julien's success would have entirely depended on the grace with which he expressed this idea and on the moment chosen for doing so. In any event, he would have emerged well, even advantageously, from a situation that was bound to appear monotonous to Mathilde.
>
> "And you no longer love me, I who adore you!" said Julien to her one day, overcome with love and unhappiness. This was about the worst blunder he could have committed. (II, 18)

The discrepancy between what might or should have happened and what actually did happen provides the double opportunity and the double satisfaction of establishing the love of the woman as well as the innocence of the hero. Surely, during this scene of anguish and embarrassment, Stendhal takes sides with Julien. The affective bond is undeniable. The omniscient author, by means of the questioning and speculative mood, sets out to explore his own past in search of conjectural compensations. He teases his hero. But the teasing serves to evoke sufferings with which the author himself is only too familiar. The conditional construction stresses the gratuitousness of this suffering, its "pure" beauty. For it is Julien's very lack of talent as a cold-blooded seducer, in other words his authenticity despite himself, that Stendhal asks us, indirectly, to admire. The mixed pleasure of reliving his own timidity and awkwardness is here coupled with the joy of glorifying the wretchedness embodied by the character. The critique of the character thus goes hand in hand with a liberating self-critique—liberating, because the author remains free to dream beyond the contingencies of autobiography, even beyond the concatenation of his own plot. He affirms his independence vis-à-vis his reader, while granting his character—as he also grants himself—the freedom to pursue his own notion of victory. The autobiographic element itself, as it is metamorphosed into the texture of fiction, functions to bring out a temporal freedom. The narrative construct permits Stendhal to fuse the lived occurrence with an ulterior interpretation, which itself remains fluid.

These ironical dialectics between the author and his characters are further intensified by dramatic struggles between the protagonists, which are characteristically suggested in military terms. Martial imagery is indeed not confined to the mock-heroic tone reminiscent of Figaro's aria "Non più andrai" (Julien, after his first tryst with Madame de Rênal, is compared to a soldier returning from parade); nor is it limited to the conventional love-symbols of attack, defense, siege, and victory. It is of course amusing to watch the inexperienced Julien confront Madame de Rênal's jewels and dresses—these "terrible instruments of feminine artillery." (I, 16) But the metaphor is significant. His readings in Napoleonic lore constantly transform the most uncontentious situation into a field of battle. This belligerent approach to reality, this notion that he must be up in arms in order not to lose his self-esteem, becomes most acute during his turbulent relations with Mathilde de La Mole, during this *commerce armé*, which forces Julien to ask himself every morning: "Will we be friends or enemies today?" (II, 10)

Nothing, in fact, could be more appropriate than this imagery of belligerence. If Julien is an assiduous reader of Las Cases, Stendhal himself has read with care, and remembered, Laclos' *Les Liaisons dangereuses*, where amorous seduction is seen as a "corps à corps" combat and where military terms such as "défensive," "rencontre," "ruse," and "petite guerre" stud the letters of Valmont and the Marquise de Merteuil. Laclos no doubt encouraged Stendhal to view love as a struggle of wills well suited to bring out the themes of energy, pride, and ideological strategy. It could be argued, of course—this would be the Marxist interpretation—that the imagery of embattlement corresponds to the diagnosis of class warfare. Does Stendhal not write that Julien's fiery glance expresses the anger of a young man "en guerre avec toute la sociéte"? (II, 13) But such an interpretation would doubtless be a misreading, for Stendhal is clearly interested, as he himself explained to his friend Salvagnoli, in "renewing the entire dialogue of love," and he was particularly proud of his treatment of the tense and highly cerebral "amour de tête."

Stendhal's great achievement is, in reality, not so much a renewal as a transposition. For he succeeded in translating into modern fiction certain elements of the Clorinda–Tancredi motif of Tasso's *Gerusalemme liberata*, which haunted him throughout his life. The notion of a love-hate relationship and the image of an amorous combat had an unquestionable hold over his imagination. In *Vie de Henry Brulard*, he recalls how the sight of the legs of his "cruel enemy" (his aunt Séraphie) filled him with desire, with what intense pleasure he imagined pressing "this implacable enemy" in his arms. Conceivably, Stendhal here echoes half-consciously the nocturnal duel in Canto 12 of *Gerusalemme liberata*:

> Tre volte il cavalier la donna stringe
> Con le robuste braccia; ed altrettante
> Da que' nodi tenaci ella si scinge,
> Nodi di fier nemico, e non d'amante.*

The terminology, especially in Part II of *Le Rouge et le Noir*, leaves no doubt about the nature of the martial metaphor that presides over Julien's relationship with Mathilde. "*Aux armes!*" he exhorts himself while planning his nocturnal ascension to Mathilde's window. As he makes plans for "the battle which is preparing," he calculates the movements of the "enemy," and undertakes an operation of "military reconnaissance" himself. Later, there is talk of a "great battle," of victories, of semivictories, and defeats. It is fascinating indeed to follow the stages of his "Parisian" love affair with Mlle. de La Mole. Alternating emotions of admiration, suspicion, contempt, desire and hate, mastery and humiliation are all part of a mechanism of action and reaction in which notions of offensive and defensive are essential movements of a psychological duel.

These tensions, which allow for no immobilization and no respite, activate at every point a sense of projection into the as-yet-unlived moment. Strangely, however—and this is one of Stendhal's subtlest achievements—restlessness and compulsiveness promote the freedom to dream. External pressures steadily maintain a contest between parallel levels of reality. The protagonists' need to find shelter from outer encroachments develops inner resources of revery and unconstraint. Often, characters involved in an appar-

---

* "Three times the cavalier the maiden grasps / In his strong arms, and thrice the maiden too, / From their tenacious knots, herself unclasps, / Knots not of lover, but of savage foe." *Jerusalem Delivered*, John Kingston James (tr.) (London: Longman, Green, Longman, Roberts, and Green, 1865), II, 49.

ently absorbing dialogue pursue an independent interior discourse. Even more successful is the suggestion of a poetic rift within the self. Coinciding but uncommunicating external events and juxtaposed but self-sufficient mental unfoldings emphasize the fundamental independence of both the unreached "other" person and the "self" whose gestures seem to belong to someone else.

One of the most arresting passages, indeed one of the supreme moments in the novel, suggests this *dédoublement*, or splitting of the self. During a verbal exchange between Julien and Mathilde in the chapter entitled "Une Loge aux Bouffes" ("A Box at the Opera"—II, 30), we hear Julien talk as he overhears himself talking, and he discovers that he sounds not only *strange* to the other but to himself as well. The passage brings out the most sophisticated and most moving qualities of Stendhal's art. The situation is viewed mostly through Julien's consciousness. By a twist of events, he gains the upper hand, and, as it is his turn to make Mathilde suffer, his pretended coldness and aloofness succeed. But her visible suffering almost melts his own determination to be strategically cruel. He barely has the courage to resist the desire to admit his love, for he knows that he will lose her as soon as he shows signs of weakness. He therefore continues talking and pretending, almost automatically, and in direct opposition to his true feelings, while his heart whispers other words to him:

> "Ah," he said to himself, as he listened to the meaningless words which his mouth was articulating, as though to foreign sounds, "if I could only cover those pale cheeks with kisses without your feeling them."

This dreamlike sequence, conveying estrangement from one's outer self, focuses on an inner reality removed from the world of actual deeds. It is the dream that has become the vital principle. The very syntax moves from general revery to specific and intimate contact, as the impersonal "those cheeks" ("ces joues") gives way to the personal pronoun "tu." The wish obscures the lived act. But even the wish is for liberation from contingency. Stendhal here achieves a poetry of silence and of unrealization, which protects and perpetuates the ability to dream. His hero, caught in himself, is freed from the vanity of giving pleasure. What he seeks is not erotic victory, but pure sensation. Tension emancipates him from submission to *amour-propre*.

Freedom Through Tension

The theme of social hostility is closely related to Stendhal's psychological themes. In the long draft of the book review he sent to his

Florentine friend Salvagnoli for publication in the *Antologia*, Stendhal stressed his desire to provide a description of the "France morale" of 1829. He was proud of his bold account of very "unlovable mores." But it is significant that what he himself considered the most remarkable section of the book, as "peinture de moeurs," was the episode in the theological seminary.[7] "*Very well* le séminaire," he jotted down approvingly in the margins of several passages as he reread that section of the novel. He was obviously pleased with his somber satire of a morally arid world of petty *arrivisme* and hypocrisy. Behind the oppressive walls of the Besançon seminary, mediocre and lazy sons of peasants, who prefer mumbling Latin words to plowing the earth, cultivate the art of hiding their uninspired greed and develop proficiency in contrite gestures. For here there exists even an art of eating a boiled egg in a holy manner. These rustic types have become a political force, or rather a political tool, for the militant Church intent on maintaining counterrevolutionary pressures and on preparing for an eventual civil war. It is quite clear that in these pages Stendhal considers himself a political diagnostician; they closely echo journalistic pieces in the *Courrier anglais* (I, pp. 184–185; IV, pp. 88–89), which point out the military training of these future "curés de campagne," their ignorance, their potential fanaticism, and their crass desire for physical well-being.

But the seminary episode also has thematic relevance. It is, after the relatively protected world of provincial Verrières, a microcosm of what Stendhal believes society is really like, a lesson in painful contact with a hostile milieu: "He considered his three hundred and twenty-one comrades as enemies." Julien's attitude is, however, not a matter of choice. He is forced into the position of "outsider" by the pressures of animosity. "I see in you something which offends the vulgar," explains the Jansenist abbé Pirard. The inevitable hatred of the "others" almost appears like a fatality weighing down on the Stendhalian hero. "*Difference engenders hatred*," concludes Julien. But the proposition could easily be inverted. Hostility produces estrangement, but it forces the individual, through separateness, into the discovery and affirmation of his independent self.

It is easy to see how such a separateness can be simultaneously a source of suffering and a fecund principle of pride and self-affirmation. Ultimately such tensions bring out the best in Stendhal's characters. Pirard himself, at first a terrifying figure of inhuman severity, achieves his true greatness through isolation and persecution. A victim of Jesuit plotting, he becomes a symbol of noble steadfastness. In the margin of the very passage evoking his selfless struggle against Marie Alacoque, the Jesuits, and his bishop, Stendhal jotted down a self-congratulatory "*very well*."

Quite appropriately, it is Pirard who gives the clearest formulation to the Stendhalian law of the happy obstacle: "If a man has merit in your eyes, place an obstacle in the way of everything he desires, and of everything he undertakes. If the merit is real, he will surely manage to overcome or get around those obstacles." (I, 29) Freedom is to be achieved through struggle with constraints; tensions can be creative and liberating.

The political themes confirm this principle of strength and resilience through resistance. Stendhal quipped that politics in a novel are like pistol shots interrupting a concert. If this is true, then the flow of Stendhalian music is constantly threatened—by remarks on class antagonisms, political discussions, observations on the Parisian nobility, echoes of recent political plots. At every point, but especially in Part II, Stendhal pulls the trigger of his metaphorical pistol. But the explosions halt nothing. On the contrary, they have a stimulating effect; they are essential to the drive of worldly ambition and to poetic dreams. In Stendhal's case, one might indeed speak of the poetry of politics. Social forces are seen as tyrannical; yet they fail to constrict the Stendhalian hero. Instead, they unleash an energy, which is in turn converted into fervor. Symbolically, the novel leads to the ultimate confrontation of Julien and the vengeful jurors who proclaim his guilt and ask for his death. But symbolically also, the trial provides a magnificent opportunity for fiery self-affirmation. In a dramatic speech to his "enemies," the jurors—a speech which, like a great theatrical performance, seems to arrest the movement of time—Julien asserts his independent spirit, and transforms a condemnation into a stoic suicide. Inequity and death thus become instruments of freedom.

Far more subtle than the dramatic affirmation of independence, and almost in contradistinction to it, a camouflaged freedom is proposed as the only truly successful defense against the evil pressures of our time. In the face of anonymous tyranny (the plight of modern man), rebellious gestures are inefficacious. The first duty of the rebel is survival, if only the survival of the spirit of rebellion. Almost prophetically, Stendhal seems to have diagnosed the despotism of a totalitarian world and the dilemmas of the oppressed spirit that chooses to "agree" in order to be able to think differently. The problem, as modern intellectuals have found out the bitter way, is how to maintain a private conscience and heretical views under oppressive regimes. Controlled dissembling may not be the noblest or most heroic weapon, but its artful practice can be made to serve noble resistance and secret liberty.

It is in this light that one must approach the complex problem of hypocrisy central to *Le Rouge et le Noir*. The terms and concepts are indeed there at the beginning of the novel (the visit to the church is "useful for his hypocrisy"); they accompany Julien to Paris ("the center of intrigue and hypocrisy"—II, I); and continue to echo in his mind during his prison meditation on death: "Talking alone to myself, and a few steps away from death, I am still playing the hypocrite . . . O you nineteenth century!" (II, 44) Paradoxically, however, the notion of hypocrisy also has a positive value. When Julien thinks of his happiness as he is about to leave for Paris, the theater of great events and of greater deeds, he imagines specifically a world of crafty schemes and of polished Machiavellian hypocrites. (I, 30) But the mental image is far from derogatory; cunning is here the very proof of energy and manly virtue. Similarly, Madame de Rênal admires Julien's talent for dissimulation. As for Mathilde, one might almost say that she takes his masterful falsehood as the clearest sign of his superiority. As she overhears a conversation in which Julien says not a word which is not a lie or a travesty of what he really believes, she is more than ever captivated by him: "What intelligence!" ("Quelle profondeur!"—II, 28)

One could invoke the Tartuffe myth, to which there are not only echoes but direct allusions throughout the novel. In church, young Julien explains to his father, he sees only God. (I, 5) To M. de Rênal, he points out that his holy vocation does not allow him to read as profane a poet as Horace. (I, 6) When perplexed about the course of action he is to adopt after Mathilde invites him to her room, he quotes lines from Molière's play, and cautions himself that Tartuffe, too, was ruined by a woman. (II, 13) And when Mathilde's pregnancy becomes known to the Marquis, who heaps execrations on the culprit, Julien's answer is supplied by a line from Le Tartuffe: "Je ne suis pas un ange . . ." ("I'm not an angel"—II, 33)

The interest of the Tartuffe myth lies not merely in the obvious theme of hypocrisy; it proposes the image of a part played out within a part. Even more significant is the fact that we are dealing here with an inverted myth. In the eyes of the Liberals under the Restoration, Molière's play assumed a militant political value. The numerous editions of the play in these years, as well as the nature of these editions, testify to the fact that it constituted an oblique, subversive weapon against the reactionary Congrégation. It is curious indeed that the very remarks concerning the military training of the antirevolutionary peasant seminarists in the Courrier anglais (I, 184–185) should appear in Stendhal's book review of Mortonval's Le Tartufe moderne. Quite clearly, the image of Tartuffe represents, in the Stendhalian context, an ambiguous symbol.

The themes of hypocrisy—one must indeed think in plural terms—encompass a hateful reality and ignoble means of fighting ignominy. The world as it is, whether in Verrières or in Paris, is filled with moral ugliness masquerading as honor. Counterfeit morality corrupts even the potentially pure, and the pressures of self-righteous public opinion choke individual values. The only way to resist victoriously is to use the infamous weapons of the enemy's hypocrisy, but to use them better. The artful, or artificial hypocrite thus has a double advantage: that of not really being a hypocrite, and that of outsmarting the evil forces that threaten his disguised spontaneity. Ultimately, the hypocrite's role becomes a means of fulfilling a moral duty and of acquiring dignity. What is at stake is the conservation of the unique qualities of the exceptional individual in the face of the immorality of conformist ethics. Freedom is thus forced to seek refuge in dissimulation.

The Discoveries of Freedom

It is not surprising that the prison theme assumes a protective and purifying value. Freedom through confinement is a paradox related to freedom through camouflage. Stendhal was, throughout his life, haunted by images of fortresses and prison cells. The Castel Sant'Angelo and the Spielberg cast their gloomy shadows across his works. There exist political reasons, no doubt: the Revolution, the Empire, the Restoration imposed their different forms of arbitrary internment. The *prison d'état* became a key symbol of modern political tyranny. Penitentiary claustration is thus viewed by Stendhal as a particularly dreadful form of human degradation. In *Le Rouge et le Noir*, Julien's first contact with prison life is the humiliating experience of having irons put on his hands. But there is also a contrary valorization; the feared prison becomes the happy prison, symbolizing self-containment and spiritual self-sufficiency. He experiences, much like Fabrice in *La Charireuse de Parme*, an unexpected at-homeness in jail. At one point, he blames himself for being hypocritical in his cell, as though there were somebody there to listen to him. (II, 44) The remark is appropriate only to the extent that it suggests the solipsistic inner monologues of Stendhal's characters, who are always their own severest judges. Characteristically, at the beginning of this chapter, Julien complains that the worst evil in prison is the inability to close one's door. No reaction could more aptly illustrate the deep delight of claustration. And no statement could be more expressive of the pride of claustration than Julien's ironic threat to Mathilde that he will exclude her from his prison: "Je cesse de te voir, je te fais fermer ma prison . . ." (II, 45)

The joyful prison is not only the locus of a happy isolation. Beyond the "amour de la solitude," Julien discovers a deeply meaningful poetry of elevation and grandiose silence. In the Gothic Besançon tower he occupies a cell at the top, and from there he enjoys, through a narrow space between two walls, a magnificent vista ("une échappée de vue superbe"). This relation between constriction and infinity is further heightened by the nocturnal silence disturbed only by the song of the osprey. (II, 36) The strange pleasure of the prison experience is not merely that of luxurious liberation from daily contingencies—a freedom from care, which brings about mastery of "l'art de jouir de la vie" and which is symbolized by Julien's delight in smoking superior Dutch cigars on top of the dungeon tower. It is the joy of meaningful tranquillity: "His soul was calm." (II, 36) And with this serenity goes a deep glance, an almost superhuman lucidity. "Julien felt strong and resolute, like a man who sees to the very bottom of his soul." (II, 44)

The image of the prison cell as a privileged place of insight and of spiritual serenity lends itself particularly to meditation on death. From Pascal to Sartre and Camus, French literature is rich in prison reveries on mortality. In fact, Julien concludes that his destiny quite logically led him to incarceration, since he was, according to the abbé Blanès's prognostication, fated to "die dreaming." Death itself becomes a pretext for self-measurement. Thus, on one occasion, Julien declares himself to be twenty degrees below the level of death. (II, 37) The high tension of this tête-à-tête with imminent nothingness raises the Stendhalian habit of taking one's own moral temperature to a tragic and even speculative level. Julien's soul at this point is almost altogether exiled to the "realm of ideas." (II, 40)

The exalted prison experience is such that Julien's happiest moments occur when he is transferred from his lofty dungeon to a dank cell reserved for prisoners awaiting execution. It is in this seemingly unpropitious setting that he lives his most intense moments of love with Madame de Rênal. The four walls of the cell become the symbol of his private world of revery, as well as of a pure and impossible love. If, at the same time, the prison imagery suggests necessary ties and inevitable separation, it is because Stendhal's imagination is repeatedly drawn to situations that stress the poetry of unrealization. Obstacles, in his fictional world, do not only propel, but also provide shelter against the snares and the corruption of erosive reality.

The prison liberation is multiple. Tired of heroic poses, freed from the compulsions of his own ambitious temperament, Julien can finally devote himself to the *present* situation; he is delivered from time. The stripping of false values allows him to relive the past, and to make of it a new present. "He could surrender himself completely to the memory of the happy days which he had once passed in Verrières or in Vergy." (II, 39) Now the "others" no longer count; he is released from their exacting glance, returned to himself, truly emancipated. Out of time and fully in possession of his own being—that is the enviable position of the Stendhalian prisoner-hero. But such self-possession can be achieved only at the end of a road. In *La Chartreuse de Parme* also, the Farnese tower and the retirement in the charterhouse occur after the worldly excursions to Waterloo and to the court of Parma. Julien understands that all his life "had been but a long preparation for unhappiness." (II, 36) But this unhappiness is turned into the most positive experience. "I no longer have anything to achieve on this earth," observes Julien in this chapter describing his arrival in jail. The expression is one of neither resignation nor sadness, but of an intuited and deeply longed-for transcendence. Immediately upon making this statement to himself, Julien falls into a deep slumber.

Ultimately, it is death itself that is the great reliever from the oppression of time. The sight of the senile abbé Chélan fills Julien with inconsolable sadness and confirms him in his death-row vocation. As has been pointed out, Julien's speech to the jurors is not so much an act of defiance with political overtones as a disguised form of suicide. That Stendhal's own imagination toyed with this notion is quite clear. M. de Frilair, the shrewd leader of the Besançon *Congrégation*, bluntly states that if the appeal is not won, his death "will be a kind of *suicide*." (II, 46) And the Jansenist confessor attending Julien informs him that unless he takes every possible step to obtain his pardon he will fall into the "awful sin of suicide." (II, 45) The suicide motif recurs indeed in a number of Stendhalian works. Octave takes poison, Mina de Vanghel shoots herself, the abbesse de Castro stabs herself; and it could easily be argued that Fabrice's almost ascetic disembodiment and death at the end of *La Chartreuse* is a particularly subtle form of self-elimination.

The typical patterns of Stendhal's imagination connect the themes of liberation with the themes of self-knowledge and self-revelation. The author pretends not to know his characters; they remain, so he claims, free to surprise him. The claim is neither a quip nor a sign of literary coquetry. The intrusive, digressive stance merely confirms that his personages are not meant to know themselves either—at least not at the outset. For Stendhal's heroes are not predetermined, despite the apparent necessity of a preexisting plot. They discover themselves existentially, through their reactions; and they even discover their reactions as a surprise.

Nothing is more revealing of this process of unconstrained discovery than the evolution of the love relationship between Julien and Madame de Rênal. When they first meet, the author makes a point of informing us that neither of them has read the novels which could trace out the part they are to play and give them a model to imitate. (I, 7) In this respect they are the antithesis of Flaubert's protagonists who have heard, read, and learned too much, and who necessarily experience desire by proxy. The innocence of Stendhal's characters is no doubt relative, but it is effective. It is perfectly logical—and thematically crucial—that they be blind to their own authenticity.

It is instructive, in this light, to compare Julien's first departure from Verrières with his second, and finally with the last meeting in jail. From suspicion to abandon, and then to full realization—that is the affective trajectory of the novel. When Julien takes leave of his mistress and enters the Besançon seminary, he completely misunderstands the meaning of her silence and frigidity. (I, 23) She appears to him as a "barely animated corpse." Concerned only with his own pride, he fails to notice the convulsive and tragic nature of her reactions. It is only retrospectively, and characteristically too late, that he is deeply moved by the "cold embraces of this living corpse." The scene suggests, through powerful understatement, a bond between worldly and transcendental love, between the temporal and the eternal orders.

The second departure, which marks the end of Part I, takes place in a climate of passion and light heartedness. The chapter comes very close to comedy, almost in a theatrical sense (there is an echo of Chérubin's window escape in *Le Mariage de Figaro*); yet these pages also penetrate new poetic and psychological depths. Madame de Rênal's sudden changes of mood, the range of her temperament, her "sudden gaiety" and impetuous movements of passion correspond to a revelation taking place in the mind of Julien: "What a superior woman!" But the revelation implies far more than the delighted appreciation of a lover. Julien has experienced this kind of revelation—almost somber in its intensity—earlier, during the sickness of Madame de Rênal's young son, when he was able to measure and to value the moral sacrifice made out of love for him. (I, 19) In the scene preceding his departure for Paris, Julien intuits something more precious still than this victory over morality and even religion (echoes of Valmont's seduction of the Présidente de Tourvel). Hidden and locked up by Madame de Rênal in one of the rooms of the house, he begins to see the beauty of uninhibited gestures and authentic responses. He is Madame de Rênal's "prisonnier" when he has this revelation. (I, 30)

It is in the real prison, however, within close range of death, that the ultimate descent into the self takes place, and Julien discovers the poetry of the privileged moment, *"l'art de jouir de la vie."* (II, 40) The atemporal delight in pure experience or sensation is not unrelated to Rousseau, and it is hardly surprising that Stendhal's clearest formulation of this mystique of the privileged moment in *Vie de Henry Brulard* ("Pour un tel moment il vaut la peine d'avoir vécu") occurs at the point of the most intense evocation of *La Nouvelle Héloïse*. But it is the privileged moment neither of an irretrievable past nor of a transitory present. At no point does Julien prove himself guilty of the sinful wish denounced by Goethe: "Verweile doch, du bist so schön!" ("O do remain, you are so beautiful!"). Protected from smugness and decay, the Stendhalian hero achieves his allegiance to happiness through a telescoping of time. The retrospective event is brought into the present; but soon after, death prevents this retrospective joy from degenerating into a commonplace satisfaction. There is a deep poetic significance to the abrupt endings of Stendhal's two major novels.

The fundamental discovery is, of course, that of identity, which only the act of living and the experience of having lived can reveal. The twin themes of father-rejection and of father-search occupy the heart of *Le Rouge et le Noir*. The myth of a new paternity not only enhances Julien in his own eyes or in the eyes of those who admired or envy him, but is also bound up with the significance of his destiny and of his freedom. Mathilde imagines that he is a glamorous "disguised prince." Elsewhere, she toys with the idea that he is the "natural son" of a country squire. (II, 9, 12) But the notion is not merely the product of an amorous and romantic mind. Julien himself chooses to believe it, and so do those who cross his path. He considers the abbé Pirard, for instance, as a new father ("j'ai retrouvé un père en vous"), and the abbé in turn suspects that the favors of the Marquis de La Mole point to a prestigious though hidden origin. (II, 1) More interesting still, the Marquis, suffering from gout, receives Julien's visits, wants him to wear a special blue suit he had made for him, and treats him as the "younger brother of the Count de Chaulnes, that is to say, the son of my friend the old Duke." (II, 7) This make-believe is more than a game. The Marquis' desire to "ennoble" Julien parallels a latent dream that all of Stendhal's characters possess: the dream of a self-wrought nobility. When the dream appears realized, when Julien has been commissioned lieutenant of hussars with the dashing name of M. le chevalier Julien Sorel de La Vernaye, he can rightfully say: "I have come to the end of my romance" ("mon roman est fini"—II, 34). There will of course be another ending, more tragic and more symbolically meaningful; but the basic revelation is clearly indicated by the first. The independently achieved identity is an answer to the filial anguish of the early chapters. "And I, too, am a kind of foundling . . ." (I, 7), he murmurs to himself at a time when he already strives to take possession of himself. But in these early pages of the novel he does not yet know that self-possession and freedom can be achieved only through a surrender to happiness.

SHOSHANA FELMAN

"Madness" in the Novels of Stendhal†

A narrow perspective [. . .] that opens up the broadest horizons.
—*Baudelaire,* Salon de 1846

What avid reader has failed to ponder Hamlet's famous reply:
—What do you read, my lord?
—Words, words, words.

It's through words that literature gives of itself to us. The literary text is nothing more than a space made of language: spoken words and silences, a meting-out of signs, a landscape of verbal forms.

In Stendhal's works, moreover, language is called upon to play a crucial role: More than one novelistic fate is shaped by something said or written—a vow, a letter, a confession, a book, and so on. In this universe, words carry exceptional status and weight. Characters listen to them uneasily, questioning themselves as they question language: " 'I've had quite a scare,' Fabrice said to himself; *hearing the sound of this word*, he came close to feeling ashamed."[1] The act of naming thus constitutes the birth of responsibility; it isn't fear in and of itself that gives rise to shame, but the naming of it, its verbal re-sounding. Language makes things happen and urges them forward. This is why Fabrice, regarding Gina, resists putting a name to his feelings:

> Because he loved her beyond all things at this moment [. . .] he vowed to himself never to tell her that *he loved her*; never would he say the word "love" in her presence.[2]

Stendhal is intensely aware of the power of words and their ability to take on a life of their own:

> There is often a *physiognomy* in how words are formulated to which no translation can do full justice,[3] we read in *La Chartreuse de Parme.*

So it was entirely reasonable that we should look for the *physiognomy* of Stendhal within the verbal landscape of his works. Setting aside all prejudices, all preconceived ideas, all prior knowledge ex-

---

† From *La "Folie" dans l'oeuvre romanesque de Stendhal* (Paris: Librarie José Corti, 1971). Translated by Margaret Flynn for this Norton Critical Edition. Reprinted by permission of the author.
1. *La Chartreuse de Parme* [*The Charterhouse of Parma*, Stendhal's 1839 novel set in Italy], p. 179. We are taking the liberty of italicizing the cited texts at our discretion. Hereafter, only Stendhal's italics will be indicated in the footnotes.
2. *Chartreuse*, p. 166. Italics Stendhal's.
3. P. 297.

ternal to the text itself, we set out, simply and strictly, to *read* Stendhal. To read wherever his words might take us as we awaited a sign from them.

And in fact, one word did give us pause: Embodying first our mindfulness of the text, then our desire to understand it, it quickly beguiled us, for—although used in countless instances—it easily goes unnoticed during a hurried reading. Emphatic and reticent, familiar and remote, it steals away as soon as it appears; effaced by the same redundancy that marks and accentuates it, this word presents an "enigmatic transparency"[4] to the critical gaze. The word we are thinking of is "madness" [*folie*], along with its entire family: "mad," "madly,"[5] and so on.

Lexical Data: Descriptive Inventory of Frequency

But why should our selection of this lexical fact be surprising? Isn't its frequency obvious? Here are the linguistic facts. "Mad" and its derivatives occur 46 times in *Armance*,[6] 122 times in *Le Rouge et le noir* [*The Red and the Black*], 144 times in *Lucien Leuwen*, and 144 times in *La Chartreuse de Parme*.[7]

* * *

The Form of Content: Attempts at Classification; The Search for a Method

* * *

LITERAL MEANING AND FIGURATIVE MEANING

In reference to the semantic content covered by a verbal signifier, a traditional criterion for classification differentiates between figurative meaning and literal meaning. This differentiation wastes no

---

4. We owe this expression to Gérard Genette, who incisively uses it to define "the distinctive nature of Stendhalian discourse." *Figures*, II (Collection "Tel Quel," Seuil, 1965), p. 192.
5. By "word," we mean a lexical unit; linguists more rigorously refer to this as a *lexeme*: "a virtual model that subsumes the entire functioning of a figure of meaning designated by a given formant, but prior to [for us, considered prior to] any manifestation in discourse, which, for its part, can only produce specific sememes." A. J. Greimas: *Sémantique structurale* [*Structural Semantics*] (Paris: Larousse, 1966), p. 51.
6. Variations add another 2 occurrences.
7. We are leaving out *Lamiel*: This is because it seemed impossible to derive a *global* assessment of any value from this outline of a novel. Indeed, *Lamiel* is not merely unfinished, as is *Lucien Leuwen*; it's a novel that was barely *begun*. The plan dated November 25, 1839, gives us an early warning of sorts: "It will get interesting," Stendhal writes, "when true love comes along" (Pléiade, *Appendice*, p. 1,031). As it happened, the novel was broken off before "true love" began.

   Since our study deals with Stendhal's major novels, we cannot, naturally, ignore *Lamiel*; as a general rule, however, and for methodological reasons, we will only refer to it for matters of detail and never for an overall perspective, as the condition of the novel does not allow this.

A Table of the Vocabulary of Madness in Stendhal's Novels

Part of Speech	Value	Number	
		Single	Plural
NOUN	Act	MADNESS	ACTS OF MADNESS
		(To do, commit) an act of madness	(To do, commit) acts of madness
	Quality	Moments Fits/episodes {of madness Night Hint A (person's) mad side	
	Quantity	(to love) unto madness	
	Persons	A madman A madwoman	Madmen Madwomen
ADJECTIVE	Attribute	To be To become To drive someone } mad To believe someone to be	
	Epithet	Nearly Completely } mad Absolutely Raving	
		Mad } pride love	

		Mad with } happiness
		              joy
		              pain
		              rage
		              worry
			Eyes
			Moments } mad with . . .

		Mad for } glory To be mad about } someone something	
		Mad as a hatter Mad as a March hare	
ADVERB	Quality Quantity	Madly (unto madness)	

time in engaging the "madness" lexeme. Let's look at the scope it assumes in the Stendhalian text.

Literally speaking, "madness" signifies a derangement of mind, a mental illness. Does this clinical use of the term exist in Stendhal's writings? Readers who, prompted by a certain critical tradition, have accustomed themselves to the somewhat inflexible image of Stendhal as a rationalist motivated by reason and enlightenment would no doubt tend to claim vehemently that it does not, pointing to the word's *erosion*, its weakening over time, its divergence from the literal meaning originally given it. Stendhal, however, is well aware of the medical scope inherent to the vocabulary of "madness." Clinical use of the term occurs more often than one might believe in the absence of a careful examination of the text. Here are three noteworthy examples that clearly use the term in a clinical sense; in all of these cases, the force of its literal meaning[8] is unfailingly eloquent:

1. *Armance*:

> It was not always at night, and not always when he was alone, that these fits of despair shook Octave. When they did, all of his actions bespoke an extreme violence, an extraordinary cruelty; if he had been anyone other than an impoverished law student without family or protectors, *he would have been locked up as a madman*.[9]

2. *Le Rouge et le noir*:
Julien has just learned that his crime was unsuccessful, whereupon the author remarks:

> Only at that moment was he freed from *the state of physical irritation and near-madness* into which he had been thrust since leaving Paris for Verrières.[1]

3. *La Chartreuse de Parme*:
Speaking of Ferrante Palla:

> It dawned on the duchess that he was *a bit mad*, but this did not alarm her [. . .]

The police will have trouble catching up with him, she thought, *he really is mad*.

> —*He's mad*, her servants told her [. . .]
> —And you never told me about these *mad things you did*, the
>   duchess said in a chiding tone [. . .]
> That day, he seemed *quite out of his head*. He said that there were people in Parma who owed him six hundred francs, and that with that amount of money he would repair his shanty, where his [. . .] children were forever catching cold.[2]

These clinical examples are not isolated ones in Stendhal's novels. Madness in the literal sense is attributed to one character after another. But the madness doesn't last; it's a passing folly. In *Le Rouge et le noir*, for example, when Fouqué sees Mathilde after Julien's execution:

8. There is, of course, less force, but nevertheless an intention toward literality when Stendhal goes so far as to *explicitly use* the literal meaning: cf. *"literally mad"* (*Leuwen*, pp. 953, 1082).
9. P. 45.
1. P. 649.
2. Pp. 363, 365, 366.

> With *wild and wandering eyes* [. . .] she had placed Julien's head on a small marble table before her and kissed it on the forehead . . .[3]

Or when, in *La Chartreuse*, Gina heads off Fabrice to save him from being poisoned:

> *Her wits astray*, she told her coachman to bring the horses to a gallop [. . .] The duchëss threw her arms around Fabrice's neck and *fainted dead away*, the episode causing all to fear first for her life, *then for her sanity*.[4]

This *fleeting* but *manifest* mode of existence of madness in the strong sense—literal insanity—is counterbalanced by a *permanent* but *latent* mode of existence of *madness held in abeyance*, poised to erupt:

"She *might go mad* and throw herself out of the window,"[5] says Julien, speaking from experience, of Madame de Rênal, whose delirious remorse caused by her son's illness he observes.

In its figurative meaning, derived from its literal meaning, the signifier "madness" does not involve a diagnosis but an image, a particular appearance (cf: "you *appear to be mad*"[6]; "the *look of madness*"[7]). This appearance is likened to actual madness through either a metaphoric or a metonymic process: by analogy or by contiguity. This shift from the literal meaning to the contiguous or to the similar is at times explicitly expressed. Cf. *Contiguity*:

"A condition *not far from madness*."[8]

"His/her behavior *bordered on the appearance of madness*."[9]
Analogy:

"*as if mad*," "*like a madman*."[1]

Characters who are called "mad" are not, medically speaking, insane; but they are *represented* "like madmen." Hence the lexical field of "madness" designates, through exaggeration, a condition of great distress wherein characters *appear to be* insane even if they are not. This is how one can be "mad with joy," can fall prey to a "mad passion" or to a "mad fancy," and "go to mad excess." Clearly, this derivative use—whether metaphoric or metonymic—of the idea of madness is the type most often seen in Stendhal, but does not overshadow the use of its literal, medical meaning.

3. P. 698.
4. P. 445.
5. *Rouge*, p. 323.
6. *Armance*, p. 67.
7. Ibid., p. 186.
8. Ibid., p. 138.
9. Ibid., p. 186.
1. Cf. *Rouge*, pp. 239, 346; *Leuwen*, pp. 951, 1034; *Chartreuse*, pp. 311, 388.

It remains to be seen whether these two uses are always so clear-cut. In some Stendhalian contexts, it is at times hard to know where the literal meaning of the idea of madness leaves off and its figurative meaning begins. Since clinical madness is both permanently in abeyance and fleeting in its manifestation, its outlines are fuzzy; it is difficult to delimit with any certainty or precision. Earlier we saw, quite clearly, the shift from the literal to the figurative meaning using explicit lexical means denoting comparison or contiguity. But the text also features a reverse shift: from the figurative to the clinical meaning.

* * *

The Tragic Ambiguity of Madness

> . . . madness, I know all of its wild joyful leaps and calamities—my burden is set down utterly.
> —*Rimbaud*, Une Saison en enfer [A Season in Hell]

THE SHATTERING OF UNEQUIVOCAL MEANING

> Humankind is so necessarily mad that not to be mad would be merely another form of madness.
> —*Pascal*

Innocence or guilt, strength or weakness, blindingly obvious error or obscure truth, retraced origin or anachronism, eternal youth or infantilism, creation or hallucination, pure meaning or pure nonsense: "Madness," in Stendhal's writings, can only be defined as a field of possibilities, a curve of varied, manifold nuances between which the Stendhalian text constantly shifts, and whose variety can at no time be reduced to an immediate, unequivocal, and transparent synthesis. Indeed, the heart of the issue resides in the rapports established between the various nuances, in the play of differences—even dissonances, as often happens—within the same idea. Here, lexical frequency creates, through the alterity within analogy, the difference that lives inside homonymy, an irreducible complexity, an unconquerable resistance. Stendhal's famously limpid style is all the more deceptive since this apparent homogeneity is radically heterogeneous. In other words, the Stendhalian text *shatters* the idea of "madness" by *perpetuating* it. At that point it becomes an open idea whose meaning is never given, whose precise signification as well as its affective overload are not set once and for all; rather, they must actualize themselves each time within a context that determines them, take ownership of themselves over a text that acts upon them.

This differential dynamism that toys with the nominal identity found in the same lexical constant causes us to experience on an involved, emotional level the writer's wearisome struggle against his own use of language, the combat of instances of language against the abstract concept of language in general.

However, the weak spot within the signifier itself becomes functional, constitutive of the signified: this infinite leakage of meaning from within language makes manifest, in the very concept of madness, the irreducibility that inhabits all logical definitions. As it shatters unequivocal meaning, deficient, approximate language calls upon the reader to use all of his/her attentiveness and intelligence; stemming any complacency—be it emotional or intellectual—it invites watchfulness through its own inadequacy. The lived experience of reading, like that of writing, brings us up against the limits of language while we are inside it; but these limits say something to us; they, too, mean something. By making us feel—and live through—the failure of rational understanding, the displacement underlying implemented language takes us to its true meaning, felt and grasped *beyond* this failure, and *through* it.

Thus, the behavior of the signifier reproduces and redoubles the status of the signified: The operations of the vocabulary of madness are such that they call on us, at the immediate level of language, to embark upon an experience akin to madness itself. Shattering the rational clarity and security of unequivocal meaning (while retaining its apparent limpidity), Stendhal's use of language makes the act of reading itself an adventurous, somewhat foolhardy, and unsettling experience. With no permanent, exhaustive, and immutable code available to it, the signifier does not transcend itself: Like madness itself, it is there, at the text's very heart, secure in its opacity, illuminating as it dissimulates, clarifying as it sows misunderstanding of a message it broadcasts over multiple wavelengths at the same time. This type of writing calls for a multilevel reading. Like the text's characters, the message itself splits in two, never to be put back together again. Forced on the reader as a choice to be made, the text simultaneously prohibits choice—by making it impossible. It all unfolds as if, in ceaselessly modifying and correcting itself inside its own semantic field, Stendhal's vocabulary of madness were merely searching for its own real meaning through internal argument.

Indeed, in the abstract dialectic played out between madness and reason, in the antagonism that pits the madman and men of reason against each other, and lastly in the struggle that contrasts the madman with society, madness by turns takes on first a positive, then a negative value. It incessantly comes up against its own contradictions. This is why all of its gestures have a dual meaning.[2] Madness is, in the deepest sense, *ambiguous*.

* * *

In *The Birth of Tragedy* Nietzsche, contemplating the sources of the tragic, echoes this ambiguous design:

> So where does tragedy come from, he asked himself;—perhaps from joy, from strength, from glowing good health, from an overflowing plenitude? [. . .] Perhaps delirium is not necessarily a symptom of degeneracy or decline [. . .] Perhaps there are—here's something for alienists to consider—neuroses of health?[3]

At once health *and* illness, madness professes to cure but remains an ever-open wound. Evoking pathos and ridicule, it is simultaneously a source of abundance and a lack. It encompasses the happiness of desire and the sorrow of need. Promising pleasures, its frustrations are everlasting. An immediate, dizzying vision of the very essence of phenomena, it manages at the same time to blind. But this blinding is "a magnificent stroke of good fortune"; it embodies the very condition for potentially achieving greatness:

Most men—according to Stendhal—experience a moment in their lives when they are capable of great things, a moment when nothing seems impossible.[4]

Madness feeds on the impossible and collides with it at the same time. It can be taken as the answer to the two main questions that Stendhal asks himself: How is humankind *true*? How is humankind *great*? But at the same time, this greatness can only be brought about through calamity; this greatness leads humankind to its downfall. Stendhal writes to Métilde:

> It is a happy heart that is warmed by the calm, careful, unwavering light of a lamp with a low flame. Of such a man we can say that he loves without inconveniencing himself or others to any great extent. *But the heart set ablaze by a volcano's fire* [. . .] *runs wild* [. . .] *and burns itself to a cinder.*[5]

The Stendhalian hero, like Empedocles, throws himself into the volcano of his own madness and is consumed. This is why, like the love on which it is predicated, madness is this path we follow along

2. Cf V. Brombert, *Stendhal et la voie oblique* [*Stendhal and the Oblique Path*] (ed.cit.), p. 19: "Stendhal's thought moves forward through antitheses; it is always aware of the dual value of the same gesture [. . .]. This is why his very choice of words is as much a challenge as it is an apology."

3. My translation.

4. *De l'Amour* [*On Love*], pp. 220–221.

5. Letter to Métilde Dembowski (Florence, July 20, 1819) *Correspondance*, vol. I, p. 981.

the edge of a *fearsome precipice*, hanging on to *perfect happiness* with our other hand.[6]

THE STENDHALIAN HERO'S TRAGIC DILEMMA

> I love *those individuals who only find out what life is as life leaves them*, because they surpass themselves [. . .]. I love the man who uses up his soul without restraint, because he gives his all and thinks not of his own preservation.
> —*Nietzsche*, Thus Spake Zarathustra

Madness's basic ambiguity poses an insoluble dilemma within Stendhal's universe. Just as the Balzacian hero must choose, in *La Peau de chagrin* [The Wild-Ass's Skin], between living life to its full intensity and self-preservation, the tragic dilemma of Stendhal's characters is that they must either *preserve themselves* or *live*. Self-preservation may be staying alive, but it is not living. For Stendhal as for Balzac, "to live is to feel alive, to experience intense sensations."[7] "Since life itself is composed only of sensations," Stendhal goes on,

> The universal inclination of all living beings is to be made aware that they are alive by experiencing the most intense sensations possible.[8]

So to be alive is to be mad. But to be mad is, by the same token, to lose oneself. To price we pay for life is living.

Hence the Stendhalian paradox of life in death. Octave, striking a "rational" attitude, tries to hold back life's movement: To spare himself pain, he swears never to fall in love. However, after suffering an apparently mortal wound in a duel, he forswears his ascetic oath and comes alive to life, love, happiness:

> *The approaching end of this life* [. . .] made him love Armance all the more [. . .]. *With death so close at hand*, he forgave himself [. . .] for going back on the oath. We die as best we can, he said inwardly; I'm dying and I've never been happier [. . .]. Octave, *to his amazement, was fully alive.*[9]

Death therefore conditions a "coming back to life."[1] But conversely, life is only possible when death is present. Similarly, Julien only accedes to life on the eve of his death. He does so through a mad gesture that is, at the precise moment when he abandons any effort at

---

6. *De l'Amour*, p. 37.
7. Ibid., p. 37.
8. *De l'Amour*, p. 288.
9. *Armance*, p. 143.
1. Ibid., p. 144. Cf. heading, p. 143. Cf. also J.-J. Rousseau: "I only began to truly live when I saw myself as a dead man" (*Confessions*, IV, Pléiade, p. 228).

self-preservation; and this access to true, real life earns him his death. With reason pushing him toward self-preservation and madness prodding him to truly live, the dialectic of reason and madness forces itself upon the novel's hero in the concrete terms of an alternative between death-in-life or finding true life in dying, between a vegetative, safe existence or an authentic living-out of life as life itself dies away.

PETER BROOKS

The Novel and the Guillotine; or, Fathers and Sons in *Le Rouge et le noir*†

The guillotine that so abruptly, perhaps unreasonably, puts an end to Julien Sorel's life and brilliant career has ever been a critical scandal, an outrage to coherent interpretation. But before using the decapitation of Julien Sorel as a focal point for critical meditation on the plot of *Le Rouge et le noir*, I would suggest briefly that *Le Rouge et le noir* may offer the first notable example of a problem in plot central to the nineteenth-century novel. If in reading Stendhal we undergo "the rites of initiation into the nineteenth century" (Levin 149), we do so largely because his novels are pervaded by a historical perspective that provides an interpretive framework for all actions, ambitions, self-conceptions, and desires; hence they offer the first decisive representations of individuals plotting their lives in response to the sociopolitical dynamics of modern times.[1] Nowhere is the issue of history more evident than in the question of authority that haunts *Le Rouge et le noir*, not only in the minds of its individual figures but in its very narrative structures. The novel represents and takes its structure from the underlying warfare of legitimacy and usurpation; its action hinges on the overriding question, To whom does France belong? This question in turn implicates and is implicated in an issue of obsessive importance in all of Stendhal's novels, that of paternity.

On reflection, one can see that paternity is a dominant issue within the great tradition of the nineteenth-century novel (extending well into the twentieth century), a principal thematic embodiment of a concern with authority, legitimacy, the conflict of

† From *PMLA* 97 (3): 348–62. Reprinted by permission of the Modern Language Association. A subsequent version of this article appears in Brooks's *Reading for the Plot: Design and Intention in Narrative* (New York: Knopf, 1984).
1. For the classic exposition of the way historical perspective pervades representation in Stendhal, see Auerbach (p. 471 in this volume).

generations, and the transmission of wisdom. Turgenev's title, *Fathers and Sons*, sums up what is at stake in a number of the characteristic major novels of the tradition: not only in *Le Rouge et le noir* but also in Balzac's *Le Père Goriot*, Mary Shelley's *Frankenstein*, Dickens' *Great Expectations*, Dostoevsky's *The Brothers Karamazov*, James's *The Princess Casamassima*, Conrad's *Lord Jim*, Gide's *Les Faux-Monnayeurs*, Joyce's *Ulysses*, Mann's *Der Zauberberg*, and Faulkner's *Absalom, Absalom!*, to name only a few of the most important texts that this conflict essentially structures. It is characteristic of *Ulysses* as a summa of the nineteenth- and early twentieth-century novel that its filial protagonist, Stephen Dedalus, should provide an overt retrospective meditation on the problem:

> Fatherhood, in the sense of conscious begetting, is unknown to man. It is a mystical estate, an apostolic succession, from only begetter to only begotten. On that mystery and not on the madonna which the cunning Italian intellect flung to the mob of Europe the church is founded and founded irremovably because founded, like the world, macro- and microcosm, upon the void. Upon incertitude, upon unlikelihood. *Amor matris*, subjective and objective genitive, may be the only true thing in life. Paternity may be a legal fiction. Who is the father of any son that any son should love him or he any son?   (207)

Stephen's theological musing on the "apostolic succession" of fatherhood strikes to the key problem of transmission: the process by which the young protagonist of the nineteenth-century novel discovers his choices of interpretation and action in relation to a number of older figures of wisdom and authority, who are rarely biological fathers—a situation that the novel often ensures by making the son an orphan or by killing off or otherwise occulting the biological father before the text brings to maturity its dominant alternatives. The son then most often has a choice among possible fathers from whom to inherit, and in the choosing—which may entail a succession of selections and rejections—he plays out his career of initiation into a society and into history and comes to define his own authority in the interpretation and use of social (and textual) codes.

Freud, in his well-known essay "Family Romances," develops the typical scenario based on the child's discovery that "pater semper incertus est": the fantasy of being an adopted child whose biological parents are more exalted creatures than his actual parents, which the child then supersedes by accepting the actual mother but creating a fantasized, illegitimate father and bastardizing siblings to establish the child's sole legitimacy. It may be significant, as Roland Barthes notes, that the child appears to "discover" the Oedipus complex and the capacity for constructing coherent narrative at about the same stage in life. For the most fully developed narratives of the child who has become a man all seem to turn on uncertainty about the father's identity, to use this uncertainty to develop the romance of authority vested elsewhere, and to test the individual's claim to personal legitimacy within a struggle of different principles of authority. In the nineteenth century, these issues touch every possible register of society, history, and fiction, and nowhere more so than in France, where the continuing struggle of revolution and restoration played itself out in dramatic political upheavals and reversals throughout the century. The nineteenth-century novel as we know it is indeed inseparable from this struggle, from the issue of authority and the theme of paternity, which provide not only the matter of the novel but its structuring force, the dynamic that shapes its plot.

From this exceedingly general sketch of how the problem of authority and paternity relates to plot, I want to return to Julien Sorel's plot by way of its end, through the curious finalities the end appears to present and the ways in which they may motivate our readings of beginning and middle. The narrator tells us, just before Julien Sorel's end, "Jamais cette tête n'avait été aussi poétique qu'au moment où elle allait tomber"—"Never had this head been so poetic as at the moment it was about to fall" (506; all translations from Stendhal are mine). The next moment of the text—the next sentence—it is all over, and the narrator is commenting on the style with which the head fell: "Everything took place simply, fittingly, and without any affectation on his part." In an elision typical of Stendhal, the climactic instant of decapitation is absent. We have the vibrations of the fall of the guillotine's blade, but not the bloody moment. The elision is the more suspect in that it is not clear that Julien's head needed to fall at all. As a traditional and rationalist criticism of Stendhal used to say, Julien's shooting of Mme de Rênal—which entails his decapitation—appears arbitrary, gratuitous, insufficiently motivated. Engaged to marry the pregnant Mathilde de la Mole, adored of her as she is adored of her father, surely Julien the master plotter, the self-declared disciple of Tartuffe, could have found a way to repair the damage done to his reputation by Mme de Rênal's letter of accusation. Those critics who try to explain Julien's act on psychological grounds merely rationalize the threat of the irrational, which is not so importantly psychological as narratological: the scandal of the manner in which Stendhal has shattered his novel and then cut its head off.[2] Still another scan-

2. Henri Martineau summarizes critical objections to the end of the novel and offers his own psychological interpretation (343–51). For another useful summary of critical commentaries on the denouement and for an attempt to remotivate Julien's acts on a rational basis, see Castex (124–55).

dal—and another elision—emerges in this ending because of the novel's chronology, which would place Julien's execution well into 1831. Yet in this novel, subtitled "Chronique de 1830," we have no mention of the most notable event of the year: the July Revolution. Indeed, Mme de Rênal in the last pages of the novel proposes to seek clemency for Julien by pleading with King Charles x, who had been dethroned for almost a year. The discrepancy is particularly curious in that the whole of Julien's ideology and career—of revolt, usurpation, the transgression of class lines—seems to beckon to and call for revolution. Is the guillotine that executes Julien—the "peasant in revolt," as he has called himself at his trial—a displaced figure for "les Trois Glorieuses," a revolution notable for having made no use of the guillotine? Is the catastrophic ending of *Le Rouge et le noir* a displaced and inverted version of the revolution that should have been?[3]

Perhaps we have begun to sketch the outlines of a problem in narrative design and intention, in plot and its legitimating authority, including history as plot, and in the status of the end on which, traditionally, the beginning and middle depend for their retrospective meaning. We can come closer to defining the problem with two statements that Julien makes shortly before the arrival of Mme de Rênal's accusatory letter. When the Marquis de la Mole has given him a new name, M. le chevalier Julien Sorel de la Vernaye, and a commission as lieutenant in the hussars, he reflects, "After all . . . my novel is finished" (444). Yet the novel—if not his, then whose?—will continue for another eleven chapters. Shortly after the statement just quoted, Julien receives twenty thousand francs from the Marquis, with the stipulation that "M. Julien de la Vernaye"—the Sorel has now been excised—will consider this a gift from his real (i.e., natural, illegitimate) father, and will donate some of it to his legal father, Sorel the carpenter, who took care of him in childhood. Julien wonders if this fiction of the illegitimate aristocratic father might not be the truth after all: "Might it really be possible, he said to himself, that I am the natural son of some great noble exiled in our mountains by the terrible Napoleon? With every moment this idea seemed less improbable to him . . . My hatred for my father would be a proof . . . I would no longer be a monster!" (446). The word "monster," as we shall see, evokes a network of references to Julien's moments of self-identification as the

---

3. Martineau establishes a careful fictional chronology of the novel in the Garnier edition (533–37). On the problem of chronology, see also Stivale. Concerning revolution and the guillotine, see Stendhal's account of his joy—at age ten—on learning of the execution of Louis XVI, an event he explicitly contrasts with the failure of the July monarchy to execute the Comte de Peyronnet and the other ministers who signed the "ordonnances de juillet," which touched off the Revolution of 1830 (*Henry Brulard* 94).

plebeian in revolt, the usurper, the hypocrite, the seducer, the Tartuffe, he who, in the manner of all monsters, transgresses and calls into question the normal orders of classification and regulation. But can illegitimacy rescue him from monstrosity, when throughout the novel illegitimacy has appeared the very essence of the monstrous? Can hatred for the legal father be a proof of innocence, that is, of the lack of monstrosity, of the lack of a need to act the hypocrite? If so, have we all along been reading, not a "Chronicle of 1830," but an eighteenth-century novel—by an author such as Fielding or Marivaux—in which the hero is a foundling whose aristocratic origins eventually will out and will offer a complete retrospective motivation—and absolution—for his desire to rise in the world: usurpation recovered as natural affinity? Legitimized by illegitimacy, Julien's plot could simply be a homecoming, a *nostos*, the least transgressive, the least monstrous of narratives.

Earlier in the novel, M. de Rênal, reflecting on his children's evident preference of Julien to their father, exclaims: "Everything in this century tends to throw opprobrium on *legitimate* authority. Poor France!" (144). The comment explicitly connects political issues of legitimacy and authority with *paternity*, itself inextricably bound up in the problem of legitimacy and authority. The shape and intention of the novel are tied closely to this network of issues. The questions of authority and legitimacy that the novel poses might be formulated first of all in the queries, What kind of novel is this? To what models of plot and explanation does it refer us? A striking example of this problem occurs early in the novel (bk. 1, ch. 9), in the episode of the "portrait in the mattress." Julien has just learned that M. de Rênal and his servants are going to restuff the straw mattresses of the house. He turns to Mme de Rênal and begs her to "save him" by withdrawing from his mattress, before M. de Rênal reaches it, a small cardboard box containing a portrait. And he also begs her not to look at the portrait; it is his "secret." The narrator, typically crosscutting from the perceptions of one character to those of another, tells us that Mme de Rênal's nascent love for Julien (of which she is still largely ignorant) gives her the heroic generosity of spirit necessary to perform what she takes to be an act of self-sacrifice, since she assumes that the portrait must be that of the woman Julien loves. Once she has retrieved the box and given it to Julien, she succumbs to the "horrors of jealousy." Cutting back to Julien, we find him burning the box, and we learn that it in fact contains a portrait of Napoleon—*l'usurpateur*, Julien names him here—with lines of admiration scratched on its back by Julien. The misunderstanding between the two characters, where neither perceives what is at stake for the other, cannot be confined to the realm of the personal: They are living in different worlds, indeed in different novels. For Mme de Rênal, the drama has to do with love and jealousy, with amorous rivalry and the possibility of adultery. She thinks she is a character in an eighteenth-century novel of manners, *Les Égarements du cœur et de l'esprit*, perhaps, or (as one of its innocents) *Les Liaisons dangereuses*. Julien, on the contrary, is living in the world of modern narrative—postrevolutionary, post-Napoleonic—which precisely throws into question the context of "manners" and the novel of manners, subverts its very possibility. Napoleon, the "usurper" in Julien's pertinent epithet, represents a different order of *égarement*, the intrusion of history into society, the reversal of a stable and apparently immutable world, that of the ancien régime, which made manners possible and necessary as social and literary codes. If, as Julien says a few chapters later, the "fatal memory" of Napoleon will forever prevent young Frenchmen like himself from being happy, the reason is that Napoleon represented the possibility of "la carrière ouverte aux talents": the legitimation of class mobility, legalized usurpation. While Julien studies not to appear a disciple of Napoleon, he manages at various times in the novel to resemble first Robespierre, then Danton, both of whom stand behind Napoleon as destroyers of the ancien régime and who, at the very least, historicized the concept of *le monde*, thus making the novel of manners, in the strict definition, impossible. The scene of the portrait in the mattress signals the impossibility of the novel of manners as Mme de Rênal understands it: questions of love and interpersonal relations no longer exist in a closed and autonomous sphere. They are menaced by class conflict as historicized in the persistent aftermath of the French Revolution.

In a number of essays and reflections over the years, Stendhal developed an explicit theory of why the Revolution had rendered social comedy—"la comédie de Molière," in his shorthand—impossible. He explains himself most fully in "La Comédie est impossible en 1836," where he argues that social comedy could work only with a unified audience, sharing the same code of manners and comportment and agreeing on what was deviant and extravagant in terms of this code. The Revolution, in destroying the society of court and salon and raising to consciousness the claims of different social classes, shattered the unity of sensibility on which Molière's effects were predicated; at a performance of *Le Bourgeois gentilhomme* in 1836, half the audience would laugh at the would-be gentleman, Monsieur Jourdain—as was Molière's intention—but the other half would admire and approve him.[4] When social class

---

4. For a fuller discussion of social comedy and the novel of manners, see Brooks, *Novel* (219–26). Stendhal's argument is largely adumbrated in *Racine et Shakespeare* (1823, 1825).

becomes the basis for political struggle, one man's object of ridicule becomes another man's serious social standard. The demonstration applies as well to the novel (as Stendhal noted in the margins of a copy of *Le Rouge et le noir*):[5] The novel of manners is itself threatened with usurpation; it cannot exclude from its pages something else, something that had best be called politics. Although Mme de Rênal has no knowledge or understanding of politics, she is living in a world where all other questions, including those of love, are eventually held hostage to the political; and this is true as well for the novel in which she figures.

Politics in *Le Rouge et le noir* is the unassimilable other, which in fact is all too well assimilated, since it determines everything: Nothing can be thought in isolation from the underlying strife between legitimacy and usurpation that polarizes the system within which all other differences are inscribed and that acts as a necessary (though I refuse to say ultimate) interpretant to any message formulated in the novel. A telling illustration of this proposition appears in chapter 18 of book 1, which describes the king's visit to Verrières and which is rich in representations of the movement from red to black, as Julien first cuts a figure in the mounted Honor Guard and then dons the cassock to assist the Abbé Chélan in the magnificent *Te Deum* at the chapel of Bray-le-Haut, which so overwhelms him that at that moment "he would have fought for the Inquisition, and in good faith" (108). It is in the midst of this religious spectacular that the narrator treacherously comments, "Such a day undoes the work of a hundred issues of Jacobin newspapers" (107). The reader who has been paying attention will understand that this undoing has been the intent and design of the religous ceremony, staged and financed by the Marquis de la Mole: it is one more political gesture in the continuing struggle to say to whom France belongs.

But if politics is the indelible tracer dye in the social and narrative codes of the novel, the very force of the political dynamic is matched by the intensity with which politics is repressed. For to admit to the force of politics is to sanction a process of change, of temporal slippage and movement forward—of history, in fact—whereas the codes of the Restoration are all overtly predicated on temporal analepsis, a recreation within history of an ahistorical past, a facsimile ancien régime that rigorously excludes the possibility of change, of revolution. Hence those who claim to be the le-

---

5. Rereading the "Bucci copy" of his novel in 1835, Stendhal noted in the margins of bk. 1, ch. 21—where Mme de Rênal has been maneuvering her husband to the conclusion that the anonymous letters come from Valenod—"Here is a scene of comedy." He then went on to lament that it could not be put on the stage and to explain why (see Garnier ed. 553).

gitimate masters of France cannot allow themselves to mention politics: The "Charter of the Drawingroom" in the Hôtel de la Mole decrees "especially that one never talk politics" (251). The result is boredom, for what has been repressed is what interests everyone most passionately and, indeed, what ultimately motivates those acts that claim ostensibly to belong to the domain of manners, since manners themselves—such an act as changing into silk stockings and slippers for dinner—are political gestures. Politics stands as the great repressed that ever threatens to break through the bar of repression. Politics, as someone calling himself "the author" puts it in a parenthetical debate with another figure called "the publisher," is like a pistol shot in the middle of a concert. Even before Julien's pistol shot shatters the ceremony of the Mass in the church at Verrières, there is a constant threat of irruption of the political into manners, a denuding of the mechanisms governing the relations of power and of persons, and of the dynamic governing history and narrative.

At stake in the play of politics and its repression is, I have suggested, the issue of legitimate authority versus usurpation; and in this opposition we find the matrix of the principal generative and governing structures of the novel. The interrelated questions of authority, legitimacy, and paternity unfold on all levels of the text: in Julien's use of models to conceive and generate his own narrative, in the problematizing of his origins and his destiny, in the overriding question of who controls the text. To treat only briefly the first of these issues, we know that from the first time Julien appears in the novel he moves in a web of bookish models, derived first of all from Las Cases's memoir of Napoleon, the *Mémorial de Sainte-Hélène*, the *Bulletins* of the Grande-Armée, and Rousseau's *Confessions*, which then are supplemented by the New Testament, which Julien has simply learned by heart, and by Joseph de Maistre's book on the papacy; to these one could add occasional references to Corneille's *Le Cid* as a model of honor and continuing citation of Molière's *Tartuffe*, another memorized text. The extent to which Julien believes in these texts varies, but so does the meaning of "belief," since he has chosen to be the *hypokrites*, the player of roles. It is significant that the Abbé Pirard will note Julien's complete ignorance of patristic doctrine: Julien's texts provide individual interpretations of models of behavior but no authoritative tradition of interpretation and conduct.

As a result, Julien continually sees himself as the hero of his own text and conceives of that text as something to be created, not simply endured. He creates fictions, including fictions of the self, that motivate action: As Hemmings has said, Julien is a "dreamer." His scenarios make him not only the actor, the feigning self, but also the stage manager of his own destiny, constantly projecting the self into the future on the basis of hypothetical plots. One of the most striking examples of such hypotheses occurs when, after receiving Mathilde's summons to come to her bedroom at one o'clock in the morning, he imagines a plot—in all senses of the term, including plot as machination, as *complot*—in which he will be seized by Mathilde's brother's valets, bound, gagged, imprisoned, and eventually poisoned. So vivid is this fiction that the narrator tells us: "Moved like a playwright by his own story, Julien was truly afraid when he entered the dining room" (335). Such fictions may even encompass the political, as when Julien immolates his last vestiges of remorse toward the Marquis—the benefactor whose daughter he is about to seduce—by evoking the fate of MM Fontan and Magalon, political prisoners of the regime: this evocation is factually accurate but of the most fictive relevance to his own case, as indeed, we may feel, are all Julien's identifications of himself as plebeian in revolt and peasant on the rise, since they do not correspond either to our perceptions of his identity or to his own identifications with more glorious models. Because the scenarist of self-conceptions cannot maintain a stable distinction between the self and its fictions, Julien must unceasingly write and rewrite the narrative of a self defined in the dialectic of its past actions and its prospective fictions.

To Julien's generation of his narrative from fictional models we can juxtapose the seriality of those figures of paternity who claim authority in his career. Julien is set in relation to a series of ideal or possible fathers, but in a curious manner whereby each father figure claims authority, or has authority conferred on him, at just the moment when he is about to be replaced. The "real" or at least legal father, Sorel the carpenter, is already well on the way to repudiation when the novel opens; his first replacement, the chirurgien-major who has bequeathed his Legion of Honor to Julien, is dead—his legacy suppressed in the movement from red to black. The paternity of the Abbé Chélan emerges in strong outline only when Julien has left him for the seminary, where the severe Abbé Pirard will eventually address Julien as *filius*. "I was hated by my father from the cradle," Julien will say to Pirard, "this was one of my greatest misfortunes; but I will no longer complain of fortune, I have found another father in you, sir" (236).[6] Yet this moment of overt recognition comes only in chapter 1 of book 2, that

6. Julien states, "[J]e ne me plaindrai plus du hasard, j'ai retrouvé un père en vous, monsieur." And the Abbé replies: "Il ne faut jamais dire le hasard, mon enfant, dites toujours la Providence." 'Never say fortune, my child, always say Providence.' Substituting "Providence" for "fortune" of course indicates a belief in an overall direction to human plots—that of the Father—which the novel as a whole tends to discredit.

is, after Julien's translation to Paris and his establishment in the
Hôtel de la Mole: precisely the moment when Pirard begins to give
way to the Marquis de la Mole, who will complicate the question of
paternity and play out its various transformations.

It is at the moment of transition from Pirard's paternity to the
Marquis' that the question of Julien's legitimation through illegitimacy is first explicitly raised—the possibility that Julien might be
the natural child of some aristocrat (perhaps hidden in the mountains of Franche-Comté during the Napoleonic wars), a circumstance that would explain what the Abbé (and later the Marquis)
see as his natural nobility. For the Abbé and the Marquis, Julien's
natural nobility is something of a scandal in the order of things,
one that requires remotivation and authorization through noble
blood, even if illegitimately transmitted. If, like the foundling of an
eighteenth-century novel or a Molière comedy, Julien were at last
to find that he had been fathered by an aristocrat, this discovery
would legitimate his exceptionality, his deviance from the normal
condition of the peasant, and show that what was working as hidden design in his destiny was, as the Abbé puts it, "la force du
sang" (233). The strength of bloodline would rewrite Julien's narrative as satisfactorily motivated, no longer aberrant and deviant,
and rescue Julien's transgressive career, and the novel's dynamic,
from the political realm by restoring them to the anodyne of manners.

A curious dialogue between the Abbé and the Marquis, two be-
lievers in paternal authority and the legitimate order, explicitly for-
mulates for the first time the theory of Julien's illegitimate nobility.
The dialogue creates a chiasmus of misunderstanding concerning
the anonymous gift of five hundred francs to Julien, as each
speaker mistakenly infers from the other's words some secret
knowledge about Julien's origins and thus makes further unfounded inferences. It is through misinterpretation and the postulation of concealment—in what is "really," so far as we know, the
absence of anything to be concealed—that Julien's noble illegitimacy begins to achieve textual status, to acquire an authorship
based on a gratuitous play of substitutes for the origin. Further re-
motivations for the origin then fall into line. The next step follows
from Julien's duel with the Chevalier de Beauvoisis, who does not
want it thought that he has taken the field of honor against a simple secretary to the Marquis; the Chevalier hence lets it be known
that Julien is the natural child of "an intimate friend of the Marquis de la Mole," and the Marquis then finds it convenient to lend,
as he puts it, "consistency" to this version. He will go on to furnish
Julien with a blue costume in addition to the secretarial black;
wearing the former, Julien will be the younger son of the old Duc

de Chaulnes (who, I note in passing, comes to be an object of hatred to Julien, a representation of repressive authority).[7] The Marquis then authorizes the Abbé Pirard "no longer to keep the secret"
of Julien's birth. The blue costume is followed by the cross (of the
Legion of Honor): the cross that the legitimate son, Norbert de la
Mole, has been demanding in vain for some eighteen months. This
process of seemingly casual ennoblement by way of illegitimacy,
motivating and promoting Julien's rise in the world through a
hidden authority, will reach its climax when the recuperated and effaced plebeian makes himself—through Mathilde's pregnancy—
into the natural son-in-law, himself continuing the bloodline, and
stands on the verge of becoming the legal son-in-law, Mathilde's
husband, the Chevalier de la Vernaye.

But I have so far said nothing about another figure of paternal
authority in the narrative: the narrator. The relation of the narrator
to Julien—and of all Stendhalian narrators to the young protagonists of his novels—is patently paternalistic, a mixture of censure
and indulgence: the narrator sets a standard of worldly wisdom that
the protagonist must repeatedly violate, yet confesses to a secret
admiration for the violation, especially for "l'mprévu" the unfore-
seeable, the moments when Julien breaks with the very notion of
model and pattern. The narrator constantly judges Julien in relation to Julien's chosen models, measuring his distance from them,
his failures to understand them, his false attributions of success to
them, and the fictionality of the constructions Julien builds from
them. As Victor Brombert has so well pointed out, the Stendhalian
narrator typically uses hypothetical grammatical forms, asserting
that if only Julien had understood such and such, he would have
done so and so, with results different from those to which he condemns himself. To take just one example, which characteristically
concerns what did not happen between Julien and Mme de Rênal:

7. The filigree of the Duc de Chaulnes in the novel presents many curiosities. The Marquis
   dubs Julien "the younger brother of the Comte de Chaulnes, that is, the son of my friend
   the old Duc" (272). Julien dispels his remorse at seducing his benefactor's daughter by
   recalling with anger that the Duc de Chaulnes has called him a "domestique" (306), a
   remark that Julien recalls again on receiving Mathilde's declaration of love (322): To be
   put in the role of Julien's father, even fictively, is to assume the burden of Julien's oedipal hatred. Mathilde, reflecting on the dishonor she is courting, mentions the Duc de
   Chaulnes as father of her official fiancé, the Marquis de Croisenois (328). Yet elsewhere
   in the novel the Duc de Chaulnes is given as the Marquis de la Mole's father-in-law, and
   after Mathilde announces her pregnancy and her determination to marry Julien, the
   Marquis thinks of passing on his peerage to Julien, since the Duc de Chaulnes has "several times, since his only son was killed in Spain, spoken of his desire to transmit his title to Norbert [de la Mole] . . ." (442). One is tempted to conclude that the shadowy
   Duc de Chaulnes, representative of the *ancien régime* and of legitimate authority, is par
   excellence the figure of paternity in the novel, pressed into service whenever Stendhal
   needs a reference to paternity. As a figure of legitimation for Julien, he is alienating, perhaps necessarily, and he may also be guilty of putting his biological son to death. And as
   a figure of paternal authority, he is curiously absent and trivial. The more one probes the
   mystery of paternity in this novel, the more mysterious it appears.

"If Mme de Rênal had had the slightest sang-froid, she would have complimented him on the reputation he had won, and Julien, with his pride set at ease, would have been gentle and amiable with her, especially since her new dress seemed to him charming" (78). Constantly referring to the worlds of misunderstanding between his characters, the missed chances and might-have-beens, the narrator repeatedly adumbrates other novels, texts of the might-have-been-written. This obtrusive narrator, master of every consciousness in the novel, claims to demonstrate why things necessarily happened the way they did, yet inevitably he suggests the arbitrariness and contingency of every narrative turn of events, how easily it might have been otherwise.

"Paternalism" is of course a highly charged concept for Stendhal—a man who used a hundred different pseudonyms; who in his letters to his sister referred to their father as "the bastard," thereby no doubt indicating his wish to consider himself illegitimate; and who once remarked that if you notice an old man and a young man together who have nothing to say to each other, you can be certain that they are father and son.[8] Encoded in his novels is always the problem of whether paternity is possible, whether there might be a father and a son who could talk to each other. The unfinished *Lucien Leuwen* comes closest to depicting a perfect father, yet even he must eventually be rejected: as Lucien says, my father wishes my happiness, but in his own manner.[9] It is a fault inherent to fatherhood that to act toward the son, even with the intent of aiding him in *la chasse du bonheur*, is inevitably to exercise an illegitimate (because *too* legitimate) control, to impose a model that claims authoritative (because authorial) status. Every Stendhal novel describes the failure of authoritative paternity in the protagonist's life and at the same time shows the narrator's effort to retrieve the failure by being himself the perfect father, he who can maintain the conversation with his son. Yet there comes a point in each novel where the protagonist must slip from under the control of the narrator-father as well.

Julien, it seems, slips from under the control of each of his figures of paternal authority when that control becomes too manifest. The paternal narrator seeks to restrain Julien, to circumscribe him through the deployment of the father's greater worldly wisdom; yet he also admires those moments when Julien kicks at the traces of

8. The remark occurs, I believe, in Stendhal's *Filosofia Nova*. On these questions, see also Starobinski (191–240). Robert André gives a detailed account of Beyle's oedipal conflict and the forms of hatred for the father presented in the novels, especially *La Chartreuse de Parme*. See also Micheline Levowitz-Treu. Henri-François Imbert perceptively discusses how Julien's search for a father relates to political questions (535–46).

9. "Oui, mon père est comme tous les pères, ce que je n'avais pas su voir jusqu'ici; avec infiniment plus d'esprit et même de sentiment qu'un autre, il n'en veut pas moins me rendre heureux *à sa façon* et non à la mienne" (*Lucien Leuwen* 1355).

narratorial control, creates the unforeseen. Julien's slippage from under the exercise of authority—his self-inventing, self-creating quality—typifies the highly metonymic character of the Stendhalian hero, a figure of unarrested, unappeasable desire that can never be anchored in a definitive meaning, even retrospectively. The entire narrative mode of Stendhal's novels is in fact markedly metonymic, indeed virtually serial, giving the impression of a perpetual flight forward, a constant self-invention at the moment and of the moment. The Stendhalian novel gives the impression of being a self-inventing artifact. What we know of Stendhal's habits of composition (particularly from the marginalia to the manuscript of *Lucien Leuwen*) suggests that he literally invented his fiction from day to day, using only the most meager of anecdotes as an armature. Each day's writing—or later, with *La Chartreuse de Parme*, each day's dictation—became an extrapolation of what the protagonist should become on the basis of what he had been and done the day before. The astonishing sense of rapidity given by these novels was matched in fact by the rapidity of their invention, their author's refusal to revise and to turn back: they are the least palimpsestic texts imaginable.[1]

On reflection, one sees that Stendhal makes curiously nonretrospective use of narrative, which would appear in its essence to be a retrospective mode, tending toward a finality that offers retrospective illumination of the whole. The Stendhalian protagonist ever looks ahead, planning the next moment, projecting the self forward through ambition: creating in front of the self, as it were, the circle of the *ambitus*, the to-be-realized. Lucien Leuwen repeatedly refers to himself as "un grand peut-être" a great perhaps, and Julien, too, in his constant becoming, eludes fixed definitions. The narrator generally seems concerned with judging the present moment, or at most the moment just past, rather than with delving into the buried past in search of time lost. Flaubert, in *L'Education sentimentale*, epitomizes the essentially retrospective nature of his own, and no doubt most, narrative when he has Frédéric Moreau, faced with the portrait of Diane de Poitiers at Fontainebleau, experience a "concupiscence rétrospective": desire oriented toward an irrecoverable past (322). Stendhal's novels, in contrast, seem to be based on a "désir prospectif": desire in and for the future. If, as Georg Lukács claims, *L'Education sentimentale* typifies the novel's organic use of time, Stendhalian time is inorganic, momentary, characterized by abruptness and discontinuity.[2] This quality may well appear para-

1. See Jean Prévost; also Gérard Genette's remarkable essay " 'Stendhal,' " which touches on a number of the questions that interest me here, and the excellent discussion of Stendhal's avoidance of closure by D. A. Miller 195–264.
2. On Stendhalian temporality, see also Genette, " 'Stendhal,' " and Georges Poulet.

doxical in a novelist so preoccupied with history, which is necessarily retrospective. Yet it accords with Stendhal's political liberalism, his belief that only the future could reconcile and resolve the contradictions of the present—and, in the process, create readers capable of understanding his novels. His venture into something resembling the historical novel, in *La Chartreuse de Parme*, is indeed accomplished by making the retrospective impulse an object of satire: the powdered wigs of the Court of Parma represent Restoration as make-believe, a ridiculous (and doomed) effort to set back the clocks of history. We might say that Stendhal's typical verb tense is the future perfect, that of the will-have-been-accomplished, a tense that allows for the infinite postponement of accomplishment. And postponement may offer one clue to the need for the arbitrary and absolute *finis* of the guillotine.

Le Rouge et le noir, in its rapid, evasive, unarrestable narrative movement, and in the narrator's games of containment and outmaneuver with the protagonist, ever tends to suggest that things might be otherwise than they are or, perhaps more accurately, that otherwise is how things are but not how they might have been. The apparently stable figure of the triangle, which René Girard found to be the basic structure of mediated desire in the novel—where *A* desires *B* because *B* is desired by *C*—lends itself, curiously, to this narrative instability and uncontrollability, since the very abstraction of the triangle figure permits a free substitution of persons at its corners. Thus, when Julien is most profoundly unhappy at his inability to make Mathilde love him with any constancy, the novel suddenly opens up its most comic episode, the courtship of the Maréchale de Fervaques according to the formula provided, along with a volume of manuscript love letters, by the absurd Russian Prince Korasoff—an episode that is an exercise in pure, that is to say empty, style. The Russian prescribes that Julien must make love to another lady—any other lady—of Mathilde's society. Julien chooses Mme de Fervaques and manages to make eloquent speeches to her by arranging himself in the drawing room so that he appears to look at her while he is gazing past her to Mathilde, the third point of the triangle. The love letters that he daily copies and delivers are so lacking in specific pertinence to their referents that when he once forgets to substitute "Paris" and "Saint-Cloud" for the "London" and "Richmond" of the original, his oversight makes no appreciable difference. Nor is their addressee of much importance: even after Mme de Fervaques has joined the dialogue and begun to answer him, he continues simply to copy the originals. The narrator comments, "Such is the advantage of the grandiloquent style: Mme de Fervaques was not at all astonished by the lack of relationship between his replies and her letters" (416).

The grandiloquent style (*style emphatique*) stands for all that Stendhal detested in such Romantic contemporaries as Chateaubriand and Victor Hugo: a grandiose inanity that was the opposite of the penetrating, denuding prose Stendhal had from childhood admired in the *philosophes* and the *Idéologues*. Julien's success in bringing Mathilde to heel is assured when she opens his desk drawer and finds there a pile of Mme de Fervaques's replies in envelopes that he has not even bothered to open. What impresses her most is not simply that he should be the sentimental choice of the grand Mme de Fervaques but that the relation should be void of content—a matter of envelopes rather than of the messages they enclose. When Mathilde falls, vanquished, at Julien's feet, her surrender is a tribute to the authority of empty style, style as pure geometry.

The emptiness generates a plenitude, for Julien's courtship of Mme de Fervaques results in Mathilde's sustained passion for Julien and in her pregnancy, a full meaning that ensures the continuity that entails all Julien's future successes—title, fortune, new name. In suggesting, through the Abbé Pirard, that Julien offer a gift "to M. Sorel, carpenter in Verrières, who took care of him in childhood" (446), the Marquis offers overt and final realization of Julien's primordial wish not to belong to his biological father. The "family romance" has, for once, come true. The elaborate fictions of Julien's legitimation through illegitimacy may correspond to Mathilde's pregnancy through elaborate and empty games of style. The episode of Mme de Fervaques is a remarkable demonstration of the instability of motivation in relation to result, a figure of the narrative's capacity to generate its significant structures from empty configurations, to institute new, authoritative governing structures in its apparently random flight forward. With Mathilde's pregnancy and Julien's dreams for the future of his son—he never conceives the child in utero as anything but a son—the past is made, retrospectively, to take on the dynastic authority that it has always lacked. By transmitting paternity and projecting it into the future, Julien can at last postulate fully the paternity that stands behind him, believe in the illegitimacy that ennobles and legitimates him. Julien at this point belongs to the Restoration, indeed stands as a figure of how Restoration is carried out: by using politics to attain a place in a system of manners that then is used to efface politics, pretending that the way things came to be as they are (by revolution and reaction, for instance) does not belong to history, that the place of each thing—and person—in the structure of things is immutable.

We have worked our way back to the end, to the moment where Julien's apparent stability, his guarantee of a nonpolitical and uneventful future, is catastrophically exploded, shattered by the pistol shot in the church of Verrières, annihilated by the fall of the blade of the guillotine. We need to return here to Julien's tentative belief in his remotivated paternity—a belief expressed in the conditional of probability (translated above): "Serait-il bien possible . . . que je fusse le fils naturel de quelque grand seigneur exilé dans nos montagnes par le terrible Napoléon? A chaque instant cette idée lui semblait moins improbable" (446)—and we need to juxtapose this belief with its "proof" in Julien's hatred for the legal father—"Ma haine pour mon père serait une preuve"—then with the comment that with this realization of the family romance he would no longer be a monster—"Je ne serais plus un monstre"—and finally with the remark, a few lines earlier, that his novel is over and the merit his alone: "Après tout . . . mon roman est fini, et à moi tout le mérite." If we can understand how hatred works to guarantee a benign origin, authorizing the political change of place and of class as necessary and nontransgressive, we still need to ask why the novel that claims to be finished continues for another eleven chapters and why these chapters stage the return of the monster.

The word "monster" is used on a few occasions in the text. It appears to refer in particular to ingratitude, especially toward figures of paternal authority, and also to erotic transgression, usurpation, class conflict, and the stance of the "plebeian in revolt," a stance that Julien tends to assume at moments of crisis (for example, Mathilde's declaration of love, his trial), perhaps because it is simplifying and political, a decisive model for action. The monster figures the out-of-place, the unclassifiable, the transgressive, the desiring, the seductive.[3] The letter that Mme de Rênal writes under the dictation of her confessor sketches a precise portrait of Julien as monster, thus provoking the catastrophe:

> Poor and avid, it is by means of the most consummate hypocrisy, and by the seduction of a weak and unhappy woman, that this man has sought to make a place for himself

---

3. Here are some examples of the use of "monster" in the novel: when Julien enters his post at the Hôtel de la Mole, the Abbé Pirard, noting the magnitude of what the Marquis is doing for Julien, says, "Si vous n'êtes pas un monstre, vous aurez pour lui et sa famille une éternelle reconnaissance" If you are not a monster, you will be eternally grateful to him and his family (235); when Julien reflects on the calumny that will attach to his name if he is killed while climbing to Mathilde's bedroom, he says to himself, "Je serai un monstre dans la posterité" 'I will be a monster for posterity' (336); when the Marquis berates him for seducing Mathilde—and Julien has just cited, in his defense, Tartuffe's "je ne suis pas un ange . . ." " 'I'm no angel'—the Marquis calls Julien "Monstre!" (434); when the Abbé Chélan comes to visit Julien in his prison cell, the Abbé addresses Julien: "Ah! grand Dieu! est-il possible, mon enfant . . . Monstre! devrais-je dire" 'Ah! Lord! is it possible, my child . . . Monster, I should say' (458). Note also this remark of Stendhal's about his relations with his own father: "J'observai avec remords que je n'avais pas pour lui une *goutte* de tendresse ni d'affection. Je suis donc un monstre me disais-je, et pendant de longues années je n'ai pas trouvé de réponse à cette objection" 'I observed with remorse that I hadn't a *drop* of tenderness or affection for him. I am thus a monster, I said to myself, and for many years I found no answer to this objection' (*Henry Brulard* 217–18).

and to become something. . . . In conscience, I am forced to think that one of his means to success in a household is to seek to seduce the most notable woman there. Covered by an appearance of disinterestedness and by phrases from novels, his sole and overriding object is to succeed in gaining control of the master of the house and of his fortune.   (448–49)

The whole letter indeed reads like an outline of *Tartuffe*, the classic story of the usurper who comes to the point of throwing the legitimate masters out of the house:

C'est à vous d'en sortir, vous qui parlez en maître: La maison m'appartient, et je le ferai connaître.

It is for you to get out, you who speak as master; The house belongs to me, and I shall make it known.

(4.7.1557–58)

This portrait of Julien has a certain truth, not only because it offers an interpretation that an unsympathetic reader might well adopt but also because it corresponds to Julien's occasional portrayals of himself as the monster. If we were looking for psychological explanations, could we not say that Julien, in attempting to kill Mme de Rênal, is seeking to kill the monster, to eradicate the person who has preserved and transmitted the monster image of himself? Perhaps he is also seeking to ensure his own eradication by assuming the monster identity—for, if he dies, the monster will die with him. Such an explanation gains plausibility when we find that Julien at his trial publicly assumes this identity, calling himself a "peasant who has revolted against the lowness of his condition" (482). In raising this political specter that everyone wants repressed, this potential for monstrous usurpation, Julien, as the Abbé Frilair points out, virtually commits suicide. It is as if he were confessing to a guilt deeper than his crime in order to make sure that full punishment would ensue. And that is one way to lay the monster to rest.

But such an "explanation" seems too easy, too smooth. It covers up and reduces the scandal of the ending, and this strikes me as a mistake, especially since Stendhal's endings constitute a chronic scandal. *La Chartreuse de Parme* collapses its set so fast that three of the four major characters are done away with in a few sentences, and two of Stendhal's important novels, *Lucien Leuwen* and *Lamiel*, never manage to get finished at all. Like his admirer André Gide, Stendhal dislikes concluding. Would it, then, be more productive to think of the Stendhalian ending as a version of what the Russian formalists called "the laying bare of the device," which here would be the very device of plotting, the need for beginning, middle, and end that in the laying bare would be shown to be both necessary and arbitrary?

I do not want to use an appeal to the *arbitraire du récit* as explanatory in itself. I do, however, want to call attention to a specific and curious intrusion of the arbitrary in the relation between the anecdote that served as source and armature for *Le Rouge et le noir* and the narrative discourse invented on the basis of the anecdote, between the "raw material" of the story and its elaborations in Julien's plot. This anecdote is strangely contextualized early in the novel itself, in condensed and displaced form, as a weird indicator of things to come. I am thinking of the moment when Julien is on his way to the Rênal house for the first time, stops in the church of Verrières for a show of prayer, and finds a scrap of newspaper, on which he reads: "Details of the execution and the last moments of Louis Jenrel, executed at Besançon the. . . ." The rest of the article is torn off. Turning the scrap over, he reads, "The first step" (25). The blood that Julien thinks he sees on the pavement (actually water from the font, colored by light coming through the crimson curtains) adds to the foreshadowing, which is somewhat crude, given Stendhal's usual practice. We seem to have the intrusion within the novel of the crime, trial, and execution of Antoine Berthet, the story that Stendhal found in *La Gazette des Tribunaux* and used as outline—a *fait-divers* covered over by the narrative discourse but only half-accommodated to its new context.[4] That Louis Jenrel is an anagram of Julien Sorel may indicate something about the partially concealed, half-assimilated status of this anecdote in the novel: the anecdote is present in the manner of a statement displaced into a corner of a dream, demanding expansion and relocation in the process of dream interpretation. How do we read the newspaper in the novel?

The ending of the novel appears to mark a new intrusion of newspaper into novel, dictating that Julien must finish in the same manner as the prototype from whom he has so markedly deviated. That is, maybe Julien shoots Mme de Rênal and goes to the guillotine *because* that original monster Antoine Berthet shot Mme Michoud de la Tour and went to the guillotine, and here my "because" does not belong to source studies or psychological explanation but

---

4. Using the terms of the Russian formalists, one could say that the *fabula* (the order of event referred to by the narrative) intrudes into the *sjužet* (the order of event in its presentation by the narrative discourse). But to do so would mean reducing the *fabula* to the bare-bones anecdote from which Stendhal worked, whereas the *fabula* is properly understood as the whole of the story to which the narrative discourse refers, the order of events that a reading of the narrative enables one to construct, an order that of course has no existence beyond this construction. What invades the narrative discourse of *Le Rouge et le noir* is distinctly heterogeneous—another order of discourse, another genre, another story.

to narratology, to a perverse logic of narrative. Julien is handed over to the guillotine because the novel is collapsed back into the anecdote, the *fait-divers*, in which it originated and from which it has diverged.[5] This turn of events may on the one hand suggest that Julien's plot, finally, is not his own to shape as he wills. On the other hand, it may suggest a more general suspicion of narrative invention, which apparently is subject to interference from outside texts—to the uncontrollable intrusion of a newspaper fragment, for example, which at the last constitutes a mortal intertext.

Saying that Julien attempts murder and suffers execution because he must be made to fulfill Berthet's scenario is of course critically perverse, but it has the advantage of not concealing the perverse relations of Stendhal's novel to Julien's. The climactic moment of *Le Rouge et le noir* may be what is known in classical rhetoric as a "metalepsis of the author": the assigning to the author of an action that should normally have been given to an agent in the text, as when one says that Vergil "makes" Dido die in book 4 of the *Aeneid*, or when Sterne or Diderot invokes the author's power to accomplish (or defer) some event in the narrative.[6] Neither Stendhal nor the narrator so overtly appears to stage-manage events—Julien's fatal act indeed inaugurates a period of diminished narratorial intervention, as we shall see—yet the effect is similar, a denuding of the very act of narrative invention. One cannot get around the problem or the effect by claiming that Julien's narrative fills in the "details" that are torn off from the newspaper story, thus providing a new, fuller motivation for the crime and the execution; for it is precisely in the details pertaining to the motives for crime and execution that the text radically frustrates us. Remotivating the text here, to make it a well-behaved, docile narrative, will always require ingenious extrapolation, classically psychological in type. It may be better to recognize that the *fait-divers* in the novel remains somewhat diverse, resisting assimilation to our usual models of seamless novelistic worlds. Although it may be perverse to read Julien's plot as motivated in its very undoing by Berthet's plot, such a reading at least forces us to face the rhetorical problem of the ending, putting before us the question of Julien's novel—whose end Julien announces before the pistol shot at Verrières—in relation to Stendhal's, with its peculiar leftover, whose status we need to determine.

5. Some earlier critics of *Le Rouge et le noir*—Léon Blum, Henri Rambaud, Maurice Bardèche—noted that Stendhal seems to insist on returning to his documentary scenario at the end; see the summary of their comments in Castex 126–27. Here again, I find the more "traditional" critics closer to the mark: they have noted real problems, though their treatment of them does not fall within the analysis of narrative that interests me here.

6. On the metalepsis of the author, see Genette's discussion of Fontanier in "Discours du récit" (244).

We may now want to knit closer ties between Julien's two remarks, "My novel is finished" and "I would no longer be a monster."
We have seen that "monster" alludes to the irrepressible presence
of class conflict and politics, which turn on the ultimate questions:
Where does legitimate authority lie? and, Who shall inherit
France? "Monster" hence connotes ambition, mobility, the desire to
rise and to change places, to be somewhere one does not belong, to
become (as by seduction and usurpation) something one cannot be
by definition (by birth). The monster is the figure of displacement,
transgression, desire, deviance, instability. Thus the monster is con-
jointly the figure of politics and of plottedness, of politics as plot
and plot as politics. Plot itself—narrative design and intention—is
the figure of displacement, desire leading to a change of position.
The plotted narrative is a deviance from or transgression of the normal, a state of abnormality and error, which alone is "narratable."
What Julien identifies as his "novel" at the moment he declares it
finished is precisely a deviant trajectory that has led him away from
the authority of his legal origins, which has deauthorized origins
and all other principles of legitimate authority, to the point where
he can postulate a new authority in the theory of natural nobility.
Yet, since that nobility, that legitimacy through illegitimacy, has
been achieved through the deviance and usurpation of a highly political career, it is ipso facto tinged with monsterism. Later in the
century, novels by Balzac, Hugo, Eugène Sue, Dickens, Dostoevsky,
and others exploit a world of the criminally deviant, as if the underworld of transgressive and dangerous social elements were the last
fund of "narratable" material in an increasingly bland social and literary system. Julien has no connection to the underworld, which
was still undiscovered in 1830; yet his plot is already criminally deviant and transgressive, politically usurpatory. Hence what must be
punished is not so much any specific act or political stance but
rather the fact of having had a plot.[7]

Can we then say that Julien Sorel is handed over to the guillotine
because he has had a plot? There must be the guillotine at the end
because there has been the novel, that strange excrescence of
telling produced by the tissue of living. The telling perpetuates itself through more telling—scenarios for its further development,
adumbrations of how it might be told otherwise—and then the simple monstrous anecdote of Antoine Berthet obtrudes again at the
end, as Stendhal's reminder (to himself, to us) that to have lived in
the divergence of plot, to have lived as the narratable, means somehow to be deviant and hence, in some cosmic narratological court,

---

7. For a more theoretical development of some of these questions, see Brooks, "Freud's
Masterplot."

to be guilty. To frame Julien's novel within his own novel—to continue beyond Julien's novel and take it to pieces—is Stendhal's way of having a plot and punishing it, of writing a novel and then chopping its head off.

The narrative "leftover" that follows Julien's shooting of Mme de Rênal presents a Julien already castrated of the desiring that creates the novelistic plot: no longer interested in ambition, he judges his whole Parisian experience to have been an error; no longer interested in Mathilde and his worldly marriage, he returns to the explicitly maternal embrace of Mme de Rênal.[8] "He never thought of his successes in Paris; he was bored with them" (471). His mode of thought and being here passes beyond the self-conceptualization and the invention of roles necessary to the plotted existence; he rejects the mediating figures essential to the creation of scenarios of desire and displacement: "One dies as one can. . . . What do *others* matter to me?" (475). Not only does Julien appear to renounce his model in these final chapters, he seems also to move beyond the control and guidance of the paternal narrator. There is far less commentary by the narrator in these chapters; indeed, his voice nearly falls silent, leaving the stage to Julien's almost uninterrupted monologue. The last four chapters (chs. 42–45), following Julien's sentencing, also lack titles and epigraphs, a departure from the rest of the novel that accords with the notable effacement of the narrator's discursiveness and dramatic presence. Julien has simultaneously moved beyond paternal authority and beyond the plotted novel. He is no longer narratable material; his novel has closed shop, and the extranovelistic perspective of its closing chapters serves to underline the disjuncture between plot and life, between Julien's novel and Stendhal's, between authoritative meaning and the violent rupture of meaning.

It is as if Stendhal had decided to enclose within *Le Rouge et le noir* the scenario for what he liked to refer to, contemptuously, as a "novel for chambermaids." Not that Julien and his plot have much to do with chambermaids, except in his social origin and in the offer, early in the novel, of Mme de Rênal's chambermaid, Elisa, as a suitable wife—an offer whose acceptance would have effectively ended the plot of ambition. We may take the "chambermaid's

8. Possessing the mother-mistress, Julien may realize a final desired confusion of origins, enacting the oedipal story according to Claude Lévi-Strauss as well as Freud. He has answered the problem of origin by its confusion, "sowing where he was sown": not only does Julien want Mme de Rênal to be mother to his unborn child, Mme de Rênal herself earlier expresses the wish that Julien were father to her children—curiously, sometimes three children and sometimes two, further confusing the question of generation and perhaps thereby further confirming Lévi-Strauss's view that the Oedipus myth tells the story of an insoluble problem. As with the postulated paternity of the Duc de Chaulnes, we are here faced with a significant confusion.

novel" more generally as the figure of seductive literature. To read a novel—and to write one—means to be caught up in the seductive coils of a deviance; to seduce, of course, is to lead from the straight path, to create deviance and transgression. Stendhal seduces us through Julien's story; then he denounces the seduction. With the fall of the blade of the guillotine, he puts an end to the artificiality of the plotted story.

Something similar, though perhaps inverse, happens to the plotting of history in Stendhal's novel. The Revolution of 1830, as I mentioned, never manages to get represented in the novel, even though in strict chronology it should be; the novel as concert waits in suspense for this historical pistol shot, which never comes. Yet the entire political dynamic of Julien's career tends toward that revolution: his personal transgression will be played out on the national theater in 1830—and then again, more savagely, in 1848 and 1871. The whole novel motivates and calls for the Revolution of 1830: it should be the forty-sixth chapter of book 2, the one beyond the last. In refusing to furnish us with that last chapter, Stendhal performs a gesture similar to his dismantling of Julien's novel, suggesting that one cannot finally allow even History to write an authoritative plot for the novel.

The issue of authority, in all its manifestations, remains unresolved. Julien achieves no final relationship with any of his figures of paternity. It is indeed Sorel the carpenter who reemerges in the place of the father at the end, and Julien attributes to him the jolly thought that the expectation of a legacy of three or four hundred louis from his son will make him, like any father, happy to have that son guillotined. The fathers inherit from the sons. As for Julien's own paternity, his plan that Mme de Rênal take care of his son—whom Mathilde will neglect—goes for naught when Mme de Rênal dies three days after he does. The fate of this son—if son it be—never is known. The novel rejects not only specific fathers and authorities but the very model of authority, refusing to subscribe to paternity as an authorizing figure of novelistic relationships. Ultimately, this refusal may be why Stendhal has to collapse his novels as they near their endings: the figure of the narrator as father threatens domination, threatens to offer an authorized version. He too must be guillotined.

The question, Who shall inherit France? is left unresolved. The question, Who shall inherit from Julien Sorel? is resolved only on the financial plane; and perhaps the victory of Sorel *père* over his son ironically represents the novelist's final and absolute paternal power to put his creatures to death. But the novel comments further on its close and perverse relation to the guillotine when Julien, in prison, recalls Danton's grammatical musings on the eve of his death: "It's singular, the verb *to guillotine* can't be conjugated in all its tenses; one can say: 'I will be guillotined, you will be guillotined,' but one doesn't say: 'I have been guillotined'" (485). For very good semantic reasons, the verb is grammatically defective: one cannot, in the first person, use it retrospectively. We encounter again, even here at the end, Stendhal's typical prospectivity, his predilection for the future perfect: "I will have been guillotined"— the tense of deferral, the tense that denies retrospective satisfaction. Deferral haunts, as well, Stendhal's relation to the "happy few" he designated as the inheritors of his message. In *La Vie de Henry Brulard*, he famously inscribes these happy few, his readers, in a future fifty or a hundred years after his time. To do so is to defer the question of readership and to temporalize the spatiality of the dialogue in which readership might be thought to consist. The uncertain reader may then, too late, want to ask of the novel why it should be thus and not otherwise: or, in the words ascribed to Beaumarchais that serve as epigraph to book 2, chapter 32: "Hélas! pourquoi ces choses et non pas d'autres?"

Works Cited

André, Robert. *Ecriture et pulsions dans le roman stendhalien*. Paris: Klincksieck, 1977.

Auerbach, Erich. *Mimesis*. Trans. Willard Trask. Garden City, N.Y.: Anchor-Doubleday, 1957.

Barthes, Roland. "Introduction à l'analyse structurale des récits." *Communications* 8 (1966): 1–27.

Brombert, Victor. *Stendhal et la voie oblique*. New Haven: Yale Univ. Press, 1954.

Brooks, Peter. "Freud's Masterplot." *Yale French Studies* 55–56 (1977–78): 280–300.

———. *The Novel of Worldliness*. Princeton: Princeton Univ. Press, 1969.

Castex, P.G. Le Rouge et le noir *de Stendhal*. Paris: Sedes, 1967.

Flaubert, Gustave. *L'Education sentimentale*. Paris: Garnier, 1964.

Freud, Sigmund. "Family Romances" [Der Familien-roman der Neurotiker]. In *Complete Psychological Works of Sigmund Freud*. London: Hogarth, 1953–59, 9:237–41.

Genette, Gérard. "Discours du récit." In *Figures III*. Paris: Editions du Seuil, 1972.

———. "'Stendhal.'" In *Figures II*. Paris: Editions du Seuil, 1969, 155–93.

Girard, René. *Mensonge romantique et vérité romanesque*. Paris: Grasset, 1961.

Hemmings, F. W. J. *Stendhal: A Study of His Novels*. Oxford: Clarendon, 1964.

Imbert, Henri-François. *Les Métamorphoses de la liberté*. Paris: Corti, 1967.

Joyce, James. *Ulysses*. New York: Random, 1961.

Levin, Harry. *The Gates of Horn*. New York: Oxford Univ. Press, 1963.

Lévi-Strauss, Claude. "The Structural Study of Myth." In *Structural Anthropology*. Garden City, N.Y.: Anchor-Doubleday, 1967, 202–28.

Levowitz-Treu, Micheline. *L'Amour et la mort chez Stendhal*. Aran: Editions du Grand Chêne, 1978.

Lukács, Georg. *The Theory of the Novel*. Trans. Anna Bostock. Cambridge: MIT Press, 1973.

Martineau, Henri. *L'Œuvre de Stendhal*. Paris: Divan, 1945.

Miller, D. A. *Narrative and Its Discontents*. Princeton: Princeton Univ. Press, 1981.

Poulet, Georges. *Mesure de l'instant*. Paris: Plon, 1968.

Prévost, Jean. *La Création chez Stendhal*. Marseille: Editions du Sagittaire, 1942.

Starobinski, Jean. "Stendhal pseudonyme." In *L'Œil vivant*. Paris: Gallimard, 1963.

Stendhal. "La Comédie est impossible en 1836." In *Mélanges de littérature*. Ed. Henri Martineau. Paris: Divan, 1933. Vol. 3.

———. *Lucien Leuwen*. In *Romans et Nouvelles*. Ed. Henri Martineau. Paris: Bibliothèque de la Pléiade, 1952, 1:760–1413.

———. *Pensées. Filosofia Nova*. Ed. Henri Martineau. Paris: Divan, 1931.

————. *Racine et Shakespeare*. Ed. Henri Martineau. Paris: Divan, 1928.

————. *Le Rouge et le noir*. Ed. Henri Martineau. Paris: Garnier, 1957.

————. *La Vie de Henry Brulard*. In *Œuvres intimes*. Ed. Henri Martineau. Paris: Bibliothèque de la Pléiade, 1955.

Stivale, Charles J. "Le Vraisemblable temporel dans *Le Rouge et le noir*." *Stendhal Club* 84 (1979): 299–313.

SANDY PETREY

Louis XVII and the Chevalier de la Vernaye: The Red, the Black, the Restoration†

No incident in Stendhal's *le Rouge et le noir* has elicited more commentary than Julien's attempt to murder Mme de Rênal. The ostensible explanation—that Mme de Rênal letter to the marquis de la Mole has irrevocably prevented Julien's marriage to Mathilde—just does not hold up. Mathilde is pregnant, and she refuses to consider an abortion. As a consequence, her father's vow never to permit her marriage is pure bluster. The marriage will certainly take place if Julien simply waits out the storm while his child's gestation continues. The end of Julien's career is in fact not Mme de Rênal's letter of denunciation but his own bloody reaction to it. A protagonist remarkable for his self-possession suddenly seems to become intent on self-destruction, a radical psychological shift that has been the subject of extensive critical speculation from the novel's original appearance to our time.

Less discussed but no less implausible than the attempted murder is its consequence, Julien's conviction, death sentence, and execution. If everything we know about Julien's character makes his crime a puzzle, everything we know about his society makes his punishment an impossibility. At the age of fourteen, Julien decided to become a priest because he saw a scrupulously honest judge deliver one shameful verdict after another in order not to incur the Church's displeasure. From that incident on, the legal system depicted in *Le Rouge et le noir* has been the tool of influential individuals rather than the agent of justice—after all, "where is the judge without a son or at least a cousin to place in society?" (217; all translations from Stendhal are my own)—and the novel's most influential characters all passionately desire Julien's acquittal. The

† From *Realism and Revolution: Balzac, Stendhal, Zola, and the Performances of History* (Ithaca: Cornell University Press, 1988), pp. 123–51. Reprinted by permission of Neohelicon/Springer. The selections from *Le Rouge et le noir* are translated from the Flammarion edition, 1968. A previous version of this essay appeared as "The Realist Speech Act: Mimesis, Performance, and Facts in Fiction" in *Neohelicon* 15.2 (September 1988): 9–29.

epigraph to the chapter that describes their machinations strongly hints that they will succeed: it narrates the liberation through bribery of a Frenchman who not only killed his sister but was guilty of another murder as well. Julien's crime, far less heinous than sororicide, should be correspondingly easier to dismiss.

When M. de Rênal, tormented by the anonymous revelation of his cuckoldry, contemplated killing his wife, he had no fear of being punished for the murder: "Whatever happens, our congregation and my friends on the jury will save me" (146). In contrast to M. de Rênal, Julien is guilty only of attempted murder. Furthermore, his friends are much more imposing than M. de Rênal's. Vigorously defending him are Mathilde de la Mole, Mme de Rênal, the all-powerful abbé de Frilair, the maréchale de Fervaques, and monseigneur l'évêque de ***, "through whom one becomes a bishop in France . . . this prelate who controlled the Church of France and made bishops" (462, 472). Yet all their efforts are futile. Julien dies on the guillotine.

Gérard Genette writes of the "contemptuous silence" with which Stendhal envelops the psychological reversal necessary for his protagonist to shoot Mme de Rênal (77). No less contemptuous is Stendhal's explanation of the social reversal necessary for a legal proceeding to conclude contrary to the wishes of Restoration notables. According to the novel's tortured motivation of its conclusion, Julien is found guilty because the abbé de Frilair makes a grievous strategic error. Instead of straightforwardly instructing the jurors he controls to vote for acquittal, he tells them to vote like their foreman, Valenod. Valenod then disobeys Frilair's explicit instructions to him in a rebellion made possible because he has already been named to the prefecture that Frilair planned to give him after the trial ended in the agreed way. Even if we ignore the implausibility of Frilair's scrupling to fix a jury in overt terms, this scenario remains outrageous. Valenod, who has just seen M. de Rênal lose the office of mayor of Verrières, knows perfectly well that Restoration officials are unmade the same way they are made. Like a mayor, a prefect has to please Church and nobility after winning office as well as while seeking it. Frilair sees acquittal as leading "to the realization of all my desires" (462), and he is not the man to forgive treachery in so important an enterprise. Valenod's tenure as prefect will undoubtedly be the shortest on record, and it is certain that he knows it. The powers that rule France and its courts are massed to assure Julien's release, and the text's effort to explain his conviction makes no concessions to credibility.

The fascinating point about this attempt to explain the inexplicable is that only in a society as vile as Restoration France would any explanation be required. What happens is actually nothing more that what is supposed to happen in a state under the rule of law: a criminal receives the punishment prescribed by statute for those guilty of his crime. The judicial procedures represented in *Le Rouge et le noir*, however, are such that it is only because of a double-cross that society treats attempted murder as attempted murder. A convoluted series of corruptions terminates as if no corruption had taken place. Furthermore, the text attributes even this accidental implementation of the legal code to actions dissociated from the modes of social coexistence described in the rest of the novel. The conclusion of *Le Rouge et le noir* is remarkable for its uncomfortable effort to motivate a radical departure from the social thematics informing what precedes it. Previously, the meaning of events was the product of a collective decision by the leaders of Church and aristocracy. At Julien's trial, the leaders of Church and aristocracy collectively decide that the defendant is blameless, but their power seems to have vanished. Suddenly, events and their consequences, a crime and its punishment, succeed one another regardless of the interpretations placed on them by characters whose hermeneutic authority is otherwise incontrovertible. Earlier, guilt and innocence were determined not by what someone did but by what socially powerful individuals said. At Julien's trial, many powerful individuals say he is innocent, but what he did remains determinant. In a staggering departure from textual precedent, *Le Rouge et le noir* ends on a character being found guilty of a crime he actually committed.

In addition to guilt and innocence, social rank acquires textually unprecedented solidity at the conclusion of *Le Rouge et le noir*. In his speech to his jury, Julien describes himself as if his peasant birth definitively established a class identity he could never hope to alter.

> Gentlemen, I do not have the honor of belonging to your class, you see in me a peasant who rebelled against his inferior situation. . . . I see men who will elect to punish in me and so discourage forever that class of young men who, born into a lower class and in some way oppressed by poverty, are fortunate enough to obtain a good education and daring enough to mix with what the pride of the rich calls society.
>
> That is my crime, gentlemen, and it will be punished with all the more severity because, as things are, I am not being judged by my peers. I do not see among the jurors any peasant who has enriched himself, I see only indignant bourgeois. [476]

The abbé de Frilair defines this speech as a declaration of class war so inflammatory that Julien's death is a kind of suicide. In Frilair's understanding, the defendant's words stimulated a "caste interest" (488) in his jurors, who voted for death in order to eliminate a grave threat to their social position.

Frilair, however, attributes to Julien's bourgeois jurors an extraordinarily disinterested devotion to the interests of the aristocracy. The contradiction is implicit in Frilair's use of "caste" to replace Julien's "class." Class is the effect of financial situation, caste the effect of birth. The latter was the basis for the Restoration's attempt to reproduce the aristocratic social organization of the ancien régime, the former the concept the bourgeoisie put forth to oppose both the ancien régime and its reproduction. Every aristocracy posits a divinely guaranteed harmony between an individual's social status and social function. God in His omniscience decides which person is suited for which task and reveals His decision through conception; from kings to beggars, every member of society *naturally* occupies the position most favorable to the divine plan. Caste implements the social organization which God Himself intends humanity to observe.

Caste consequently condemns the bourgeoisie to eternally subaltern functions, and the jurors come from the bourgeoisie. Their "caste interest" is at loggerheads with their class interest. Although Julien's speech does indeed subvert the caste principles of Restoration aristocracy, his listeners are not the beneficiaries but the victims of those principles. It is not nobles who sit in judgment but, as Julien said, "only bourgeois," only members of the Third Estate whose interests are thwarted by social equation of birth with worth. The subtitle of *Le Rouge et le noir* is *Chronique de 1830*, chronicle of the year when the French bourgeoisie's resentment against the ideology of birth produced a revolution for the sake of exactly the kind of class mobility Julien claims as a right. The abbé de Frilair's argument that twelve bourgeois jurors understood that claim as a threat to their most vital interests presumes a political docility about to be violently repudiated by the rest of France's middle class. Although Julien does in fact sound like Figaro, his audience consists of Jourdains rather than Almavivas, and bourgeois gentlemen do not normally see a capital offense in the contention that a man can rise above the position to which he was born.

Julien's demand that oppressed young men be allowed to ascend the social scale is strikingly similar to the bourgeois ideology that prepared the Revolution of 1789 as well as to the bourgeois frustration that produced the Revolution of 1830. If one wanted a brief summary of the speech with which Julien supposedly threatened the bourgeoisie with political doom, it would be hard to improve on the question with which Sieyès opened *Qu'est-ce que le tiers état?*, his famous pamphlet in favor of the bourgeoisie's political exaltation: "What are they asking for? To become SOMETHING." Besides asking its readers to believe that irresistible political influence is powerless to save Julien from the guillotine, the conclusion of *Le Rouge et le noir* defines archetypically bourgeois sentiments as anathema to archetypically bourgeois characters. Julien's fatal speech should not affront but stroke his listeners' "caste interest."

The career of the jury's foreman, Valenod, has mounted an attack on caste at least as vigorous as Julien's. Like the defendant, the chief juror began life as one of "that class of young men . . . born into a lower class and in some way oppressed by poverty." And, like the defendant, the chief juror endured the resentment of his fellows after he rose above the place assigned him by birth. Although Valenod and M. de Rênal exploit Verrières together, the aristocratic mayor benefits from an indulgence denied his plebeian accomplice. "People were jealous of the mayor, the liberals had grounds for complaint; but after all he was noble and made for a superior position, whereas M. Valenod's father had not left him six hundred livres of income. People who had taken pity on the apple-green suit everyone saw him wearing in his youth had been forced to come to envy his Norman horses, his gold chains, his clothes straight from Paris, all his current prosperity" (162). Since Valenod is no more "noble and made for a superior position" than Julien, it is hardly credible that he and his jurors would interpret a classically bourgeois defense of upward mobility as a seditious act so threatening to the bourgeoisie that its perpetrator must be put to death. Julien's speech is nothing more than a development of the bourgeoisie's preferred rallying cry, *careers open to talents*.

Even Frilair's strictures about Julien's speech are irreconcilable with his own biography. Like Valenod, Frilair is a perfect illustration of the upward mobility he supposedly finds intolerably threatening. "Twelve years earlier, M. l'abbé de Frilair had come to Besançon with the tiniest of trunks which, according to reports, contained all he possessed. Now he was one of the department's richest property owners" (217). The men who are represented by the text as provoked to frenzy by Julien's speech have in fact lived out each of the principles the speech defends. What they experience as a personal affront could more logically be understood as a statement of personal solidarity.

In yet another apparent concession to the class sensitivities of his jurors, Julien addresses them as Julien Sorel, peasant son of a Jura carpenter, whereas he has every right to speak as M. le chevalier de la Vernaye, lieutenant in the fifteenth hussars regiment, "one of the most brilliant in the army" (444). Although this new name comes from the marquis de la Mole's determination that his daughter not marry a commoner, its validity is unimpeachable. Strong documentary evidence attests not only to Lieutenant de la

Vernaye's identity but to his outstanding previous service as second lieutenant.

Julien Sorel begins to address his bourgeois jury with this sentence: "Gentlemen, I do not have the honor of belonging to your class." Lieutenant de la Vernaye has full authority to reverse the terms: "Gentlemen, you do not have the honor of belonging to my class." That it is the peasant Sorel rather than the knighted la Vernaye who takes the floor is among the least understandable components of a denouement consistently indifferent to comprehensibility. Even more than Julien's crime, his trial and execution stand apart from the preceding portion of the novel. If we take the final chapters' lack of titles and epigraphs as a formal correlative to the substantive disparities that distinguish them from the seventy-four chapters that come before, each with its own title and epigraph, then the point of dissociation is precisely the trial and verdict.

Julien's speech and death sentence thus constitute a stark line of demarcation within *Le Rouge et le noir*. On one side of the line, Restoration ideology is a fictitious construct; on the other, it appears to describe real social practices with real collective adherence. Judicial procedures that were unconnected to facts now culminate in the outcome prescribed by law; bourgeois characters who were contemptuous of the idea that "noble" and "made for a superior position" were synonymous expressions now react with horror to an attack on that synonymy; men who have themselves *become* rich and powerful abruptly believe that riches and power should belong only to those *born* with them; a character who despised his peasant family and all it stood for now vindicates his peasant condition with passionate pride. In the aberrant conclusion to *Le Rouge et le noir*, a crime is a crime regardless of who exonerates the criminal, a peasant is a peasant despite documentary proof of his nobility, and the philosophy of caste describes an immutable fact of life accepted by those it would oppress as well as those it glorifies. In each instance, social discourse accurately represents reality and appears thoroughly referential. The Austinian constative is irrelevant to a world where social identity is not a conventional creation but an objective given, and it is in just such a world that Julien Sorel is condemned to death. Words that did things have lost their ability to perform, and the things words say have become passive descriptions of the way things are.

But the anomalous character of the referential discourse concluding *Le Rouge et le noir* foregrounds the constative discourse preceding it. The text insistently dissociates the collective processes making Julien a criminal from those making him the chevalier de la Vernaye, a radical ideological break that highlights what precedes as well as what follows. In one of the novel's crucial chapters (II, 8), Mathilde de la Mole observes the most brilliant representatives of her age at the ball in the hôtel de Retz. The titles, honors, and decorations she sees strike her as so many shams; none signifies anything except itself, none actually represents reality, each is glaringly performative. The only "decoration" that is the consequence of its bearer's behavior is the death sentence pronounced on Count Altamira in his South American homeland. Only here is a word attached to a thing, only here does language designate something outside itself. " 'The only thing I see distinguishing a man is a death sentence,' thought Mathilde . . . 'a title of baron, of vicomte, is bought; a cross is given; my brother just got one, what did he do? A rank is obtained' " (296). Three passive verbs—*is bought, is given, is obtained*—embody the passive nature of the Restoration's distinguishing marks. All decorations are assumed to be referential because they theoretically recognize merit previously displayed, all are actually constative because they express nothing beyond the force that accompanies and succeeds their utterance.

The chapter narrating Mathilde's insight is entitled "Which Decoration Distinguishes?" In semiotic terminology, that question would read "Which sign refers?" For an Austinian formulation, take "Which name is not a performance?" All the titles that, according to Restoration ideology, designate the divinely guaranteed nature of the world in fact do nothing more than activate a conventional agreement. Only a death sentence reliably denotes an action. The death sentence concluding *Le Rouge et le noir* appears in a text that has already defined the sentence as unique among signs for indicating rather than creating facts.

But the final death sentence is not unique in its immediate context, where the signs of social rank have the same substance as the classification of criminal behavior. Lieutenant de la Vernaye ("a rank is obtained") represents himself as a peasant, and his jurors confirm that no other representation would be acceptable. The objective fact of birth authoritatively establishes the linguistic form of identity. Earlier, the existence of the chevalier de la Vernaye compellingly illustrated Mathilde's thesis that only a death sentence has referential validity in her society. At Julien's trial, the chevalier vanishes, and birth acquires the same determinant impact as death.

Before the trial, referential language is so alien to Restoration discourse that the word "fact" is indistinguishable from the word "fiction." Facts remain factual regardless of who believes them, fictions depend on their reader's connivance. Just such connivance is the sine qua non of what Stendhal's Restoration accepts as a fact. For example, the norms of aristocratic society restrict dueling to social peers. When Julien's duel with the chevalier de Beauvoisis violates those norms, the violation is eliminated by instantaneous verbal creation of equality in rank. "That very evening, the chevalier de Beauvoisis and his friend repeated everywhere that this M. Sorel, who was by the way a perfect young man, was the natural son of one of the marquis de la Mole's intimate friends. This fact passed without difficulty" (282). The ease with which this *fact* passed prefigures that establishing the chevalier de la Vernaye's nobility and military experience. After "public opinion declared in his favor" (444), M. de la Vernaye's status is secure. He ceases to be the peasant Julien Sorel with precisely the same smoothness manifest when the peasant Julien Sorel later ceases to the the chevalier de la Vernaye. Because words do not describe the world but only stimulate a conventional interpretation, designation of a fact requires nothing more than manipulation of public opinion.

The interaction of social identity and performative semantics in *Le Rouge et le noir* perhaps receives its clearest formulation soon after Julien takes up his secretarial duties in Paris. When the marquis de la Mole, confined to his room by gout, wants to treat his secretary as an equal, he gives him a blue suit. Dressed in black, Julien is a secretary; dressed in blue, he is the son of a duke. "My dear Sorel, allow me to make you the gift of a blue suit; when it pleases you to wear it and to come to my rooms, you will be, in my eyes, the younger brother of the comte de Chaulnes, which is to say the son of my friend the old duke" (283–84). This stratagem preserves the form of orthodox social relations by assuring that a tone of equality is adopted solely between individuals holding the same rank. At the same time, it turns the standard view of the basis for social relations on its head. It is not rank that authorizes a tone of equality but a tone of equality that establishes rank. Signs do not reflect but originate the condition they articulate. In spectacular fashion, Julien's blue suit epitomizes the production of concrete referents from arbitrary signs characteristic of social interaction in *Le Rouge et le noir*.

Austin's originative condition for a felicitous performative is a conventional procedure having conventional effect. The marquis de la Mole's instructions institute the conventional procedure as a visit in a blue suit and specify the conventional effect in unequivocal terms: "You will be, in my eyes, the younger brother of the comte de Chaulnes." As legitimate son of the duc de Chaulnes, as illegitimate son of another friend of the marquis de la Mole, and as the chevalier de la Vernaye, Julien manifests the central social theme in *Le Rouge et le noir*: identity identifies nothing except the conventions observed by those who recognize it. Stendhal's Restoration is a performative universe.

Le Rouge et le noir incorporates a graduated series of links between the blatant artificiality of the identity conferred by Julien's suit and the concealed artificiality of identities conferred by other social conventions. On Julien's return from England, the marquis de la Mole presents him with a cross and redefines the procedures that will bring forth an aristocrat from a secretary. "I no longer want to have you abandon your black suit, and I'm accustomed to the more amusing tone I've taken with the man wearing the blue suit. Until further notice, this is understood: when I see this cross, you will be the younger son of my friend the duc de Chaulnes." (288). The status conferred by a blue suit depended on a convention observed by only two men. That conferred by the cross is ratified by the whole of French society. In a clear echo of Mathilde's insight into the performative force of all decorations, her father uses the cross to change the world by changing a name. As Julien notes with intense satisfaction, the change is extensive. Every facet of his interaction with the marquis varies according to the signifiers he puts on.

This move from blue cloth to a coveted decoration also goes from a semiprivate agreement to a universally observed convention. The development continues until it absorbs every form of identification in *Le Rouge et le noir*. Who is the marquis de la Mole? A man other people treat as if they had said to him what he says to Julien, "You will be, in my eyes, the marquis de la Mole." In *Le Rouge et le noir*, the marquis' noble birth inherently confers nothing more substantial than Julien's blue suit. Both marks of identity are significant only because society agrees on what they signify. During the revolutionary decades before the Restoration—the decades that Stendhal's notables devote their lives to repressing—France proved in blood and fire that what nobility means is not a natural fact but a social custom. When customs changed, nobility became a capital crime instead of a cardinal virtue. To be born a marquis and to wear a blue suit are identical insofar as each accords status only because someone else recognizes the status it accords. Whether aristocratic blood or a new color of clothes, any mark of social position is an empty signifier. The signified attached to it is historically not eternally determined.

The impossibility of distinguishing between the status attached to aristocratic parents and that attached to a different suit is implicit in the bloodline that Julien acquires by wearing blue. In the marquis's words, Julien becomes the son of the duc de Chaulnes, who is also the father of the marquise de la Mole (250). The marquis therefore not only ennobles Julien but makes him his own brother-in-law and the uncle of Mathilde and Norbert. A blue suit puts Julien into both of the families whose "natural" superiority the marquis de la Mole should have the greatest interest in preserving.

Instead, the marquis recapitulates the text in which he appears by equating the natural with the conventional, a suit of clothes with blood and marriage, at the base of social order. The duc de Chaulnes, "well known for his aristocratic prejudices" (250), is the archetypal proponent of a referential understanding of social titles. The text's predilection for collapsing referents into conventions is apparent in the duc de Chaulnes's central role in a stunning display that titles are the opposite of what he wants to believe.

The play with conventional alteration of Julien's paternity in *Le Rouge et le noir* reminds contemporary readers of Jacques Lacan. For Lacan, the immense symbolic function attached to the Name of the Father depends on the Name's dissociation from procreative reality: the capacity "to observe the real is precisely that which has not the slightest importance in the matter" of paternity's social definition (*Écrits*, 199). Because it institutes humanity's symbolic articulation of its universe, the Name of the Father is essential even in tribes that do not understand the male contribution to reproduction, and "it is certainly this that demonstrates that the attribution of procreation to the father can only be the effect of a pure signifier" (199). To meet the needs of a pure signifier, a blue suit serves as well as patrilineal descent.

But in realist fiction, the signifier can fulfill its social responsibility only if its purity is concealed and it is assumed to convey not an arbitrary but an inalienable signified. The marquis de la Mole cannot change the way he treats Julien without mediating the change through a new identity; the Name requires the Father, the blue suit the duc de Chaulnes. The constative semantics of *Le Rouge et le noir* achieves conventional effect only when conventional procedures define signs as referential. Dressed in black, Julien expresses the same emptiness as when he is dressed in blue. The clothes of an aspirant to the priesthood alter his "perfect unbelief" (284) no more than the clothes of an aristocratic dandy alter his peasant birth. Nevertheless, his heavenly father furnishes a signified at least as substantial as the duc de Chaulnes. The protagonist of *Le Rouge et le noir* continuously demonstrates that the two fundamental institutions of the Restoration, the Church and the aristocracy, are erected on emptiness yet convey absolute plenitude. The characters of *Le Rouge et le noir* continuously do for themselves exactly what the regime of Louis XVIII and Charles X did for itself, convert quintessentially performative operations into incontrovertibly referential truths.

The Restoration's restoration of the connection between the Name and the Father, the signifier and the referent, was its most urgent historical task. Because the French Revolution had exposed the signs of Church, monarchy, and aristocracy as formal exercises in vacuous expression, the pure signifier lost its capacity to structure social existence. As a result, the reconstituted Bourbon regime sought to obliterate France's memory of the void behind language in order to reestablish signs' perfect referential validity. The marquis de la Mole could not treat Julien as an equal without previously making him the son of a duke; other members of France's dominant class could not feel confident of identity without previously assuming that the names articulating social status were infallible expressions of reality. If the names and reality were in contradiction, it was reality that had to adapt.

I take the literary play with signs and referents in *Le Rouge et le noir* to be a faithful analogue to the historical work with signs and referents characteristic of the Restoration. Both the novel and the age furnish a sustained, monumental display of verbal creativity successfully masquerading as verbal reference. The Restoration's first sovereign, Louis XVIII, took his name through a process indistinguishable from that which made Julien Sorel the son of the duc de Chaulnes. From Louis I in the fourteenth century to Louis XVI in the eighteenth, France's monarchs assumed their regal numerals on assuming their throne. Kingly titles were the outward sign of an actual fact, a name granted on the occasion of an event. The son of Louis XVI never assumed the throne and consequently never became Louis XVII; two years after his father was guillotined, he died as a citizen rather than a monarch. "Louis XVII" is the signifier in all its purity, unpolluted by attachment to anything except other signifiers.

Yet the Restoration began by converting that pure signifier into the name of a person who ruled. Immediately after his nephew's death, the brother of Louis XVI took the title of Louis XVIII in retroactive affirmation that the semiotic sequence of French monarchs faithfully represented an immutable historical succession. Like Julien's entry into the duc de Chaulnes's family, the referential value of "Louis XVII" at first rested only on a semiprivate agreement, that accepted by the dwindling number of aristocratic émigrés who remained with the exiled French court during its hapless treks across Europe. Like the empty decorations that Mathilde observed at the hôtel de Retz, however, the royal stature of a pitiful child became an objective truth when the Bourbons regained the throne in 1814. As was the case with "chevalier de la Vernaye," all that was required for "Louis XVII" to generate a referent was the acquiescence of public opinion. A dead child became the king of France through institution of a conventional procedure with the predominant conventional effect of annihilating objective reality in order to invigorate social beliefs.

Le Rouge et le noir accomplishes its most direct historical reference through multifarious demonstrations that reference is always a historical fabrication. Julien's black suit, blue suit, and shifting fathers are so many chronicles of an age in which signs produce something from nothing because their interpreters' lives depend on it. The performative onomastics of *Le Rouge et le noir* represents the performative history of the Restoration, a regime that made its founding document—the Charter of 1814—into a storehouse of precedents for the exuberant creativity of the signs identifying Julien. In fact an indispensable reaction to the French people's resistance to full reinstitution of the Old Regime, the Charter of 1814 nevertheless defined itself as the free, unconstrained gift of Louis XVIII to his people. In the charter's preamble, the king presents what he is writing as a simple continuation of his predecessors' immemorial commitment to the liberty of their subjects. The charter names the kings whose work it prolongs as Louis le Gros, Saint Louis, Philippe le Bel, Louis XI, Henri II, Charles IX, and Louis XIV, a list obliterating not only the Revolution but most other discontinuities in French history as well. From the twelfth through the nineteenth centuries, France's kings are an integral whole; the charter responds not to the Declaration of the Rights of Man but uniquely to "the example of the kings our predecessors" and "the venerable monuments of ages past." "By uniting older times and modern times," "by thus seeking to reconnect the chain of the ages," the charter made unbroken repetition the program of a nation.

The charter's most stupefying use of language to change history is its final words: "Given in Paris, in the year of grace 1814 and the eighteenth year of our reign." While "given" factualizes the fiction of Louis' power *not* to give what his subjects demand, dating the charter in the nineteenth year of his reign makes the difference between fact and fiction officially indeterminable. The first eighteen years of Louis XVIII's reign, like all the years of Louis XVII's, exist solely in the words naming them. They entered history on entering language and in the process severed political truth from historical reality. The clause with which *Le Rouge et le noir* narrates Julien's first acquisition of an aristocratic identity is perfectly applicable to the Restoration's acquisition of political power; "this fact passed," and the definition of a "fact" became whatever a community chose to make it. What was historically eighteen years of powerless exile became linguistically eighteen years of absolute power.

How do human beings survive under a monarch who uses language to destroy facts? By taking care never to use language to express those facts. To return to Lacan, Restoration discourse was an arduous effort to conceal the absence of the Father by venerating the presence of the Name, and the safest way to prevent denotational slips was to make sure that language remained endlessly repetitive. Since the goal of the Restoration was to convince itself that the world its words established was actually there, reference to a different world was rigorously prohibited. Instead of referring to what was, conversation could only repeat what was heard; language was socially acceptable in direct proportion to its alienation from social reality. The boredom Auerbach brilliantly situates at the core of *Le Rouge et le noir* is the effect of a speech community's determination to use language in such a way that it can never say anything. "The slightest living idea seemed obscene. Despite the correct tone, the perfect decorum, the desire to please, boredom was visible on every face. The young men who came to pay their respects, afraid of mentioning something that might suggest a thought or reveal some forbidden reading, fell silent after a few truly elegant comments on Rossini and the day's weather" (*Le Rouge et le noir*, 265). Stendhal's epigraph to the chapter entitled "Ways of Acting in 1830" is "Speech was given to man to conceal his thought." The route to success in 1830 is mapped by the epigraph to another chapter (II, 28): "He got by through calling what was white black and what was black white." And through calling the Directorate and Empire the first eighteen years of Louis XVIII's reign.

The criterion of linguistic propriety in *Le Rouge et le noir* is total hostility to linguistic reference. "Afraid of mentioning something that might suggest a thought," Stendhal's characters are condemned to say only what they know has already been said. An unprecedented choice and arrangement of words evokes the unthinkable possibility that social organization might diverge from precedent as well; expressing a thought not universally shared introduces the revolutionary concept that people do not unanimously agree that Louis XVII ruled France. Since the Restoration depended for its survival on the belief that what always had been was still and would always be, the conversations it authorized were interminable reiteration of the already said.

Before the French Revolution, the word *revolution* assured return of the old; afterward, it proclaimed creation of the new. The Restoration directed its campaign against the Revolution toward eradicating just this sort of change in sense, and the only way to immobilize sense is to assure that the signs expressing it remain inert. The effect was the stultifying dinners in the hôtel de la Mole, with conversation restricted to an exchange of words chosen because their exchange has already been certified harmless. "Readymade sentences suited the mind of the lady of the house quite well" (260), and her guests share her predilection. The dominant class's compulsion to expunge innovation from existence acquires the textual form of a shared revulsion at innovation in speech.

Henri Lefebvre has characterized our own time as the age of a general eclipse of "referentials"; the words we most respect appear not to refer to the world but only to reproduce themselves. Long before Lefebvre, Stendhal defined the Restoration through an analogous gulf between speech and reference. Although love and death must figure among the ultimate human referentials, Stendhal's Restoration transforms both into rote ceremonies enacted apart from existential involvement. "In Paris love is the son of novels" (66), its expression a frozen discourse changing every twenty years "according to the currently fashionable pastime" (316). Death scripts are equally constrictive. For Mathilde, "the duel is now nothing but a ceremony. Everything about it is known beforehand, even what you're to say as you fall" (333). Death in social upheaval leaves no more room for improvisation than death during social rites. "Well then! Say the Revolution started up again. What roles would Croisenois and my brother play? It's written beforehand. Sublime resignation" (320). If one wanted to summarize socially acceptable behavior in Le Rouge et le noir, it would be hard to improve on Mathilde's variant phrasing of a single idea: "Everything about it is known beforehand . . . it's written beforehand." Decency demands immobility; in a society committed to the belief that history must be repetitive, life and death become applications of a precedent. Imprévu is a dirty word throughout Le Rouge et le noir because whatever is not written in advance threatens apocalypse.

The Charter of 1814 took pains to express Louis XVIII's solidarity with "the example of the kings our predecessors . . . the venerable monuments of ages past." Under the regime founded by the charter, the past's monuments circumscribe individual experience as tightly as political institutions. So thorough is social prohibition of everything except repetition that even Mathilde's will to flout prohibitions leads to a different form of repetition. She first understands her attraction to Julien through Manon Lescaut, La Nouvelle Héloïse, and Lettres d'une religieuse portugaise (317), then comes to love through Boniface de la Mole and Marguerite de Navarre. Like Louis XVIII invoking the memory of Louis le Gros and Louis le Grand, Mathilde defines her life through her affinity with the dead. The origin of the Restoration was a monarch's assertion that he was repeating the past, that of Mathilde's love her desire to follow his example.

In his priestly black suit, the atheist Julien Sorel is a living exemplification of the barrier between signs and reference in Le Rouge et le noir. The career the atheist follows exemplifies one of the barrier's corollaries: because signs that do not denote can only repeat, expert repetition is the surest means of social advancement. Julien's

meteoric ascent is due to his unique talent for making the already
written work for him.

The two key decisions in Julien's life are to study for the priesthood and to make Mathilde definitively his. The former takes him
to the Rênal household and then out of Verrières, the latter makes
him the chevalier de la Vernaye and opens the way to wealth and
power. Each decision is a farcical commentary on Restoration repetition: Julien's career begins in memorization and culminates in
copying. His vertical move from the depths to the summit of society
occurs because of a horizontal move from one set of dead words to
another, from the New Testament and *Du pape* to letters written by
a Russian to a woman Julien has never seen. The narrative armature of *Le Rouge et le noir* is a serial display of its protagonist's ability to use language so that it refers neither to external reality nor to
internal sensations. Horatio Alger of the Restoration, Julien goes
from rags to riches by recognizing that society listens most intently
to what was said in another time and at another place.

Julien's first script is of course Scripture itself. "To win over the
old priest Chélan, on whom he saw his future to depend, he had
memorized the entire New Testament in Latin, he also knew the
book *Du pape* by M. de Maistre and believed in one as little as
the other" (49). By definition, memorized language is unrelated to
the situation in which it is repeated and to the inner state of its
speaker. Julien's conviction that the New Testament was nonreferential even at the time of its composition makes its estrangement
from reality absolute. The words that do things in the Restoration
are those which have no potential for saying things. Only static language produces a dynamic career.

Repetition of the New Testament begins to work miracles for
Julien at the Rênal household and continues to do so at Valenod's.
In the second theater, the audience's ecstasy increases with its inability to understand anything being said: " 'When will these fools
get tired of hearing this biblical style they don't understand at all?'
he thought. But on the contrary this style amused them with its
strangeness, they laughed at it" (161). The full measure of glory attaches to mastery of language that has shed its pragmatic potential;
in a world where reference could be fatal, free-floating signifiers offer the exhilaration of continued life—"they laughed at it." Repetition, recitation, Restoration—a major historical concern of *Le
Rouge et le noir* is with collective euphoria in response to all discourse in which reference is unutterable.

Julien begins his rise by memorizing not only the New Testament
but also Joseph de Maistre's *Du pape*, one of the crucial ideological
documents of the Restoration. Commenting on Latin in the liturgy,
Du pape makes explicit and grave what *Le Rouge et le noir* leaves

implicit and comic, the vital importance of protecting language from human manipulation if rulers are to survive. "As for the people properly so called, if they do not understand the words, so much the better. Respect is enhanced, and the mind loses nothing. He who does not understand understands better than he who understands poorly. . . . From every imaginable point of view, religious language should be placed beyond the domain of men" (131; translations from Maistre are my own). With language "beyond the domain of men," human dominion over meaning vanishes as well. The rapt adoration elicited by Julien's content-free recitations is the effect of a society's unconscious sensation that representational language is its mortal enemy.

The man Julien calls "my M. de Maistre" (265) understood quite well that antirepresentational language is indistinguishable from absolute truth if no one challenges it. In *Le Rouge et le noir*, social identity is not referential but constative; in *Du pape*, papal infallibility is not descriptive but prescriptive. "It is in fact absolutely the same thing, in practice, not to be subject to error and not to be subject to accusations of error" (119). That the first eighteen years of Louis XVIII's reign were nonexistent matters not at all "in practice" if his subjects confirm their participation in his reign's nineteenth year. For the Restoration as seen by both Maistre and Stendhal, the referents that matter are not those which underlie language but those which follow it. The constative function addresses not what was but what will be.

The second set of holy writings responsible for Julien's triumphs consists of the fifty-three numbered letters transcribed so as to win Mathilde de la Mole by wooing Mme de Fervaques. Recall how those letters enter the text. Julien, in abject despair because of Mathilde's latest rejection, confides in the Russian prince Korasoff, whose advice is that Julien pretend to love someone else. When Julien replies that he lacks the will and the wit to sustain the necessary correspondence, Korasoff supplies him with a full set of letters written by another Russian during a seduction attempt in England some time earlier. For my purposes, the interesting point about this provenance is that it resonates with the Restoration's historical mission no less than the Bible and Maistre's *Du pape*. Written by one Russian and given to Julien by another, Korasoff's letters also connect the nineteenth century to the eighteenth as if the Revolution had never taken place: "Russians copy French behavior, but always fifty years late. They are now in the century of Louis XV" (*Le Rouge et le noir*, 394), which is to say the age Louis XVIII attempted to resuscitate.

Julien's use of this Russian correspondence almost seems to be designed as a textbook illustration of how language can communicate without the slightest pretense of referring. According to the celebrated schema in Jakobson's "Linguistics and Poetics," the six factors in an act of verbal communication are the addresser, the addressee, the context to which they refer, the contact between them, the code they use, and the message they send. The first three factors—addresser, addressee, and referential context—constitute the connections between language and the extralinguistic world, and those are precisely the factors eliminated during Julien's correspondence. As addresser, Julien does not exist. Transcribing automatically and unconsciously, he is a passive means for words to move from one sheet of paper to another. The first letter literally puts him to sleep, the rest figuratively do the same. "What he copied struck him as so absurd that he ended up transcribing line by line without thinking of meaning" (408). As addressee, Julien is even less present than as addresser. Even though he does so without thinking, he does at least write and, albeit unconsciously, legitimately functions as addresser. He does not read at all, however, and the addressee function is completely absent from his communication with Mme de Fervaques. Without even opening them, he throws the letters addressed to him into a drawer and continues to send his letters in numerical order as if no response had intervened.

When the addresser is unconscious and the addressee uninterested, the referential context is nonexistent. One of the letters Julien copies alludes to London and Richmond. "Without thinking of meaning," he reproduces the allusion without realizing that he should substitute "Paris" and "Saint-Cloud." The astonishing aspect of this farcical gaffe is not that Julien so easily explains it away when Mme de Fervaques confronts him but that it is apparently the only reference to reality in the whole, immensely long correspondence. Page after page, letter after letter written in England by a Russian to a Quaker serve without alteration to express Julien's devotion to a Catholic in Paris.

The starkly antireferential character of Julien's successful wooing has special importance because of the wooing's place in the novel. The most crucial single moment in Julien's ascendent career is his decision to employ Korasoff's letters according to the accompanying instructions. It is uniquely because of the letters that Julien conquers Mathilde and uniquely because of the conquest that he becomes the chevalier de la Vernaye. The paradox is that this critical juncture in the classic realist plot, the Parisian success of a young man from the provinces, is also the point of greatest disjuncture between language and its classic realist function, representation of a reality prior to and independent of its writing. As the novel reiterates with Rabelaisian verve, the sender of Julien's letters to

Mme de Fervaques is a purely textual creation, the product rather than the producer of the words he writes. Barthes's comments in "The Death of the Author" on modern literature's substitution of a "scriptor" for an author apply without adaptation to Julien's effacement during his transcription of the letters which are to make his fortune: "The modern scriptor is born simultaneously with the text, is in no way equipped with a being preceding or exceeding the writing, is not the subject with the book as predicate; there is no other time than that of the enunciation, and every text is eternally written *here and now*" (145). Identical to Barthes's modernist achievements, Julien's letters are pure inscription without expression, pure textuality without reference, pure writing without authorship.

In *La Carte postale*, Jacques Derrida uses correspondence's necessary detachment from its author and recipient to exemplify writing's escape from origins, destinations, and reference. Julien's correspondence with Mme de Fervaques is in this sense an exemplary Derridean moment. Korasoff's friend Kalisky has his letters copied before delivering them to his Quaker. Korasoff receives a copy of the copy, Julien a copy of the copy of the copy, Mme de Fervaques a copy of the copy of the copy of the copy. Moreover, even the "original" letters have no more referential value than their multiple reproductions. Not only did Kalisky make no effort to write what he actually felt, he also recognized that writing's principal purpose is simply to exist as writing: "The first forty letters were intended only to secure forgiveness for the daring decision to write" (*Le Rouge et le noir*, 409). The act that produces the chevalier de la Vernaye is total submission to words that represent a void.

In another Derridean twist, the episode with Mme de Fervaques makes speech as unreliable as writing. Everything Julien says to the maréchale is actually intended for Mathilde, nothing he says to Mathilde represents anything he actually feels. Julien's first step toward winning Mme de Fervaques's heart is to speak in such a way that London, Paris, and all other words become interchangeable and indistinguishable. "He grew so animated that Mme de Fervaques could no longer understand what he was saying. This was a first step forward" (405). The gibberish addressed to Mme de Fervaques reaches Mathilde, its alternate destination, only on condition that whatever remains comprehensible be obviously untrue: " 'The more what I say is false, the more she'll like me,' thought Julien" (408). This insight is among the novel's most succinct statements of the inverse correlation between language's referential validity and performative force in Restoration society. In order for words to do something, they must categorically refuse to say anything.

When writing to Mme de Fervaques, Julien is an unresistant

medium through which language passes as if there were no one there. When speaking to Mathilde, his absence is just as pure. The emotions he feels for Mathilde are so intense that their description slips into the Romantic rhetoric Stendhal spent much of his life trying to keep out of his prose; for example, Julien is "penetrated by love to the most intimate recesses of his heart. Never had he worshipped her to such an extent" (420). Despite this fervor, however, Julien speaks as if he felt nothing at all. He conquers Mathilde "while listening to the sound of the empty words his mouth was saying as he would have listened to an alien noise" (420). The empty sounds coming from his mouth are the oral equivalent of the empty letters copied by his hand. Both estrange language from the circumstances in which it is produced and from the subjectivity of its producer. Whether seducing in Paris or when reciting the Bible in Verrières, the language that works is language that abnegates the referential function.

Yet Mme de Fervaques instantaneously sees through Julien's letters to an indubitable, incontrovertible referent. She reads what he writes as the direct manifestation of solid identity which permits no misinterpretation. "It's impossible not to perceive devotion, extreme seriousness, and much conviction in the prose of this young priest; he will display the gentle virtue of Massillon" (407). The assurance with which Mme de Fervaques discerns reality where there is none may be connected to her need for others to do for her what she does for Julien. At the summit of a community based on contempt for bourgeois values, she owes her position to bourgeois activity. As a result, she too requires signs that create identity instead of denoting it. "Her whole life seemed to have no object other than to make everyone forget that she was the daughter of an *industrialist*" (396). "Up to the time she saw Julien, Mme de Fervaques's greatest pleasure had been to write the word *maréchale* beside her name" (415). The italics are Stendhal's, and the two italicized words are in contrary relation to the world. *Industrialist* names reality, *maréchale* its social representation, and Mme de Fervaques's life-long struggle is to assure that the latter transcends the former. When she immediately penetrates Julien's letters to grasp the concrete substance they depict, she replicates the process through which she wants her fellows to identify her. Writing *maréchale* is her equivalent to Julien copying Kalisky. Both exercises in the free play of signifiers become referentially unimpeachable because their readers assume them to be so.

In Derrida's *La Carte postale*, the correspondent brought into being through a collection of verbal signs dissolves through the same semiotic interaction that gave him life. In Stendhal's *Le Rouge et le noir*, signs' products are incomparably more solid. Although writing

maréchale beside her name is Mme de Fervaques's private amusement, public performance of the same fatuous enterprise creates
the powerful woman who distributes the most important positions
in the Church of France. Analogously, Julien's correspondence with
the maréchale exemplifies what Barthes discussed in "Death of the
Author," written documents irrevocably severed from any preexisting personality. In conversation with Mathilde, while listening to
the words that come from his mouth as if they came from somewhere far away, Julien proclaims that the speaker is as dead as the
author. But Mme de Fervaques falls in love with the writer of the
borrowed letters, Mathilde with the speaker of the alien words. To
designate the entity that exists solely within writing, Barthes invents a neologism undefiled by previous use to refer to reality, *scriptor*. To designate the human being whose linguistic production is
followed by full integration into the world, Stendhal chooses a
name with daunting referential force, M. le chevalier de la Vernaye.
As Mathilde understood at the duc de Retz's ball, the emptiness
prior to declaration of social identity is irrelevant to the fullness
that follows it. Like Louis XVII, the chevalier de la Vernaye acquires historical substance at the same time he attains linguistic
form.

The distinction between Barthes's scriptor and Stendhal's chevalier—not what precedes writing but what succeeds it—is analogous
to the difference between realist and modernist fiction. Realism
uses words to convey the impression of reality, modernism to convey the impression of words. Although neither genre escapes the
iron law of representation, according to which the representing
medium inevitably dominates the thing represented, realism enacts
the fact that collective conventions can effectively abolish the distance between reality and representation. In *Du Pape*, immunity
from accusations of error is in practice exactly the same thing as infallibility. In *Le Rouge et le noir*, immunity from accusations of
falsehood is in practice exactly the same thing as truth. Stendhal's
invention of Julien Sorel, society's invention of the chevalier de la
Vernaye, and Restoration history's invention of Louis XVII are com-
parably persuasive demonstrations that verbal production and social reality are in no sense mutually exclusive.

All of Julien's many identities have a double textual character. At
first unfounded, ungrounded, and void, they nevertheless become
founding, grounding, and complete when a collectivity accepts the
names given them as authentically referential. It is the second moment in this sequence that distinguishes realism from the modernist genres that followed it and leads to an intriguing question. If
realist narrative is consistently concerned with the historically specific conventions that make signs appear to refer, is there a sense in

which realism—like modernism—embodies the verbal operations it also represents? Modernist experiments confound the reader with words while showing characters universally confounded with words. Does realist fiction analogously make words do for the reader what they do for *its* characters, assume referential authority while simultaneously denying that this authority is based on reference?

In the case of *Le Rouge et le noir*, the answer is an unqualified yes. Readers of this novel must begin by going through a process identical to that which produces the duc de Chaulnes's younger son, the blatant display of signs' unqualified arbitrariness. Yet Stendhal's readers, like his characters, immediately learn that signs' arbitrariness is immaterial to their representational power. What precedes the realist discourse of *Le Rouge et le noir*? Not only the facts of the Restoration but also a triple demonstration that the connection between discourse and facts is never reliable. The novel's title and its first two epigraphs detach language from reality as insistently as Julien's letters to Mme de Fervaques and his speech to Mathilde. That a quintessentially representational novel follows these introductory instances of antirepresentational dissemination makes the novel as a whole a perfect figure for its major social theme: reference, never immanent to language itself, is always reliable within the confines of a language community.

"Le rouge et le noir" denotes nothing. Or rather it denotes everything its readers want it to. Like the color of Julien's suits, the color of his novel has no referent until the addressee supplies one. Like the Marquis de la Mole, we readers have obligingly supplied referents and thus have assured that the red and the black convey a sense as firm as the blue. Stendhal's critics have for a century and a half been doing for the title given to his novel precisely what his characters do for the titles given to them, that is, attach a representational function to words that have none. "Red" and "black" have been taken to refer to the army and the Church, political liberalism and ecclesiastical reaction, and the colors on a roulette wheel with the same groundless certainty displayed when society ratifies the chevalier de Beauvoisis's decision that Julien Sorel is the illegitimate son of one of the Marquis de la Mole's noble friends. Critic Henri Martineau's announcement of what the title really means has the depth of conviction apparent when Beauvoisis' friends defend the legitimacy of his duel. In both cases, a fact passes even though it is demonstrably not a fact. "The red indicates Julien's republicanism as the black designates ecclesiastical circles. There can be no more obscurity except for those who enjoy surrounding classic works with clouds that they themselves produce for the pleasure of bursting through them" (346). To attach so unequivocal a meaning to so equivocal a title does *for* the text what is repeatedly done *in* it, interpret words as the names of things when they are actually nothing more than the names of words. The truth of "le rouge et le noir," as of *Le Rouge et le noir*, is that the truth of language is whatever its users attribute to it.

The novel's epigraph extends the demonstration to the truth of truth. "*La vérité, l'âpre vérité*. Danton" is the same kind of self-deconstructing syntagm as André Breton's "soluble fish," for Danton never said "La vérité, l'âpre vérité." The bitter truth is consequently that there is no such thing as truth if we take the word to mean objective facts independent of their representation. Like Stendhal's title, his epigraph has become in critical writings the opposite of what it is in his text. The truth the novel will express is not language's referential but its performative force.

After a nonreferential title and an antireferential epigraph, the text proper begins by detaching language from meaning as well as reference. The epigraph to Chapter I, Part I of *Le Rouge et le noir* is

> Put thousands together
> Less bad,
> But the cage less gay.
> HOBBES

Not only did Hobbes never say any such thing, but this English quotation means that Stendhal's monolingual readers reach his text across mysterious, impenetrable foreign words. Bilingual readers are no better off. What "Hobbes" said is as senseless to native speakers of English as to those who know no English at all. Put thousands of what together? Does "less bad" refer to the thousands or to their coming together? What kind of cage is it, and what is less bad about its being less gay? Like the novel's title, the epigraph to its first chapter conveys no meaning except what its readers create for it.

The necessity of producing its meaning may help explain why the first chapter's epigraph is printed as a poetic excerpt when Hobbes never wrote poetry. Etymologically and teleologically, poetry is verbal creation rather than verbal reference. After a title designating nothing and an apostrophe to truth with an untrue attribution, *Le Rouge et le noir* gives language the form canonically associated with autonomous verbal expression. Stendhal opens his novel with three different instances of a linguistic form that repels all efforts to determine its origin, its purpose, and its sense.

Then comes language that has stood as a faithful description of reality for more than a hundred and fifty years. "Put thousands together Less bad, But the cage less gay. HOBBES" segues into "The small village of Verrières could pass for one of the prettiest in

Franche-Comté" and the classic realist narrative of human experience in a precise sociohistorical milieu. A tripartite antirepresentational exercise prepares the novel that inaugurated the golden age of Western literature's exemplary representational form; three demonstrations that "realist literature" is a contradiction in terms introduce five hundred pages in which realist literature became a historical fact.

Le Rouge et le noir thus does for itself just what it does for Julien and the society in which he lives: it converts farcical displays of language's irremediable alienation from reality into compelling proof that language is reality's direct and unmediated expression. Mme de Fervaques reads Kalisky's letters and identifies Julien with Massillon, Stendhal's critics read *Le Rouge et lè noir* and identify Julien with Antoine Berthet. The grounds for the identifications are unimportant; what matters is that in each case an actual human being emerges from words that obviously contain no such thing. Danton did not say "La vérité, l'âpre vérité," 1814 was not the nineteenth year of Louis XVIII's reign; nevertheless, scholastic manuals such as P.-G. Castex and P. Surer's confidently use Stendhal's epigraph to state the essence of his novelistic accomplishment and Louis XVIII got away with his idiosyncratic counting practices. The great mimetic achievement of *Le Rouge et le noir* is its reproduction of the great mimetic achievement of the Restoration, establishing the sensation of extrasemiotic reality through signs that have no descriptive value of any kind.

The most nearly explicit articulation of the novel's *mise en abîme* of its own spurious representationality comes at the end of the ascendant phase of its protagonist's career. When Julien Sorel, a purely verbal creation, becomes the chevalier de la Vernaye, a purely verbal creation, he understands his success as the conclusion of a novel: " 'After all,' he thought, 'my novel is over, and it's due to me alone' " (442). Like the most skillful of realist authors, Julien has taken empty words and produced the plenitude of a being accepted as real by all his readers. His novel has ended because the realist illusion has triumphed.

The red, the black, and the Restoration thus name not a work of fiction and its actual referent but a single, unitary vision of how sense is made. The historical semantics of realist fiction represents a universe in which meaning—to return to Barthes's "Death of the Author"—does not precede but does exceed the signs expressing it. The Restoration itself was based on a series of verbal strategies preceded by twenty-five years of turbulent demonstrations that they could be nothing more than exercises in autotelic textuality. But those strategies worked. The Restoration exceeded its originative assertion that the Revolution and Empire were unconnected to the reality of France and acquired a solid place in history. The multiple ways in which the peasant Julien Sorel acquires a solid place in aristocratic society are so many commentaries on a world in which solidity could be nothing more than a matter of convention. Canonical readings of Julien's novel make it clear that solidity and convention have continued to form our most basic understanding of what is real in realism.

ALISON FINCH

The Sense of an Ending in Stendhal's *Le Rouge et le Noir*†

Vivre isolé! . . . Quel tourment! . . .

Je deviens fou et injuste, se dit Julien en se frappant le front. Je suis isolé ici dans ce cachot; mais je n'ai pas *vécu isolé* sur la terre; j'avais la puissante idée du *devoir*. Le devoir que je m'étais prescrit, à tort ou à raison . . . a été comme le tronc d'un arbre solide auquel je m'appuyais pendant l'orage; je vacillais, j'étais agité. Après tout je n'étais qu'un homme . . . mais je n'étais pas emporté.

C'est l'air humide de ce cachot qui me fait penser à l'isolement . . .

Et pourquoi être encore hypocrite en maudissant l'hypocrisie? Ce n'est ni la mort, ni le cachot, ni l'air humide, c'est l'absence de madame de Rênal qui m'accable. Si, à Verrières, pour la voir, j'étais obligé de vivre des semaines entières, caché dans les caves de sa maison, est-ce que je me plaindrais?

L'influence de mes contemporains l'emporte, dit-il tout haut et avec un rire amer. Parlant seul avec moi-même, à deux pas de la mort, je suis encore hypocrite . . . O dix-neuvième siècle!

. . . Un chasseur tire un coup de fusil dans une forêt, sa proie tombe, il s'élance pour la saisir. Sa chaussure heurte une fourmilière haute de deux pieds, détruit l'habitation des fourmis, sème au loin les fourmis, leurs œufs . . . Les plus philosophes parmi les fourmis ne pourront jamais comprendre ce corps noir, immense, effroyable: la botte du chasseur, qui tout à coup a pénétré dans leur demeure avec une incroyable rapidité, et précédée d'un bruit épouvantable, accompagné de gerbes d'un feu rougeâtre . . .

. . . Ainsi la mort, la vie, l'éternité, choses fort simples pour qui aurait les organes assez vastes pour les concevoir . . .

Une mouche éphémère naît à neuf heures du matin dans les grands jours d'été, pour mourir à cinq heures du soir; comment comprendrait-elle le mot *nuit*?

Donnez-lui cinq heures d'existence de plus, elle voit et comprend ce que c'est que la nuit.

Ainsi moi, je mourrai à vingt-trois ans. Donnez-moi cinq années de vie de plus, pour vivre avec madame de Rênal.

† From *The Art of Reading: Essays in Memory of Dorothy Gabe Coleman*, edited by Philip Ford and Gillian Jondorf. Cambridge: Cambridge French Colloquia, 1998, p. 125–34. Reprinted by permission of the editors.

Et il se mit à rire comme Méphistophélès. Quelle folie de dis-
cuter ces grands problèmes!
　　　　　　　—Stendhal, *Le Rouge et le Noir*, Part II, Chapter 44[1]

'Live in isolation! . . . what torment! . . .
　'I'm going mad, I'm being unfair,' Julien said to himself, striking
his forehead. 'I'm isolated here in this cell; but I haven't *lived isolated* on earth; I had the powerful idea of *duty*. The duty I set myself, whether wrongly or rightly . . . has been like a solid tree-trunk
against which I leaned during the storm; I wavered, I was agitated.
After all, I was only human . . . but I wasn't swept away.
　'It's the damp air of this cell that makes me think of isolation . . .
　'And why still be hypocritical at the very moment I'm cursing
hypocrisy? It's not death, not the cell, not the damp air, it's Mme
de Rênal's absence that's crushing me. At Verrières, if in order to
see her I'd had to live weeks on end hidden in the cellars of her
house, would I have complained?
　'The influence of my contemporaries is winning,' he said out
loud and with a bitter laugh. 'Alone, speaking to myself, two steps
away from death, I'm still a hypocrite . . . Oh, nineteenth century!
　'. . . A hunter fires a shot in a forest, his prey falls, he rushes
forward to seize it. His shoe knocks into an anthill two feet high,
destroys the ants' dwelling, scatters afar the ants, their eggs . . .
the most philosophical of the ants will never be able to understand that black, immense, frightful body: the hunter's boot, that
has all of a sudden penetrated their home with incredible speed,
and preceded by a dreadful noise, along with sprays of reddish
fire . . .
　'Thus death, life, eternity, very simple things for anyone who
has vast enough organs to conceive them . . .
　'At the height of summer, a mayfly is born at nine in the morning, then to die at five in the evening; how would it understand
the word *night*?
　'Give it another five hours' existence, it will see and understand
what night is.
　'So it is for me, I'll die at the age of twenty-three. Give me another five years' life, to live with Mme de Rênal.'
　And he began to laugh like Mephistopheles. 'What madness:
discussing these great problems!'

Critics have often commented on the speed of the endings of both
Le Rouge et le Noir and *La Chartreuse de Parme*—whether to blame
or praise. They point to the brevity of Stendhal's remarks about
Julien's execution ('Jamais cette tête n'avait été aussi poétique
qu'au moment où elle allait tomber. [. . .] Tout se passa simple-
ment, convenablement et de sa part sans aucune affection' (p. 697),
'Never had that head been so poetic as at the moment it was to fall.
[. . .] Everything went off simply, fittingly and on his side without

1. Stendhal, *Romans et nouvelles*, Bibliothèque de la Pléiade, ed. H. Martineau (Paris: Gallimard, 1952), I. 691–2. In this passage, emphases and suspension points are Stendhal's
or the editor's; in all succeeding quotations, emphases are mine unless otherwise indicated, and '[. . .]' are mine if enclosed in brackets.

any affectation'); and they cite the summary dispatching of characters on the last page of *La Chartreuse*.[2] This abruptness is undeniable. However, the above extract from Julien's meditations in prison (about eight pages from the end of the novel) shows—obviously—that a summum does not have to be at the literal close of a work.

What is most immediately noticeable about this sequence is that it has a deliberate concentration of imagery unusual in Stendhal. Within a page, there are three separate and clearly signalled images, somewhere between metaphor, analogy, and fable: duty as the trunk of a solid tree against which to lean during the storm; death as a hunter's boot destroying an anthill; life as the existence of a mayfly. These images are not in themselves as original or bold as the kind of figurative writing we might find in Balzac or Proust, and all would seem to be adapted from other writers. Duty as a tree is a simile suggested by the Mme de Duras whose novels *Olivier* and *Édouard* helped Stendhal with the plots of *Armance* and *Le Rouge*.[3] The hunter image derives from Goethe's *Faust*, and Martineau traces the mayfly image back to Diderot.[4] But Stendhal recharges all of them; here, as often, he is turning apparently 'easy' adoption of others' usages into his own mode of allusive writing. (A similar process is apparent not only in his well-known plagiarisms but also in his use of common hyperbole or his swoops into a raconteur's colloquialisms.)

2. Thus, J. Prévost, in *La Création chez Stendhal* (Paris: Gallimard, 1951), says: 'Par un excès de soudaineté et tout en énonçant le fait, il nous en dérobe la peine physique. L'exécution de Julien [. . .] est glissée en une ligne au milieu de pensées tout étrangères à l'échafaud. Cette vitesse souveraine, cette sorte d'euthanésie littéraire [. . .] reparaîtra [. . .] à la fin de la *Chartreuse*' (p. 323). ('By means of an excessive suddenness and at the same time stating the fact, he takes away from the reader the physical distress of that fact. Julien's execution [. . .] is slipped in: one line in the midst of thoughts that could not be more foreign to the idea of the scaffold. This sovereign swiftness, this as it were literary euthanasia [. . .] reappears at the end of *La Chartreuse*.') Prévost goes so far as to say that once Julien has reached the height of his ambitions (the betrothal to Mathilde and the accompanying change in social status), the reader 'ne trouve plus guère qu'un sec résumé de la vie du héros' (p. 333) ('finds barely more than a dry summary of the hero's life'). M. Wood, in *Stendhal* (London: Elek, 1971), remarks that events towards the end of the novel are recounted with 'extreme terseness', that the writing is 'extremely strange' (p. 85), and that 'At moments of crisis he simply will not tell us how his heroes feel, or how we are to respond' (pp. 85–6). R. Pearson, on the other hand, takes a subtler view, bringing out 'the aesthetic benefit of abrupt conclusion' in *Stendhal's Violin: A Novelist and his Reader* (Oxford: Clarendon, 1988), p. 241.

3. In the unpublished but widely circulated *Olivier*, the impotent hero complains he has no sense of 'Devoir', 'Duty' (Duras's capitalisation) and that 'Plus misérable que le roseau, je plie et ne me relève pas' ('More wretched than a reed, I bend and do not rise up again') (C. de Duras, *Olivier ou le secret*, texte inédit établi, présenté et commenté par D. Virieux (Paris: Corti, 1971), p. 155). (There are shades of La Fontaine, of course, in both the Duras and the Stendhal images.) Virieux points out that Stendhal uses almost verbatim another metaphor from this same work in *Armance* (p. 147, n. 45).

4. Soon after Faust first appears, he complains: 'I am not like a god! Too deeply now I feel / This truth. I am a worm stuck in the dust, / Burrowing and feeding, where at last I must / Be crushed and buried by some rambler's heel' (Goethe, *Faust*, tr. D. Luke (Oxford: Oxford University Press, 1987), Part One, ll. 652–5). For the mayfly image, see p. 692, n. 1.

In part, this recharging is achieved by Stendhal's through-composing of the images. All rural pictures, each modulates into the following one: the tree of the first becomes the forest of the second; the helpless insects of the second become the ephemeral insect of the third. More substantially, the recharging is achieved through the immediate context; through the resonances Stendhal sets up between the images and other parts of the novel; and through the explicit questions raised as to how to verbalise the un-verbalisable. As is well known, such questions recurrently amused and troubled the mature Stendhal.[5] But here they are put in their most extreme form, since Julien is groping toward expressing not just feelings about death but, impossibly, the experience itself.

Thus, leaning against a tree suggests a clinging not just to duty but to life—an attempt to find shelter against an elemental force, the death that could 'emport[er]' one ('sweep one away'). The hunter image emphasises this helplessness before death in a more brutal, urgent, and undignified mode. Julien is now no doubt at-tempting to imagine what his own death by guillotine will be like. The 'corps noir, immense, effroyable' ('black, immense, frightful body') is not only a symbolic figure of death, but is also imprecise enough to evoke the appearance of the erected guillotine. The 'bruit épouvantable' and the 'incroyable rapidité' ('dreadful noise', 'incredible speed') (especially 'incredible' with the adjective preced-ing the noun, unusual in French) are Julien's way of conceptualis-ing the falling blade; the sprays of reddish fire are the spurting of the blood, and the pain as the nerves are assailed in an unimagin-ably explosive shock. (The phonetic patterning in this paragraph—[p] and [f]—denser than usual in Stendhal, intensifies the climax.)

The mayfly image does more than re-emphasize the incompre-hensibility of death: its barely sketched-out physicality implies a yearning to have a little longer to enjoy sensation. Like other writers, Stendhal suggests this simple savouring of sensation through the pleasures of a summer's day, starting with the freshness of the morn-ing, 'neuf heures du matin' ('nine in the morning'). (And Julien, still a young man, is in the 'summer' of his life.) The 'night' which the mayfly cannot know is complex. Not merely death and the idea of death, it is also here the continuation of life, more particularly life with Mme de Rênal. ('Donnez-lui cinq heures d'existence de plus, elle voit et comprend ce que c'est que la nuit. [. . .] Donnez-moi

---

5. See, for example, his marginal notes to *Lucien Leuwen* and key comments in the *Vie de Henry Brulard* (not least the famous last sentence 'On gâte des sentiments si tendres à les raconter en détail': 'One spoils such tender feelings if one recounts them in detail') (*Œuvres intimes*, Bibliothèque de la Pléiade (Paris: Gallimard, 1955), p. 395). Pearson brings out the importance for Stendhal of suggestion, as opposed to statement, at many points in his *Stendhal's Violin*, and especially in his concluding chapter 'Reverie' (pp. 266–75).

cinq années de vie de plus, pour vivre avec madame de Rênal.' ('Give it another five hours' existence, it will see and understand what night is. [. . .] Give me another five years' life, to live with Mme de Rênal.') Night suggests, then, a long, intimate eroticism. This final image in fact concludes Julien's meditations: there are now (after this extract) a few brief thoughts, followed very shortly by the end of the chapter with its last sentence, 'Julien se sentait fort et résolu comme l'homme qui voit clair dans son âme' (p. 693) ('Julien felt strong and resolute like a man who understands himself'). The image is able to be conclusive precisely because it is a synthesising one, combining fear of death with love for a partner.

Stendhal, then, reanimates these three images through their immediate, and urgent, setting. They also recapitulate wider structures of the novel. First, they allude to the title, echoed in the 'noir' and 'rougeâtre' ('black' and 'reddish') of the hunter image: here is how both colors are about to end. Second, the hunter's gunshot echoes Julien's shooting of Mme de Rênal: now he is to be 'shot'.[6] Third, the country scenes evoked show Julien finally rejecting the urban not just in deed and thought but more involuntarily, too, in imagination. Fourth, the forest and mayfly refer indistinctly back to the summer days near the beginning when Julien and Mme de Rênal chased butterflies in the orchard with the children, preparing perhaps the shortly following memory of these scenes at the moment of his execution: 'Les plus doux moments qu'il avait trouvés jadis dans les bois de Vergy revenaient en foule à sa pensée et avec une extrême énergie' (p. 697).[7] ('The sweetest moments he had once encountered in the Vergy woods crowded back into his thoughts and with extreme energy'.)

More generally, Julien's stress on the difficulties of understanding contrasts with the feats of empty intelligence that his virtuoso memory had allowed him to perform earlier. Girard claims that many outstanding novelists show their heroes, at the moment of death, not just undertaking a retrospective assessment, but undergoing a moral transformation: hatred gives way to love, pride to humility.[8] As in Constant and Flaubert, then, reflections about language and understanding have moral implications, and can create a special sense of tragedy.

6. We might also see here a connection with Stendhal's half-joking, half-serious comments on other pistol-shot disturbances (politics in the novel are like the pistol-shot at the concert): they are the ultimate disruption—and yet, are they? Dissonance has its part in aesthetic structures.

7. In the early sequence there are no fewer than three pitying references within two paragraphs to the fate these butterflies meet: they are twice said to be 'pauvres': 'poor'; finally, 'On les piquait sans pitié' (p. 263) ('they were pitilessly pierced with pins') (like Julien himself?).

8. R. Girard, *Mensonge romantique et vérité romanesque* (Paris: Grasset, 1961); as well as Stendhal, Girard cites Tolstoy, Proust, and others (e.g. pp. 234, 296–8).

Still at a general level, we may, too, find in the hunter figure a culmination of the historical and political considerations that permeate *Le Rouge*. Hunting has clear social meanings in this novel, where it is almost always an upper-class activity. Underlings like Julien may participate, but it is led by nobles such as M. de Rênal (pp. 273, 335–6) or by the king (p. 602). And here the hunter is 'higher' on the scale of creation than the ants he unwittingly treads on. So this is a picture of low-status creatures being destroyed by a well-equipped high-status creature who has already proved his ability to rule nature, having just successfully shot an animal. We know already that Julien has been condemned to death in part because he is a proletarian who has dared to leave his class. He has of course played a part in his own punishment by himself outlining this class-based analysis at his trial; but even if he had not, the conditions for his condemnation were already there, with the presence of Valenod who is jealous of Julien both sexually and socially. Now, in the figure of the hunter, we have a suggestion that Julien is being crushed not only by a penal code but also by a class system.

This interpretation is reinforced when we look at other uses in *Le Rouge* of key words in this passage, and contrast them with frequency and usage in *La Chartreuse*. Would Dorothy Gabe Coleman have approved of resorting to word-frequencies and concordances in close readings? Possibly not; she was too alive to the complexities of syntax and tone, and too wary of the potential aridity of formalism, to resort to such mechanical devices as a way of analysing her favourite works. But, keenly aware as she also was of patterning in poetry, she might not have entirely rejected tools that allow one to see structures which, deliberate and visible in verse, are normally diffuse and hidden in the novel. We can use the concordance of *Le Rouge* and *La Chartreuse* to trace briefly the fortunes of two lexical fields in the hunter image—it is important to have some means of comparison, since frequencies for one work only do not tell us much on their own.[9]

Let us, then, look at 'haut' ('high'), with its range of meanings from physical to figurative—appearing here in the anthill 'haute de deux pieds' ('two feet high'); and at the *chasseur/chasser* group (*hunter/hunt*), taking *chasser* in both its main French meanings of 'to hunt' and 'to banish'.

The anthill, only 'haute de deux pieds' ('two feet high') already conveys the insignificance of human achievement, and we are quite consciously ready to identify it with the social 'heights' encountered over the preceding 500 pages. Looking at the concordance, we find what we were not, however, likely to be so consciously aware of:

9. All figures in the following discussion are taken from my *Concordance de Stendhal*: Le Rouge et le Noir *et* La Chartreuse de Parme, *Compendia*, vol. 13 (Leeds: Maney, 1991).

that there are far more figurative uses of *haut* in *Le Rouge* than in *La Chartreuse*: high rank, high opinions of x or y, high sense of morality, lofty thoughts. In addition, *hauteur* (in French, *haughtiness* as well as *height*), and the associated word *hautain* (*haughty*), are used more often in *Le Rouge*.[1] So, by the time we reach the two-foot-high anthill, we bring to the word 'haute' not just pictures of physical height, but other images of moral and social height which this novel, markedly more than *La Chartreuse*, slowly draws together by its use of *haut* in other contexts. The cumulative *hauts*, *hauteurs*, and *hautains* come together at not only obvious thematic levels but also subliminal lexical ones. They reinforce here the idea of a catastrophic destruction of all kinds of control and aspiration, from the sublime to the silly.

Hunters appear in *La Chartreuse* as well as in *Le Rouge*, but with differences in usage. Whereas in *La Chartreuse* the noun *chasseur/s* always denotes 'real' characters, in *Le Rouge* the single use of the word before the two in this passage comes—as here—only in a figure of speech. (Julien is at a certain point 'content comme un chasseur' (p. 346) ('happy as a hunter') discovering a plain full of game.) Therefore, there is a surprise here—this final hunter is almost as much of an intrusion into the lexis of the novel as his foot is into the anthill. When we look at the verb *chasser*, other complexities emerge. *Le Rouge* uses this verb rather more often than *La Chartreuse*, never to mean hunting of animals, but almost always as 'chasing someone away', banishing them—from, say, one's house or salon.[2] Such fears of chasing away or banning haunt Julien and determine many of his actions. In the seminary, he thinks that after Pirard's departure 'le parti du *Sacré-Cœur* va me dégrader et peut-être me *chasser*' (p. 409), ('the *Sacred Heart* party is going to demote me, perhaps *send me away*');[3] newly arrived in the Mole household, he finds Mathilde's brother unexpectedly charming: 'Est-il possible, se dit-il, que ce soit là l'homme dont les plaisanteries offensives doivent me *chasser* de cette maison!' (p. 449) ('Can it be,' he thought, 'that this is the man whose offensive jokes were destined

---

1. The two novels are almost exactly the same length, so raw frequencies will tell us all we need to know; they do not have to be expressed as percentages or put through the unnecessarily complicated tests of stylometrics. (See my 'Excitement and Astonishment in *Le Rouge et le Noir* and *La Chartreuse de Parme*', *Essays in French Literature*, XXVI (1989), 21–37, n. 8; and 'The Imagery of a Myth: Computer-Assisted Research on Literature', *Style*, XXIX (1995), 530–40.) In the following groups of figures, those for *Le Rouge* will always come first.
   Haut/e/s/es: 119, 90. Of these, literally high or tall: 26, 50; figuratively high (thoughts, class, morality, etc.): 65, 34. (The other uses occur in, e.g., phrases meaning "loud," "high colour", etc.) *Hauteur/s*: 36, 26. Of these, literally high or tall: 8, 9; meaning 'haughtiness': 28, 17. *Hautain/e*: 18, 6.
2. Other uses (few) would be, e.g., 'to banish an illusion/to banish boredom'.
   Chasser: 27, 21; of these 0, 3 refer to a 'real' hunt. *Chasse*: (noun) 9, 15; of these 8, 15 refer to a 'real' hunt. *Chasseur/s*: (noun) 3, 14. (Early in *La Chartreuse*, some of these *chasseurs* are members of the *chasseurs* military division.)
3. Stendhal's/editor's emphasis in '*Sacré-Cœur*'.

to drive me out of this house!'); and when Mathilde proposes revealing her pregnancy to her father, 'Mais,' says Julien, 'il me *chassera* avec ignominie!' (p. 625) ('But he'll send me away in ignominy!'). After such uses, we at last come upon what is by far the most physically realised embodiment of chasing or hunting in the novel: the hunter with the frighteningly noisy gun, the heavy black boot, the greedy grasping of his fallen prey. ('Il s'élance pour la saisir.' ('He rushes forward to seize it.')) We are, by now, predisposed to see in this particular *chasseur* an embodiment of everything that has had the potential to *chasser* in the other sense, culminating with the 'exiling' of Julien himself and the crushing of his anthill edifices.

Pulling related meanings into the net in this way will strike some as far-fetched, others as exciting, depending on their estimation of the power of the signifier; we might cautiously conclude that it would be as wrong to dismiss entirely the case for subliminal links as to overstate it. At any rate, analysed with a combination of the naked eye and the mechanical help of the concordance, this passage shows that the shortly following 'real' end of *Le Rouge et le Noir* is irreducibly elliptical still, of course—but is not foreshortened. It can afford to be brief because it refers back to this meditation, thus subsuming a prolonged network of associations. As we see here, the teleology which many critics view as a hallmark of the nineteenth-century novel can be unexpectedly dispersed in its nature.

The passage is significant at levels other than those of these three well-foregrounded images. Julien's final Mephistophelian laughter arises from his sudden recognition that he is trying to make a bargain—with whom? ('Donnez-moi cinq années de vie de plus [. . .]' ('Give me another five years' life [. . .]').) He has, perhaps, always been a version of Faust, as the adoption of Goethe's worm/rambler metaphor suggests.[4] But he now becomes both Faust and a devil possessed of all-powerful rhetoric. For Julien has just performed a linguistic trick as clever as any of Mephistopheles's: through his mayfly analogy, he has turned the night of death into a night of sensuous enjoyment. As a multilateral Faust/Mephistopheles, then, Julien can appreciate the dramatic ironies that may quasi-aesthetically present themselves at the approach of death. (His laugh is comparable to Bette's silent savouring, on her death-bed, of the Hulots' still-firm conviction that she is 'l'ange de la famille' ('the family angel'); even now, she does not disabuse them: dramatic irony, of the kind the author himself enjoys, is preferable to the revelation her earlier self might have desired.)[5]

---

4. See above, n. 4.
5. Balzac, *La Cousine Bette* (Paris: Librairie Générale Française, 1963), p. 442. Julien's Mephistophelian laugh and his earlier 'rire amer' ('bitter laugh') also have a role in Stendhal's life-long search to define and create varying modes of comedy. Some thirty

The reflections on the damp air of the cell, and on the influence of contemporaries, create other kinds of ambiguities. Julien at first claims that physical and cultural environment *do* affect the tenor and content of one's thoughts and feelings, even at those supreme moments when unclouded thought ought to be possible. But he then affirms that one can escape both the physical environment and the 'contemporary' hypocrisy apparently forced upon one: 'Ce n'est ni la mort, ni le cachot, ni l'air humide, c'est l'absence de madame de Rênal qui m'accable' ('It's not death, not the cell, not the damp air, it's Mme de Rênal's absence that's crushing me'). However, Julien's own interpretation here is perhaps too simple: when, a few pages later, he leaves his cell for execution, Stendhal writes: 'Le mauvais air du cachot devenait insupportable à Julien. Par bonheur, le jour où on lui annonça qu'il fallait mourir, un beau soleil réjouissait la nature [. . .]. Marcher au grand air fut pour lui une sensation délicieuse [. . .]. Allons, tout va bien, se dit-il, je ne manque point de courage' (p. 697) "The bad air in the cell was becoming unbearable for Julien. Luckily, the day he was told he must die, a fine sun shone down joyously on nature [. . .]. Walking in the open air was delicious to him [. . .]. 'Come, it's all going well,' he said to himself, 'I'm not lacking in courage.' ") The air of the cell was not so immaterial after all; at any rate, the reader is left in uncertainty on this point—an uncertainty which shows (if it still needed showing) that the nineteenth-century novel is not monolithic in its presentation of surroundings and causes.

The narrative pace of this passage is both atypical and typical of Stendhal. This is not a rapidly moving sequence, yet in Stendhal reflection and impetus are not incompatible: even here, unobtrusively, there is that illusion of events being pushed along, or collapsed into each other, that he creates so often elsewhere.[6] Action is fast—the storm might 'emport[er]' one ('sweep one away'),

---

years previously, he had started to puzzle over how to reconcile the laughable with the *odieux* (the *odious*); here is one example of the blending he often does achieve in his mature works. See his comments on his own attempts at drama in *Théâtre* (Paris: Le Divan, 1931) (e.g. on his play *Les Deux Hommes*, written 1803–4: II. 178; or on *Letellier*, first version written 1804–5: III. 18, 270).

6. For decades, critics have been trying to define this illusion, often seeking to express it through rather belle-lettrist metaphors of their own. To take only two examples from among very many, in the 1930s C. Du Bos remarks that 'Le style de Stendhal, c'est l'action d'un cheval de race' ('Stendhal's style is the movement of a thoroughbred horse') (*Approximations*, Deuxième Série (Corrêa, 1932), p. 2); in the 1950s, J.-P. Richard writes that '*Le Rouge* halète. C'est le roman d'un coureur qui oublie de reprendre souffle [. . .]. Le miracle demeure *La Chartreuse*: surprise d'un récit dont l'écoulement souple est nerveux comme une véhémence'.) ('*Le Rouge* pants. It is the novel of a runner forgetting to draw breath [. . .]. The miracle is still *La Chartreuse*: a surprise, a narrative whose supple flow is nervously vehement' ('Connaissance et tendresse chez Stendhal', in *Littérature et sensation* (Paris: Seuil, 1954), p. 102). R. Pearson comments sanely on this area in *Stendhal's Violin*; see the chapter 'Time and Imagination in *Le Rouge et le Noir*', especially the section 'The Passage of Time', pp. 102–7.

the hunter *rushes* to *seize* his prey ('s'élance', 'saisir'), and his boot penetrates the anthill with, as we have seen, 'incroyable rapidité' ('incredible speed'). The mayfly image too—that of the astonishingly short life snuffed out—is more than just an echo of a Romantic topos. It is an extreme example of the elided time-scale that creates the narrative speed *in excelsis* of Stendhal's two best novels. Five years become five hours; a life becomes a day.

Furthermore, Julien's meditation, rather than taking on an air of grave development, passes quickly from one idea to the next; these ideas, whether low-key or passionate in tone, are not formally structured but slip, apparently casually, from one point to another, then back again, in a mode characteristic of Stendhal. For example, the conclusion drawn after the paragraph about the hunter ('Ainsi la mort, la vie', etc. ('Thus death, life'), seems to be the moral of the fable, but it does not even have a main verb, and then, surprisingly, we come to another analogy, that of the mayfly. So we jump from illustration to conclusion back to illustration, in a manner which is at once disjointed and supple. This approach mirrors Julien's own many-pronged effort to come to terms with his situation, and also represents one way the mind works—dartingly and obliquely.

This brings us back to the most self-reflecting implications of this passage: the exceptional value it gives to metaphorical and analogical thinking. Stendhal's strictures against Chateaubriand's style, and against even Balzac's excesses and affectations, have made commentators, not unjustifiably, focus on his economies and ironies; they have been inclined to think that he does not 'believe in' figurative language.[7] In fact, Stendhal does use such language more than is sometimes realised, and when he does it is, as I have shown, both unpretentious and powerful. However, what is really unusual about this passage is not so much its density *per se* of figures of speech, but its interweaving of these figures with a discussion of the limits of understanding. Stendhal, far from being a 'metaphor-hater', is, at this near-final point, suggesting that there are certain feelings and thoughts that can be approached *only* by way of figurative language. The 'sense of an ending' could scarcely be more resonant than in this passage.[8]

---

7. For example J. Attuel, who, in *Le Style de Stendhal: Efficacité et romanesque* (Paris: Nizet, 1980), tends to reproduce this view 'from the horse's mouth' without question (e.g. p. 345). A much subtler discussion is to be found in A. Jefferson, *Reading Realism in Stendhal* (Cambridge: Cambridge University Press, 1988), e.g. pp. 93, 99.
8. I of course borrow my key phrase from F. Kermode's *The Sense of an Ending* (Oxford: Oxford University Press, 1967).

LISA G. ALGAZI

The Quest for the Mother: A Psychoanalytic Feminist Reading of *The Red and the Black*†

Whatever happened to Julien's mother? This question, long pondered by readers and students of Stendhal, lies at the heart of Julien's quest for acceptance and, finally, love in the arms of the two mother-mistresses in *The Red and the Black*, Mme. de Rênal and Mathilde. Only Julien's social ambition rivals his unconscious longing for maternal affection as his prime motivation, and in the end, in the sanctuary of his prison cell, it is the latter that triumphs. In this essay I propose a psychoanalytic feminist approach to understanding the role of the mother in *The Red and the Black* and its relevance to a critical analysis of the text as a whole. To this end I examine Stendhal's ambiguous portrayal of the maternal figure and its implications both for Julien and for future generations of French women.

The Representation of Mothers: From Christian Tradition to Psychoanalysis

Traditional maternal imagery in the Western Christian tradition tends to revolve around the sacred figure of the Virgin Mary, the mother of Christ whose example all women should follow. In keeping with this image the ideal mother has traditionally been represented as a chaste and selfless extension of her (mostly male) offspring, dedicated solely to their care and nurturing, to the total exclusion of her own needs and desires. In maternal representations in French literature from Rabelais to Rousseau, women who become mothers are automatically excluded from the realms of sexuality and active selfhood of any kind, leaving only their capacity to mother as the central expression of their identities as women. Most often, they become accessories to the hero, mere props that help to explain the personality and character of the protagonist.

With the rise of psychoanalytic theory came a new understanding of this traditional vision of motherhood and its underlying symbolic mechanisms, starting with Freud's theories on the preœdipal stage

† From *Approaches to Teaching Stendhal's* The Red and the Black, eds. Dean de la Motte and Stirling Haig (New York: Modern Language Association of America, 1999), pp. 130–38. Reprinted by permission of the publisher. The selections from *The Red and the Black* in English are from the Norton edition, 1968. The selections in French are from Garnier-Flammarion edition, 1964. Subsequent analysis of the maternal figure in *The Red and the Black* appears in Algazi's *Maternal Subjectivity in the Works of Stendhal* (Edwin Mellen Press, 2001).

of child development and the sexual nature of the relationship between the (male) infant and the mother. Later theorists have modified Freud's concepts to create an image of the mother as a refuge from the patriarchal world, representing a state of being that both precedes and supercedes patriarchal society. According to the French psychoanalyst Jacques Lacan, the symbolic, or the realm of language, is essentially patriarchal, because of the privileged position of the phallus as transcendental signifier. The law of the father represents the law of a phallic society where no thought can exist outside language and no language can exist without assuming the preexistence of the phallus. As a complementary realm to the symbolic in Lacan's theory of child development, the Imaginary represents the early infant period when there is no distinction between subject and object, self and other, and the child experiences a symbiotic relationship with the mother's body; its identity and its mother's merge and become inseparable.

This blissful period, when the child's world seems free of contradictions or uncertainties, ends when the child becomes aware of the father and the outside world represented by the father: the preestablished structure of social and sexual roles that make up the family and society and that Lacan calls the symbolic order. When the child enters the symbolic order, learning language and differentiating the self, it becomes a part of a world radically different from that in which it had existed with its mother. The blurry boundaries of the Imaginary and the womblike peace of life before language fade as the child begins its new life in the public realm controlled by the father and those like him. French feminist and psychoanalytic theorist Julia Kristeva (*Soleil*) sees the period of child development before the interference of the father as a possible source of prelinguistic communication. The sensual, wordless language between mother and child becomes *le sémiotique*, drawing on the rhythms of the merging bodies and the strength of the instinctive drives expressed between mother and infant. For Kristeva this special time before patriarchal intervention allows both mother and child to experience a world free from the strictures of patriarchal law, of the law of language, of the symbolic. It is such a world to which Julien wishes to return, and his quest will lead him from the provinces to Paris to a provincial prison, where he finally finds his *sémiotique* with his quintessential woman, Mme de Rênal.

Mme de Rênal, Mother and Savior

The Red and the Black revolves around a motherless hero, leaving the maternal role in Julien's development conveniently open. From the moment he arrives at the Rênals' home to take up his tutoring duties, we find an abundance of metaphors for birth, or rebirth: Julien's symbolic bath in the fountain, his wet hair, and his unsure manner all lead Mme de Rênal to treat him like a lost child and take him under her maternal wing. Her first words to him, "Que voulez-vous ici, mon enfant?" 'What do you want here, my child?' (48; 21; l.6) begin their relationship on a more intimate footing than the reserved Mme de Rênal would normally tolerate with a stranger, particularly a man. Neither her convent education, which the narrator describes as worthless, nor her experience with loud and abrupt men such as her husband and his friends has prepared her for this encounter with a sensitive, effeminate young peasant who seems to her more like a shy young girl than the authoritarian, mean-tempered brute she had expected. Overwhelmed with relief, she welcomes Julien as an addition to her family, thinking that he will be a friend to her eldest son, who is not much younger than Julien.

As Julien settles into the routine of educating the young sons of this aristocratic family, his privileged relationship with the mistress of the house becomes ever more intimate, as she takes charge of his social education much as he teaches her sons their Latin. For Mme de Rênal, this tender interest in someone other than her children is a new and strange experience; her emotional universe had previously been confined to maternal love, as befitted a good Catholic wife and mother. Her innocence in affairs of the heart and her tendency to treat Julien like a son blinds her to the enormity of her transgression, allowing her to step outside the traditional limits of motherhood to feel and act on her own desires. In contrast to earlier literary portrayals of mothers who strayed from the chaste ideal, however, the author does not censure Mme de Rênal for neglecting her children as she slowly evolves from Julien's surrogate mother to his passionate mistress. On the contrary, her transformation provides Julien with both his missing mother figure and a means of escape into the imaginary world of the prison. As Mme de Rênal becomes more active in protecting and nurturing her lover-son, Julien slowly realizes that the key to his happiness lies in her love, not in social recognition or power; the return to the presymbolic maternal space gives him more pleasure than any of the worldly gifts that his other mistress, Mathilde, can offer.

After Julien tries to kill her, Mme de Rênal defies patriarchal religion and propriety by defending her attacker, using all her new-found self-assurance in her efforts to bring about his pardon. However, these efforts are and must be in vain: as a woman and mother, she has no power over the symbolic order. Only in the maternal space of the prison can she control the life of her lover-son, just as she brought him food and water when he was temporarily imprisoned in her bedroom. Her appearance in his cell, and the contrast between her un-self-conscious devotion and Mathilde's ostentatious displays, renew Julien's will to live:

> [I]l fut éveillé par des larmes qu'il sentait couler sur sa main. Ah! c'est encore Mathilde, pensa-t-il à demi éveillé. [. . .] Ennuyé de la perspective de cette nouvelle scène dans le genre pathétique, il n'ouvrit pas les yeux. [. . .] Il entendit un soupir singulier; il ouvrit les yeux, c'était Mme de Rênal.
> —Ah! Je te revois avant que de mourir, est-ce une illusion? s'écria-t-il en se jetant à ses pieds. [. . .] Sache que je t'ai toujours aimée, que je n'ai jamais aimé que toi.　　　(537–38)

> [H]e was awakened by tears which he felt trickling on his hand.
> Ah! It's Mathilde again, he thought, still half asleep. [. . .] Bored by the prospect of another scene in the pathetic vein, he did not open his eyes. [. . .] He heard an unusual sob; he opened his eyes, it was Mme. de Rênal.
> —Ah! So I can see you again before I die, or is it an illusion? [. . .] You must know that I've always loved you, I never loved anyone but you.　　　(393–94; 2.43)

His claim that he never loved anyone but her is an indication of his redefinition of love since the time of his imprisonment: Julien finally understands the value of maternal passion and the futility of *l'amour-vanité*, as Stendhal calls the vainglorious, self-conscious infatuation that he distinguishes from sincere and natural passion (*l'amour-passion*). Only in prison does Julien recognize that his infatuation with Mathilde had more to do with vanity and ambition than with his own emotions; belatedly, he grasps the full extent of Mme de Rênal's maternal devotion, entrusting his fate and that of his unborn son to her care. In the midst of their lovemaking Julien tells her: "songe [. . .] qu'il faut que tu vives pour mon fils, que Mathilde abandonnera à des laquais [. . .]" You must suppose [. . .] that you are required to live for my son, whom Mathilde will abandon to the care of lackeys [. . .]' (440; 395; 2.43). His perception of Mathilde's inability to mother becomes the determining factor in his preference for the englobing efficacy of his surrogate mother, Mme de Rênal.

Sacrificing her reputation and her religion to her desire, Mme de Rênal achieves total separation from the authority of the father, returning to the prison against both her confessor's wishes and her husband's explicit orders. Exceeding even the efforts of the wealthy and aggressive Mathilde, Mme de Rênal obtains permission to see Julien twice a day, and the two lovers treasure their last moments together in his little cell, finally isolated from the petty interferences of the symbolic by the walls of the patriarchal prison. Within this protected maternal space, Mme de Rênal becomes Julien's mother once more, protecting him from his jailers and living from day to day in a blissfully symbiotic harmony that not even their time in the woods of Vergy had granted them. United at last with his adored mother-mistress, free of the distractions of the symbolic order, Julien finally finds the happiness that had eluded him in his frantic pursuit of masculine ambitions:

> [I]l vivait d'amour et sans presque songer à l'avenir. Par un étrange effet de cette passion, quand elle est extrême et sans feinte aucune, Mme de Rênal partageait presque son insouciance et sa douce gaieté.
> —Autrefois, lui disait Julien, quand j'aurais pu être si heureux pendant nos promenades dans les bois de Vergy, une ambition fougueuse entraînait mon âme dans les pays imaginaires. [. . .] Non, je serais mort sans connaître le bonheur, si vous n'étiez venue me voir dans cette prison.   (552–53)

> [H]e was living on love and almost without a thought for the future. By a strange effect of this passion when it is at its height and perfectly sincere, Mme de Rênal almost shared in his indifference and gentle gaiety.
> —In the old days, Julien told her, when I could have been so happy during our walks through the forest at Vergy, smoldering ambition dragged my soul way into imaginary lands. [. . .] No, I should have died without ever knowing happiness if you had not come to see me in this prison.   (405; 2.45)

Living in such complete harmony that they share the same feelings and thoughts, the two lovers spend their precious last days together in a presymbolic paradise, interrupted only by periodic unwelcome visits of the rejected mistress, Mathilde. After Julien's execution, while Mathilde is occupied with the disposition of his mortal remains, Mme de Rênal continues her pattern of maternal devotion to her lover at the expense of her own children: in spite of her promise to live for the sake of Julien's son, three days after his death, "elle mourut en embrassant ses enfants" 'she died in the act of embracing her children' (556; 408; 2.45).

MATHILDE DE LA MOLE, OR THE MATERNAL FAILURE

Julien's preference for Mme de Rênal's real maternal passion over Mathilde's self-conscious infatuation demonstrates his willingness to sacrifice all the things he had once thought important—career, wealth, social status—for the pleasure of a nostalgic return to the original mother-child realm of blissful unity, beyond the reach of the patriarchal structures that have continually oppressed and excluded him. His nostalgia for such an extrasymbolic bond cannot be satisfied by the cold Mathilde, even though she is carrying his child. While her actions demonstrate her untiring devotion to her lover, she ultimately cannot fulfill Julien's emotional and psychological needs, because of an essential lack. What is this lack that defines, by opposition, the ideal Stendhalian woman? Both Mme de Rênal and Mathilde are mothers, at least in the physiological sense. Both use every means available to help Julien in his struggle against patriarchal society. Finally both women sacrifice the most precious possession of any respectable nineteenth-century Frenchwoman, their reputations, to their love for Julien, defying their families and their social peers to help him.

The real difference lies in Julien's perception of the maternal role and of Mathilde's inability to fulfill that role. For Julien, the moment when he discovers the sublime nature of unconditional love comes when Mme de Rênal's youngest son, Stanislas, falls ill. Mme de Rênal's conviction that she will be damned for all eternity because of her adultery, as well as her continuing love for Julien in spite of this conviction, melts the core of Julien's skeptical heart:

> La méfiance et l'orgueil de Julien, qui avait surtout besoin d'un amour à sacrifices, ne tinrent pas devant la vue d'un sacrifice si grand, si indubitable et fait à chaque instant. Il adorait Mme de Rênal. [. . .] Leur bonheur était désormais d'une nature bien supérieure, la flamme qui les dévorait fut plus intense.
>
> (137)

> Julien's suspicion and anxious pride, which required above all a love built on sacrifice, could not hold out against a sacrifice so vast, so unquestionable, so continual. He adored Mme. de Rênal. [. . .] Henceforth their happiness was of a finer grain; the passion that devoured them was more intense. (93; 1.19)

Julien's first meeting with Mathilde gives a very different picture. Although Mathilde is described as weak and pale, the narrator notes that her voice "n'a rien de féminin" '[is] short, sharp, completely unfeminine' (291; 220; 2.7). Despite the feminine frailty of her body, her spirit is masculine. When Julien first sees her, he compares the haughty Mathilde with his image of womanhood based on his experience with Mme de Rênal and subsequently denies her womanhood, faithful to the ideal created by the maternal devotion of the only woman he has ever known. On his next encounter with Mathilde, he repeats his disapproval of Mathilde's lack of femininity: "Julien lui trouva [. . .] l'air dur, hautain et presque masculin" 'Julien [. . .] decided she looked hard, arrogant, almost masculine' (283; 198; 2.3). His instinctive revulsion for this hybrid of masculine and feminine traits will be temporarily over-come by a surge of vanity, only to resurface at the end of the novel in his rejection of Mathilde's unwelcome attentions.

Where Mathilde shows enthusiasm only for intellectual plea-sures, Mme de Rênal overflows with "natural" passions, as Julien reflects when he first encounters Mathilde: "Quand les yeux de Mme de Rênal s'animaient, c'était du feu des passions [. . .]" 'When Mme de Rênal's eyes grew animated, it was with the fire of passion. [. . .]' (280; 196; 2.2). Mathilde seems vain and artificial in com-parison, causing Julien to regret the loss of his beloved surrogate mother.

> Quelle différence avec ce que j'ai perdu! quel nature char-mant! quelle naïveté! Je savais ses pensées avant elle, je les voyais naître, je n'avais pour antagoniste, dans son coeur, que la peur de la mort de ses enfants; c'était une affection raisonnable et naturelle, aimable même pour moi qui en souf-frais. J'ai été un sot. Les idées que je me faisais de Paris m'ont empêché d'apprécier cette femme sublime.
> Quelle différence, grand Dieu! et qu'est-ce que je trouve ici? de la vanité sèche et hautaine, toutes les nuances de l'amour-propre et rien de plus.   (338)

What a difference from the woman I have lost! what natural charm there! What simplicity! I knew her thoughts before she did herself; I saw them forming in her mind; within her heart my only opponent was her fear that her children might die; it was a sensible and natural affection, such that even I, who suf-fered from it, found it admirable. I've been a fool. My imagin-ings about Paris prevented me from appreciating that glorious woman.

What a difference, good God! And what do I find here? Van-ity, dry and arrogant, every conceivable variety of self-approval, and nothing else.   (242; 2.10)

Where Mme de Rênal possesses all the qualities of Julien's ideal woman, including the maternal passions that he calls "raisonnable et naturelle [et] aimable," Mathilde has nothing but vanity and pride. This assessment of his preference for the sincere woman with the capacity for maternal affection explains his eventual rejec-tion of Mathilde and his return to the security of Mme de Rênal's arms and the charms of the imaginary.

In the midst of their stormy relationship Mathilde suddenly dis-covers that she is expecting a child. From the first she treats her pregnancy as a tool, to expedite her ambition of marrying Julien. She joyously informs her lover of her condition, adding: "N'est-ce pas une garantie? Je suis votre épouse à jamais" 'Isn't this a guarantee? I am your wife forever' (475; 347; 2.32). In her coldly calculating manner, she views the unborn child dispassionately, determined to use her pregnancy to manipulate her father. Seeing a chance for her own advancement in the potential glory of her lover, Mathilde will stop at nothing to satisfy their mutual ambition; her pregnancy fills her with joy, not for sentimental reasons, but because it gives her the opportunity to sacrifice her reputation to her lover and at the same time to bind Julien to her forever. This strategy, although reminiscent of Julie's premarital pregnancy and miscarriage in Rousseau's *La Nouvelle Héloïse*, meets with greater success: M. de La Mole, after his initial outrage and much deliberation, actually gives Julien both a noble title and a commission as lieutenant in the army. Just as his daughter had hoped, M. de La Mole prefers to safeguard the family honor by elevating Julien, since the pregnancy makes their marriage unavoidable.

While Mathilde uses her pregnancy as a bargaining tool in the negotiations with her father, however, Julien thinks only of the welfare of his future son. Never doubting that the child will be a boy, he dreams of his future nurturing role as a father, which suddenly gives purpose to his life and his ambitions. When he offers his life to the marquis de La Mole as just retribution for his daughter's dishonor, he does so reluctantly, thinking, "J'aime la vie. [. . .] Je me dois à mon fils" 'I am fond of life. [. . .] I have a duty to my son' (481; 351; 2.33). His earlier ambitions take on a more generous air as his thoughts dwell on the future of his son: "Lorsqu'elle apprit à Julien qu'il était lieutenant de hussards, sa joie fut sans bornes. On peut se la figurer par l'ambition de toute sa vie, et par la passion qu'il avait maintenant pour son fils" 'When she told Julien he was a lieutenant of hussars, his joy knew no bounds. It can be estimated from the ambition of his whole life, and from the passion that he was now feeling for his new son' (491; 359; 2.34). In the dynamics of the couple the traditional roles are now completely reversed: Mathilde tends to the business of social and financial success, leaving Julien to dream about the future of their child in an effort to compensate for Mathilde's obvious lack of interest in mothering. To Mathilde, motherhood becomes a means of coercion, which she employs most effectively against the prejudices and plans of her aristocratic father. Indeed, Mathilde as future mother would have accomplished her goal of union with an ennobled Julien, if not for the fatal intervention of Mme de Rênal's letter and its reminder of the attraction of the maternal bond.

After his imprisonment, Julien longs for "une tendresse simple, naïve et presque timide," 'a simple, a naive and almost timid approach' (516; 378; 2.39), adjectives that remind him of Mme de

Rênal and that indicate the essential qualities lacking in the hypocritical, glory-seeking, and aggressive Mathilde. Julien's infatuation
with Mathilde was a child of his vanity, a product of mimetic desire
that overcame his initial resolution that she would never be a
woman in his eyes. When Mathilde bravely attempts to intervene
on his behalf during his imprisonment, Julien seems more shocked
than grateful, preoccupied with his thoughts of Mme de Rênal. His
love for Mathilde begins and ends with his worldly ambition; once
he is liberated from that driving ambition by the prospect of death,
his love for her (*l'amour-vanité*) fades overnight, replaced by an all-
consuming passion for his ideal woman, Mme de Rênal.

Mathilde fails to measure up to Julien's standards of femininity
in part because of her numerous "masculine" traits. In many respects Mathilde is androgynous; she is denied Julien's moment of
glory not because of her gender, which the narrator repeatedly describes as masculine, but because of her sex. In fact Mathilde
seems even more aggressive and ambitious than Julien, seeing her
motherhood, that much-praised sacred female occupation, only as
a tool with which to manipulate her father, while her lover thinks of
the welfare of the unborn child. Afraid for the safety of his only offspring, Julien expresses his lack of confidence in its mother's feminine and maternal capacities, saying to Mathilde even before his
reunion with his first mistress:

> J'ai une grâce à vous demander [. . .] mettez votre enfant en
> nourrice à Verrières, Mme de Rênal surveillera la nourrice.
> [. . .] La mort de mon fils serait au fond un bonheur pour
> l'orgueil de votre famille, c'est ce que devineront les subal-
> ternes. La négligence sera le lot de cet enfant du malheur et de
> la honte. [. . .]
>
> Il se trouvait de nouveau vis-à-vis cette idée si choquante
> pour Mathilde: Dans quinze ans Mme de Rênal adorera mon
> fils, et vous l'aurez oublié.   (518–20)

> I have a favor to ask of you [. . .] put your child out to nurse at
> Verrières; Mme. de Rênal will keep an eye on the nurse. [. . .]
> The death of my son would gratify the pride of your family, and
> that's what the flunkies will guess about it. Neglect will be the
> lot of this child of misery and shame. [. . .]
>
> He found himself once more face-to-face with this idea
> which so distressed Mathilde: in fifteen years, Mme. de Rênal
> will adore my son, and you will have forgotten him.
>   (379–80; 2.39)

Concerned about the child's welfare, Julien entrusts his son's care
to Mme de Rênal, having no doubt of *her* capacity to mother. During his long hours of self-examination in the lonely prison cell,

Julien passes judgment on Mathilde, thinking: "On peut devenir sa-vant, adroit, mais le cœur! . . . Le cœur ne s'apprend pas" 'You may become learned, you may become shrewd, but the heart! . . . the heart can't be trained' (535; 391; 2.42). In spite of Mathilde's ac-complishments, Julien implies that she lacks some instinctive qual-ity that cannot be taught. His repeated references to Mathilde's indifference to their child, coupled with his total rejection of her attentions, suggest the importance of maternal instinct for the motherless Julien and thus the reason for his rejection of Mathilde in favor of the essential mother figure, Mme de Rênal. A failure as a mother, Mathilde must also be a failure as Julien's mistress and protector; only a maternal figure can re-create the peace and har-mony of the imaginary for a weary Julien searching for a respite from the harsh symbolic order that has condemned him.

Julien's quest for the mother, then, ends in prison, where he finds at long last the symbiotic unity of unconditional maternal love with Mme de Rênal. Julien's own mother, perhaps dead as a result of his birth (a common occurrence in early-nineteenth-century France), haunts him, yet her absence leaves him conveniently free to play the son of a wealthy and beautiful surrogate mother with whom he is free to act out his incestuous filial desire in the privi-leged space of the imaginary. In this Romantic passion play Mme de Rênal becomes both more aware of her own selfhood through her desire for her lover and more selflessly devoted to him, opening the door to a new version of the traditional maternal image, one in which the mother and the woman are allowed to coexist, defying the tradition of maternal purity in favor of a new maternal ideal.

In *The Red and the Black* Stendhal creates a space in which women who mother can exist as free individuals, not only as moth-ers. Although the author dooms Mathilde's attempts at selfhood to failure because they stray completely from the feminine roles of mistress and mother, Mme de Rênal's discovery of maternal self-determination provides a new and attractive option to women who wish to combine traditional and nontraditional gender roles. By studying this space and recognizing it for the unique, however ephemeral, innovation it is, readers of Stendhal can better under-stand the attitudes and ideals that influence Western culture's defi-nition of womanhood and can begin to explore possible avenues of escape from the strictures of traditional gender identity.

SUSANNA LEE

The Red and the Black: Navigating the Secular World†

In 1830, the question of what sort of explanatory narratives were viable or believable was much at the fore of French cultural consciousness. For one, political posturing since the Revolution had compromised the notion of an absolute truth, of a definitive version of how the world is and how it should be. The ideological rationales of the ancien régime gave way to those of the Revolution, were then revived, and then phased out once more. Within the Restoration period, laws were introduced and then abandoned, then introduced again.[1] The multiplicity of confessions, allowed by the Revolution's nominal separation of church and state, was compromised in 1814 and resuscitated in 1830. These continuous mutations, and the various justifications mounted to sustain them, put in question the entire notion of a final truth or formula. Meanwhile, in the philosophical-spiritual domain, secular modes of understanding were coming increasingly to dominate religious modes. Positivist philosophies moved to replace religion as a means of explanation, to replace sacred forces with social forces, God with science, fate with biological determinism. Given these substitutions and the political and legal turbulence of the Restoration, God as a means of explanation began to seem both archaic and somewhat disingenuous. In the midst of these evolutions was published Stendhal's *The Red and the Black* (*Le Rouge et le noir*).

The historical particulars of 1830, recounted in *Le Rouge*, are emblematic of the tensions intrinsic to the idea of secularism. *Le Rouge et le noir*, like a world without a master plot, both embodies and inspires a number of explanatory narratives. But it also underscores the arbitrariness and ultimate insufficiency of all these narratives—at a historical moment when, for reasons political, eco-

---

† From *A World Abandoned by God: Narrative and Secularism* (Lewisburg: Bucknell University Press, 2006), pp. 22–43. Reprinted by permission of the University of Nebraska Press. The selections from *The Red and the Black* in English are from the Norton edition, 1968. The selections in French are from the Garnier edition, 1950. A previous version of this essay appeared as " 'Il ne faut jamais dire le hasard, mon enfant, dites toujours la Providence': Sense and Coincidence in *Le Rouge et le noir*" in *French Forum* 28.2 (Spring 2003): 35–55.

1. In 1814 came an order to close restaurants and stores during services, and another dictating that those living on church parade routes must raise certain banners when the procession passed. In 1825, Charles X insisted on a *cérémonie du sacre*, but as René Rémond writes, this ceremony "inspires more derision than fervor, and its failure underlines the irremediably archaic character of Restoration pretenses" (Rémond, *Religion et société en Europe: Essai sur la secularisation aux XIXe et XXe siècles*, 13). Translations mine, when not otherwise attributed.

nomic, and philosophical, organization is most desired. It undermines even those modes of narrative production that do not seem
to be "productions" at all, such as science, psychology, the logical
discernment of cause and effect, intuition, as well as biblical narratives and the idea of destiny. In an environment in which problems
of who or what (if anything) structures the world had a particular
philosophical as well as political import, this novel, in the name of
realism, carefully undermines the viability of all explanatory narratives. In an ironic subversion suitable to the historical moment, it
radically undermines the theoretical bases of secular culture as
well as the convictions of the ecclesiastics, and, in so doing, questions the nature and function of narrative.

The transition to secularism poses the problem of where meaning is to be situated: in the outside world, within the domain of the
mind, or somewhere in between. This is the problem to which
Hegel (among others) responded when he tried to reconcile freedom and the "demands of union with cosmic spirit," or the opposition between mind and world as the source of meaning. As Charles
Taylor writes, "A disenchanted world is correlative to a self-defining
subject, and the winning through to a self-defining identity was accompanied by a sense of exhilaration and power, that the subject
need no longer define his perfection or vice, his equilibrium or
disharmony, in relation to an external order. With the forging of
this modern subjectivity there comes a new notion of freedom, and
a newly central role attributed to freedom, which seems to have
proved itself definitive and irreversible."[2]

The question of what drives Julien Sorel's ascent and descent
stands at the base of Le Rouge plot criticism. Critics generally recognize that Julien does not ascend the social scale on his own
steam but rather on a tide of outside forces. For Miller, Brombert,
Blin, and others, those outside forces mean the social machine, the
vicissitudes of Restoration culture, and the sentimental caprices of
others.[3] It is de Rênal's love and not Julien's strategies that produces his amorous success. It is Chélan who puts Julien in Besançon, the Marquis via Pirard who brings him to Paris, this
marquis' boredom that invents the blue suit, and Mathilde's unplanned pregnancy that turns him into the chevalier de La Vernaye.
The "outside forces" that decide Julien's existence can also be read
as forces of the unconscious (Felman, Crouzet) or, should Julien in

---

2. Taylor, Hegel, 9.
3. D. A. Miller points out: "The world of Le Rouge et le noir is defined by little else than an
   incessant play of conspiratorial forces. Yet Julien's adaptation is strikingly dysfunctional.
   The paranoia is nearly always misplaced, and the progress from Verrières to Besançon to
   Paris depends less on Julien's actual schemes of advancement than on lateral, unforeseen developments" (Miller, Narrative and Its Discontents, 196).

fact be the son of an aristocrat, of some biological determinism. But these outside forces, it is worth noting, have in common an element that embodies both the pursuit and the subversion of explanatory apparatuses. This is the force of chance.

When Julien is with the Rênals, he is chosen to ride at the head of the king's parade. It constitutes a moment of great pride for Julien, particularly at the instant when he barely escapes falling into the mud: "His joy exceeded all measure when, as they passed by the old rampart, the noise of the little cannon caused his horse to shy out of line. By great good luck [*par un grand hasard*], he did not fall off, and from that moment on he felt himself a hero."[4] "From that moment on": his pride comes from the fact that he remains on the horse. But in fact, the subtle intrusion of *hasard* contradicts Julien's understanding of the moment as his own creation and explicitly dissipates the notion of personal agency. The act cannot be entirely "heroic" when it is as much an enactment, an intrusion from without, as an act; and yet, the incident contributes to Julien's sense of his competence and his place in the world. What is more, it contributes to others' sense of him: At dinner with the Valenod, the guests admire him: "These fine gentry, who knew Julien only by reputation and from seeing him on horseback when the king of _____ came to town, were his most enthusiastic admirers" (112; 141).

Hasard, again and again, intervenes at the precise moments when Julien is most proud of his competence, most sure of himself. In the salon with Mme. de Fervaques, for instance, the narrator writes: "He had taken an action, he was less miserable; his eyes fell by accident [*par hasard*] on the Russia-leather briefcase in which Prince Korasoff had placed the fifty-three love letters that were his gift to Julien" (328; 404). And then, on the next page, the narrator reveals that "accident [*le hasard*] had revealed to Julien the path to eloquence" (329; 405). It is true that Julien has acted, that he has done something. But chance has twice intervened to carry Julien through that course of action, handing him both eloquence in the salon and the turn of the head that enables him to remember the letters. Again, though, the eloquence that chance makes accessible inspires Fervaques to admire Julien, and Julien to admire himself. Here, there is a sense that the personal triumph is neither. Indeed, the idea of the personal is complicated, as chance intrudes on the very parameters of Julien.

In his study of chance in nineteenth-century fiction, David Bell

---

4. Stendhal, *The Red and Black*, 81; in the French edition, *Le Rouge et le noir*, 102. Further references to both editions will be cited in the text by page number with the English listed first, followed by the French.

underscores the importance of the auspicious (chance) occasion. He writes, "What the strategist forgets or neglects is quite simply the fortuitous nature present at the founding of the law, the unpredictable propensities that gave the law its particular shape and signal its temporary (because nonoriginary) status."[5] Chance produces space, signifies opportunity: Bell describes Stendhal's characters (in *La Chartreuse* in particular) as strategists or tacticians according to their understanding of this freedom.[6] In *Le Rouge*, chance is both the foundation of the plot and the condition of narrative: the sign, as it were, under which the novel is set. Chance places the narrative on a continuous circular pursuit of meaning that becomes, for character and reader, the principal concern of the novel.

The Epic Force of Chance

To more precisely cast the use of chance in *Le Rouge*, I turn to Georg Lukács's account of the transition from the epic to the novel. This transition, as he recounts it in *The Theory of the Novel*, turns on the character's dependence on outside forces:

> Achilles or Odysseus, Dante or Arjuna—precisely because they are guided along their paths by gods—realise that if they lacked this guidance, if they were without divine help, they would be powerless and helpless in the face of mighty enemies. The relationship between the objective and subjective worlds is maintained in adequate balance: the hero is rightly conscious of the superiority of the opposing outside world; yet despite this innermost modesty he can triumph in the end because his lesser strength is guided to victory by the highest power in the world.[7]

In the epic, the "highest power in the world" sustains the hero, who in turn depends upon that power to guide his path. That "highest power" acts both as a spiritual guide for the character and as a cement that unifies the narrative—that connects the episodes to one another and the epic character to the world of action. In the novel, though, this cement comes undone and the nature of the protagonist's path turns suddenly solitary: "The first great novel of world literature stands at the beginning of the time when the Christian God began to forsake the world; when man became lonely and could find meaning and substance only in his own soul, whose home was nowhere; when the world, released from its paradoxical anchorage in a beyond that is truly present, was abandoned to its

5. Bell, *Circumstance: Chance in the Literary Text*, 59.
6. Ibid., 79.
7. Lukács, *The Theory of the Novel*, 98.

immanent meaninglessness."[8] The novelistic world is thus one in which the spiritual connection of the hero to the outside world is dissolved, in which the "highest power in the world" (the gods of the epic) gives way to an "immanent meaninglessness." The novelistic character, or a character in a world without God, responds to this meaninglessness by generating a meaning or substance of his or her own: "The inner importance of the individual has reached its historical apogee: The individual is no longer significant as the carrier of transcendent worlds, as he was in abstract idealism, he now carries his value exclusively within himself."[9]

In turning to *The Theory of the Novel*, I mean to discuss the characters' dependence on or independence from outside forces as Lukács does, in spiritual terms. The transferal of "value" from the outside to the inside could be read as a rite of passage or as a gesture of pride, but Lukács narrates it as a response to a world situation. In the preface to *The Theory of the Novel*, he declares the stakes of his discussion by pointing out that for Hegel "Art becomes problematic precisely because reality has become nonproblematic. The idea put forth in *The Theory of the Novel*, although formally similar, is in fact the complete opposite of this: The problems of the novel form are here the mirror-image of a world gone out of joint. This is why the 'prose' of life is here only a symptom, among many others, of the fact that reality no longer constitutes a favourable soil for art. . . . And this is not for artistic but for historico-philosophical reasons."[1] Michael Holzman reads the moment in the preface when Lukács writes that "the author was not looking for a new literary form, but, quite explicitly, for a 'new world' " (20), with this statement: "That 'new world' was as little social as literary, and if it was not as specifically sectarian as that of Lukács' friend Buber, it was most certainly religious."[2] Holzman then speaks of reading *The Theory of the Novel* "as a wish, as, in a way, a novel or a fantasy, a search through literary history for exactly those lost Blessed Ages, for immanence, for God."[3]

Based on the schematic criteria that Lukács outlines, Julien Sorel fits the description of a novelistic character, both in his ideo-

8. Ibid., 103.
9. Ibid., 117.
1. Ibid., 17.
2. Holzman, *Lukács's Road to God: The Early Criticism against its Pre-Marxist Background*, 126–27. Holzman also explicates the opening lines of Lukács's book ("Blessed are those Ages when the starry sky is the map of all possible paths . . .") (29), describing them as "something of an incantation" (119). And then: "We should not find it unusual that the genesis of *The Theory of the Novel* was an ethical situation, not a literary question. The beginning of *The Theory of the Novel* shows that the book's proper end is not the understanding of a few novels, or even of the nature of literary creation as such, but rather how one might best approach the ethical problems of living in an 'age of absolute sinfulness' " (130).
3. Ibid., 129.

logical and his historical positions. For one, Julien has an incredulous disposition, a suspicion of institutional religion, a sense that
the Church is nothing but a profitable business, and a mistrust of
ecclesiastics. What is more, he resists the notions of God and transcendence in a more fundamental sense. He believes that what
happens around him—his social circumstances, the conduct of
others, the decisions that are made for him—is not the work of
God, not an indication of the world as it is meant to be, not about
a cosmic master plan, but about social mores and rules, rules
whose uniformity is born of artificial manipulation rather than divine ordinance. This belief pushes Julien to position himself as a
manipulator and a climber, qualities that he admires in Napoleon.
He sees his successes as his own doing ("the credit is all mine") and
remains contemptuous of superstition, even his own. He embodies
romantic irony as René Bourgeois describes it: "Romantic irony . . .
is a philosophical disposition, wherein the world is a theater on
which one must play one's role quite deliberately, keeping in mind
another universe, one born of the imagination, which stands at
once in opposition to and in correspondence with the first."[4] In *Le
Rouge*, we can understand these opposing worlds as the outside
context as Julien understands it and the inner landscape within
which he operates. As the narrator writes, "Julien . . . had sworn an
oath never to say anything except what seemed false to him" (114;
143); he has promised that the part played on the outside stage will
be held at a distance from his inner feelings.

On the one hand, his is the ironic disposition of a cynical mind
under Restoration culture, where the entire political structure can
be read as a theater with rapidly changing sets and costumes. But
more profoundly, Julien's is a secular disposition, a strategic self-
sufficiency created for a world without an intrinsic or sacred order,
without God. Restoration culture, as critics have observed, resem-
bles an elaborate mise-en-scène, but one without substantial connection to some spiritual force.[5] And when there is no guidance,
and thus no substantial source of meaning and direction, the
moment comes when the character "carries his value exclusively
within himself." Kierkegaard outlines this transposition of meaning
from the world into the character in *Either/Or*. "Our age . . . must
turn the single individual over to himself completely in such a way
that, strictly speaking, he becomes his own creator."[6] Unfortunately,

---

4. Bourgeois, *L'ironie romantique: Spectacle et jeu de Mme de Staël à Gérard de Nerval*,
   107. For Lukács, "Irony gives form to the malicious satisfaction of God the creator at
   the failure of man's weak rebellions against his mighty, yet worthless creation and, at the
   same time, to the inexpressible suffering of God the redeemer at his inability to re-enter
   that world. Irony, the self-surmounting of a subjectivity that has gone as far as it was
   possible to go, is the highest freedom that can be achieved in a world without God" (93).
5. Cf. Sandy Petrey, *Realism and Revolution*.
6. Kierkegaard, *Either/Or*, 121.

as repeated intrusions of chance demonstrate, the world Julien inhabits is not entirely novelistic, in Lukács' sense of the word, and
does not turn Julien completely over to himself, but rather contains
a subtle residue of epic structure. Personal freedom and the concept of action must be rethought when chance intrudes (and in this
novel chance moments *are* presented as intrusions) on individual
agency. When, in the episode where Julien holds Mme. de Rênal's
hand ("Julien thought it was his *duty* to make sure that the hand
was not withdrawn when he touched it" (42; 51, italics in text]),
the narrator writes that Julien "had found, almost by accident
[*presque par hasard*], enough blind courage to take a single action"
(44; 54), *hasard* comes in to contradict the sense of duty. "Almost"
shifts the locus of compulsion, of duty, placing Julien somewhere
between free choice and unconscious beholdenness to another dimension. Another such intervention, and in some sense the most
subversive to Julien's sense of success, appears in the episode that
leads him to declare: "My novel is finished, and the credit is all
mine. I was able to make myself loved by that monster of pride, he
thought, glancing at Mathilde; her father cannot live without her
nor she without me" (359; 444, tm).[7] Here again, though, chance
has intervened. In that victorious moment in the library, when
Julien "makes himself loved by that monster of pride" ("So there
she is, that proud beauty, at my feet!" [338; 418]), the narrator
writes, "Only accident [*le hasard tout seul*] had brought about this
outburst" (339; 419). Again and again, an active and independent
hasard orchestrates Julien's experiences: "A lucky accident [*Un
heureux hasard*] brought Julien into the presence of M. Valenod"
(51; 64); "As luck would have it [*Le hasard voulut que*], Abbé de
Frilair was on duty that evening" (164; 204); "The singular person
whom chance [*le hasard*] had rendered absolute mistress of all his
happiness" (296; 365); "The excesses of zeal, of which chance [*le
hasard*] had made him the witness" (313; 385, tm).

When chance has a substantial hand in his success, Julien,
though he alone is accountable for his actions, cannot claim responsibility, anymore than Achilles or Odysseus can claim sole responsibility for their victories. With the support of chance, as
Lukács would put it, Julien "can triumph in the end because his
lesser strength is guided to victory by the highest power in the
world." But whereas this guidance is fundamental to the epic, it
becomes doubly subversive in this chronicle of manipulation and
studied orchestration. In Homer, the gods were there to under-
write the virtues of Achilles or Odysseus, not to compromise them.
Chance in *Le Rouge*, though, functions not to guide Julien but to

---

7. Here and elsewhere, the abbreviation "tm"—translation modified—indicates my alterations of the English version.

intrude on and dismantle his fantasies of autonomous manipulation at precisely those moments when the fantasies are at their pinnacle. This inscrutable force prevails at the moments when Julien becomes most enthusiastic about his own value, giving Bourgeois' ironic world another dimension, that of chance, superimposed on and trumping Julien's vision (he carries "exclusively within himself" a value that in fact comes from without). But even more ironic is that this inscrutable force is that of chance: the precise antithesis of fate, of epic structure, of everything that made Lukács's epic world a secure and meaningful arena in which to operate.

Chance and the Autonomous Subject, or the Double Bind of Secularism

Sandy Petrey places chance in a political context by finding in it an embodiment of the arbitrary, performative, and content-free nature of Restoration ideology and laws. In a more abstract sense, chance embodies the spiritual situation of a culture from which transcendence has departed but in which secular logic has not taken root. Chance reminds (or threatens) Julien and the reader that an entire alternatise world stands outside the realm of human machinations and interpretations. In contrast to the providentialist reading of history that precedes the Restoration, chance dismantles or contradicts the predication of causal chains, of determinism, of all manner of modes of reason, secular and religious, because it renders cause, linear narration, and understanding largely immaterial.[8] The result is a sort of vacuum, a relentless orchestrated failure of modern (and ancient) epistemological strategies that places Julien in a double predicament. On the one hand, the repeated intrusions of chance deprive Julien of the autonomous existential certitude that Lukács finds in the novelistic hero. On the other hand, because the principle of chance is not in fact a principle, not a conferrer of meaning, and furthermore because Julien does not even see chance in operation, the narrative is denied the organic structure and seamless direction that Lukács finds in the epic. When Julien decides to go riding, writes the narrator, "acting only on himself and not at all on Mathilde's mind or heart, he was leaving up to chance [*au hasard*] the disposition of his own destiny" (296; 365). And yet, we know by this time that the disposition of Julien's own destiny is up to chance no matter what he does and no matter how he envisions his actions.

This chronicle of 1830 traces cultural and individual responses

8. Joseph de Maistre, *Soirées de Saint Petersbourg, Considérations sur la France*, and so on.

to the transition to a nonreligious consciousness. In order to do
this, the novel creates that space of transition, creates the particular semiepic and semisecular 1830 that it chronicles. This, again, is
the same space of transition to which Hegel responded when he
tried to reconcile freedom and the "demands of union with cosmic
spirit." Writes Charles Taylor, in a description reminiscent of
Lukács and Kierkegaard:

> From the standpoint of the autonomous, finite subject, the
> larger course of events which affects him is distinguished from
> what he does as what happens to him: his fate. This fate is
> quite distinct from himself, in the sense that it is not at all an
> expression of him, something one can only find in what he
> does. From this point of view, that of separation, the injunc-
> tion of an earlier time to reconcile oneself to fate, to come to
> see its necessity and hence make peace with it, can only be un-
> derstood as a call to surrender, not as an invitation to deeper
> insight. But the course of things is in some sense an expres-
> sion of cosmic spirit; and hence to see it as quite other is to
> define oneself in opposition to cosmic spirit. On the other
> hand, to be united to infinite spirit, even more to see oneself as
> its vehicle, would be to recognize in one's fate an expression of
> a reality from which one could not dissociate oneself.[9]

Le Rouge casts chance as a metaphor for this ambivalence about
connection to the outside world and, what is more, casts fiction as
the arena for its dramatization. Julien follows the directions of
chance like the ancient Stoic's dog tied to the wagon; and yet, he
has neither the Stoic's attitude of resigned submission nor the
Hegelian's deep understanding of the wagon's course and its logic.
Implied in the intrusions of chance, which both comprise and undo
the "Chronicle of 1830," is an ironic ambivalence about the transition to a secular world. This chronicle expresses on the one hand a
desire to be rid of the constraints of the philosophical and ontological structures of the past and, on the other hand, a reluctance to
abandon those form-giving structures.

Living in Limbo: Chance and Providence

Chance, as we said, prevents the reader from situating meaning
solidly within the world of action or within the world of the mind.
The characters, too, seem to sense this problematic function and
are much occupied with negotiating the cosmic (or random) spirit
of the outside world. Julien regards such spirits with a mistrust that

9. Taylor, *Hegel*, 79.

morphs into philosophical detachment: "Hitherto, he had been angry only with his destiny [*le hasard*] and with society" (62; 78); "A poor devil like me, dropped by fate [*par le hasard*] in the lowest rank of society, will never get a chance like this again" (270; 333). And, before he meets his father for the last time: "Chance [*le hasard*] has placed us near one another on the earth" (398; 496). While Julien maintains a sort of brave denial, Mathilde on the other hand sees chance as a fairy godmother: "What could she want? Fortune, noble birth, intelligence, beauty (as everyone kept telling her and as she believed herself) had been piled on her by the hand of fate [*les mains du hasard*]. Such were the thoughts of the most envied heiress of the Faubourg Saint-Germain" (250; 309). And again: "Between Julien and me there is no contract to be signed, no lawyer, everything is heroic, everything is up to the free play of chance [*tout sera fils du hasard*]" (252; 311). And then, bemoaning the modern age: "A man's life was one continual train of dangers [*hasards*]. Nowadays civilization has eliminated danger [*a chassé le hasard*], and the unexpected never happens" (265–66; 327). In the end, there is no great distinction between the respective superstitions of these characters, for the chance that Julien and Mathilde ponder (or welcome or fear) is eclipsed by the narrative chance that actually acts upon them.

While Julien embraces the idea of being his own creator and Mathilde enjoys being the favored daughter of chance, the ecclesiastics, on the other hand, want to weave chance into a sacred narrative of destiny. At the beginning of the second part of the novel, Julien has left the seminary for the Hôtel de La Mole. He declares to the abbé Pirard, "My father hated me ever since I was in the cradle; it was one of my greatest griefs; but I shall no longer complain of fortune [*je ne me plaindrai plus du hasard*], I have found another father in you, sir" (191; 236). To this, " 'Very well, very well,' said the abbé in some embarrassment; then he recalled [*rencontrant fort à propos*] a timely expression from his days as director of the seminary: 'you must never speak of fortune, my child, always say Providence instead [*il ne faut jamais dire le hasard, mon enfant, dites toujours la Providence*]' " (191; 236, tm). Julien has no response to this statement and the narrator no comment.

Pirard's replacement of chance with Providence exemplifies the sort of narrative production, or reduction, that Bell decried in his examination of chance. When Pirard insists on Providence, having "recalled a timely expression of the seminary director," he does not stipulate that his bond with Julien in particular is the work of Providence. He insists instead, in a semantic gesture that seems almost instinctual, that Julien should substitute Providence for chance in every case. Pirard's principled rejection of Julien's way of speaking comes from a long-lived and powerfully developed theoretical point of view, but his manner of articulating it, I would propose, does not so much replace chance with Providence as absorb the one into the other. Pirard, in his capacity as seminary director (and thus as former seminarian who learned from his seminary director, who in turn learned from another, etc.), intends a spiritual paternalism, but in the end, he seems only to fob his student off with a slogan—a slogan that seems surprisingly rote and insubstantial in its application.

Helmut Thielicke writes in *Nihilism*: "Accident is the 'other side' of fate itself," and, "Fate and chance are the same thing, only seen from different sides."[1] Thielicke's book starts, tellingly, with a consideration of "nihil" and "ism," or nothingness (nihil) and absoluteness of position (ism), and the collapse of chance into fate can be read in connection with this reconciliation. When, in the second part of *Le Rouge*, Mme. de Fervaques makes a cryptic comment about love, Julien thinks: "Either that means nothing or it means everything. These are some of the secrets of language that will be forever hidden from us poor provincials (333; 412)." One of the secrets of language that looms in the *hasard-Providence* episode, in the Fervaques episode, and in the rest of *Le Rouge* is the intimate connection—and in a sense the ultimate interchangeability—between meaning everything and meaning nothing. If *a* is *b*, goes the mathematical principle, then *b* is *a*, and while Pirard's substitution intends to minimize chance in favor of Providence, it simultaneously and unintentionally elides the distinction between these propositions. If Providence is a vehicle of meaning and chance a repository of meaninglessness, in other words, then the replacement of chance with Providence brings meaning and meaninglessness into a precariously close proximity. Chance become Providence gains a sudden significance, a sudden substance, but by the same token, that Providence that once was chance retains the sense or shade of meaninglessness—a meaninglessness that, in this novel, continues to surface.

Providence and the Business of Narrative Production

Pirard's substitution of chance for Providence is a testament both to the need for and the futility of narratives: the scramble for the condensation of chance into Providence, of disorder into order, and the continual appearance of more chance, more disorder, to be so condensed. On the one hand, the facile emptiness of the substitution is important for the criticism of Restoration politics that sub-

1. Thielicke, *Nihilism*, 58.

tends this narration. During the Restoration, as Petrey described: "The characters of *Le Rouge et le noir* continuously do for themselves exactly what the regime of Louis XVIII and Charles X did for itself, convert quintessentially performative operations into incontrovertibly referential truths."[2] Among those performative operations was the insertion of the discourse of sacred order into social and historical narratives.[3] Aside from its political resonance, though, and aside from its critical implications for the Church and its discourse, Pirard's substitution presents the taming of chance, by whatever means, as an act of narrative production, and vice versa. At the start of the chapter entitled: "A Plot [*Un Complot*]," the narrator inserts this epigraph: "Random words, accidental encounters [*des rencontres par effet du hasard*] turn into conclusive evidence in the mind of an imaginative man, if he has a bit of fire in his heart" (256; 317). *Le Rouge et le noir* both demands and chronicles the production of narrative strands, the synthesis of "random words" into a chain—for the characters and for the reader. At the same time, it impedes that same production with a deliberate series of disparate elements that both demand and resist connection.

The entire plot of *Le Rouge*, indeed, constitutes a sort of mosaic on which any structure remains a false imposition and in which the search for first causes must remain unsatisfied. Writes Victor Brombert, "Rapid shifts of point of view, calling for several layers of simultaneous interpretation, almost totally abolish explicatory transitions."[4] For Shoshana Felman, these "rapid shifts" permeate the novel's lexicon: "Taking apart (yet with apparent lucidity) rational clarity and the security of univocal meaning, Stendhalien language makes reading itself an adventuresome experience, risky and uncomfortable."[5] And not just paragraphs and words, but the entire narrative comprises various disembodied sections—of bounds from one episode to another, from one moment to another. In the episode of the secret note, the narrator compares politics in the novel to a pistol shot in a concert ("The noise is shattering without being forceful. It doesn't harmonize with any of the other instruments" [304; 376]). To continue this musical comparison, the world of *Le Rouge* can be read as a discordant orchestra; without what Brombert called explicatory transitions, the novel resonates not so much as a symphonic whole as a compendium of various

2. Petrey, *Realism and Revolution*, 135.
3. One example of this performative weaving can be found in Charles X's aforementioned insistence on a *cérémonie du sacre* in 1825, to ennoble both himself and the Church. This gesture, essentially a ceremonial replacement of *hasard* with *Providence*, did not so much resuscitate as devalue the sacred. Another such ceremonial conversion was found in the 1814 ordinances cited earlier. These ordinances seemed not to be an expression of divine order, but rather a clumsy and random fabrication of it—a misguided desire to turn *hasard* into *Providence*.
4. Brombert, *Stendhal: Fiction and the Themes of Freedom*, 68.
5. Felman, *La "Folie" dans l'oeuvre romanesque de Stendhal*, 146.

melodies, one on top of the other. The cacophonous composition of scenes—for instance, the introduction of Falcoz and Giraud; the episode of the secret note and Castanède's inexplicable opposition to the note's delivery; the adjudication scene and the visit of Geronimo; the encounter with Don Diego Bustos, introduced and then abandoned; the continuous alterations in sentiment; Julien's love for Mme. de Rênal, then for Mathilde, then, suddenly, once more for Mme. de Rênal—produce this discordance. So does the continued focus on the present, which Michel Crouzet names the "perpetual discovery which would be the law of the narrative,"[6] and which Brombert described as crucial not just to the narration but to the characters' experience: "Stendhal's heroes discover themselves existentially, through their reactions; and they even discover their reactions as a surprise."[7]

The novel's simultaneous demand for and resistance to consolidation finds further articulation in its continuous erasure of memory. For instance, once at the Rênal house: "[Julien] forgot everything, including his purpose in coming" (22; 25). When M. de Rênal goes away, "[Mme. de Rênal] had quite forgotten his existence" (40; 48). Further on, Julien: "If he had stopped seeing M. de Rênal, in a week he would have forgotten him, his house, his dogs, his children, and his whole family" (50; 62). Norbert meets Julien and the next morning "had forgotten his existence" (199; 246, tm). As for his sister, when Julien returns from Strasbourg: "Mathilde had almost forgotten him" (325; 400). On the one hand, these persistent erasures serve to undermine the sentimental bases of romanticism: there can be no permanent adoration when the brain and heart have no retention. But more than this, these erasures undermine the sense of a narration that builds. Crouzet's comparison with the surrealists is perhaps the most apt, for the novel is comprised of these suspensions, bounds from one moment to the other—moments that enter into one another, act on one another, obscure one another, but resist composition and condensation, resist conversion into Providence or even into a reasonable narrative.

The fundamental disembodiment that permeates this novel contradicts the sense that understanding is cumulative, and in so doing undermines the predictive and explicatory function of the past. It also turns the process of reading into an exercise in connecting dots that resist connection. Given these leaps and gaps and interruptions, any synthesis would necessarily be an imposition, and an incomplete one. Readers would necessarily, as Carol Mossman proposes, "extract one series of messages while ignoring the other."[8] At

6. Crouzet, *Le Rouge et le noir: Essai sur le romanesque Stendhalien*, 63.
7. Brombert, *Stendhal: Fiction and the Themes of Freedom*, 95.
8. Mossman, *The Narrative Matrix*, 25.

best, the narrator indicates, the mind can generate possible narratives, none of which are complete and none of which come close to
encompassing the world in its disconnection and disorder. We can
consider for instance the shooting of Mme. de Rênal and the punishment that ensues, about which D. A. Miller said: "Each separate
motive on its own merits is insufficient, and all the motives taken
together do not command a cohesive psychological case."[9] The various plot elements that lead up to the shooting can each be made to
make sense, but resist an encompassing narrative. The marquis re-
acting to Mme. de Rênal's letter, for instance, can read as the moral
father outraged at Julien's conduct, or, alternatively, as the hypocritical aristocrat pleased at the excuse to banish the peasant. As
for Julien, he can represent the jealous lover furious with the
Church, the parvenu obsessed with Mathilde, the lover obsessed
with Mme. de Rênal, the son obsessed with Mme. de Rênal, the
paranoiac worried about his reputation, the egomaniac who does
not want to be misunderstood, or the self-destructive madman. The
death sentence, finally, can be read as bourgeois vengeance on the
upstart peasant, Valenod's punishment of his rival, the result of
Frilair's clumsiness, the simple intrusion of judicial principle, a
senseless aberration, and so on. The entire scene, if not the entire
novel, reads as a complicated compendium of intersecting and superimposed circles, stories, and readings. Like the sort of children's
book that divides into horizontal sections so that the head of a bear
can rest on the body of a horse and the legs of a chicken, *Le Rouge
et le noir* encourages such curious combinations and resists a con-
densing explanatory narrative.

　　We know that the transition to secularism poses the problem
of where meaning is to be situated, within the character or in
the outside world. Chance, both as a dramatic instrument and as a
narrative principle, precludes a harmonic vision of the outside
world. It turns what Lukács named "the highest power in the
world" into a largely amorphous force and so encourages what Taylor described as "disenchantment." And as cited earlier, Lukács
wrote that the "individual, no longer significant as the carrier of
transcendent worlds . . . now carries his value exclusively within
himself." Julien, a novelistic hero ("my novel is finished") certainly
seems to want the novel to be about him ("the credit is all mine"),
as do readers; *Le Rouge* is often called a psychological novel. But
it is important to see that the strand of psychological interpretation in this novel, like all its strands of interpretation, is systematically broken or blurred at important points by a disorder that
intrudes on the subject from within and without. This blurring un-

9. D. A. Miller, *Narrative and Its Discontents*, 219.

dermines the conceptual parameters of character and also impedes the "winning through to self-identity" even in the midst of disenchantment.

Chance, the Unconscious, and the Dead End of Self-revelation

Some readers propose that chance, in such sentences as "he had had almost by accident [*par hasard*] the blind courage to act" and "accident [*le hasard*] had revealed to Julien the path to eloquence" could be read as indicating the operation of the unconscious rather than the epic intrusion of another dimension.[1] This reading is entirely possible, but not as valuable an instrument of comprehension as it seems. One problem is that aside from moments in which chance could be read as code for the unconscious, it is connected in other instances to a force outside (it would be hard for instance to declare that Julien's unconscious made him remain on the horse); so even the operation of the unconscious would not disable the other sorts of chance that intrude upon him. Another more fundamental problem is that chance, no matter what it is and where it is situated, has already been placed in an ironic contradiction with Julien's understanding, his sense of character, his pride. Therefore, even when we read certain moments of chance to mean that Julien's unconscious is in operation, the fact remains that that unconscious is inaccessible to him, unassimilable, enigmatic. Nineteenth-century psychological discourse, in fact, long describes the unconscious less as an integral part of one's character than as an inscrutable alternative dimension. Henri Ellenberger's *The Discovery of the Unconscious* traces the history of this dimension. Of Schopenhauer, he writes, "man is an irrational being guided by internal forces, which are unknown to him and of which he is scarcely aware."[2] Carus described an unconscious that "is turned toward the future and toward the past but does not know of the present."[3] (This idea could be read as an oracular description of the psyche, an alternative to *Le Rouge*'s focus on chance and Providence.) Carus focused, as Jung would, on the unbeholdenness of the unconscious to constraints of time, space, and direct experience. Von Hartmann understood the unconscious in terms of an energy force, as a "highly intelligent though blind dynamism underlying the visible universe"[4] and Nietzsche conceived of psychic energy as being dammed up and discharged in the same way as physical energy.[5] Darwin situates this energy in the

---

1. Cf. Felman, *La "Folie" dans l'oeuvre romanesque de Stendhal*, and Crouzet, "Julien Sorel et le Sublime."
2. Ellenberger, *The Discovery of the Unconscious*, 208.
3. Quoted in Ellenberger, 207.
4. Ibid., 210.
5. Ibid., 273.

nervous system, but echoes the sense that it constitutes an independent mechanism: "Certain actions which we recognize as expressive of certain states of the mind are the direct result of the constitution of the nervous system, and have been from the first independent of the will, and, to a large extent, of habit."[6]

In the course of the century, the unconscious replaced the supernatural as principal character in scenes of drama and madness. Chevreul, in experiments with divining rods and pendulums, attributed to unconscious thoughts and movements phenomena that had been previously attributed to "spirits."[7] Bergson and Janet (both of whom, as Ellenberger writes, "revealed their deep-seated preoccupation with religion late in life"),[8] wrote of the automatic nature of unconscious reasoning. Freud would later describe the instincts as "representatives of all the forces originating in the interior of the body and transmitted to the mental apparatus" and, in a more poetic moment, as "an urge inherent in organic life to restore an earlier state of things;[9] he also introduced the concept of displaceable or sublimated energies.[1] Georg Groddeck, demonstrating that writings on the unconscious used the discourse of the supernatural well into the twentieth century, insisted that "man is animated by the Unknown, that there is within him . . . some wondrous force which directs both what he himself does, and what happens to him. The affirmation 'I live' is only conditionally correct, it expresses only a small and superficial part of the fundamental principle, 'Man is lived by the It.' "[2]

In their readings of *Le Rouge*, Shoshana Felman and Michel Crouzet cite the unconscious, much as Bell cites chance, as an obstacle rather than a key to planned understanding. Felman describes Julien's actions in terms of madness, defining madness as a "derangement, a mental sickness,"[3] and as senselessness with respect to an established order: "Madness is relative: it is senseless with respect to sense, which denies it and is then denied by it in turn."[4] Crouzet writes, "This [the sublime] is the dimension from which I want to study Julien Sorel: this character [*personnage*], but is he in fact a character, he whom one cannot grasp without interpreting, without mutilating, this non-character [*non-caractère*] endlessly covered and described in contradictions. His only coherence comes perhaps not from a psychological but from a poetic reading,

---

6. Darwin, *The Expression of the Emotions in Man and Animals*, 66.
7. Ellenberger, *The Discovery of the Unconscious*, 313.
8. Ibid., 354.
9. Freud, *Beyond the Pleasure Principle*, 34–36.
1. Ibid., 44.
2. Groddeck, *The Book of the It*, 16.
3. Felman, *La "Folie" dans l'oeuvre romanesque de Stendhal*, 33.
4. Ibid., 88.

where he could be understood for his effects. The sublime would be that constant that gives him, in his brilliance and incoherence, a formal definition."[5] And then: "Psychoanalysis, perhaps because it misrepresents or flattens the Sublime, seems deadly for this concept-form so suited to romantic modernity."[6] The unconscious, as fountain of ideas and images, retains the element of the inexplicable or uncontainable. It is not surprising, since psychology is a form of narrative, that the introduction of the science of the mind, as well as of narrative production, accompanies the fading of the sacred master plot. But the unconscious, as we see, like generated narratives, like the replacement of chance with Providence, does not elucidate enigma, but rather transposes it. Psychoanalysis, like psychoanalytic criticism, resonates thus as a Band-Aid over an abyss, for whether Julien throws himself in a fit of madness or is pushed by a cosmic hand, the rise of the unconscious as Stendhal frames it here functions as a Trojan horse returning the vast unreadable to the modern world.

Let us consider the disclosure of Julien's character that operates in the course of the novel. From the start, the narrator predicates a distinction between the character Julien discloses to the outside world and the character that he in fact is (the distinction described in Bourgeois' romantic irony). This distinction, underscored in the numerous references to hypocrisy, to role-playing, to the desire to "rely only on those parts of my character that I've thoroughly tested" (37; 59), to "never . . . say anything except what seemed false to him," suppose a "him" obscured under the charade—a character conscious of a core concealed within. In the Hôtel de La Mole, Julien is employed as a scribe: He copies the words of the marquis. This occupation, which is also emblematic of his modus operandi (Julien has previously copied Napoleon, Rousseau, Molière, etc.), rests on the distinction between the scripted and unscripted on which the narrator has insisted from the start. In a sense, the entire Hôtel de La Mole is about that distinction and about speculation on what Julien would do in spontaneous moments, in the absence of mimesis, deception, verbatim recitations, and other calculated performances. Critics have commented on the value and substance in this obscured spontaneous Julien. For instance, for D. A. Miller: "The moments when plots falter coincide with moments when Julien seems most closely in touch with himself, at a primary level of being."[7] And for Brombert: "[Julien] is persistently wrong about his feelings and, above all, charmingly un-

5. Crouzet, "Julien Sorel et le Sublime," 91.
6. Ibid., 105.
7. D. A. Miller, *Narrative and Its Discontents,* 196

aware of his real qualities."[8] These comments and the narrator's insinuations presume that there is a fundamental Julien, a primary
level that can be uncovered. This focus is appropriate to the historical moment; character, as Lukács said, stands as the nucleus of
modern fiction, and much of the novel seems to maintain this principle.

For months, Julien is unable to transcend the Hôtel de La Mole,
unable to depart. In London, he is praised for his "cool expression,
a thousand miles from the sensation of the moment" (222; 276, italics in text). And even in Strasbourg he continues to copy, only
this time from Korasoff and not the marquis. However, within the
frame of his mimetic occupation, there are moments when Julien
can escape, when he eludes the bounds of calculation and mimesis.
And these moments, curiously, invariably produce senselessness
rather than a comprehensible core. The first instance of unplanned
originality appears in Julien's first series of copies: "The marquis
entered, glanced at the copies, and noted with amazement that
Julien wrote *cela* with two *l*'s, *cella*" (195; 241). This spontaneous
nonsense word becomes a signature feature of Julien: At dinner, the
marquis introduces him as "my secretary, and he writes *cela* with
two *l*'s" (196; 243). But this signature feature, this first departure
from the script, in this scene, in this house, and in French, has no
meaning. As Jared Stark points out, the unscripted Julien (the two
l's indicate the presence of Julien Sorel, *sur-l*, Sorel) is the embodiment of senselessness.[9]

Another moment of spontaneous revelation comes when Julien
draws a sword on Mathilde—an action that is instantly cut short
(the sword, no more than the pen, can function as an instrument of
self-expression in the house of La Mole). Another such instance is
when Julien discusses Napoleon with Mathilde (abandoning one
script to discuss another), and another is when he declares his adoration for her. But the final and most important such moment is his
response to Mme. de Rênal's letter. When this document arrives,
Julien runs from the house, never to return, no longer the scribe.
This is his most spontaneous action and it is also, significantly, his
most unreadable. From the moment he steps out of the house, his
actions are dramatic, erratic, and peculiar. The narrator writes: "On
this swift journey he was unable to write to Mathilde, as he had intended to do; his hand formed nothing on the paper but illegible
scrawls [*traits illisibles*]" (362; 449). Unable to read or represent himself as other than the manipulated and mediated character
that he was in the Paris mansion, Julien cannot make sense. This

---

8. Brombert, *Stendhal: Fiction and the Themes of Freedom*, 99.
9. I thank Jared Stark.

predicament continues in Verrières at the arms merchant, where Julien "had great difficulty in making him understand he wanted a pair of pistols" (362; 449). Not a word is said from Paris to the church, and the gun transaction seems to be enacted almost without human participation. The inauthentic and mimetic structure of the house of La Mole is broken and the "unscripted" Julien is released. From the Hôtel de La Mole to the shooting in Verrières, Julien is positioned to move from the mimetic to the spontaneous, from the calculated to the natural, from the surface to the nucleus. But when he does move thus, there is nothing to read.

This progression of incidents—the duties as scribe, the restrictions, and then the moment of spontaneous action—prepare the gradual disclosure of what Miller named the "primary level." And yet, the wordless shooting of Mme. de Rênal is the most incomprehensible action in the entire novel. What does this action articulate? What is being revealed? For some it is a frustration with God, who had "stolen" Mme. de Rênal. For others it is the loss of Mathilde. For some it is the fact that his actual character is exposed, or that his actual character is discounted. Just as during the parade, chance (Providence) intruded at the moment he became a hero, here that outside force (madness, chance, the unconscious, romantic obsession) intrudes at the moment he is to express himself, at the moment the story becomes, in the most fundamental sense, about him. If indeed this is the core of Julien, the essence of his character, a "winning through to a self-defining identity," it is a core or an identity that announces nothing but its unreadable nature. The road from La Mole to Verrières undoes what it pretends to reveal, sending the reader to search elsewhere for an explanatory chain.

Louis Jenrel, or the Oracle

What Lukács named the "highest power in the world" has morphed into chance, and thus loses its form-giving power. Its constant presence, however, precludes "the inner importance of the individual" from "reaching its historical apogee." Though the individual is supremely important to himself and to the reader, intrusions from without continue to undermine his discoveries and determine his movements. Lucidity, once proclaimed, is denied and individual vision remains incomplete. Because this is so, though, because both Julien and the reader are systematically blocked in the pursuit of understanding, we should consider the place of the narrator in this spiritual and epistemological limbo. After all, the intrusion of chance and coincidence, the superimposition of various dimensions of action, the subversion of predictions, and the complication of character readings depend on third-person narration. When the marquis introduces Julien as the secretary "whom I've just added to my staff, and propose to make a man of, if that [*cella*] can be done" (196; 243), his pun, his senselessness, has to be spelled out. In the coach to Verrières, it is the confusion in Julien's writing (*traits illisibles*) that indicates his internal chaos. On the one hand, then, the narrator stands as reporter for a disordered world. On the other hand, the incomplete nature of the individual vision extends to this narrator, making him a participant in rather than a dominator of the culture he documents. The narrator occupies an uncertain space between mastery and subversion of mastery, between the pronouncement of last words and the retraction or substitution of those last words, between postulation of first causes and erasure of those causes.

In order to examine the role of the narrator, and by extension of narrative production, we must turn to the piece of paper that Julien finds in the church on his way to the Rênal house. For though it seems that there exists no absolute word, no superstructure to this world, there is a slender formal element that in some sense decides, or seems to decide, the course of the entire narrative: a subtle Providence, as it were, in the form of the oracle: "He found the church dark and deserted . . . All alone in the church, he took a seat in the finest pew. It bore M. de Rênal's coat of arms. On the lectern, Julien noted a scrap of printed paper, set out there as if for him to read. He glanced at it and saw: *Details of the execution and last moments of Louis Jenrel, executed at Besançon, on the*____The paper was torn. On the other side were the first words of a line: *The first step . . .*" (20; 25, italics in text). The oracle, if we can name it that, has most commonly been read as a fanciful detail, rather than as a fundamental force in the plot. Michal Peled Ginsburg writes, "At first sight it seems as if this piece of paper functions as an oracle announcing, at the very beginning, what will inevitably happen at the end . . . At the end of the novel we should be able to recognize how 'the first step' started a chain of events that led with some logic and necessity to the last step—the violent murder attempt and the execution. But this reading is totally unconvincing. Why would the totally formal resemblance between Julien Sorel and Louis Jenrel (their names are anagrammatic—a formal resemblance that Julien does not even fully grasp) predict a similarity in their fates? . . . In other words, the oracle-text is presented as almost pure form, as empty of content as possible."[1]

The principal objection here is that there is no reason to read

1. Ginsburg, "On Not 'Yielding a Return': Plot and the Concept of Freedom in *The Red and the Black*," 99.

this paper as an oracle, that an anagram in a church with blood-colored curtains does not constitute a prediction, much less point to a causal chain. Ginsburg's objection, entirely valid, brings us back—and it seems that this was the narrator's intention—to the notions of Providence and chance. In some sense, as an explanatory narrative, the oracle embodies the uselessness of explanatory narratives, but this uselessness, this ultimate fusion of chance with Providence, is, I would propose, the point of the novel. The oracle ends—or rather eludes—the search for a line of reasoning through insertion of a causal or at least predictive chain of the sort common in the epic. But even if the paper is not an oracle, even if it is just a coincidence, the fact remains that the shooting and execution would be no more or less assimilable, no more or less explicable as a pure mundane coincidence than as an oracular prediction. In the end, what matters is the fundamentally unassimilable nature of the shooting, the sense that it originates or is readable only in another, ever elusive dimension.

The ultimate fusion of chance and Providence sets in motion an eternal circle of perception similar to that embodied in Julien's prison meditations—a circle of reason and senselessness, first causes and multiple causes, or causes and coincidences. On the one hand, this circle derides the production of master plots, or derides the mind that is prepared to read coincidence as oracle. And this derision in turn undercuts all the master plots that have ever been produced, all the cosmic reasons that have been located and used as explanations from time immemorial, by virtue of its emptiness, its thin presence. On the other hand, because the fact remains that Julien does come to the same end as Louis Jenrel, because the slim formal element that is the oracle-coincidence is the closest we come to a prediction of that "unpredictable" execution, the intrusion of the oracle implies in some sense that a master plot cannot be avoided. This second scenario constitutes a particularly radical act for Restoration culture and a particularly anachronistic epistemological subversion. While readers ponder sources and reasons, while Restoration politicians and ecclesiastics claim an understanding of God's will, while Machiavellian manipulators orchestrate their social ascents ("Nowadays civilization has eliminated danger [le hasard], and the unexpected never happens"), this novel introduces a real Providence, a master cause. The real Providence is the one that no one (character) sees, or that no one (reader) can believe. During the Restoration, as Petrey described, the answer to the question "why" is often absent. But here, that "why" is resuscitated—taken out of the hands of politicians, ecclesiastics, and parvenus, and placed, in some strange sense, in the hands of God. Throughout this novel, the more Restoration politics fabricate a vision of the world, the more the real world recedes. Conversion of chance into Providence seems only to generate more chance, and the more characters (and readers) come to understand the "entire story," the more the "entire story" is displaced. This displacement, I propose, (re)inserts an element of the enigmatic in a culture that depends on and values pure manipulation. If the Restoration means a disingenuous free-for-all, then the oracle represents a fantasy of retribution, of transcendent order, of a means to make truth visible and dominant—a fantasy, ironically, of Providence.

Stendhal: A Chronology

1747   Birth in Grenoble of Chérubin Beyle, son of Pierre Beyle, procurator in Parliament.

1757   Birth in Grenoble of Henriette Gagnon, daughter of Doctor Henri Gagnon.

1781   Marriage of Chérubin Beyle, attorney-in-training at the Parliament of Grenoble, to Henriette Gagnon.

1783   On January 23, Henri Beyle is born at rue des Vieux-Jésuites, in Grenoble. Two sisters are born later: Pauline (1786) and Zénaïde (1788).

1790   On November 23, his mother dies.

1791   Henri Beyle is sent to stay with his maternal uncle Romain Gagnon at Les Échelles, in the Savoie region.

1792   In December, Abbot Raillane is hired as Henri Beyle's tutor. "Raillane's Tyranny" continues until August 1794.

1793   On May 15, Chérubin Beyle is imprisoned for the first time; his name had been added to the list of local suspects on April 26. He will be released briefly on two occasions, then reincarcerated, and released permanently on July 24, 1794 (6 Thermidor according to the Revolutionary calendar).

1796   On November 21, Henri Beyle begins his studies at the École Centrale de Grenoble, which opened its doors on the same day.

1797   Death of Séraphie Gagnon (born 1760), Henri's heartily disliked aunt; he gives thanks to God.

1799   On October 30, following three years of successful studies at the École Centrale de Grenoble and graduating with a first-place prize in mathematics, Henri departs for Paris. He abandons his plan to participate in the entrance examinations for the École Polytechnique. He takes up lodgings in a town house [hôtel] at the intersection of rue de Bourgogne and rue Saint-Dominique, then takes a room at the quincunx at Les Invalides between rue Saint-Dominique and rue de Grenelle, then takes another room facing rue du Bac. In late December, dispirited and ill, he is taken in by his cousins the Darus at rue de Lille, at the corner with rue de Bellechasse.

1800   Pierre Daru, Inspector of Reviews and General Secretary of War, uses his influence to secure him a position in the ministry offices as a supernumerary. On June 10, Henri Beyle joins him in Milan, in the reserve army commanded by the First Consul. On October 23, he is posted as a sublieutenant in the Sixth Dragoon Regiment. He begins to keep a journal.

1801   On February 1, appointed aide-de-camp to General Michaud, Henri spends time in Lombardy; as the year draws to a close, however, he is granted sick leave and travels to Grenoble.

1802   In Grenoble, Henri Beyle falls in love with Victorine Mounier, whom he joins in Paris in April. He takes lodgings in rue Neuve-Augustin (now known as rue Saint-Augustin). In July, he resigns from the army. He plans to devote himself to literature, brushes up on his Italian, starts learning English, haunts Parisian theaters, drafts ideas for tragedies, and maps out an epic poem, *La Pharsale* [*Pharsalia*]. He falls in love with his young cousin Adèle Rebuffel and, with the girl's mother, makes plans for their future together.

1803   Henri, who, since November 24, 1802, has been staying at the Hôtel de Rouen, rue d'Angivilliers, near the Louvre, continues to read voraciously and works on a comedy, *Les Deux Hommes* [*The Two Men*]. Lives *la vie galante* in Paris. In June, with his money running out, he returns to Grenoble.

1804   Tired of Grenoble, he returns to Paris via Geneva on April 8. He stays at Hôtel de Rouen, then at rue de Lille with his friend Barral, finally at rue de la Loi (rue de Richelieu). Lively correspondence with his sister Pauline. He starts work on a new comedy, *Letellier*, and discovers Destutt de Tracy's *Idéologie*. He is introduced to Mademoiselle Duchesnois from the Théâtre-Français. At the end of the year, he meets a young tragedienne, Mélanie Guilbert, called Louason, through the actor Dugazon.

1805   In love with Mélanie Guilbert, who has been hired for an engagement at the Grand Théâtre de Marseille, he leaves Paris with her in May and rejoins her in late July following another stay in Grenoble. He works in the import-export house of Charles Meunier, first at rue Paradis, then at rue du Vieux-Concert (now known as rue Venture).

1806 Henri Beyle leaves Marseille in May, spends June in Grenoble, and returns to Paris on July 10, where he moves back in at rue de Lille. He renews his ties with Pierre Daru, who has been appointed Councillor of State and Intendant General. On October 16, he leaves for Prussia with Pierre's brother, Martial Daru, and, on October 27, enters Berlin in Napoleon's wake. Appointed Provisional Deputy War Commissar, takes up his post in Brunswick.

1807 Following a mission to Paris in January, Henri returns to Brunswick, where he leads a busy life with occasional excursions and longer journeys. He pays court to Wilhelmine de Griesheim (Mina). He reads Shakespeare and Goldoni.

1808 His stay in Brunswick continues: work-related activities, high-society life, reading, hunting parties. He works on a *Tableau de Brunswick* [*Portrait of Brunswick*] and a *Histoire de la guerre de succession d'Espagne* [*History of the Spanish War of Succession*]. Recalled to Paris, he returns there on December 1.

1809 Henri Beyle moves into the Hôtel de Hambourg, rue Jacob. He leaves Paris in April in order to be under the direct orders of Intendant General Pierre Daru. He meets up with him in Strasbourg and accompanies him to Vienna, which he enters on May 13. His enjoyable stay in the Austrian capital is cut short in July for a brief mission to Hungary. Pierre Daru is appointed Count of the Empire. In November, Henri Beyle begins to woo Countess Alexandrine Daru, who has come to Vienna for a one-month stay.

1810 After a stay in Linz, Henri Beyle returns to Paris in January and stays at rue du Colombier (now rue Jacob). On August 1, he is appointed Auditor of the Council of State; on the 22nd, he is appointed Inspector of the Accounts, Buildings, and Furniture of the Crown. This marks the beginning of an exceptional period in his life. In October, he moves to rue Neuve-du-Luxembourg (now rue Cambon).

1811 Henri enjoys glittering high-society life in Paris, where he mixes with the most notable figures of the Empire period. Begins a liaison with Angéline Bereyter, an actress at the Opéra-Buffa (Théâtre-Italien). Count Daru is appointed Secretary of State. On May 31, at Bécheville, near Meulan, he declares his love to the countess, who does not yield to his advances but retains her friendship for him. On August 29, he leaves for Italy, traveling through Montbard, Dijon, Dole, Morez, and Geneva. In Milan, arriving there on September 7, he obtains the favors of Angela Pietragrua (Gina), whom he had met eleven years earlier. Continuing his travels, he visits Bologna, Florence, Rome, Naples, Ancona, and Parma. Leaving Milan, he returns to France in November. Deeply impressed by his journey, he starts work, with Lanzi as his inspiration, on *Histoire de la peinture en Italie* [*History of Italian Painting*] and outlines a *Vie de Michel-Ange* [*Life of Michelangelo*].

1812   Henri Beyle misses Milan and finds Paris dull. He is granted permission to join the Grande Armée in Russia and leaves on July 23. He is present at the battle of Moskowa, enters Moscow and remains there for a month (from September 14 to October 16), leaving along with the army.

1813   Henri returns to Paris on January 31 and stays there, at rue Neuve-du-Luxembourg, until April 19. He is disappointed at being passed over for appointments as prefect, counsel and baron, and for knighthood in the Legion of Honor: "I'm back at square one." He is ordered to leave for Germany, takes part in the Saxony Campaign, is present at the battle of Bautzen; in June and July, he stays at Sagan, in Silesia, working as a provincial administrator: "I rule, but like all kings, I yawn a bit while doing so." Ill, he seeks treatment in Dresden then returns to Milan on September 7, by way of France. Spends time in Como and Venice. He returns to Paris in late November via Turin and Mont-Cenis.

1814   In January, placed under the command of Senator Count de Saint-Vallier, Henri Beyle organizes, in Grenoble, the defense of the Dauphiné region. Ill throughout the following month, he is allowed to return to Paris following a mission to Chambéry. He remains in Paris from March 27 to July 20. He participates in the allied troops' entrance and signs the Council of State declaration recognizing the Bourbons' return to power, but the auditor corps is done away with. He expects a position to come his way but eventually becomes discouraged. He then decides to move to Italy, leaving Paris on July 20, stopping in Milan, Genoa, Pisa, Florence, Bologna, Parma, and Milan again; for the next seven years, Milan will become his "headquarters." Further amorous entanglements with Angela Pietragrua.

1815 His first book, on Haydn, Mozart, and Métastase, is published in Paris under the pseudonym Louis-Alexandre-César Bombet. He sets up his household in Milan. Gina prevents him from going back to Paris upon Napoleon's return, which he learns of on March 6. He ends his relationship with her as the year draws to a close.

1816 Beyle leads a high-flying life highlighted by evenings at La Scala. From April 5 to April 19, he spends time in Grenoble, where he witnesses the collapse of the Bonapartist conspiracy fomented by Jean-Paul Didier, as well as the ensuing repression. Back in Milan, he is introduced to the liberal circle of Monsignor de Breme, meets Lord Byron, discovers the *Edinburgh Review*, and begins to ponder the issue of "romanticism." In December, he travels to Rome.

1817 A travel-filled year—to Rome (January), Naples (February), and Rome again; returns to Milan on March 4. Then, on April 9, leaves for France: Grenoble (April), Paris (May–July), London (first two weeks of August) and back to Paris. Returns to Milan on November 21, after spending time in Grenoble and Thuellin with his sister Pauline Périer-Beyle, newly widowed; she accompanies him to Italy. In quick succession Henri publishes (using his initials) his *Histoire de la peinture en Italie*, followed by (using the name Monsieur de Stendhal, cavalry officer) *Rome, Naples et Florence en 1817*.

1818 Remains in Milan (except from April 9 to May 6, for a stay in Grenoble to attend a trial involving his sister's financial interests; she does not return with him to Italy upon its conclusion). In August, excursions in the Brianza region, to Lake Como in October, and to Varese in November. The month of March marks the beginnings of his ardent love for Métilde Dembowski, née Viscontini. He works on a *Vie de Napoléon* [*Life of Napoleon*].

1819 Henri Beyle, mad with passion, follows Métilde to Volterra (June) and to Florence, where he spends forty days (June–July). In Bologna, he learns that his father died on June 20: on August 10, he reaches Grenoble and remains there until September 14; debts are Chérubin Beyle's only legacy. On the eve of his departure, he participates in the election of Abbot Grégoire, a liberal candidate for a deputy seat in the Isère region.

Stays in Paris from September 18 until October 14. Returns to Milan via Geneva. On December 29, he comes up with the initial idea for his treatise *De l'Amour* [*On Love*].

1820   Milan. A trip to Bologna and Mantua from March 19 to March 30; stays in Varese for the month of August. Completes the *De l'Amour* treatise. It is widely rumored by Milan's liberals that he is a government agent.

1821   Back in favor among the liberals, but suspected of carbonarism by the government, Henri Beyle realizes that he must leave Milan. In despair, he bids farewell to Métilde and returns to France in June. From October 19 to November 21, he spends time in London. Upon returning to Paris, he finds the manuscript of his treatise *De l'Amour*, which had gone missing at the Strasbourg post office a year earlier.

1822   Henri Beyle, a Parisian once more, resides in the Hôtel des États-Généraux, rue Sainte-Anne, during the spring season; when summer arrives, he moves to the Hôtel des Lillois, rue de Richelieu, where he becomes romantically involved with the singer Giuditta Pasta. This ushers in a very social, man-about-town period. He spends a great deal of time at the salon of the Tracys, rue d'Anjou-Saint-Honoré. He also is a regular at the houses of Cuvier, Delécluze, Madame Cabanis, Countess Beugnot, Baron Gérard, and others. On August 17, *De l'Amour* is published in two volumes. On November 1 he begins his collaboration with *New Monthly Magazine*, published in London. He will later be a contributor to other English reviews, which will ensure him a decent income.

1823   January–October: Paris. On March 8, the first *Racine et Shakespeare*, a manifesto in favor of "romanticism," goes on sale. On October 18, he again departs for Italy, via Geneva; he spends time in Genoa, Florence, Rome. On November 15, his *Vie de Rossini* [*Life of Rossini*] goes on sale.

1824   January: Rome. February: Florence, Bologna, Parma. The remainder of the year is spent in Paris, at 118, rue du Faubourg-Saint-Denis; then, as of September 15, at 10, rue Richepanse, at the corner of rue Duphot. In May, he forms a liaison with Countess Clémentine Curial, the daughter of Count Beugnot (Menti).

1825   Paris. On March 19, the second *Racine et Shakespeare* appears in bookstores; in December, the anti–Saint-Simonian pamphlet *D'un Nouveau Complot contre les industriels* [*On a New Anti-Industrialist Plot*] is published. Métilde Dembowski dies in Milan on May 1.

1826 January–June: Paris. Spends the summer in England. Upon his return, breaks off his affair with Countess Curial to his great distress. Drafts *Armance*.

1827 January–July: Paris, where he lodges at rue Le Peletier, near the Opéra, then at rue d'Amboise. On February 24, the second edition of *Rome, Naples et Florence* (drawn up the previous year) is published. On July 20, he again leaves for Italy (Genoa, Naples, Ischia, Rome, Florence). In August, *Armance* appears in print.

1828 Arriving in Milan on New Year's Eve, Henri Beyle is immediately expelled. After a stay at Lake Maggiore, he returns to Paris on January 29 and moves into the Hôtel de Valois, rue de Richelieu. A year marked by financial belt-tightening follows, during which he loses his military pension and his work for English periodicals dries up. He is appointed Deputy Auditor of Heraldry for the Seals Commission: The position is purely honorific.

1829 January–September: Paris. He finishes work on *Promenades dans Rome* [*Walks in Rome*], which will appear in print on September 5. During the spring, he is romantically linked to Alberte de Rubempré (Alberthe, Madame Azur or Sanscrit). With the involvement turning sour, by way of consolation he starts off, on September 8, on a long trip in the south of France (Bordeaux, Toulouse, Carcassonne, Barcelona, Montpellier, Marseille, and Grenoble). During the night of October 25–26, in Marseille, he develops an embryonic set of ideas for *Julien*, later to become *Le Rouge et le noir* [*The Red and the Black*]. Returning to Paris in early December, he learns that his friend Adolphe de Mareste has supplanted him in the affections of Alberte de Rubempré. On December 13, his novella, *Vanina Vanini*, is published in the *Revue de Paris*.

1830 In January he finishes another novella, *Mina de Vanghel*. Giulia Rinieri, whom he met three years earlier, confesses her love for him; she becomes his mistress on March 22. On April 8, contracts with Levavasseur for the novel he is writing, whose final title, *Le Rouge et le noir*, is decided upon in early May; he labors away at it busily until July. On July 28, he is de-

lighted to witness the progress of the insurrection from
his window. He is expecting a prefecture from the new
regime; Minister of the Interior Guizot denies him this,
along with a consulary position, which is later granted
to him by Count Molé, Minister of Foreign Affairs. Appointed to the post on September 25 in Trieste, he
writes to Giulia's guardian on November 6 to ask for
her hand in marriage; he receives a response only after
much time has passed. He leaves France the same day;
Le Rouge et le noir is published, in two volumes, a week
later. He takes up his post on November 26 but, following a stay in Venice, he learns on December 24 that the
Austrian government has refused him the exequatur (a
document recognizing foreign consular officers).

1831   Henri Beyle resides in Trieste awaiting a ruling from
Paris on his fate; he spends a month in Venice, from
January 20 to February 19. Appointed to Civita-
Vecchia, he returns to his post on April 17, the Holy
See grants him the exequatur. He travels frequently to
Rome. In August–September, he spends several weeks
in Florence after a stop in Siena.

1832   Spends roughly a third of the year at Civita-Vecchia
and another third in Rome. He makes a mission to An-
cona (March) and pleasure trips to Naples (January), to
Siena and Florence (August), to the Abruzzi region
(October), and again to Siena, where Giulia lives
(October–November). He writes *Souvenirs d'égotisme*
[*Memoirs of an Egotist*].

1833   January–August: Rome and Civita-Vecchia (three
weeks in Siena in January–February, ten days in Florence in May–June). On June 20, Giulia Rinieri weds
her cousin Giulio Martini. Spends leave time in Paris
(Hôtel de Valois) from September 11 to December 4;
returns via Geneva, Lyon, Marseille, Nice, Genoa, and
Florence: During a steamboat trip down the Rhine, he
meets George Sand and Alfred de Musset, who are
traveling to Venice.

1834   Rome and Civita-Vecchia. Henri Beyle pays frequent
visits to Count and Countess Cini, who live at Castel
Gandolfo. He starts work on the novel that is eventually to become *Lucien Leuwen*.

1835   Rome and Civita-Vecchia (a trip to Bologna and
Ravenna from October 8 to November 8). In January, he is awarded the cross of the Legion of Honor for
literary achievement. He dictates *Lucien Leuwen*

(June–September), which is destined to remain incomplete; then, on November 23, he begins to write *Vie de Henry Brulard* [*Life of Henry Brulard*].

1836   January–April: Rome and Civita-Vecchia. He continues to work on *Vie de Henry Brulard*. Finally granted the leave he has ardently desired for a number of years, he returns to Paris on May 24 (Hôtel de la Paix, rue du Mont-Blanc, at chaussée d'Antin); this period of leave is to last three years, thanks to the protection of Count Molé, now Council President. In November, he begins work on *Mémoirs sur Napoléon* [*Memoirs on Napoleon*], which he will abandon the following year.

1837   Paris (a trip from May 25 to July 5: La Charité-sur-Loire, Bourges, Tours, Nantes, Le Havre, Rouen; he also appears to have taken another trip, to Brittany and to the Dauphiné region, during August–September). In the *Revue des Deux Mondes*, he publishes two "Italian tales," *Vittoria Accoramboni* (March 1) and *Les Cenci* [*The Cenci Family*] (July 1); he begins *Mémoires d'un touriste* [*Memoirs of a Tourist*]. New addresses in Paris: Hôtel Favart, place des Italiens (March), then rue Caumartin (July).

1838   Henri Beyle retains his ties to Paris but, in order to write a follow-up volume to *Mémoires d'un touriste* (the first edition of which was to be published on June 30), he travels extensively throughout France, Switzerland, Germany, Holland, and Belgium from March 11 to July 22; this is followed by another trip, to Belgium and Normandy, from October 12 to November 2. In the *Revue des Deux Mondes*, he publishes a new Italian tale, *La Duchesse de Palliano* [*The Duchesse of Palliano*] (August 15), begins *L'Abbesse de Castro* [*The Abbess of Castro*], and, from November 4 to December 26, writes *La Chartreuse de Parme* [*The Charterhouse of Parma*].

1839   January–June: Paris. He moves into a new town house at rue Godot-de-Mauroy. *L'Abbesse de Castro* is published in two parts in *La Revue des Deux Mondes* (February 1 and March 1); *La Chartreuse de Parme* goes on sale on April 6. He sketches out ideas for various novellas and develops the main ideas for *Lamiel*. He leaves Paris on June 24 but only returns to his post on August 10, after leisurely travels in Switzerland and Italy. He spends the end of the year in Rome and at Civita-Vecchia (taking a trip to Naples with Mérimée from October 20 to November 9). He works on *Lamiel*, his final novel, which, like *Lucien Leuwen*, will remain unfinished.

1840   Rome and Civita-Vecchia. He courts a mysterious "Earline," who is probably Countess Cini. He revises *La Chartreuse de Parme* and continues work on *Lamiel*. In July, then in August–September, spends time in Florence, where he renews contact with Giulia. On October 15, he reads Balzac's article on *La Chartreuse de Parme* in the *Revue parisienne*.

1841   January–October: Rome and Civita-Vecchia (two brief stays in Florence in August and October): On March 15, he suffers a stroke from which he slowly recovers. He is granted sick leave and returns to Paris on November 8. He stays at Hôtel de l'Empire, rue Neuve-des-Grands-Augustins (now rue Daunou), then at Hôtel de Nantes, rue Neuve-des-Petits-Champs (today, rue Danielle-Casanova).

1842   Paris. Resumes literary activity (*Lamiel, Suora Scolastica*). He suffers another stroke on rue Neuve-des-Capucines, on March 22 at 7 P.M. Transported to his lodgings, he dies on March 23 at 2 A.M. without regaining consciousness. Following a religious service at the Church of the Assumption, he is buried at Montmartre Cemetery on March 24.

Selected Bibliography

• indicates a work included or excerpted in this Norton Critical Edition.

• Algazi, Lisa. *Maternal Subjectivity in the Works of Stendhal*. Edwin Mellen Press, 2001.
• Auerbach, Erich. *Mimesis: The Representation of Reality in Western Literature*. Trans. Willard R. Trask. Princeton, NJ: Princeton University Press, 1953.
  Blin, Georges. *Stendhal et les problemes du roman*. Paris: Corti, 1978.
• Brombert, Victor. *Stendhal: Fiction and the Themes of Freedom*. New York: Random House, 1968.
• Brooks, Peter. *Reading for the Plot: Design and Intention in Narrative*. New York: Knopf, 1984.
• Felman, Shoshana. *La "Folie" dans l'oeuvre romanesque de Stendhal*. Paris: Librairie José Corti, 1971.
• Girard, René. *Deceit, Desire, and the Novel*. Trans. Yvonne Freccero. Baltimore: The Johns Hopkins University Press, 1965.
  Imbert, Henri-François. *Variétés beylistes*. Paris: Champion, 1995.
  Landry, François. *L'Imaginaire chez Stendhal: Formation et expression*. Paris: L'Age d'Homme, 1983.
• Lee, Susanna. *A World Abandoned by God*. Lewisburg, PA: Bucknell University Press, 2006.
  Lukacher, Maryline. *Maternal Fictions: Stendhal, Sand, Rachilde, and Bataille*. Durham, NC: Duke University Press, 1994.
  Miller, D. A. *Narrative and Its Discontents: Problems of Closure in the Traditional Novel*. Princeton, NJ: Princeton University Press, 1981.
  Mossman, Carol, *The Narrative Matrix: Stendhal's Le Rouge et le noir*. Lexington, KY: French Forum Publishers, 1984.
• Petrey, Sandy. *Realism and Revolution: Balzac, Stendhal, Zola and the Performances of History*. Ithaca, NY: Cornell University Press, 1988.
  Prévost, Jean. *La Création chez Stendhal*. Paris: Mercure de France, 1951.
  Richard, Jean-Pierre. *Stendhal-Flaubert: Littérature et sensation*. Paris: Seuil, 1970.
  Talbot, Emile. *Stendhal Revisited*. New York: Twayne Publishers, 1993.